METHODS IN COMPUTATIONAL PHYSICS

Advances in Research and Applications

Volume 9

Plasma Physics

Methods in Computational Physics

Advances in Research and Applications

1 STATISTICAL PHYSICS
2 QUANTUM MECHANICS
3 FUNDAMENTAL METHODS IN HYDRODYNAMICS
4 APPLICATIONS IN HYDRODYNAMICS
5 NUCLEAR PARTICLE KINEMATICS
6 NUCLEAR PHYSICS
7 ASTROPHYSICS
8 ENERGY BANDS OF SOLIDS
9 PLASMA PHYSICS

METHODS IN COMPUTATIONAL PHYSICS

Advances in Research and Applications

Edited by

BERNI ALDER

Lawrence Radiation Laboratory
Livermore, California

SIDNEY FERNBACH

Lawrence Radiation Laboratory
Livermore, California

MANUEL ROTENBERG

University of California
La Jolla, California

Volume 9

Plasma Physics

1970

ACADEMIC PRESS

NEW YORK AND LONDON

COPYRIGHT © 1970, BY ACADEMIC PRESS, INC.
ALL RIGHTS RESERVED
NO PART OF THIS BOOK MAY BE REPRODUCED IN ANY FORM,
BY PHOTOSTAT, MICROFILM, RETRIEVAL SYSTEM, OR ANY
OTHER MEANS, WITHOUT WRITTEN PERMISSION FROM
THE PUBLISHERS.

ACADEMIC PRESS, INC.
111 Fifth Avenue, New York, New York 10003

United Kingdom Edition published by
ACADEMIC PRESS, INC. (LONDON) LTD.
Berkeley Square House, London W1X 6BA

LIBRARY OF CONGRESS CATALOG CARD NUMBER: 63-18406

PRINTED IN THE UNITED STATES OF AMERICA

Contributors

Numbers in parentheses indicate the pages on which the authors' contributions begin.

THOMAS P. ARMSTRONG, *University of Kansas, Lawrence, Kansas* (29)

HERBERT L. BERK, *Lawrence Radiation Laboratory, University of California, Livermore, California* (87)

CHARLES K. BIRDSALL, *Electrical Engineering and Computer Science Department, University of California, Berkeley, California; Consultant, Lawrence Radiation Laboratory, Livermore, California* (241)

JACK A. BYERS, *Lawrence Radiation Laboratory, University of California, Livermore, California* (259)

JOHN M. DAWSON, *Princeton University, Plasma Physics Laboratory, Princeton, New Jersey* (1)

ROLLIN C. HARDING, *Lawrence Radiation Laboratory, Livermore, California* (29)

R. W. HOCKNEY,* *NASA, Langley Research Center, Hampton, Virginia* (135)

JOHN KILLEEN, *Lawrence Radiation Laboratory, Livermore, California and Department of Applied Science, University of California, Davis, California* (259, 421)

GEORG KNORR, *The University of Iowa, Iowa City, Iowa* (29)

A. BRUCE LANGDON, *Electrical Engineering and Computer Science Department, University of California, Berkeley, California* (241)

H. RALPH LEWIS, *University of California, Los Alamos Scientific Laboratory, Los Alamos, New Mexico* (307)

KENNETH D. MARX, *Sandia Laboratory, Livermore, California and Department of Applied Science, University of California, Davis, California* (421)

DAVID MONTGOMERY, *The University of Iowa, Iowa City, Iowa* (29)

R. L. MORSE, *University of California, Los Alamos Scientific Laboratory, Los Alamos, New Mexico* (213)

H. OKUDA, *Electrical Engineering and Computer Science Department, University of California, Berkeley, California* (241)

D. E. POTTER, *Imperial College, London, England* (339)

KEITH V. ROBERTS, *U.K. Atomic Energy Authority, Culham Laboratory, Culham, Abingdon, Berkshire, England* (87, 339)

* *Present address*: IBM Watson Research Center, Yorktown Heights, New York.

Preface

Interest in plasma physics has greatly increased in the last two decades primarily because of the problems connected with the controlled thermonuclear power program and with the geomagnetic environment. In both of these areas experimentation is difficult and expensive, hence any theoretically gained understanding is highly desirable. Because the theoretical study of plasmas involves the mathematically very difficult problem of dealing with the collective behavior of many charged particles, the computer has become an essential tool in solving the equations, although the calculations themselves are quite complex. This is true of either of the two numerical approaches that have been developed; the particle simulation method and the solution of the continuum equations.

The particle method is versatile but time consuming. A one-dimensional version is given in the chapter by Dawson, and two-dimensional versions are described in the chapters by Hockney, Morse, and Birdsall *et al.* By solving stepwise the simultaneous equations of motion of the individual charged particles in the presence of magnetic and electric fields, valuable details of the behavior of plasmas are obtained, including the occurrence of instabilities. On the other hand, the continuum methods have yielded, with relatively little computer time and the use of realistic boundary conditions, calculations in agreement with experiments on plasma machines. This is particularly true under conditions where particle collisions dominate, as illustrated in the chapters by Roberts and Potter, and Marx and Killeen. In general, the computational technique that is used in the continuum case is the finite difference method of solution of the hydrodynamic-like equations which have added complexity due to the presence of magnetic and electric fields. In the collisionless (Vlasov) case, however, and so far only in one dimension, two specialized numerical techniques have been applied which are presented in chapters by Armstrong *et al.*, and Berk and Roberts.

Future developments in both more efficient numerical methods and faster computers should lead to ever more realistic plasma calculations, including three-dimensional ones. Regretfully, application of the numerical techniques presented here to the very similar problem of stellar dynamics could not be considered because of space limitations.

January, 1970　　　　　　　　　　　　　　　　　　　　　　BERNI ALDER
　　　　　　　　　　　　　　　　　　　　　　　　　　　　　　SIDNEY FERNBACH
　　　　　　　　　　　　　　　　　　　　　　　　　　　　　　MANUEL ROTENBERG

Contents

CONTRIBUTORS v
PREFACE vii
CONTENTS OF PREVIOUS VOLUMES xiii

THE ELECTROSTATIC SHEET MODEL FOR A PLASMA AND ITS MODIFICATION TO FINITE-SIZE PARTICLES
John M. Dawson

I. Introduction... 1
II. The Electrostatic Sheet Model.................................. 2
III. Investigations with Finite-Size Particles..................... 16
References... 27

SOLUTION OF VLASOV'S EQUATION BY TRANSFORM METHODS
Thomas P. Armstrong, Rollin C. Harding, Georg Knorr, and David Montgomery

I. Introduction... 30
II. The Fourier–Fourier Expansion.................................. 35
III. The Fourier–Hermite Expansion................................. 55
IV. Extension of the Fourier–Hermite Expansion..................... 74
V. Summary and Suggested Future Directions......................... 82
References... 84

THE WATER-BAG MODEL
Herbert L. Berk and Keith V. Roberts

I. Introduction... 88
II. Physical Properties of Step-Function Distributions............. 90
III. Numerical Methods... 100
IV. Numerical Stability of the Leapfrog Scheme..................... 111
V. Numerical Experiment of the Bump-on-Tail Instability............ 116
Appendix I. Continuous Distribution as the Limit of a Step Function........ 126
Appendix II. Analysis of Synchronization Method................... 129
References... 133

THE POTENTIAL CALCULATION AND SOME APPLICATIONS
R. W. Hockney

I. Introduction	136
II. Direct Methods	139
III. Iterative Methods and Convergence	164
IV. The Arbitrary Force Law	176
V. Some Computer Models	181
VI. Applications in Particle Models	184
Appendices	202
References	210

MULTIDIMENSIONAL PLASMA SIMULATION BY THE PARTICLE-IN-CELL METHOD
R. L. Morse

I. Introduction	213
II. Fluid PIC Simulation of Axisymmetric Plasma Guns	214
III. Collisionless PIC	224
References	239

FINITE-SIZE PARTICLE PHYSICS APPLIED TO PLASMA SIMULATION
Charles K. Birdsall, A. Bruce Langdon, and H. Okuda

I. Introduction	241
II. General Theory for a Model of Finite-Size Particles	243
III. Scattering Cross Section	248
IV. Fokker–Planck Drag and Diffusion Coefficients for a Cloud Plasma	252
V. The Effect of Using a Spatial Grid	254
VI. Historical Note	265
VII. Conclusions	257
References	257

FINITE-DIFFERENCE METHODS FOR COLLISIONLESS PLASMA MODELS
Jack A. Byers and John Killeen

I. Introduction	259
II. Numerical Solution of the Vlasov Equation	260
III. Low-Beta Plasma Models Using the Guiding-Center Drift Equations	282
References	305

APPLICATION OF HAMILTON'S PRINCIPLE TO THE NUMERICAL ANALYSIS OF VLASOV PLASMAS

H. Ralph Lewis

I. Introduction	307
II. Lagrangian Description of the Physical System	311
III. Derivation of Approximation Schemes from Hamilton's Principle	320
IV. Specialization to a Finite Number of Particles	325
V. Application to the Cold Two-Stream Instability with a Continuum of Particles	332
Appendix A. Gradients with Respect to Position and Velocity	335
Appendix B. Formulas for L and H in the General Case	337
References	338

MAGNETOHYDRODYNAMIC CALCULATIONS

Keith V. Roberts and D. E. Potter

I. Introduction	340
II. Magnetohydrodynamic Models	345
III. Difference Methods	360
IV. One-Dimensional Codes	387
V. Two-Dimensional Codes	391
VI. Calculations on the Plasma Focus Experiment	398
VII. A Three-Dimensional Code	414
VIII. Concluding Remarks	416
References	417

THE SOLUTION OF THE FOKKER–PLANCK EQUATION FOR A MIRROR-CONFINED PLASMA

John Killeen and Kenneth D. Marx

I. Introduction	422
II. Mathematical Formulation Which Describes the Collisional Behavior of a Plasma	424
III. One-Dimensional (Isotropic or Pseudoisotropic) Problems	429
IV. Two-Dimensional (Nonisotropic) Problems	441
V. Nonisotropic Problems with Spatial Dependence of the Magnetic Field	467
Appendix A. Transformation of the Fokker–Planck Equation to (v, θ) Coordinates and Specialization to a Two-Component Plasma	481
Appendix B. Derivation of "Simpson's Rule" Quadrature Formula for Unequal Intervals	484
Appendix C. Other Methods of Calculating g	485
Appendix D. Solution of the Difference Equations	486
References	489
AUTHOR INDEX	491
SUBJECT INDEX	497

Contents of Previous Volumes

Volume 1: Statistical Physics

The Numerical Theory of Neutron Transport
Bengt G. Carlson

The Calculation of Nonlinear Radiation Transport by a Monte Carlo Method
Joseph A. Fleck, Jr.

Critical-Size Calculations for Neutron Systems by the Monte Carlo Method
Donald H. Davis

A Monte Carlo Calculation of the Response of Gamma-Ray Scintillation Counters
Clayton D. Zerby

Monte Carlo Calculation of the Penetration and Diffusion of Fast Charged Particles
Martin J. Berger

Monte Carlo Methods Applied to Configurations of Flexible Polymer Molecules
Frederick T. Wall, Stanley Windwer, and Paul J. Gans

Monte Carlo Computations on the Ising Lattice
L. D. Fosdick

A Monte Carlo Solution of Percolation in the Cubic Crystal
J. M. Hammersley

AUTHOR INDEX—SUBJECT INDEX

Volume 2: Quantum Mechanics

The Gaussian Function in Calculations of Statistical Mechanics and Quantum Mechanics
Isaiah Shavitt

Atomic Self-Consistent Field Calculations by the Expansion Method
C. C. J. Roothaan and P. S. Bagus

The Evaluation of Molecular Integrals by the Zeta-Function Expansion
M. P. Barnett

Integrals for Diatomic Molecular Calculations
Fernando J. Corbató and Alfred C. Switendick

Nonseparable Theory of Electron-Hydrogen Scattering
A. Temkin and D. E. Hoover

Estimating Convergence Rates of Variational Calculations
Charles Schwartz

AUTHOR INDEX—SUBJECT INDEX

Volume 3: Fundamental Methods in Hydrodynamics

Two-Dimensional Lagrangian Hydrodynamic Difference Equations
William D. Schulz

Mixed Eulerian-Lagrangian Method
R. M. Frank and R. B. Lazarus

The Strip Code and the Jetting of Gas between Plates
John G. Trulio

CEL: A Time-Dependent, Two-Space-Dimensional, Coupled Eulerian-Lagrange Code
W. F. Noh

The Tensor Code
G. Maenchen and S. Sack

Calculation of Elastic-Plastic Flow
Mark L. Wilkins

Solution by Characteristics of the Equations of One-Dimensional Unsteady Flow
N. E. Hoskin

The Solution of Two-Dimensional Hydrodynamic Equations by the Method of Characteristics
D. J. Richardson

The Particle-in-Cell Computing Method for Fluid Dynamics
Francis H. Harlow

The Time Dependent Flow of an Incompressible Viscous Fluid
Jacob Fromm

AUTHOR INDEX—SUBJECT INDEX

Volume 4: Applications in Hydrodynamics

Numerical Simulation of the Earth's Atmosphere
Cecil E. Leith

Nonlinear Effects in the Theory of a Wind-Driven Ocean Circulation
Kirk Bryan

Analytic Continuation Using Numerical Methods
Glenn E. Lewis

Numerical Solution of the Complete Krook-Boltzmann Equation for Strong Shock Waves
Moustafa T. Chahine

The Solution of Two Molecular Flow Problems by the Monte Carlo Method
J. K. Haviland

Computer Experiments for Molecular Dynamics Problems
R. A. Gentry, F. H. Harlow, and R. E. Martin

Computation of the Stability of the Laminar Compressible Boundary Layer
Leslie M. Mack

Some Computational Aspects of Propeller Design
William B. Morgan and John W. Wrench, Jr.

Methods of the Automatic Computation of Stellar Evolution
Louis G. Henyey and Richard D. Levée

Computations Pertaining to the Problem of Propagation of a Seismic Pulse in a Layered Solid
F. Abramovici and Z. Alterman

AUTHOR INDEX—SUBJECT INDEX

Volume 5: Nuclear Particle Kinematics

Automatic Retrieval Spark Chambers
J. Bounin, R. H. Miller, and M. J. Neumann

Computer-Based Data Analysis Systems
Robert Clark and W. F. Miller

Programming for the PEPR System
P. L. Bastien, T. L. Watts, R. K. Yamamoto, M. Alston, A. H. Rosenfeld, F. T. Solmitz, and H. D. Taft

A System for the Analysis of Bubble Chamber Film Based upon the Scanning and Measuring Projector (SMP)
Robert I. Hulsizer, John H. Munson, and James N. Snyder

A Software Approach to the Automatic Scanning of Digitized Bubble Chamber Photographs
Robert B. Marr and George Rabinowitz

AUTHOR INDEX—SUBJECT INDEX

Volume 6: Nuclear Physics

Nuclear Optical Model Calculations
Michael A. Melkanoff, Tatsuro Sawada, and Jacques Raynal

Numerical Methods for the Many-Body Theory of Finite Nuclei
Kleber S. Masterson, Jr.

Application of the Matrix Hartree-Fock Method to Problems in Nuclear Structure
R. K. Nesbet

Variational Calculations in Few-Body Problems with Monte-Carlo Method
R. C. Herndon and Y. C. Tang

Automated Nuclear Shell-Model Calculations
S. Cohen, R. D. Lawson, M. H. Macfarlane, and M. Soga

Nucleon-Nucleon Phase Shift Analyses by Chi-Squared Minimization
Richard A. Arndt and Malcolm H. MacGregor

AUTHOR INDEX—SUBJECT INDEX

Volume 7: Astrophysics

The Calculation of Model Stellar Atmospheres
Dimitri Mihalas

Computational Methods for Non-LTE Line-Transfer Problems
D. G. Hummer and G. Rybicki

Methods for Calculating Stellar Evolution
R. Kippenhahn, A. Weigert, and Emmi Hofmeister

Computational Methods in Stellar Pulsation
R. F. Christy

Stellar Dynamics and Gravitational Collapse
Michael M. May and Richard H. White

AUTHOR INDEX—SUBJECT INDEX

Volume 8: Energy Bands of Solids

Energy Bands and The Theory of Solids
J. C. Slater

Interpolation Schemes and Model Hamiltonians in Band Theory
J. C. Phillips and R. Sandrock

The Pseudopotential Method and the Single-Particle Electronic Excitation Spectra of Crystals
David Brust

A Procedure for Calculating Electronic Energy Bands Using Symmetrized Augmented Plane Waves
L. F. Mattheiss, J. H. Wood, and A. C. Switendick

Interpolation Scheme for the Band Structure of Transition Metals with Ferromagnetic and Spin-Orbit Interactions
Henry Ehrenreich and Laurent Hodges

Electronic Structure of Tetrahedrally Bonded Semiconductors: Empirically Adjusted OPW Energy Band Calculations
Frank Herman, Richard L. Kortum, Charles D. Kuglin, John P. Van Dyke, and Sherwood Skillman

The Green's Function Method of Korringa, Kohn, and Rostoker for the Calculation of the Electronic Band Structure of Solids
Benjamin Segall and Frank S. Ham

AUTHOR INDEX—SUBJECT INDEX

The Electrostatic Sheet Model for a Plasma and its Modification to Finite-Size Particles

JOHN M. DAWSON

PRINCETON UNIVERSITY
PLASMA PHYSICS LABORATORY
PRINCETON, NEW JERSEY

I. Introduction	1
II. The Electrostatic Sheet Model	2
A. The One-Species Model	3
B. The Numerical Method for Following the Motion of the One-Species, One-Dimensional Plasma	4
C. Numerical Methods for Solving the Two-Species Sheet Model	7
D. Noise and Collisional Phenomenon for the Sheet Model	10
E. Collisional Emission and Absorption of Longitudinal Waves	14
III. Investigations with Finite-Size Particles	16
A. The Finite-Size Particle Model	17
B. Investigation of Fluctuations about Thermal Equilibrium	22
C. The Weak Cold Beam for Finite-Size Particles	24
D. Use of Different Size Charges on the Particles	26
References	27

I. Introduction

ONE OF THE OLDEST and most versatile of the one-dimensional models for numerical investigation of plasmas is the sheet model. This model was first used to investigate electrostatic effects, plasma oscillations, the kinetics of one-dimensional plasmas, and the two-stream instability (Buneman, 1959; Dawson, 1962a, 1962b; Smith and Dawson, 1963; Eldridge and Feix, 1962). In this paper, we will discuss the electrostatic sheet model. The emphasis will be on the methods used to handle these problems on the computer and on a number of problems that are encountered (for example, noise). However, actual codes will not be given.

More recently, the sheet model has been modified by allowing motion in the plane of the sheets, as well as perpendicular to them (Hasegawa and Birdsall, 1964; Shanny et al., 1962; Langdon and Dawson, 1967). This modification allows the inclusion of magnetic effects and the inclusion of

Fokker–Planck-type collisional effects (by a Monte Carlo method). With these modifications, cyclotron waves (Hasegawa and Birdsall, 1964), radiation effects (Langdon and Dawson, 1967), and Harris-type instabilities (Byers and Grewal, 1968) (associated with monoenergetic velocity distributions) have been studied. While these latter modifications are quite interesting and broad in scope, we shall not deal with them here, since to do them justice would take us too far afield.

II. The Electrostatic Sheet Model

There are two electrostatic sheet models, the one-species and the two-species models. The one-species model (Dawson, 1962a) considers a plasma composed of a large number of identical charge sheets embedded in a fixed uniform neutralizing background (see Fig. 1). The sheets are all constrained

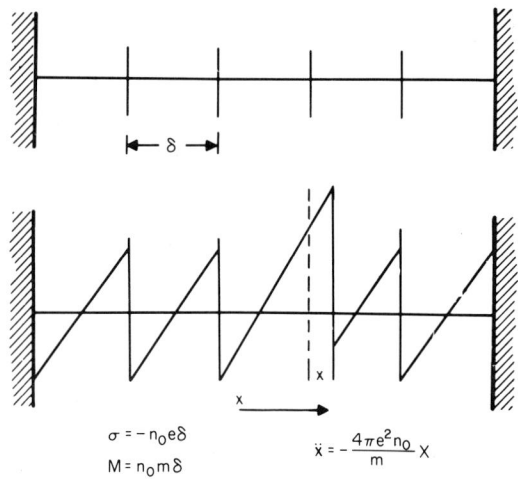

FIG. 1. Sheet model.

to be perpendicular to, say, the x axis, and are allowed to move freely in the x direction. They are allowed to pass freely through each other.

The two-species model (Smith and Dawson, 1963; Eldridge and Feix, 1962) consists of both positively and negatively charged sheets. The sheets are again constrained to be perpendicular to, say, the x axis, and are allowed to move only in the x direction. They are allowed to pass freely through each other. The charges on the sheets are equal and opposite, but their masses are taken to be different. Generally the mass ratio is not taken to be as large as 2000 to 1, because, in that case, the computer spends all its time computing what the fast-moving electrons are doing. Typically, mass ratios in the range of 10's to 100's are used, and one attempts to scale the results for realistic mass ratios.

We shall begin by discussing the one-species model.

A. THE ONE-SPECIES MODEL

For the one-species model, there exists an equilibrium situation, with the sheets at rest. In this equilibrium situation, the sheets are equally spaced, and the average electric field that a sheet feels is zero, as is shown in Fig. 1. At each sheet, the electric field jumps by $-4\pi\sigma$ (Gauss' law); $-\sigma$ is the charge per unit area. Between the sheets, the electric field varies linearly with distance, due to the background charge. The equilibrium separation of the sheets (δ) is n_0^{-1}, where n_0 is the density of the neutralizing background.

If one of the sheets (say, the ith sheet) is displaced from its equilibrium position by a distance x_i, it passes over an amount of positive charge $\sigma n_0 x_i$ per unit area. By Gauss' law, the electric field which the sheet sees is $4\pi n_0 \sigma x_i$, and its equation of motion is

$$m\ddot{x}_i = -\sigma E = -4\pi n_0 \sigma^2 x_i$$

or

$$\ddot{x}_i = -\omega_p^2 x_i \tag{1}$$

$$\omega_p^2 = 4\pi n_0 \sigma^2/m.$$

Equation (1) is simply the equation for an harmonic oscillator, and its solution is

$$x_i(t) = x_i(0) \cos \omega_p t + (\dot{x}_i(0)/\omega_p) \sin \omega_p t \tag{2}$$

$$\dot{x}_i(t) = \dot{x}_i(0) \cos \omega_p t - \omega_p x_i(0) \sin \omega_p t. \tag{3}$$

Each sheet oscillates independently of all the others at the plasma frequency.

Equation (1) and the solution given by Eqs. (2) and (3) hold only if the sheet does not cross another. If a crossing does take place, the electric field jumps by $-4\pi\sigma$, and the acceleration undergoes a sudden jump. This situation is the same as if the sheets had interchanged equilibrium positions. Thus, the equation of motion for a sheet is

$$\ddot{x}_i = -\omega_p^2 X_i \tag{4}$$

where x_i is the sheet's position and X_i is its displacement from an instantaneous equilibrium position.

It is now possible to construct a second-one-dimensional plasma model that is entirely equivalent to the one just described. Suppose that, instead of having sheets that pass freely through one another, we had perfectly elastic sheets. It is a property of perfectly elastic collisions between identical particles in one dimension that the particles simply exchange velocities. This leads to the same situation that results from the particles passing through each other. The only difference between the end results is the names we give to the particles.

It is possible to build a mechanical model of the one-dimensional plasma. It consists of a number of identical pendulums, each with an elastic ball at its end. These are lined up and constrained to oscillate only along this line of centers.

One can illustrate a number of properties of one-dimensional plasmas with this model. For example, if the first pendulum is pulled aside and released so as to strike the second, it will give its velocity to the second, the second in turn will give its velocity to the third, and so on. A pulse thus moves through the pendulums. When a pendulum strikes its neighbor it gives up its velocity, but not its displacement. Thus, the pulse leaves the pendulum behind it in a displaced state and they start to oscillate. This is equivalent to the excitation of a plasma oscillation by a fast sheet moving through a plasma.

B. The Numerical Method for Following the Motion of the One-Species, One-Dimensional Plasma

We wish to solve Eq. (4) for the sheets, correcting the orbit for crossings of neighboring sheets. When a sheet crosses a neighbor the acceleration jumps by

$$\Delta \ddot{x} = \pm \omega_p^2 \delta \tag{5}$$

where δ is the interparticle spacing, and the $+$ sign is to be used if the sheet crossed was initially on the right, while the minus sign is to be used if it was on the left.

Let the particles be ordered according to their occurrence along x. Now if no crossing takes place, then the solution of Eq. (4) is given by

$$\dot{x}_i(t + \Delta t) = \dot{x}_i(t) \cos \omega_p \Delta t - \omega_p X_i(t) \sin \omega_p \Delta t \tag{6}$$

$$x_i(t + \Delta t) = x_i(t) + \dot{x}_i(t) \sin \omega_p \Delta t - X_i(t)(1 - \cos \omega_p \Delta t). \tag{7}$$

The code computes these noncrossing positions and checks whether any crossings have taken place; that is, it checks if

$$x_i(t + \Delta t) > x_j(t + \Delta t) \quad \text{for } j > 1. \tag{8}$$

(Remember that the particles are ordered in x). If it finds that such a crossing has taken place, it computes the time of crossing by first finding the chords to the two orbit curves in the x, t plane, and then computing the crossing times for these (see Fig. 2). This first approximation to the crossing time, t_{c1}, is given by

$$\Delta t_{c1} = \Delta t \frac{x_j(t) - x_i(t)}{x_j(t) - x_i(t) + x_i(t + \Delta t) - x_j(t + \Delta t)}. \tag{9}$$

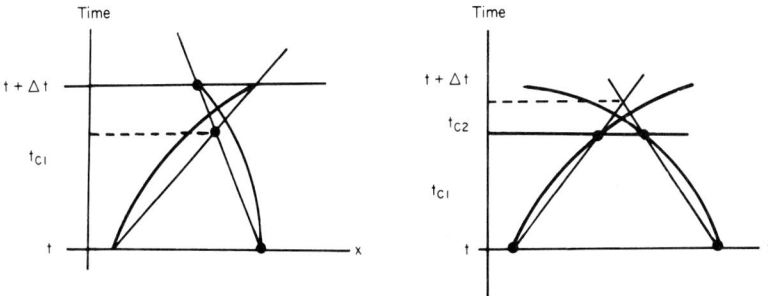

FIG. 2. Crossing figure.

The code next computes the positions of the two particles at this predicted crossing time from the noncrossing orbits. It then computes the chords through the points at t and t_{c1} and finds their crossing time, t_{c2}. This time is used as the correct crossing time. The effect of earlier crossings (if any) during Δt is not included. If two particles crossed before time t, due to corrections to their orbits from crossings in the previous time interval, this t_{c2} will be negative, and the method will find a correction. The orbits of the particles are corrected by adding the constant acceleration $\pm \omega_p^2 \delta$ to their motion over the remainder of the time step, the sign depending on the order of crossing.

The earliest version of this code attempted to calculate the motions without taking into account corrections for crossings during Δt. Even with time steps so short that the probability of one sheet crossing another was small, it was found that the energy drifted down at an unacceptable rate, the rate being roughly

$$(\Delta E/E)_{\text{per } \omega p^{-1}} = \omega_p \Delta t \tag{10}$$

where Δt is the time step. Not only is this rate rather large, but it improves only as the first power of Δt. By including the first crossing correction, conservation of energy improved as Δt^2 and was about three orders of magnitude better for $\omega_p \Delta t = 0.05$ and $n\lambda_D = 10$. By including the second correction to the crossing time, a further improvement of two orders of magnitude in the energy conservation was obtained for $\omega_p \Delta t = 0.05$ and $n\lambda_D = 10$. The increase in running time due to this last correction was negligible (perhaps 1%) and was more than compensated for by our ability to use larger time steps for a given accuracy.

In addition to energy checks, an old version of the code without the second correction to the crossing time was checked for time reversibility. The motion of a system of 9 sheets was reversed and found to retrace its path within an accuracy of one part in 10^3 (all orbits were this accurate) over a period of 6 oscillations ($\omega_p t = 36$). For this case, there were about 2.5 particles per Debye length.

If the particles are arranged in the order in which they occur in x, then in checking for crossings we need only check nearby particles in the table (hence, nearby particles in x). There is a maximum x separation that particles can have and still cross in a time step. This is given by

$$\Delta x_{\max}(i) = [v_{-\max} + v(i)] \Delta t \qquad (11)$$

where $\Delta x_{\max}(i)$ is the maximum distance we must look ahead for a crossing with particles i, $-v_{-\max}$ is the maximum negative velocity of any particle, $v(i)$ is the velocity of the ith particle, and Δt is the time step. We check only ahead (in x) for crossings, since crossings from behind will have been picked up earlier as we move through the table. The maximum negative velocity is updated every ω_p^{-1}.

If this method is to be efficient, the particles must be ordered according to their position in x. This is achieved by counting the number of times a sheet crosses one to its right and subtracting from this the number of times it is crossed by one to its left. This number gives the number of spaces the particle must be advanced (or moved back) in the table. [All tables of pertinent data (positions, velocities, particle identity) are so ordered.] For each crossing a particle experiences from the right, another particle experiences one from the left. Thus, the sum of the total number of crossings (counting those from the right as positive and those from the left as negative) must be zero, and this is used as a check on the codes. Further, this procedure results in a unique ordering for the particles, and no two particles should fill the same place in the table. This is used as a second check on the code.

The boundaries are handled as follows. A set of image charges is included at each end. A sufficient number of these charges is included so that a particle inside the system cannot overrun the last image particle in one time step. If we desire a reflecting boundary condition, then the image particles are mirror images (equal distance from the boundary, but with negative velocity) of the particles immediately adjacent to the boundary. If we desire periodic boundary conditions, then the images are identical to the particles at the other end of the system except for the fact that they are displaced by plus or minus L (L is the length of the system); the sign depends on which end of the system we are considering. The motions of the last few image particles may not be correct, but this is not important since they are replaced by new images at the end of each time step.

The code is generally run at an average of between one half and one crossing per particle per time step. Energy is conserved to about one part in 10^5 for about 40 time steps if there are 20 particles per Debye length. The code requires roughly 2×10^{-4} sec per particle per time step on an IBM 360/65. Generally, diagnostics such as computation of the velocity distribution function, the Fourier transform of the electric field, and phase space plots for the particles are included. These can consume an appreciable amount of time depending on what is included.

C. NUMERICAL METHODS FOR SOLVING THE TWO-SPECIES SHEET MODEL

The two-species sheet model (Smith and Dawson, 1963) consists of two types of sheets with equal but opposite charges and different masses. These sheets are constrained to be perpendicular to, say, the x axis and are allowed to pass freely through each other.

The equation of motion of a sheet is

$$\ddot{x}_i = (\sigma_i/m_i)E_i \tag{12}$$

where E_i is the average electric field at sheet i (i refers to the order in x). Between crossings, E is a constant, and the orbit of i is given by

$$x_i = x_{io} + v_{io}t + \sigma_i E_i t^2/2m_i. \tag{13}$$

Likewise, the orbit of a neighboring particle is

$$x_j = x_{jo} + v_{jo}t + \sigma_j E_j t^2/2m_j \tag{14}$$

where $j = i \pm 1$. Since the charge on a sheet is $\pm\sigma$, by Gauss' law E_j must equal $E_i \pm 4\pi\sigma$, the $\pm$ sign depending on the sign of the charge on i. The crossing time for i and j is obtained by equating x_i and x_j, or is given by

$$(x_{io} - x_{jo}) + (v_{io} - v_{jo})t + (\sigma_i E_i/2m_i) - (\sigma_j E_j/2m_j)t^2 = 0. \tag{15}$$

Solving for t gives

$$t = \frac{\Delta v \pm (\Delta v^2 - 4\Delta a\,\Delta x)^{1/2}}{2\Delta a} \tag{16}$$

where

$$\Delta x = x_{io} - x_{jo},$$

$$\Delta v = v_{io} - v_{jo}, \tag{17}$$

$$\Delta a = (\sigma_i E_i/2m_i) - (\sigma_j E_j/2m_j). \tag{18}$$

It is possible that particles i and j never cross, or that the time of crossing is very large so that they cross other particles in the meantime. However, it is always true that crossing can take place only between instantaneously neighboring particles.

Now we may advance the system, crossing by crossing, recording a particle's position and velocity at the time of its last crossing. We make a list of crossing times for particles crossing their nearest neighbors. The two particles with the shortest crossing times are crossed. After crossing these particles, new crossing times are computed for them with respect to their new neighbors. The old crossing times involving these particles are deleted, and the new crossing times are inserted in the crossing table at the appropriate places.

In order to make the above method efficient so that it does not require a prohibitive amount of computer time, a number of tricks are used. First, the crossing times are inserted in the crossing table in the order in which they occur, so that the next crossing is that one given at the beginning of the table. In order to facilitate entering crossing times in the table, the first few digits of the crossing time are used to address its position in the table. To prevent the need for rearranging the whole crossing table or moving a large number of crossing times in the table when a new one is inserted, the table is made much larger than the total number of crossing times (we used a factor of about 10), so that it contains mostly empty spaces. Thus, when a new crossing time is inserted, it will generally go in an empty space. If there is a crossing time in that space, then it is compared with the one to be inserted, and they are placed in the table in the proper order. If the existing entry must be moved, it will generally be only one space because of the large amount of empty space.

Since we cannot keep an infinitely long crossing table, we must decide on the maximum credible crossing time for neighbors. If the time is longer than this, then one or the other of the particles will be crossed by a third particle before the predicted crossing takes place. The maximum credible crossing time is determined on the basis of probability arguments. The rate of crossing which a particle with velocity v experiences is roughly

$$n(v^2 + v_T{}^2)^{1/2} = dN_c/dt = \dot{N}_c \tag{19}$$

where N_c is the number of crossings the particle has experienced, n is the density, and $v_T{}^2$ is the mean square random velocity (in this expression we have used the rms velocity relative to other particles in place of the average relative velocity that would apply). Now the probability that the particle does not experience a crossing in a time interval τ is

$$P(\text{no crossing}) = \exp[-\dot{N}_c \tau]. \tag{20}$$

The maximum crossing time kept in the table is chosen so that P is extremely small, generally of the order of 10^{-8} to 10^{-9}. (The minimum value of $\dot{N}_c$ may be used to compute τ; a τ of the order of twenty times the mean crossing time must be used.) Such a small value of P is required because in a system containing several thousand sheets, each of which makes several thousand crossings during a run, one must ensure that an actual crossing is not overlooked. Because of this, most of the crossing times are concentrated near the top of the table. In order that space be available at the top of the table for insertion of new crossing values, one must take this into account. This situation might be improved by leaving a block of a few spaces at the end of the table to accommodate crossing times greater than 6 or 7 times the average crossing time, but it would complicate the logic for the use and updating of the table and has not been done by us.

As mentioned above, in order to speed the insertion of entries into the crossing table, the first few digits of the crossing time are used as the address. As one proceeds in time the size of the crossing times get larger and larger, and hence the address of the entries become larger and larger. If the crossing table is not to be too large, we must compensate for this. This is done by making the table circular, with the distance around the circle equal to the maximum interval over which a crossing must be considered. A flag is put at the position of the last crossing time considered. This time is subtracted from the new crossing times, and the first few significant figures then determine its location in the table relative to the last crossing.

Boundary conditions are handled by putting image particles at the ends of the system. For reflecting boundary conditions, mirror images of the two end particles are inserted at the mirror points from the two ends. For periodic boundary conditions, images of the opposite ends are inserted at the appropriate locations.

The above method of advancing the system, crossing by crossing, is essentially as accurate as the machine and is quite fast. For the machine used, energy was conserved to ten significant figures over long times ($\omega_p t \approx 100$; the machine has 12 significant figures). The calculation took about one minute per ω_p^{-1} for 1000 electrons and 1000 ions on a CDC 1604, which is several orders of magnitude slower than present fast machines. The calculation time scales like the number of particles times the number of particles per Debye length. The one disadvantage is that a large amount of storage is needed for the crossing table. At the time that the code was written, this was not serious, since the computing time essentially limited the size of the system that could be considered.

It would be possible to use this crossing time method for the one-species problem. One must solve the transcendental equation

$$\delta = (x_i - x_{i+1}) \cos \omega_p t_c + ([\dot{x}_i - \dot{x}_{i+1}]/\omega_p) \sin \omega_p t_0 \tag{21}$$

in calculating crossing times for neighboring particles (δ equals the interparticle spacing). On the other hand, it is possible to use the approximate crossing time method used on the one-species model for the two-species model. The latter has been done and works well (it is essentially as fast and conserves energy to about four significant figures over runs with $\omega_p t \approx 100$).

D. Noise and Collisional Phenomenon for the Sheet Model

Because the sheet model consists of discrete particles, a collision-type phenomenon occurs in it. Every time a sheet crosses another, it experiences a jump in the force it feels, and its orbit is changed. These jumps lead to collisional-type effects which may mask the effects one is trying to investigate. If we are to make use of the code, it is important to understand these effects. These effects are also of interest in their own right, as they relate to the kinetic theory of plasmas. Much of this theory can be checked in detail on this model (Dawson, 1962a; 1963; Smith and Dawson, 1963; Eldridge and Feix, 1962; Feix, 1967; Birmingham et al., 1965).

When the standard kinetic theory of plasmas that includes only the two-particle correlation function is applied to the one-species sheet model, it predicts that all stable distribution functions are time-independent. It is relatively easy to understand this result on physical grounds. Consider two identical particles in one dimension which initially have velocities v_1 and v_2. Let them interact. After this interaction they will have velocities $\tilde{v}_1$ and $\tilde{v}_2$. Now, by conservation of energy and momentum, there are two conserved quantities. The only possible values of $\tilde{v}_1$ and $\tilde{v}_2$ that conserve the energy and momentum are

$$v_1 = \tilde{v}_1 \qquad v_2 = \tilde{v}_2 \qquad (22)$$

or

$$v_1 = \tilde{v}_2 \qquad v_2 = \tilde{v}_1. \qquad (23)$$

In either case the distribution function is not changed.

One might expect that in a plasma where many particles are interacting simultaneously, these two conservation laws would not contain the whole story. However, the theory treats all interactions as weak, and hence, so far as it is concerned, the effects are additive (assuming uncorrelated or random encounters). The effect of one collision on another is taken negligible, and the conservation relations still freeze the result. Actually, in simultaneous encounters, one encounter affects the other, and so there should be some collisional effect.

These points were checked by a numerical experiment on the one-species sheet model. The actual rate of relaxation to Maxwellian was determined (Dawson, 1963). The problem investigated was that of the time development of a distribution which initially had the square profile shown in Fig. 3. The

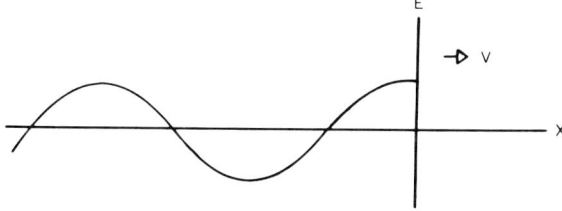

Wake of a fast sheet

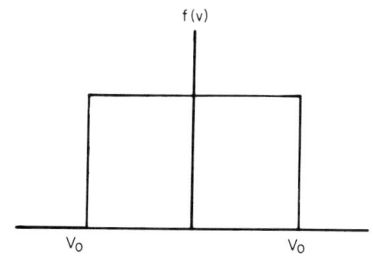

Initial velocity distribution

FIG. 3. Square $f(v)$.

initial velocity of a particle was obtained by computing a random number that had a uniform probability of lying anywhere between -1 and 1 and then multiplying this number by v_0. A number of different v_0's were used to determine the dependence of the time development on the kinetic energy or number of particles per Debye length $[\lambda_D = (v^2)^{1/2}/\omega_p, (v^2) = \frac{1}{3}v_0^2$ is the mean square velocity]. The initial positions were chosen to be equally spaced. During the first plasma oscillation, Debye shielding clouds develop around each of the particles. The formation of these clouds requires some energy, and as a result there is a short period of rapid adjustment that rounds off the corners of the distribution. After this initial adjustment, the distribution evolves very slowly. Figure 4 shows the time development of the velocity distribution for the case

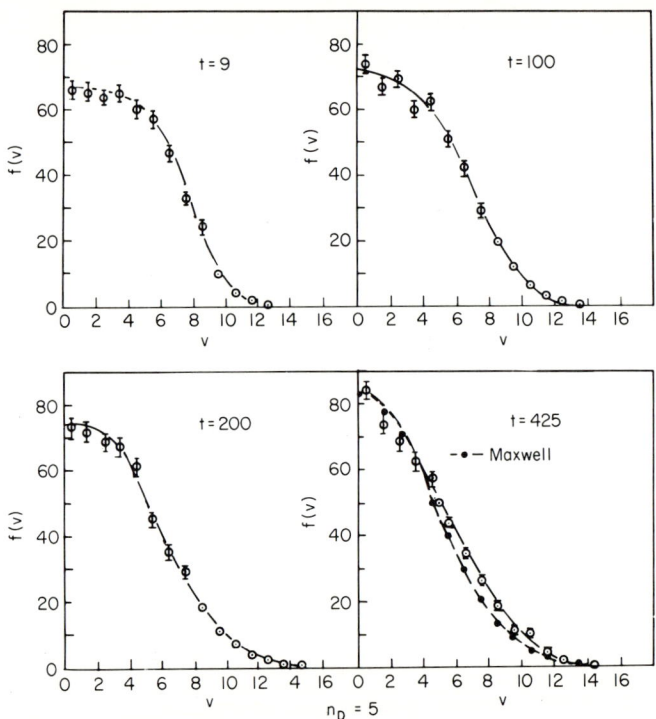

FIG. 4. Time development of π dia.

of 5 particles per Debye length. The first figure shows the situation just after the transient; the other figures show how the distribution evolves toward a Maxwellian. It is essentially reached by $\omega_p t = 425$. This time is much longer than the time required for a group of singled-out particles to acquire the background distribution; this latter time is only $10\,\omega_p^{-1}$.

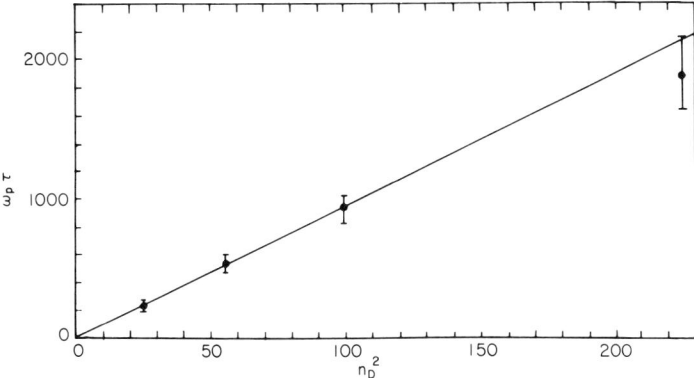

FIG. 5. Relaxation time vs $(n\lambda_D)^2$.

Figure 5 shows a plot of the relaxation time vs $(n\lambda_D)^2$ as determined from such calculations. We see that the relaxation time is proportional to $(n\lambda_D)^2$. This indicates that the simultaneous interaction of three particles gives rise to the relaxation, since the relaxation time due to two-particle interactions would be proportional to $n\lambda_D$ if it did not cancel out. At the present time, there is no theoretical calculation that predicts this relaxation, although it is possible to estimate a relaxation time that is of the right order of magnitude from the emission and absorption of waves by particle encounters.

One interesting point which was found was that the distribution function undergoes rapid random fluctuations about a mean distribution which gradually drifts toward a Maxwellian. The fluctuations in the number of particles with velocities in a small range about zero are shown in Fig. 6. The rapid

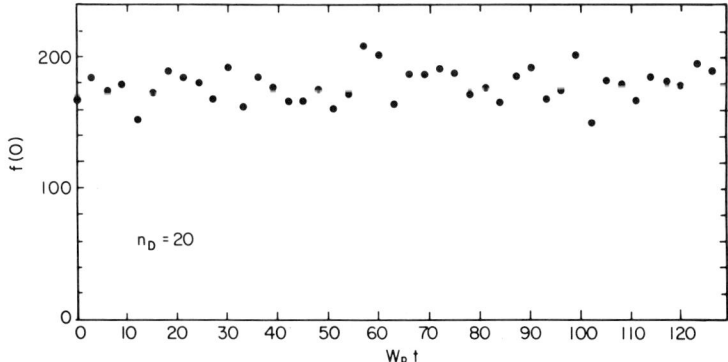

FIG. 6. Fluctuation in $f(v)$.

fluctuations are clearly visible. These fluctuations result from the constant exchange of energy between the electric field and the particle kinetic energy. Although this exchange is constantly going on, it is such that it produces very little systematic change. This shows that the fact that the distribution relaxes slowly results from a very subtle balance, and thus the calculation provides an important test of the kinetic theory of plasmas.

E. Collisional Emission and Absorption of Longitudinal Waves

In the last section we saw that two-particle encounters do not alter the distribution function for a one-species, one-dimensional plasma, and that the actual relaxation of the distribution to a Maxwellian is very slow indeed. One might conclude from this that collisional effects will be of no importance to sheet model calculations. However, this is not so, since collisions can affect one quantity differently from another. During the course of investigations on the sheet model, this was indeed found to be the case. An important example is that of collisional emission and absorption of longitudinal waves.

When two charged particles encounter each other, their mutual acceleration gives rise to the emission of electromagnetic waves. Likewise, the acceleration also leads to the emission of longitudinal waves. This emission of longitudinal waves can also take place in a one-species, one-dimensional plasma.

One might ask: If two-particle encounters in the sheet model do not lead to thermalization of a distribution function, how can they lead to the emission and absorption of plasma waves? The answer is the following. The lack of relaxation due to two-particle encounters was a consequence of the conservation of energy and momentum. For the case of emission and absorption of a wave a third element is present—the wave—which also contains energy and momentum, and so the conservation laws no longer fully determine the outcome. A theory for the emission of longitudinal waves has been developed (Birmingham *et al.*, 1965, 1966) which involves the acceleration of two particles and their shielding clouds when they encounter each other This theory is essentially identical to the theory used to describe weak turbulence in a plasma. Thus, a check of this theory of wave emission also provides a check of weak turbulence theory, at least for the low levels of waves that are encountered here.

The theory for the emission of longitudinal waves was checked on the one-species sheet model (Dawson *et al.*, 1969). The emission encountered here is analogous to that from electron–electron collisions (like particle encounters). Figure 7 shows a plot of the emission *vs* wave number (inverse of the wavelength). The curve is the one predicted by theory. The points are those

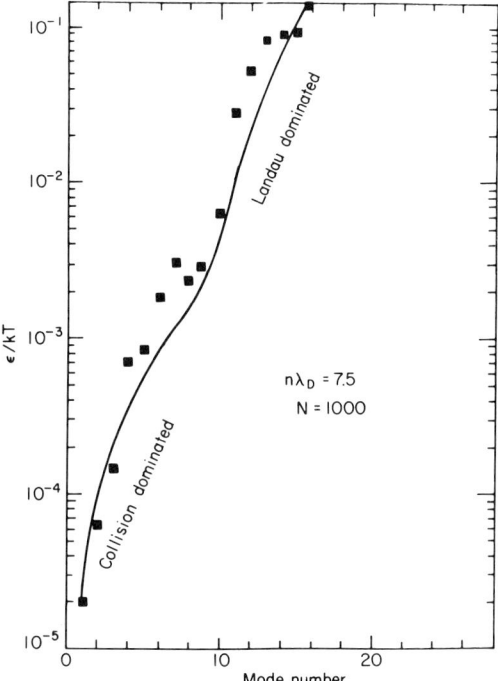

FIG. 7. Emissivity *vs* mode number.

obtained from a numerical experiment on a system of 1000 particles with 7.5 particles per Debye length. The agreement is quite good, the emission varying over three orders of magnitude.

Closely related to the emission of waves due to particle encounters is the absorption of waves due to particle encounters. The collisional absorption of waves may be found from the emission because of the fact that the emission and absorption must lead to thermal equilibrium, where each mode of oscillation has an energy kT. Figure 8 shows a plot of the damping time for waves against wave number (number of wavelengths which fit in the system). The system contained 1000 sheets and had 7.5 particles per Debye length. The solid curve is the theoretical one and is the sum of the two dashed curves marked "collisional damping" and "Landau damping." The collisional damping curve is that predicted by the collisional theory just discussed. The damping that is shown in the curve labeled Landau damping does not have its origin in collisions, but rather arises from the absorption of energy by particles moving at the phase velocity of the wave.

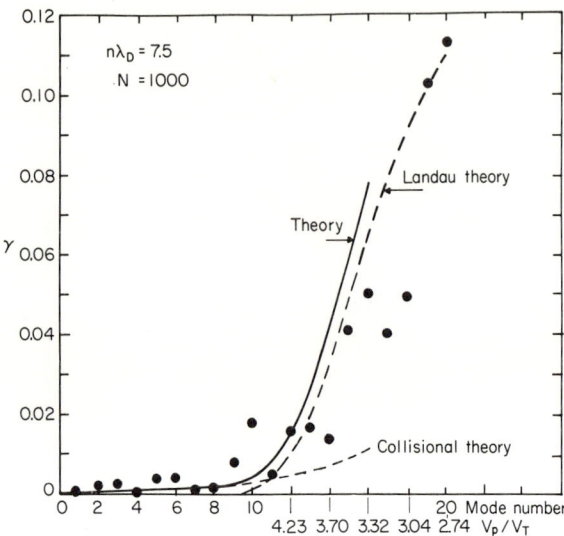

Fig. 8. Damping *vs* mode number.

III. Investigations with Finite-Size Particles

In order to overcome the collisional effects associated with sheets, some alternate models would be useful. Basically, we are not interested in the detailed particle motions, but rather in the gross collective motions which involve many degrees of freedom. It should be possible to model a plasma in such a way that we correctly treat its gross behavior while eliminating the detailed behavior associated with particle encounters.

There have been a number of attacks on this problem. The one which might seem the most straightforward is to solve the Vlasov equation numerically. This has been done and with some success (Kellogg, 1965; Armstrong, 1967; Feix and Grant, 1967; Berk and Roberts, 1967). However, there is a basic difficulty which limits all such approaches to following the motion for a finite time (Armstrong, 1967; Berk and Roberts, 1967). The Vlasov equation really describes a system with an infinite number of degrees of freedom (an infinite number of particles). As long as the distribution function has a relatively simple form, so that it can be described by a few parameters, one can follow its development. However, if the distribution function develops a complex structure so that a large number of parameters (of the order of a few thousand) are required, then the finite size of the computer again becomes a constraint, and we can no longer follow the detailed motion. Since the distribution function generally develops this complex structure (probably for all cases we are interested in doing numerically), this problem cannot be avoided. When this point is reached one must throw away some of the information (one must simplify the distribution function) in order to proceed. Whatever mathematical method one uses to smooth the distribution function, one is never sure of its physical consequence. Such smoothing is somewhat akin to collisions for the discrete particle model. However, it is entirely numerical in nature, depending on the smoothing procedure, and its effects on the results will require analysis (either theoretically or experimentally).

The particle approach to plasma simulation automatically limits the information the machine must handle to that which is required to specify the particle motion. If the enhanced collisional effects can be sufficiently reduced, then this method offers a natural, and physically appealing, method for such limitation. The remaining collisional effects can be understood and taken into account by physical arguments which are already generally well understood.

A number of authors have reduced the collisional effects by smoothing the field due to the particles (Hockney, 1966; Birdsall and Fuss, 1968; Morse, 1968). Hockney has made such smoothing by dividing r space into a number of cells and then computing the fields as if all the particles in one cell were at its center. He ignores the interaction of particles within one cell with each other, thus cutting off the interaction at small distances. Birdsall (Birdsall and Fuss, 1968) has modified Hockney's method by distributing the charge in a cell on its corners. The particle-in-cell method of Morse (1968) is equivalent to Birdsall's charge sharing.

All these methods use a mathematical prescription for smoothing the potential, and this is roughly equivalent to smoothing out the interaction for close encounters. However, all these methods suffer from the same difficulty as smoothing the distribution function for the Vlasov calculation: the mathematical smoothing procedure introduces effects whose consequences are not completely understood. One can eliminate such doubts only by a detailed investigation of the model's behavior (both theoretically and experimentally).

The gross behavior presumably does not depend in a critical way on the detailed motions of all the particles. It should be determined by a number of macroscopic parameters. The number of such parameters may be large, but it should be much less than the number of particles. If this is not true, then we have no hope of describing the plasma. If this is true then there should be a method for keeping the essential information and eliminating the great mass of details which are unimportant. The particle-in-cell method achieves this by using a finite number of particles and of cells.

A. THE FINITE-SIZE PARTICLE MODEL

We have started another approach to this problem. Since we are primarily interested in the long-wavelength collective motions of the plasma, we should keep only these modes in the calculation. Thus, we should keep only Fourier modes with wavelengths longer than some minimum wavelengths. This can be done simply by dropping the electric fields for wavelengths shorter than those considered important. Thus, we could take the electric field due to a particle to be given by the finite Fourier sum

$$E(r) = 4\pi\sigma \sum_{k_{min}}^{k_{max}} \frac{i\mathbf{k}}{k^2} \exp[i\mathbf{k} \cdot (\mathbf{r} - \mathbf{r}_i)]. \qquad (24)$$

Here k_{max} and k_{min} are determined by the shortest and longest wavelengths we are interested in, r is the position of the particle, and σ is its charge. Generally k_{max} should be of the order of λ_D^{-1} where λ_D is the Debye length and k_{min} is determined by the size of the system; k_{min} is of the order of R^{-1}, where R is the radius of the system.

Now if we take the electric field to be that given by Eq. (24) then the electric field will have oscillations in it as illustrated in Fig. 9 for the one-

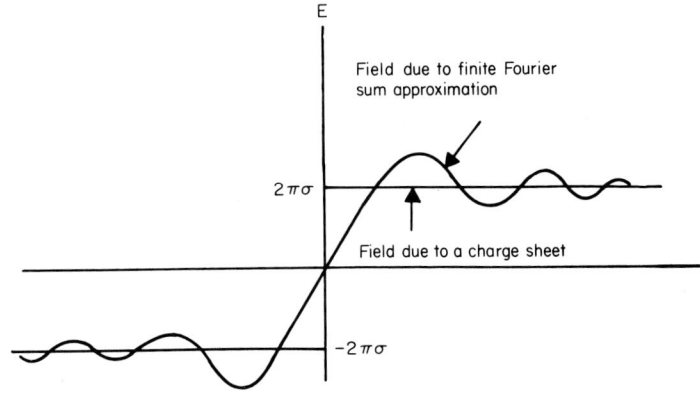

FIG. 9. E field vs x.

dimensional case. Such oscillations of the field are undesirable and can be eliminated (Langdon, 1967). We need not choose the field to be of the form (24) but may take it instead to be of the form

$$E(r) = 4\pi\sigma \sum_{k_{min}}^{k_{max}} \frac{i\mathbf{k}}{k^2} f(k) \exp[i\mathbf{k} \cdot (\mathbf{r} - \mathbf{r}_i)] \qquad (25)$$

where $f(k)$ is a form factor. One appropriate choice of $f(k)$ is $\exp[-k^2 a^2 / 2]$. We now recognize that if k_{max} had been infinite, Eq. (25) would have been the electric field produced by the Gaussian distribution of charge

$$\rho(r) \propto \sigma \exp[-(r - r_i)^2/2a^2]. \tag{26}$$

Thus, Eq. (26) would be the field due to a finite-size particle of dimensions a. If $k_{max}^2 a^2$ is large, then all the terms in the infinite sum for k greater than k_{max} are small, and the finite sum gives an adequate approximation to the field of such a particle. Since the field from such a particle is smooth and does not oscillate, this will be essentially true for the finite sum.

We now restrict ourselves to the one-dimensional case and consider the interaction between particles with charge densities given by

$$\rho(x) = \frac{-\sigma \exp[-(x - x_i)^2/2a^2]}{\sqrt{2\pi} a} \tag{27}$$

where x_i is the position of the center of the cloud and $-\sigma$ is its total charge. Fourier analizing the charge density, we have

$$\rho(k) = \frac{-\sigma \exp[-k^2 a^2/2 + ikx_i]}{\sqrt{2\pi}} \tag{28}$$

while $E(k)$ is given by

$$ikE(k) = \frac{-4\pi\sigma \exp[-(k^2 a^2/2) + ikx_i]}{\sqrt{2\pi}}. \tag{29}$$

The force on particle i due to particle j is given by

$$F_{ij} = \int_{-\infty}^{\infty} E_j(x)\rho_i(x) \, dx$$

$$= \frac{2\sigma^2 i}{\sqrt{2\pi} a} \int dk \, dx \, \frac{\exp[ik(x_j - x) - (k^2 a^2/2) - (x - x_i)^2/2a^2]}{k} \tag{30}$$

$$F_{ij} = 2\sigma^2 i \int \frac{\exp[ik(x_i - x_j) - k^2 a^2]}{k} \, dk. \tag{31}$$

This force has the same functional form as the E field at x_i due to a particle at x_j with half-width $\sqrt{2}a$ and a charge σ.

Now, since we must work with a finite set of terms, we replace the force law by the finite Fourier sum

$$F_{ij} = F_0 \sum_{k_{\min}}^{k_{\max}} \frac{\exp[-k^2 a^2] \sin k(x_j - x_i)}{k} \tag{32}$$

where $k = 2\pi n/L$, n is an integer, L is the length of the system. This force is periodic with period L and is equivalent to considering an infinite set of identical systems end to end. The system is overall neutral because the field is periodic. This is equivalent to having a fixed stationary neutralizing background.

The force on particle i due to all other particles is given by

$$F_i = m\ddot{x}_i = \sum_{k_{\min}}^{k_{\max}} \frac{A \exp[-k^2 a^2]}{k} \left\{ \sin kx_i \sum_j \cos kx_j - \cos kx_i \sum_j \sin kx_j \right\} \tag{33}$$

(the i term may be included in the j sums because there is no self-force of i on itself).

To advance the particle in time, we assume that during a time step the force can be computed as if the particles move with a constant velocity. We further assume that $k_{\max} v_i \Delta t$ is small or that a particle moves only a small fraction of the shortest wavelength considered. Thus, we approximate Eq. (33) by

$$m\ddot{x}_i = \sum_{k_{\min}}^{k_{\max}} \frac{A \exp[-k^2 a^2]}{k} \left\{ [\sin kx_i(t)(1 - \tfrac{1}{2}k^2 v_i^2(t)\tau^2) + kv_i(t)\tau \cos kx_i(t)] \right.$$

$$\cdot \left[\sum_j \cos kx_j(t) \right] - [k\tau \sin kx_i(t) + k^2 v_i \tau^2 \cos kx_i(t)]$$

$$\cdot \left[\sum_j v_j(t) \sin kx_j(t) \right] - [\tfrac{1}{2}k^2\tau^2 \sin kx_i(t)] \cdot \left[\sum_j v_j^2(t) \cos kx_j(t) \right]$$

$$- [\cos kx_i(t)(1 - \tfrac{1}{2}k^2 v_i^2(t)\tau^2) - kv_i(t)\tau \sin kx_i(t)] \cdot [\sum \sin kx_j(t)]$$

$$- [k\tau \cos kx_i(t) - k^2 v_i(t)\tau^2 \sin kx_i(t)] \cdot \left[\sum_j v_j(t) \cos kx_j(t) \right]$$

$$\left. + \tfrac{1}{2}k^2\tau^2 \cos kx_i(t) \sum v_j^2(t) \sin kx_j(t) \right\}. \tag{34}$$

Here t is the time at the beginning of a time step and τ is the time elapsed during the time step; only terms up to second order in τ have been kept. Equation (34) can be integrated to yield the velocity and position of the particles.

Equation (34) looks relatively complex, and one may wonder if we are losing rather than gaining by this technique. In this connection we should note the following. First the sums on j are independent of i and can be evaluated for all particles once and for all. Each sum on j must be evaluated for every k considered. Thus if there are N particles and M modes, we must evaluate αNM terms, where α is a constant of proportionality determined by the number of j sums (there are six in this case). Likewise, in advancing the particles we must evaluate βM terms for each particle which gives βMN terms to find. Thus, the time for the whole calculation is proportional to MN. If we had to compute the particle interactions directly (pair by pair), the calculation would be proportional to $N^2/2$. Thus, if M is much smaller than the number of particles, we gain over direct interaction calculations by this technique. In general, we wish to keep only a few modes, the long-wavelength collective modes which are important to the problems under investigation. Thus, M should be much smaller than N. Furthermore, since the particles must represent the full distribution function in phase space, whereas the modes only have to represent the r space part of the disturbance, we need many more particles than modes.

By including the time dependence of the particle positions in Eq. (34), we complicate the calculation. However, by doing this we greatly improve the accuracy of the method and allow ourselves to take larger time steps which more than compensate for the added computation. Without doing this, energy conservation for the system was very poor. By including it we conserve energy to about one part in 10^3, over times of the order of $100\, \omega_p^{-1}$. We have recently found that by using the leap frog method for positions and velocities, much of the advantage of including the time in this expression is obtained.

For the same number of particles and the number of modes as grid points used in the methods of Hockney (1966), Birdsall (1968), and Morse (1968), the above method is slower (their calculation time scales like $\alpha N + \beta M^2$, where M is the number of grid points). However, it is possible to modify this procedure by using a combination of r space and k space grids so as to make the number of computations proportional to $N + \beta M^2$. We have done some preliminary calculations of this type, and substantial time saving is achieved and the accuracy appears to hold up. Since this method involves following exact dynamics of particles interacting through a modified Coulomb potential, many physical checks on the calculations, such as conservation of energy and momentum, can be applied.

B. Investigations of Fluctuations about Thermal Equilibrium

The first problem we investigated with the finite-size particle model was the fluctuations about thermal equilibrium to see if they behave as expected. Figure 10 shows a plot of the amplitude of the rms electric field fluctuations *vs*

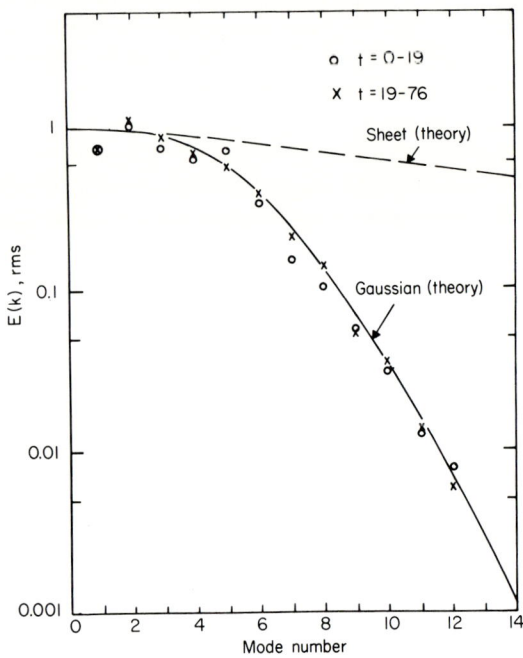

FIG. 10. Rms E field *vs* mode number.

mode number for charge clouds with $a = 2\lambda_D$ (λ_D is the Debye length), and with $k_{max} \lambda_D$ equal to 2. The solid curve is the theoretically predicted curve for Gaussian charge clouds. This curve is predicted from the formula

$$P(E_k)\, dE_k \propto \exp[-\psi_k(E_k)/KT]\, dE_k \tag{35}$$

where $P(E_k)$ is the probability of finding the electric field in dE_k about the value E_k, and ψ_k is the work required to create the fluctuations E_k; ψ_k is given by

$$\psi_k = \frac{E_k^2 L}{16\pi}(1 + k^2 \lambda_D^2 \exp[k^2 a^2]). \tag{36}$$

(L is the length of the system.) The first term on the right is the energy in the electric field, the second term is that required to deform the gas of cloud centers isothermally to the required density fluctuation.

The average value of $E_k^2 L$ obtained from Eqs. (35) and (36)

$$\left\langle \frac{E_k^2 L}{2\pi} \right\rangle = \frac{KT}{2\{1 + k^2 \lambda_D^2 \exp[k^2 a^2]\}}. \tag{37}$$

We see that $\langle E_k^2 \rangle$ is strongly reduced if $k^2 a^2$ is greater than one.

The upper dashed curve in Fig. 10 is that predicted for sheets, i.e., a equals zero. The points are those obtained from the numerical experiment. They agree quite well with the theoretically predicted values. There are some deviations for small mode numbers, but this is most likely due to the fact that the initial conditions do not start these modes out with energy KT, and they take a long time to relax to their thermal value (the averages used here are time averages). As can be seen from Fig. 10, the theoretical fluctuations at long wavelength are hardly affected by the use of finite-size particles, while those at short wavelengths are strongly suppressed as expected. We have run other cases with different values of a and always find similar agreement.

Another interesting thing we can do is derive the dispersion relation for the finite-size particle model. The collisionless Boltzmann equation for these particles is given by

$$\frac{\partial f}{\partial t} + v \frac{\partial f}{\partial x} + \frac{F}{m} \frac{\partial f}{\partial v} = 0 \tag{38}$$

where $f(x, v)$ is the distribution function of cloud centers and velocities. The force on the particles is obtained by integrating $E(\xi)\rho(\xi, x)$ over ξ, x is the position of the center of the charge cloud,

$$F(x) = 4\pi\sigma^2 i \int \frac{dk \exp[-ikx - k^2 a^2]}{\sqrt{2\pi} k} \int f(k, v) \, dv. \tag{39}$$

This is the same expression one obtains for point particles except for the factor $\exp[-k^2 a^2]$. If we linearize Eq. (38) and Fourier analyze Eqs. (38) and (39) in space and time, we obtain

$$f(k, \omega) = \frac{iF(k, \omega) \, \partial f_0/\partial v}{m(\omega + kv - i\varepsilon)} \tag{40}$$

$$kF = 4\pi\sigma^2 \exp[-k^2 a^2] \int f(k, v) \, dv. \tag{41}$$

Here ε is a small damping which has been added to determine the direction of integration around the poles. Substituting Eq. (40) into Eq. (41) we obtain the dispersion relation

$$1 = \frac{4\pi\sigma^2}{mk} \exp[-k^2 a^2] \int \frac{\partial f_0/\partial v \, dv}{(\omega + kv - i\varepsilon)}. \tag{42}$$

This is the same as the usual dispersion relation except for the factor $\exp[-k^2 a^2]$. Thus, the long-wavelength modes are unaffected, while the short-wavelength modes are strongly modified.

C. The Weak Cold Beam for Finite-Size Particles

The second problem we investigated was the instability caused by a weak cold beam passing through a warm plasma. For this experiment, systems containing 1000 particles were used; one fifth of them were in the beam. There were twenty particles per Debye length, the beam was cold and had a velocity of four times thermal velocity (the velocities of all particles are shifted so there is no net current). Runs were made with particles of one half, one, and

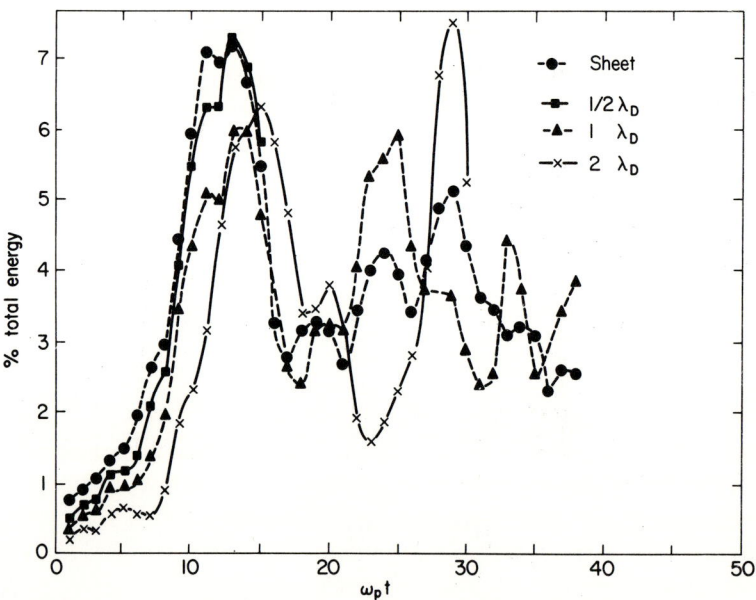

FIG. 11. Electric field energy for two stream instability; comparison for different size particles.

two Debye lengths for their half-widths ($a = 1/2\, \lambda_D$, λ_D, $2\lambda_D$). For all three runs, the initial positions and velocities were the same. A short run was made with the sheet model with identical initial conditions for comparison.

Figure 11 shows plots of the total electric field energy for these four runs. For the sheet case and the 1/2 Debye length particles, there is quite close agreement. For the one Debye length particles, there is still pretty good agreement though some differences appear. However, an appreciable part of this difference can be attributed to the electric field energy in the short-wavelength modes which are suppressed in this case. A rough correction can be made by adding the initial deviation in electric field energy between the $a = \lambda_D$ case and the sheet case, to the $a = \lambda_D$ case. This will ccount for about half the difference at the time of the first peak.

When one comes to the two Debye length size particles, a qualitative change takes place, in that the first peak in the electric field energy is appreciably reduced and shifted to a later time, and the second peak is much larger. This difference is probably due to the fact that the size of the particle affects the growth rate of mode three. Table I lists the growth rates for all four cases for modes 1–4.

TABLE I

GROWTH RATES FOR MODES 1–4 VARIOUS PARTICLE SIZES

a/λ_D	Mode Number			
	1	2	3	4
0	0.163	0.255	0.250	0.148
0.5	0.163	0.255	0.243	0.125
1.0	0.163	0.250	0.220	0.058
2.0	0.162	0.233	0.114	0.002

Figure 12 shows phase space plots of the particle positions for $t = 0$ and $t = 15$. The initial conditions are the same for all cases so that the $t = 0$ plot for $a = \lambda_D/2$ would apply to all cases. The plots for $\lambda_D/2$ and $1\lambda_D$ are strikingly similar, both as to the number of vortexes formed and their shape at $\omega_p t = 15$. For the case of $a = 2\lambda_D$, however, only two vortexes are formed, and thus there is a qualitative difference. This more or less shows that mode three was effectively stabilized by the finite size of the particle, and that this led to the qualitative difference in electric field energy between this case and the others. If more modes had been unstable, say 5 to 10, it is likely that the difference would not have been so great.

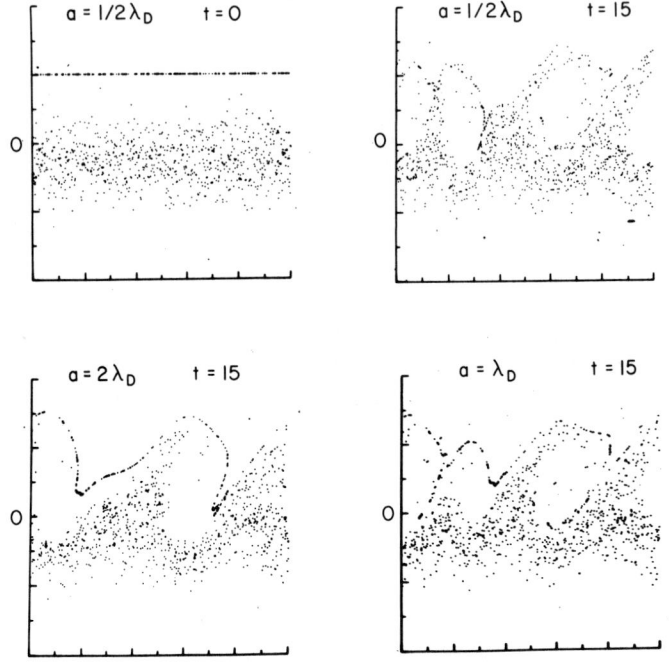

Fig. 12. Vortexes in XV space.

D. Use of Different Size Charges on the Particles

There is one further modification of this model which we have been investigating. Let us imagine that we have a number of species of particles with charges $-Q_\sigma$ and masses M_σ (σ denotes the species). We take Q_σ/M_σ to be the same for all species. Now the Vlasov equations for this system of particles are

$$\frac{\partial f_\sigma}{\partial t} + \mathbf{v} \cdot \frac{\partial f}{\partial \mathbf{r}} - \frac{Q_p}{M_\sigma} \mathbf{E} \cdot \frac{\partial f_\sigma}{\partial \mathbf{v}} = 0 \tag{43}$$

$$\mathbf{\nabla} \cdot \mathbf{E} = -4\pi \left\{ \sum_\sigma Q_\sigma \int f_\sigma \, d\mathbf{v} - en_0 \right\} \tag{44}$$

where en_0 is a fixed uniform neutralizing background (here we are considering point particles, but the whole analysis could be done almost as easily for finite size particle). Now let us define a new distribution function $F(v)$ by

$$F(r, v, t) = \sum_\sigma \frac{Q_\sigma}{e} f_\sigma(r, v, t) \tag{45}$$

where e is some basic smallest charge unit considered. If we multiply Eq. (43) by Q_σ/e and sum over all σ, then we obtain

$$\frac{\partial F}{\partial t} + \mathbf{v} \cdot \frac{\partial F}{\partial \mathbf{v}} - \frac{e}{m} \mathbf{E} \cdot \frac{\partial F}{\partial \mathbf{v}} = 0 \qquad (46)$$

while Eq. (44) is

$$\nabla \cdot \mathbf{E} = -4\pi \left\{ e \int F \, dv - e n_0 \right\}. \qquad (47)$$

These are the usual Vlasov equations for a single species of particles. At the Vlasov level, the system behaves the same as a single species plasma.

Now the advantage of using such a system is that, in many problems, most of the particles form a background medium which oscillates in response to a few particles (for example, a bump in the tail of the distribution function). All the computers time is spent in following the mass of particles which are not doing anything interesting. By the above procedure, we could replace the bulk of the particles by a few hundred particles which have perhaps a charge $100\,e$, while the particles in the interesting regions of phase space might be represented by a few thousand particles with charge e. This gives us the equivalent of many more particles. Before this can be done, collisional effects with the massive particles must be reduced to an acceptable value. Collisional effects are, of course, not included in the Vlasov description. This is where the use of finite size particles will greatly help us. This procedure should also be useful in one, two, and three dimensions. We have carried out some preliminary investigations on this method, and they look promising. However, much more work is required to determine its limitations and strength.

ACKNOWLEDGEMENTS

The author is deeply indebted to efforts of many people who made this article possible. He should particularly like to acknowledge the efforts of Dr. C. Smith, who largely developed the two-species code, the efforts of Drs. C. G. Hsi, R. Shanny, and W. L. Kruer, who developed the finite-size particle model and the multispecies charge model, and the efforts of H. Fallon and the Computing Group of the Princeton Plasma Physics Laboratory, without whose help the calculations could not have been performed.

This work was performed under the auspices of the U.S. Atomic Energy Commission Contract No. AT(30-1)-1238.

Use was made of the computer facilities supported in part by National Science Foundation Grant NSF-GP 579.

REFERENCES

ARMSTRONG, T. P. (1967). *Phys. Fluids* **10**, 1269.
BERK, H. L., and ROBERTS, K. V. (1967). *Phys. Fluids* **10**, 1595.
BIRDSALL, C. K., and FUSS, D. (1968). *Bull. Am. Phys. Soc.* **13**, 283.

BIRMINGHAM, T., DAWSON, J., and OBERMAN, C. (1965). *Phys. Fluids* **8**, 297.
BIRMINGHAM, T., DAWSON, J., and KULSTRUD, R. (1966). *Phys. Fluids* **9**, 2013.
BUNEMAN, O. (1959). *Phys. Rev.* **115**, 503.
BYERS, J., and GREWAL, M. (1968). *Proc. APS Topical Conf. Numerical Simulation of Plasma*, Sept. Paper D3, University of California, Los Alamos, N.M.
DAWSON, J. (1962a). *Phys. Fluids* **5**, 445.
DAWSON, J. (1962b). *Nucl. Fusion*, 1962 *Suppl., Part 3*, 1033.
DAWSON, J. M. (1963). *Phys. Fluids* **7**, 419.
DAWSON, J., SHANNY, R., BIRMINGHAM, T. (1969). *Phys. Fluids* **12**, 687.
ELDRIDGE, O. C., and FEIX, M. (1962). *Phys. Fluids* **5**, 1307.
FEIX, M. R. (1967). *Symp. Comp. Simulation Plasma and Many-Body Problems*, NASA SP-152, p. 3. Williamsburg, Virginia, April 19–21.
FEIX, M. R., and GRANT, F. C. (1967). *Symp. Comp. Simulation Plasma and Many-Body Problems*, NASA Report SP-153, p. 151. Williamsburg, Virginia, April 19–21.
HASEGAWA, A., and BIRDSALL, C. K. (1964). *Phys. Fluids* **7**, 1590.
HOCKNEY, R. W. (1966). *Phys. Fluids* **9**, 1826.
KELLOGG, P. J. (1965). *Phys. Fluids* **8**, 102.
LANGDON B., and DAWSON, J. (1967). *Symp. Comp. Simulation Plasma and Many-Body Problems*, NASA SP-153. Williamsburg, Virginia, April 19–21.
LANGSON, A. B. (1967). This was suggested to the author in a private communication.
MORSE, R. L. (1968). Private communication.
SHANNY, R. A., DAWSON, J. M., and GREENE, J. M. (1962). *Phys. Fluids* **10**, 1281.
SMITH, C., and DAWSON, J. (1963). Princeton University Plasma Physics Laboratory, Report Matt-151.

Solution of Vlasov's Equation by Transform Methods

THOMAS P. ARMSTRONG

UNIVERSITY OF KANSAS, LAWRENCE, KANSAS

ROLLIN C. HARDING

LAWRENCE RADIATION LABORATORY, LIVERMORE, CALIFORNIA

GEORG KNORR

THE UNIVERSITY OF IOWA, IOWA CITY, IOWA

DAVID MONTGOMERY

THE UNIVERSITY OF IOWA, IOWA CITY, IOWA

I. Introduction	30
A. Statement of the Problem	30
B. Computational Difficulties	33
C. Relation to Other Models	34
II. The Fourier–Fourier Expansion	35
A. The Fourier–Fourier Transforms as a Natural Solution to Computational Problems	35
B. Representation; Boundary and Initial Conditions	39
C. Summary of Results	45
D. Questions of Accuracy	53
III. The Fourier–Hermite Expansion	55
A. Representation and Initial Conditions	55
B. Truncation Difficulties	65
C. Modification to Include "Collisions"	69
D. Brief Summary of Results	71
IV. Extension of the Fourier–Hermite Expansion	74
A. The Extension to Include External Fields	74
B. Calculations with Inhomogeneous Equilibria	77
C. Hybrid Models	81
V. Summary and Suggested Future Directions	82
References	84

I. Introduction

A. Statement of the Problem

THERE IS PROBABLY NO BRANCH OF PHYSICS in which it has become clearer that computer methods have an indispensable role to play than in plasma physics. This is because of three facts which have become evident:

(1) The dynamical equations of plasma physics are simple to write down, being essentially the Maxwell equations for electromagnetic variables and classical equations of motion for the mechanical variables.

(2) These dynamical equations, though structurally simple, are impossible to solve analytically, being highly nonlinear and involving infinite numbers of degrees of freedom.

(3) The gross macroscopic behavior of a plasma exhibits a wealth of regularities and collective modes of motion which are often recognizable from numerical data, even though they are difficult or impossible to prove analytically in a satisfying way.

The application of numerical analysis to plasma physics divides itself rather naturally at the outset into two substantially different formulations: we may call them direct-particle *simulation* and the continuum *equation of motion* method.

Simulation proceeds from a model in which the dynamics of discrete charged masses (in one, two, or three dimensions) are followed by solving the individual particle equations of motion. The fields are regularly recalculated from the particle positions and velocities, and the system evolves self-consistently. The majority of numerical calculations on plasmas have been of the simulation variety. These are discussed at length elsewhere in this volume.

A specific example of the *equation of motion* method is what we shall be concerned with in this article. This method proceeds from a point one step removed from the exact microscopic dynamics of the particles, solving instead a set of continuum equations. These continuum equations have been arrived at by some sort of smoothing process in which the distribution of the discrete particles which really make up a plasma has been approximated by some kind of smooth, continuous variable (fluid variable or distribution function). Thus while the equation of motion method performs the averaging first and then computes the dynamical evolution, the simulation approach performs the two operations in the reverse order.

It is of little purpose to advocate one method over the other; each provides information that would be difficult to obtain any other way. In favor of the simulation method is the fact that the discrete particle encounters, which govern all the irreversible physical processes, are represented in a realistic way; this is very hard to do with the continuum descriptions. (Anyone knowledgable in plasma physics has only to imagine the difficulty in following the development of pair correlations, say, from their equations of motion in order to appreciate the content of this statement.) Against this advantage is the fact that the charge in a computer model of a plasma is never so finely subdivided as the charge in a real plasma. One deals with thousands of particles in attempting to simulate systems containing, say, 10^{17} or 10^{18}. This fact has the consequence that the "noise," or nonsystematic fluctuation in the field quantities (which approaches zero, the more finely subdivided is the charge) is often much larger than the corresponding quantity in a real plasma. If one is not careful, it may get so large as to swamp the supposedly macroscopic, systematic effects that one thinks one is seeing.[1]

The main advantage to the equation of motion method, in our opinion, lies in the fact that it is much easier to make detailed comparisons with analytical theory and such results as may be extracted from it. *Essentially all of analytical plasma theory consists of approximate solutions to continuum equations.* The most useful single function of the equation of motion method may be that of testing and suggesting these analytical approximations.

The system of equations developed in this article consists of *Vlasov's equation* for the electron distribution function $f(x, v, t)$,

$$Df/Dt \equiv \partial f/\partial t + v(\partial f/\partial x) - E(\partial f/\partial v) = 0; \qquad (1)$$

and *Poisson's equation* for the electric field $E(x, t)$,

$$\partial E/\partial x = 1 - \int_{-\infty}^{\infty} f \, dv. \qquad (2)$$

This pair of equations is a highly idealized description of a plasma under the following assumptions and approximations:

(1) The positive ions (present in all plasmas) are taken to be immobile and uniformly distributed;

(2) the negative charges (electrons) are assumed to be subdivided infinitely finely, with constant charge-to-mass ratio and charge per unit volume;

---

[1] An example from the theory of a one-dimensional sheet plasma might be in order. The statistical theory of an equilibrium one-dimensional plasma shows that the ratio of mean-square fluctuation in the electrostatic plasma field to the thermal energy density is of the order of the so-called "plasma parameter." For a laboratory plasma, this is usually as small as, say, 10^{-4} or 10^{-5}; in sheet model simulations, it has usually been of the order of 1/20 or so.

(3) all disturbances of the plasma from the spatially uniform state are one-dimensional;

(4) only electrostatic forces between the charges are taken into account.

For convenience, all quantities in these two equations are displayed in natural dimensionless units.[2] The basic unit of time t and velocity v are the reciprocal of the so-called electron plasma frequency ω_p and the electron thermal velocity. Lengths x are measured in units of the ratio of these, the so-called Debye length. The electron distribution $f = f(x, v, t)$ and electric field $E = E(x, t)$ are also dimensionless. Any graduate-level text in plasma physics (e.g., Montgomery and Tidman, 1964) can be consulted for further discussion of the physical significance of these various quantities; we shall not go deeper into the matter here.

It can be fairly said that a thorough qualitative understanding of the solutions of Eqs. (1) and (2), subject to various initial and/or boundary conditions, is a necessary, though not sufficient, condition for an understanding of plasma behavior.

By the *initial value problem*, which we shall mainly be concerned with here, we mean that we give $f(x, v, 0)$ (often periodic in x) and compute $f(x, v, t)$ and $E(x, t)$ for $t > 0$. We usually assume no source of charge at $x = \pm\infty$, so that (2) determines $E(x, t)$ uniquely from $f(x, v, t)$. The initial value problem is conceptually simpler than the *boundary value problem* (which we get, roughly, by interchanging the roles of x and t in the initial conditions), so that most of the work has ignored the boundary value problem. It is, however, much in need of attention at this time.

There are various initial configurations for which $E(x, t)$, the electric field, has a tendency to oscillate with decreasing amplitude (Landau, 1946). These configurations are said to be *Landau damped* (for a detailed mathematical treatment, see Saenz, 1965).

In other situations, the integral $\int E^2 \, dx$ has a tendency to oscillate and *grow*. These situations are said to be *unstable*. The unstable $\int E^2 \, dx$ must eventually cease to grow, since the total energy

$$\mathscr{E} = \tfrac{1}{2} \int E^2 \, dx + \tfrac{1}{2} \int f v^2 \, dx \, dv \tag{3}$$

[2] The system before it has been nondimensionalized is:

$$\frac{\partial f}{\partial t} + v \frac{\partial f}{\partial x} - \frac{e}{m} E \frac{\partial f}{\partial v} = 0, \qquad \frac{\partial E}{\partial x} = 4\pi e n_0 (1 - \int f \, dv),$$

where f is the distribution function of electrons (probability per unit x-space per unit v-space) and E is the electric field. n_0 is the average electron and ion density/unit x, $-e$ is the electronic charge, and m is the electronic mass. The nondimensionalization described in the text leads to Eqs. (1) and (2).

is a constant of the motion for Eqs. (1) and (2), and both terms in $\mathscr{E}$ are positive semidefinite.

Perhaps the two most important effects of a physical character to be extracted from Eqs. (1) and (2) are the nonlinear evolution of Landau damping and instabilities. Both phenomena can be predicted from linearized versions of the Vlasov–Poisson system, but both are intrinsically nonlinear.

B. Computational Difficulties

One difficulty more than any other inhibits the application of numerical analysis to Eqs. (1) and (2): the tendency of $f(x, v, t)$ to develop *steep gradients* in the x, v plane as the time t increases. This can be seen as follows. Equation (1) is an expression of the constancy of the electron distribution $f(x, v, t)$ along the particle trajectory $x(\tau), v(\tau)$, defined by

$$\frac{dx(\tau)}{d\tau} = v(\tau), \qquad \frac{dv(\tau)}{d\tau} = -E(x(\tau), \tau). \tag{4}$$

It is a well-known feature of particle motion in a field (E, say) that two points $x_1(\tau), x_2(\tau)$ in general move far apart for large values of τ, even though $x_1(0)$ and $x_2(0)$ lay initially close together. If we prescribe smooth initial values for $f(x, v, 0)$ [in the sense that nearby points in the x, v plane have only slightly differing values of $f(x, v, 0)$], this means that these nearby points will in time move far apart, carrying their initial values of f with them. Similarly, their new near neighbors will in some cases have come from quite different locations and have brought quite different values of f along with them. This implies the existence of increasingly large values of $\partial f/\partial v$, and consequently a need for greater and greater precision in computing f.

This effect is in fact present in the equation for free streaming particles,

$$\partial f/\partial t + v(\partial f/\partial x) = 0;$$

its solution $f(x, v, t) = f(x - vt, v, 0)$ has, by inspection, secularly increasing v derivatives.

In principle, other, subtler effects can also move particles far apart in velocity space. To discuss this point, we need to resolve the electric field $E(x, t)$ into Fourier components ("plane-wave" decomposition), so that

$$\frac{dv(\tau)}{d\tau} = -E(x(\tau), \tau) = -\sum_{k,\omega} E(k, \omega) e^{i[kx(\tau) - \omega \tau]}. \tag{5}$$

Without specifying under what circumstances $E(x, t)$ can be so decomposed, we remark that it follows from a detailed consideration of the orbit theory involved in Eqs. (4) and (5) that particle trajectories are strongly affected only by those Fourier components $E(k, \omega)$ for which v lies within a velocity interval

$$\Delta v \cong \pm 2[E(k, \omega)/k]^{1/2}$$

of the *phase velocity* ω/k. This interval in velocity space is customarily called the *trapping width* of the wave $E(k, \omega)$. Particle orbits can only readily cross that region of v space that is spanned by the overlapping trapping widths of waves. If this region is large, then nearby velocity points can also wander far apart, and large values of $\partial f/\partial x$ are ultimately to be expected as well as large values of $\partial f/\partial v$.

In the numerical calculations performed so far on Eqs. (1) and (2), the large $\partial f/\partial v$ effect has been more important than large $\partial f/\partial x$. But, ultimately, as the spectral representations $E(k, \omega)$ are allowed to become more complex, both problems are expected to come in. There are arguments that for small or moderate departures from spatial uniformity, the $\partial f/\partial v$ limitation will always be the more severe, and as will be seen, we have found it to be so in practice.

C. Relation to Other Models

We have already remarked on the relation to the discrete "simulation" approach. There have been three basic lines of attack on Eqs. (1) and (2) of which we are aware. We may call these the *water bag* model, the *direct* solution, and the *transform* method. The primary purpose of this article is to discuss two *transform* methods of solution. First, however, we shall remark briefly on the first two.

In the *water bag* model, one essentially follows the particle orbits (4), making use of the constancy of f. Some especially convenient initial conditions are assumed: f is assumed initially constant inside a few simple regions of the x, v plane, and zero elsewhere. Since the orbits (4) can never cross, following points on the boundary of these simple regions solves (1) completely, for f retains its initial value and remains zero outside. (Poisson's equation is simple enough in one dimension that it is not difficult to recalculate E at each step.) This method has been used by Nielsen et al. (1959), by DePackh (1962), and by Berk and Roberts (1967a,b, and this volume). Its advantages are considerable information per computing dollar and conceptual simplicity. Its disadvantages are that the aforementioned steep phase-space gradients develop and the boundaries of the phase space regions rapidly become ragged. It is difficult to argue that they can be systematically smoothed without destroying the accuracy of the calculation. One is restricted mostly to phenomena in which the interesting physics occurs during the first few plasma periods.

The only *direct solutions* of which we are aware are due to Knorr (1961) and Kellogg (1965). Kellogg's computation assumes mobile ions and follows both Vlasov equations directly on an x, v grid. It is difficult to assess the utility of this method, since similar problems have not been considered by either of of the other methods to our knowledge. The tendency towards steep gradients of f results in numerical instabilities which are not easy to overcome. Further work is needed in order to validate this method.

The *transform method* is motivated partially by an attempt to eliminate partial differentiation in favor of algebraic operations in (1) and (2). Both $\partial/\partial x$ derivatives can be eliminated by a Fourier transformation in x. Two different transformations in v have been used: the Fourier transform in v and the Hermite (Gram–Charlier) transform in v. The details of these two approaches are what this article is about.

A brief outline of the rest of the article follows. In Section II, the Fourier–Fourier transformation scheme due to Knorr (1963a,b) is presented. In Section III, the Fourier–Hermite transformation scheme originated by Armstrong (1966, 1967) and Armstrong and Montgomery (1967, 1968, 1969) is discussed. Section IV concerns a generalization of the Armstrong scheme due to Harding (1968a,b) to include *external* electric fields in the problem.

The relevance of the Fourier–Hermite transformation to the Vlasov–Poisson system was discovered independently and explored by Grant and Feix (1967a,b) and by Sadowski (1967). For further numerical computations along these lines, see also the reference list at the end of this article.

II. The Fourier–Fourier Expansion

A. The Fourier–Fourier Transforms as the Natural Solution to Computational Problems

As has been mentioned in Section I, the usual difference methods, when applied directly to the Vlasov equation break down after a few plasma periods. We want to look now somewhat more closely into the reasons for this failure because the Fourier–Fourier transform is a rather simple and straightforward artifice to avoid this breakdown.

First of all, we have made the Vlasov equation dimensionless by introducing ω_p^{-1} as the time scale where $\omega_p = (4\pi e^2 n_0/m)^{1/2}$ is the plasma frequency. If in addition we choose some thermal velocity as unit for the velocities, the scaling length becomes $v_{th} \omega_p^{-1} = \lambda_d$, which is just the "Debye length." The electric field is then measured in units of $4\pi e n_0 \lambda_d$.

In these dimensionless units, we can write our basic equation, describing an electron plasma and a homogeneous, smeared-out ion background as in Eqs. (1) and (2). The distribution function f is normalized to unity such that

$$\frac{1}{L}\int_0^L dx \int_{-\infty}^{+\infty} dv\, f(x, v, t) = 1 \tag{6}$$

where L is the length of the plasma considered.

For our purpose of demonstrating the inadequacy of the conventional computing methods, it is already sufficient to consider the linearized version of Eqs. (1) and (2):

$$\frac{\partial f_1}{\partial t} + v \frac{\partial f_1}{\partial x} - E_1(x, t) \frac{\partial f_0(v)}{\partial v} = 0,$$

$$\frac{\partial E_1(x, t)}{\partial x} = -\int_{-\infty}^{+\infty} f_1(x, v, t)\, dv. \tag{7}$$

In deriving Eq. (7), we have assumed that $f(x, v, t) = f_0(v) + f_1(x, v, t)$, $E = E_1(x, t)$, and neglected terms of second order in f_1, E_1. Because the system (7) is linear, we may now introduce an explicit space dependence

$$\begin{Bmatrix} f_1(x, v, t) \\ E_1(x, t) \end{Bmatrix} = \begin{Bmatrix} f_k(v, t) \\ E_k(t) \end{Bmatrix} e^{ikx},$$

which reduces our system to the form:

$$\frac{\partial f_k}{\partial t} + ikv f_k - E_k \frac{\partial f_0(v)}{\partial v} = 0, \qquad ikE_k(t) = -\int_{-\infty}^{+\infty} f_k(v, t)\, dv. \tag{8}$$

We can now immediately write down a formal solution for the distribution function f_k, which is given by

$$f_k(v, t) = \int_0^t e^{-ikv(t-t')} E_k(t') \frac{\partial f_0}{\partial v}\, dt' + g_k(v) e^{-ikvt}. \tag{9}$$

The second term clearly represents the initial conditions. $g_k(v)$ must be a function the moments of which exist. When we take any moments of f_k to arrive at macroscopic quantities, such as density, momentum, etc., the Riemann–Lebesgue lemma assures us that

$$\lim_{kt \to \infty} \int_{-\infty}^{+\infty} dv\, v^n g_k(v) e^{-ikvt} = 0.$$

If $g_k(v)$ is a holomorphic function which goes to zero exponentially for large v, the integral goes to zero even exponentially fast (compare Titchmarsh, 1937). If we take for $g_k(v)$ an entire function which is regular in the whole complex plane, the integral will go to zero faster than exponentially for large kt. This is, for example, the case for a Maxwellian.

Because of this behavior, the term is omitted in the usual applications. However, it is seen from Eq. (9) that this term is in no way small compared with the first term. This is certainly so for small times; for stable plasmas, for which the electric field does not grow exponentially, this statement holds for all times.

An experimental proof that this term actually represents a real phenomenon has been given by the detection of echo effects (Gould *et al.*, 1967; O'Neil and Gould, 1968). For general reference, the reader is referred to Backus (1960).

Furthermore, it must be recalled that this term determines the overall asymptotic nature of the solution for large times. Only if $g(v)$ satisfies certain conditions of analyticity may we expect an exponential decay or growth of the Landau type for the electric field. If these conditions of "smoothness" are not satisfied, then the solution may display almost any behavior (Weitzner, 1963, 1964).

That Landau damping (or exponential growth in the case of an instability) is by no means the general behavior of the solution can be seen without any mathematics by the following reasoning: Assume that we have computed the solution of Eqs. (1) and (2) up to some time T and also assume that this solution exhibits an exponential decay of the electric field. We use now the resulting distribution at $t = T$ with all velocities reversed as a new initial condition for a new run effectively reversing the time. The result will be that we find now an exponential growth of the electric field until we come to $t = T$. Then the growth will flatten off and will change over into an exponential decay. The reason for this behavior is, of course, that the Vlasov equation in its original as well as in its linearized form is invariant with respect to a reversal in time and velocity. Thus, the second run is just the inverse of the first run.

Not only in analytic theory, but also in numerical computation does the second term on the right side of Eq. (9), which represents the initial conditions, prove itself a trouble-maker. It has already been said that its absolute value is comparable to the first term on the right-hand side of Eq. (9). It represents oscillations of frequency kt in velocity space. If we try to represent the distribution function by its numerical values in a grid in x, v space with spacings Δx and Δv, then these oscillations will be quite inadequately described by, say, six points per oscillation.

In order to describe the distribution function in velocity space, we have to extend the domain in v to, say, four times the thermal velocity, so that $-4 \leq v \leq +4$. Also assume that we have $N = 200$ points available in that interval. Then we find that $\Delta v = 1/25$.

It follows that after time $t/2\pi = 1/(6\Delta vk)$, the result of the computation must deteriorate because the oscillations can no longer be adequately represented by the grid.

In numerical computations concerned with Landau damping, one is quite constrained in the available wavenumbers. If we choose them too small, the damping will be unnoticeable during a time of about 100 plasma periods. On the other hand, if we choose k large, Landau damping will be very strong, and the electric field will decay too fast. So the computations confine the range of k to $\frac{1}{4} \leq k \leq \frac{1}{2}$.

For $k = \frac{1}{2}$ we find $t/2\pi = 8$. This means that after eight plasma oscillations the numerical solution will no longer describe the solution of the Vlasov equation. This failure has been experienced by several authors (Knorr, 1961; Kellogg, 1965). If it were possible to transform the Vlasov equation from x, v space into some other coordinates, such that in the new coordinates the initial conditions do not exhibit an oscillation with a frequency increasing in time, it would be much easier to cope with a numerical integration of the Vlasov equation.

Such a transformation does indeed exist. It is a Fourier transformation in velocity space.

Assume for simplicity that $g(v)$ has the form $g(v) = (2\pi)^{-1/2} \exp(-v^2/2)$. Then the second term in (9) transforms into

$$\int_{-\infty}^{+\infty} g(v) \exp(iktv + iyv)\, dv = \exp[-\tfrac{1}{2}(kt + y)^2]. \tag{10}$$

Clearly, the oscillatory character has disappeared altogether. The result is a smooth Gaussian, the center of which is located at $y_0 = -kt$. We are facing now another difficulty, however, if we want to represent this term numerically. We can only represent a finite interval in y, say $-y_{\max} \leq y \leq y_{\max}$. After a time $t = y_{\max}/k$, we shall have lost an appreciable fraction of the information about this term because it will have disappeared from our computing matrix. There is, however, an important difference: It is true that we lose information about this term after some time, but this does not ruin the computation of the other terms. It has been seen that in linear theory the term in question becomes unimportant after some time when we compute macroscopic quantities. So we may hope that also in nonlinear theory the neglect of this term for large times is not too stringent. However, care must be taken: If we intend to compute echo effects, we must choose $y_{\max}$ large enough so that the term remains well represented during the time the echoes occur.

B. Representation; Boundary and Initial Conditions

1. *Representation*

For the purpose of studying wave propagation in infinite and finite plasmas it is convenient to decompose Eq. (1) first into a Fourier series in x. We write:

$$f(x, v, t) = \sum_{n=-\infty}^{+\infty} f_n(v, t) \exp(ink_0 x),$$

$$E(x, t) = \sum_{n=-\infty}^{+\infty} E_n(t) \exp(ink_0 x). \tag{11}$$

The f_n and E_n are obtained by the inversion formulas:

$$f_n(v, t) = \frac{1}{L} \int_0^L f(v, x, t) \exp(-ik_0 nx)\, dx, \qquad k_0 = \frac{2\pi}{L},$$

$$E_n(t) = \frac{1}{L} \int_0^L E(x, t) \exp(-ik_0 nx)\, dx, \qquad n = 0, \pm 1, \pm 2 \cdots.$$

When we insert these equations into Eq. (1), we obtain:

$$\frac{\partial}{\partial t} f_n(v, t) + ink_0 v f_n - \sum_{q=-\infty}^{+\infty} E_q \frac{\partial}{\partial v} f_{n-q}(v, t) = 0. \tag{12}$$

Poisson's equation and the second Maxwell's equation take the form:

$$-ink_0 E_n(t) = \int_{-\infty}^{+\infty} f_n\, dv; \qquad -\frac{\partial}{\partial t} E_n(t) = \int_{-\infty}^{+\infty} v f_n\, dv. \tag{13}$$

This representation is perfect for a bounded plasma; for an infinite plasma, however, it is an approximation because we always have to settle for a minimum wavenumber k_0. This, however, turns out to be no serious restraint. Another point of minor importance is that all E_n for $n \neq 0$ are uniquely determined; not however E_0. E_0 represents the instantaneous average electric field in the plasma. For an infinite plasma this is caused by charge accumulation at $\pm$ infinity; for a finite plasma it is caused by external boundary conditions. (An example would be a plasma in a condenser when a potential difference is maintained between the condenser plates.)

From now on we consistently put $E_0 = 0$. With this condition our system is completely equivalent to Eqs. (1) and (2).

We now apply the Fourier transform in v, defined by the relations:

$$F_n(y, t) = \int_{-\infty}^{+\infty} f_n(v, t) \exp(ivy)\, dv,$$

$$f_n^i(v, t) = \int_{-\infty}^{+\infty} F_n(y, t) \exp(-ivy)\, \frac{dy}{2\pi}.$$

The Vlasov equation takes now the form:

$$\frac{\partial F_n(y, t)}{\partial t} + nk_0 \frac{\partial F_n(y, t)}{\partial y} + iy \sum_{-\infty}^{+\infty} E_q(t) F_{n-q}(y, t) = 0. \tag{14}$$

Poisson's equation and the second Maxwell's equation become:

$$-ink_0 E_n(t) = F_n(0, t); \qquad \frac{\partial}{\partial t} E_n(t) = +i \frac{\partial}{\partial y} F_n(0, t). \tag{15}$$

An advantage of the Fourier–Fourier transform (and of the Fourier–Hermite expansion as well) is that the integral over the distribution function in Poisson's equation disappears and there remains only an algebraic relation between E and F.

We can represent the transformed distribution function $F_n(y, t)$ by a matrix; n characterizes the rows and the discretized y the columns of the matrix. Equation (15) tells us that the density and electric field are given by the column vector $y = 0$ of the F matrix.

It is convenient for the numerical procedure to introduce $w = k_0^{-1} y$ instead of y, and to combine Eq. (14) and Poisson's equation:

$$\frac{\partial}{\partial t} F_n(w, t) + n \frac{\partial}{\partial w} F_n(w, t) = w \sum_{q=-\infty}^{+\infty} \frac{1}{q} F_q(0, t) F_{n-q}(w, t). \tag{16}$$

This is our final system which will be programmed.

The characteristics of Eq. (16) are straight lines with a slope $1/n$ (the time axis pointing upward):

$$t - t' = (1/n)(w - w').$$

We may integrate along these characteristics and obtain a formal solution for F_n:

$F_n(w, t)$

$$= F_n(w - nt, 0) + \sum_{q=-\infty}^{+\infty} \int_0^t (w - ns) q^{-1} F_q(0, t - s) F_{n-q}(w - ns, t - s) \, ds. \quad (17)$$

If we forget for the moment about the sum term, we see that the shape of $F_n(w, t)$ is the same as for $t = 0$, but displaced along the w axis. If in a numerical program we make the time step $\Delta t = \Delta w$, then this displacement can be performed exactly numerically. In other words, we have integrated the first two terms of Eq. (16) exactly. What is left is to find a suitable numerical routine for the sum terms in Eq. (17).

As the characteristics of Eq. (16) run out of the areas of known quantities, the first set of values for $t + \Delta t$ has to be obtained by extrapolation. In an iterative step values are improved so that the truncation error becomes $O[(\Delta t)^2]$.

It is perhaps worthwhile to remark that these computations were performed on a computer with a total storage capacity of only 4000 words for both program and storage space. Utmost economy was mandatory and only programs with one matrix $F_n(w, t_0)$ stored at a time could be considered.

$F_n(w, t)$ is in general complex and when programming, we have to split up Eq. (16) into its real and imaginary part. As $f(x, v, t)$ is real, there is a reality condition for F_n:

$$F_n(w, t) = F^*_{-n}(-w, t); \quad (18)$$

it is thus possible to eliminate the imaginary part of F_n when we compute the real part of F_n for positive and negative n and w.

The fact that $f(x, v, t)$ is positive definite can be represented only as a very complicated condition on the characteristic function (Cramér, 1966), and so far no use of the condition in numerical computations seems to have been made.

It should be noted that the use of a Fourier transform in all variables of a probability distribution is well known in mathematical statistics. It is called there "the characteristic function." It derives its importance from the fact that the characteristic function of a sum of independent random variables is equal to the product of their characteristic functions.

The application to the numerical computation of distribution functions, however, seems to have been a novelty when it was first done in 1963.

2. *Conservation Laws*

The system (1) and (2) is a conservative system for which certain conservation laws hold. The most important are conservation of particle number, momentum, and energy.

The constancy of particle number is expressed by

$$\frac{\partial}{\partial t} F_0(0, t) = 0, \quad \text{or} \quad F_0(0, t) = 1, \tag{19}$$

which is obtained from Eq. (16) for $w = 0$ and $n = 0$.

When we differentiate Eq. (16) with respect to w, we find for $w = 0$ and $n = 0$, because of the symmetry of the sum:

$$\frac{\partial}{\partial t} \frac{\partial}{\partial w} F_0(w, t)\big|_{w=0} = 0, \tag{20}$$

which is the conservation of momentum.

When we finally differentiate Eq. (16) twice with respect to w and make use of the relations in Eq. (15), we find:

$$\frac{\partial}{\partial t} \left[-\frac{1}{2} k_0^2 \frac{\partial^2 F(w, t)}{\partial w^2}\bigg|_{w=0} + \sum_{n=1}^{\infty} E_n(t)^2 \right] = 0. \tag{21}$$

The first term is the kinetic energy of the particles and the second is the energy in the electric field.

3. Truncation

The sum in Eq. (16) or Eq. (17) extends from minus to plus infinity and the question arises as to what error is introduced if the sum is truncated. Assume that we have neglected all terms with $n \geq N + 1$ and that we have the relation $F_n = O(\varepsilon^n)$, either as the initial condition or for some later time.

The interaction term

$$\sum_{q=-\infty}^{+\infty} (w/q) F_q(0, t) F_{n-q}(w, t)$$

which couples the different modes will then contain terms of the order $\varepsilon^{|n-\nu|+|\nu|}$, i.e., $\varepsilon^{2\nu-n}$ for $\nu > n$. The largest error which will be made comes from the first neglected term for which $\nu = N + 1$. It is of the order ε^{2N+2-n}. Because $F_n = O(\varepsilon^n)$, the relative error with respect to F_n will be $\varepsilon^{2(N+1-n)}$. It is seen that the error increases with the order n of the harmonic and is $O(\varepsilon^2)$ for $n = N$. It has been tacitly assumed that these errors do not accumulate as time goes on and so vitiate the estimate. We can, however, see directly from the numerical results how good our assumptions still are. It turns out that, in most cases, it is sufficient to consider just a few harmonics. It is, for example, easy for stable oscillations to keep the second harmonic always two or even more orders of magnitude below the level of the first harmonic. For unstable cases, the second harmonic was coupled to the first harmonic and exhibited a growth rate twice as large as the first harmonic. Thus, when the instability leveled off it had grown as large as a tenth or a third of the amplitude of the first harmonic. This then indicates that some inaccuracy is introduced by the truncation.

We have to introduce another truncation because of the finiteness of the interval in w. As we have seen above, we shall always have terms which move to the boundary of the matrix and then simply get lost. An example is shown in Fig. 3. This loss of information seems to be an unavoidable feature of the integration of the Vlasov equation. Fortunately, truncation does not introduce any numerical instability. On the other hand, truncation of the matrix in the Fourier–Hermite expansion results in numerical difficulties (compare Section III). The error introduced by this truncation can be determined experimentally and will be dealt with in Section II.D.

4. Boundary Conditions

For a simulation of an infinite plasma, the decomposition of $f(x, v, t)$ into a Fourier series already guarantees periodic boundary conditions. However, $F_n(w, t)$ will be complex. Because of $F_n(-w, t) = F_n^*(w, t)$, the computation can be limited to positive n. Such a scheme has been used to study the nonlinear behavior of single moving waves.

If we are interested in saving computation costs, we can start with symmetric initial conditions:

$$f(x, v, 0) = f(-x, -v, 0). \qquad (22)$$

It is easy to show that then for all later times, the distribution function will retain this symmetry. In F space, Eq. (22) is written as

$$F_n^*(w, t) = F_{-n}(-w, t).$$

This, combined with the reality condition Eq. (18), results in

$$F_n(w, t) = F_n^*(w, t), \quad \text{or} \quad \text{Im } F_n(w, t) = 0.$$

The imaginary part of F is identically zero and we save a factor of two in computation time—apart from facilitating the programming.

We pay for this, however. The symmetry implies that for any wave which is traveling to the right, say, we also have one which is traveling to the left.

If we study an instability of the "bump on the tail" type, we shall always have two bumps on two tails, etc. The electric field will be a standing wave, which will periodically almost vanish. In order to compare the results of such a calculation with simple concepts like trapped particles, etc., it will be necessary to invoke arguments, such as, that two waves are weakly coupled, which are not completely evident in a highly nonlinear regime where the density modulation is large.

The boundary condition at $w = +w_{max}$ has been taken to be simply $F_n(\pm w_{max}, t) = 0$. This seems to be the simplest and best way to deal with problem. All other boundary conditions are likely to induce numerical instabilities.

5. Initial Conditions

Principally, any initial condition which can be represented with adequate accuracy in F space may be used. We give here an enumeration of particular initial conditions which have been used with success.

For stable waves, the symmetric condition

$$f(x, v, 0) = (2\pi)^{-1/2} \exp(-\tfrac{1}{2}v^2)(1 + A \cos k_0 x) \tag{23}$$

describes a standing damped wave. The typical behavior can be seen in Fig. 1(a–d). By using different amplitudes A and wavenumbers k_0, the variation of Landau damping and Landau damping as functions of amplitude and wavelength can be studied.

To study two stream instabilities, one may take two Maxwellians, displaced with respect to each other:

$$\begin{aligned}f(x, v, 0) = &(2\pi)^{-1/2}(1 - A) \exp[-\tfrac{1}{2}(v + v_s)^2] \\ &+ (2\pi)^{-1/2}(A/\sqrt{\sigma}) \exp[-(1/2\sigma)(v + v_s - v_p)^2](1 + \epsilon \cos k_0 x).\end{aligned} \tag{24}$$

f is always normalized.

In this formula, we may vary the ratio of the particle numbers in the two streams given by $(1 - A)/A$, the ratio of the corresponding temperatures $1/\sigma$, and the gap between the two beams in velocity space v_p. v_s is actually a dummy variable, determining only the Galilean frame from which we observe the instability. It can be adjusted in such a way that the electron plasma as a whole is at rest, or that the resulting electric field appears as a standing wave. Note that when the resulting electron current does not vanish, it is compensated automatically by an equal and opposite ion current due to the condition $E_0 = 0$. Moreover, a different v_s was used to check the Galilei invariance of the program (compare Section D).

A typical result is shown in Fig. 4(a) and (b). A more or less large amount of time is spent before the solution grows definitely exponentially. Also the exponential growth is not of real interest, because it is well described by linear theory. One could save computation time if one chose as initial condition a distribution function which corresponds to the linear solution of the problem. One can then save an appreciable portion of the run in Fig. 4 and concentrate on the area where the electric field has reached its maximum.

C. Summary of Results

We first discuss the results concerning the nonlinear damping of stable distributions. Initial condition Eq. (23) has been used throughout. Typical results are shown in Fig. 1(a)–(d). The figures are ordered according to the initial amplitude of the electric field which is given by $E(t=0) = A/k_0$. In Fig. 1(a) we observe Landau damping of the first harmonic which persists unchanged during the time of the computation. This corresponds completely to the linear theory. Increasing the initial field by decreasing k_0 leads to Fig. 1(b). It is seen that now Landau damping has become very weak, illustrating the fact that the range of k in numerical calculations is limited. A close examination of Fig. (1b) shows, however, that the damping decrement seems to decrease. This is borne out more clearly in Fig. 1(c) where, again, $E(t=0)$ has been increased and the damping decrement clearly decreases near $t = 30$.

In Fig. 1(d), we observe the development of a plateau of the electric field. This reminds us of the quasilinear theory (Vedenov et al., 1962; Drummond and Pines, 1964; Bernstein and Engelmann, 1966), where a plateau of the electric field is also obtained. The quasilinear theory deviates in its assumptions drastically from the numerically computed cases discussed here, the most important assumptions being: (1) a continuous wave spectrum, (2) $\gamma/\omega_p \ll 1$, and (3) $\gamma > 0$, i.e., we are dealing with a weak instability.

It should be remarked, however, that an extension of the quasilinear theory to the stable case has been suggested by Bernstein and Engelmann (1966).

All three conditions are not satisfied by the numerical computation, so that detailed comparison is not possible.

The quasilinear theory arrives at a diffusion equation in velocity space for the homogeneous distribution function f_0 which has the effect that f_0 is flattened in the environment of the phase velocity $V_{\rm ph}$ of the wave. For $t \to \infty$, a horizontal plateau of f_0 is predicted for this domain of velocity space. Comparing the numerical results with the quasilinear theory (see Section III), we also observe a flattening of the distribution function, but it is not exactly at the phase velocity and it may be superimposed by a wave-like pattern. On

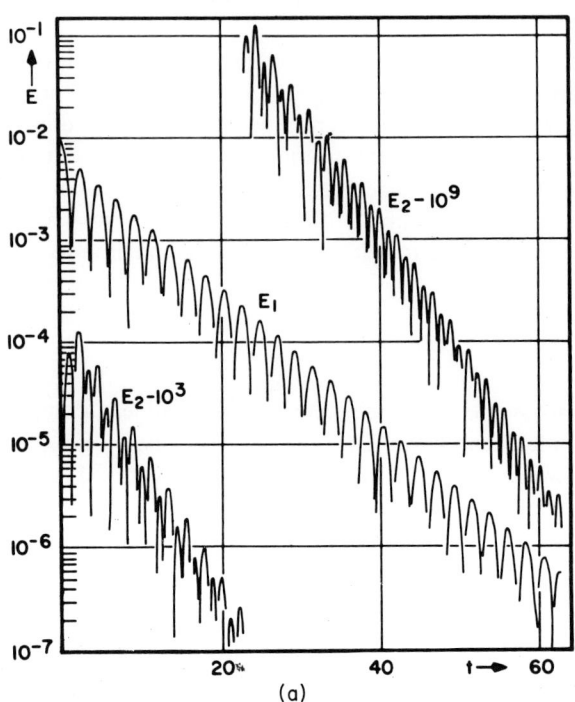

(a)

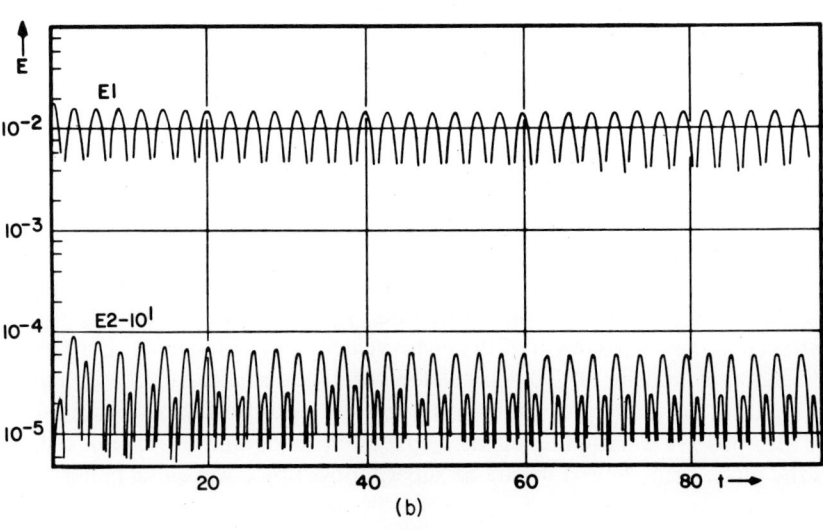

(b)

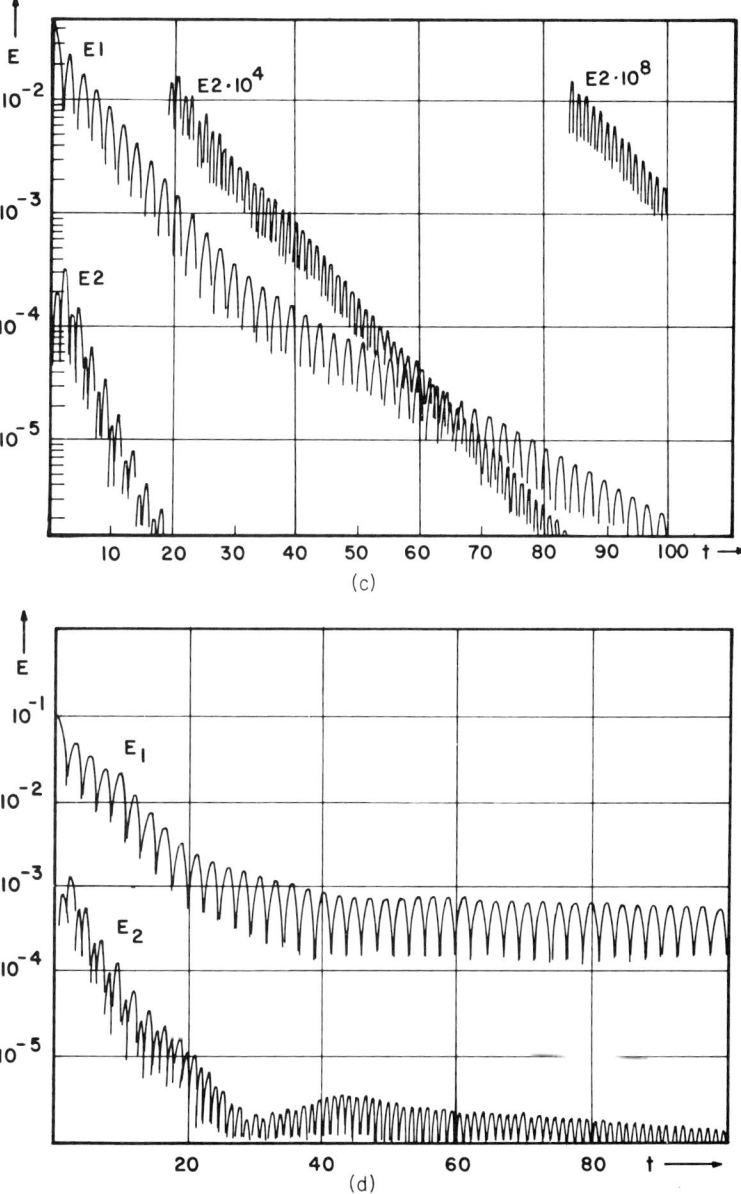

FIG. 1(a)–(d). Electric field (on a logarithmic scale) versus time for a standing stable wave. Wavenumber k and amplitude A refer to the initial conditions of Eq. (23). $E(t=0) = A/k$ is the initial field.

	a	b	c	d
$E(t=0)$	0.02	0.04	0.1	0.2
A	0.01	0.01	0.05	0.1
k	$\frac{1}{2}$	$\frac{1}{4}$	$\frac{1}{2}$	$\frac{1}{2}$

the average, however, it can be seen that the particles close to V_{ph} are accelerated for the stable case and thus take away energy from the wave.

These remarks apply to a weakly unstable plasma where the density modulation is small ($\Delta n/n \ll 1$) and the trapping of particles is not yet important.

For strongly nonlinear cases ($\Delta n/n \sim 1$), we expect a behavior which no longer resembles the quasilinear theory. Such a case is shown in Fig. 2

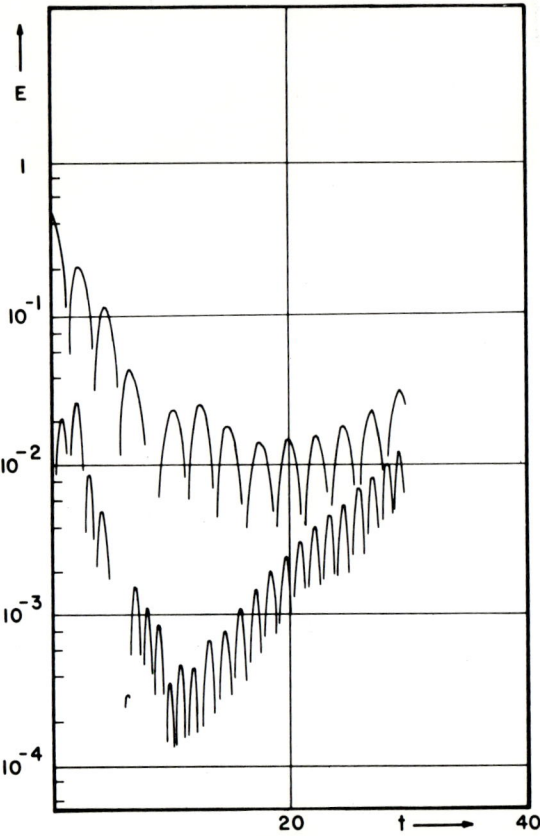

FIG. 2. Strongly nonlinear standing wave. The initial conditions are as in Fig. 1, but $k = \frac{1}{2}$ and $A = \frac{1}{2}$.

where $k = \frac{1}{2}$ and $A = \frac{1}{2}$. The diffusion is so strong that the plasma, so to speak, creates its own instability. Initially, the plasma is strongly damped, but then, after $t = 18$, it starts to grow again. In this case, trapped particles probably play an important role.

A typical plot of the characteristic function is shown in Fig. 3 corresponding to the former case of Fig. 1(d). Figure 3(a) shows the characteristic function

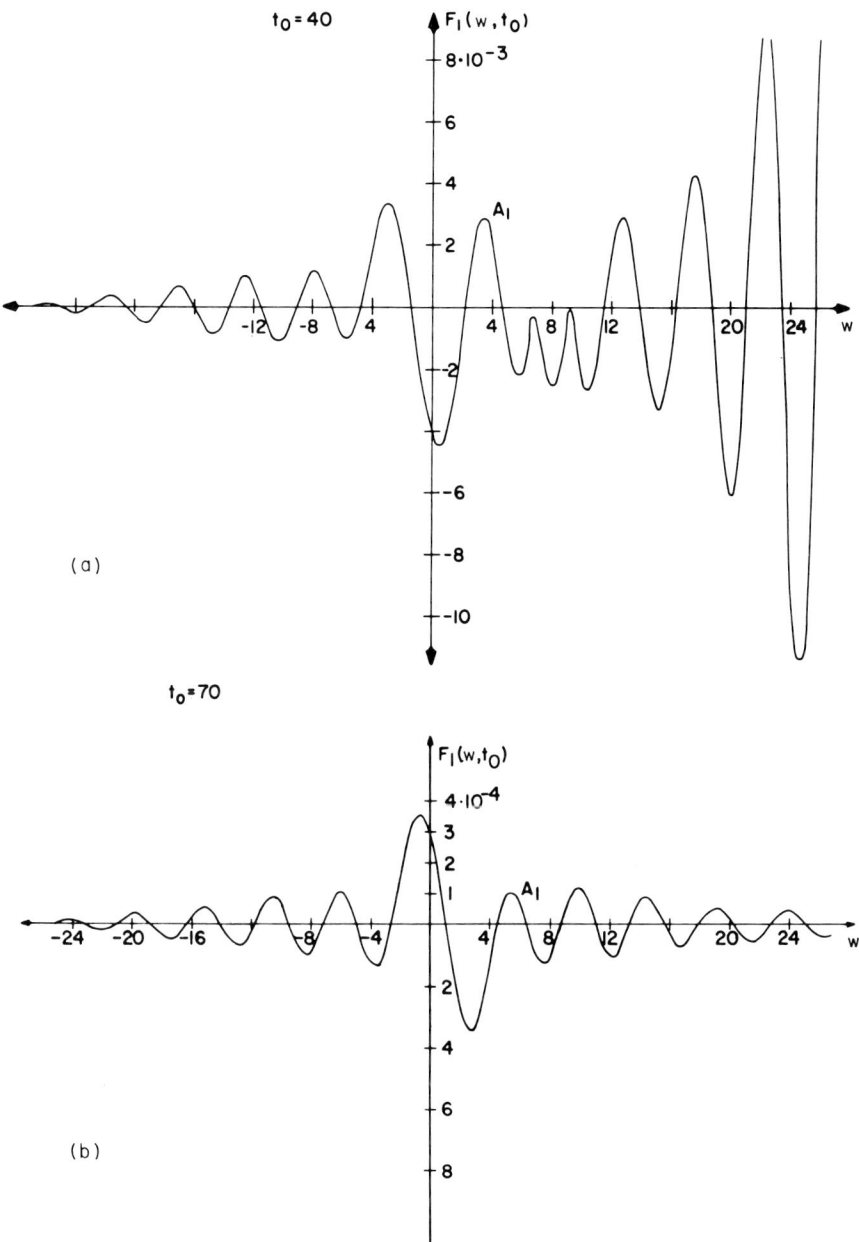

FIG. 3. The characteristic function $F_1(w, t_0)$ for (a) $t_0 = 40$ and (b) $t_0 = 70$. Note that $F_1(0, t_0)$ is proportional to the instantaneous electric field.

of the first harmonic for $t = 40$. We see that the values in the neighborhood of w_{max} are much larger than in the rest of the interval. At $t = 70$, the function has its peak for small w.

The second harmonic is always at least two orders of magnitude smaller than the first, indicating that taking into account only two harmonics is here an excellent approximation for the Vlasov equation. The damping of the second harmonic is about twice as large as the damping of the first harmonic. This shows that the second harmonic is coupled to the first, which is also evident from some analytic considerations (Knorr, 1963a,b). This behavior is, however, contrary to the assumptions of the quasilinear theory, according to which all harmonics are coupled to f_0 only and not to each other.

Figure 4 shows typical behavior for a two-stream instability. It has been created by the initial conditions of Eq. (24). Very clearly, three quite different phases can be distinguished. During the first part, no instability can be discerned. The electric field oscillates more or less randomly. This is the region where many solutions of the linear dispersion function contribute to the electric field. In Fig. 4(a), E_1 drops at $t = 3!$ to an order of magnitude below its initial value.

After some time, a clearly exponential rise sets in. Now the most unstable solution of the dispersion function dominates all others. This growth finally must level off. We see that the electric field fluctuates on a quite high level. It may be called a first approach to a turbulent state of a plasma. At $t = 60$ and after, E_2 has come to within a factor of 3 to the level of E_1. It would have been desirable to have more harmonics available to be assured that the solutions obtained represent exactly the Vlasov equation. The obtained level of the excitation is again given by order of magnitude by the quasilinear theory, as is borne out by a closer examination (Knorr, 1963a).

A look at the plots of the characteristic functions shows that they drop to zero toward the boundaries of w much faster than in the stable case (compare Fig. 5). This is to be expected because now the first term on the right-hand side of Eq. (9) overpowers the second. In Fig. 6 the phases of the first and second harmonics of the electric field are plotted. Because of relation (18), we can write:

$$F_{\pm n}(0, t) = |F_n(0, t)| \exp(\pm i\varphi_n(t)).$$

Combining this and Eqs. (12) and (15), we can write the electric field as:

$$E(x, t) = 2/k_0 \sum_{n=1}^{\infty} |F_n(0, t)/n| \sin[nk_0 x + \varphi_n(t)].$$

Thus, $\varphi_n(t)$ is directly the phase of the electric field. The phase velocity is

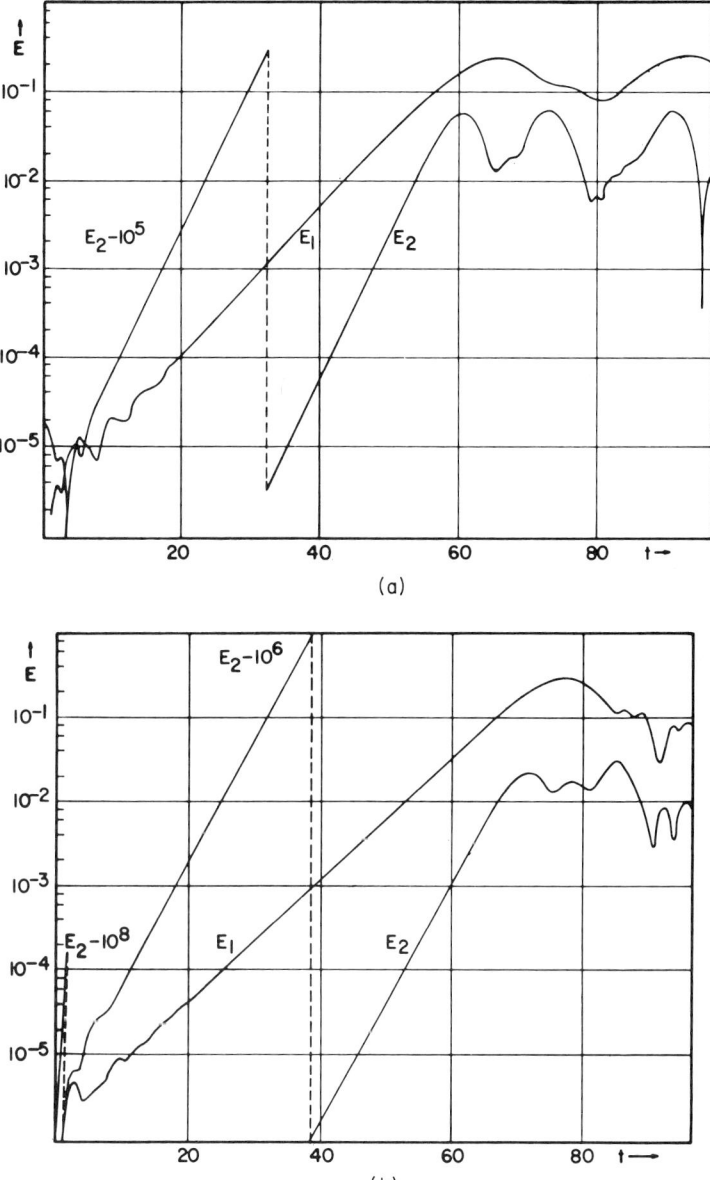

FIG. 4(a) and (b). Plot of the electric field versus time for an unstable initial condition as in Eq. (24). The parameters are:

	a	b
k	$\frac{1}{4}$	$\frac{1}{4}$
A	$\frac{1}{2}$	$\frac{1}{8}$
v_p	4.2	5
σ	1	1

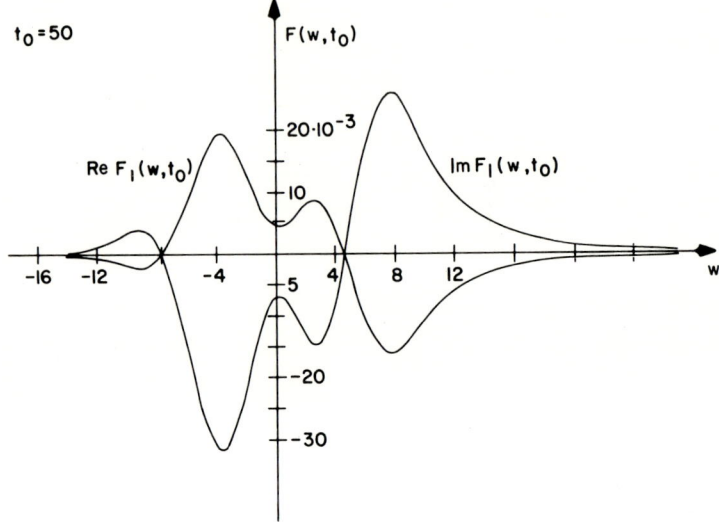

FIG. 5. The characteristic function $F_1(w, t_0)$ for $t_0 = 50$ for the case of Fig. 4(a). Contrary to Fig. 3(a), the function vanishes at all times at the boundaries.

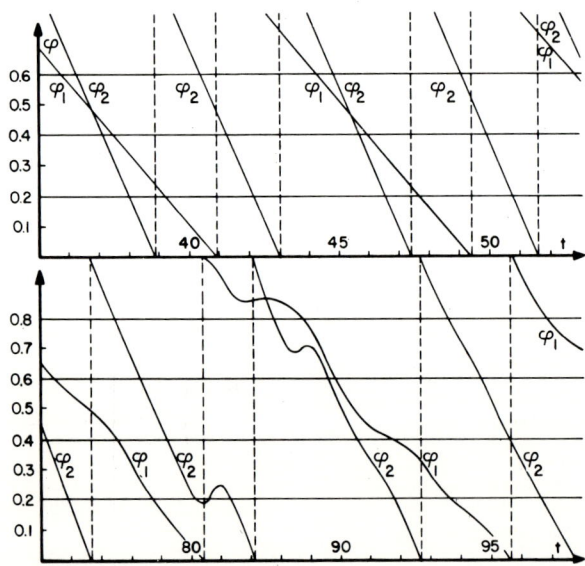

FIG. 6. The phase φ_n of $E_n(x, t) = E_n^0(t) \sin[nk_0 x + \varphi_n(t)]$ for $n = 1, 2$ for an unstable initial condition corresponding to Fig. 4(b).

given by $V = -i\varphi_n(t)/nk_0$. During the period of the exponential growth, φ_1 and φ_2 are linear functions of t as expected from linear theory. For later times ($80 < t < 100$), this is no longer so. After periods where $\varphi_{1,2}$ grow approximately linear with time, there are sudden jerky motions. The phase velocity changes its sign and after about one plasma period returns to its original value. Questions as to how this behavior can perhaps be described as a random process, how it depends on the number of harmonics present in the plasma, and if these effects are caused by trapped particles, have not yet been explored.

D. Questions of Accuracy

As far as questions of accuracy are concerned, it must be kept in mind that the computer program does not represent the full nonlinear Vlasov equation, but a system different from it because the infinite number of harmonics has been truncated. The extent to which the truncated system represents the Vlasov equation has been discussed previously in Section B.

For the remaining question of how accurately the computer program solves the truncated system, there are several tests available:

(1) the choice of different step sizes in time and in w;
(2) time reversal;
(3) use of conservation theorems; and
(4) invariance with respect to Galilei transformations.

(1) When we decrease the finite differences in time and w, the computer solution should converge toward the actual solution of system (16). Also, the conservation of energy should be satisfied better and better. Figure 7 shows three runs where Δt is 0.1, 0.2, and 0.4. The corresponding initial conditions are exactly the same. We observe that the total energy of the electric field is very much the same except for a phase lag for the larger time-steps. The change of the total energy decreases roughly by a factor of 10 when the time-step is reduced by a factor of 2.

(2) The system of Eq. (16) is time reversible. If we change the sign of w, the system should return exactly to its initial condition. Due to the numerical inaccuracies, however, it does not do this. The amount of deviation may then serve as a check of the numerical errors introduced.

It has been seen above that in a numerical integration of the Vlasov equation, there is necessarily associated a loss of information, and we cannot expect the system to return exactly to its initial conditions after a time-reversal. Nevertheless, for not too large times, this method can be used as a very valuable check.

(3) The most extensively used check was the constancy of the energy.

The conservation of particle number is already automatically satisfied by the fact that $F_0(0, t) = 1$ is built into the program. The total energy, however, is the sum of kinetic energy and energy in the electric field and does change in time. Figure 7 shows that for an unstable case, the change in total energy is

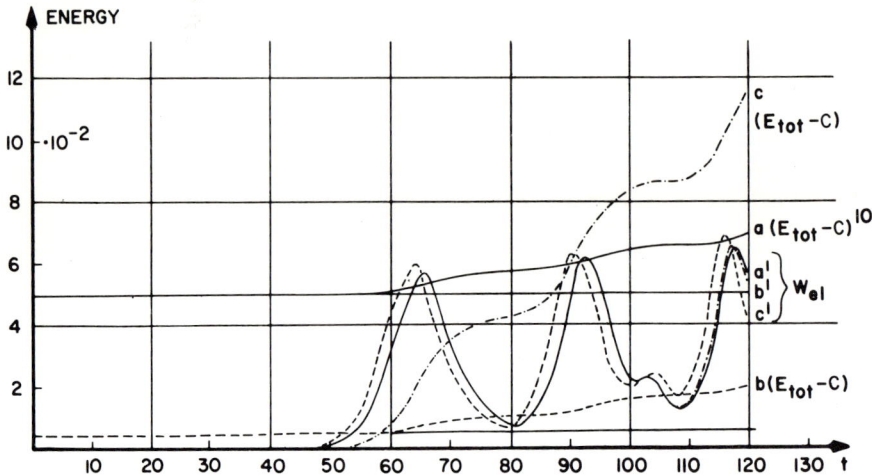

FIG. 7. Plot of the total electric field energy and total energy versus time for three different time-steps. The total energy should remain constant. It is seen that the change in total energy is reduced by roughly a factor of 10 if the time-step Δt is decreased by a factor of 2. To plot the total energy, the constant $C = 2.70$ had to be subtracted. The parameters are:

	a	b	c
Δt	0.1	0.2	0.4

much smaller than the growth of the electric energy which in turn is only a small part of the total energy. We find from Fig. 7 that $\Delta\mathscr{E}/W_{el} = 3.3 \times 10^{-2}$ and $W_{el}/\mathscr{E} = 2 \times 10^{-2}$. $\mathscr{E}$ is the total energy of the system and W_{el} is the peak energy in the electric field.

(4) The use of a Galilei transformation as check of accuracy is based on the following: if we view the plasma at $t = 0$, characterized by $F_n(w, 0)$ from a different Galilean frame moving with speed v_s with respect to the laboratory system, the initial conditions transform into $F_n(w, 0) \exp(iv_s k_0 nw)$. Thus, the computer "sees" a completely different initial condition. The amplitudes of the electric field are invariant and should be the same for both initial conditions. Runs of the same physical initial conditions, but seen from different Galilean frames, showed no difference up to $t = 30$. For $t > 30$, a small phase difference of the electric field developed, whereas the amplitudes remained constant to an amazing degree.

III. The Fourier–Hermite Expansion

A. Representation and Initial Conditions

When the distribution function is expanded in Fourier series in space and Gram–Charlier (Hermite) series in velocity, the nonlinear Vlasov equation is reduced to an infinite set of first-order ordinary nonlinear differential equations for the expansion coefficients (Weissglas, 1962; Engelmann et al., 1963; Armstrong, 1966, 1967; Grant and Feix, 1967a; Sadowski, 1967; Harding, 1968a,b; Crownfield and Broaddus, 1963). Although some results can be obtained analytically by linearizing in small spatial perturbations and invoking a closure condition to eliminate the higher Hermite coefficients (cf. Weissglass, 1962; Engelmann et al., 1963; Grant and Feix, 1967a), our interest is in using the Gram–Charlier expansion in order to obtain a representation of the nonlinear Vlasov equation in a form convenient for numerical integration. Accordingly, this treatment will emphasize the application and computational experience using the Fourier–Hermite expansion technique and the reader is referred to Grant and Feix (1967a,b) for mathematical subtleties not discussed here.

In the following treatment, we consider specifically the case of a one-dimensional electron plasma with a uniform, smeared-out neutralizing ion background described by the Vlasov and Poisson equations (1) and (2). The distribution function is expanded as:

$$f(x, v, t) = \sum_{n=-\infty}^{\infty} \exp(ink_0 x) \sum_{m=0}^{\infty} \exp(-v^2/2) h_m(v) Z_{mn}(t), \quad (25)$$

where x, v, and t are the previously defined dimensionless variables, $k_0 = 2\pi/L$ is the fundamental (discrete) wavenumber, and

$$h_m(v) = \frac{(-1)^m \exp(v^2/2)}{((2\pi)^{1/2} m!)^{1/2}} \frac{d^m}{dv^m} \exp(-v^2/2)$$

is the orthonormal Hermite polynomial of degree m. Several recursion properties of $h_m(v)$,

$$v h_m(v) = (m+1)^{1/2} h_{m+1}(v) + m^{1/2} h_{m-1}(v), \quad (26)$$

$$\frac{d}{dv} h_m(v) = v h_m(v) - (m+1)^{1/2} h_{m+1}(v) = m^{1/2} h_{m-1}(v), \quad (27)$$

are used in reducing the Vlasov equation to

$$\frac{d}{dt} Z_{mn}(t) + ink_0 \{m^{1/2} Z_{m-1,n} + (m+1)^{1/2} Z_{m+1,n}\}$$

$$+ m^{1/2} \sum_{q=-\infty}^{\infty} E_{n-q} Z_{m-1,q} = 0, \qquad (28)$$

$$m = 1, 2, 3, \ldots, \qquad n = 0, \pm 1, \pm 2, \ldots,$$

and

$$\frac{d}{dt} Z_{0n}(t) + ink_0 Z_{1,n} = 0, \qquad n = 0, \pm 1, \pm 2, \pm 3, \ldots. \qquad (29)$$

The Fourier components of the electric field $E_n(t)$ where

$$E(x, t) = \sum_{n=-\infty}^{\infty} \exp(ink_0 x) E_n(t), \qquad (30)$$

are obtained from Poisson's equation as

$$E_n(t) = \frac{i(2\pi)^{1/4}}{nk_0} Z_{0,n}(t), \qquad n \neq 0 \qquad (31)$$

and

$$E_0(t) = 0. \qquad (32)$$

The condition for reality of $f(x, v, t)$ requires that

$$Z_{mn}(t) = Z^*_{m,-n}(t). \qquad (33)$$

Perfectly reflecting boundaries are used which lead to (Montgomery and Gorman, 1962; Gartenhaus, 1963):

$$f(x, v, t) = f(-x, -v, t), \qquad (34)$$

$$E(x, t) = -E(-x, t), \qquad (35)$$

if these relations are imposed at $t = 0$. It follows from Eq. (34) that

$$Z_{mn}(t) = (-1)^m Z_{m,-n}(t) \tag{36}$$

and from Eq. (35) that

$$E_n(t) = -E^*_{-n}(t). \tag{37}$$

Combining Eqs. (33) and (36) results in

$$Z_{mn}(t) = (-1)^m Z^*_{mn}(t)$$

or

$$\begin{aligned} \operatorname{Re} Z_{mn}(t) &= 0, & m &= 1, 3, 5, 7, \ldots \\ \operatorname{Im} Z_{mn}(t) &= 0, & m &= 0, 2, 4, \ldots \end{aligned} \tag{38}$$

Using Eqs. (31) and (37) we obtain $\operatorname{Im} Z_{0,n}(t) = 0$ consistent with Eq. (38). From Eq. (38) it can be seen that the Z_{mn} are either purely real or purely imaginary so that Eqs. (28) and (29) can be interpreted as referring to the real parts for even order and the imaginary parts for odd order m of Z_{mn}. We have

$$\frac{dZ_{mn}}{dt}(t) = (-1)^m \left[nk_0 \{ m^{1/2} Z_{m-1,n} + (m+1)^{1/2} Z_{m+1,n} \} \right.$$
$$\left. + m^{1/2} \sum_{q=-\infty}^{\infty} E_{n-q} Z_{m-1,q} \right], \quad m, n = 0, 1, 2, 3, \ldots, \tag{39}$$

and

$$E_n(t) = \operatorname{Im} E_n(t) = \frac{(2\pi)^{1/4}}{nk_0} Z_{0,n}(t). \tag{40}$$

Now if one specifies $f(x, v, 0)$, which in turn determines all the $Z_{mn}(0)$'s one can solve Eqs. (39) and (40) by simply integrating forward in time. The system of Eqs. (39) and (40) is infinite and must be truncated before numerical integration can be done. Section B describes the possible inaccuracies arising from truncation; for now we simply assume that

$$Z_{m,n}(t) = 0, \quad \text{for} \quad m > M \quad \text{or} \quad n > N,$$

and obtain a finite system of equations to which standard numerical procedures can be applied.

Examples of various forms of initial conditions $f(x, v, 0)$ which have been studied are:

$$f(x, v, 0) = \frac{\exp(-v^2/2)}{(2\pi)^{1/2}} (1 + \epsilon \cos k_0 x), \tag{41}$$

which yields Landau damping of the initially excited stable k_0 and the $2k_0$, $3k_0, \ldots$, nonlinearly excited waves;

$$f(x, v, 0) = v^2 \frac{\exp(-v^2/2)}{(2\pi)^{1/2}} (1 + \epsilon \cos k_0 x), \tag{42}$$

which represents a strongly unstable counterstreaming electron plasma that has growing waves if $|k_0| < 1$ (Grant and Feix, 1967a);

$$f(x, v, 0) = \frac{\exp(-v^2/2)}{(2\pi)^{1/2}} (h_0(v) + (2/3)^{1/2} h_4(v))(1 + \epsilon \sum_{n=1}^{8} \cos nk_0 x), \tag{43}$$

which corresponds to the "bump-on-the-tail" situation (cf. Drummond and Pines, 1962; Vedenov et al., 1962) of tenuous, high velocity beams of particles flowing through a relatively more dense background plasma in which, for sufficiently small k_0, several waves are unstable.

All of the situations described above require only a few nonzero elements of the matrix $Z_{mn}(t)$ initially. The class of velocity distributions which can be represented in Gram–Charlier series is limited to those for which $f(v) \to 0$ at least as fast as $v^n \exp(-v^2/2)$. For example, Cauchy distributions of the form

$$f(v) = A/(v^2 + b^2)^n$$

are not conveniently representable. That is not a serious limitation of this method because velocity distributions of physical interest do decrease sufficiently rapidly.

Because the numerical problem has been reduced to that of integrating a set of differential equations (39) of the form

$$dZ_{mn}(t)/dt = G_{mn} Z \tag{44}$$

where $Z = \{Z_{mn}\}$ and G_{mn} is a nonlinear algebraic matrix operator, several standard Runge–Kutta or predictor–corrector techniques can be applied. We chose to use a fourth-order Runge–Kutta method as outlined by Gill (1951) because of the ease of starting the calculation and of changing the time-step Δt as compared to predictor–corrector methods. The fourth-order method required the evaluation of the right-hand side of Eq. (44) at four points in each Δt interval. Consequently, provision in the computer storage had to be made for storing each of the four subintervals in a matrix of the dimension $6N$, where use has been made of the fact that only the $m \pm 1$ rows are necessary to compute $\dot{Z}_{mn}$. Gill's algorithm was rewritten in a form to eliminate the need to store the Z matrix itself at all four subinterval points; as can be seen below, only the most recent evaluation of Z is needed. The algorithm used is as follows:

Denote $Z_{mn}^l(t) = Z_{mn}^l(j\,\Delta t)$ as $Z_{mn}^l(j)$ where j labels the interval Δt and l the subinterval. We have

$$Z_{mn}^0(j) = Z_{mn}^4(j-1),$$
$$Z_{mn}^1(j) = Z_{mn}^0(j) + \tfrac{1}{2}(\Delta t)G_{mn}^0 Z_{mn}^0(j),$$
$$Z_{mn}^2(j) = Z_{mn}^1(j) + \Delta t\{(-1 + (\tfrac{1}{2})^{1/2})G_{mn}^0 Z_{mn}^0(j)$$
$$+ (1 - (\tfrac{1}{2})^{1/2})G_{mn}^1 Z_{mn}^1(j)\},$$
$$Z_{mn}^3(j) = Z_{mn}^2(j) + \Delta t\{(\tfrac{1}{2} - (\tfrac{1}{2})^{1/2})G_{mn}^0 Z_{mn}^0(j) \qquad (45)$$
$$- G_{mn}^1 Z_{mn}^1(j) + (1 + (\tfrac{1}{2})^{1/2})G_{mn}^2 Z_{mn}^2(j)\},$$
$$Z_{mn}^4(j) = Z_{mn}^3(j) + \Delta t\{\tfrac{1}{6}G_{mn}^0 Z_{mn}^0(j) + \tfrac{1}{3}(1 + \sqrt{2})G_{mn}^1 Z_{mn}^1(j)$$
$$- \tfrac{2}{3}(1 + (\tfrac{1}{2})^{1/2})G_{mn}^2 Z_{mn}^2(j) + \tfrac{1}{6}G_{mn}^3 Z_{mn}^3(j)\},$$
$$Z^0(j+1) = Z^4(j), \quad \text{etc.}$$

For the problems considered, the truncation error of Gill's method was found to be insignificant compared to other inaccuracies in the procedure and no attempt was made to improve the basic algorithm, Eqs. (45), with the inclusion of truncation error minimizing terms. In typical runs, the truncation error estimates were of the same order as the roundoff errors.

Several successively more complicated FORTRAN computer codes have been written utilizing the methods outlined above; a simplified function diagram is shown in Fig. 8. The current version of the code has flexibility to allow selection by means of the input data cards:

(1) arbitrary input Z_{mn} matrix;
(2) output list options, including Z_{mn}, $f(x, v, t)$, $E(x, t)$, etc.;
(3) graphical output;
(4) truncation procedures.

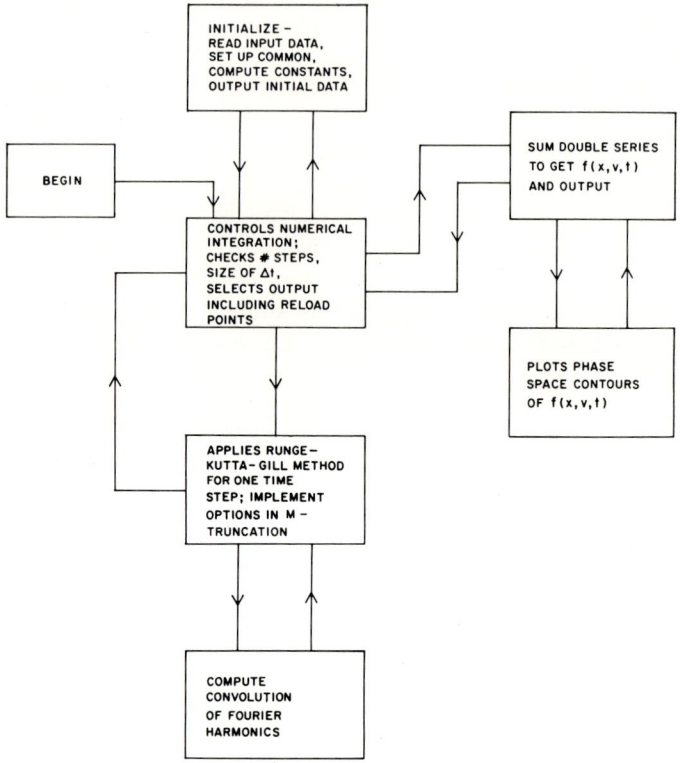

FIG. 8. Simplified function diagram of generalized Fourier–Hermite code.

In addition, the size of Δt is automatically reduced as necessary to maintain numerical stability. The code requires about $M(N+3) + 262N + 2500$ words of common storage plus about 2500 words. Typical values of M,N are 100, 3; 500, 9. For the problems studied thus far, the limiting factor has been processor time and not storage. The nature of the computations is such that for large M and N, the time required for an iteration goes approximately as MN^2. Figure 9 shows plots of the time required per iteration unit M for various versions of the code which have been run on various machines. Comparing curves A and B shows the factor of 4 cost in time required to use a generalized Fourier convolution term which is necessarily less efficient than one written specifically for a given value of N. Curves C, D and E correspond to substantially identical codes run on three different machines. Comparing curves E and F shows the approximate 60% increase in time required for double vs. single precision arithmetic.

The reliability and accuracy of the codes have been checked in various ways:

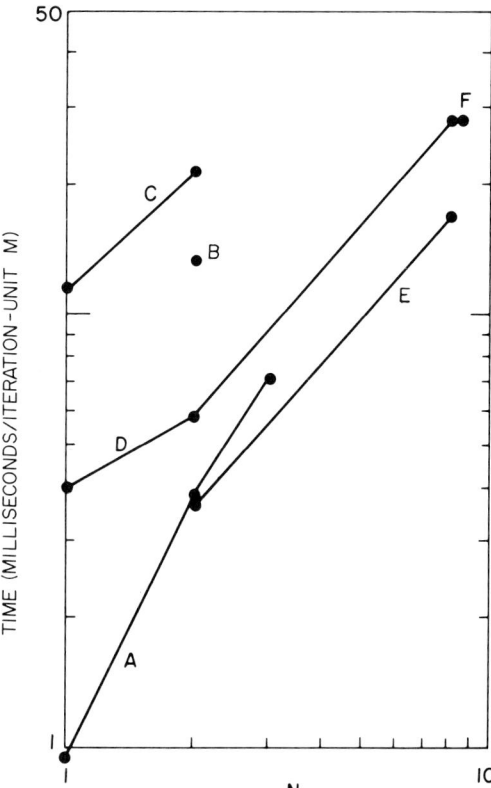

FIG. 9. Computing time required for various machines and versions of the Fourier–Hermite program. A: IBM 7044, Fourier convolution explicitly written out for each N, e.g., one source code for $N = 2$, another for $N = 3$, etc. B: IBM 7044, Fourier convolution generalized, one source code runs any N. C: English Electric K.D.F.-9 optimized version using generalized convolution. D: G.E 625, same code as C. E: IBM 360-65, same code as C. F: I.B.M 360-65, double-precision version of E. To obtain total run time for given N, multiply by M times the number of iterations required.

(1) by comparison with linearized analytic theory in instances where perturbations are small;

(2) by comparison with the exact analytic solutions of the free-streaming ($E = 0$) problem as discussed in Section B;

(3) by integrating forward and then backward in time (Eqs. (1) and (2) are exactly reversible in time);

(4) by computing the total energy which is conserved by Eqs. (1) and (2) (the total particle number is exactly conserved as a result of the form of the transformed equations); and

(5) by comparing runs of different M, N, and Δt.

Not all of the checks listed above are done for any particular case; hence we will cite results from various runs.

The linearized analytic theory of stable plasma oscillations obtains the result that $E_n(t) \propto \exp[i\omega(nk_0)t]$, where t is large enough for the initial value effects to have disappeared. If $n = 1$, $k_0 = 0.5$, the analytic results are Re $\omega = 1.416$, Im $\omega = 0.1534$, and the numerical results are Re $\omega = 1.412$, Im $\omega = 0.153$; the results are in agreement to the precision with which the analytic results are known from the approximate solutions of the dispersion relation. The strictly exponential behavior of $E_1(t)$ is illustrated in Fig. 10.

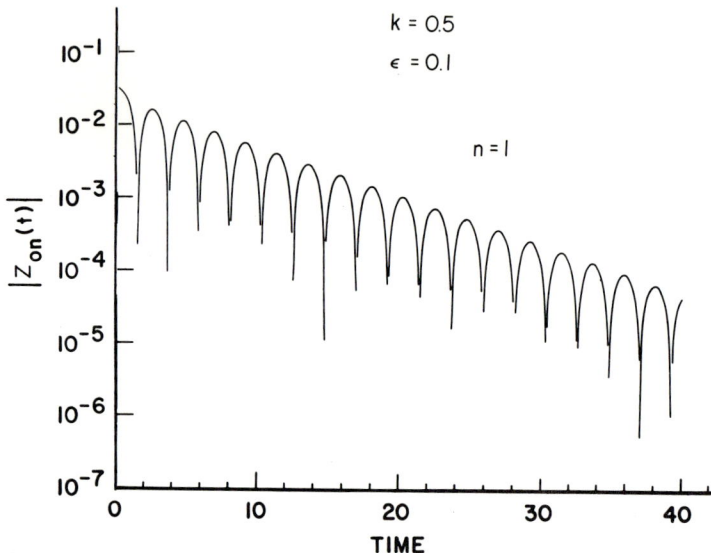

FIG. 10. Plot of $\log|Z_{01}(t)|$ versus t for the linearized $N = 1$ case showing exponentially damped electron plasma oscillations. (After Armstrong, 1967.)

The equation describing the free-streaming flow of a neutral gas [obtained by setting $E = 0$ in (25)] develops the troublesome large gradients in velocity as will be discussed in Section B. Although the free-streaming equation has properties which make it difficult to integrate numerically, the exact analytic solution for all time is easily obtained. If we use initial conditions of the form (41), the exact solution for the Z_{mn}'s is:

$$Z_{mn}(t) = \frac{(ink_0 t)^m \epsilon}{((2\pi)^{1/2} m!)^{1/2} 2} \exp\left(-\frac{(nk_0 t)^2}{2}\right), \quad n = \pm 1, \ m = 0, 1, 2, 3 \ldots,$$

$$Z_{mn}(t) = 0, \quad n \neq \pm 1.$$

(46)

This solution is compared in Table I and Fig. 11 with the solution obtained by

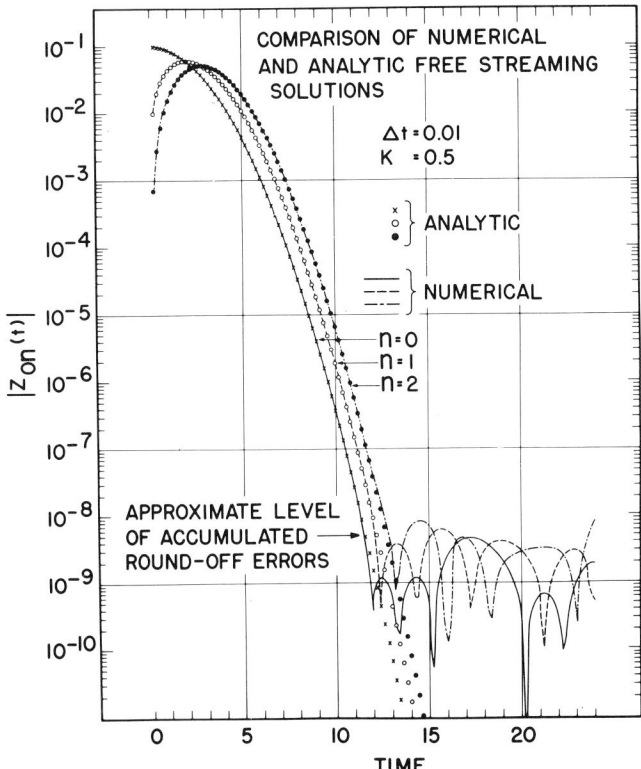

FIG. 11. Comparison of numerical and analytic solutions of free-streaming equation for $Z_{0n}(t)$, showing the level of roundoff and truncation errors.

TABLE I

COMPARISON OF ANALYTIC AND NUMERICAL FREE-STREAMING SOLUTIONS

	Z_{01}			
Time	Numerical	Analytic	Deviation	Iterations
0	$0.31580938 \times 10^{-1}$	$0.315809380 \times 10^{-1}$	0.00	0
2	$0.19154749 \times 10^{-1}$	$0.191548077 \times 10^{-1}$	-5.87×10^{-8}	80
4	$0.42739932 \times 10^{-2}$	$0.427401530 \times 10^{-2}$	-2.21×10^{-8}	160
6	$0.35082764 \times 10^{-3}$	$0.350832540 \times 10^{-3}$	-4.90×10^{-9}	240
8	$0.10592985 \times 10^{-4}$	$0.105952250 \times 10^{-4}$	-1.24×10^{-9}	320
10	$0.11814119 \times 10^{-6}$	$0.117692000 \times 10^{-6}$	$+4.50 \times 10^{-10}$	400
12	$0.10854431 \times 10^{-8}$	$0.480977060 \times 10^{-9}$	$+6.04 \times 10^{-9}$	480

numerically integrating Eq. (39) with all E_q's $= 0$. The observed discrepancies are of the same order as the expected accumulated roundoff errors.

As a check of reversibility in time of the numerical solutions, an unstable case Eq. (42) was integrated forward and then backward 800 time steps (20 ω_p^{-1}). The final result for the charge density $Z_{01}(0)$ differed by 0.29% from the initial value, a level of error typical of all the Z_{mn}'s. The error is several hundred times larger than that expected from truncations and roundoff and is thought to be associated with the process of truncating in the m index for this run.

In a recent run using the unstable "bump-on-tail" initial conditions, Eq. (43), the total energy was conserved to one part in 10^8 over a 65 ω_p^{-1} run. By comparison, approximately 3% of the initial particle kinetic energy went into wave growth. The total energy is, however, relatively insensitive to significant errors in $f(x, v, t)$ which do not extend over a large phase area. In this case, total energy was very well conserved despite the fact that $f(x, v, t)$ went slightly *negative* in a small phase area. The fact that $f(x, v, t)$ went negative in several spots was not unexpected in this run because the $f(x, v, 0)$ was initially zero on the lines of $v^2 = 3$ and if the errors in computing f are random, half of the $f(x, v, 0)$ which starts out zero goes slightly negative. The negative spots in f are not believed to have affected the precision of the desired information $E_n(t)$.

A universal test of the precision of a numerical solution is its sensitivity to the size of the finite difference used, in this case Δt. Table II gives a summary of points of comparison for a particular run. Although estimates for the truncation error in Runge–Kutta methods are necessarily crude, the discrepancies in Table II seem to be larger than one would expect from randomly accumulated truncation errors and are of the magnitude consistent with a direct

TABLE II

COMPARISON OF Z_{01} OBTAINED WITH DIFFERENT Δt FOR $k = 0.5$, $\varepsilon = 0.1$

Time	Z_{01}		Deviation (%)
	$\Delta t = 0.025$	$\Delta t = 0.0125$	
0	$0.31580938 \times 10^{-1}$	$0.31580938 \times 10^{-1}$	0.0
5	$0.10228778 \times 10^{-1}$	$0.10228960 \times 10^{-1}$	0.00080
10	$0.23269353 \times 10^{-2}$	$0.23268939 \times 10^{-2}$	0.0017
15	$-0.18966850 \times 10^{-3}$	$-0.18967476 \times 10^{-3}$	0.0033
20	$-0.35462848 \times 10^{-3}$	$-0.35463134 \times 10^{-3}$	0.00081
25	$-0.33775979 \times 10^{-3}$	$-0.33774903 \times 10^{-3}$	0.0032

accumulation of errors. Even so, the level of uncertainty in the solutions illustrated by Table III is well within the allowable range for any known application.

Further discussion of errors, especially those arising from the truncations in the Fourier and Hermite series, is deferred to Section B. As a final comment on the performance of the computer codes, it should be noted that the analysis has centered on the information contained in the $Z_{0,n}$ (gives electric field) and $Z_{2,0}$ (gives particle kinetic energy) coefficients because those quantities are of greatest physical interest. Other elements could be studied with approximately similar results, except that those elements near the boundaries of the matrix the errors are significantly larger than those quoted. Fortunately, when the matrix is sufficiently large, the effect of the boundary elements on the physically interesting information in the matrix is apparently small.

B. Truncation Difficulties

It is easily seen that Eqs. (39) and (40) do not form a closed system in either the Fourier index n or the Hermite index m. The nonlinear term arising from $E(\partial f/\partial v)$ couples each Fourier mode to an infinite number of other modes and the convective term arising from $v(\partial f/\partial x)$ couples each Hermite index to the one above and below. We consider first the effect of the truncation of the Fourier series.

The requirement that $f(x, v, t)$ and $E(x, t)$ be expandable in strongly convergent Fourier series limits the class of initial conditions for which this method is appropriate to those where at least the initial state is nearly homogeneous, e.g.,

$$\varepsilon = Z_{0,1}(0)/Z_{0,0}(0) \quad \text{sufficiently small.}$$

Shock-like or sheath problems would require a different set of basis functions for the spatial expansion (cf. Leavens, 1967). The customary linearized analytic solution of Eqs. (39) and (40) considers the fate of small perturbations about a homogeneous initial state. That procedure provides the basis for studying the effect of the Fourier truncation in the nonlinear problem. It is found numerically that if the $n = 1$ wave is initially excited in a stable (Landau damped) case with amplitude ε, then the nth harmonic is excited nonlinearly to amplitude $O(\varepsilon^n)$. The desired precision in the numerical solutions is obtained by choosing the initial ε, k_0 set and running the problem with several increasing values of N until the changes (at fixed time) in the quantities of interest, usually the E_n's, are smaller than the allowable inaccuracies. Table III gives a comparison of the $Z_{01}(t)$ and $Z_{02}(t)$ obtained from identical stable initial conditions, Eq. (41) with $k_0 = 0.5$, $\varepsilon = 0.25$, and using $N = 2$

TABLE III

COMPARISON OF SECOND- AND THIRD-ORDER RESULTS, $k = 0.5$, $\varepsilon = 0.25$

Time	Z_{01}		Deviation (%)	Z_{02}	
	Second	Third		Second	Third
0	$0.78952347 \times 10^{-1}$	$0.78952347 \times 10^{-1}$	0.0	0.0	0.0
5	$0.22993276 \times 10^{-1}$	$0.22987347 \times 10^{-1}$	0.026	$0.34944769 \times 10^{-3}$	$0.33626417 \times 10^{-3}$
10	$0.45308043 \times 10^{-2}$	$0.45328011 \times 10^{-2}$	0.044	$0.58144960 \times 10^{-4}$	$-0.64013374 \times 10^{-4}$
15	$0.31100715 \times 10^{-2}$	$0.31371019 \times 10^{-2}$	0.861	$0.73193859 \times 10^{-5}$	$0.26057195 \times 10^{-4}$

and $N = 3$ in successive runs. In this case, one naively expects discrepancies as large as $O(\varepsilon^3) = 1.6\%$ to appear. In fact the changes in $Z_{01}(t)$ were less than $O(\varepsilon^3)$ and in $Z_{02}(t)$ much greater; the comparison is complicated because the introduction of the third harmonic disturbs the phase of the second. If more precise information on the second harmonic is needed, a run using $N = 4$ would be necessary to establish the convergence. The primary obstacle to running with large numbers of Fourier harmonics is processor time which increases $\propto N^2$.

In the case of unstable initial conditions, N is chosen such that the desired convergence is obtained at limiting amplitude. Usually if N includes two or more linearly stable waves, the convergence is adequate. Our experience has been that the truncation of the Fourier series presents much less serious difficulties than that of the Hermite series in the problems considered to date.

The troublesome large velocity derivatives of $f(x, v, t)$ arising from the convection term in Vlasov's equation are evident in the solution of the free-streaming equation (46); the remarks we shall make now are based on the free-streaming equation but are also appropriate for the plasma case. The mth coefficient grows as $t^m \exp(-(nk_0 t)^2/2)$ to a maximum (or minimum) value of

$$Z_{mn}^{\max} = i^m \frac{\varepsilon}{2} \frac{(m)^{m/2}}{(2\pi m!)^{1/2}} \exp\left(\frac{-m}{2}\right), \tag{47}$$

which reduces for large m to

$$Z_{mn}^{\max} \doteq \frac{i^m \varepsilon}{2(2\pi)^{1/2}} \exp(-m). \tag{48}$$

The time at which the mth coefficient attains its maximum (or minimum) value is

$$t = \sqrt{m}/nk_0, \tag{49}$$

and the rate at which the coefficient attaining its maximum value moves toward larger m is

$$dm_{\max}/dt = 2nk_0 t \tag{50}$$

where m has been treated as a continuous variable. Equations (48)–(50), show that the tendency is for coefficients at large m to grow, and that the "velocity" with which the initial disturbance applied at low m numbers increases with t. Whenever the boundary M is chosen, the coefficients at the boundary will grow large by the time $t = \sqrt{M/nk_0}$. The contribution of $Z_{M+1,n}(t)$ to the $Z_{M,n}(t)$ can not simply be ignored because $Z_{M+1,n}(t)$ and $Z_{M-1,n}(t)$ are large and of opposite sign, nearly canceling each other out in the expression for $Z_{M,n}(t)$ [c.f. Eq. (39)]. One is therefore obliged to adopt one of several options:

(a) Stop the computation at some time $t \leq \sqrt{M/nk}$; choose M large enough to obtain solutions for the desired time.

(b) Make use of the property of (39) that $Z_{m,n}$ only involves $Z_{M+1,n}$ and $Z_{M-1,n}$ and reduce M by one unit at each time-step beginning at $t = \sqrt{M/nk_0}$. One can gain an additional $M \Delta t$ interval of time and retain accurate solutions.

(c) Prevent $Z_{M,n}$ from ever growing large by introducing some artificial term into Eq. (1) to "smooth out" the steep velocity derivatives (cf. Grant and Feix, 1967a,b, and Section C)

(d) Accurately estimate $Z_{M+1,n}(t)$ from the $Z_{M,n}$, $Z_{M-1,n}$, $Z_{M-2,n}$, etc. by some extrapolation procedure.

We have used (a)–(c) with success for various problems and although considerable effort was put into (d), no satisfactory (numerically stable) extrapolation procedure has yet been found. In the application of the (a)–(c) options, the current version of the code economizes by computing all the Z_{mn}'s up to the value of m when a series of the Z_{mn}'s falls below some predetermined absolute value. This feature provides for very rapid computation while the Z matrix is initially small.

From the form of Eq. (39) it can be seen that as M increases Δt should be reduced for numerical stability. Taking a rough, finite difference approximation to (39) we have (setting $E \equiv 0$),

$$\Delta Z_{mn}/\Delta t \doteq \delta m^{1/2} nk_0 Z_{m,n}, \qquad (51)$$

where $\delta = (Z_{m+1,n} - Z_{m-1,n})/Z_{m,n}$. If $\Delta Z_{mn}/Z_{mn}$ is to be small, we need $\delta m^{1/2} \Delta t n k_0$ small. δ is in practice a fairly small number; hence, if $m^{1/2} \Delta t n k_0 \leq 1$, the numerical stability should be satisfactory. This criterion is found to work well.

Finally, we illustrate the effect on $f_n(v, t)$ of neglecting the higher order Hermite coefficients. Figure 12 shows a plot of the $n = 1$ distribution function for a case where 960 terms of the Hermite series are retained as compared to a case with 360. The series represents the actual solution obtained in a case where the number of Hermite coefficients was allowed to increase as necessary. As can be seen from the figure, the $M = 360$ series yields nearly the same $f_n(v, t)$ as does the $M = 960$ series. Whether the 360-term series is adequate

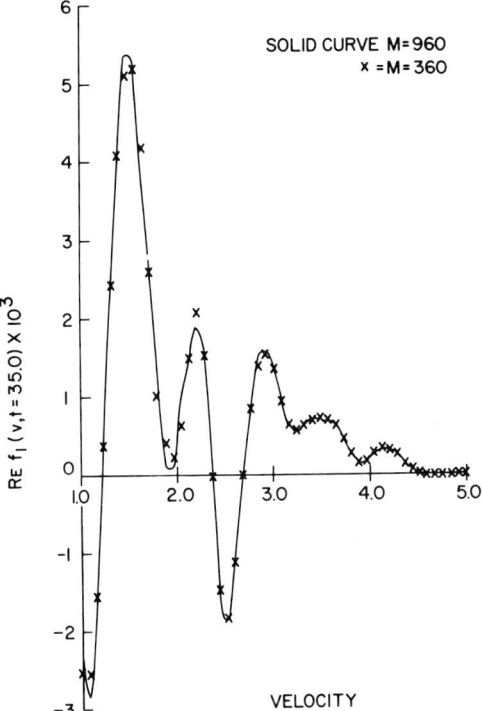

FIG. 12. Comparison of Re $f_1(v, t = 35.0)$ obtained from 960 and 360 terms of the Hermite series in a representative case. Note the good agreement throughout velocity space.

depends on how precisely the shape of $f_n(v, t)$ must be computed. In the case shown, $M = 360$ would have been adequate. The remaining 600 coefficients were retained as "insurance" against the propagation of anomalous information generated at the boundary back into the matrix. If computing time is at a premium or if one needs less precise information on $f_n(v, t)$, the value of M can be reduced.

C. Modification to Include "Collisions"

In this section we will follow closely the treatment of Grant and Feix (1967a,b). The introduction of a term on the right-hand side of Eq. (1) to produce the velocity space smoothing effect of collisions is one way to solve the difficulty of an unbounded increase in Hermite polynomials required to represent the $f(x, v, t)$. The "collision" terms which can be used in one dimension and which for one species are artificial, are not intended to accurately represent real collisions between discrete particles.

One form which has been used is the Bhatnagar–Gross–Krook model:

$$(\delta f/\delta t)_c = -v_c\{f(x, v, t) - n(x)\exp(-v^2/2)\}. \tag{52}$$

If $n(x) = N$ const, then $f(x, v, t)$ tends toward a spatially uniform Maxwellian, and if $n(x) = \int f(x, x, t)\,dv$, then $f_n(v, t)$ tends toward a Maxwellian. The representation of Eq. (52) in the Fourier–Hermite expansion is:

$$\begin{aligned}(\dot{Z}_{mn})_c &= -v_c Z_{mn}(t), & m &\neq 0, \\ (\dot{Z}_{0n})_c &= -v_c\{Z_{0n}(t) - N\} & &\text{if } n(x) \text{ is const,} \\ (\dot{Z}_{0n})_c &= 0 & &\text{if } n(x) = \int f(x, v, t)\,dv.\end{aligned} \tag{53}$$

This form of collision term is unselective in Hermite space, acting on nearly all coefficients equally. There is no tendency to smooth out the fine-scale wrinkles in $f(x, v, t)$ preferentially.

A more effective term is the simplified Fokker–Planck term (Lenard and Bernstein, 1959; Taylor and Comisar, 1963; Chandrasekhar, 1943) of the form

$$\left(\frac{\delta f}{\delta t}\right)_c = v_c\left\{\frac{\partial(vf)}{\partial v} + \frac{\partial^2 f}{\partial v^2}\right\} \tag{54}$$

represented by

$$(\dot{Z}_{mn}(t))_c = -v_c m Z_{mn}(t) \tag{55}$$

(cf. Grant and Feix, 1967a,b) which causes higher Hermite coefficients to be selectively suppressed. Grant and Feix (1967b) show that if $Mv_c \sim O(1)$, the the introduction of Eq. (55) into Eqs. (28) and (29) avoids the breakdown of the representation at $t = \sqrt{M/Nk_0}$; collision effects, however, become predominant after a time $t = 1/v_c \doteq M$. The time for which one can study approximately collisionless phenomena is extended from $t = \sqrt{M/Nk_0}$ to M. If $Nk_0 < 1/\sqrt{M}$, it would obviously not be desirable to use the collision term at all. For stable initial conditions, the effect of the collisions is to add to the Landau damping. The behavior of Re ω and Im ω from the linearized Fourier–Hermite expansion as functions of v_c and M is shown in Fig. 13. In the nonlinear case, the collision term competes with the waves in interacting with the distribution function; the collisions tend to maintain $f_0'(v = \omega/k) < 0$, while the nonlinear wave interaction tends to make $f'(v = \omega/k) \to 0$. Hence, where

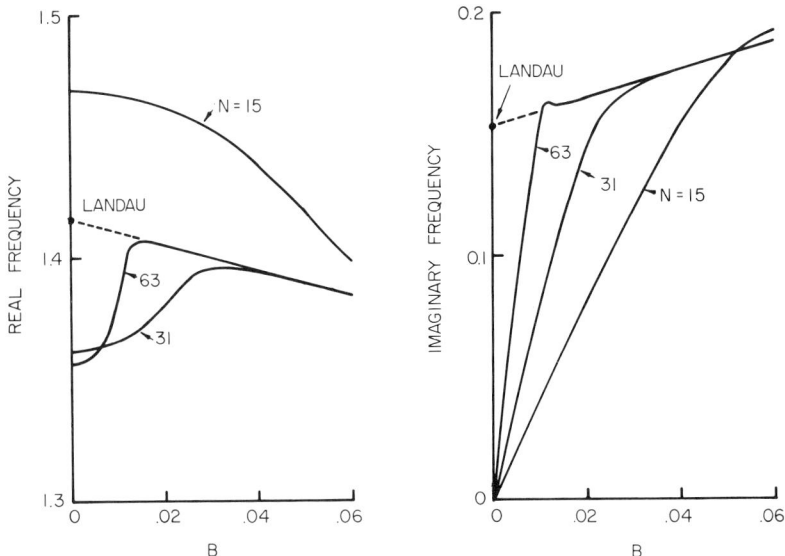

FIG. 13. Convergence of linearized Fourier–Hermite results for real and imaginary ω to the Landau results as functions of the collision frequency B and the number (N, in this case) of Hermite coefficients retained. Note that $NB \sim 1$ recovers the Landau result. (After Grant and Feix, 1967b.)

the shape of $f_0(v)$ is important to the effects which are of interest in the problem, the influence of a collision term should be carefully examined.

A comparison of $E_1(t)$ obtained with and without a collision term of the form of Eq. (54) for unstable initial conditions [Eq. (42)] is shown in Fig. 14. No qualitative changes were introduced by the collision term. In this case the limiting amplitude of $E_1(t)$ and the nature of the state of the system were the desired information, and the use of the collision term allowed a significant saving of computer time.

Denavit *et al.* (1968) have studied in detail the collision term of Eq. (54), employing analytical and numerical methods.

D. Brief Summary of Results

This section presents a necessarily cursory survey of the problems to which the Fourier–Hermite or a closely related method has been applied. Most of the attempts have apparently met with success insofar as providing some new insight into significant physical problems. The order in which the problems are discussed should not be taken to reflect our assessment of their relative importance, but rather the approximate order in which the results appeared. It is also our intention to credit all the contributors to each problem

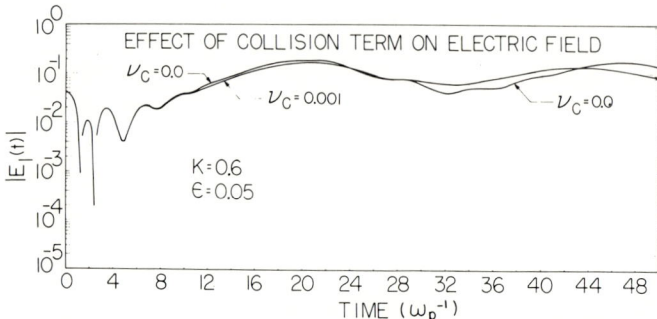

FIG. 14. Plot of $\log|E_1(t)|$ versus t in an unstable case showing the effect of the collision term on the time development of E_1. (After Armstrong and Montgomery, 1967.)

who used orthogonal polynomial expansions, and we apologize in advance for any oversight of work with which we may not be acquainted. The following list enumerates the relevant problems:

(1) *Nonlinear Landau damping in a stable plasma*

Large amplitude waves are excited in a Maxwellian plasma and the subsequent damping and nonlinear interaction of waves with the $f(x, v, t)$ are examined. It is found that initial damping is faster than the Landau rate and is probably due to strong trapping of resonant particles by the wave. The number of particles below the phase velocity in $f_0(v, t)$ decreases and, above the phase velocity, increases in agreement with the resonant particle interaction picture. The damping decrement $\gamma(t)$ decreases with time, becoming much smaller than the linear value at large times if the initial excitation is sufficiently large. The most important nonlinear terms in Vlasov's equation for determining the time development of the electric field are apparently the terms $E_1(\partial f_{-1}/\partial v) + E_{-1}(\partial f_1/\partial v)$ which produce a second-order change in $f_0(v, t)$. A successful nonlinear analytic theory based on the above assumption has been given (Gary, 1967), which obtains $\gamma(t_a), f_0(v, t_a)$ where t_a is an asymptotic time. Contributions to this problem have been made by Armstrong (1966, 1967), Grant and Feix (1967a,b), and Sadowski (1967).

(2) *The strongly unstable counterstreaming plasma*

An initial condition representing two interpenetrating electron streams (cf. Eq. 42) in a periodic system short enough so that only the $n = 1$ wave was unstable was integrated. N was chosen to include some stable harmonics to assure convergence of the Fourier series. The results of numerical calculation have shown that nonlinear effects cause the growth to cease after a small fraction of the stream energy has been converted to electric field energy, and that the system approaches an inhomogeneous equilibrium in the long time regime. Contributions to this problem are due to Armstrong (1966, 1967), Grant and Feix (1967a), and Armstrong and Montgomery (1967).

(3) *The one-dimensional plasma diode*

This problem is appropriate for inclusion here because it is a method of solving the Vlasov equation with the periodic boundary condition relaxed. The technique which Lomax (1967) chose to use involves the expansion of the distribution function in Laguerre polynomials. Diode characteristics have been obtained by this technique.

(4) *The effect of an externally applied electric field on an electron plasma*

This problem is fully discussed in Section IV.

(5) *Plasma wave echoes*

Crownfield and Broaddus (1968) have applied the Fourier–Hermite method to cases where two excitations are applied to a stable plasma at different times. According to analytic theories (O'Neill and Gould, 1968) an "echo" wave appears at a later time. The shape of the envelope of the echo wave and the dependence of the amplitude on the excitation amplitude and delay are in agreement with analytical predictions. The echo wave appears despite the fact that the electric fields in both the applied excitations have Landau damped away. The excitations produce undamped contributions to the distribution function which can become phase coherent and give rise to the echo wave. The introduction of a small number of "collisions," which affect the undamped part of the distribution function, greatly reduces the amplitude of the echo (Hinton and Oberman, 1968; O'Neil, 1968). Preliminary numerical results with collisions agree with the expectations of analytic theory. Future studies are planned to investigate the large amplitude regime.

(6) *Nonlinear ion acoustic waves*

This problem is expanded in Section IV,C.

(7) *Weakly unstable "bump-on-tail" instability*

The methods outlined in Section A have recently been applied (Armstrong and Montgomery, 1969) to initial conditions of the form given by Eq. (43). This case represents two tenuous electron beams (at $\pm V_{\text{drift}}$) interpenetrating a more dense background plasma. The specific intent of the choice of initial conditions was an attempt to elucidate the range of applicability of the quasi-linear theory (Drummond and Pines, 1962; Vedenov, *et al.*, 1962; Bernstein and Engelmann, 1966) which purports to apply to weak instabilities of this type. Eight waves were computed of which four were linearly unstable ($n = 2, 3, 4, 5$); $n = 1$ was essentially stable and undamped, while $n = 6, 7, 8$ were strongly damped. As expected, the nonlinear processes caused the "hole" in the distribution function between the background plasma and the stream to fill in; a result not expected from quasilinear theory was the dominance in the large amplitude state of the wave with the largest growth rate. Over four-fifths of the electrostatic field energy at maximum amplitude was concentrated in the most strongly unstable wave. The dominance of the single wave was attributed to the fact that the waves were initially excited at a level about a factor of 20 below the limiting amplitude, and the fastest growing wave simply outgrew the others. The trapping width of the largest wave overlapped the phase velocities of the other unstable waves; hence, the largest wave was able to "turn off" the other waves nonlinearly. It is now surmised as a result of this study that in order for customary quasilinear theory to be applicable, the initial excitation must not be too much smaller than the limiting amplitude.

IV. Extension of the Fourier–Hermite Expansion

With suitable modifications, the basic Fourier–Hermite expansion described in Section III can be used to solve more general versions of the nonlinear Vlasov–Poisson system. Extensions to two dimensions are discussed in another article in this volume; in this section we shall consider only additions to the one-dimensional model.

In Sections IV,A and IV,B we extend the model to include electric fields, time varying or stationary, that are assumed to be maintained by forces external to the electron plasma. The extension to a plasma of mobile ions and electrons is discussed in Section IV,C. The high ratio of ion mass to electron mass leads to a much slower time scale for phenomena associated mainly with ion motion, as compared to the time scale of phenomena associated mainly with electron motion. For this reason the electron motion is handled differently, and the model described is called a *hybrid model*.

A. The Extension to Include External Fields

The basic electrostatic phenomena in an electron plasma have characteristic lengths of the order of the electron Debye shielding length and frequencies of the order of the electron plasma frequency. Situations do occur in experiments, however, where phenomena are not directly related to these scales. These situations can be investigated in the Fourier–Hermite representation by providing for electric fields or potentials that are maintained independent of the activity of the plasma. We shall call these independent fields "external fields" to distinguish them from fields calculated self-consistently from the electron distribution, and shall regard them as being known functions of position and time.

1. Inclusion of External Fields

The distribution of electric charge in the system determines the electric field E (or, equivalently, the potential ϕ) through Poisson's equation

$$-\frac{\partial^2 \phi}{\partial x^2} = \frac{\partial E}{\partial x} = 1 - \int_{-\infty}^{\infty} f \, dv \tag{56}$$

where the right-hand side gives the total charge density. As used in this article the "1" is the normalized uniform density of the immobile ion background, and the velocity integral of the electron distribution gives the charge density due to the electron plasma.

To simulate the effect of an external field or potential in our system, we merely add to the right-hand side of (56) an "equivalent source charge density" which in vacuum would give rise to the desired external field or potential. We shall call this added charge density ρ_{ext} and regard it as a known function of x and t. The solution of the coupled equations, Vlasov's and Poisson's, proceeds as before, but now we are in a sense solving a boundary value problem rather than a pure initial value problem.

The new term in Poisson's equation is Fourier-analyzed into components $\rho_n(t)$ and upon substitution into the Fourier-analyzed Poisson equation leads to the following replacement for Eq. (31):

$$E_n(t) = \frac{i(2\pi)^{1/4}}{nk_0} (Z_{0n}(t) - \rho_n(t)), \qquad n \neq 0.$$

Thus the external source charge density is specified by its Fourier coefficients $\rho_n(t)$ which are given functions of time for any particular situation that we wish to calculate.

In a plasma experiment one usually does not control charge densities or electric fields directly, but instead one controls the electric potential on various surfaces within or surrounding the plasma. In particular, we set out to simulate an experiment (Decker and Hirshfield, 1967) in which a series of annular disks were evenly spaced along the axis of, and perpendicular to, a plasma column. The potentials on the disks were made to oscillate sinusoidally in time at a high frequency with the potentials on adjacent disks being 180° out of phase.

The equivalent source charge density for this potential is a series of Dirac δ-functions of alternating sign with $\sin \omega_0 t$ time dependence. The Fourier coefficients ρ_n of the δ-function charge density are nonzero only for odd n and are equal for all odd n.

Because of limitations of computing time and core storage it was necessary to limit most of our calculations to only three Fourier components for f, namely $n = 0, 1$, and 2. Thus, for the δ-function distribution only the $\rho_1(t)$ component of ρ_{ext} could be used. This is not a severe limitation since most of the physics is represented by the evolution of the first two Fourier components, $f_0(v, t)$ and $f_1(v, t)$, of the electron distribution.

This does illustrate that distribution function calculations may be more expensive than direct particle simulation if it is desired to study the development of a large number of modes simultaneously. On the other hand, expansion method calculations can be completely collisionless and can give the perturbed distribution function accurately at very low signal levels. A comparable reduction in collisional and statistical noise in direct particle simulations would require a very large number of particles.

2. *Time Dependent External Fields*

Response of the electron plasma to an oscillating external field was measured over two frequency ranges: $\omega_0 \gtrsim \omega_{\text{pe}}$ and $\omega_0 \ll \omega_{\text{pe}}$. Here ω_{pe} is the electron plasma frequency.

(a) $\omega_0 \gtrsim \omega_{\text{pe}}$. In these calculations the object was to measure the amplitude, frequency, and phase of the electron response to the external (driving) field and to observe the resultant modification of the distribution function. We wished to compare these items quantitatively as the driving amplitude was increased above the level at which nonlinear effects appear. The nonlinear effects are of the same nature as those described in Section III (arising physically from trapping of particles by the electric field), but were much harder to study in the earlier nondriven case because the perturbed field damped quickly and trapped particles were quickly freed.

Results of one calculation are shown in Fig. 15. The curves labeled $n = 1$ and $n = 2$ are the absolute values of the first and second Fourier coefficients of the part of the total electric field due only to the plasma electrons (that is, the external field has been subtracted from the total field). The curve labeled K.E. shows the percent increase in the total kinetic energy of the electrons. For the first 17 time units, the trapped electrons gain energy from the driving field: for the next 15 time units, they yield most of that energy. In contrast to

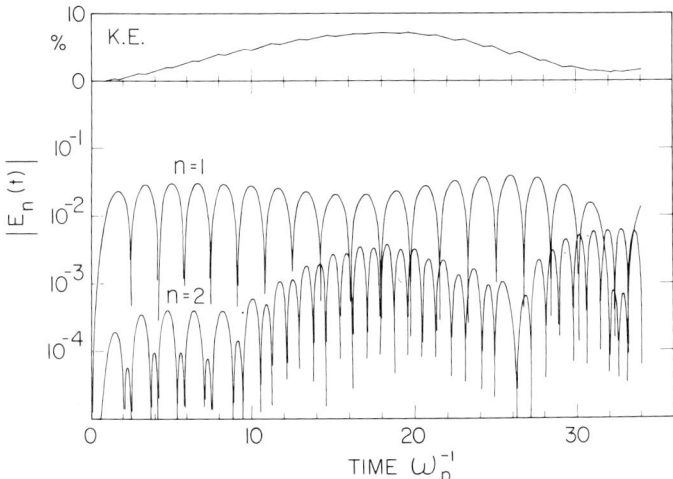

FIG. 15. Result of calculation of response of an electron plasma to an externally driven electric field. Curves $n = 1$ and $n = 2$ give the absolute value of the first and second Fourier components of the particle electric field. The curve labeled K.E. shows the percent increase in the total electron kinetic energy. The sinusoidal driving field had wavenumber $k_0 = 0.916$, frequency $\omega_0 = 1.923$, and amplitude $\rho_1 = 0.0458$. Particle electric field plus driving field gives the total electric field.

the situation of Section III, total energy is *not* conserved here because the external field is not calculated self-consistently.

(b) $\omega_0 \ll \omega_{pe}$. In these calculations the external field was chosen to represent a perturbation in the ion background charge density oscillating much slower than an electron plasma oscillation. The purpose was to see whether the electrons would modify their velocity and spatial distribution in such a way as to maintain a constant ratio of pressure

$$(P \equiv \int_{-\infty}^{\infty} v^2 f(x, v, t)\, dv) \quad \text{to number density} \quad (n \equiv \int_{-\infty}^{\infty} f(x, v, t)\, dv).$$

It was found that the ratio did not vary more than about 2% when the oscillating background perturbation was 15%.

B. Calculations with Inhomogeneous Equilibria

Except for those situations with unstable initial conditions in Section III. equilibria for the calculations described have been spatially homogeneous, It has been known for some time (Bernstein *et al.*, 1957; Harris, 1957) that Eqs. (1) and (2) have time-independent solutions which involve inhomogeneous electric fields. Analytical investigations of the stability of various inhomogeneous equilibria have been made by Montgomery (1960), Low (1961), Pearlstein (1964), Freidberg (1965), and Knorr (1968). Here we describe a numerical study (Harding, 1968a,b) of Landau damping of perturbations about a particular type of inhomogeneous equilibrium.

In our dimensionless units the constant of motion for an electron is its total energy, $\xi = v^2/2 - \phi(x)$, the sum of its kinetic and potential energy. Any function f of this constant of motion solves Vlasov's equation. If $f(v^2/2 - \phi(x))$ and $\phi(x)$ are determined self-consistently from Poisson's equation, then we have an inhomogeneous equilibrium. Let us construct such an equilibrium.

We choose $\rho_{ext} = \varepsilon \cos k_0 x$ (independent of time) as our inhomogeneous background charge density and let the distribution be

$$f(x, v) = a/(2\pi)^{1/2} \exp(-v^2/2 + \phi(x)). \tag{57}$$

Now we must use f and ρ_{ext} in Poisson's equation and solve for $\phi(x)$.

Consider solutions for $\phi(x)$ that require only the first terms in a Fourier cosine expansion:

$$\phi(x) = A_1 \cos k_0 x + A_2 \cos 2k_0 x + A_3 \cos 3k_0 x + \cdots$$

with $|A_1| \gg |A_2| \gg |A_3|$, etc., and pick A_1 small enough such that the exponential series $\exp \phi = 1 + \phi + \phi^2/2 + \cdots$ also converges rapidly. Using these expansions and (57) in Poisson's equation and retaining terms through order (A_1^3) leads to a set of relations involving A_1 and k_0:

$$a = \frac{1}{1 + A_1^2/4}, \quad A_2 = \frac{-aA_1^2/4}{a + 4k_0^2}, \quad A_3 = \frac{-aA_1}{24} \cdot \frac{A_1^2 + 12A_2}{a + 9k_0^2}, \tag{58}$$

$$\varepsilon = 2\rho_1 = A_1(a + k_0^2) + aA_1(A_1^2 + 4A_2)/8.$$

Since the velocity distribution is assumed Maxwellian [that is, $f(v)$ is proportional to $\exp(-v^2/2)$], it is easy to solve for the nonzero equilibrium matrix elements Z_{01}, Z_{02}, and Z_{03} for any chosen k_0, A_1 pair. [Z_{00} is always $(2\pi)^{-1/4}$.]

The predicted equilibrium coefficients Z_{0n} are then used as initial values to see how well they represent a time-independent solution of Eq. (28). For an intermediate pair of values, $A_1 = 0.1$ and $k_0 = 0.5$, the coefficient Z_{01} was found to oscillate with an amplitude on the order of 0.01% about the predicted equilibrium value. In two or three trials it was possible to reduce the oscillation to 0.0006% by adjusting the starting value by about 0.001%.

(The calculations were done on an IBM 7044 which does 8-digit arithmetic, and terms involving f_3 were not calculated.) The predicted values were even better for smaller k_0. These small remaining oscillations can be considered to be an effective background noise level for this computer model of the inhomogeneous equilibrium. The "tuning" procedure is thus desirable to lower the noise level as far as possible so that small perturbations from the equilibrium can be followed for longer times as they damp down into the noise level.

With an equilibrium set of coefficients Z_{00}, Z_{01}, and Z_{02} verified for a given k_0, inhomogeneous Landau damping is measured by using an initial value of $Z_{01}(\text{perturbed}) = 1.05 Z_{01}(\text{equilibrium})$. The perturbation electric field is $E_{1(\text{pert})} = E_{1(\text{particles})} - E_{1(\text{equilibrium})}$. For these small perturbations, nonlinear effects are unimportant and the amplitude of the perturbation decreases exponentially with time until it gets down near the background noise level. That is, $E_{\text{pert}}(t) = E_{\text{pert}}(0) \exp(-\gamma t)$ where γ is a constant for linear Landau damping. The result of a sample calculation with a relatively large γ is shown in Fig. 16. For a homogeneous equilibrium with $k_0 = 0.50$, the linear Landau-damping decrement is 0.154. The sample calculation used $k_0 = 0.50$ and an

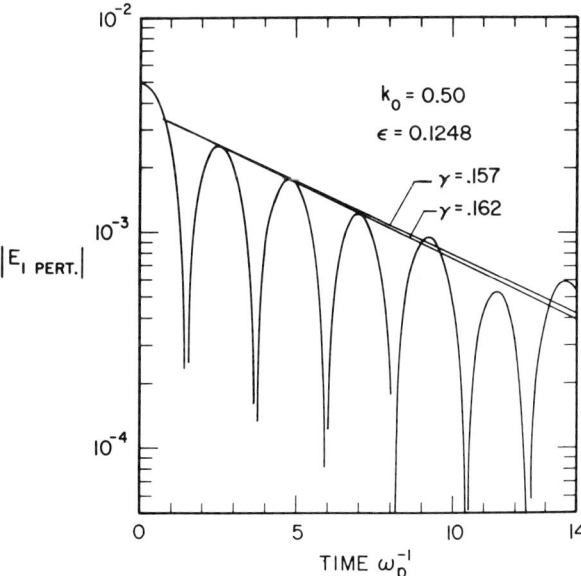

FIG. 16. Damping of a perturbation on a spatially nonuniform equilibrium to illustrate measurement of the damping decrement γ for the case with wavenumber $k_0 = 0.50$ and inhomogeneity $\varepsilon = 2\rho_1 = 0.125$. Difference in slopes for the two straight lines indicates the uncertainty in γ as $E_{1(\text{pert})}$ approaches the background noise level.

inhomogeneity of $\varepsilon = 2\rho_1 = 0.125$. From the semilogarithmic plot we measure $\gamma \simeq 0.160$ for the short time before $E_{1(\text{pert})}$ damps to the background level.

The damping decrement γ was measured in this way for several wavenumbers k_0 with the same inhomogeneity (as measured by A_1) and for several degrees of inhomogeneity at certain k_0. It was found that γ increased relative to the *homogeneous* damping decrement as the degree of inhomogeneity was increased and that the increase was more rapid at smaller k_0 in agreement with a theory of inhomogeneous damping (Jackson and Raether, 1966). Although the theory did not apply in complete detail to the case calculated, the measured increase in γ was in remarkable agreement with the increase predicted using the theory. This agreement is shown in Fig. 17.

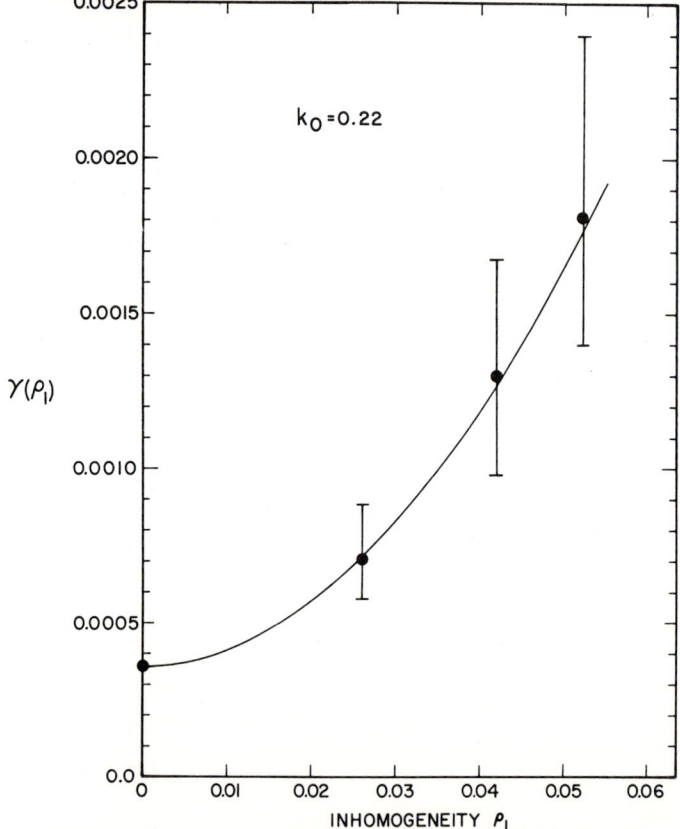

FIG. 17. Landau damping decrement γ as a function of increasing inhomogeneity ρ_1 for $k_0 = 0.22$. The theoretical curve (based on Jackson and Raether, 1966) assumes that the eigenfunction of the electric field is the Mathieu function $se_2(k_0 x, q)$ where $q = 4\rho_1/(3k_0^2)$.

C. Hybrid Models

1. *Nonlinear Ion Waves*

The major obstacle to any Vlasov numerical calculation for a two species plasma is the vastly different time scale for electron and ion motion. For realistic mass ratios, the electrons would have to be followed through about 40 times as many oscillations as the ions. Consequently it is difficult to obtain even a few ion oscillations with the electrons treated rigorously. This difficulty can be circumvented in two ways: by making m_i/m_e and, hence, the time scales more comparable or by setting $m_e = 0$. We describe here a model suggested by Doucet (1967) for the electron contribution to the charge density, which can be combined with Eqs. (1) and (2) (written for ions) in order to study ion Landau damping or growth in the presence of an electron background. Following the development of Armstrong and Montgomery (1968), the model for the electrons is to treat them as a massless fluid with an adiabatic equation of state. That leads to a relation between ϕ and n_e

$$\frac{T_i}{T_e} \phi(x, t) = \frac{\gamma}{\gamma - 1} \{n_e(x, t)^{\gamma - 1} - 1\} \tag{59}$$

where T_i is the ion temperature, T_e is the electron temperature, γ is the exponent ($\neq 1$) in $P_e = P_0(V_0/V)^\gamma$, the units are dimensionless ion units, and $\phi \equiv 0$ when $n(x, t) = 1$, uniform. One now desires $n_e(x, t)$ or its Fourier components in order to put it into Poisson's equation (Eq. 2) which couples the electrons to the ions. The right-hand side of Eq. (59) can be expanded in a power series and the linear term retained.
Let

$$\delta n_e(x, t) = n_e(x, t) - 1 \quad \text{then} \quad \delta n_e(x, t) \doteq (T_i/\gamma T_e)\phi(x, t) \tag{60}$$

where δn_e has no spatially uniform part and, hence, no $n = 0$ Fourier component. If $\gamma = 2$, Eq. (60) is exact; if $\gamma = 1$, Eq. (60) is still appropriate, although Eq. (59) is not. Notice that the $n_e(x, t)$ term is obtained without having to numerically integrate the electron equation of motion.

Now one rewrites the Eqs. (30) and (31) to correspond to ions with the effect of the electrons appearing in Eq. (31) as:

$$E_n(t) = \frac{-i(2\pi)^{1/4} Z_{0n}(t)}{(nk_0 + T_i/\gamma T_e nk_0)}, \quad n \neq 0. \tag{61}$$

The form of Eq. (61) immediately shows that the ion wave behavior will approach the electron wave case if T_e or nk_0 is large, and will be very different if nk_0 is small. The remainder of the numerical procedure is identical with the electron wave case except that Eq. (61) replaces Eq. (31). Although all the computations are not yet finished, preliminary results show that the nonlinear development of stable ion waves in the regime $T_i = T_e$ in this model is qualitatively similar to that of electron waves. Some important effects of the electron dynamics such as electron Landau damping are not recovered in this model and it remains to be determined how far the model can be pushed.

V. Summary and Suggested Future Directions

This article has been intended as a state-of-the-art survey of existing methods of solving Vlasov's equation numerically. Simply by virtue of the fact that the calculations described have been restricted to the one-dimensional and spatially periodic, it is immediately clear that only a beginning has been made on the total problem, and that much remains to be done. We now try to identify the achievements, in qualitative physical terms, that in our opinion have come out of the computations. We also offer some suggestions and speculations about future work.

Most of the worst difficulties associated with solving Vlasov's equation by approximate analytical means are connected, as mentioned in the Introduction of Section I, with our inability to calculate particle trajectories in the parts of velocity space which lie near the phase velocities of waves. (Other parts of the phase plane can be treated adequately by perturbation theory). In the computational schemes described, the computer has no more difficult a time calculating in this region of phase space than any other. It can be said that most of the distinctively nonlinear effects which have emerged so far from the numerical calculations are intimately associated with this region of strong interaction between particles and waves. We can now claim to have a good qualitative understanding of "nonlinear Landau damping," the evolution of the "two-stream" instability (in the presence of a limited number of unstable waves), and the echo phenomenon. It is likely that not many qualitatively new one-dimensional phenomena (with the important exception of fully developed turbulence, involving many unstable wave numbers) remain to be discovered other than these. In our opinion, the investigation of parametric resonance phenomena (see, for example, Dubois, 1968) is not a notably promising area for computer investigations in one-dimensional Vlasov plasmas.

A new breakthrough would be required to treat one-dimensional problems in which the requirement of spatial periodicity had been lifted—all the solutions described so far depend upon spatial periodicity in a crucial way. A number of nonperiodic problems await such a breakthrough: the development of shocks, the dynamics of sheath formation, the nonlinear response of a Vlasov plasma to a periodic signal impressed at one point in space, and the evolution of discontinuities, to name a few. One can only hope breakthroughs will be forthcoming which will allow inroads to be made on these important problems.

A larger area where it is certain that some of the existing methods can be generalized straightforwardly is that of two-dimensional spatially periodic Vlasov plasmas. This converts the number of independent variables from three to either four or five, and thus considerably increases the requisite amounts of computer time. Since the more ambitious one-dimensional problems still strain current computer budgets (as of 1969), this project is bound to be somewhat futuristic, but is nonetheless an inevitability, both because computers continue to grow faster and more flexible, and because there is no other visible method of acquiring accurate data on the behavior of nonlinear two-dimensional Vlasov plasmas uncontaminated by discrete particle effects.

It is immediately apparent that the Vlasov–Poisson system in two dimensions can be solved in the Fourier–Hermite representation of Section II. It is further obvious that the inclusion of *magnetic fields* and *transverse fields* provides no obstacles: the equations governing the evolution of the matrix elements for the distribution function are again first-order ordinary differential equations in the time. There are now going to be either three or four indices instead of two, but the methods of computation are undoubtedly going to be qualitatively the same.

Very probably, the Fourier–Fourier transform techniques can be adapted as well. Somewhat more care will be necessary, however, since even in one dimension, one still has *partial* differential equations to solve.

Exciting physical effects are expected to result from the two-dimensional calculations in the absence of a magnetic field, due to the increased geometrical possibilities for particles to see components of the electric fields as practically time independent in their own rest frames, and thus interact strongly with them. The condition for such a strong interaction in two (or three) dimensions is

$$\omega \cong \mathbf{k} \cdot \mathbf{v},$$

which is clearly much less restrictive than the one-dimensional condition.

$$\omega \cong kv.$$

In particular, the prospect of the energization of particles to velocities much faster than the fastest phase velocity, $\{\omega/|\mathbf{k}|\}_{\max}$, is intriguing.

The inclusion of magnetic fields, which is in principle straightforward, broadens the range of expected qualitatively different physical phenomena, leading to the cyclotron resonance of particles with waves whose frequencies bear approximately rational relations to the gyrofrequencies ($n\omega_{\text{wave}} + m\omega_{\text{particle}} \cong 0$, where m and n are integers). The longitudinal electrostatic resonance described in this article will of course also be present, and doubtless some hybrid types of resonance involving both kinds of effects simultaneously, the details of which remain to be thought through.

In summary, we can say with some confidence that transform solutions of Vlasov's equation have shown themselves capable of extracting considerable information about the nonlinear behavior of plasmas in a rather clean-cut way. With some confidence, we can also assert that we are near the beginning, rather than the end, of these explorations.

Acknowledgments

We wish to acknowledge Professors B. Hubbard, P. J. Kellogg, and D. Pfirsch for helpful discussions during the course of these investigations.

Financial support for the computations reported here have come from several sources. Most of the work done at the University of Iowa, by Armstrong, Harding, and Montgomery, was supported by grants NGR-16-001-043 and NsG 233-62 from the National Aeronautics and Space Administration. Most of the work of Knorr was done while at the Max Planck Institut für Physik und Astrophysik in Munich, Germany. The work of Armstrong has been supported in part by the Culham Laboratory, Culham, Abingdon, Berks., in England, and in part by University of Kansas research grant 3035-5038 in recent months. Harding has been supported in part by a postdoctoral fellowship from Lawrence Radiation Laboratory, Livermore, California.

The help of the Computer Center personnel at the University of Iowa has been invaluable, as has help from the Culham Laboratory computational group and the University of Kansas computer center.

References

Armstrong, T. P. (1966) Univ. of Iowa Res. Rept. No. 66-34. Ph.D. Thesis, Univ. of Iowa, Iowa City.
Armstrong, T. P. (1967). *Phys. Fluids* **10**, 1269.
Armstrong, T. P., and Montgomery, D. C. (1967). *J. Plasma Phys.* **1**, 425.
Armstrong, T. P., and Montgomery, D. C. (1968). *Proc. APS Topical Conf. on Numerical Simulation of Plasma, Sept. 18–20, 1968*. Los Alamos Sci. Lab. Rept. No. LA-3990, Los Alamos, New Mexico.
Armstrong, T. P., and Montgomery, D. C. (1969). Univ. of Iowa Res. Rept. No. 69-10. Univ. of Iowa, Iowa City, Iowa. (To appear in *Phys. Fluids*).
Backus, G. (1960). *J. Math. Phys.* **1**, 178.
Berk, H. L., and Roberts, K. V. (1967a). *Phys. Fluids* **10**, 1595.
Berk, H. L., and Roberts, K. V. (1967b). *Phys. Rev. Letters* **19**, 297.
Bernstein, I. B., and Engelmann, F. (1966) *Phys. Fluids* **9**, 937.
Bernstein, I. B., Greene, J. M., and Kruskal, M. D. (1957). *Phys. Rev.* **108**, 546.

CHANDRASEKHAR, S. (1943). *Rev. Mod. Phys.* **15**, 1.
CRAMÉR, H. (1966). "Mathematical Methods of Statistics," Chap. 10. Princeton Univ. Press, Princeton, New Jersey.
CROWNFIELD, F. R., and BROADDUS, T. (1968). *Bull. Am. Phys. Soc. Ser. II* **12**, 1515.
DECKER, J. F., and HIRSHFIELD, J. L. (1967). *Proc. Conf. Phys. Quiescent Plasmas, Jan. 10–13, 1967, Frascati*, Vol. II, p. 475. Assoc. Euratom-Comitato Naz. per l'Energia Nucl., Rome.
DENAVIT, J., DOYLE, B. W., and HIRSCH, R.H. (1968). *Phys. Fluids* **28**, 2241.
DEPACKH, D. C. (1962). *J. Electron Control* **10**, 139.
DOUCET, H. (1967). Private communication.
DRUMMOND, W. E., and PINES, D. (1962). *Nucl. Fusion Suppl. Pt. 3*, 1049.
DRUMMOND, W. E., and PINES, D. (1964). *Ann. Phys.* **28**, 478.
DUBOIS, D. F. (1969)., *Proc. Summer School on Statistical Physics of Charged Particle Systems. Kyoto, Japan.* "Statistical Physics of Charged Particle Systems" (R. Kubo and T. Kihara, eds.). Syōkabō and W. A. Benjamin, Inc., Tokyo and New York.
ENGELMANN, F., FEIX, M., MINARDI, E., and OXENIUS, J. (1963). *Phys. Fluids* **6**, 266.
FREIDBERG, J. P. (1965). *Phys. Fluids* **8**, 1031.
GARTENHAUS, S. (1963). *Phys. Fluids* **6**, 451.
GARY, S. P. (1967). *Phys. Fluids* **10**, 570.
GILL, S. (1951). *Proc. Cambridge Phil. Soc.* **47**, 96.
GOULD, R. W., O'NEIL, T. M., and MALMBERG, J. H. (1967). *Phys. Rev. Letters* **19**, 219.
GRANT, F. C., and FEIX, M. R. (1967a). *Phys. Fluids* **10**, 696.
GRANT, F. C., and FEIX, M. R. (1967b). *Phys. Fluids* **10**, 1356.
HARDING, R. C. (1968a). *Phys. Fluids* **11**, 2233.
HARDING, R. C. (1968b) Ph.D. Thesis, Univ. of Iowa, Iowa City, Iowa.
HARRIS, E. G. (1957). *Bull. Am. Phys. Soc.* **2**, 67.
HINTON, F. L., and OBERMAN, C. (1968). *Phys. Fluids* **11**, 1982.
JACKSON, E. A., and RAETHER, M. (1966). *Phys. Fluids* **9**, 1257.
KELLOGG, P. J. (1965). *Phys. Fluids* **8**, 102.
KNORR, G. (1961). *Z. Naturforsch.* **16a**, 1320.
KNORR, G. (1963a). Rept. MPI/PA-14/63. Rept. of the Max Planck Inst. für Physik und Astrophysik, Munich.
KNORR, G. (1963b). *Z. Naturforsch.* **18a**, 1304.
KNORR, G. (1968). *Phys. Fluids* **11**, 885.
LANDAU, L. D. (1946). *J. Phys. USSR* **10**, 25.
LEAVENS, W. M. (1967). *Phys. Fluids* **10**, 2708.
LENARD, A., and BERNSTEIN, I. B. (1958). *Phys. Rev.* **112**, 1456.
LOMAX, R. J. (1967). NASA Publ. SP-153. Clearinghouse for Federal Scientific Information, Springfield, Virginia.
LOW, F. E. (1961). *Phys. Fluids* **4**, 842.
MONTGOMERY, D. C. (1960). *Phys. Fluids* **3**, 274.
MONTGOMERY, D. C. (1969). *Proc. Summer School on Statistical Phys. of Charged Particle Systems, Kyoto, Japan.* "Statistical Physics of Charged Particle Systems" (R. Kubo and T. Kihara, eds.). Syōkabō and W. A. Benjamin, Inc., Tokyo and New York.
MONTGOMERY, D. C., and GORMAN, D. (1962). *Phys. Fluids* **5**, 947.
MONTGOMERY, D., and TIDMAN, D. A. (1964). "Plasma Kinetic Theory." McGraw-Hill, New York.
NIELSEN, C. E., SESSLER, A. M., and SYMON, K. R. (1959). *Proc. Intern. Conf. on High Energy Accelerators, Sept. 14–19, 1959, Geneva*, p. 239. CERN, Geneva.
O'NEIL, T. M. (1968). *Phys. Fluids* **11**, 2420.
O'NEIL, T. M., and GOULD, R. W. (1968). *Phys. Fluids* **11**, 134.

PEARLSTEIN, L. D. (1964). *Phys. Fluids* **7**, 1461.
SADOWSKI, W. L. (1967). NASA Publ. SP-153. Clearinghouse for Federal Scientific Information, Springfield, Virginia.
SAENZ, A. W. (1965). *J. Math. Phys.* **6**, 859.
TAYLOR, E. C., and COMISAR, G. G. (1963). *Phys. Rev.* **132**, 2379.
TITCHMARSH, E. C. (1937). "Introduction to the Theory of Fourier Integrals," Chap. 1, Para. 1.27, p. 44. Oxford Univ. Press, London and New York.
VEDENOV, A., VELIKHOV, E., and SAGDEEV, R. (1962). *Nucl. Fusion Suppl. Pt.* **2**, 465.
WEISSGLAS, P. (1962). *Plasma Phys.* (*J. Nucl. Energy Pt. C*) **4**, 329.
WEITZNER, H. (1963). *Phys. Fluids* **6**, 1123.
WEITZNER, H. (1964). *Phys. Fluids* **7**, 476.

The Water-Bag Model*

Herbert L. Berk
LAWRENCE RADIATION LABORATORY
UNIVERSITY OF CALIFORNIA, LIVERMORE, CALIFORNIA

and

Keith V. Roberts
U.K. ATOMIC ENERGY AUTHORITY
CULHAM LABORATORY, CULHAM, ABINGDON, BERKSHIRE, ENGLAND

I. Introduction 88
II. Physical Properties of Step-Function Distributions 90
   A. Free Energy 91
   B. Debye Shielding 92
   C. Plasma Oscillations 93
   D. Motion of a Test Charge 97
   E. Two-Stream Instability 97
   F. Phase-Space Vortices 100
III. Numerical Methods 100
   A. Integral Representation of Coordinates and Velocities 102
   B. Chaining 104
   C. Calculation of the Electric Field 105
   D. Trimming of Contours 107
   E. Calculation of the Mean Distribution Function 109
IV. Numerical Stability of the Leapfrog Scheme 111
   A. Odd and Even Phase Spaces 111
   B. Computational Instability 112
   C. Synchronous and Antisynchronous Modes 113
   D. Generalized Dispersion Relation 114
   E. Synchronization of the Contours 116
V. Numerical Experiment of the Bump-on-Tail Instability 116
   A. Equilibrium and Linear Analysis 116
   B. Hole–Wave Interaction 118
   C. Nonlinear Evolution 118
   D. Trimming 118
   E. Hybrid Model 119
Appendix I. Continuous Distribution as the Limit of a Step Function 126
Appendix II. Analysis of Synchronization Method 129
References 133

---

* This work was supported jointly by the U.S. Atomic Energy Commission and the U.K. Atomic Energy Authority.

I. Introduction

THE VLASOV EQUATION DESCRIBES the motion of an ideal incompressible fluid in a 2N-dimensional (**q**, **p**) phase space where **q** and **p** are N-dimensional canonical coordinate and momentum vectors. The configuration of this phase fluid is represented by a distribution function $f(\mathbf{q}, \mathbf{p})$ which evolves with time according to the equation

$$\frac{df}{dt} \equiv \frac{\partial f}{\partial t} + \mathbf{V} \cdot \frac{\partial f}{\partial \mathbf{q}} + \mathbf{F} \cdot \frac{\partial f}{\partial \mathbf{p}} = 0, \tag{1}$$

where $\mathbf{V} = d\mathbf{q}/dt$ and $\mathbf{F} = d\mathbf{p}/dt$. The force per unit mass **F** is obtained by solving a field equation and may be determined partly by external sources and partly by internal sources that are functionals of f itself, so that one can talk of a "self-interacting" phase fluid (Berk et al., 1969).

The fluid picture is particularly clear for the case $N = 1$, since a continuous distribution $f(x, v)$ can then be represented graphically by contours of constant in the two dimensional (x, v) phase plane (Fig. 1). The contours C_j move with

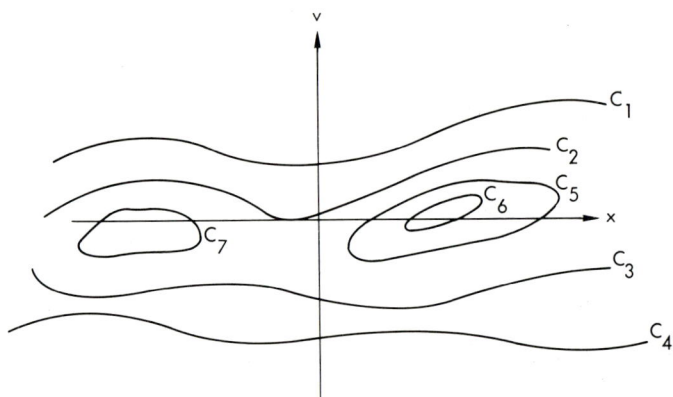

FIG. 1. Contour representation of a continuous or a step-function distribution in phase space.

the fluid and preserve their topology as the system evolves, so that no crossing or smearing occurs; and furthermore, the area enclosed between any two contours is an invariant of the motion. Each point (x_i, v_i) on a contour obeys the "particle" equations

$$dx_i/dt = v_i, \quad \text{and} \quad dv_i/dt = \alpha_i(x_i, v_i, t). \tag{2}$$

The example discussed in this paper is that of a two-dimensional electron phase fluid neutralized by a uniform positive background charge. The acceleration $\alpha = (e/m)E(x, t)$ is independent of density and is due to an electric field E that satisfies Poisson's equation:

$$\frac{d}{dx}\left(\frac{e}{m}E\right) = \omega_p^2\left[\frac{1}{2\overline{V}}\int_{-\infty}^{\infty} f\,dv - 1\right], \qquad (3)$$

where $\omega_p^2 = (4\pi n_0 e^2)/m$, e is the electronic charge (which has a negative value), m is the electronic mass, n_0 is the mean particle density, and $2\overline{V}$ is a normalization factor. Subsequently we shall write $(e/m)E$ simply as $E = -\partial\phi/\partial x$.

Several methods for solving the coupled Vlasov–Poisson equations (1) and (3) have been described in the literature (NASA Rept., 1967; Los Alamos Rept., 1968). Since Eq. (1) is a partial differential equation, perhaps the most straightforward approach is to use a two-dimensional difference scheme with a rectangular mesh in (x, v) space, a method adopted in four dimensions by Killeen and Rompel (1966). This type of calculation is simple but lengthy, since several thousand mesh points are required, and truncation errors will lead to some numerical diffusion even if a fourth-order-accurate difference scheme is employed (Roberts and Weiss, 1966). Most workers have used some variant of the particle model originally developed by Buneman (1959) and Dawson (1962), which simulates the continuous phase fluid by a discrete set of points. The local density of these points in a small region of the phase plane defines an approximation to $f(x, v)$ that can be used in Eq. (3) to evaluate the charge distribution; and their motion according to Eqs. (2) gives a graphic picture of the fluid flow (Morse and Neilson, 1968; Dawson et al., 1968), although some numerical diffusion results from the random electric fields caused by statistical fluctuations in the charge density. More exact solutions of the coupled Vlasov–Poisson equations have been obtained, at a considerable cost in computer time, by expansion in terms of Fourier components and orthogonal polynomials (Knorr, 1963; Armstrong, 1967).

An alternative method of following the evolution of the system is to track each contour curve C_j (Berk and Roberts, 1967a). At each time t the configuration of the contours determines the charge density $\int f\,dv$ so that $E(x)$ can be computed from Eq. (3). With $E(x_i)$ and v_i determined, Eq. (2) is then used to find a new configuration at time $t + dt$.

This method is particularly tractable if the distribution function is specified exactly by only a finite number of curves, which is true for generalized step-function distributions consisting of regions of constant f, separated by boundaries on which f changes discontinuously. The diagram in Fig. 1 can just as well represent this case, with only the curves separating the different f regions being represented in the figure. Once these boundary curves are known, the distribution is precisely determined, and it is not necessary to follow fluid points inside the regions even though they may be undergoing complicated motions. It will be shown in Section III how to construct the charge density for an arbitrary boundary configuration. We shall find it convenient to refer to these boundaries simply as "contours," since they have the same general properties; in fact, they correspond to regions of the phase plane where many contours coalesce.

Dory (1962) was the first to use this numerical technique to investigate nonlinear properties of the negative-mass instability, and Woods (1969) has used it to describe particle trapping in Astron. The term "water-bag model" was introduced by De Packh (1962) in an analytic calculation of the behavior of electron beams, in which a bounded region of uniform density evolved as an incompressible fluid in phase space, like a blob of water inside a deformable, perfectly elastic container.

The curves become stretched and distorted as the motion proceeds, and our program therefore adds extra points in order to maintain accuracy. Eventually the calculation terminates due either to slowness of the computation or to lack of storage space, but until this point is reached the water-bag technique is capable of considerable accuracy at a small cost in computer time, and therefore it provides a useful addition to the other methods that are available.

II. Physical Properties of Step-Function Distributions

Although the evolution of a step-function distribution is simple to calculate, a detailed investigation of such systems is only warranted if their physical properties are similar to those of the continuous distributions that occur in real plasmas. This is true for phenomena that depend mainly on the overall shape of the distribution function, rather than on its precise details. In this case, a more thorough understanding of the physics can often be obtained by studying a step-function distribution, since it is easier to isolate the contributions of individual regions of phase space. By way of illustration, we present in this section a graphical interpretation, stimulated by our nonlinear computations with the water-bag model, of topics such as free energy (Gardner, 1963; Fowler, 1964), Debye shielding, plasma oscillations, test-particle motion, and the thermal two-stream instability.

Although these illustrations provide considerable insight into the nonlinear behavior of two-dimensional phase fluids, caution should be used in extending this to four- or six-dimensional fluids ($N = 2$ or 3), which are much less well understood. In ordinary hydrodynamics, for example, it is known that there are important qualitative differences in the turbulent behavior of incompressible fluids in two and three dimensions. Correspondingly, some of the phenomena described in this paper may not generalize to higher-dimensional cases.

A. Free Energy

The total energy of the phase fluid is proportional to

$$\frac{1}{2} \iint f v^2 \, dx \, dv + (2V/\omega_p^2) \int (E^2/2) \, dx, \qquad (4)$$

and must remain invariant as the system evolves. Both terms in Eq. (4) are determined by the configuration of the contours C_j; and the kinetic energy term may be compared to the gravitational potential energy of a system of incompressible liquids of constant but different densities (such as oil and water), with v^2 playing the part of the height coordinate. If $\partial f/\partial v^2 < 0$ (oil floating on water), the phase fluid is stable and its free energy is said to be zero, while if $\partial f/\partial v^2 > 0$, it may be able to lose kinetic energy by an incompressible interchange motion (analogous to the Rayleigh–Taylor instability of a liquid boundary), in which dense regions "fall" toward the x axis as shown in Fig. 2, giving up their energy to the electric field, while regions of lower density move in the opposite direction. This is the origin of the thermal two-stream instability to be discussed in Section II,E. This gravitational

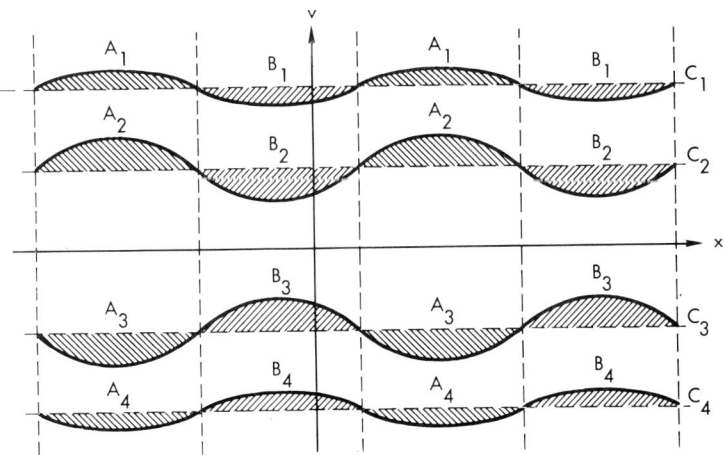

FIG. 2. Phase-space contours for a two-stream instability.

analogy is not exact, however, since the condition $\partial f/\partial E < 0$ is sufficient but not necessary for stability, and we shall later meet stable configurations in which it is not satisfied.

B. DEBYE SHIELDING

Debye shielding may also be represented graphically. Figure 3 exhibits

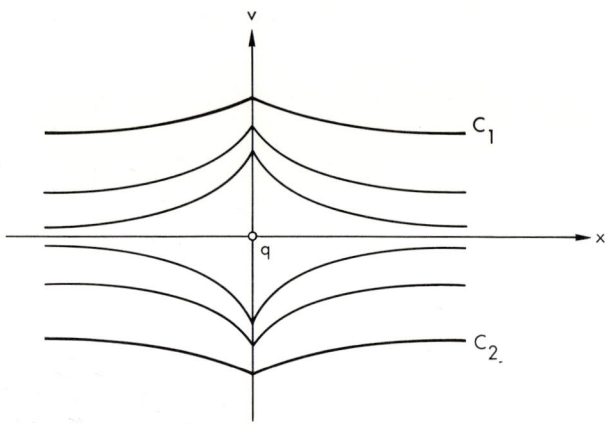

FIG. 3. Phase-space contours that develop due to Debye shielding of a positive charge q.

the stationary pattern of equal-energy contours

$$\mathscr{E} \equiv \tfrac{1}{2}v^2 + \phi = \text{constant} \tag{5}$$

that is set up in response to a positive point charge q. For a step-function distribution, f is constant between the contours C_1 and C_2. Points on the upper contour C_1 move to the right and are attracted to the charge q, so that the velocity $v_1(x)$ increases and C_1 rises as it approaches q and falls as it departs. A corresponding situation occurs for the lower curve C_2. This deformation causes an increase in the charge integral

$$\int f\,dv = f[v_1(x) - v_2(x)], \tag{6}$$

and hence the negative charge density is largest close to q and decreases to the equilibrium value far from q. Trapped particles are taken into account automatically, provided that f is everywhere constant. This buildup of background charge is just the Debye shielding that cancels the electric field at a large distance. If q were negative the contours would be depressed rather than raised, but the effect of shielding is quite similar. For sufficiently small perturbations Eq. (1) gives

$$\delta \mathscr{E} \equiv \overline{V} \, \delta v + \phi = 0, \tag{7}$$

so that for a symmetrical configuration $\delta \int f \, dv = -(2\phi)/\overline{V}$ and Poisson's equation (3) becomes

$$d^2\phi/dx^2 - (\omega_p^2/\overline{V}^2)\phi = 4\pi q, \tag{8}$$

with the solution

$$E = -2\pi q Sg(x) \exp(-|x|/\overline{V}), \tag{9}$$

where

$$Sg(x) = 1, \quad x > 0, \quad \text{or} \quad Sg(x) = -1, \quad x < 0.$$

Debye shielding can be described in much the same manner for continuous distributions, with the thermal velocity replacing $\overline{V}$.

C. Plasma Oscillations

Figure 4 shows two stable distributions that are monotonic functions of

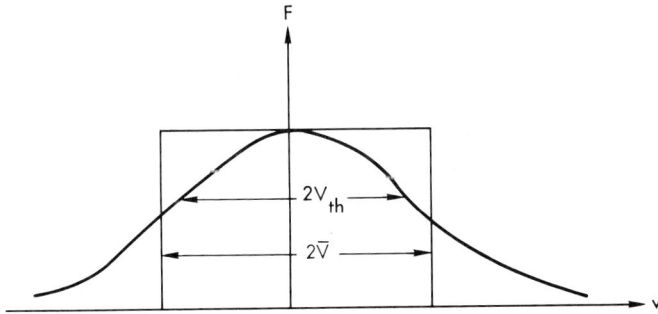

FIG. 4. Two stable distribution functions: a continuous and a step-function distribution.

energy: a continuous distribution and a step-function distribution. In the electrostatic problem each gives rise to dispersive waves, commonly called plasma oscillations. The dispersion relation for a step-function is

$$\omega^2 = \omega_p^2 + k^2 \overline{V}^2, \tag{10}$$

where ω is the radian frequency and k is the wavenumber; and this relation is exact. For a continuous (Maxwell) distribution the dispersion relation is approximated by

$$\omega^2 = \omega_p^2 + 3k^2 v_{th}^2, \tag{11}$$

provided that the phase velocity $v_{ph} \equiv \omega/k \gg v_{th}$. The waves can be represented graphically by oscillations of the f contours in the (x, v) plane (analogous to oscillations of a liquid surface or interface), which transform energy from kinetic to electrostatic form and vice versa.

Plasma oscillations can be described approximately by a set of fluid equations with the ideal gas law

$$v_{th}^2 n^{-3} = \text{constant},$$

where

$$v_{th}^2 = \int dv\, v^2 f(v, x),$$

and it has recently been demonstrated by Betrand and Feix (1968) that for the step-function distribution shown in fig. 4 these equations are exact, provided that the phase space contours remain single-valued functions of x.

Although the dispersion relations (10) and (11) are quite similar, there is an important physical difference between the two models. Linear oscillations of a step-function distribution last indefinitely, while those of a continuous distribution decay due to Landau damping. This difference arises from the detailed local structure of the continuous distribution function, since if $\partial f/\partial v^2 < 0$ in the neighborhood of the phase velocity v_{ph} of the wave, a steady incompressible interchange motion can occur, which raises denser fluid to higher velocity while decreasing the velocity of the less dense fluid. Within the limits of a linearized description, this "resonant" region of the fluid, therefore, continually absorbs energy from the wave.

If the initial amplitude of the wave is sufficiently large, this energy absorption may saturate after a finite time (O'Neil, 1965; Armstrong, 1967), and then the nonlinear response of a continuous distribution can be similar to that of a step function. To see this, we discuss the phase-space contours that are induced by finite-amplitude plasma oscillations, first for step functions and then for continuous distributions. Figure 5 shows the stationary f contours in the reference frame of a wave with phase velocity v_{ph}, which can equally well be thought of as the fluid streamlines or as contours of

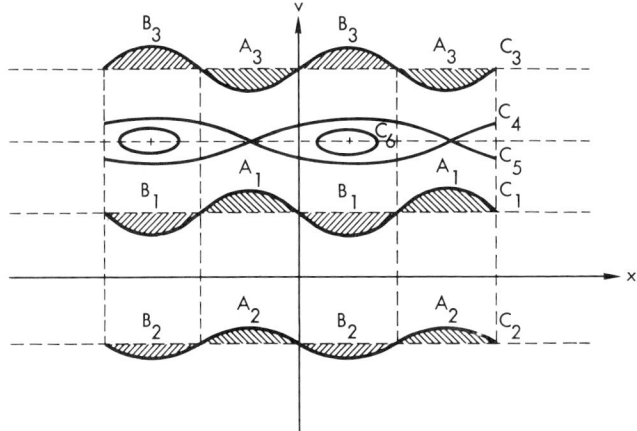

Fig. 5. Phase-space contours for stationary plasma oscillations.

constant energy $\mathscr{E} = \tfrac{1}{2}v^2 + \phi$. In the laboratory frame the whole contour pattern translates uniformly to the right.

In the case of a step-function distribution the lower curves C_1 and C_2 represent the boundaries of the fluid, and the phase velocity of the wave lies outside this region. The curves C_3–C_6 are therefore "virtual" constant-energy contours, not occupied by particles. C_1 is more deeply modulated than C_2, since the particles on C_1 interact for a longer time with a given phase of the wave. Specifically, the interaction time is inversely proportional to the Doppler-shifted frequency $\omega - kv = k(v_{\text{ph}} - v)$, and the modulation amplitudes $\delta v_{1,2}$ are given by

$$\delta v_{1,2} = \left| \frac{E}{k(v_{\text{ph}} - v)} \right|. \tag{12}$$

There is less area enclosed in the B-labeled regions of the wave than in the A regions, so that the B phases that have a deficiency of electrons are positively charged, while the A phases are negatively charged.

The individual particles on the contours continually exchange energy with the wave, since they sample different phases at the local Doppler-shifted frequency. However, it is apparent from the diagram that the total kinetic energy of the perturbed system in the laboratory frame must be greater than the original equilibrium energy, since a sinusoidally perturbed contour can be constructed from the initial equilibrium by transferring fluid from regions B_1 and A_2 to A_1 and B_2, respectively, while conserving the area invariant. In addition there is a positive field energy $(2\bar{V}/\omega_p^{\,2}) \int (E^2/2)\, dx$ that must be added to the system.

With some modifications the same picture can be used for continuous distributions, although now a continuum of contours must be considered. Though it is no longer so obvious from the diagram, the B regions where the contours have troughs for $v < v_{\text{ph}}$ are negatively charged, and the A regions are positively charged. The phase-space region $v > v_{\text{ph}}$ tends to reverse this trend, but will not be very effective for a distribution that falls exponentially with v^2, such as a Maxwellian. As before, one can show that the average kinetic energy in the laboratory frame increases as the result of the perturbation. In Appendix I we prove these statements by considering a generalized step function with many infinitesimal steps and then finding the continuum limit.

Another important region in Fig. 5 lies between the contours C_4 and C_5, where fluid circulates in the trough of the wave at a trapping frequency that is approximately $\omega_T \approx (kE)^{1/2}$. To reach this state from the initial equilibrium, the trapped fluid has to absorb energy from the wave, since in the perturbed state f contours such as C_6 straddle the level $v = v_{\text{ph}}$, while the original equilibrium f has larger values for smaller v. The redistribution of fluid requires that in the mean the larger f values rise and the smaller fall. In Appendix I it is shown that the kinetic energy density difference $\Delta \mathscr{E}_{\text{kin}}$ between the perturbed and the equilibrium states in the trapped band is

$$\Delta \mathscr{E}_{\text{kin}} \approx (\Delta v)^3 v \frac{\partial f}{\partial v}, \tag{13}$$

where Δv is the velocity width of the band that is given by $(\Delta v)^2 \approx E/k$.

In a transient situation when an electric field E_0 is initially present with wavenumber k, the resonant band will absorb energy in an attempt to reach a stationary state. If this is to be achieved before the electric field has decayed away, the initial field energy density $\sim (\overline{V}/\omega_p^2) E_0^2$ must be greater than the energy required to form the trapped particle structure. This inequality requires

$$E_0 \gtrsim \frac{\omega_p^2}{|k|} \left(\frac{\partial f}{\partial v^2} \right)_{v_{\text{ph}}} v_{\text{ph}}^2 = \frac{1}{\pi} \left| k v_{\text{ph}}^2 \gamma \frac{\partial \varepsilon_R}{\partial \omega} \right| = \frac{1}{\pi} \left| \frac{\omega^2 \gamma}{k} \frac{\partial \varepsilon_R}{\partial \omega} \right|, \tag{14}$$

where

$$\gamma = \frac{\omega_p^2}{k^2} \left(\frac{\partial f}{\partial v} \right)_{v_{\text{ph}}} \bigg/ \frac{\partial \varepsilon_R}{\partial \omega}$$

is the linear damping rate, ε_R is the real part of the dielectric function for real ω, and for plasma oscillations $\partial \varepsilon_R / \partial \omega \approx 2/\omega_p$. Rearranging terms, we find that the condition to achieve a stationary state with a finite field amplitude present is

$$(kE_0)^{1/2} \equiv \omega_T > \gamma. \tag{15}$$

Thus, if we have a small but finite electric field that satisfies inequality (15), a steady wave should be maintained for a continuous as well as for a step-function distribution.

D. Motion of a Test Charge

There is an exotic superfluidity effect that occurs with a simple step-function distribution ($f \neq 0$, $|v| < \overline{V}$) when the test charge moves with a speed $|v| < \overline{V}$ through the plasma. In general, the drag D on a particle moving with velocity v is given by

$$D \propto \int dk \, \frac{\text{Im}[\varepsilon(k, kv)]}{k \, |\varepsilon(k, kv)|^2} + \sum_\alpha \frac{\pi}{[k_\alpha(\partial\varepsilon/\partial\omega)(k_\alpha, k_\alpha v)(v - v_g)]} \tag{16}$$

where $\varepsilon(k, \omega)$ is the dielectric function, $\varepsilon(k_\alpha, k_\alpha v) = 0$, for k_α real and

$$v_g = -\left[\frac{\partial\varepsilon}{\partial k} \bigg/ \frac{\partial\varepsilon}{\partial\omega}\right]_{k=k_\alpha}.$$

For a step-function distribution, Im $\varepsilon = 0$, and therefore a drag will only occur if the velocity of the test particle is equal to the phase velocity of a natural mode of oscillation. From Eq. (11) we see that $|\omega/k| > \overline{V}$, and therefore there is no drag if $|v| < \overline{V}$. For $|v| > \overline{V}$, the test charge continually excites Cerenkov radiation, which propagates away, so that it loses energy and slows down.

This superfluid behavior is not a general characteristic of continuous distributions. The test charge induces a local interchange motion in phase space that interacts with the local velocity gradient of f, so that it always tends to slow down if $\partial f/\partial v^2 < 0$. [Note that Im $\varepsilon \propto \partial f/\partial v^2$ in the first term of Eq. (16).]

E. Two-Stream Instability

The use of a generalized step function to describe the interaction between two interpenetrating thermal beams is another example where insight into linear and nonlinear development has been obtained (Berk and Roberts, 1967a,b,c). Figure 6 shows two distribution functions that can represent the equilibrium for a two-stream instability, and in Fig. 2 the phase-space contours for the step-function distribution are illustrated. The distribution is constant between the contours C_1 and C_2 and between C_3 and C_4 and is zero elsewhere.

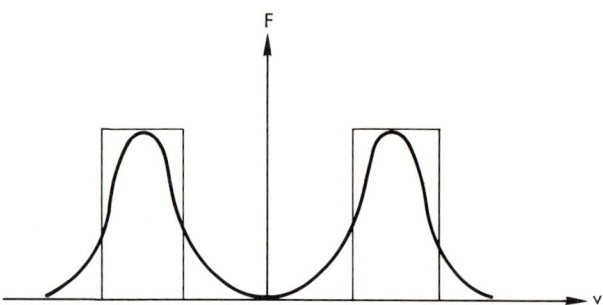

FIG. 6. Two distributions that represent a thermal two-stream instability.

Consider a sinusoidal perturbation with zero phase velocity. A perturbed configuration that maintains the area invariants can be constructed from the initial equilibrium configuration by displacing fluid from the A regions at the inner curves into the B regions and, similarly, fluid from the B regions at the outer curves into the A regions. Since the inner curves are more deeply modulated than the outer curves, they dominate the response of the system, and in the limiting case of marginal stability, it follows from Eq. (12) that the loss of kinetic energy is proportional to $1/v_2 - 1/v_1$, where v_1 and v_2 are the velocities of the outer and inner curves, respectively.

Instability can only arise if it is possible to find a perturbation of the equilibrium that leaves the total energy unchanged. In the case discussed here, the loss of kinetic energy at the inner curves as the fluid "falls" from region A to region B is balanced partly by a gain in electric-field energy and partly by the kinetic-energy gain at the outer curves; and for this two-stream problem an unstable mode whose linear state has the character of Fig. 2 does indeed develop.

For two thermal beams, the outer curves play only an incidental role in the instability. From the character of the velocity modulation of the outer curves [Eqs. (7) and (12)], it is seen that they attempt to shield the charges produced by the inner curves, as explained in Section II,B. However, the further away they are in velocity space, the less effective is the shielding, as Eq. (8) shows. To the extent that the outer curves can be neglected altogether, the system is entirely described by the cavity in phase space between curves

C_2 and C_3. Hence this problem can be viewed as the evolution of a cavity in an electron phase fluid, and it has been shown (Berk *et al.*, 1969) that it is exactly equivalent to the evolution of a one-dimensional gravitational system whose step-function distribution is constant between C_2 and C_3 and zero elsewhere.

Figure 7 exhibits the nonlinear state of the two-stream problem achieved

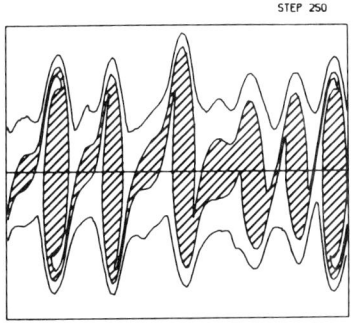
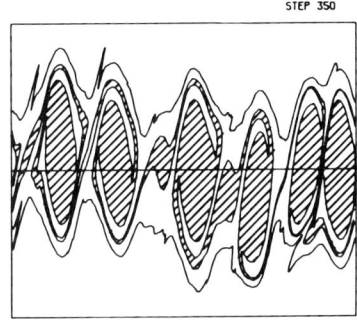
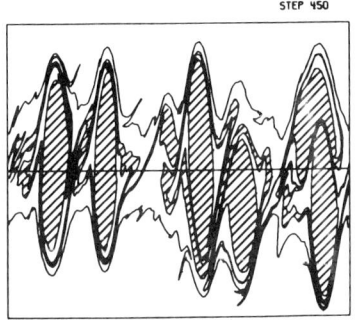

FIG. 7. Hole formation in two-stream instability.

in a computer experiment (Berk and Roberts, 1967c). The cavity has coalesced into stable structures in phase space that are analogous to one-dimensional stars (Hohl and Feix, 1966). In the limit that the outer contours can be neglected, analysis of a single hole shows that it is stable. However, an array of holes is expected to be unstable, because the holes should attract one another. In Fig. 7 there is an example of two hole structures in the process of coalescing due to this attractive force. The presence of the outer curves does not substantially change the interpretation, since they only shield the attractive force; and the system shown in Fig. 7 can therefore be thought of as a set of gravitating stars attracting each other with a Debye (or meson) potential that satisfies an equation similar to Eq. (8). Apart from thin spikes, Fig. 7 shows that the two outer curves behave adiabatically and merely shield the positive charges of the holes, in contrast to the nonadiabatic behavior of the inner curves.

The description given here for the two-stream instability applies equally well when continuous distributions are used, and similar results have been obtained in other computer experiments (Armstrong, 1967; Morse and Neilson, 1968).

F. PHASE-SPACE VORTICES

Because a hole is positively charged, it generates a potential well that traps electrons with neighboring velocities, so that the phase fluid in the vicinity of the hole circulates in a clockwise sense; and in a computer-generated movie film that follows the motion of particles each hole appears like a vortex in the fluid (Berk and Roberts, 1967c). Thus, vortices in phase space attract one another, and it is interesting that the same phenomenon occurs for vortices of finite size in a real incompressible fluid in two dimensions. Numerical experiments are currently in progress to study this effect.

III. Numerical Methods

In our numerical calculation, each contour C_j is approximated by a chain of Lagrangian points $P_{j,i}$ linked to each other by straight-line segments, as indicated in Fig. 8. Adjacent points must remain sufficiently close to one

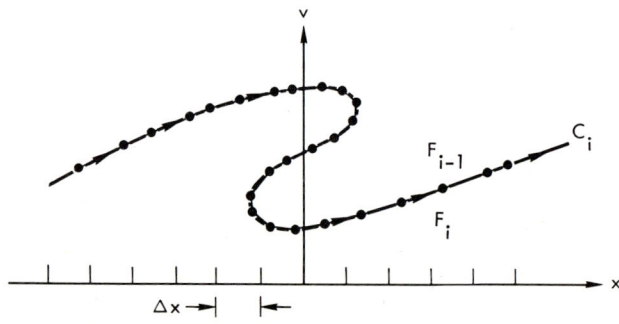

FIG. 8. Numerical approximation of a continuous contour. Points are connected by line segments, and arrows indicate direction of chaining.

another in order for the sum of the elementary trapezoidal areas to approximate accurately the invariant area within the contour. A list-processing technique, described in Section III,B, is used to insert or remove points if segments along a contour stretch or contract too much in the course of the calculation.

The points $P_{j,i}$ are represented by fixed-point integers, since the processing of coordinates is then particularly efficient in problems with periodic boundary conditions. The fluid in the upper half of the phase plane moves steadily to the right since $v > 0$, while the fluid in the lower half-plane moves steadily to the left, giving a horizontal shearing motion. Thus a curve that initially lies entirely within the fundamental period $0 \leq x < L$ can eventually cross the left or right boundaries several times. By using an integer representation for the coordinates one can project the position of a point $P_{j,i}$ back to the fundamental period simply by masking out the period number that is stored in the most significant bits of the coordinate word. This means that it is not necessary to test each particle to see whether it has crossed a period boundary. A more detailed discussion is given in Section III,A.

The electric field is determined from Poisson's equation, or from its integrated form, which is Gauss' law:

$$\begin{aligned}
E(x_{m+1} - x_m) &= \frac{\omega_p^2}{2\bar{V}} \left[\int_{x_m}^{x_{m+1}} dx \int f \, dv - \Delta x \right] \\
&= \frac{\omega_p^2}{2\bar{V}} \left[\sum_j \Delta f_j \int_{x_m}^{x_{m+1}} dx \, v_j(x) - \Delta x \right] \\
&= \frac{\omega_p^2}{2\bar{V}} \left[\sum_j \Delta f_j A_j(x_{m+1}, x_m) - \Delta x \right],
\end{aligned} \qquad (17)$$

where $\Delta f_j = f_j - f_{j-1}$ is the discontinuity in f due to the jth contour and $A_j(a, b)$ is the signed area enclosed between contour j and the x axis in the interval between points $x = a$ and $x = b$ ($a > b$).

The points x_m determine a fixed Eulerian grid and divide the phase plane into vertical strips $x_m \leq x < x_{m+1}$ of equal thickness Δx. To determine the electric field from Eq. (17) it is necessary to calculate the area $A_{j,m}$ enclosed between each contour j and the x axis in each Eulerian strip m. This is performed by scanning the points on C_j in order and determining the trapezoidal area associated with each pair of adjacent points. If the area encompasses more than one Eulerian strip, then partial areas are allocated to each of the strips. Without any additional check this method automatically processes any arbitrary contour configuration correctly, including curves with multiple values of v for a given x, and it is exact for polygonal contours.

Once the fields at the Eulerian points x_m have been determined, the field at each Lagrangian point $P_{j,i}$ is obtained by linear interpolation between the endpoints of the Eulerian interval in which the point x_i lies. The contour configuration is then incremented in time by using a second-order-accurate leapfrog scheme:

$$x_i[(n + 1) \Delta t] = x_i[(n - 1) \Delta t] + 2v_i[n \Delta t] \Delta t,$$
$$v_i[(n + 1) \Delta t] = v_i[(n - 1) \Delta t] + 2E_i[n \Delta t] \Delta t. \quad (18)$$

This scheme is examined in Section IV, where it is shown to contain a weak computational instability that can be stabilized by periodically synchronizing the contours associated with the odd and even time steps.

A useful diagnostic is the mean distribution function $(1/L) \int f(x, v) \, dx$ at a given instant. This is obtained by a simple scanning operation, in much the same manner as the charge distribution is determined. A discussion is given in Section III,E.

A disadvantage of our integration method is that contours can elongate indefinitely. As already mentioned, we can maintain accuracy by inserting points wherever they are needed, but eventually the storage space is exhausted or the computation becomes too slow, and the run must then be terminated. One method of avoiding this catastrophe is to "trim" the phase diagram by removing the very thin filamentary regions that tend to develop and rejoining the broken ends of the curves. Storage locations belonging to sections of curve that have been removed are then added to a common pool, and the calculation can continue. In a computer facility with an interactive on-line display this trimming operation would provide a user with the fascinating option of altering the contour topology from time to time while he watched the numerical experiment develop. In Section III,D we describe the trimming operations that are now implemented, and in Section V we exhibit a calculation where trimming has been used.

A. Integral Representation of Coordinates and Velocities

The coordinates and velocities of points on the contours are represented by integers. The system has period L, so that each computer point with coordinate (x_i, v_i) actually stands for an infinite set of physical points with coordinates

$$(x_i + \lambda L, v_i), \quad \lambda = 0, \pm 1, \pm 2, \cdots. \quad (19)$$

We divide each period into $L = 2^l$ Eulerian intervals of unit length, where l is an integer, and use separate parts of the coordinate word to represent:

(a) the period,
(b) the Eulerian interval m, within this period,

(c) the position within the interval.

This is achieved by writing

$$X = Ax + P = A(\lambda L + m + f/A) + P, \tag{20}$$

where

$$0 \leq f < A, \quad 0 \leq m < L, \quad A = 2^a, \quad L = 2^l, \quad P = 2^p.$$

Typical values for a 48-bit computer word[1] are $a = 30$, $l = 6$, $p = 46$. The purpose of the large integer p is to make sure that the stored coordinate X always remains positive, however far the point moves, so that the arithmetic is independent of the representation that is used for negative numbers on a specific type of computer. There are several advantages in using powers of 2. For example, it is easy to use masking operations in FORTRAN, where these are available, or to convert to assembly language to make the critical sections of the program faster; and octal dumps are readily interpreted. The exponent a determines the accuracy with which the coordinate can be defined. There is some room for adjustment between the three parts (a), (b), and (c) of the word, but in practice this method can be as accurate as one that uses floating-point numbers.

At the start of the calculation, all the points are in the initial period ($P \leq X < P + AL$), and they are then allowed to move freely according to the difference equations

$$\begin{aligned} X_i[(n+1)\,\Delta t] &= X_i[(n-1)\,\Delta t] + V_i[n\,\Delta t], \\ V_i[(n+1)\,\Delta t] &= V_i[(n-1)\,\Delta t] + R_i[n\,\Delta t], \end{aligned} \tag{21}$$

where V and R are integers that represent $2v\,\Delta t$ and $4r\,\Delta t^2$, respectively, r being the acceleration. This scaling avoids all unnecessary multiplications. After some time, most of the points will have left the initial period at one or other of the boundaries $x = 0, L$ and will have moved into an adjacent period. However, there is no need to test for this escape (which would cost computer time), since in order to calculate the charge density, electric field, and particle acceleration we simply project the coordinates into the fundamental period $0 \leq X < AL$ by masking out all but the $a + l$ least significant bits. This can be

---

[1] The program was developed on the CDC 3600 at the University of California, San Diego, and has been adapted for the ICL KDF9 at the Culham Laboratory. Both of these machines have 48-bit words. It is also used on the CDC 6600 at the Lawrence Radiation Laboratory, Livermore, with a 60-bit word. The three versions of FORTRAN are very similar.

done in the FORTRAN dialects used by the statement

$$\text{IXFUND} = \text{IXTRUE} . \text{AND} . \text{MASK} \tag{22}$$

where MASK $= 2^{a+1} - 1$, IXTRUE is the true coordinate, and IXFUND is the position within the fundamental period. This masking facility is very useful for Vlasov and other particle problems, as well as for character manipulation; and it is unfortunate that it is not available on all machines, nor in ASA FORTRAN.

To calculate the Eulerian interval in which a point lies, a FORTRAN integer division is used. Since the divisor is a power of 2, this is equivalent to a logical right shift by a places, which eliminates the fractional part of the coordinate. In assembly language the standard MASK and SHIFT operations would be employed. Evidently the equations of motion (21) occupy a small fraction of the total computer time. The major fraction is required for calculating the charge distribution, which is discussed in Section III,C.

B. Chaining

Two types of curves have currently been implemented: those that form closed loops in the phase plane (type 1) and those that run continuously from $x = -\infty$ to $x = +\infty$ (type 0). Each type of curve is defined by a chain of successive points:

$$(x_B, v_B), (x_\alpha, v_\alpha) \cdots (x_\rho, v_\rho), (x_E, v_E), \tag{23}$$

where B and E define the beginning and the end of the chain. For a type 1 chain the successor to (x_E, v_E) is (x_B, v_B); for a type 0 chain it is $(x_B + L, v_B)$, where L is the periodicity length. We adopt the convention that the closed loops (type 1) always have a clockwise direction, while the endless curves (type 0) are directed towards the right. This convention is invariant under topological transformations of the phase plane, but when curves are cut up and then fitted together to form new closed loops it may be necessary to reverse the direction of some of the broken pieces (Section III,D).

The points are stored in random core locations

$$l_B, l_\alpha, \ldots, l_\rho, l_E. \tag{24}$$

There is a successor function

$$S(l') = l'' \tag{25}$$

that defines the storage location l'' of the point that follows l' in the chain, and three arrays b_j, e_j, n_j that define, respectively, the locations of the first and last points on curve j and the number of points. All unused points are linked together to form curve o, the "free-space" list, which is specified by b_o, e_o, n_o.

As the motion proceeds, each curve becomes more and more stretched out and it is necessary to add extra points if accuracy is to be maintained. We can insert a point γ between α and β by writing

$$l_\gamma := b_o, \quad b_o := S(b_o), \quad n_o := n_o - 1, \quad n_j := n_j + 1 \tag{26}$$

(remove the first point of the free-space list and assign it to curve C_j), and

$$S(l_\alpha) := l_\gamma, \quad S(l_\gamma) := l_\beta \tag{27}$$

(insert the new location between l_α and l_β in the chain). The new point γ is placed at the midpoint of the segment (α, β); i.e., in general,

$$X_\gamma := \tfrac{1}{2}(X_\alpha + X_\beta), \quad V_\gamma := \tfrac{1}{2}(V_\alpha + V_\beta). \tag{28}$$

Some care is needed if the segment happens to be (E, B), but we need not discuss this here.

A point β lying between α and γ on curve j can be removed, and the location added to the free-space list, by writing:

$$S(l_\alpha) := l_\gamma, \quad n_j := n_j - 1, \quad S(e_o) := l_\beta, \quad e_o := l_\beta, \quad n_o := n_o + 1. \tag{29}$$

C. Calculation of the Electric Field

To calculate the charge density it is necessary to evaluate the integral

$$\int f(x, v)\, dv \tag{30}$$

as a function of x. Because the phase plane has been divided into regions of constant density, $f(x_0, v)$ is a step function of v for each x_0. Let the contour C_j separate two regions R_j, R_{j-1} with phase densities f_j, f_{j-1}, with R_j on the right when C_j is traversed in the positive sense, and define

$$\Delta f_j = f_j - f_{j-1}. \tag{31}$$

Suppose that C_j crosses the vertical line $x = x_0$ at an arbitrary number (possibly zero) of points $v_{j,q}$ and define $S_{j,q} = 1$ if it crosses in the direction of x increasing, -1 otherwise. Then

$$f(x_0, v) = -\sum_j \sum_q \Delta f_j \, \theta(v - v_{j,q}) S_{j,q}, \qquad (32)$$

where $\theta(v)$ is the Heaviside step function

$$\theta(v) = 1, \quad v > 0, \qquad \theta(v) = 0, \quad v < 0, \qquad (33)$$

and the integral becomes

$$f(x_0, v) = \sum_j \sum_q \Delta f_j \, v_{j,q} S_{j,q}. \qquad (34)$$

In the calculation we assume that each curve is a polygon; and we are required to evaluate the integral

$$\int dv \int_{x_m}^{x_{m+1}} dx \, f(x,v) \qquad (35)$$

over each interval

$$x_m \leq x \leq x_{m+1}, \qquad 0 \leq m < L. \qquad (36)$$

By adding extra points wherever a segment crosses one of the vertical boundaries of the intervals, we can express each term (35) as a sum over all subsegments that lie within the interval (36); i.e.,

$$\sum_{\text{subsegments}} \Delta f_j(x'' - x')\{(v'' + v')/2\}, \qquad (37)$$

where x'' is the successor of x' (allowing for the extra points). It is easy to verify that Eq. (37) gives the correct result for all possible configurations of the segment.

The computational procedure is therefore very simple: We scan along each curve in the positive sense and determine the x intervals in which the two endpoints of each segment lie by masking and integer division, as explained in Section IIIA. Each interval occupied by the segment is then credited with an additional amount of charge according to formula (37), which is evaluated in floating-point form.

For polygonal curves this calculation of the total charge within each

Eulerian interval is exact, apart from rounding errors. The electric field at each interval boundary is then calculated from the integral formula

$$(\Delta E)_m = 4\pi(Q_m - q_0), \tag{38}$$

where Q_m is the charge in the mth interval, q_0 is a uniform positive background charge that is adjusted to make the total charge exactly zero, and

$$-(\Delta E)_m = (d\phi/dx)_{m+1} - (d\phi/dx)_m. \tag{39}$$

Eq. (39) is also exact, but in order to impose the periodicity condition

$$\phi(L) - \phi(0) \equiv -\int_0^L E \, dx = 0, \tag{40}$$

we must assume that $E(x)$ varies linearly across each Eulerian interval. This approximation is also needed to calculate the electric field at the Lagrangian points x_i for insertion in Eq. (18).

Altogether, therefore, there are two minor sources of error in calculating the electric fields at each time step. First, we have assumed that the curves C_j are polygons, but this property cannot be preserved with time since straight segments tend to distort. Second, we have assumed that $E(x)$ can be obtained by linear interpolation from the values on the Eulerian grid, whereas in fact it has a more complicated structure in which d^2E/dx^2 changes from one constant value to another at every point x_i. The first type of error is minimized by increasing the number of Lagrangian points on the contours, and the second by increasing the number of Eulerian intervals. There is a third source of error in calculating the motion of the contours, which depends on the time step Δt, and this is discussed in Section IV.

D. Trimming of Contours

In the course of a run, two contours or two portions of the same contour often approach one another until a negligible area is enclosed between them over a finite length. Then the two curves have become a single "diploid" curve, and it is wasteful to scan this twice. If the f values on either side of the diploid curve are identical, then the system is unaltered when the diploid section is removed altogether.

Figure 9 illustrates three cases in which a diploid can form. The diagram shown in Fig. 9(a) is somewhat easier to process and will be discussed first. In this case, one alters the chaining on C_1 by connecting point C to point D and creates a new closed curve beginning with point A and terminating with

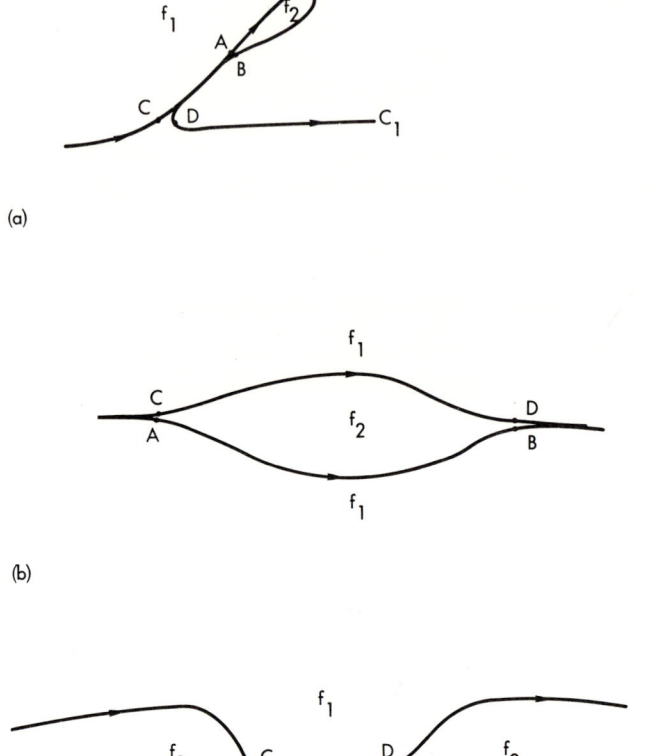

FIG. 9. Three cases of contour coalescence.

point B. The points between C–A and B–D are no longer needed and are added to the free-space list.

In Fig. 9(b) the diploid points to the left of A, C and to the right of D, B can be added to the free-space list. In addition it is necessary to create a closed curve whose points are chained in a clockwise direction, so that the linkage between points A and B must be reversed. In the program, the statement CALL REVLINK(IA, IB) will reverse the linkage between the points A and B with serial numbers IA and IB, respectively; and we may then link A to C and D to B.

One additional complication remains, since the coordinate values between A and C and between D and B may differ by a multiple of the periodicity L

of the calculation. A call to subroutine MASCUR(IC) will arrange for the coordinates on the newly formed curve IC to vary in a continuous manner.

Figure 9(c) shows a third case, in which the diploid curve now separates two regions 1 and 3, with different f values, that were not originally adjacent to one another. In this case we can discard the portion C–D, connect C to A and B to D, reverse the linkages as appropriate, and introduce a new "type 2" curve that joins the points A and B of two other contours and has $\Delta f = f_3 - f_1$. This facility has not yet been implemented.

E. CALCULATION OF THE MEAN DISTRIBUTION FUNCTION

It is often of interest to evaluate the mean distribution function

$$\bar{f}(v) = L^{-1} \int f(x, v)\, dx = L^{-1} \int dx \sum_j \Delta f_j \theta[v - v_j(x)]. \tag{41}$$

In practice it is most efficient to determine $d\bar{f}(v)/dv$ and then integrate with respect to v. From Eq. (41) we find

$$\begin{aligned}
\frac{d\bar{f}}{dv} &= L^{-1} \sum_j \Delta f_j \int dx\, \delta[v - v_j(x)] \\
&= L^{-1} \sum_j \Delta f_j \int dv_j \frac{dx(v_j)}{dv_j} \delta(v - v_j) \\
&= L^{-1} \sum_j \Delta f_j \int \frac{dx}{dv_j} dv_j.
\end{aligned} \tag{42}$$

To evaluate this sum numerically we divide the phase plane into a set of $2N$ horizontal Eulerian strips of width Δv, as shown in Fig. 10. For each contour C_j, a "mean slope"

$$(dx/dv)^j_{v_{n+1/2}}$$

is associated with the nth horizontal strip centered at $v_{n+1/2} = (n + \tfrac{1}{2})\,\Delta v$, $(-N \leq n \leq N - 1)$, according to

$$(dx/dv)^j_{v_{n+1/2}} = (\Delta x/\Delta v)^j_{v_{n+1/2}} = \sum_{\substack{\text{all}\\\text{subsegments}}} [x(\beta) - x(\alpha)]/\Delta v, \tag{43}$$

where $x_j(\beta)$ and $x_j(\alpha)$ are the coordinate values of C_j where it intersects the

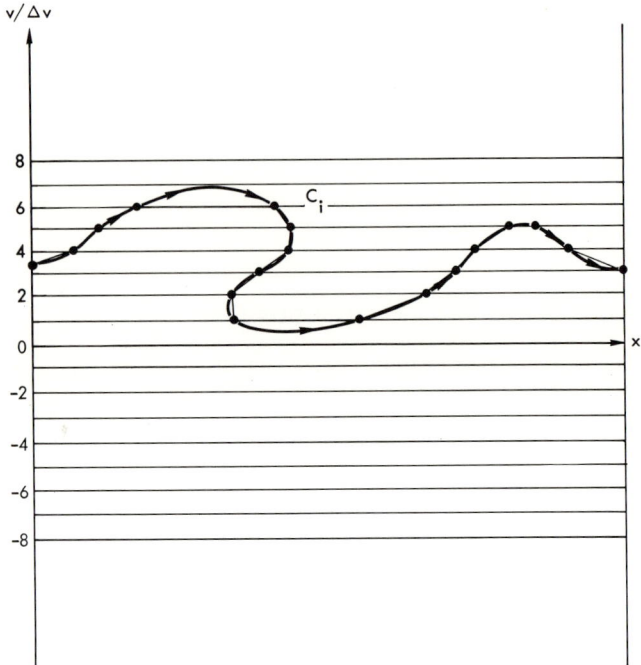

FIG. 10. Approximation of contour configuration used to calculate $\bar{F}(v)$.

boundaries of the strip. As the contour is scanned in the direction of the linkage, α is reached before β.

In practice we construct the elementary slopes by scanning the Lagrangian points on each contour in order and determining, by a masking operation, to which horizontal strip each point belongs. If the successor x'' of x' lies in the same strip, the coordinate difference $(x'' - x')$ is added to the current value of Δx for this strip. If they lie in adjacent strips, the intersection point x''' is found by interpolation, and the differences $(x''' - x')$ and $(x'' - x''')$ are added to the current values of Δx for the respective strips. In addition the code treats more general cases, where more than one horizontal boundary separates a pair of Lagrangian points or where the points lie outside the range of the velocity grid.

The result of this scan is to determine $(\Delta x/\Delta v)^j_{v_{n+1/2}}$ for any contour configuration. The mean distribution $\bar{f}(v_n)$ can then be constructed from the sum

$$\bar{f}(v_n) = L^{-1} \sum_j \Delta f_j \sum_{p=-N}^{n-1} (\Delta x/\Delta v)^j_{p+1/2}, \qquad -N \leq n \leq N. \qquad (44)$$

This calculation takes longer than and is not as accurate as the charge evaluation. However, it is only used for diagnostic purposes and is not performed at each time step.

IV. Numerical Stability of the Leapfrog Scheme

The Lagrangian contour points satisfy the particle equations of motion (2), and at first glance it might appear that the problem of solving Vlasov's equation by computing the motion of these points should be similar to that of moving individual particles in a many-particle code. In either case it seems beneficial to stagger the positions, velocities, and accelerations in order to achieve second-order accuracy in the time integration. Thus in particle codes with velocity-independent forces, the acceleration at time $t = n\,\Delta t$ can be used to increment the velocity from $(n - \frac{1}{2})\,\Delta t$ to $(n + \frac{1}{2})\,\Delta t$, and this velocity can then be used to increment the position from $n\,\Delta t$ to $(n + 1)\,\Delta t$. Specifically, the difference scheme is:

$$v_i[(n + \tfrac{1}{2})\,\Delta t] = v_i[(n - \tfrac{1}{2})\,\Delta t] + E[x_i(n\,\Delta t), n\,\Delta t]\,\Delta t,$$
$$x_i[(n + 1)\,\Delta t] = x_i[n\,\Delta t] + v_i[(n + \tfrac{1}{2})\,\Delta t]\,\Delta t. \tag{45}$$

This scheme is feasible because the charge density needed to calculate E at time t depends solely on the positions $x_i(t)$ and not on the velocities, which therefore need not be available at this time. With the water-bag model, however, the charge density is computed from a contour configuration that involves both the position and the velocity coordinates at the same instant of time, and it would appear that a more elaborate difference scheme is needed[2].

A. Odd and Even Phase Spaces

A choice that maintains second-order accuracy is a leapfrog scheme in which two phase spaces are employed; an odd-parity space S_o in which both position and velocity coordinates are defined at odd times $(2n + 1)\,\Delta t$, and an even-parity space S_e in which they are defined at even

---

[2] It has recently been pointed out to us by K. Symon that the charge integral $\int f\,dv$ can be evaluated from a set of velocity coordinates displaced by $\Delta t/2$, since according to the first Eq. (45), all contours at a fixed position x shift uniformly in the vertical direction. As a consequence, Eq. (45) can also be used for the water-bag model and preserves second order accuracy in Δt. This property was not realized when we originally developed our code, and we used instead the leapfrog scheme discussed in this section.

times $2n\,\Delta t$ ($n = 0, 1, 2, \ldots$). The even space determines the motion of contours in the odd space and vice versa, and the difference equations are:

$$\begin{aligned}
x_o[(2n+1)\,\Delta t] &= x_o[(2n-1)\,\Delta t] + 2v_e(2n\,\Delta t)\,\Delta t, \\
v_o[(2n+1)\,\Delta t] &= v_o[(2n-1)\,\Delta t] + 2E_e(2n\,\Delta t)\,\Delta t, \\
x_e[(2n+2)\,\Delta t] &= x_e(2n\,\Delta t) + 2v_o[(2n+1)\,\Delta t]\,\Delta t, \\
v_e[(2n+2)\,\Delta t] &= v_e(2n\,\Delta t) + 2E_o[(2n+1)\,\Delta t]\,\Delta t,
\end{aligned} \quad (46)$$

where the subscripts o and e denote odd and even parities, respectively.

B. Computational Instability

A difficulty with many leapfrog schemes is that spurious motions may develop, since there are twice as many degrees of freedom in the numerical integration as in the physical problem. In our model we have two associated curves C_o and C_e to represent each physical contour, as shown in Fig. 11;

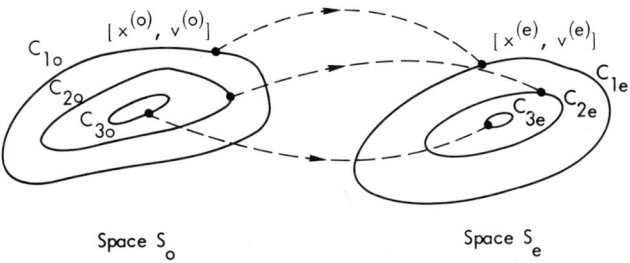

FIG. 11. Conjugate odd- and even-parity spaces. The configuration in S_e is used to increment the configuration in S_o and vice versa.

and every point (x_o, v_o) corresponds to a conjugate point (x_e, v_e) on C_e. From a contour configuration $C_{o,e}$ one calculates the fields $E_{o,e}$ at the Lagrangian positions $x_{o,e}$ and then uses $v_{o,e}$ and $E_{o,e}$ to increment $x_{e,o}$ and $v_{e,o}$. In the limit $\Delta t \to 0$ this coupled system will reproduce the original system if the contours C_o and C_e are initially exactly synchronized with one another. However, any misalignment may lead to completely spurious motions, which after a finite time can cause large departures from the true state.

In a difference scheme where Δt is finite, C_o and C_e are not defined exactly at the same instant nor are they moved in precisely the correct way. Consequently, one cannot expect them to remain aligned for all time. Asynchronous motions are bound to arise, and to prevent the development of large misalignments between the two sets of curves it is necessary to synchronize them periodically by averaging the conjugate coordinates.

In the plasma problem we find that the asynchronous motion leads to a weak linear computational instability that is similar to the physical Jeans instability of the corresponding gravitational configuration, and which is independent of Δt in first approximation. Interestingly enough, the asynchronous motion of the real gravitational problem is not so severe, since it gives rise to stable computational modes similar to plasma oscillations.

We now analyze the asynchronous instability in a quantitative manner and describe the synchronization method now used. A more detailed discussion is given in Appendix II. Since the instability is present in the limit $\Delta t \to 0$, we first study this simpler case by introducing a set of differential equations.

C. Synchronous and Antisynchronous Modes

Consider an equilibrium configuration in which the distribution function is represented by N horizontal contours C_j with $v_j(x) = V_j = \text{const}$, and the jump in f on each contour is $\Delta f_j = f_j - f_{j-1}$. In equilibrium the odd and even contours are exactly synchronized.

The linearized equations of motion that describe a perturbation of this equilibrium are:

$$\left[\frac{\partial}{\partial t} + V_j \frac{\partial}{\partial x_j}\right] \delta x_j^{(o,e)} = \delta v_j^{(e,o)}, \tag{47}$$

$$\left[\frac{\partial}{\partial t} + V_j \frac{\partial}{\partial x_j}\right] \delta v_j^{(o,e)} = E^{(e,o)}(x_j), \tag{48}$$

$$\frac{\partial E^{e,o}}{\partial x} = \frac{\omega_p^2}{2\bar{V}} \sum_j \Delta f_j \, \delta v_j^{e,o}, \tag{49}$$

where "δ" refers to the departure of the curves from their initial state.

Because these equations are symmetrical, their solutions can be separated into two independent classes: the synchronous modes with

$$\begin{Bmatrix} \delta x_j^o \\ \delta v_j^o \\ E^o \end{Bmatrix} = \begin{Bmatrix} \delta x_j^e \\ \delta v_j^e \\ E^e \end{Bmatrix} = \begin{Bmatrix} \delta x_j^+ \\ \delta v_j^+ \\ E^+ \end{Bmatrix}, \tag{50}$$

and the antisynchronous modes with

$$\begin{Bmatrix} \delta x_j^o \\ \delta v_j^o \\ E^o \end{Bmatrix} = -\begin{Bmatrix} \delta x_j^e \\ \delta v_j^e \\ E^e \end{Bmatrix} = \begin{Bmatrix} \delta x_j^- \\ \delta v_j^- \\ E^- \end{Bmatrix}. \tag{51}$$

The equations for each class are:

$$\left[\frac{\partial}{\partial t} + V_j \frac{\partial}{\partial x_j}\right] \delta x_j^\pm = \pm \delta v_j^\pm, \tag{52}$$

$$\left[\frac{\partial}{\partial t} + V_j \frac{\partial}{\partial x_j}\right] \delta v_j^\pm = \pm E^\pm(x_j), \tag{53}$$

$$\frac{\partial E^\pm(x)}{\partial x} = \frac{\omega_p^2}{2\bar{V}} \sum_j \Delta f_j\, \delta v_j^\pm(x). \tag{54}$$

Notice that Eqs. (53) and (54) are independent of Eq. (52) and form a closed set. In the antisynchronous case these two equations are invariant to the transformation $E^- \to -E^-$, $\omega_p^2 \to -\omega_p^2$, which changes them to the equations used for the physical Jeans instability.

D. Generalized Dispersion Relation

Because the equations are linear and describe the perturbations of a spatially homogeneous system, we can Fourier analyze and write the solutions in the form $A(x, t) = A(k) \exp(-i\omega t + ikx)$. If this form is substituted into Eqs. (53) and (54), the following generalized dispersion relation is obtained:

$$1 \mp \frac{\omega_p^2}{2k^2\bar{V}^2} \sum_{j=1}^N \Delta f_j \bigg/ \left(\frac{\omega}{k\bar{V}} - u_j\right) \tag{55}$$

where the upper sign applies to the synchronous mode and the lower sign to the antisynchronous mode, $2\bar{V} = \sum \Delta f_j V_j$, and $u_j = V_j/\bar{V}$. This relation describes all the linearized physical and computational modes.

In the special case $N = 2$, $V_1 = -V_2 = \bar{V}$, the dispersion relation is

$$\omega^2 = \pm \omega_p^2 + k^2 \bar{V}^2, \tag{56}$$

which is easy to analyze. The upper sign corresponds to physical plasma oscillations, while the lower sign gives a computational Jeans instability if $|k| < \bar{V}/\omega_p$. This result is a general property of distributions that are monotonically decreasing functions of v^2. (For the step-function model, this implies that $\Delta f_j > 0$ when $V_j > 0$, and $\Delta f_j < 0$, when $V_j < 0$.) In the general case, the presence of instability can be inferred from an investigation of the diagram of

$$G(\zeta) = \sum_{j=1}^N \Delta f_j/(\zeta - u_j) \tag{57}$$

shown in Fig. 12, where $\zeta = \omega/k\bar{V}$ is the phase velocity. Since the dispersion relation (55) is

$$\pm \frac{k^2 \bar{V}^2}{\omega_p^2} = \sum_{j=1}^{N} \Delta f_j \bigg/ \left(\frac{\omega}{k\bar{V}} - u_j\right) = G\left(\frac{\omega}{k\bar{V}}\right), \quad (58)$$

the roots of the dispersion relation correspond to the intersections of $G(\omega/k\bar{V})$ with a horizontal line. This line lies in the upper half-plane for synchronous case and in the lower half-plane for the antisynchronous case. For the monotonic type of distribution corresponding to Fig. 12, we see that there are

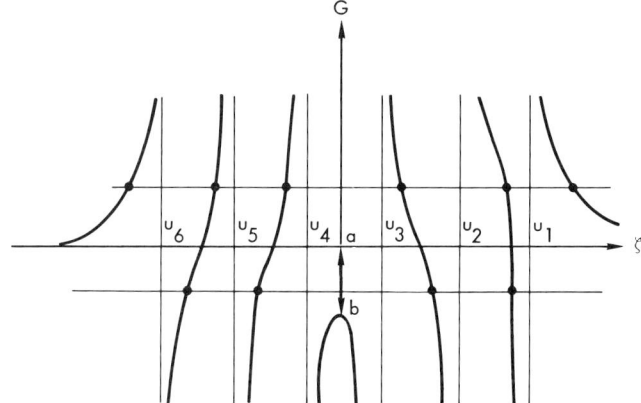

FIG. 12. Schematic diagram of $G(\zeta)$. The unstable band lies in the gap $a-b$.

N real roots for all values of k^2 in the synchronous case. In the antisynchronous case two roots are missing in the band $0 < k^2 < k_0^2$, where $k_0^2 \approx \omega_p^2/\bar{V}^2$. These two roots are in the complex (ω/k) plane and correspond to the two complex roots one finds from Eq. (56). Nonmonotonic distributions may be analyzed in a similar way.

It may be mentioned that Eq. (56) is a general relation if one integrates the Vlasov equation by the leapfrog scheme. In the continuum limit it has the form

$$1 \mp \frac{\omega_p^2}{k^2 \bar{V}} \int dv \, \frac{\partial f}{\partial v} \bigg/ (\omega - kv) = 0. \quad (59)$$

As far as the numerical applications are concerned, the gravitational instability is a weak computational mode, since a difference scheme can be incremented many time steps [of order $(\omega_p \Delta t)^{-1}$] before the asynchronous behavior is important. Hence a periodic, but infrequent, synchronization of the odd and even contours is enough to quench the unwanted unstable motion.

E. Synchronization of the Contours

In most of the numerical experiments the following synchronization procedure was used. Suppose that at some point in the calculation, the positions, velocities, and accelerations on both the odd-parity contours at time $(2n + 1)\,\Delta t$ and the even-parity contours at time $2n\,\Delta t$ are known. The asynchronous component is then filtered out by constructing the following average variables associated with time $(2n + \frac{1}{2})\,\Delta t$:

$$\bar{x}_j[(2n + \tfrac{1}{2})\,\Delta t] = \tfrac{1}{2}\{x_j[(2n + 1)\,\Delta t] + x_j(2n\,\Delta t)\},$$
$$\bar{V}_j[(2n + \tfrac{1}{2})\,\Delta t] = \tfrac{1}{2}\{V_j[(2n + 1)\,\Delta t] + V_j(2n\,\Delta t)\}, \quad (60)$$
$$\bar{E}[(2n + \tfrac{1}{2})\,\Delta t] = \tfrac{1}{2}\{E[(2n + 1)\,\Delta t] + E(2n\,\Delta t)\}.$$

A new set of contour pairs is then created by incrementing the coordinates by an amount $\pm \Delta t/2$ in time using a simple Taylor expansion:

$$x_i\begin{bmatrix}(2n + 1)\,\Delta t \\ 2n\,\Delta t\end{bmatrix} = \bar{x}_i \pm \bar{V}\frac{\Delta t}{2} + \frac{\bar{E}(\Delta t)^2}{8},$$
$$V_i\begin{bmatrix}(2n + 1)\,\Delta t \\ 2n\,\Delta t\end{bmatrix} = \bar{V}_i\Delta t \pm \frac{\bar{E}(\Delta t)^2}{2}. \quad (61)$$

A more complete discussion is given in Appendix II.

V. Numerical Experiment of the Bump-on-Tail Instability

We now present some results of a numerical integration of the bump-on-tail instability of a plasma. This problem has recently been investigated by other workers (Morse and Neilson, 1968; Dawson et al., 1968) using different methods.

A. Equilibrium and Linear Analysis

The initial unstable equilibrium distribution is shown in Fig. 13. The parameters defining this equilibrium are $V_j = (1.0, 0.75, 0.5, 0.25, 0.05, -1.0)$; $f_j = (0.4, -0.2, 0.2, 0.3, 0.3, -1.0)$; $\omega_p\,\Delta t = 0.05$; $\bar{V}\,\Delta t/\Delta x = 1/8$ and $\Delta x/L = 1/64$, where $2\bar{V} = \sum V_j\,\Delta f_j = 1.44$, L is the periodicity length, Δx the Eulerian grid interval, and Δt the time step.

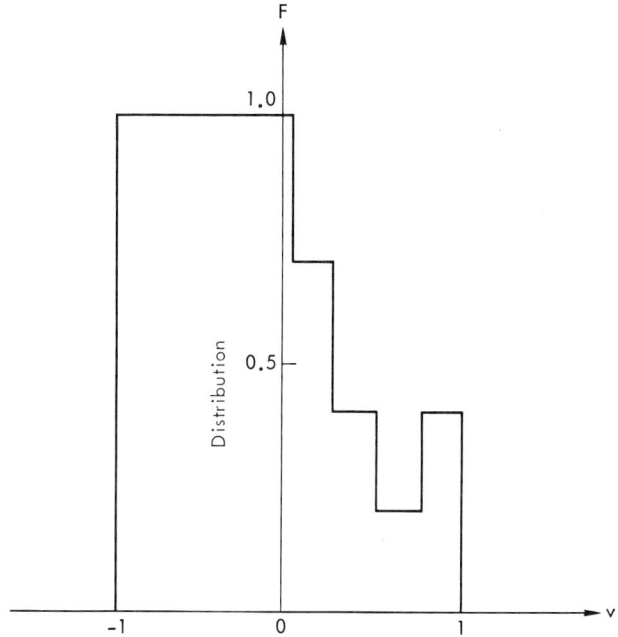

FIG. 13. Equilibrium bump-on-tail distribution.

A center-of-mass velocity has been imposed in order to make the velocities of the two outer contours comparable with one another. Clearly the instability results from an incompressible interchange of the phase fluid between regions 1 and 2. For convenience we have chosen f_1 and f_3 so that Lagrangian points can be removed in regions where contours C_2 and C_3 happen to coalesce.

Linear stability analysis shows that there are five unstable wavenumbers $k_n = (2\pi n)/L$, and the real frequencies ω_R and growth rates γ of these modes are presented in Table I.

TABLE I

FREQUENCY OF OSCILLATION OF UNSTABLE MODES

Wavenumber index, n	ω_R/ω_p	γ/ω_p
1	0.18	0.038
2	0.35	0.072
3	0.50	0.096
4	0.64	0.100
5	0.79	0.078

B. Hole–Wave Interaction

There is an important qualitative difference between the bump-on-tail distribution and the two-stream instability of two equal interpenetrating beams. In the two-stream problem the unstable modes exist only due to the presence of a cavity, and they would be completely absent if the cavity were filled. For the bump-on-tail distribution, however, the system could still support waves at a phase velocity equal to the velocity of the cavity even if it were filled in. Thus in the nonlinear state of the two-stream instability, we saw that when holes develop they tend to move as independent particles. The holes attract each other, but since there is little viscosity due to the background fluid the rest of the plasma plays only a passive role. With the bump-on-tail instability we expect holes to develop that can then interact with the waves of the main system. In our description of the numerical experiment we shall indicate where we think interesting behavior arises from this hole–wave interaction.

C. Nonlinear Evolution

Figure 14 presents the phase-space evolution of the bump-on-tail instability. The uppermost contour was excited at $t = 0$ with random amplitudes and phases of the eight longest wavelengths of the system. Steps 100 and 250 show the instability still in its linear stage. Notice that the most fully developed pulse tends to have the highest velocity. This may be an example of Čerenkov plasma radiation emanating from the developing hole. As it forms, the hole can excite the plasma waves of the main system, and this causes energy to propagate away so that the exciting source must lose energy. Because the source is a hole with negative mass, loss of energy causes it to rise in velocity space. In this experiment the Čerenkov radiation lasts only a finite time, since the periodic boundary conditions allow the radiation to overtake the original source and then reinteract with it.

By step 500 we see that five distinct holes have formed (initially there were five unstable modes). "Umbilical cords" are forming, and one hole (the first to develop) has a faster velocity that the others. At step 650 the fastest hole is about to overtake the next one and is beginning to distort its shape, although the configuration of the other holes has not changed substantially. Figure 15 shows that the spatially averaged distribution at step 650 has formed a plateau in the region of the holes.

D. Trimming

By step 800 several umbilical cords have completely coalesced, and at this stage the diagram was trimmed. Figures 14(f) and (g) show the phase diagram before and after the trimming operation. At step 1000 the two interacting holes have essentially fused together, and at this stage an additional trimming operation was performed. The calculation was stopped at step 1150, after about ten full plasma periods. It appears at this stage that, except for a small "spray," the holes are tending to align themselves in a lattice-like structure, probably as the result of the hole-wave interaction, although further investigation will be needed to understand this mechanism. The mean distribution function still maintains its plateau, so that the presence of holes in phase space is not inconsistent with the quasi-linear principle that the bump-on-tail distribution forms a plateau in the steady state (Vedenov et al., 1961; Drummond and Pines, 1962). However, this calculation could not be described by quasi-linear theory, since trapping rather than velocity-space diffusion dominates the nonlinear properties of the system.

E. Hybrid Model

We see that to continue the experiment it is necessary to trim the turbulent region frequently. To avoid this complication, a hybrid program is being

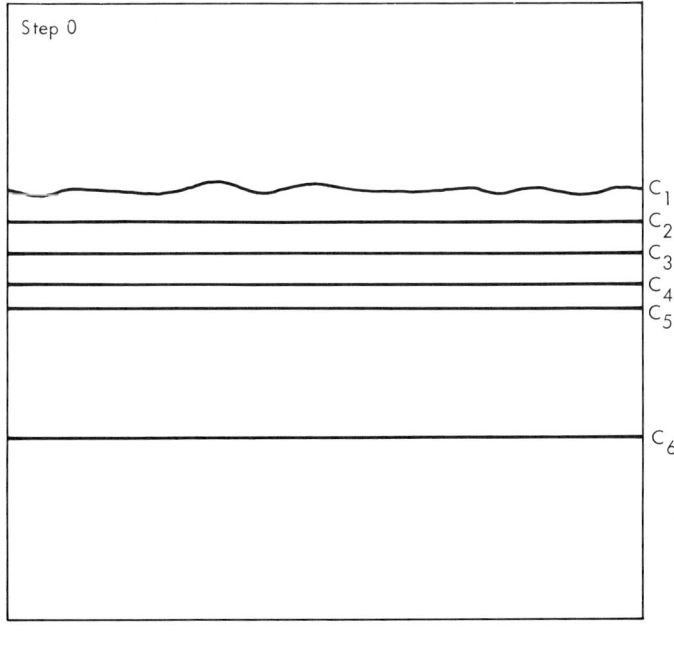

(a)

Fig. 14.(a)–(i) Phase space evolution of bump-on-tail instability.

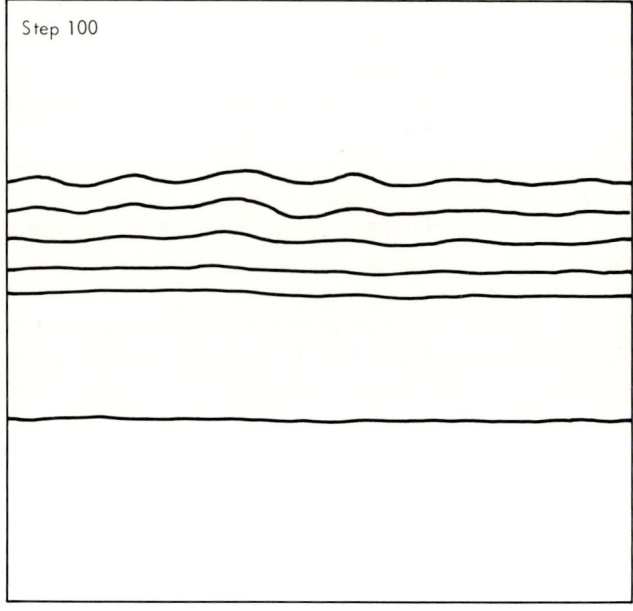

(b)

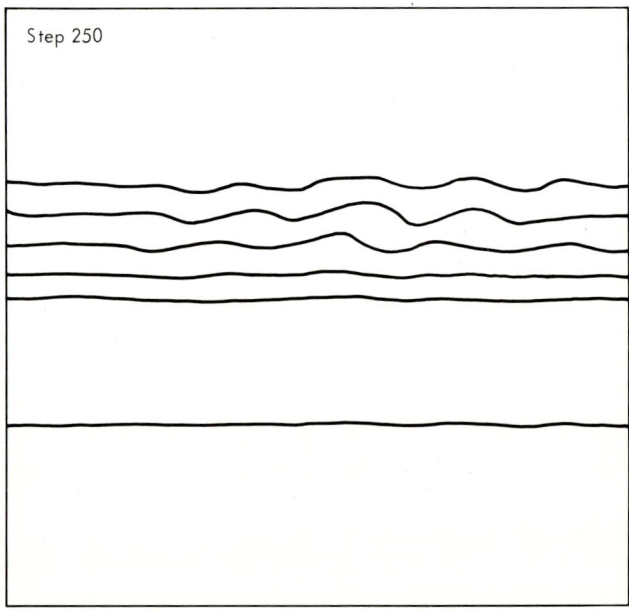

(c)

THE WATER-BAG MODEL   121

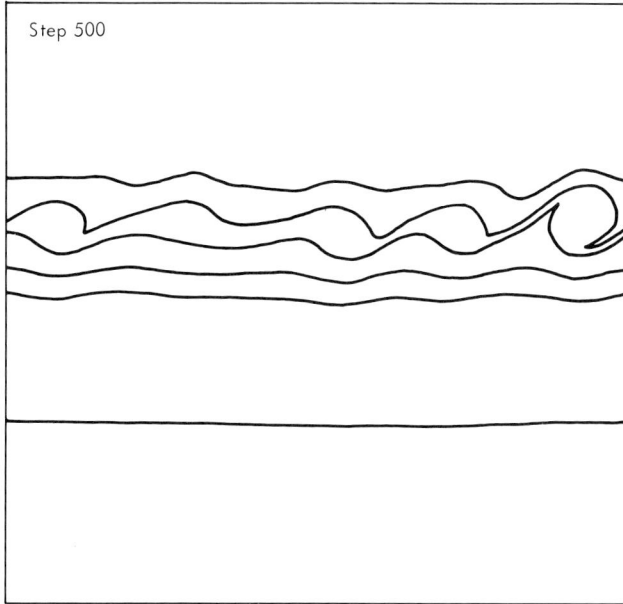

(d)

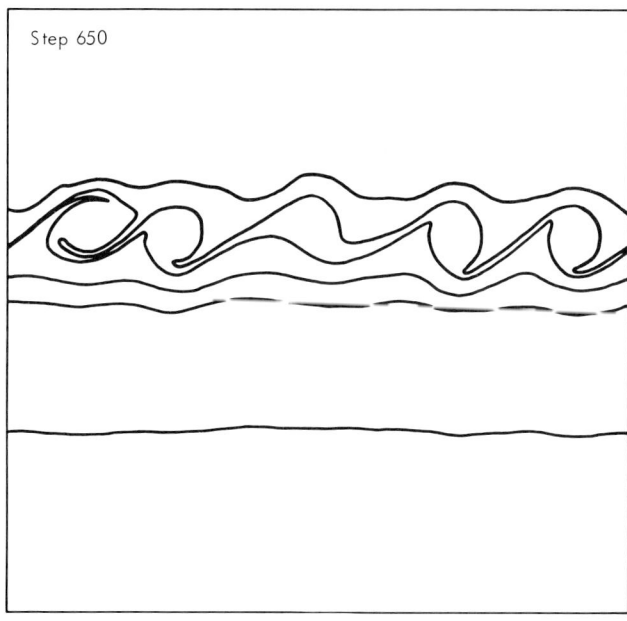

(e)

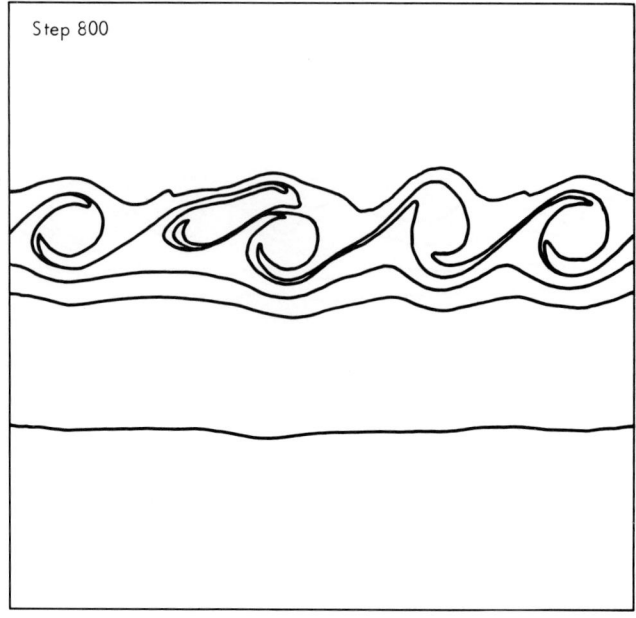

(f)

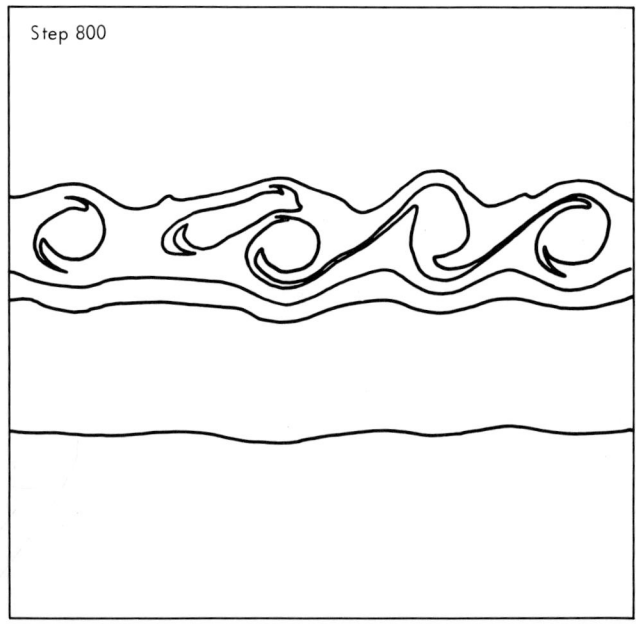

(g)

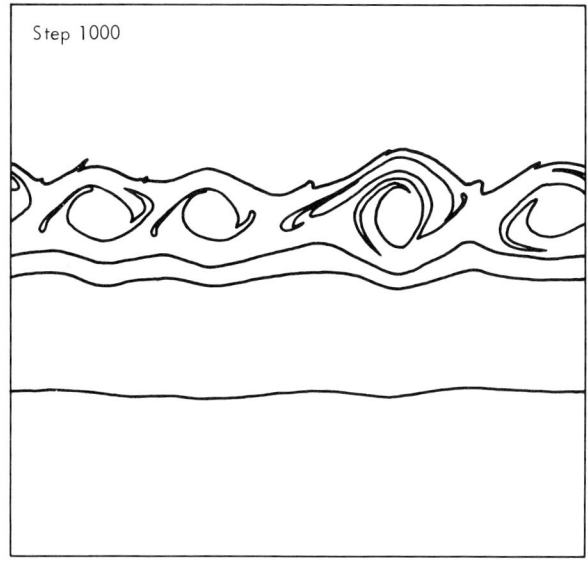

(h)

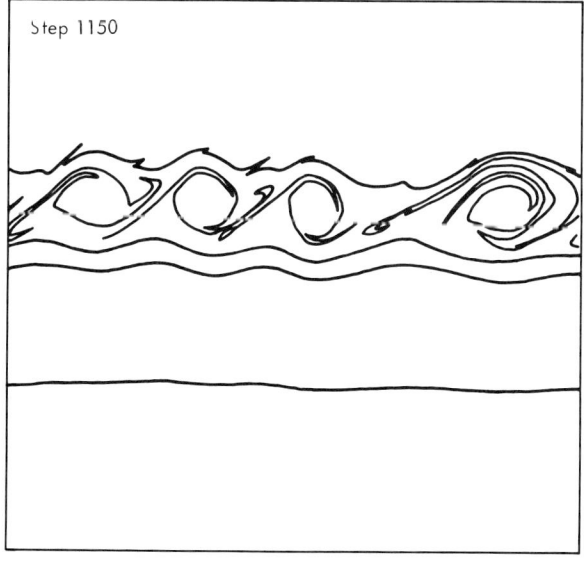

(i)

developed in which particles and step-function contours are followed simultaneously.

It appears from the numerical experiment discussed here that only the resonant contours break into turbulent motion and that the nonresonant contours (with the partial exception of the uppermost contour) undergo only laminar flow in phase space. Hence the nonresonant contours could be followed indefinitely with only a small number of Lagrangian points. The particle method could then be used to describe the fluid contained in the resonant layer. Figure 16 illustrates such a hybrid distribution, in which the "weight" of the individual particles is chosen to be negative so that the particles can represent the holes.

This hybrid model requires a modification in the way the system is incremented in time. For the step-function distribution we still have a set of odd- and even-parity contours that are incremented by the leapfrog scheme of Eq. (46). For the point particles, however, only one set of phase coordinates is needed; and as discussed at the beginning of Section IV it is convenient to associate the position of each particle with the integral times $n \, \Delta t$ and the velocities with half-integral times $(n - \frac{1}{2}) \, \Delta t$. This allows the total charge to be

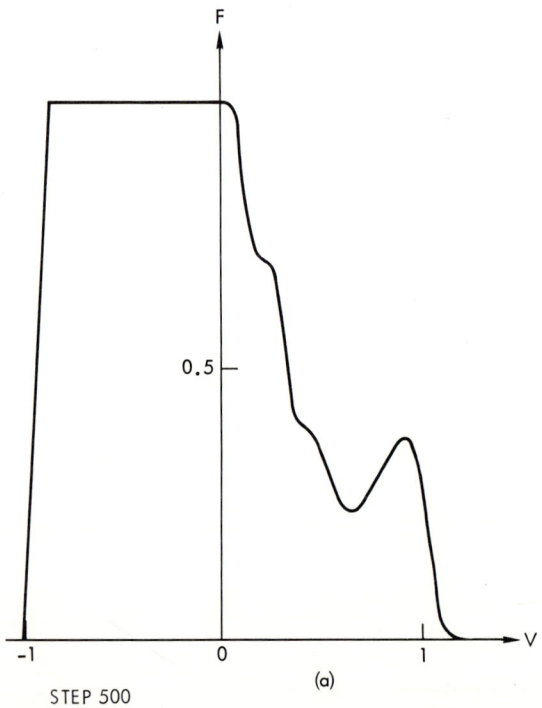

STEP 500

FIG. 15.(a)–(c). Evolution of mean distribution function for bump-on-tail instability.

THE WATER-BAG MODEL

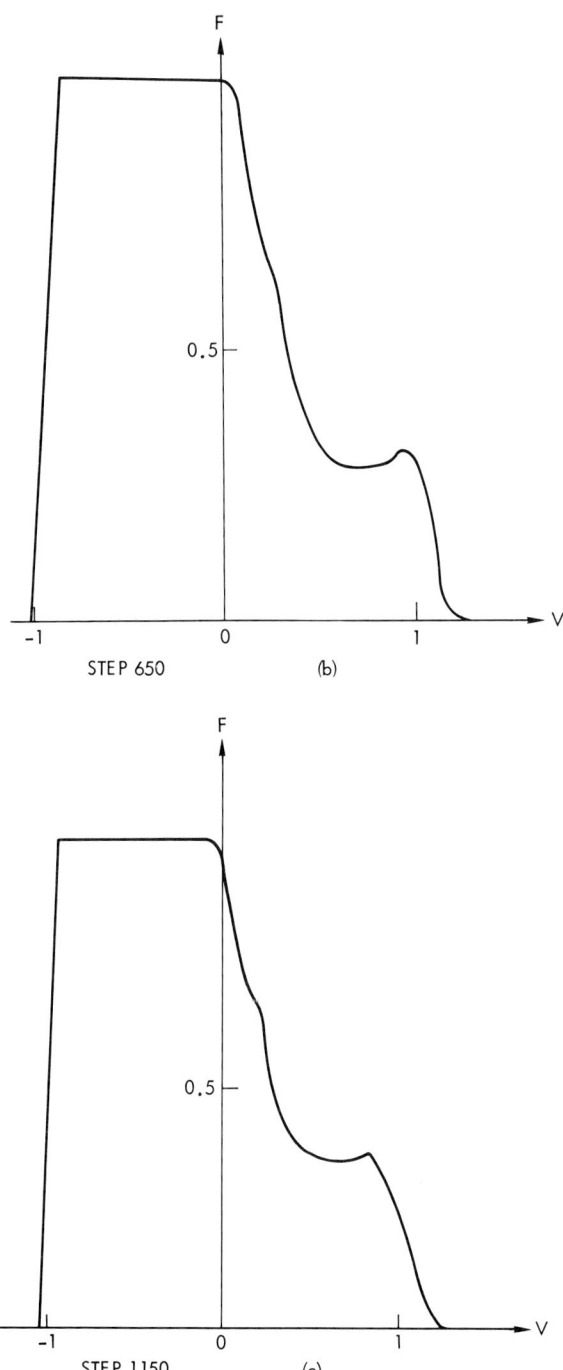

STEP 650 (b)

STEP 1150 (c)

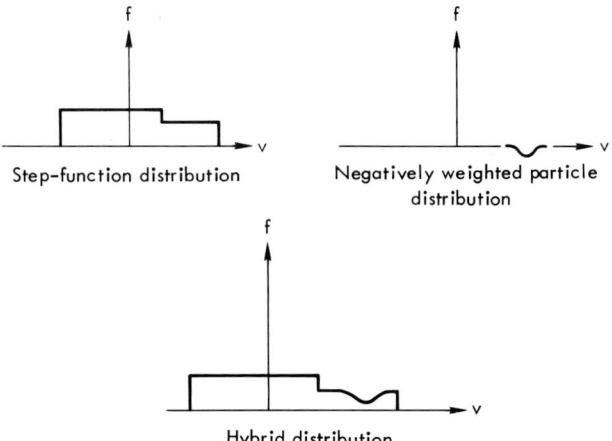

Fig. 16. Hybrid distribution function.

evaluated at each integral time, as required by both parts of the calculation. Then at each step the Lagrangian points on the contours of the current parity move from $(n-1)\,\Delta t$ to $(n+1)\,\Delta t$, while all the individual particles at coordinates $\{x[n\,\Delta t],\ v[(n-\tfrac{1}{2})\,\Delta t]\}$ are incremented to $\{x[(n+1)\,\Delta t],\ v[(n+\tfrac{1}{2})\,\Delta t]\}$ according to Eq. (45).

The hybrid model should provide excellent statistics for those problems in which the dynamics of a limited region of phase space is important, and we hope to carry out a numerical experiment with this model soon.

Appendix I. Continuous Distribution as the Limit of a Step Function

The close analogy between the dynamics of continuous and step-function distributions can be studied by treating the continuous function as the limiting case of a step function, as shown in Fig. 17. The limit is taken by letting

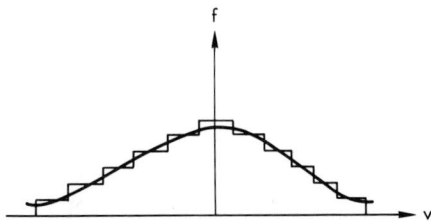

Fig. 17. Continuous distribution and its step-function approximation.

$\Delta f \to 0$ and $\Delta v \to 0$ while keeping $\Delta f/\Delta v \to -\partial f/\partial v$ finite. It has been shown (Berk and Book, 1969) that if the dielectric function of a continuous distribution is given by

$$\varepsilon_R(k, \omega) + i\varepsilon_I(k, \omega), \tag{62}$$

where ε_R and ε_I are real functions of ω and k, then the dielectric function of the corresponding step-function distribution with finite Δv is:

$$\varepsilon_R(k, \omega) - \cot(\omega/k \, \Delta v)\varepsilon_I(k, \omega) + \theta[(k \, \Delta v/\omega)^2]. \tag{63}$$

The physical difference between the two cases arises because a step contour with velocity $v \doteq \omega/k$ cannot be exactly resonant with one of the natural modes of oscillation of the system, so that the energy transfer will be reversed after a time $t \approx 1/k \, \Delta v$. However, the structure of Eq. (63) guarantees that for $t \ll 1/k \, \Delta v$, the responses of the two systems are nearly identical (Baldwin and Rowlands, 1966).

Except for the contours near the wave phase velocity, we can recover the steady-state continuum response as a limit of a step-function response. The excluded region in phase space encompasses those contours that are trapped by the wave. Hence the following discussion applies only to those contours whose equilibrium velocity v satisfies the inequality $(v - \omega/k)^2 \gg E/k$.

In section II we saw that the shapes of the perturbed contours C_j and the values of the Δf_j determined the elementary density contributions from each contour in space. Similarly, in a continuous distribution the shape of each contour of constant f and the associated $\partial f(v)/\partial v$ determines the elementary density contributions. For an equilibrium distribution, the density contribution from a phase element Δv embracing a velocity contour $v = v_0$ is $\Delta v f(v_0)$. When v is modulated in space, the elementary density contribution is then

$$\begin{aligned}\Delta v \, \delta f(v_0, x) &= \{f[v(x)] - f(v_0)\} \Delta v \\ &= \delta v(x) \frac{\partial f(v_0)}{\partial v} \Delta v \\ &= \frac{E_0 \cos(kx - \omega t)}{(\omega - kv_0)} \frac{\partial f(v_0)}{\partial v} \Delta v,\end{aligned} \tag{64}$$

where $\delta v(x) = E(\omega - kv_0)^{-1} \cos(kx - \omega t)$ is the linear response to an electric field $E_0 \sin(kx - \omega t)$. The expression for the perturbed density contribution from a contour of a step function is

$$\delta n_i = -\frac{E \cos(kx - \omega t)}{(\omega - kv_i)} \Delta f_i, \tag{65}$$

and we see that Eq. (64) is the limiting case of Eq. (65).

The kinetic energy density contributed to the perturbed system by each contour can likewise be constructed by considering the continuous distribution as the limit of a step-function distribution. The kinetic energy for a step-function distribution is given by

$$T = \frac{1}{2}\int dv\, v^2 f(v) = \frac{1}{6}\sum_i v_i^3 \Delta f_i. \tag{66}$$

Hence the contribution from each contour to the perturbed kinetic energy δT_i is given by

$$\delta T_i = \tfrac{1}{2}[v_i^2\, \delta v(x) + \delta v_i^2(x)v_i]\,\Delta f_i + \theta(\delta v_i^3). \tag{67}$$

If the mean kinetic energy is then constructed by averaging over all space, we find:

$$\delta \overline{T}_i \equiv \frac{1}{2}\int_0^L dx\, \delta T_i = \tfrac{1}{2}v_i(\delta\bar{v}_i)^2\,\Delta f_i$$

$$= \frac{1}{4}\frac{E_0^2 v_i\,\Delta f_i}{(\omega - kv_i)^2}, \tag{68}$$

where $\delta v_i(x)$ has been expressed in terms of the electric field.

Summing $\delta\overline{T}_i$ over all contours, we obtain the standard expression for the wave energy δW:

$$\begin{aligned}
\delta W &= \frac{\omega_p^2}{2\overline{V}}\sum_i \delta\overline{T}_i + \frac{1}{2L}\int dx\, E^2(x) \\
&= \frac{E_0^2}{4}\left[1 + \frac{\omega_p^2}{2k\overline{V}}\sum_i \frac{\Delta f_i\, kv_i}{(\omega - kv_i)^2}\right] \\
&= \frac{E_0^2}{4}\left[1 - \frac{\omega_p^2}{2k\overline{V}}\frac{\partial}{\partial\omega}\sum_i \frac{\Delta f_i(kv_i - \omega + \omega)}{\omega - kv_i}\right] \\
&= \frac{E_0^2}{4}\frac{\partial}{\partial\omega}\left[\omega\left(1 - \frac{\omega_p^2}{2k\overline{V}}\sum_i \frac{\Delta f_i}{\omega - kv_i}\right)\right], \tag{69}
\end{aligned}$$

where we have used the relation $\sum \Delta f_i = 0$.

Taking the continuum limit of Eq. (69), we then find:

$$\delta W = \frac{E_0^2}{4} \frac{\partial}{\partial \omega} \left[\omega \left(1 - \frac{\omega_p^2}{2k^2 \bar{V}} P \int \frac{dv(\partial f/\partial v)}{v - \omega/k} \right) \right]$$

$$= \frac{E_0^2}{4} \frac{\partial}{\partial \omega} [\omega \varepsilon_R(\omega, k)], \tag{70}$$

where P denotes principal part; and this is the standard expression for the wave energy that has been obtained by directly adding the contributions of each region of velocity space.

To obtain the kinetic energy associated with an interchange of two neighboring contours Δv apart, we simply use the expression given in Eq. (68) [substitute Δv for $\delta v_i(x)$] and sum over the contours enclosed in Δv. Since the perturbed energy on each contour is proportional to $(\Delta v)^2$ and the contours lie in a band Δv, the perturbed energy is proportional to $(\Delta v)^3$, and we readily obtained the expression given in Eq. (13) of the text.

Appendix II. Analysis of Synchronization Method

To examine the synchronization scheme in more detail, we now consider the linear solution of Eq. (47) in the limit $\Delta x \to 0$, but Δt finite. The analysis is similar to the $\Delta t \to 0$ case, and one finds that the linearized modal response can be expressed as:

$$\delta x_j(n\,\Delta t) = -\int dk \, \exp[ikx_j^{(o)}] \sum_\alpha \left[\frac{\mathscr{E}_\alpha^+(k)}{\sin^2 \Omega_{j\alpha}^+} \exp(-in\Omega_{j\alpha}^+) \right.$$

$$\left. + \frac{(-1)^n \mathscr{E}_\alpha^-(k)}{\sin^2 \Omega_{j\alpha}^-} \exp(-in\Omega_{j\alpha}^-) \right],$$

$$\delta v_j(n\,\Delta t)\,\Delta t = i \int dk \, \exp[ikx_i^{(o)}] \sum_\alpha \left[\frac{\mathscr{E}_\alpha^+(k)}{\sin \Omega_{j\alpha}^+} \exp(-in\Omega_{j\alpha}^+) \right. \tag{71}$$

$$\left. + \frac{(-1)^n \mathscr{E}_\alpha^-(k)}{\sin \Omega_{j\alpha}^-} \exp(-in\Omega_{j\alpha}^-) \right],$$

$$E(n\,\Delta t, x_j)(\Delta t)^2 = \int dk \, \exp[ikx_j^{(o)}] \sum_\alpha [\mathscr{E}_\alpha^+(k) \exp(-in\Omega_{j\alpha}^+)$$

$$+ (-1)^n \mathscr{E}_\alpha^-(k) \exp(-in\Omega_{j\alpha}^-),$$

where

$$\Omega_{j\alpha}^{+} = [\omega_\alpha{}^{+}(k) + kv_j]\,\Delta t, \qquad \Omega_{j\alpha}^{-} = [\omega_\alpha{}^{-}(k) + \pi/\Delta t + kv_j]\,\Delta t,$$

and both $\omega_\alpha{}^{+}$ and $\omega_\alpha{}^{-}$ obey the dispersion relation

$$1 - \frac{\omega_p{}^2\,\Delta t}{2k\bar{V}} \sum_j \frac{\Delta f_j}{\sin[(\omega_\alpha - kv_j)\,\Delta t]} = 0. \tag{72}$$

If $\omega\,\Delta t \ll 1$, the solution of Eq. (72) differs from Eq. (55) by $\theta[(\omega\,\Delta t)^2]$.

To determine the quantitative effect of synchronization, the modal expansion given in Eq. (71) can be substituted into the filtering operations given by Eq. (60). The mean coordinates $\delta\bar{x}$, $\delta\bar{v}\,\Delta t$, and $\delta\bar{E}\,\Delta t^2$ are then found to be:

$$\delta\bar{x}_j = -\int dk\,\exp[ikx_j^{(0)}] \sum_\alpha \left\{ \frac{\mathcal{E}_\alpha{}^{+}(k)}{\sin^2 \Omega_{j\alpha}^{+}} \exp[-i(2N+\tfrac{1}{2})\Omega_{j\alpha}^{+}] \right.$$
$$\left. \times \cos(\Omega_{j\alpha}^{+}/2) - i\frac{\mathcal{E}_\alpha{}^{-}\,\sin(\Omega_{j\alpha}^{-}/2)}{\sin^2 \Omega_{j\alpha}^{-}} \exp[-i(2N+\tfrac{1}{2})\Omega_{j\alpha}^{-}] \right\},$$

$$\delta\bar{v}_j\,\Delta t = i\int dk\,\exp[ikx_j^{(0)}] \sum_\alpha \left\{ \frac{\mathcal{E}_\alpha{}^{+}(k)}{\sin \Omega_{j\alpha}^{+}} \exp[-i(2N+\tfrac{1}{2})\Omega_{j\alpha}^{+}] \right. \tag{73}$$
$$\left. \times \cos(\Omega_{j\alpha}^{+}/2) - i\frac{\mathcal{E}_\alpha{}^{-}}{\sin \Omega_{j\alpha}^{-}} \exp[-i(2N+\tfrac{1}{2})\Omega_{j\alpha}^{-}] \sin(\Omega_{j\alpha}^{-}/2) \right\},$$

$$\overline{E(x_j)}(\Delta t)^2 = \int dk\,\exp[ikx_j^{(0)}] \sum_\alpha \{\mathcal{E}_\alpha{}^{+}(k)\exp[-i(2N+\tfrac{1}{2})\Omega_{j\alpha}^{+}]$$
$$\times \cos(\Omega_{j\alpha}^{+}/2) - i\mathcal{E}_\alpha{}^{-}\exp[-i(2N+\tfrac{1}{2})\Omega_{j\alpha}^{-}]\sin(\Omega_{j\alpha}^{-}/2)\}.$$

Notice that this operation has filtered the antisynchronous component and has projected a remnant amplitude $\mathcal{E}_\alpha{}^{-}\sin(\Omega_{j\alpha}/2)$ into the synchronous state. If we now use Eq. (61) to construct a new set of contours and we assume that the remnant can be neglected, we find that the new superposition of eigenmodes is given approximately by:

$$\delta x_j = -\int dk\,\exp[ikx_j^{(0)}] \sum_\alpha \left\{ \frac{\mathcal{E}_\alpha{}^{+}\exp(-in\Omega_{j\alpha}^{+})}{\sin^2 \Omega_{j\alpha}^{+}} [1 + \theta(\Omega^4)] \right.$$
$$\left. + \frac{(-1)^n\theta(\Omega^3)}{\sin^2 \Omega_{j\alpha}^{+}} \mathcal{E}_\alpha{}^{+} \exp(-in\Omega_{j\alpha}^{-}) + \frac{(\Omega^{+})^2 \mathcal{E}_\alpha{}^{+}}{4\sin^2 \Omega_{j\alpha}^{+}} \right\}, \tag{74}$$

$$\delta v_j \, \Delta t = i \int dk \, \exp[ikx_j^{(o)}] \sum_\alpha \left\{ \frac{\mathscr{E}_\alpha^+ \exp(-in\Omega_{j\alpha}^+)}{\sin \Omega_{j\alpha}^+} [1 + \theta(\Omega^4)] \right.$$
$$\left. + \frac{(-1)^n \theta(\Omega^3)}{\sin \Omega_{j\alpha}^+} \mathscr{E}_\alpha^+ \exp(-in\Omega_{j\alpha}^-) \right\}, \qquad (74)$$

$$E(x_j)(\Delta t)^2 = \int dk \, \exp[ikx_j^{(o)}] \sum_\alpha \{\mathscr{E}_\alpha^+ \exp(-in\Omega_{j\alpha}^+)[1 + \theta(\Omega^4)]$$
$$+ (-1)^n \theta(\Omega^3) \mathscr{E}_\alpha^+ \exp(in\Omega_{j\alpha}^-)\}.$$

Now the amplitude of the new antisynchronous mode is $\theta(\Omega^3)$, while the amplitude of the synchronous mode is unaltered within an error $\theta(\Omega^4)$. In addition, the synchronization scheme has introduced a displacement mode whose amplitude is

$$(\delta x_k) = \frac{(\Omega^+)^2}{4} \frac{\mathscr{E}^+}{\sin^2 \Omega_{j\alpha}^+}.$$

This mode is obtained by translating the equilibrium contours horizontally, without any vertical motion. In the linear theory of spatially homogeneous configurations that is presented here, this displacement can be neglected, since there is no electric field associated with this motion. However, in nonlinear motion or in spatially dependent equilibrium problems, this mode may be of more importance.

The optimum rate of synchronization is determined by minimizing the error introduced per time step. Initially, the amplitude of the antisynchronous mode is approximately $(\Omega^+)^3 \approx (\omega_p \, \Delta t)^3$. If the modes are synchronized after N steps, this amplitude grows to the level $(\omega_p \, \Delta t)^3 \exp(N\omega_p \, \Delta t)$, whereupon it is filtered and a remnant $(\omega_p \, \Delta t)^4 \exp(N\omega_p \, \Delta t)$ is projected into the synchronous mode. The average error per time step, ER, is then:

$$\mathrm{ER} = (\omega_p \, \Delta t)^5 \frac{\exp(N\omega_p \, \Delta t)}{N\omega_p \, \Delta t}.$$

This expression is minimized when $N = 1/\omega_p \, \Delta t$, whereupon

$$\mathrm{ER}_{\min} = (\omega_p \, \Delta t)^5 e. \qquad (75)$$

In obtaining this estimate it was assumed that the displacement mode could be neglected. However, since most of our numerical applications are for nonlinear problems, we probably should consider that the displacement mode introduces a distortion error $\theta[(\omega_p \Delta t)^2]$ into each synchronization. In this case the average error per time step is then:

$$\text{ER} = \frac{(\omega_p \Delta t)^3}{N\omega_p \Delta t} = \frac{(\omega_p \Delta t)^5}{N\omega_p \Delta t} \exp(N\omega_p \Delta t);$$

and ER is minimized when

$$N \approx -\frac{2 \ln(\omega_p \Delta t)}{(\omega_p \Delta t)}, \quad \text{and} \quad \text{ER}_{\min} \approx -\frac{(\omega_p \Delta t)^3}{2 \ln(\omega_p \Delta t)}. \tag{76}$$

An alternate synchronization scheme has been devised that can remove the asynchronous remnant to $\theta(\Omega^3)$, although the synchronous component is distorted by an amount $\theta(\Omega^2)$. Such a scheme is probably desirable when treating spatially dependent structures.

In the new scheme, instead of filtering first, the contours of both parities are interpolated to a set of coordinates at a common time $t = (2N + \frac{1}{2}) \Delta t$:

$$\begin{aligned}
x_j^{(o)}[(2N + \tfrac{1}{2}) \Delta t] &= x_j[(2N + 1) \Delta t] - v_j(2N \Delta t) \Delta t/2, \\
v_j^{(o)}[(2N + \tfrac{1}{2}) \Delta t] &= v_j[(2N + 1) \Delta t] - E(2N \Delta t, x_j) \Delta t/2, \\
x_j^{(e)}[(2N + \tfrac{1}{2}) \Delta t] &= x_j(2N \Delta t) + v_j[(2N + 1) \Delta t] \Delta t/2, \\
v_j^{(e)}[(2N + \tfrac{1}{2}) \Delta t] &= v_j(2N \Delta t) + E[(2N + 1) \Delta t, x_j] \Delta t/2.
\end{aligned} \tag{77}$$

The antisynchronous components are then filtered by taking the average of these coordinates:

$$\bar{x}_j = \tfrac{1}{2}[x_j^{(o)} + x_j^{(e)}], \qquad \bar{v}_j = \tfrac{1}{2}[v_j^{(o)} + v_j^{(e)}]. \tag{78}$$

These new coordinates determine a new charge density so that an electric field $\bar{E}[(2n + \tfrac{1}{2}) \Delta t]$ can be determined. Equation (61) can then be used to obtain a new set of contours at $2N \Delta t$ and $(2N + 1)t$.

The modal analysis of this scheme shows that the synchronous mode is distorted by $\theta(\Omega^2)$. An antisynchronous component whose amplitude is $\theta(\Omega^3)$ is established after each synchronization, and this antisynchronous amplitude projects into the synchronous mode a remnant amplitude

$$\Omega^3 \cdot \Omega^3 \exp(N\Omega) \approx (\omega_p \Delta t)^2 \exp(N\omega_p \Delta t).$$

The error per time step is then:

$$\text{ER} \approx \frac{(\omega_p\,\Delta t)^3}{N\omega_p\,\Delta t}\,[1 + (\omega_p\,\Delta t)^4 \exp(N\omega_p\,\Delta t)]$$

The optimum $N \equiv N_{\text{opt}}$ and minimum error for this scheme is then:

$$N_{\text{opt}} \approx -4\ln(\omega_p\,\Delta t)/\omega_p\,\Delta t, \qquad \text{ER}_{\text{min}} \approx (\omega_p\,\Delta t)^3/4\ln(\omega_p\,\Delta t). \tag{79}$$

This is a slight improvement from the expression given in Eq. (76). These error estimates have not as yet been tested in numerical calculations.

ACKNOWLEDGMENTS

We would like to thank Professors Harold Grad and Harold Weitzner for their kind hospitality at the Courant Institute of New York University, where part of this work was written.

REFERENCES

ARMSTRONG, T. P. (1967). *Phys. Fluids* **10**, 1269.
BALDWIN, D. E., and ROWLANDS, G. (1966) *Phys. Fluids* **9**, 2444.
BERK, H. L., and BOOK, D. L. (1969). *Phys. Fluids* **12**, 649.
BERK, H. L., and ROBERTS, K. V. (1967a). *Symp. Computer Simulation of Plasma and Many Body Problems, Williamsburg.* NASA Rept. SP-153, p. 91.
BERK, H. L., and ROBERTS, K. V. (1967b). *Phys. Fluids* **10**, 1595.
BERK, H. L., and ROBERTS, K. V. (1967c). *Phys. Rev. Letters* **19**, 297.
BERK, H. L., NIELSEN, C. E., and ROBERTS, K. V. (1959). Phase space hydrodynamics of equivalent nonlinear systems: Experimental and computational observations. Rept. UCRL-71438, Lawrence Radiation Lab. Livermore, California.
BETRAND, P. and FEIX, M, R. (1968). *Phys. Letters* **28A**, 68,
BUNEMAN, O. (1959). *Phys. Rev.* **115**, 503.
DAWSON, J. M. (1962). *Phys. Fluids* **5**, 445.
DAWSON, J. M., HSI, C. G., and SHANNY, R. (1968). *Proc. APS Conf. Numerical Plasma Simulation of Plasma, Los Alamos.* Los Alamos Rept. LA-3990, p. A1.
DE PACKH, D. C. (1962). *J. Electron Contr.* **10**, 13a.
DORY, R. A. (1962). Midwestern Univ. Res. Assoc. Rept. 654.
DRUMMOND, W. E., and PINES, D. (1962). *Nucl. Fusion Suppl. Pt. 3*, 1049.
FOWLER, T. K. (1946). *Phys. Fluids* **7**, 249.
GARDNER, C. S. (1963). *Phys. Fluids* **6**, 839.
HOHL, F., and FEIX, M. (1966). *Phys. Letters* **22**, 432.
KILLEEN, J., and ROMPEL, S. L. (1966). *J. Comp. Phys.* **1**, 29.
KNORR, G. (1963). *Z. Naturforsch.* **18a**, 1304.
Los Alamos Rept. LA-3990 (1968). *Proc. APS Conf. Numerical Plasma Simulation of Plasma, Los Alamos.*
MORSE, R. L., and NEILSON, C. W. (1968). *Proc. APS Conf. Numerical Plasma Simulation of Plasma, Los Alamos,* Los Alamos Rept. LA-3990, p. A4.
NASA Rept. SP-153 (1967). *Symp. Computer Simulation of Plasma and Many Body Problems, Williamsburg.*

O'NEIL, T. (1965). *Phys. Fluids* **8**, 2255.
ROBERTS, K. V., and WEISS, N. O. (1966). *Math. Comp.* **20**, 272.
VEDENOV, A. A., VELIKOV, E. P., and SAGDEEV, R. Z. (1961). *Nucl. Fusion* **1**, 82.
WOODS, C. H. (1969). Interaction of a Vlasov System with dissipative structures. Rept UCRL-71302. Lawrence Radiation Lab. Livermore, California. (To be published in *Plasma Phys.*)

The Potential Calculation and Some Applications

R. W. Hockney[1]

NASA, LANGLEY RESEARCH CENTER
HAMPTON, VIRGINIA

I. Introduction	136
II. Direct Methods	139
A. Program Specification	139
B. Fourier Analysis Routine	141
C. Hockney's FACR Method	146
D. Buneman's DCR Method	155
E. The Optimum FACR(l) Method	160
F. The Inclusion of Electrodes	162
G. The Removal of Boundaries	163
III. Iterative Methods and Convergence	164
A. The SOR Process	164
B. The Cyclic Chebyshev Method	167
C. Random Error Study	169
D. Influence of the Good Guess	170
E. Convergence Criteria	173
IV. The Arbitrary Force Law	176
A. Doubly-Periodic Systems	176
B. Isolated Systems	178
V. Some Computer Models	181
VI. Applications in Particle Models	184
A. Pros and Cons of Particle Models	184
B. Plasma Physics	187
C. Electron Devices	190
D. High B-Field and Vortex Flow	192
E. Galactic Simulations	194
Appendices	202
A. The Subroutine FOUR67	202
B. The Subroutine POT1	202
C. The Subroutine POT3	202
References	210

[1] *Present address:* IBM Watson Research Center, Yorktown Heights, New York.

I. Introduction

THE SIMULATION OR MODELING of physical systems on a computer has become a practical method of investigating the properties of such diverse things as plasmas, galaxies of stars, and fluid vorticity. The calculation of the field (usually via the potential) is a critical part of most numerical simulations. In the case of a plasma model, one may be required to derive the electrostatic potential from a known charge distribution, (Hockney, 1966b) and, if the self-magnetic field is important, also the components of the vector potential from the components of the current distribution. Similarly in hydrodynamics, one may wish to derive the streamfunction from the vorticity distribution (Fromm and Harlow, 1963) or in gravitation the gravitational potential from the mass distribution, (Hockney, 1967b). In all these cases the potential function ϕ is related to the source distribution ρ by Poisson's equation

$$\frac{\partial^2 \phi}{\partial x^2} + \frac{\partial^2 \phi}{\partial y^2} + \frac{\partial^2 \phi}{\partial z^2} = -4\pi\rho(x, y, z). \tag{1}$$

This problem of calculating the potential arises both in Lagrangian particle models, in which the potential field is used to accelerate a large number of individual particles, and in Eulerian models, in which average quantities, such as pressure and velocity, are advanced on a fixed mesh. The rapid and accurate calculation of the potential from a given source distribution is difficult and time consuming. In fact, it is often the bottleneck in attempts to reduce the cycle time of a simulation. We devote our attention here exclusively to this problem.

While the solution of the truly three-dimensional problem is possible (Birdsall and Kamimura, 1966), we restrict consideration here to a simpler problem. However, many of the techniques discussed have a natural extension to three dimensions. The case considered is that in which the source distribution is given at the points of a regular two-dimensional (x, y) mesh, and the potential is to be obtained at the same points. In the first instance, we assume there is no variation of the source in the third dimension z and the problem reduces to the solution of Poisson's equation in two dimensions; namely,

$$\frac{\partial^2 \phi}{\partial x^2} + \frac{\partial^2 \phi}{\partial y^2} = -4\pi\rho(x, y). \tag{2}$$

In Section II, a finite difference approximation to Poisson's equation is used and advantage is taken of the special form of these difference equations to reduce the computational effort.

This two-dimensional calculation gives a finite-difference approximation to the potential due to a collection of infinitely long rods, in which each rod makes a contribution to the potential at each point on the mesh approximately proportional to the logarithm of its distance to that point. As a generalization, we describe in Section IV a Fourier transform technique which can solve the case where the interaction potential is other than logarithmic; in fact, it may be arbitrarily prescribed. In this method, the potential at a mesh point is regarded as the sum of contributions from all other mesh points according to a given law of interaction. The finite convolution theorem is then used to evaluate the double sum. If the interaction is taken as the reciprocal of the distance, we are considering the potential due to a system of point charges lying in a plane. This is of particular importance in the gravitational simulation of a galaxy of stars which to a good approximation may be considered as a collection of point stars moving in a plane.

Edge effects in a finite-length plasma can be approximately included by considering the interacting charges to be finite-length rods or to have some assumed z-dependence of charge density. In either case, the interaction potential can be calculated and used in the calculation of the potential. In another application it might be appropriate to represent a plasma as a collection of "dressed" ions, each with their own Debye cloud and a potential of interaction proportional to $r^{-1} \exp(-r/\lambda_D)$.

Since the interaction potential can be quite arbitrary, one can also calculate the potential field due to a collection of molecules as is required in the study of molecular dynamics (Gentry, *et al.*, 1965). Furthermore, if the truncation error due to using a finite-difference approximation to Poisson's equation in the problem of interacting infinitely long rods is too much, then one can always make the interaction potential exactly a logarithm and obtain the *exact* solution of the *differential* equation. One would, of course, always do this if it were not for the fact that the Fourier transform method is slower and uses more storage than the method for solving the finite-difference form of Poisson's equation.

There is a problem, too, with boundary conditions, the Fourier transform technique being best suited to the solution of a doubly periodic system of charges with no physical electrodes. The presence of electrodes, even around the rectangular edge of the system, requires precalculating a large capacity matrix and using it to calculate the required surface charges on the electrodes. This requires solving the doubly-periodic problem twice, hence, doubling the computing time.

An isolated system of charges (no electrodes anywhere) with an arbitrary interaction potential can be solved by the Fourier transform technique at the expense of using four times the storage and four times the computer time than is required for the doubly periodic case with no electrodes. Hence, the choice of technique for a particular problem is influenced by many factors, particularly the law of interaction, the boundaries, and the importance of truncation error.

In the case that the two-dimensional form of Poisson's equation relates the potential to the charge distribution, we describe a family of direct methods for the solution of the difference equations. A popular alternative is to use an iterative method of solution, and these are discussed in Section III. Iterative methods are simple to program and are better suited to problems with complicated boundary shapes or electrodes. Furthermore, one is attracted by the fact that a "good guess" to the solution is always available in the form of the potential distribution at the last timestep. The snag with iterative methods is that one never knows for sure if one is taking enough iterations to reduce the error by a reasonable amount. This is an important consideration because quite small changes in potential can cause large changes in particle orbits and because it is common practice to take about ten times fewer iterations than the theory of iterative processes predicts may be necessary.

The theory of the point *successive overrelaxation* (SOR) iterative technique is well developed, and sharp upper bounds on the magnitude of the error are available as a function of the number of iterations. These results are quoted partly as a warning because the guaranteed rates of convergence for large meshes are very, very slow indeed.

For example, on a 128 × 128 mesh, 233 iterations are required for the SOR technique to guarantee the reduction of the error to one percent of its initial value, and during the first 20 iterations, the error may increase to 30 times its initial value! The fact that far fewer iterations (usually 20 or less) are normally taken, apparently with satisfactory results, can only be due to the influence of the "good guess." We give some results of the error decay for sample problems for which the exact solution is known when starting with both good and bad guesses. These results do not encourage one to use iteration when the direct method can be used, since the latter can obtain the *exact* solution of the *difference* equations in the time of five or six SOR iterations. On the other hand, there may be no alternative to the iterative techniques if the boundary conditions are complicated. Unfortunately, it is difficult to make general statements on the influence of the good guess since the shape of the initial error vector depends on the charge distribution in a particular problem, and this will change from step to step through a calculation. If, on the other hand, one avoids this difficulty by taking a number of iterations that theory guarantees will produce a certain error reduction regardless of the goodness of the guess (say a modest one percent), then the computer time required becomes prohibitively long.

In Section V we give a brief description of a typical particle model which includes a potential calculation. Cycle times for such a model are given for a variety of computers. In Section VI we discuss the application of such particle models to a number of physical problems, pointing out the difficulties which are encountered. Tested computer programs are given in Section VII.

II. Direct Methods

The simplest finite-difference approximation to Poisson's equation in two dimensions is that obtained from the "five-point" difference formula; namely,

$$\frac{(\phi_{s-1,t} - 2\phi_{s,t} + \phi_{s+1,t})}{HX^2} + \frac{(\phi_{s,t-1} - 2\phi_{s,t} + \phi_{s,t+1})}{HY^2} = -4\pi\rho_{s,t}, \quad (3)$$

$$0 < s < NX, \quad 0 < t < NY.$$

Hockney (1965) described a fast direct method using Fourier analysis for the solution of these equations. In that paper, computer times and operation counts were given for an IBM 7090 program which solved the difference equation on a 48 × 48 mesh in 0.88 sec. We will describe here a new and more general program (called POT1), written and timed on the CDC 6600 and IBM 360/67 computers.

A. Program Specification

The calculation is performed on a rectangular (x, y) mesh $(NX \neq NY)$ where the mesh spacing may be unequal $(HX \neq HY)$. The number of points being computed may be either $(N - 1)$, N, or $(N + 1)$, depending on the boundary conditions, but in any event, N is restricted to a power of 2 ($NX = 2^{IQX}$, $NY = 2^{IQY}$). This restriction simplifies the program for Fourier analysis, particularly when fast Fourier transform (FFT) methods are used (Cooley and Tukey, 1965; Gentleman and Sande, 1966; Cochran et al., 1967). It also simplifies the process of recursive cyclic reduction in step (c) of the Poisson solver. Three different boundary conditions are permitted in the x-direction, selected by the value of $IBCX$, and similarly, three different boundary conditions are permitted in the y-direction, selected by $IBCY$. All nine possible combinations of these boundary conditions are possible. The possible boundary conditions are given by:

$IBCX = 1$. The potential has given values placed on $\phi_{0,t}$ and $\phi_{NX,t}$ before entry to the subroutine POT1. The routine converts the charges $q_{1,t}$ to $q_{NX-1,t}$, initially given on mesh-points 1 to $NX - 1$, to values of potential.

$IBCX = 2$. The field is zero at $s = 0$ and $s = NX$. The condition is obtained by assuming the symmetry $\phi_{1,t} = \phi_{-1,t}$ and $\phi_{NX+1,t} = \phi_{NX-1,t}$. The routine converts the charges $q_{0,t}$ to $q_{NX,t}$, initially given on mesh-points 0 to NX, to values of potential.

$IBCX = 3$. All variables are periodic in x. That is to say, $\phi_{-s,t} = \phi_{NX-s,t}$. The routine converts the charges $q_{0,t}$ to $q_{NX-1,t}$, initially given on mesh-points 0 to $NX - 1$, to values of potential.

There are similar definitions for $IBCY = 1, 2, 3$.

The required inputs to the program are values of IQX, IQY, HX, HY, $IBCX$, $IBCY$, together with the charge distribution, and in the case that $IBC = 1$, the given values of the potential. The mesh for an example problem with $IQX = 4$, $IQY = 3$, $IBCX = 3$, $IBCY = 1$ is shown in Fig. 1.

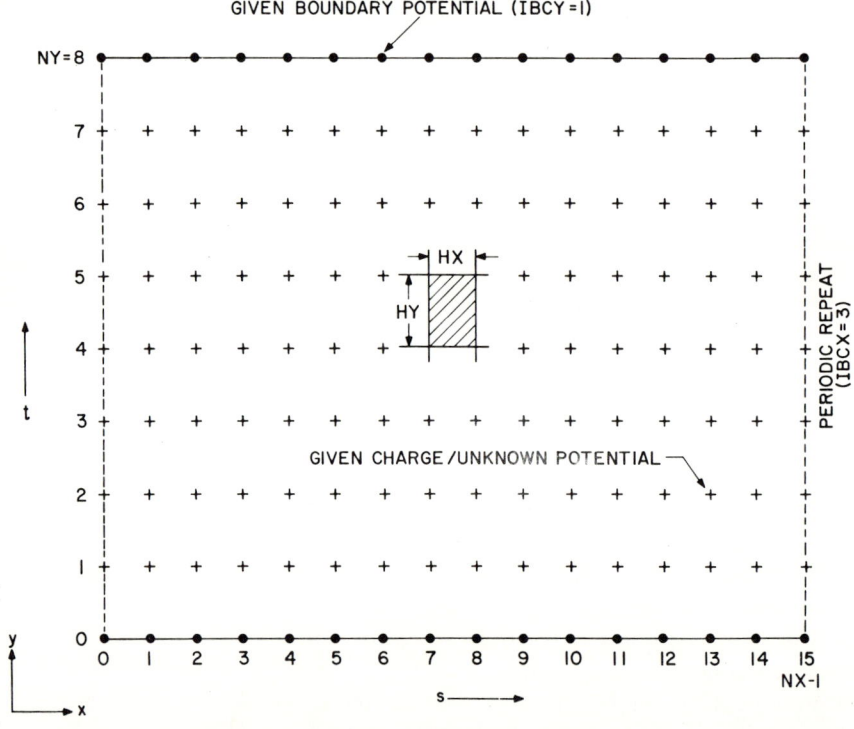

FIG. 1. An example problem solved by the subroutine POT1. The mesh repeats periodically in the x-direction ($IBCX = 3$) and has given boundary values in the y-direction ($IBCY = 1$). The number of mesh points differs in x and y ($IQX = 4$, $IQY = 3$) and the basic cell of the mesh is rectangular ($HX \neq HY$). Initially, potential values are given on the solid-circular mesh points and values of charge on the crossed points. The subroutine replaces the given charge by the potentials at the crossed points.

B. FOURIER ANALYSIS ROUTINE

The basis of all but one of the direct methods for solving the potential problem is the finite Fourier transform. Hence, we describe first the subroutine FOUR67 which has been written to perform a real transform on n real data values.

The principle of the method goes back to Runge (1903) and involves grouping the terms in the defining series which are multiplied by the same factor first, before performing the multiplication. The process of grouping involves only additions and subtractions and may be viewed as the folding of the data values and adding or subtracting the values that then lie on top of each other. A systematization of this folding was given by Hockney (1966a). The FORTRAN IV code for FOUR67 is given in Appendix A. The folding of the data is performed by the subroutines TFOLD and TFOLD1. The folding is continued as long as the symmetry of the sine functions permit, at which stage the harmonic components may be expressed as series of much reduced length. There is now no avoiding the multiplications present in the reduced series. The reduced series are evaluated recursively by the subroutine KFOLD in a manner analogous to the fast Fourier transform algorithms. The subroutine FOUR67 has two parameters IQ and IBC, which specify, as follows, the number of points involved and the boundary conditions in an analogous way to the definitions given for the parameters of POT1.

$IBC = 1$. Sine analysis or synthesis is defined by

$$Y_k = \sum_{s=1}^{n-1} Z_s \sin\left(\frac{\pi s k}{n}\right), \qquad 1 \leq k \leq n-1. \tag{4}$$

Fourier analysis followed by Fourier synthesis yields $n/2$ times the initial values.

$IBC = 2$. Cosine analysis or synthesis is defined by

$$Y_k = \sum_{s=0}^{n} E(s,n)^2 Z_s \cos\left(\frac{\pi s k}{n}\right), \qquad 0 \leq k \leq n, \tag{5}$$

where

$$E(i,j) = \begin{cases} 1/\sqrt{2}, & \text{if } i = 0, \\ 1, & \text{otherwise.} \end{cases}$$

Fourier analysis followed by Fourier synthesis yields $n/2$ times the initial values.

$IBC = 3$. Periodic analysis is defined by

$$Y_k = 2\sum_{s=0}^{n-1} E(k, n/2) Z_s \cos\left(\frac{2\pi sk}{n}\right), \qquad 0 \le k \le n/2,$$

$$Y_k = 2\sum_{s=0}^{n-1} Z_s \sin\left(\frac{2\pi s(k - n/2)}{n}\right), \qquad n/2 + 1 \le k \le n - 1.$$

(6)

$IBC = 4$. Period synthesis is defined by

$$Y_s = 2\sum_{k=0}^{n/2} E(k, n/2) Z_k \cos\left(\frac{2\pi sk}{n}\right)$$

$$+ 2\sum_{k=n/2+1}^{n-1} Z_k \sin\left(\frac{2\pi s(k - n/2)}{n}\right), \qquad 0 \le s \le n - 1.$$

(7)

Periodic analysis followed by periodic synthesis yields $2n$ times the initial values.

The folding of the data values is performed by the subroutine TFOLD according to the definitions

$$Z_s^{(t+1)} = Z_s^{(t)} - Z_{m-s}^{(t)}, \qquad Z_{m-s}^{(t+1)} = Z_s^{(t)} + Z_{m-s}^{(t)}, \qquad s = 0, 1, \ldots, m/2 - 1. \quad (8)$$

The effect of folding on input values consisting of pure harmonics (and any input is a linear combination of these) is shown in Fig. 2. We consider the periodic case ($IBC = 3$). The first folding separates the sine from the cosine harmonics. Subsequent folding on both the sine and cosine harmonics gradually separates the harmonics into groups. First one has the odd harmonics, then those with k of the form two times an odd number, then four times an odd number, eight times an odd number, and so on. When no further folding can be performed on an harmonic, it is of the form of either

$$\sum_{s=0}^{h-1} a_s \sin\left(\frac{\pi}{2} \cdot \frac{ks}{h}\right), \qquad \text{or} \qquad \sum_{s=0}^{h-1} a_s \cos\left(\frac{\pi}{2} \cdot \frac{ks}{h}\right), \qquad 0 < k(\text{odd}) < 2h. \quad (9)$$

These summations are of much reduced length compared to the original and span an odd number of $\pi/2$ in the argument of the sine or cosine.

The reduced summations are evaluated by a recursive procedure similar in spirit and speed to the fast Fourier transform algorithms. It is, however, different in detail and was devised in order to evaluate the real summations (9) over an odd number of $\pi/2$ directly, rather than going via complex summations over an integral number of 2π that are evaluated by the fast Fourier transform algorithms.

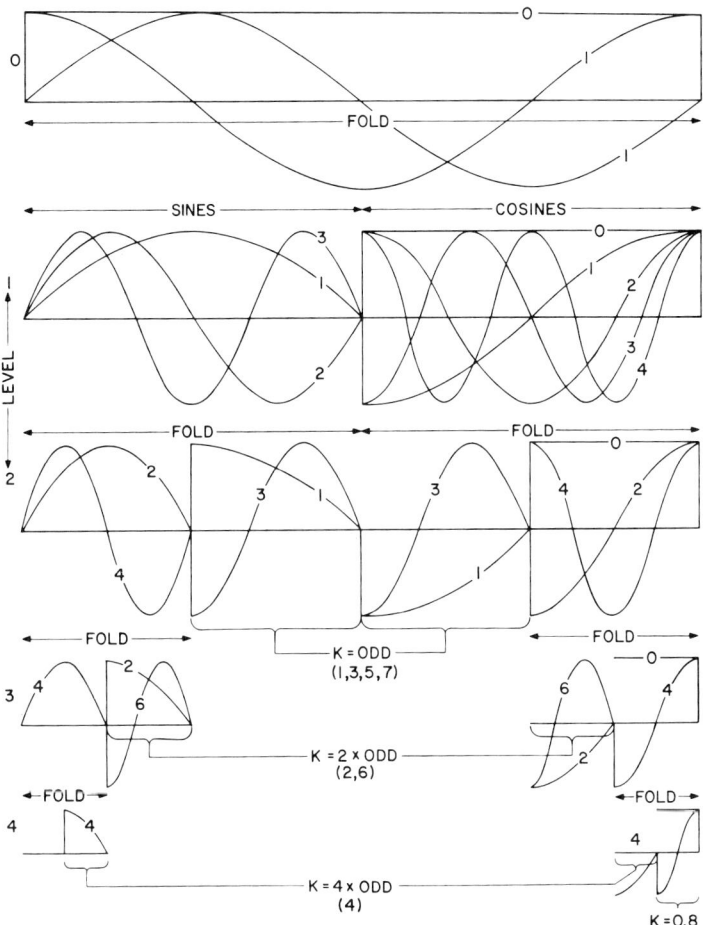

FIG. 2. Separation of the harmonics by folding. The figure shows the changing contents of the array Z for a periodic analysis on 16 points. To avoid confusion only the first few harmonics are sketched at each level.

Let us define the recurrence relations:

$$S_r^{(t+1)}(k) = S_r^{(t)}(k) + \{\cos(\theta)S_{r+h/(2m)}^{(t)}(k) + \sin(\theta)C_{r+h/(2m)}^{(t)}(k)\},$$
$$S_{r+h/(2m)}^{(t+1)}(4m - k) = -S_r^{(t)}(k) + \{\text{as above}\},$$
$$C_r^{(t+1)}(k) = C_r^{(t)}(k) + \{\cos(\theta)C_{r+h/(2m)}^{(t)}(k) - \sin(\theta)S_{r+h/(2m)}^{(t)}(k)\}, \quad (10)$$
$$C_{r+h/(2m)}^{(t+1)}(4m - k) = C_r^{(t)}(k) - \{\text{as above}\},$$
for $t = 0, 1, \ldots, T-1$, where $T = \log_2 h$.

The following quantities depend on the level of recursion t,

$$m = 2^t, \qquad \theta = \pi k/(4m),$$

and the relations are applied for

$$r = 0, 1, \ldots, h/m - 1, \quad \text{and} \quad 1 \le k(\text{odd}) \le 2m - 1.$$

The initial conditions are given by the contents of $S_r^{(0)}(1)$ and $C_r^{(0)}(1)$. If $S_0^{(0)} = S_h^{(0)} = 0$, the solution to the recurrence is

$$S_0^{(T)}(k) = \sum_{s=0}^{h-1} (S_{h-s}^{(0)}(1) + C_s^{(0)}(1)) \sin\left(\frac{\pi}{2} \cdot \frac{ks}{h}\right),$$

$$C_0^{(T)}(k) = \sum_{s=0}^{h-1} (-S_{h-s}^{(0)}(1) + C_s^{(0)}(1)) \cos\left(\frac{\pi}{2} \cdot \frac{ks}{h}\right), \qquad 1 \le k(\text{odd}) \le 2h - 1. \quad (11)$$

By a suitable choice of the initial conditions, any of the required summations can be obtained. In the case of periodic conditions, the sine and cosine summations for a particular set of harmonic numbers can be obtained together with one use of the recurrence relations.

The recurrence relations are implemented in the subroutine KFOLD, and Fig. 3 shows the manner in which the variables in storage are combined at different levels in the recurrence. At all levels, the new values overwrite the old.

The number of real arithmetic operations (an operation is any of $+$, $-$, $\times$, $\div$) required for a Fourier analysis of N real data values is as follows:

Sine transform:

$$IBC = 1, \qquad 5N \log_2 N - 8N + 6, \qquad N \ge 4.$$

Cosine transform:

$$IBC = 2, \qquad 5N \log_2 N - 8N + 12, \qquad N \ge 4.$$

Periodic transform:

$$IBC = 3 \text{ or } 4, \qquad 2.5N \log_2 N - 3.5N + 2 \log_2 N + 5, \qquad N \ge 8.$$

However, it will be sufficiently accurate to use only the first two terms of these expressions in subsequent estimates.

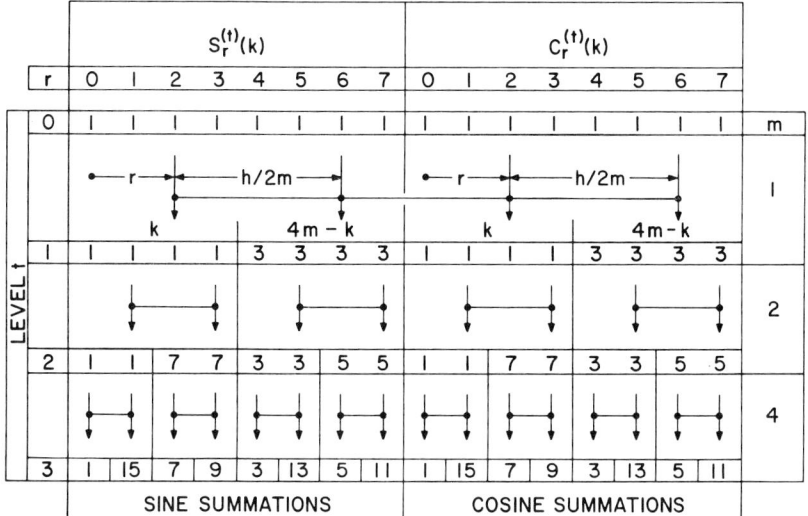

FIG. 3. Development and storage of the summations for different values of k during the recursive use of the Eqs. (10). The integers in the central part of the figure are the values of k of the summations at different levels, and the arrows indicate the positions of the partial summations that are combined at each level.

The operation count for periodic conditions can be compared with that for the regular fast Fourier transform reported by Cooley et al. (1967). The count obtained from this report for N real data points is $2.5\, N \log_2 N - 1.25N$ real arithmetic operations, showing that FOUR67 may be a marginal improvement on the regular algorithm for an analysis of real data. However, this advantage may be lost in practice due to the extra complexity of the algorithm.

Recent developments in the fast Fourier transform, described to the author by J. W. Cooley, indicate that the sine and cosine transforms need take no longer than the periodic transform. In this case the operation counts and times given later for the solution of Poisson's equation with periodic boundary conditions may be taken to apply to all boundary conditions.

The time taken on the CDC 6600 for a periodic analysis using subroutine FOUR67 is given (to 5%) by $(2N \log_2 N + 500)$ μsec and the measured time for an analysis on 1024 points was 0.021 sec. To obtain this computing speed, it was necessary to code the most important subroutines in machine code (actually the COMPASS assembly language). The all-FORTRAN version of the subroutine ran 5.7 times slower and took 0.125 sec for the same case.

Table I shows the computer time required for a Fourier analysis ($IBC = 3$) on different numbers of data points, and Table II gives the computer time for 1024 points with the different possible boundary conditions.

TABLE I

COMPUTER TIME (SEC) FOR A PERIODIC FOURIER ANALYSIS ($IBC = 3$) FOR DIFFERENT NUMBERS OF POINTS USING SUBROUTINE FOUR67

	CDC 6600		IBM FORTRAN IV[a]	
n	COMPASS	FORTRAN	360/67	Error
32	7.57×10^{-4}	—	3.64×10^{-3}	2.9×10^{-6}
64	1.32×10^{-3}	6.00×10^{-3}	7.46×10^{-3}	3.6×10^{-6}
128	2.42×10^{-3}	1.20×10^{-2}	1.58×10^{-2}	3.4×10^{-6}
256	4.90×10^{-3}	2.40×10^{-2}	3.40×10^{-2}	5.8×10^{-6}
512	1.01×10^{-2}	5.20×10^{-2}	7.44×10^{-2}	6.2×10^{-6}
1024	2.15×10^{-2}	1.06×10^{-1}	1.61×10^{-1}	7.4×10^{-6}

[a] Using H-level compiler option 2 on the model 67-1 machine.

TABLE II

COMPUTER TIME (SEC) FOR FOURIER ANALYSIS AND SYNTHESIS FOR DIFFERENT BOUNDARY CONDITIONS ON 1024 POINTS USING SUBROUTINE FOUR67

IBC	6600[a]	360/67[b]
1	0.170	0.281
2	0.170	0.281
3	0.106	0.161
4	—	0.166

[a] CDC FORTRAN IV.
[b] FORTRAN IV code; level H option 2 compiler on the model 67-1 machine.

C. HOCKNEY'S FACR METHOD

The Fourier Analysis/Cyclic Reduction (FACR) direct method is based on performing a Fourier analysis in one direction (say the x-direction), followed by the solution of the harmonic equations in the other direction, using cyclic reduction. If the boundary conditions are simple enough, as they are for cases defined for the subroutine POT1, then sines and cosines are the eigenfunctions of the operator and the harmonic equations are uncoupled. The harmonic equations can then be solved separately and rapidly. Hence, the algorithm is as follows: Fourier analyze the given charge distribution to obtain the harmonic components of the charge. Given the harmonic components of the charge, solve the harmonic equations for the harmonic components of the potential. The desired potential is then obtained by Fourier synthesis.

For simple boundary conditions in y (similar to those in x), it would be possible to Fourier analyze also in the y-direction and still obtain uncoupled equations for the harmonics. We prefer, however, to restrict the Fourier analysis to one direction for two reasons. First, one finds that the number of arithmetic operations is about 50% greater if a double Fourier analysis is used. Second, more general problems may be solved if there is no Fourier analysis in the second direction. For example, one can solve Poisson's equation by the FACR method in (r, z) and (r, θ) coordinates if one restricts Fourier analysis to the z and θ coordinates, respectively; however, we will not pursue this further here. Poisson's equations in these coordinates are:

$$\frac{\partial^2 \phi}{\partial z^2} + \frac{\partial^2 \phi}{\partial r^2} + \frac{1}{r}\frac{\partial \phi}{\partial r} = -4\pi\rho(r, z),$$

$$\frac{\partial^2 \phi}{\partial \theta^2} + r^2 \frac{\partial^2 \phi}{\partial r^2} + r\frac{\partial \phi}{\partial r} = -4\pi r^2 \rho(r, \theta). \tag{12}$$

When the FACR method is applied to the difference equations, the number of arithmetic operations may be further reduced by making use of the two-cyclic property of the difference equations. This property enables one to eliminate all reference to variables on the odd lines of the mesh. This process, which we call Odd/Even reduction, produces a set of equations for the even lines of the mesh which are more complicated than the original. The even-line equations, however, have the same symmetry as the original equations and may be solved by Fourier analysis as already described. After the solution on the even lines is found, the solution on the odd lines is obtained by solving the original odd-line equations. These may be solved independently since the solution on the intermediate even lines has already been obtained.

To simplify the mathematical description of the method, we shall assume that the mesh is square ($HX = HY$), and that the boundary conditions are periodic in the x-direction and given values in the y-direction. The original difference equations may then be written

$$\boldsymbol{\phi}_{t-1} + A\boldsymbol{\phi}_t + \boldsymbol{\phi}_{t+1} = -4\pi\boldsymbol{\rho}_t HX^2 = \mathbf{q}_t, \qquad 0 < t < NY, \tag{13}$$

where the vectors $\boldsymbol{\phi}_t$ and $\mathbf{q}_t$ are the potential and right-hand side for the tth row of the mesh

$$\boldsymbol{\phi}_t = \begin{pmatrix} \phi_{0t} \\ \phi_{1t} \\ \vdots \\ \phi_{NX-1,t} \end{pmatrix}, \quad \mathbf{q}_t = \begin{pmatrix} q_{0t} \\ q_{1t} \\ \vdots \\ q_{NX-1,t} \end{pmatrix}. \tag{14}$$

The matrix A specifies the five-point difference operator

$$A = \begin{pmatrix} -4 & 1 & 0 & \cdot & \cdot & \cdot & 0 & 1 \\ 1 & -4 & 1 & & & & & 0 \\ 0 & 1 & & & & & & \cdot \\ \cdot & & \cdot & & \cdot & & & \cdot \\ \cdot & & & & & & & \\ \cdot & & & & & 1 & & 0 \\ 0 & & & & 1 & -4 & 1 \\ 1 & 0 & \cdot & \cdot & \cdot & 0 & 1 & -4 \end{pmatrix}. \quad (15)$$

The unknowns related by a single equation are indicated by the circles in Fig. 4(a) in which the even lines are shown as solid lines and the odd lines are dashed lines.

We now describe the steps of the FACR algorithm.

1. *Odd/Even Reduction*

Consider the three neighboring equations

$$\begin{aligned} \phi_{t-2} + A\phi_{t-1} + \phi_t &= \mathbf{q}_{t-1}, \\ \phi_{t-1} + A\phi_t + \phi_{t+1} &= \mathbf{q}_t, \qquad t \text{ even}, \quad (16) \\ \phi_t + A\phi_{t+1} + \phi_{t+2} &= \mathbf{q}_{t+1}. \end{aligned}$$

Multiplying the middle even-line equation by $-A$ and adding, one obtains:

$$\phi_{t-2} + (2I - A^2)\phi_t + \phi_{t+2} = \mathbf{q}_t^*, \qquad t \text{ even}, \quad (17)$$

where the modified right-hand sides on the even lines are

$$\mathbf{q}_t^* = \mathbf{q}_{t-1} - A\mathbf{q}_t + \mathbf{q}_{t+1}, \qquad 0 < t(\text{even}) < NY. \quad (18)$$

Equations (17) are the new equations which relate unknowns on the even lines only. The unknowns related by a single equation are indicated by the circles in Fig. 4(b). The process of Odd/Even reduction means the formation of the modified right-hand side $\mathbf{q}_t^*$ on all the even points using Eq. (18). The modified right-hand side overwrites the original as it is formed.

The modification is performed by the subroutine RHSE and the number of operations required is

$$2.5 \, NX \, NY. \quad (19)$$

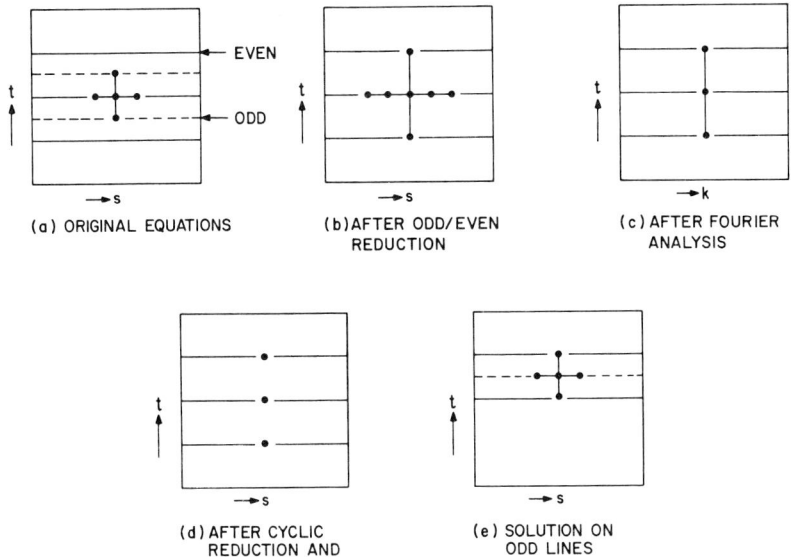

FIG. 4. The different stages of the FACR algorithm. The circles show the positions of the variables related at each stage; even lines are the solid lines and odd lines are dashed lines.

2. *Fourier Analysis on Even Lines*

A real finite Fourier analysis is performed on the even-line equations according to the transformation:

$$\phi_{s,t} = \tfrac{1}{2}\phi^c_{0,t} + \tfrac{1}{2}\phi^c_{NX/2,t}(-1)^s \\ + \sum_{k=1}^{NX/2-1} \left\{ \phi^c_{k,t} \cos \frac{2\pi ks}{NX} + \phi^s_{k,t} \sin \frac{2\pi ks}{NX} \right\}, \qquad (20)$$

where the harmonic components are given by

$$\begin{aligned}\phi^c_{k,t} &= \frac{2}{NX} \sum_{s=0}^{NX-1} \phi_{s,t} \cos \frac{2\pi ks}{NX}, \\ \phi^s_{k,t} &= \frac{2}{NX} \sum_{s=0}^{NX-1} \phi_{s,t} \sin \frac{2\pi ks}{NX},\end{aligned} \qquad (21)$$

with analogous expressions for $q^*_{s,t}$, $q^{c*}_{k,t}$, $q^{s*}_{k,t}$.

This transformation is exact and involves no truncation of an infinite Fourier series. It is simply a linear matrix transformation on the original data.

Substituting the expansion (20) into the even-line Eqs. (17) and using the finite orthogonality relations of the harmonics, one obtains

$$\phi_{k,t-2} + \lambda_k \phi_{k,t} + \phi_{k,t+2} = q^*_{k,t}, \quad t \text{ even,} \quad (22)$$

where ϕ and q^* refer to either the sine or cosine harmonic, and

$$\lambda_k = -2\left(8 - 8\cos\frac{2\pi k}{NX} + \cos\frac{4\pi k}{NX}\right). \quad (23)$$

Because the chosen sines and cosines are the eigenvectors of the matrix A, Eqs. (22) are NX independent sets of $NY/2$ equations, one set for each of the NX harmonics ($NX - 1$ sine harmonics and $NX + 1$ cosine harmonics). The variables related by these equations are shown in Fig. 4(c).

This step is performed by the subroutine FOUR67 and the number of operations required is

$$0.5 \ NX \ NY [2.5 \log_2 NX - 3.5]. \quad (24)$$

3. Recursive Cyclic Reduction

The harmonic equations may be abbreviated to

$$\phi_{t-2} + \lambda \phi_t + \phi_{t+2} = q_t, \quad t \text{ even,} \quad (25)$$

where the asterisk and the subscript k have been dropped. These equations form a tridiagonal system and are solved by the recursive application of the process of cyclic reduction. This method was devised in collaboration with Professor G. Golub and is superior to Gauss elimination for the case that the boundary conditions on Eqs. (25) are periodic, since it avoids the storage of one auxiliary vector. For the case of given value conditions or zero-slope conditions, it is probably no better than Gauss elimination, but we use it so that a single subroutine does all cases.

Reference to alternate variables in Eq. (25) can be eliminated by the same process as used in the Odd/Even step. One need only replace the matrix A by the scalar λ in Eqs. (16)–(18). Originally there are $NY/2$ unknowns (even-line values only), and after one reduction, one has $NY/4$ unknowns. The reduced equations are still tridiagonal and of the same form as the original. The only difference is that the value of the central coefficient changes. Thus, this process of cyclic reduction may be repeated recursively to give equations for $NY/8$ unknowns, $NY/16$ unknowns, and finally a single equation.

If we let l be the level of reduction, then the equations at that level are

$$\phi_{t-2^l} + \lambda^{(l)} \phi_t + \phi_{t+2^l} = q_t^{(l)}, \quad t = 2^l \text{ step } 2^l \text{ until } NY - 2^l, \quad (26)$$

and the recurrence formulas for the central coefficient and right-hand side are

$$\lambda^{(l+1)} = 2 - (\lambda^{(l)})^2, \qquad q_t^{(l+1)} = q_{t-2^l}^{(l)} - \lambda^{(l)} q_t^{(l)} + q_{t+2^l}^{(l)}, \tag{27}$$

with the starting values

$$\lambda^{(1)} = \lambda_k, \qquad q_t^{(1)} = q_{t,k}^*. \tag{28}$$

The final equation, reached when $l = L = \log_2 NY - 1$, relates the unknown at $t = NY/2$ to those at $t = 0$ and $t = NY$. The latter two points have known values from the boundary conditions. Hence, the center value is found by division from

$$\phi_{NY/2} = (q_{NY/2}^{(L)} - \phi_0 - \phi_{NY})/\lambda^{(L)}. \tag{29}$$

For the case that the boundary conditions are periodic or zero slope, the reduction process is taken a further level to $l = L = \log_2 NY$. The symmetry of the boundary conditions is then used to solve for the values at the boundaries.

For $IBCY = 3$ at $l = \log_2 NY$, one has

$$\phi_{-NY} + \lambda^{(L)} \phi_0 + \phi_{NY} = q_0^{(L)},$$

but $\phi_0 = \phi_{-NY} = \phi_{NY}$ by periodicity; hence,

$$\phi_0 = q_0^{(L)}/(\lambda^{(L)} + 2).$$

If, on the other hand, $IBCY = 2$, then one has equations for both ϕ_0 and ϕ_{NY} at $l = \log_2 NY$. These are

$$\phi_{-NY} + \lambda^{(L)} \phi_0 + \phi_{NY} = q_0^{(L)}, \qquad \phi_0 + \lambda^{(L)} \phi_{NY} + \phi_{2NY} = q_{NY}^{(L)}.$$

However, from the condition of zero slope at $t = 0$ and NY, we have that $\phi_{-NY} = \phi_{NY}$ and $\phi_{2NY} = \phi_0$; hence,

$$\lambda^{(L)} \phi_0 + 2\phi_{NY} = q_0^{(L)}, \qquad 2\phi_0 + \lambda^{(L)} \phi_{NY} = q_{NY}^{(L)}.$$

The solution to these equations is

$$\phi_0 = (\lambda^{(L)} q_0^{(L)} - 2q_{NY}^{(L)})/((\lambda^{(L)})^2 - 4), \qquad \phi_{NY} = (-2q_0^{(L)} + \lambda q_{NY}^{(L)})/((\lambda^{(L)})^2 - 4).$$

Having found the values on the boundaries, the central value is found in the same way as before. Having found the central and boundary values, the remaining intermediate values are fitted in by the recursion

$$\phi_t = (q_t^{(l)} - \phi_{t-2^l} - \phi_{t+2^l})/\lambda^{(l)} \quad \text{for} \quad \begin{cases} l = L-1, \ldots, 1, \\ t = 2^l \text{ step } 2^{l+1} \text{ until } NY - 2^l. \end{cases} \quad (30)$$

Only known values, just calculated at the previous deeper level, appear on the right-hand side.

For the case that there are no given values anywhere on the boundary ($IBCX, IBCY \neq 1$), the set of equations for the zero cosine harmonic, $\phi_{0,t}^c$ ($0 < t < NY$), is singular. One of these equations is redundant, since for these conditions there is an additional physical requirement for a solution of the Poisson problem, namely, that the total charge in the interior of the region is zero. The potential itself is then undetermined to a constant, and an additional linear constraint can be arbitrarily imposed on the solution. For convenience in the subroutine POT1 we chose

$$\phi_{0,0}^c = 0, \quad \text{if} \quad IBCY = 3, \quad \text{and} \quad \phi_{0,0}^c + \phi_{0,NY}^c = 0, \quad \text{if} \quad IBCY = 2.$$

This implies that the level of the potential is adjusted to make the average potential zero on the line $t = 0$ (or the lines $t = 0$ and $t = NY$ if $IBCY = 2$). If the total charge on the mesh does not happen to be zero, the solution to POT1 implies that a constant charge has been added to make the total charge zero. The constant charge is added to all points on the bottom row ($t=0$) if $IBCY=3$, or to all points on the top and bottom rows ($t=0$ and NY) if $IBCY=2$.

The number of operations required for the solution of a set of n equations by cyclic reduction is approximately $6n$. Since only the even lines are involved, the total number of operations is

$$3\, NX\, NY. \quad (31)$$

The equations are solved in the subroutine CRED.

4. Fourier Synthesis on Even Lines

The solution of Eqs. (25) by recursive cyclic reduction has determined the values of all the harmonic amplitudes of the potential on the even lines of the mesh. A Fourier synthesis is performed on the even lines by the subroutine FOUR67 to obtain the values of the potential on the even lines.

The number of operations required is

$$0.5\, NX\, NY[2.5 \log_2 NX - 3.5]. \quad (32)$$

The stage indicated by Fig. 4(d) is reached.

5. Solution on the Odd Lines

The solution for the potential on the odd lines can be found from the original odd-line equations (13) by putting the known values of the neighboring even lines on the right-hand side.

The equations are

$$A\phi_t = q_t - \phi_{t-1} - \phi_{t+1}, \qquad t \text{ odd.} \tag{33}$$

Since A is a tridiagonal system of the form (25) with $\lambda = -4$, the cyclic reduction subroutine CRED may be used again to solve for the values on the odd lines. Before this can be done, the right-hand side must be formed. This is done by the subroutine RHSO. The total number of operations required to determine the potential values on the odd lines is thus

$$4 \, NX \, NY. \tag{34}$$

6. Total Operations

The total operations are

$$2.5 \, NX \, NY [\log_2 NX + 2.4]. \tag{35}$$

We note that the total number of operations is proportional to the number of mesh points ($NX \, NY$) except for a very insensitive dependence on the logarithm. Taking $NX = NY = 128$ and 2 μsec per operation, we obtain 3.8×10^5 operations and 0.77 sec. The measured time on the CDC 6600 is 0.75 sec.

The above estimate is for periodic conditions in the x-direction ($IBCX = 3$) and is the most favorable for the application of Fourier analysis. For given values or zero gradient conditions ($IBCX = 1$ or 2), the time required for the Fourier analysis stage is approximately doubled and the number of operations becomes

$$5 \, NX \, NY \lceil \log_2 NX + 0.3 \rceil. \tag{36}$$

However, as previously mentioned, it is believed that improvements are possible to the Fourier analysis routine which will reduce this figure close to that required for $IBCX = 3$.

7. Total Storage

In all the processes 1–5, the new values calculated can overwrite the values from which they were derived. Hence, the main storage required is the mesh itself of $NX \, NY$ points. In addition, $3 \, NX$ auxiliary storage (the arrays Y, Z, INDEX, SI) is used by the Fourier analysis routine and a further NX is

TABLE III

COMPUTER TIME AND ERROR FOR DIFFERENT BOUNDARY CONDITIONS ON A 128 × 128 MESH USING SUBROUTINE POT1

IBCX	IBCY	CDC 6600[a]		IBM 360/67[b]	
		Sec	Error[c]	Sec	Error[c]
1 or 2	1	0.91	2.0×10^{-12}	4.71	0.8×10^{-4}
	2	0.94	2.2×10^{-12}	4.85	2.2×10^{-4}
	3	0.93	1.4×10^{-12}	4.79	1.2×10^{-4}
3	1	0.75	1.6×10^{-12}	3.53	1.2×10^{-4}
	2	0.77	3.7×10^{-12}	3.64	1.9×10^{-4}
	3	0.76	1.4×10^{-12}	3.58	3.2×10^{-4}

[a] In COMPASS assembly code.
[b] FORTRAN IV level H opt $= 2$ compiler on the model 67-1 machine.
[c] The difference in the error reflects the difference in the single precision word length of the two computers.

required to store a coefficient for each harmonic (the array AKX), in all

$$NX\,NY + 4\,NX \text{ computer words.} \qquad (37)$$

8. *Computer Time*

Table III gives the computer time for all nine possible boundary conditions for a 128 × 128 mesh. The error is the maximum deviation between a known exact solution to the difference equations and the solution obtained by the

TABLE IV

COMPUTER TIME REQUIRED TO SOLVE 2D POISSON EQUATION BY THE FACR METHOD FOR DIFFERENT-SIZED MESHES, FOR $IBCX = 3$, $IBCY = 1$, USING SUBROUTINE POT1

Mesh	CDC 6600[a]		IBM 360/67[b]	
	Sec	Error	Sec	Error
32 × 32	0.056	1.7×10^{-13}	0.219	4.5×10^{-5}
64 × 64	0.196	4.4×10^{-13}	0.879	6.5×10^{-5}
128 × 128	0.746	6.7×10^{-13}	3.527	1.1×10^{-4}
256 × 256	2.954	—	14.539	5.4×10^{-4}

[a] COMPASS assembly code.
[b] FORTRAN IV level H opt $= 2$ compiler on the model 67-1 machine.

subroutine POT1. The exact solution ranged in value from $-\frac{1}{2}$ to $+\frac{1}{2}$. The measured error is approximately 500 times the rounding error on the CDC 6600. This is about what we would expect from the random addition of 3.8×10^5 rounding errors[2] since $\sqrt{(3.8 \times 10^5)} = 618$.

Table IV gives the computer time for one set of boundary conditions as a function of the mesh size. The computer time is slightly less than linear with the number of mesh points. A good rule of thumb is that the solution time is 50 μsec per mesh point.

D. BUNEMAN'S DCR METHOD

1. *The Algorithm*

The Double Cyclic Reduction (DCR) method is an interesting extension to the process of Odd/Even reduction which has been given by Buneman (1968). He observes that the equations for the even lines may also be reduced to equations for every fourth line and these in turn may be reduced to equations for every eighth line, and so on. Finally one ends up with an equation for a single line. This equation is solved and the solutions to the remaining lines are found by solving the reduced equations appropriate to each level of reduction. This algorithm avoids any need for Fourier analysis and leads to a very short computer program, but, as we shall see, it does not give the fastest program.

Let us, for convenience, redefine the original difference equations for a line of the mesh as

$$\phi_{j-1} - B^{(0)}\phi_j + \phi_{j+1} = -2\mathbf{p}_j^{(0)}, \tag{38}$$

where $B^{(0)}$ is the tridiagonal matrix with coefficients $\{-1, 4, -1\}$ and $\mathbf{p}_j$ is proportional to the known right-hand side.

One stage of Odd/Even reduction leads to a new set of equations on the even lines

$$\phi_{j-2} - B^{(1)}\phi_j + \phi_{j+2} = -2\mathbf{p}_j^{(1)}, \tag{39}$$

where $B^{(1)} = (B^{(0)})^2 - 2I$ and $\mathbf{p}_j^{(1)} = B^{(0)}\mathbf{p}_j^{(0)} + \mathbf{p}_{j-1}^{(0)} + \mathbf{p}_{j+1}^{(0)}$.

The new Eq. (39) is of the same form as Eq. (38) and hence the process may be repeated recursively with

$$\phi_{j-2^l} - B^{(l)}\phi_j + \phi_{j+2^l} = -2\mathbf{p}_j^{(l)} \tag{40}$$

$$\begin{aligned} B^{(l+1)} &= (B^{(l)})^2 - 2I, \\ \mathbf{p}_j^{(l+1)} &= B^{(l)}\mathbf{p}_j^{(l)} + \mathbf{p}_{j-2^l}^{(l)} + \mathbf{p}_{j+2^l}^{(l)} \end{aligned} \quad \text{for} \quad l = 0, 1, \ldots, \log_2 n \tag{41}$$

[2] For $N = 128$, there are 3.8×10^5 arithmetic operations.

where l indicates the level of reduction and n the original number of lines.

The reduction step of the algorithm is to form modified right-hand sides, $\mathbf{p}_j^{(l)}$, according to the relation (41) until only a single equation is left. The lines related at different levels in the reduction are shown in Fig. 5 for the case of 16 points.

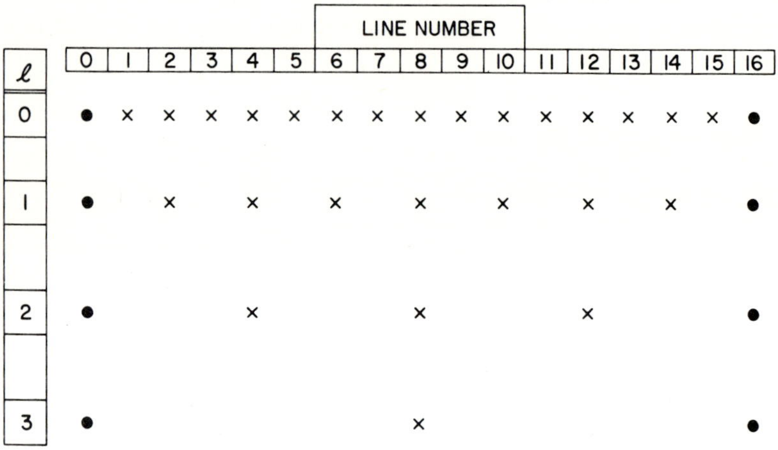

FIG. 5. The lines related at different levels of reduction in the DCR algorithm. Unknown lines are indicated by the crosses and the known boundary values by circles.

The expansion step of the algorithm is to form the solution of Eqs. (40) recursively as follows:

$$\phi_j = (B^{(l)})^{-1}[2\mathbf{p}_j^{(l)} + \phi_{j+2^l} + \phi_{j-2^l}], \quad \text{for} \quad l = \log_2 n, \ldots, 0, \quad (42)$$

where it will be observed that the potentials on the right-hand side are known values calculated at the previous deeper level.

The matrices $B^{(l)}$ fill up with nonzero elements rapidly ($B^{(0)}$ is tridiagonal, $B^{(1)}$ is five diagonal, $B^{(2)}$ is nine diagonal, and so on) and hence the number of operations required to solve an equation increases as the level increases. Considerable simplification is achieved, however, by observing that $B^{(l)}$ can be factored into a product of 2^l tridiagonal matrices as follows:

$$B^{(0)} = \text{tridiagonal with coefficients } \{-1, 4, -1\}.$$

Consider first

$$B^{(1)} = (B^{(0)})^2 - 2I = (B^{(0)} + \sqrt{2}I)(B^{(0)} - \sqrt{2}I),$$

the product of two tridiagonals. Now consider,

$$B^{(2)} = (B^{(1)})^2 - 2I = (B^{(1)} + \sqrt{2}I)(B^{(1)} - \sqrt{2}I)$$
$$= ((B^{(0)})^2 - (2 - \sqrt{2})I)((B^{(0)})^2 - (2 + \sqrt{2})I). \quad (43)$$

Hence,

$$B^{(2)} = (B^{(0)} + \sqrt{(2 - \sqrt{2})}I)(B^{(0)} - \sqrt{(2 - \sqrt{2})}I)$$
$$\times (B^{(0)} + \sqrt{(2 + \sqrt{2})}I)(B^{(0)} - \sqrt{(2 + \sqrt{2})}I)$$

the product of four tridiagonals. Clearly, the process repeats and all that is necessary is to generate and store the central coefficients of the factor matrices. The upper and lower diagonal are always -1. A general form for such factorizations is given by Buzbee et al. (1969).

The central coefficient of $B^{(l)}$ grows rapidly and is of the order 4^{2^l}. For $l = 7$, which would occur on an 128×128 mesh, the central coefficient is of the order 10^{78} and overflow will occur on some computers (for example, the IBM 360 series with a real number maximum of $\sim 10^{75}$). In any event, overflow will occur for fairly modest n on any existing computer if the built-in real number format is used. (Overflow on the CDC 6600 with a real number maximum of $\sim 10^{307}$ will occur for 512×512 points). One might consider storing the exponent as a separate integer and writing special purpose floating point subroutines for multiplication, but it is better to use a revised form of the recurrence relation which involves multiplications by the inverse of B instead of B itself. Underflow rather than overflow then occurs, but this presents no problem since most computer systems automatically replace an underflowed number with an exact zero, and proceed with the calculation.

The revised recurrence used by Buneman (1968) is to form during reduction at each level the variable

$$\mathbf{p}_j^{(l+1)} = (B^{(l)})^{-1}[2\mathbf{p}_j^{(l)} - \mathbf{p}_{j-h}^{(l-1)} \quad \mathbf{p}_{j+h}^{(l-1)} + \mathbf{p}_{j-2h}^{(l)} + \mathbf{p}_{j+2h}^{(l)} - \mathbf{p}_{j-3h}^{(l-1)} + \mathbf{p}_{j+3h}^{(l-1)}]$$
$$+ [\mathbf{p}_j^{(l)} - \mathbf{p}_{j-h}^{(l-1)} - \mathbf{p}_{j+h}^{(l-1)} + \mathbf{p}_{j-2h}^{(l)} + \mathbf{p}_{j+2h}^{(l)}], \quad (44)$$
$$\text{for} \quad l = 1, \ldots, \log_2 n, \quad \text{where} \quad h = 2^{(l-1)},$$

with

$$\mathbf{p}_j^{(1)} = (B^{(0)})^{-1}[2\mathbf{p}_j^{(0)}] + [\mathbf{p}_{j-1}^{(0)} + \mathbf{p}_{j+1}^{(0)}], \quad \text{for} \quad l = 0. \quad (45)$$

A slightly simpler form of this recurrence can be used if one has available separated meshes for the charge and potentials.

The unknown potentials are solved during expansion by the recurrence

$$\phi_j = (B^{(l)})^{-1}[2\mathbf{p}_j^{(l)} + \phi_{j-2h} + \phi_{j+2h}] + [\mathbf{p}_j^{(l)} - \mathbf{p}_{j-h}^{(l-1)} - \mathbf{p}_{j+h}^{(l-1)}], \quad (46)$$
$$\text{for} \quad l = \log_2 n, \ldots, 1, \quad \text{where} \quad h = 2^{(l-1)}.$$

Here, again, at all stages the potentials appearing on the right-hand side are known values. For $l = 0$, one uses the original equations

$$\phi_j = (B^{(0)})^{-1}[2\mathbf{p}_j^{(0)} + \phi_{j-1} + \phi_{j+1}]. \quad (47)$$

These relations (44)–(47) can be shown to be algebraically identical with the simpler relations (41) and (42). A further attraction of the new recurrence is that both the contraction and expansion recurrences are of the same form (namely, $B^{-1}P + Q$) and can use many computer instructions in common.

At each stage of reduction and expansion, it is necessary to solve 2^l tridiagonal systems of equations. Each tridiagonal system is solved by recursive cyclic reduction as explained in Section II,C,3. As with the FACR method, the DCR method requires only one mesh, which is used both for the given charges and the unknown potentials.

2. Operation Count and Speed

Let us consider a mesh of n lines each of m points long. Counting the operations in the reduction and expansion stages at the lth level together, one must evaluate the square brackets in Eqs. (44) and (46) and the additions between them on $n/2^l$ lines. This requires $18mn/2^l$ operations. Summing from $l = 1, \ldots, \infty$, one has (to better than 1% for $n > 128$) $18mn$ operations.

At the lth level, one must solve $2^{(l-1)}$ tridiagonal systems twice (once during reduction and again during expansion) for each line. The solution of one tridiagonal set of equations takes approximately $6m$ operations. The solution of all the systems at the lth level takes $2 \times 6m \times 2^{(l-1)} \times n/2^l = 6mn$ operations. The number of levels required depends on the boundary conditions in the x-direction. For given values on the boundary ($IBCX = 1$), one requires $\log_2 n - 1$ levels and for periodic conditions ($IBCX = 3$), $\log_2 n$.

The total number of operations for the DCR method is, therefore,

$$\begin{aligned} 6nm[\log_2 n + 2], & \quad \text{for} \quad IBCX = 1, \\ 6nm[\log_2 n + 3], & \quad \text{for} \quad IBCX = 3. \end{aligned} \quad (48)$$

The corresponding counts for the FACR method are from Section II,C,6.

$$\begin{aligned} 5nm[\log_2 n + 0.3], & \quad \text{for} \quad IBCX = 1, \\ 2.5nm[\log_2 n + 2.4], & \quad \text{for} \quad IBCX = 3. \end{aligned} \quad (49)$$

It is also interesting to include the operation counts for the "poor man's Poisson solver" (Boris and Roberts, 1969). This is the obvious method of a double Fourier analysis followed by a division, followed by a double Fourier synthesis. This is trivial to program given a library routine for Fourier analysis. We will call this the DFA method and the number of operations required is, ignoring the division,

$$10nm[\log_2 nm - 3.2], \quad \text{for} \quad IBCX = IBCY = 1,$$
$$5nm[\log_2 nm - 2.8], \quad \text{for} \quad IBCX = IBCY = 3. \quad (50)$$

The above comparison shows that for large n, the FACR method is potentially twice as fast as the DCR method for periodic conditions, but only 20% faster for given values. The DCR method is potentially three times faster than the DFA method for given-value conditions and 50% faster for periodic conditions.

Some of these differentials are lost due to bookkeeping operations which have been ignored. The DCR method gains significantly over FACR in this respect due to the simplicity of the program. Buneman's DCR program, which was kindly lent to the author, contains 59 FORTRAN instructions (in 2464 bytes) in the Poisson solving loop in a single subroutine. This is to be compared to 428 FORTRAN instructions (in 11,120 bytes) and 14 subroutines in Hockney's FACR program POT1. The general conclusions based on operational counts are borne out rather well by the measured computer times given in Table V.

TABLE V

COMPARISON BETWEEN DIFFERENT DIRECT METHODS FOR SOLVING THE POISSON DIFFERENCE EQUATION[a]

Mesh	DCR[b]	FACR[c]	FACR[d]	DFA[e]
32 × 32	0.297	0.219	0.265	0.529
64 × 64	1.363	0.879	1.113	2.155
128 × 128	6.152	3.527	4.711	9.021
256 × 256	27.488	14.539	20.187	38.359

[a] Time in seconds on the IBM 360/67-1 machine using all FORTRAN programs compiled with the level H, OPT = 2 compiler.
[b] Buneman's subroutine *XYPOIS* with $IBCX = 1$, $IBCY = 1$.
[c] Subroutine POT1 with $IBCX = 3$, $IBCY = 1$.
[d] Subroutine POT1 with $IBCX = 1$, $IBCY = 1$.
[e] Subroutine POT3 with $IBCX = 3$, $IBCY = 3$.

3. Choice of Algorithm

When solving large problems on a computer with a large memory size, the FACR algorithm would probably be preferred. The larger memory requirement could be accommodated and the user would gain the speed advantage of between 20% and 90%, which on large problems could mean the saving of a substantial amount of computing time. The DCR algorithm comes into its own on the small computer with limited memory capacity (for example, an IBM 1800 configuration with 4096 words of storage or an IBM 1130 with 8000 bytes of storage), since it provides probably the only direct algorithm that can be fitted into such systems. The problems to be solved on small computers are in any case small, so that the longer solution time for the DCR algorithm is of little importance.

E. THE OPTIMUM FACR(l) METHOD

We shall now generalize the FACR method to include l levels of Odd/Even reduction before Fourier analysis is performed and use the notation FACR(l) for such a method. Section II describes the FACR(1) method with one stage of reduction, and the DCR method can be considered an FACR($\log_2 n$) method. In addition, the FACR(0) method, the FACR method without the use of Odd/Even reduction has been used by Veronis (1966) in connection with a problem in wind-driven ocean circulation.

Since we have seen that FACR(1) takes fewer operations than DCR and it is easy to see that it takes fewer than FACR(0), the question arises as to whether there is an optimum level of reduction.

The optimum level will be shown to be $l = 1$ or 2, and there will be no overflow problems if we use the simple recurrences (41) and (42) for the reduction. We shall consider an ($n \times m$) mesh in (x, y) coordinates as before with Fourier analysis in the x-direction.

The modification of the right-hand side according to Eq. (41) takes $1.5nml + nm[1 - 2^{-l}]$ operations. This leaves $m/2^l$ equations to be solved by Fourier analysis and cyclic reduction at the cost of $2nm[2.5 \log_2 n - 3.5n]/2^l$ and $6nm/2^l$ operations. The expansion stage takes $2nm[1 - 2^{-l}]$ operations for the formation of the right-hand sides and $3nml$ for the solution of the tridiagonal systems.

The total number of operations per mesh point in the FACR(l) method is:

$$3 + 4.5l + (5 \log_2 n - 4)/2^l. \tag{51}$$

Figure 6 gives a plot of the operations per mesh point against the level of reduction l for a typical mesh with $n = 128$. A shallow minimum is obtained at two levels of reduction, and it is estimated that the introduction of a further

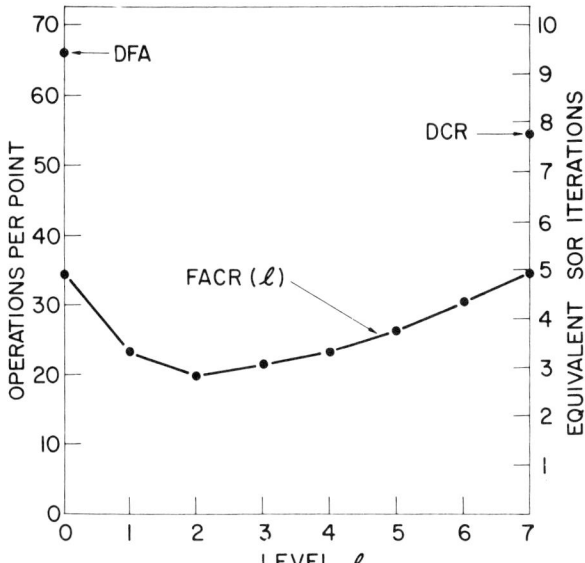

FIG. 6. The number of operations per point for the FACR(*l*), DFA and DCR algorithms on a 128 × 128 mesh. The equivalent number of SOR iterations is also given (assuming the most favorable value of seven operations per point per iteration). In all cases, the most favorable boundary conditions for each algorithm are chosen. Note the minimum number of operations at $l = 2$.

level of reduction into the subroutine POT1 could introduce up to a 10% increase in speed.

The optimum level of reduction clearly depends on the relative efficiencies of the Fourier analysis and cyclic reduction subroutines that are being used. The key question is whether it is faster to solve the equations $B^{(l)}x = b$ by Fourier analysis or by cyclic reduction. As l increases and the matrix $B^{(l)}$ fills up with nonzero elements, Fourier analysis becomes a more and more suitable method of solution. Once Fourier analysis has been chosen at the level l, one has the FACR(l) algorithm. During the development of the original FACR(1) algorithm on the IBM 7090 (Hockney, 1965), Golub and Hockney discussed the desirability of a further stage of Odd/Even reduction; however, it was rejected since careful timing of the Fourier analysis and cyclic reduction routines then available showed that the FACR(2) algorithm would have been slower.

The FACR(l) type of algorithm can be applied to more general equations than those considered here. A comprehensive mathematical account of such generalizations is given by Buzbee *et al.* (1969) in a description of the CORF family of algorithms (the cyclic odd/even reduction and factorization method).

Some workers (e.g., Birdsall and Fuss, 1968) have found it advantageous to use the nine-point difference approximation to Poisson's equation (Forsythe and Wasow, 1960, p. 194). This has a much smaller truncation error than the five-point formula and its use may be important when fairly coarse meshes are employed. The direct techniques described above may be used on the nine-point equations. The amount of computation is greater and hence the solution times will be longer than those quoted above for the five-point approximation.

F. The Inclusion of Electrodes

The direct methods which have just been described for the solution of Poisson's equation may appear to have rather limited application, particularly to electron gun simulation, since electrodes are not permitted in the interior of the region, although, of course, they may form the boundaries to the problem. One way around this restriction (Hockney, 1968b) is to precalculate a capacity matrix C, say, which relates the potential and charge on a number of points in the interior. These points are to be electrodes held at given potentials and the purpose is to calculate the surface charge which is induced on the electrode by the surrounding space charge. The solution is then obtained by solving Poisson's equation twice, as follows. First, Poisson's equation is solved with zero charge on the electrode points and the error in the potential at the electrode points from the desired values is recorded. This error when multiplied by the capacity matrix and negated gives the desired surface charge on each electrode point. Poisson's equation is solved again with the surface charge present and the solution is now correct everywhere in the region including the electrode points.

To find the capacity matrix, one first forms the inverse capacity matrix, $A = C^{-1}$. Each column of A is obtained by putting unit charge on each electrode point in turn (with zero charge on all the other electrode points), and solving Poisson's equation. The potential values on the electrode points form the elements of the column of A. The capacity matrix is formed by inversion of A and this limits the application of the method to 100–200 points on the CDC 6600. The capacity matrix is symmetric so that the storage required is $l(l + 1)/2$ for l electrode points. Since the capacity matrix depends only on the geometry of the problem and not on the space charge distribution, it may be calculated once and for all at the beginning and stored. The time to multiply the error by the capacity matrix is negligible, hence, the computer time required for determining the potential is doubled if electrodes are included in this fashion. It is possible to make refinements to this procedure if the electrodes do not pass through the mesh points.

If the number of electrode points is too large to permit the calculation and storage of a capacity matrix, the surface charge can be adjusted iteratively in response to the local error at the electrode point, with the solution of Poisson's equation still being obtained by a direct method. Alternatively, direct methods may be abandoned entirely, the whole mesh being adjusted by an iterative method. Iterating only on the electrode points has the advantage of concentrating the error in the potential near the electrodes and hence away from the space charge, whereas iterating over the whole mesh spreads the error more uniformly and hence tends to put more error in the beam region of an electron gun.

When the potential is given along the boundary of the region ($IBC = 1$), it is often convenient to reduce this case to one in which the given potential is zero. This may be done by adding a layer of equivalent charge to all mesh points within one mesh distance of the boundary. The modified charge on these these points is given by

$$q_c^* = q_c - \phi^*, \tag{52}$$

where q_c is the original charge and ϕ^* is the given value of the potential at the boundary. On substituting Eq. (52) into the difference equation with zero values assumed on the boundary, one sees that the correct equation is being solved.

G. The Removal of Boundaries

The solution of Poisson's equation in a region requires the presence of electrodes at known potentials around the boundaries of the region or the assumption of symmetry conditions at the boundaries. Hence, the solution of Poisson's equation is an ideal method when such conditions actually exist. However, there are problems where it is desired to know the potential due to an isolated system of charges in the absence of any electrodes or symmetry. The boundary condition is now only that the potential varies at infinity in the correct manner (logarithmically in a 2D problem). An efficient method of solving this problem is to calculate the correct potential around the boundary of a region, using some other technique, and then fill in the interior of the region using the Poisson solver which now has provided for it the necessary boundary values. This technique has been used in a simulation of an isolated galaxy of rod stars by Hockney (1967b) and by Hohl (1968a,b).

The values of the potential on the boundary are obtained from the expansion:

$$\phi(Z) = \text{Re}\left[a_0 \log_e(R/L) + \sum_{l=1}^{\infty} a_l/(lZ^l)\right], \tag{53}$$

where $Z = X + iY$ are the coordinates on the boundary referred to an origin at the center of the rectangle and $R = (X^2 + Y^2)^{1/2}$. L is an arbitrary constant conveniently taken to be a side of the rectangle.

This expansion is valid provided none of the charges reach the boundary, and, in practice, we limit the summation to twelve terms. The complex coefficients a_l in the expansion are obtained by taking the various moments of the charge distribution according to the definition

$$a_l = \sum_{s=1}^{NX-1} \sum_{t=1}^{NY-1} \{(s - NX/2)HX + i(t - NY/2)HY\}^l q_{s,t}. \tag{54}$$

Since the summation is performed over a regular mesh, symmetry may be used to reduce the number of arithmetic operations. If $NX = NY = N$, there is eightfold symmetry, and the number of operations required to evaluate $l_{\max}$ coefficients can be reduced to $(2l_{\max} + 3)N^2$. The evaluation of the series at the boundary points takes $10l_{\max}N$ operations. With $l_{\max} = 12$, $N = 48$, the total number of operations is 6.8×10^4. Taking 20 μsec as the average arithmetic operation time on the IBM 7090, the calculated time for the calculation of the boundary values is 1.35 sec. The measured time was 1.4 sec. Thus, this apparently simple correction to the boundary takes 1.6 times as long as the solution to Poisson's equation in the whole of the interior. However, the boundary adjustment method is still quicker than the Fourier transform method, which is to be described later, by a factor of about 2.8 and uses a great deal less storage (see Section IV, B and Table VII).

III. Iterative Methods and Convergence

Iterative methods for the solution of Poisson's equation are popular because they are simple to program. Also, one feels intuitively that the most is being made of the available information, since the potential of the last time-step is available as a good guess to start the iteration on the present step. We summarize below the known results for convergence for the most-used method, that of successive overrelaxation by points (SOR).

A. The SOR Process

Let us take as a test problem the solution of Poisson's equation in a square region with a zero potential given around the boundary. This region is covered by an $n \times n$ mesh, and the five-point difference equation is used:

$$\phi_{i-1,j} + \phi_{i+1,j} + \phi_{i,j-1} + \phi_{i,j+1} - 4\phi_{i,j} = -4\pi\rho_{i,j}h^2 = q_{i,j}, \\ \text{for } 1 \leq i, \; j \leq n-1, \tag{55}$$

where $\phi_{i,j} = 0$ for $i = 0$ or n, or $j = 0$ or n. This is the so-called "model problem" which has been studied much in the literature of numerical analysis. It has the advantage that exact analytic expressions are available for eigenfunctions, convergence rates, and error norms. The results that we quote are due to many authors, notably Young, Varga, Kahan, Golub, Sheldon, and are taken from Varga (1962) and from Forsythe and Wasow (1960).

The SOR process consists of sweeping the mesh point by point in a systematic way, making corrections to the potential at each point. Two meshes are required, one for the right-hand side $q_{i,j}$, and the other for the values of $\phi_{i,j}$. This contrasts with the direct method which requires only one mesh. At each point, one first calculates the residual,

$$R = \phi_{i-1,j} + \phi_{i+1,j} + \phi_{i,j-1} + \phi_{i,j+1} - 4\phi_{i,j} - q_{i,j}, \tag{56}$$

using the values of ϕ at the center and neighboring points. Depending on the way the mesh is swept, some of these values may already have been changed in this iteration. In any case, the latest value is always stored on the mesh. The new value at the point being corrected is defined from

$$\phi_{i,j}^{\text{new}} = \phi_{i,j}^{\text{old}} + (\omega/4)R, \tag{57}$$

where ω is the overrelaxation factor which may be adjusted to improve the convergence of the process. For the model problem one can show (Varga, 1962, p. 111) that the best asymptotic convergence is obtained if $\omega = \omega_b$, where

$$\omega_b = 2/[1 + (1 - \mu^2)^{1/2}], \qquad \mu = \cos \pi/n. \tag{58}$$

In order to study convergence, we define the root-mean-square error (proportional to the L_2 norm) after the tth iteration as

$$\|\varepsilon^{(t)}\| = \left(\sum_{i,j=1}^{n-1} (\phi_{i,j}^{(t)} - \phi_{i,j}^*)^2 \right)^{1/2} \bigg/ (n-1), \tag{59}$$

where $\phi_{i,j}^*$ is the exact solution of the difference equations. The error vector at the tth iteration may be considered as the result of a matrix operation $M^{(t)}$ acting on the initial error vector $\varepsilon^{(0)}$; i.e.,

$$\varepsilon^{(t)} = M^{(t)} \varepsilon^{(0)}. \tag{60}$$

For some processes, such as SOR, $M^{(t)}$ is the result of repeating t times the same operation, hence, $M^{(t)} = (M^{(1)})^t$. In other processes, such as the Chebyshev method, $M^{(t)}$ is a polynomial in $M^{(1)}$.

Taking the norm of both sides, one has

$$\|\boldsymbol{\varepsilon}^{(t)}\| = \|M^{(t)}\boldsymbol{\varepsilon}^{(0)}\| \leq \|M^{(t)}\| \, \|\boldsymbol{\varepsilon}^{(0)}\|. \tag{61}$$

Hence, $\|M^{(t)}\|$ is a sharp upper bound on the factor by which the initial error is reduced after t iterations. This guarantees two things. First, it guarantees that regardless of the initial guess (and, therefore, $\boldsymbol{\varepsilon}^{(0)}$), the norm of the error is reduced at least by $\|M^{(t)}\|$ after t iterations. Unfortunately, it also guarantees that there exists some initial guess for which the factor of reduction is only $\|M^{(t)}\|$.

To show how disappointing this result is, we plot $\|M^{(t)}\|$ against t in Fig. 7

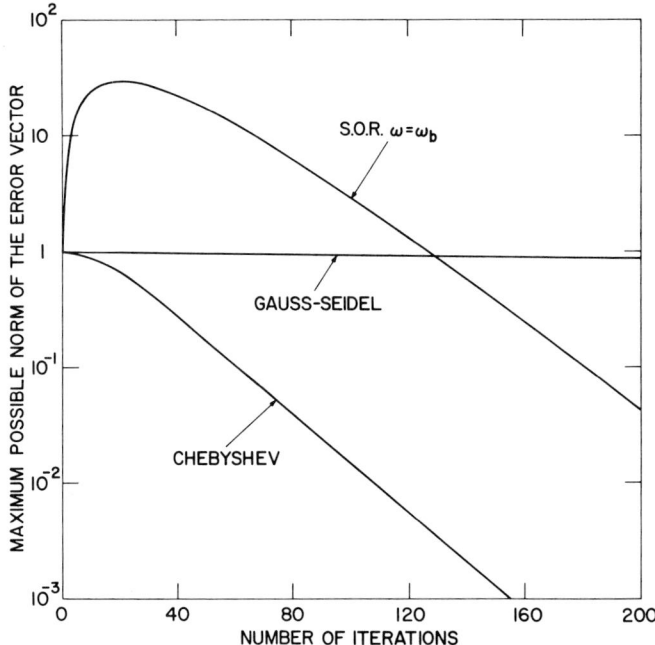

FIG. 7. Theoretical error bounds for the variation of the maximum possible norm of the error vector (relative to its initial value) with the number of iterations, for the SOR, Gauss–Seidel, and Chebyshev methods, on a 128 × 128 mesh using Odd/Even ordering.

for the SOR process on a 128 × 128 mesh, when the points are taken in odd/even ordering during the iteration. In this ordering, all the odd points [those for which $(i + j)$ is odd] are corrected first and then all the even points. This is like taking first all the white squares and then all the black squares of a checker board. For this case, $\|M^{(t)}\|$ may be calculated analytically (Varga, 1962, p. 152),

$$\|M^{(t)}\| = \left\{\frac{2t}{\mu} + \left(\frac{4t^2}{\mu^2} + 1\right)^{1/2}\right\}(\omega_b - 1)^2, \tag{62}$$

where $\mu = \cos \pi/n$.

Figure 7 shows that for a mesh of 128 × 128 points, the error may grow to 30 times its initial value during the first 20 iterations and that it can take $n\,(=128)$ iterations to reduce the error to its initial size. To ensure an error reduction of one percent requires 233 iterations and to ensure 10^{-6}, 432 iterations. These figures are to be compared with the direct method which will obtain the solution with an error of $\sim 10^{-12}$ in the time of five and six SOR iterations.

The results will be different if the points are corrected in other than the odd/even order. It is more usual and simpler to correct the points line by line, in the same way as one reads the words on a page of a book (sometimes called the "typewriter ordering"); however, the author does not know an analytic result for $\|M^{(t)}\|$ in this case.

A program has been written for the SOR process on the CDC 6600. The inner loop of the program was carefully coded in COMPASS assembly code and is contained entirely in the eight-word instruction stack of the CDC 6600. The execution time on a 128 × 128 mesh is 0.154 sec per iteration. This probably represents a best case since no logic was included in the loop to determine the maximum residual, a feature that would certainly be included in a production program in order to estimate the error. The inclusion of such logic would have further slowed down the program by making the inner loop exceed the instruction stack. We have seen (Table III) that the direct method can solve the difference equations in 0.75 to 0.94 secs depending on the boundary conditions. Thus the direct method solves the difference equations in the time of 5 or 6 SOR iterations.

B. The Cyclic Chebyshev Method

The guaranteed error decay can be improved by many orders of magnitude by using a slight variation of the odd/even SOR process. The only difference is that in this cyclic Chebyshev method, the value of ω, the overrelaxation factor, is changed every half iteration, according to the following scheme (Varga, 1962, p. 141),

$$\begin{aligned}
\omega^{(0)} &= 1, \\
\omega^{(1/2)} &= 1/(1 - \tfrac{1}{2}\mu^2), \\
\omega^{(t+1/2)} &= 1/(1 - \tfrac{1}{4}\mu^2\omega^{(t)}), \qquad t = \tfrac{1}{2}, 1, \tfrac{3}{2}, \ldots, \infty.
\end{aligned} \tag{63}$$

The first half iteration is defined as the first sweep over the odd points of the mesh, the second half iteration as the first sweep over the even points, the third half iteration as the second sweep over the odd points, and so on. One may show that $\omega^{(\infty)} = \omega_b$, so the process is SOR with the overrelaxation factor varying from 1 to ω_b. In both the SOR and Chebyshev methods, the final asymptotic rate of error decay is the same, a factor of $\omega_b - 1$ per iteration.

For a 128 × 128 mesh, $\omega_b = 1.9521$, and hence asymptotically, the error norm is reduced by a factor 0.95 per iteration. However, the guaranteed initial rate of decay is far superior in the Chebyshev method as can be seen in Fig. 7 for a 128 × 128 mesh.

For the cyclic Chebyshev method, one has (Varga, 1962, pp. 152, 139),

$$\|M^{(t)}\| = (\|P_{2t-1}\|^2 + \|P_{2t}\|^2)^{1/2}/2^{1/2}, \tag{64}$$

where

$$\|P_t\| = (\omega_b - 1)^{t/2} \frac{2}{1 + (\omega_b - 1)^t}.$$

One can show that $\|M^{(t)}\|$ always decreases as t increases and, for $n = 128$, the asymptotic rate of convergence is guaranteed after $n/4$ iterations. A one percent error reduction is guaranteed after 108 iterations, and a 10^{-6} reduction after 295. However, even with this improved convergence, one can only guarantee error reduction by the factor 0.96 in a time equivalent to the use of the direct method.

One can intuitively see the reason why approximately $n/2$ iterations are required before the asymptotic rate of convergence is established, in the special case of a single charge at the extreme right-hand side of the mesh. By considering where changes are made on the mesh at each iteration, one can see that for the case of odd/even ordering, it takes $n/2$ iterations before any changes whatsoever are made to the points near the left edge of the mesh due to this single charge.

The fact that iterative methods are used successfully by many authors (Fromm, 1964; Hohl, 1968a,b; Chorin, 1968) indicates that the initial error vectors that are met in practice are usually not the worst ones. Nevertheless, the above worst cases can arise and serve as warning against the use of iterative techniques without a proper investigation of the error decay in the particular problem being solved. In order to assess the convergence that is likely to arise in actual problems, we have considered two cases, that of random errors and that of the error arising due to the motion of a bar of charge. In the latter case, we investigate the influence of the good and bad initial guess.

C. Random Error Study

The use of three meshes in the random error study is illustrated in Fig. 8. A random distribution of potential ϕ^* is first generated on the first mesh. On a second mesh, the charge distribution q which would generate ϕ^* is found by differencing using the difference equation

$$q_{i,j} = \phi^*_{i-1,j} + \phi^*_{i+1,j} + \phi^*_{i,j-1} + \phi^*_{i,j+1} - 4\phi^*_{i,j}. \tag{65}$$

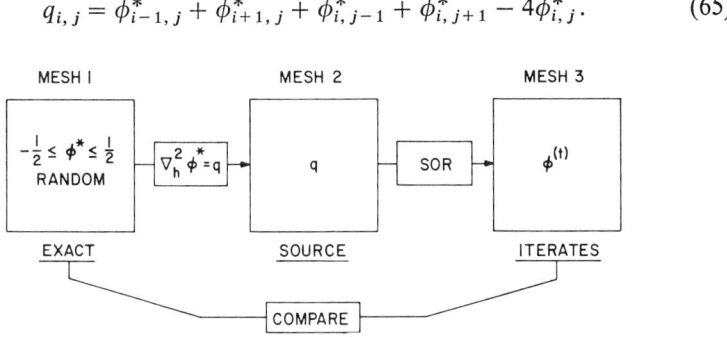

FIG. 8. The use of three meshes during the random error test. ∇_h^2 stands for the finite difference approximation for the Laplacian [Eq.(65)].

Hence, ϕ^* is the exact solution of the difference equation for the charge distribution q. The iterative procedure is now used on a third mesh to generate successive approximations to the solution, $\phi^{(t)}$, say. We have taken $\phi^{(0)} \equiv 0$, hence the initial distribution of error is random. Since the exact solution of the difference equation is known, the RMS norm of the error may be calculated at every iteration. This is plotted for various iterative procedures in Fig. 9.

We first observe that for SOR with $\omega = \omega_b$, the error decays at about the asymptotic rate after a small initial growth. If, however, we use SOR with $\omega = 1$, thus converting it to the Gauss–Seidel iteration with no overrelaxation, the initial error decay is much more rapid, the error decaying by an order of magnitude in the first six iterations. Subsequently, however, the error decay becomes hopelessly slow, the asymptotic rate of error decay per iteration for Gauss–Seidel being a factor of $\mu^2 = \cos^2 \pi/n$ per iteration. For a 128 × 128 mesh, this is a factor of 0.9949 per iteration which is to be compared with a factor of 0.95 per iteration if $\omega = \omega_b$ is used. At the asymptotic rate (Forsythe and Wasow, 1960, p. 283), the Gauss–Seidel procedure requires $2.3n^2/\pi^2$ (=4000 if $n = 128$) iterations for the reduction of the error by a factor 10, compared with $2.3n/2\pi$ (=47 if $n = 128$) iterations for SOR with $\omega = \omega_b$. This shows how pathologically slow convergence can be when a substantial sized mesh is used and how important it is to use the best value of ω in the SOR process if substantial error reduction is required.

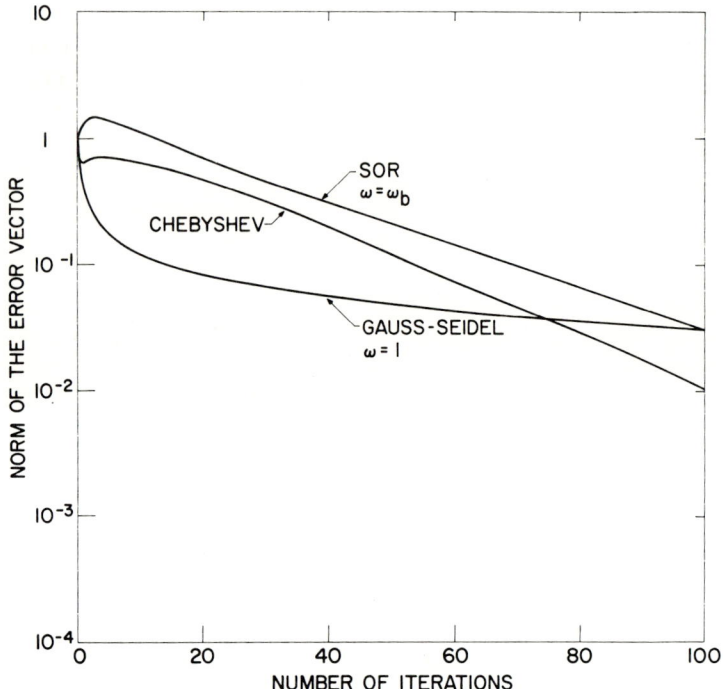

Fig. 9. Variation of the norm of the error vector with the number of iterations for a random initial error on a 128 × 128 mesh using the SOR, Gauss–Seidel, and Chebyshev methods.

We have seen that as regards the initial rate of error decay, $\omega = 1$ is superior to $\omega = \omega_b$, but as regards the asymptotic rate of decay $\omega = \omega_b$ is vastly superior to $\omega = 1$. This suggests that the Chebyshev method which smoothly varies ω from 1 to ω_b might combine with merits of both values of ω. The third curve of Fig. 9 shows that for random errors, the Chebyshev method is indeed superior to SOR. Curiously enough, both Chebyshev and SOR are worse than Gauss–Seidel for the first 80 iterations. This is probably a special feature of the random error case. It does not, for example, apply to the more realistic error distribution considered in Section D. Since the Chebyshev method is such a trivial variation of the SOR process and has superior error decay properties, there seems to be no reason for using the straight SOR process.

D. Influence of the Good Guess

In a typical plasma simulation, some charge will move about a mesh distance in a timestep of the calculation. We, therefore, took as a simple test example the case of a bar of charge, two mesh distances wide, which moves sideways one mesh distance during a timestep. This example also simulates reasonably the motion of an arm of a galaxy in a gravitational model.

The mesh taken is defined by the indices $0 \le i, j \le 128$, with the boundary condition that $\phi_{i,j} = 0$ if $i = 0$ or 128, or $j = 0$ or 128. Initially, unit charges are placed on mesh points $i = 63$, $j = 32$–96, and $i = 64$, $j = 32$–96, thus placing the bar of charge just left of the center. The Chebyshev method is then used, starting from $\phi \equiv 0$ as an initial guess, to obtain the potential. Five-hundred iterations were taken at which time the maximum residual was reduced to 10^{-9}, and the theory of norms guarantees that the error reduction is at least 10^{-11}. This is regarded as the exact solution.

The bar is now moved one mesh distance to the right, as illustrated in Fig. 10, and hence occupies columns $i = 64$ and 65. The exact solution to this new

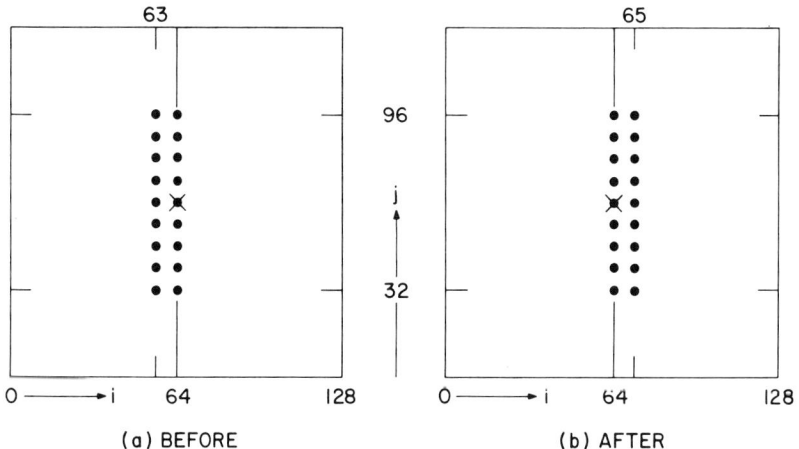

FIG. 10. Position of the charges before and after the motion of a bar of charge one mesh distance from left to right. The before and after positions have reflective symmetry about the center line $i = 64$. A cross marks the field test point.

distribution of charge is known since it is the previously computed solution reflected about the center column $i = 64$. The test consists of iteration to determine the new potential distribution starting from $\phi \equiv 0$ (a "bad" guess) or from the potential previously calculated for the bar in its old position (a "good" guess). Since the exact solution is known, the error norms can be calculated.

In Fig. 11 we plot the norm of the error divided by the norm of the exact solution versus the number of iterations. The results show that the Chebyshev method is the best. The rate of decay of the error for this method is approximately the same for the good and bad guesses and follows closely the norm

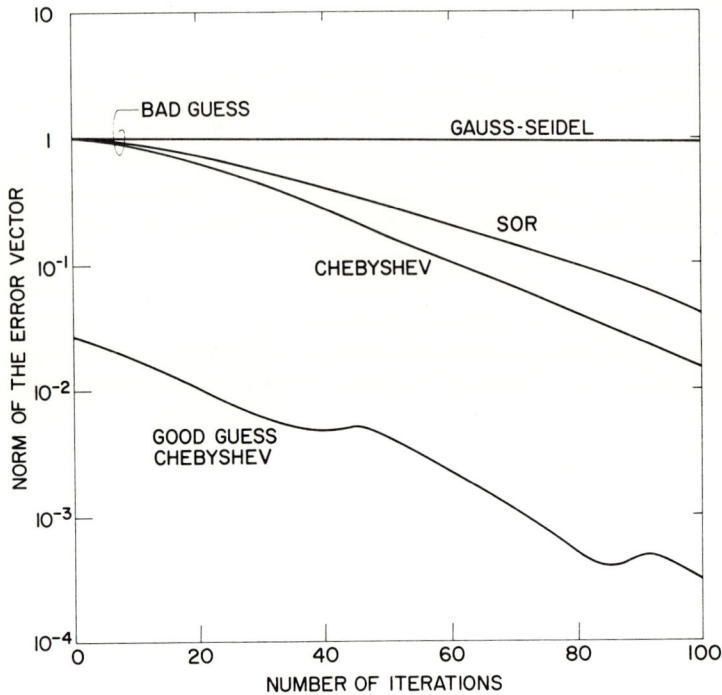

FIG. 11. Variation of the norm of the error vector with the number of iterations when a bar of charge moves one mesh distance for good and bad starting guesses on a 128 × 128 mesh.

limit of Fig. 7. Six iterations with a good guess produces an error decay factor of only 0.78, 57 iterations are required to reduce the error to one-tenth of its initial value, and 105 iterations are required for a reduction to 1%. The corresponding figures for the error decay starting with a bad guess are 0.95 reduction in 6 iterations and a reduction to one-tenth in 61 iterations.

Although the initial rate of error decay is somewhat better for the good guess, the main difference between the good and bad guess results is that the initial size of the error in the good guess is only 1/40 of that for the bad guess. We can estimate the effect of continually introducing errors at each step, and only reducing the error by a modest amount at each step by treating all vectors as scalars in the following crude argument.

Suppose an error α is introduced at each step and that the error reduction per step is by a factor λ. Then,

$$\varepsilon^{(0)} = \alpha, \qquad \varepsilon^{(1)} = \alpha\lambda + \alpha,$$

and after t timesteps,

$$\varepsilon^{(t)} = \alpha[\lambda^t + \lambda^{t-1} + \cdots + \lambda + 1] \tag{66}$$
$$= \alpha(1 - \lambda^{t+1})/(1 - \lambda). \tag{67}$$

Hence, $\varepsilon^{(\infty)} = \alpha/(1 - \lambda)$ since $\lambda < 1$.

If in our example we only take six iterations per step, then $\lambda = 0.83$ and $\varepsilon^{(\infty)} = 6\alpha$. Hence, the error finally in the system is six times the error committed per step, or in our case where $\alpha = 1/40$, an error of 15%.

A spot-check has also been made on the field at the center of the system $i = 64, j = 64$. As the bar moves, this field should reverse direction, and, since it is the field acting on elements of the bar, it is particularly important that this be calculated correctly. The relative error in the field at the center decays quite rapidly for both good and bad guesses. In both cases the relative error is 10^{-1} after about 4 iterations, 10^{-2} after about 25 iterations, and 10^{-3} after about 100 iterations. In this case the "good" guess results are somewhat worse than those for the "bad" guess, presumably because the zero field assumed as the "bad" first guess is closer to the solution than the reversed field from the last timestep which is used as the "good" first guess.

E. CONVERGENCE CRITERIA

We have seen that it is rarely possible to carry on an iterative process for the number of iterations that will guarantee that the error is reduced by a substantial factor. In practice it is more usual to carry on an iteration until some convergence criteria is satisfied. Since the exact answer is not known, no direct measure of the true error is available and the error must be estimated from the size of measurable quantities, such as the size of the residuals or the changes in the solution from the last iteration. We consider both cases below.

Consider for simplicity that the iterative processs has settled down so that there is one dominant error vector with a real eigenvalue λ. For SOR with $\omega = \omega_b$, all eigenvalues have the same modulus of $\omega_b - 1$. Two of these are real. Let $\boldsymbol{\phi}^{(t)}$ be the tth iterate and $\boldsymbol{\varepsilon}^{(t)}$ be the true error at the tth iteration. Then the change during the tth iteration is

$$\boldsymbol{\Delta}^{(t)} = \boldsymbol{\varepsilon}^{(t+1)} - \boldsymbol{\varepsilon}^{(t)} = (\lambda - 1)\boldsymbol{\varepsilon}^{(t)}. \tag{68}$$

Hence,

$$\boldsymbol{\varepsilon}^{(t)} = (\lambda - 1)^{-1}\boldsymbol{\Delta}^{(t)}, \tag{69}$$

or

$$\|\boldsymbol{\varepsilon}^{(t)}\| = |(\lambda - 1)|^{-1} \|\boldsymbol{\Delta}^{(t)}\|. \tag{70}$$

For 128 × 128 mesh, $\omega_b = 1.9521$ and $\lambda = 0.9521$; therefore,

$$\|\mathbf{\epsilon}^{(t)}\| = 20\|\mathbf{\Delta}^{(t)}\|. \tag{71}$$

Thus, in this case, the true error is 20 times the change made during the iteration. Therefore, for this size mesh, it is important to set the required tolerance on $\mathbf{\Delta}^{(t)}$ at least ten times more severe than the required accuracy in the solution. It is also clear that the slower the convergence (the more mesh points there are and the closer λ is to 1), the easier it is to satisfy a convergence criteria based on the value of $\mathbf{\Delta}$. In the limit of an iterative process that does not improve the initial guess at all, then any criterion based on the size of $\mathbf{\Delta}$ is satisfied in one step even though the guess may bear no relation at all to the true solution.

It is rather more satisfactory to base the criteria on the extent to which the given equations are satisfied, namely the size of the residuals, than merely on changes made during the iterative process. However, even here the situation is not a happy one. Let the finite difference equations for an $n \times n$ mesh be represented by

$$A\mathbf{\phi}^* = \mathbf{\rho}, \tag{72}$$

where $\mathbf{\phi}^*$ is the exact solution for the charges $\mathbf{\rho}$ and A is the $n^2 \times n^2$ matrix with one row for each of the n^2 equations of the mesh. Then the residual vector at the tth iteration is defined as

$$\mathbf{R} = A\mathbf{\phi}^{(t)} - \mathbf{\rho}, \tag{73}$$

and the true error is

$$\mathbf{\epsilon}^{(t)} = \mathbf{\phi}^{(t)} - \mathbf{\phi}^*. \tag{74}$$

Hence,

$$\mathbf{R} = A\mathbf{\epsilon}^{(t)}, \tag{75}$$

and taking norms of both sides,

$$\|\mathbf{R}\| \leq \|A\| \|\mathbf{\epsilon}^{(t)}\|. \tag{76}$$

Also, one has

$$\mathbf{\phi}^* = A^{-1}\mathbf{\rho}, \tag{77}$$

and
$$\|\boldsymbol{\phi}^*\| \leq \|A^{-1}\| \|\boldsymbol{\rho}\|, \tag{78}$$

or
$$\|\boldsymbol{\rho}\| \geq \|A^{-1}\|^{-1} \|\boldsymbol{\phi}^*\|. \tag{79}$$

Dividing Eq. (76) by Eq. (79), one obtains
$$\frac{\|\mathbf{R}\|}{\|\boldsymbol{\rho}\|} \leq \|A\| \|A^{-1}\| \frac{\|\boldsymbol{\varepsilon}^{(t)}\|}{\|\boldsymbol{\phi}^*\|}. \tag{80}$$

Similarly, one may show
$$\frac{\|\boldsymbol{\varepsilon}^{(t)}\|}{\|\boldsymbol{\phi}^*\|} \leq \|A\| \|A^{-1}\| \frac{\|\mathbf{R}\|}{\|\boldsymbol{\rho}\|}, \tag{81}$$

and combining these,
$$\frac{1}{K} \frac{\|\mathbf{R}\|}{\|\boldsymbol{\rho}\|} \leq \frac{\|\boldsymbol{\varepsilon}^{(t)}\|}{\|\boldsymbol{\phi}^*\|} = K \frac{\|\mathbf{R}\|}{\|\boldsymbol{\rho}\|}, \tag{82}$$

where K is defined as the condition number of the matrix A,
$$K = \|A\| \|A^{-1}\|. \tag{83}$$

For the model Poisson problem with known eigenvectors and taking $n = 128$,
$$K = \frac{\cos(n-1)\pi/n - 1}{\cos \pi/n - 1} \simeq \frac{4n^2}{\pi^2} \cong 6400. \tag{84}$$

Hence,
$$\frac{1}{6400} \frac{\|\mathbf{R}\|}{\|\boldsymbol{\rho}\|} \leq \frac{\|\boldsymbol{\varepsilon}^{(t)}\|}{\|\boldsymbol{\phi}^*\|} \leq 6400 \frac{\|\mathbf{R}\|}{\|\boldsymbol{\rho}\|}, \tag{85}$$

and to be sure that the relative error in the solution is less than, say, 10^{-3}, one must set the criterion such that the norm of the residual must be 10^{-7} of the norm of the charge vector. It is important to realize that the equality signs in the above relation can be realized for particular choices of the vectors ρ, ϕ^*, $\varepsilon^{(t)}$, R, and thus it is clear that tests based on the size of the residuals can be very insensitive indeed, particularly for large numbers of mesh points.

There seems to be no satisfactory way of knowing when to stop an iteration. One feels intuitively that one need not be bound by theoretical results which are based on worst cases that perhaps will not occur in practice. In fact, it is common practice to ignore the theoretical results on convergence, by taking, for example, 6–7 iterations only with a criterion of $\Delta < 10^{-3}$. Even so, physically sensible results appear to be obtained. But this is not satisfactory and as we have seen above, small changes from iteration to iteration or small residuals do not guarantee that the solution has comparable accuracy even by several orders of magnitude. The best solution to the problem is obviously to use a direct method of solution if one can.

IV. The Arbitrary Force Law

We now discuss the Fourier transform techniques which can be used when the force (or potential) of interaction is arbitrary. These techniques have been developed independently by a number of people, including the author, Miller and Prendergast (1968), and G. Rybicki.

The problem is to calculate the potential on a rectangular mesh (here assumed to be a square $n \times n$ mesh for simplicity) due to a distribution of particles given on the same mesh. The particles will be spoken of as "charges," but this does not mean that the interaction between them is necessarily the interaction between charges.

A. Doubly-Periodic Systems

Any function $f_{s,t}$ defined on the mesh is assumed to repeat periodically in both directions outside the region of definition, $0 \leq s, t \leq n - 1$. The double finite Fourier transform of such a function may then be defined as

$$\hat{f}_{k,l} = \sum_{s,t=0}^{n-1} f_{s,t} \exp\left(-\frac{2\pi i}{n}(sk+tl)\right). \tag{86}$$

Then the Fourier expansion of the original function is

$$f_{s,t} = \frac{1}{n^2} \sum_{k,l=0}^{n-1} \hat{f}_{k,l} \exp\left(\frac{2\pi i}{n}(sk+tl)\right). \tag{87}$$

These relations for the finite Fourier transform may be verified by making use of the orthogonality relation

$$\sum_{s=0}^{n-1} \exp\left(\frac{2\pi i s}{n}(k-l)\right) = n\delta_{k,l}.$$

The potential at the mesh point (a, b) may be defined as a direct summation over contributions from charges at all the other mesh points, from the expression

$$\phi_{a,b} = \sum_{s,t=0}^{n-1} q_{s,t} F_{a-s, b-t}, \tag{88}$$

where $q_{s,t}$ is the charge on mesh point (s, t). The interaction between charges is described by the potential $F_{c,d}$ which is the potential at the point (c, d) due to a unit charge at the origin $(0, 0)$. This potential is arbitrary except that, like everything else, it is periodically repeated in both directions outside the region of definition.

The number of operations required to compute the potential at all mesh points from the definition (88) will be a small multiple of n^4. Taking the most favorable view that F has been precalculated and stored, the number of operations would be n^4. For $n = 128$ and 2 μsec/operation, the computer time required is nine minutes. This is to be compared with $10n^2 \log_2 n$ and 2.4 sec for the Fourier transform method which is to be described. Although economies can be made in the summation method, by approximating and using a graded set of meshes (Hohl and Hockney, 1969), the programs still run slower than the exact solution using the Fourier transform method.

Introducing the transform of the interaction potential F into Eq. (88), one has

$$\phi_{a,b} = \frac{1}{n^2} \sum_{s,t=0}^{n-1} q_{s,t} \sum_{k,l=0}^{n-1} \hat{F}_{k,l} \exp\left(\frac{2\pi i}{n}\{(a-s)k + (b-t)l\}\right), \tag{89}$$

and rearranging terms,

$$\phi_{a,b} = \frac{1}{n^2} \sum_{k,l=0}^{n-1} \hat{F}_{k,l} \left\{\sum_{s,t=0}^{n-1} q_{s,t} \exp\left(-\frac{2\pi i}{n}(sk + tl)\right)\right\} \exp\left(\frac{2\pi i}{n}(ak + bl)\right). \tag{90}$$

The term in braces is the definition of the transform of q; hence,

$$\phi_{a,b} = \frac{1}{n^2} \sum_{k,l=0}^{n-1} \hat{F}_{k,l} \hat{q}_{k,l} \exp\left(\frac{2\pi i}{n}(ak + bl)\right). \tag{91}$$

Comparing (91) with the definition of the Fourier transform, one has the result that

$$\hat{\phi}_{k,l} = \hat{F}_{k,l}\hat{q}_{k,l}. \tag{92}$$

This result is the finite analog of the convolution theorem, that the Fourier transform of the convolution of two functions is the product of their Fourier transforms. Here the potential is the convolution of the charge distribution with the interaction potential.

Hence, the potential due to any doubly periodic array of charges with an arbitrary potential of interaction can be found. First, the desired doubly periodic interaction potential F is written on a mesh for a unit charge at the origin. The Fourier transform $\hat{F}$ of this interaction potential is found and stored. This calculation need be done only once. During each timestep of a simulation, a charge distribution q is obtained on a second mesh. The double Fourier transform $\hat{q}$ of this distribution is found, and this may overwrite the original charge distribution q. The Fourier transform of the charge is multiplied by the Fourier transform of the interaction potential to give the Fourier transform of the potential distribution. The potential distribution due to the original charge distribution is then obtained by a double Fourier synthesis. All operations on the second mesh may overwrite each other and the total storage required is approximately $2n^2$.

It should be noted that in some simple cases the transform F does not need the storage n^2. For a general isotropic interaction potential depending only on the distance between interacting charges, $\hat{F}_{c,d} = \hat{F}_{d,c}$ and hence only $n(n+1)/2$ numbers need be stored.

A double Fourier transform on an $n \times n$ mesh of real numbers can be performed in $5n^2[\log_2 n - 1.4]$ operations. The total number of operations is, therefore, $10n^2[\log_2 n - 1.3]$. For $n = 128$, this is 0.92×10^6 operations which at 2 μsec operation is 1.84 sec. The measured time on the CDC 6600 was 1.85 sec.

B. Isolated Systems

The Fourier transform method which has been described will solve a doubly periodic system of charges with an arbitrary form of interaction. No conductors or boundaries are permitted in the system and if these are present, the capacity matrix method, which was described in connection with the solution of Poisson's equation, must be used. Sometimes it is desired to study an isolated cloud of charge or, in the case of a gravitational model, an isolated galaxy.

The method may be adapted to isolated systems if one is prepared to use only one-quarter of the available mesh points for the charge distribution, say, the bottom left-hand corner, defined by $0 \le s, t \le n/2$. The charge distribution over the remaining three-quarters of the system is made identically zero. Taking the interaction of point charges as an example, an interaction potential is constructed as follows:

$$\left. \begin{array}{l} F_{c,d} = (c^2 + d^2)^{-1/2} \\ F_{n-c,d} = F_{c,n-d} = F_{n-c,n-d} = F_{c,d} \\ F_{0,0} = 1 \end{array} \right\} \quad \begin{array}{l} 0 \le c, d \le n/2 \\ c + d \ne 0. \end{array} \quad (93)$$

When this potential is repeated periodically, one sees that the correct r^{-1} potential for a point charge at the origin is obtained within the region $-n/2 \le c, d \le n/2$. At the boundary of this region there is a cusp and outside the region the potential is incorrect, However, if we use only the bottom left-hand corner for the charge distribution and only use the potential in this region, the correct potential for an isolated system is obtained. The potential outside the bottom left-hand corner is incorrect, containing as it does all the unphysical cusps of the interaction potential. But this does not matter since this potential is never used. The use of the mesh for an isolated system is illustrated in Fig. 12.

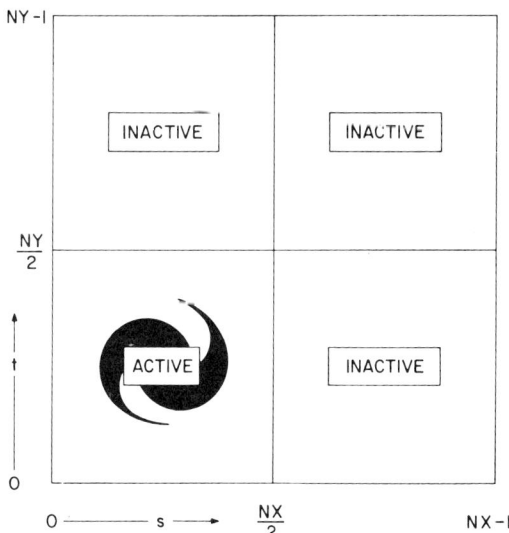

FIG. 12. The use of the potential mesh for calculations on an isolated system. Only the active quarter of the mesh may be used for charges or masses. The remaining inactive regions are required during the calculation.

This method gives the exact potential (except, of course, for rounding error) over a square (or rectangular) array of mesh points. If there are $N \times N$ charge mesh points given, then the calculation must be performed on a $2N \times 2N$ mesh requiring a storage of $8N^2$ (four times the storage of the doubly periodic system[3]). Since the computer time is roughly proportional to the number of points used in the calculation, the computer time is also four times that for a doubly periodic system. This method for isolated systems appears to be wasteful of both computer time and storage. It is to be expected that further economies can be made.

A subroutine, POT3, has been written for an isolated system using the Fourier transform technique and the measured execution times are given in Table VI.

TABLE VI

COMPUTER TIME (SEC) FOR DIFFERENT-SIZE MESHES (SUBROUTINE POT3)

Mesh points[a]		CDC 6600[b]		IBM 360/67[c]	
Periodic	Isolated	COMPASS	FORTRAN IV	FORTRAN IV	Error
32 × 32	16 × 16	0.132	0.354	0.529	—
64 × 64	32 × 32	0.494	1.524	2.155	6.6×10^{-6}
128 × 128	64 × 64	1.854	6.618	9.021	6.7×10^{-6}
256 × 256	128 × 128	7.542	28.708	38.359	7.6×10^{-6}

[a] Mesh points available for the charge distribution and the corresponding potential distribution.
[b] Central processor time, includes all time for calculation except for input and output.
[c] Level H, opt = 2 compiler on the model 67-1 machine.

The FORTRAN IV code for POT3 is given in Appendix C. Execution times on the CDC 6600 are given for this program compiled using the FORTRAN version 2.1 compiler, and for a program with the inner loops of the Fourier analysis routine programmed in the COMPASS assembly code. Both programs were run under the Langley Research Center SCOPE 3.0 operating system and the times were measured by calling the library subroutine SECOND(T) before and after execution of the potential solver. The difference in the time is taken as the execution time and is probably accurate to two milliseconds. The convenience of programming completely in FORTRAN on the CDC 6600 is seen to cost a factor of between 3 and 4 in execution time. Times are

---

[3] This can be reduced to $5N^2$ by using the symmetry in the function $\hat{F}_{c,d}$.

also given for the FORTRAN IV program run on the IBM 360/67 using the Level *H* option 2 compiler.

Table VII gives a comparison of the storage and execution times required

TABLE VII

MEASURED COMPUTER TIME REQUIRED ON A 128 × 128 MESH FOR DIFFERENT SYSTEMS

System	CDC 6600[a] (CPU Sec)	Storage[b]
Infinite rods via Poisson	0.75	16 K
Isolated rod charges[c]	1.82	16 K
Periodic point charges	1.85	32 K
Isolated point charges	6.68	80 K

[a] FORTRAN control but inner loops in COMPASS assembly code.

[b] Storage required for main 2D meshes, not including program and minor temporary storage. $K = 1024$.

[c] Using the boundary adjustment method followed by the solution of Poisson's equation. The computer time is estimated from operation counts.

to solve for the potential on a 128 × 128 mesh for various conditions and force laws. The times are for the COMPASS-coded routine.

V. Some Computer Models

The potential calculations described above have been used in the computer simulation of plasmas (Hockney, 1966b; Byers, 1966), space charge flow (Wadhwa *et al.*, 1965; Yu *et al.*, 1965; Levy and Hockney, 1968; Hockney, 1968b), and galaxies (Hockney, 1967b, 1968c; Hohl and Hockney, 1969; Hockney and Hohl, 1969). Some of these applications are described in more detail in Section VI.

In these models the coordinates (positions and velocities) of a large number of interacting particles are stored in the computer and advanced stepwise in time. First, the particle coordinates are inspected one by one, and a charge distribution is built up on a fixed mesh according to the position of each particle. The potential on this same mesh is found by one of the methods described above. The particles are then advanced for a short timestep by integrating Newton's law of motion using the local electric field. This field is obtained from the potential mesh by differencing. A new set of positions and velocities are obtained and the cycle is repeated.

The quantities stored for each particle are the present position $X^{(t)}$, $Y^{(t)}$ and the distance moved during the last timestep $DX^{(t-DT/2)}$, $DY^{(t-DT/2)}$, which is proportional to the velocity. These quantities are advanced using the simplest difference approximation to Newton's laws of motion; namely,

$$DX^{(t+DT/2)} = DX^{(t-DT/2)} + AX^{(t)}DT^2, \quad X^{(t+DT)} = X^{(t)} + DX^{(t+DT/2)}, \tag{94}$$

and similarly for the y-components. This central difference scheme is symmetric in time and accurate to third order in DT. Here $AX^{(t)}$ is the acceleration at time t, obtained by differencing the potential. If the charge to be accelerated lies in the (i,j) cell of the mesh, we use the approximation:

$$AX^{(t)} = (q/m)(\phi_{i-1,j} - \phi_{i+1,j})/2H, \tag{95}$$

and similarly for the y-component. (q/m) is the charge-to-mass ratio of the particle.

All the scale factors appearing in Eqs. (94) and (95) can be absorbed into the charge that is inserted onto the mesh for each particle. If this charge q^* is taken as

$$q^* = q\, DT^2/(2Hm),$$

then the potential ϕ^* appearing on the mesh will be similarly scaled. Thus,

$$\phi^* = \phi\, DT^2/(2Hm).$$

Then Eq. (94) becomes simply

$$DX^{(t+DT/2)} = DX^{(t-DT/2)} + \phi^*_{i-1,j} - \phi^*_{i+1,j}.$$

In a similar fashion, any scale factors appearing in the potential solver can be absorbed in the charge q^*.

Table VIII gives the breakdown of the cycle time for a number of different 2D models with infinitely long rod particles, and Table IX gives the cycle time for a number of different models with an arbitrary force law.

In all cases the only force considered was the electric field. The presence of a magnetic field would increase the time for the acceleration step. In all but the one case noted, the entire calculation is performed in the available core store of about 100,000 60-bit computer words. For this to be possible, it was necessary to pack into one computer word the x- and y-positions and the x- and y-velocities of a particle, using 15 bits for each item of information.

TABLE VIII

2D MODELS SOLVING THE FIELD VIA POISSON'S EQUATION USING SUBROUTINE POT1
(TIME IN CPU SEC)[d]

Computer	IBM 7090	CDC 6600		IBM 360/67
No. of particles	2000	10,000	50,000	50,000
MESH	48 × 48	64 × 64	128 × 128	128 × 128
RHO[a]	in ACCN	0.19	0.87	2.98
POT[b]	0.88	0.20	0.75	3.72
ACCN[c]	1.22	0.57	2.83	10.68
Cycle	2.10	0.96	4.45	17.38

[a] Time to form charge distribution on mesh from the particle positions.
[b] Time to solve for the potential.
[c] Time to accelerate the particles.
[d] Central Processor Unit time. The time for the arithmetic exclusive of any input and output.

The position, in units of the mesh distance, was recorded in fixed point to six binary places and the velocity, in units of mesh distance divided by timestep, to 13 binary places.

When using such limited precision in recording the velocities, care must be taken not to use too *short* a timestep. The timestep taken must be long enough so that the change of velocity in a step is larger than the minimum velocity that can be recorded.

TABLE IX

ARBITRARY FORCE[a] MODELS CALCULATING THE FIELD BY THE FOURIER TRANSFORM
TECHNIQUE USING SUBROUTINE POT3 (TIME IN CPU SEC)

Computer	CDC 6600 (COMPASS coded)			IBM 360/67[d]
No. of particles	10,000	50,000	50,000[c]	100,000
MESH[b]	32 × 32	64 × 64	128 × 128	64 × 64
RHO	0.19	0.87	0.87	5.97
POT	0.49	1.85	7.54	9.24
ACCN	0.57	2.83	2.83	21.37
Cycle	1.25	5.56	11.24	36.58

[a] Actually for point charges moving in a plane.
[b] ($n \times n$) mesh quoted is for an isolated system. The same applies for a ($2n \times 2n$) doubly periodic system.
[c] Required the storage of particle coordinates on a disk backing store. Time does *not* include transfer time to and from disk.
[d] In-core calculation with FORTRAN IV level H opt $= 2$ compiler using the model 67-1 machine with LCS storage.

Boris and Roberts (1969) have used packing differently. They store (X, Y) in one word and (DX, DY) in another. The acceleration is obtained from the mesh and packed as $(AX\ DT^2, AY\ DT^2)$. The new velocity is then obtained by adding the packed acceleration vector to the packed velocity vector and the new position vector by adding the packed velocity vector to the old position vector. By adding packed words, the number of arithmetic operations is halved and the number of computer instructions is reduced.

Using these techniques, Boris and Roberts have been able to accelerate 50,000 particles in 7.2 sec on the English Electric KDF9 (similar in storage and speed to the IBM 7090), and feel that the times for the acceleration step in Tables VIII and IX could be reduced by a significant factor if vector addition techniques were used. By careful buffering, using three buffers, they are able to store coordinates on magnetic tape without loss of speed and hence make the KDF9 look like a machine with a fast memory of several million words.

VI. Applications in Particle Models

As has already been mentioned, the problem of solving for the potential may arise both in particle models and Eulerian models. In the former, the system is represented by calculating the individual motion of a large number of representative particles, while in the latter, the partial differential equations representing a fluid approximation are solved on a fixed mesh in space. In either case the potential due to a given source distribution must be found in order to determine the forces acting on the system. We shall limit ourselves here to the discussion of a variety of applications in particle models and refer the reader to other articles for a discussion of Eulerian models.

A. Pros and Cons of Particle Models

The maximum number of particles that can be moved on present-day computers (e.g., the CDC 6600 or IBM 360/91) is of the order of 10^5. This is still six orders of magnitude below the number of plasma particles in even a small volume of a plasma device or the number of stars in a galaxy. Hence, it is inevitable that each representative particle in a computer model carries with it the charge and mass of about 10^6 electrons or ions, and the computer particle is best regarded as the center of gravity of a cloud of electrons or ions with dimensions equal to the cell size of the space mesh. But, unfortunately, ions and electrons in a plasma do not go around in clouds the size of the computer programer's cell size, and most of the problems associated with the use of particle models arise from this grossly exaggerated lumpiness of the model.

1. Noise and Fluctuations

Due to this lumpiness, both the binary collison rate and the mean-squared electric field fluctuations are enhanced over their values for a real plasma by a factor equal to the number of ions or electrons in the cloud. Hence, it is particularly important to be able to estimate these effects and show that they are small compared to the phenomena being investigated.

In addition, the finite size of the timestep and space mesh used in particle models gives rise to random error fields and a lack of energy conservation. It is well known that random fields in a real plasma cause stochastic heating of the plasma (Shapiro, 1965; Sturrock, 1966; Puri, 1966). Invariably the kinetic energy of a particle model is observed to increase for the same reason. Recently Birdsall and Fuss (1968) have proposed smoothing procedures to reduce this effect.

2. Collisional Effects

In a computer plasma, just as in a physical plasma, the relative importance of binary collisional effects and collective effects is measured by the number of particles in a Debye square N. Taking the plasma period τ_p as the characteristic time for collective action and the collision time τ_{coll} as characteristic of binary effects, one has

$$\tau_{coll} = (N/K)\tau_p.$$

The value of K depends on the particular method of estimation used and on the precise definition of collision time, whether it is the slowing down time due to momentum transfer, the relaxation time for energy exchange, or the expectation value of the time for a test particle to be deflected by 90°. In any event, it seems that K lies between one and ten for rod models. Although some estimates of collisional and noise effects have been made (Hockney, 1966b) and confirmed by measurement (Hockney, 1968a), much theoretical work needs to be done to put the subject on a satisfactory basis. A start has been made in this direction by Birdsall et al. (1968).

3. Limitations of Space Scale

Assuming K of about 10, this means that if one wishes to study a collisionless plasma phenomenon for 100 plasma periods, one will need about 1000 particles per Debye square. Hence, with 10^5 particles available, it is only possible to study a region about $10\lambda_D$ square. Since many experimental situations cover distances of many thousands of Debye lengths, particle models are best suited to the study of sheath regions or in situations where the phenomenon is not affected by a distortion of the Debye length.

4. Limitations on Time Scale

In order to follow the motion of each particle in the simulation, it is necessary to integrate Newton's laws of motion. This has to be done in an explicit fashion with a timestep shorter than the shortest time constant in the system. This usually means taking about 10 timesteps per electron plasma period. With a cycle time of, say, 30 seconds per timestep and three hours computing in a typical calculation, one has a study of 360 electron plasma periods. For a hydrogen plasma this corresponds to only nine ion plasma periods. Hence, most particle model calculations are performed with an artificial ion-to-electron mass ratio of 64 or 16, giving a study of 45 or 90 ion plasma periods, respectively.

5. Particle Models

The advantage of a particle model is that it simulates, within the limits of the physical interactions which are included, all the properties of a physical plasma. Effects of inertia and the finite size of the Larmor radius are included without difficulty, and there is no problem with the interpenetration of beams, which gives rise to a multivalued velocity field in a fluid approach. In the latter respect, the particle model has the same flexibility as a finite difference solution of the Boltzmann equation in phase space. This approach exchanges a paucity of particles for a very coarse division of the four-dimensional phase space. This method has been adopted by Killeen and Rompel (1966), who divide phase space into an $81 \times 12 \times 19 \times 9$ ($=160,000$) mesh in z, r, v_z, v_r in a simulation of the E-layer in the Astron fusion device.

An interesting alternative approach, in which the individual bits of the computer memory are used to indicate the presence or absence of a particle in a cell of phase space, has been used in a galaxy simulation by Miller and Prendergast (1968), on a typical $256 \times 256 \times 50 \times 50$ mesh for x, y, v_x, and v_y.

6. Fluid Models

Fluid equations are derived from the Boltzmann equation by taking moments over velocity space and assuming an equation of state. A manageable set of partial differential equations is obtained for the macroscopic quantities of density and average velocity, at the expense of suppressing certain physical effects, which are present in a particle model. Changes in shape of the velocity distribution and velocity space instabilities cannot be described nor can problems involving the interpenetration of beams or large Larmor radius for these give rise to unrepresentable velocity fields. If, in addition, quasi-neutrality is assumed, as in the case of an MHD[4] model, then inertial effects

---

[4] MagnetoHydroDynamic.

of the electrons and electron plasma oscillations are suppressed. With a sensible and valid set of approximations, fluid models can usually come much closer to the simulation of actual physical apparatus than can particle models. On the other hand, particle models are clearly more suitable for studying basic plasma phenomena on a microscopic scale.

We shall now describe a variety of applications of particle models to different areas of physics.

B. PLASMA PHYSICS

A particle model has been used to study the transport of plasma across a fixed external magnetic field (Hockney, 1966b; Hockney, 1967a). It is often observed in physical experiments that this transport is orders of magnitude larger than is expected to arise from collisions between the plasma particles. The purpose of the computer simulation was to see if this effect of anomalously high diffusion could be reproduced.

Figure 13 shows the time development of one computer experiment. Electrons and ions, displayed in the top left and right squares of each picture, respectively, are injected with a half-maxmillian velocity distribution from the top of a square region. The system repeats periodically from left to right and the bottom side of the square represents the wall of the containing vessel. A strong magnetic field is applied perpendicular to the region. The gyroradius of both ions and electrons is less than the distance to the wall, so that in the absence of any other effects there is no transport of plasma to the wall. The scaling is such that neither gyroradius can be considered small, and this situation would be difficult to study in any but a particle-type model.

The system is, however, unstable and a flute forms in the electron distribution. This is seen at $t = 500$ and is very obvious at $t = 800$. The effect of the flute on the electrostatic potential is seen in the perspective view of the potential surface in which the wall is toward the reader. At $t = 800$ a strong wave in the potential surface is seen. The electric fields of this wave are parallel to the wall and drive the plasma to the wall via the $\mathbf{E} \times \mathbf{B}/\mathbf{B}^2$ drift of charged particles in a magnetic field.

We have already said that particle models grossly exaggerate collisional effects and that collisional effects produce diffusion of plasma across a magnetic field; hence the use of a particle model to study diffusion needs some justification. The experiments being described were conducted on an IBM 7090 with a maximum 2000 plasma particles available and scaled such that there were about ten particles per Debye square. In these conditions it was found that all the particle transport could be attributed to collisional effects near the injection plane, but that for most of the region, and particularly near the wall, the transport was all attributable to the potential wave. A crucial experiment

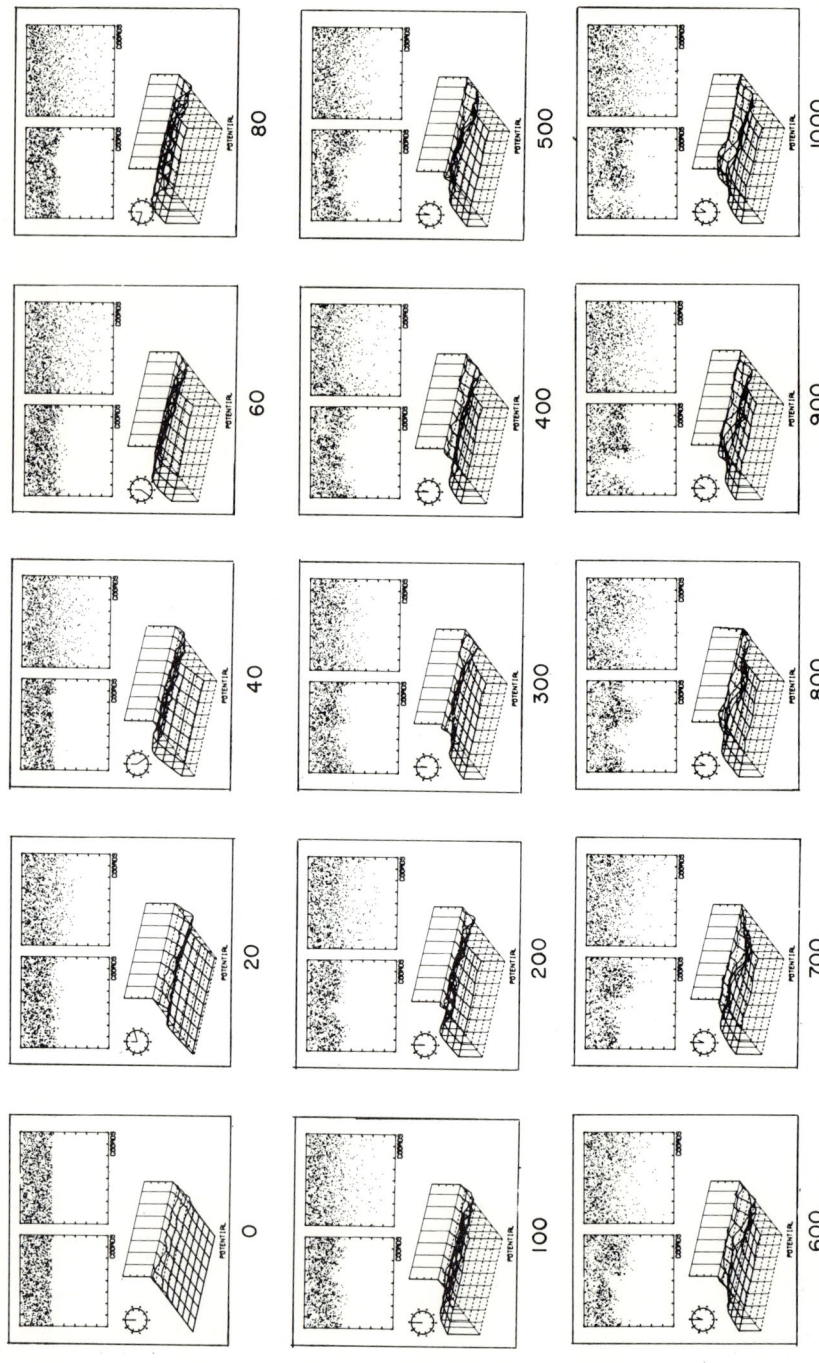

Fig. 13. Still frames from a movie of the computer simulation of anomalous plasma diffusion across a magnetic field. The electron positions are at the top left and the ions at the top right. Note the formation of a flute in the electron distribution and the growth of a wave on the potential distribution which is shown in projection at the bottom.

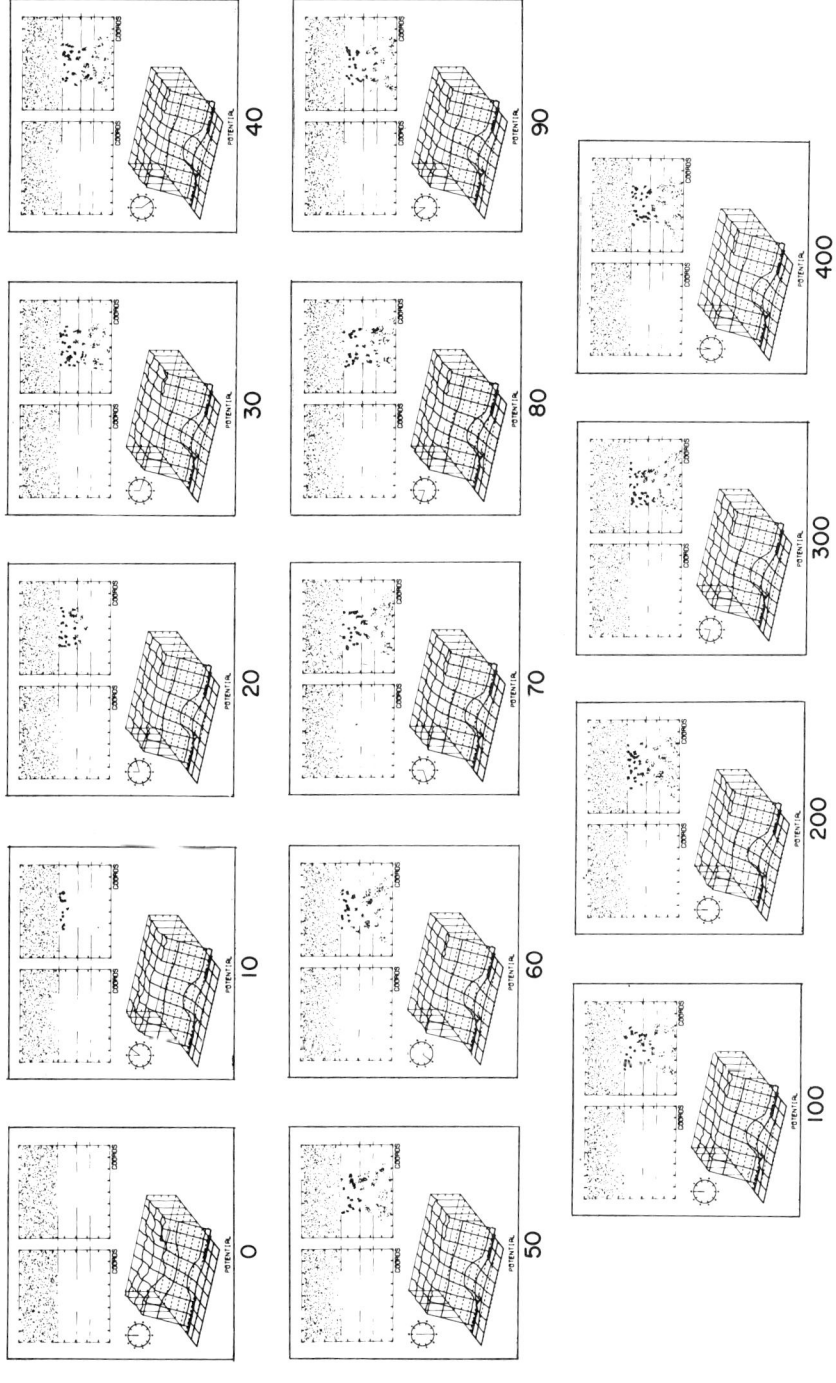

FIG. 14. Simulation of an ion gun. A plasma occupies the top third of the region with electrons shown at the top left and ions at the top right. Ions are extracted from the plasma by a series of electrodes which produce the potential distribution shown at the bottom. The ions are split into ten parts as they enter the ion beam.

was made to confirm this conclusion, in which the potential wave was artificially suppressed and the transport was thereby reduced to a few percent of its former value. On a third-generation computer with the capability to move 100,000 particles, experiments can be conducted in which collisional effects are quite negligible.

The calculation was performed on a 48 × 48 space mesh. With 1200 particles the timestep was 1.73 sec on an IBM 7090 without display.

C. Electron Devices

1. *Ion Gun Simulation*

Figure 14 shows the time development of a simulation of a plasma ion gun. The top third of the square region contains a plasma out of which a beam of ions is extracted by a series of electrodes. The electrodes were held at given potentials by the capacity matrix method described in Section II,F. In addition, it was necessary to detect when any particles hit an electrode surface, to record this event, and to remove the particle from the model. The calculation of these events is very time consuming since, in principle, every particle must be tested for possible interception with every electrode. This time is reduced somewhat by only doing these tests on particles that are within a certain distance of the electrodes. This avoids testing most of the particles that lie in the interior of the plasma region.

A problem with density variation was encountered, the density in the region of the ion beam being only one-hundredth of the density in the plasma. If all the computer particles had been given the same charge and mass, then practically all the particles would have been used in the plasma region and the beam region would have had hardly any particles. To alleviate this problem, a class of light ions was included to simulate the beam, each with one-tenth the charge and mass of the particles in the plasma. When a plasma particle crossed into the beam region of the model, it was divided into ten light ions spread slightly about the original particle. The resulting clusters of particles can be seen being drawn out of the plasma from step 10 onwards. Even with this strategem, the description of the beam region was unsatisfactorily coarse in the results with 2000 particles shown in Fig. 14. However, results with 100,000 on a third-generation computer would be satisfactory.

2. *Virtual Electrodes in a Cylinder*

Two-dimensional computer experiments have been performed on the behavior of charged particles when injected into an evacuated cylinder (Hockney, 1968b). For certain currents of injection, stable virtual electrodes

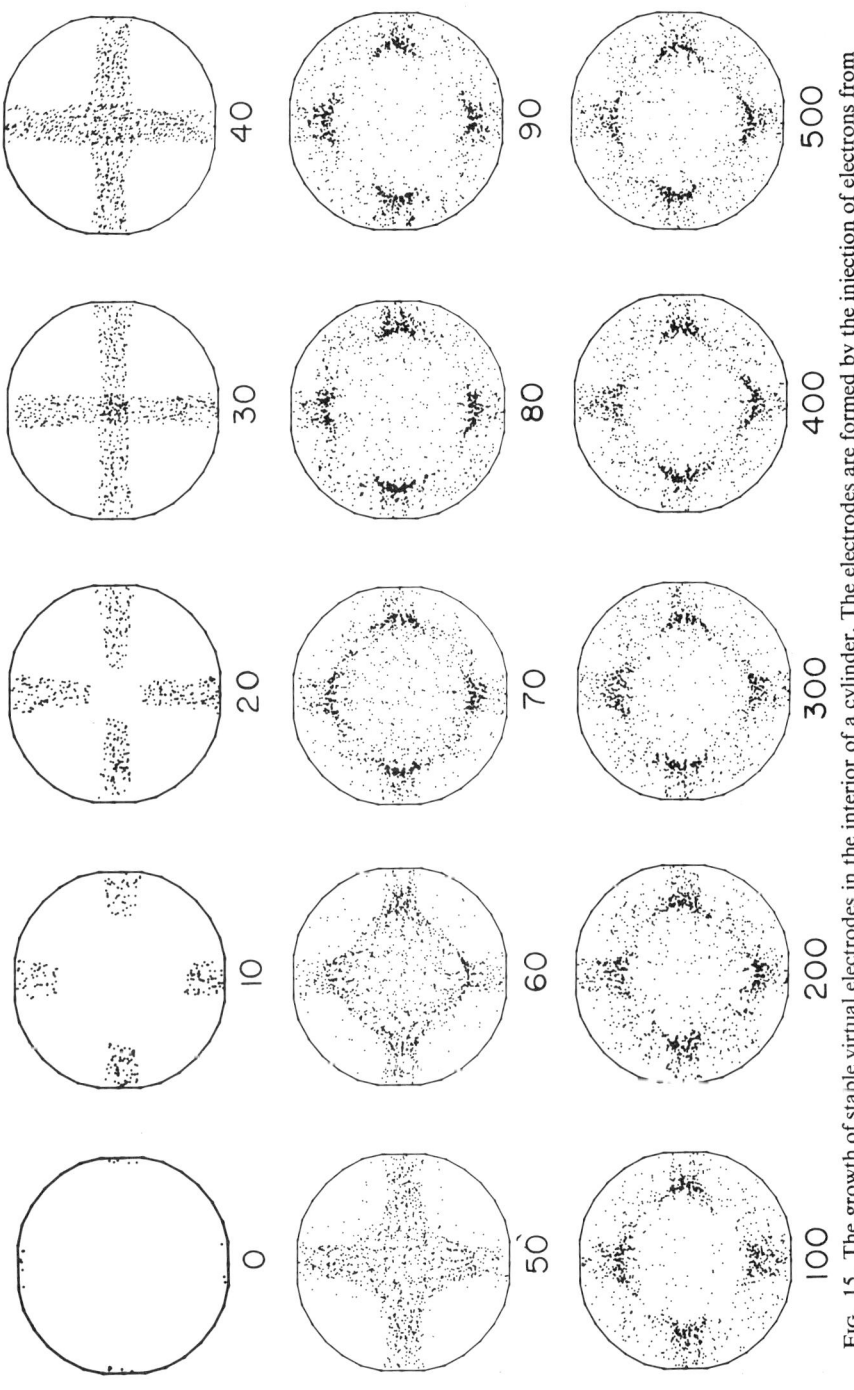

Fig. 15. The growth of stable virtual electrodes in the interior of a cylinder. The electrodes are formed by the injection of electrons from four separate guns. One single particle transit time is about 50 time units.

are formed in the interior. The stability of such electrodes is of importance to the operation of certain electrostatic containment devices for controlled thermonuclear fusion, reported by Hirsch (1967).

Figure 15 shows the time evolution in a case where the current was injected from four separate guns. Initially, the injected electrons pass right across the system ($t = 0$ to $t = 40$). At $t = 50$ the space charge of electrons already in the system becomes sufficient to slow down and eventually to return injected particles to a place on the wall near to their point of injection. By $t = 70$ a stable cloud of electrons (a virtual electrode) has formed opposite each gun and the injected particles from each gun splay out in the form of a fountain. The computer simulation was able to show the stability of the virtual electrode for at least eight single-particle transit times.

This example demonstrates more than any of the others the usefulness of a particle model. The geometry and nonlinearity of the problem precludes the use of analysis, and the complex interstreaming of the electron beams (the type of interstreaming changing with time) would preclude the use of a fluid model. Furthermore, the fact that only a single species of particle is present avoids the problems over time scale which often occur with particle models.

The potential calculation was performed on a 48×48 mesh square and the potential was held to approximately zero on a cylinder by using the capacity matrix method. A timestep took 4 sec on an IBM 7090. This includes the time to generate a magnetic tape for subsequent plotting on a Stromberg Carlson 4020 microfilm recorder.

D. High B-Field and Vortex Flow

Computer experiments have been performed to study the stability and nonlinear development of low density electron beams in a strong magnetic field by Levy and Hockney (1968). This work was motivated by a new concept of a heavy-ion accelerator, the HIPAC, in which ions fall into a deep potential well, the well being produced by electrons which are suspended in a strong magnetic field (Janes *et al.*, 1966).

Figure 16 shows a simulation of a linear version of this device. The system repeats periodically from left to right and the electrostatic potential is held to zero on the top and bottom sides of the square. There is a strong magnetic field perpendicular to the region which holds a beam of electrons in the center of the region (the gyroradius of the electrons is small compared with the beam and apparatus dimensions). The self-electrostatic field of the beam is in opposite directions for the electrons lying above and below the center line. Hence, the $(\mathbf{E} \times \mathbf{B})/B^2$ drift of the electrons is also opposite above and below the center line. This gives rise to a shear in the velocity distribution.

Linear analysis shows that if the beam is thinner than about one-fifth of

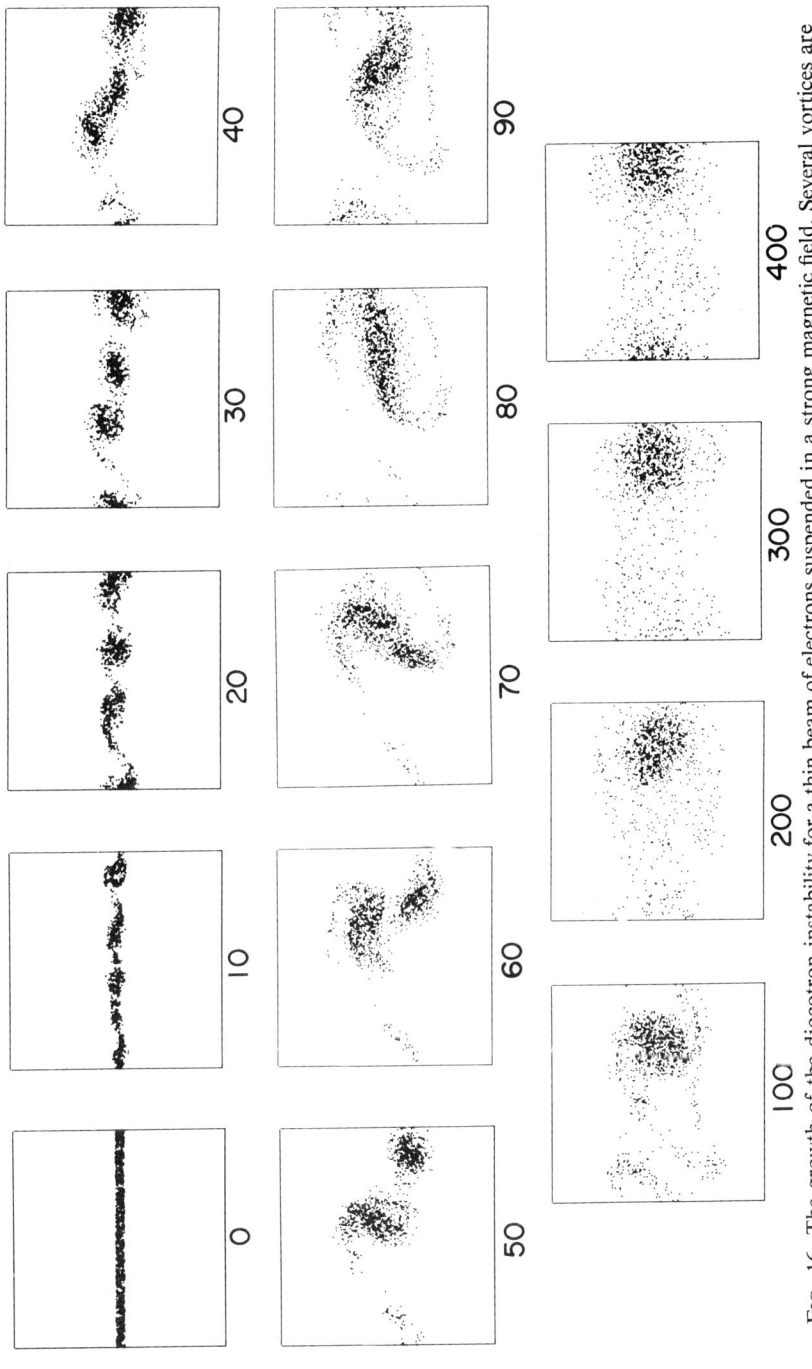

FIG. 16. The growth of the diocotron instability for a thin beam of electrons suspended in a strong magnetic field. Several vortices are formed which coalesce into a single vortex whose amplitude is limited by nonlinear effects. No electrons reach the top and bottom walls. The system repeats periodically from left to right.

the repeat length, the system is unstable to the formation of vortices. Figure 16 shows the case for a particularly thin beam in which several wavelengths are unstable. The $m = 3$ mode has the greatest growth rate and three vortices are initially formed ($t = 30$), after which these coallesce into two vortices ($t = 60$), and finally into a single stable vortex ($t = 100$–400).

This result is interesting in that it shows that an unstable situation is not necessarily disasterous, since no electrons have reached the walls of the vessel. The linear growth regime ($t = 0$ to $t = 30$) can be predicted theoretically and the calculated growth rates agree well with those observed in the computer model. The computer model has the advantage that it predicts the large-amplitude nonlinear behavior that would be difficult to obtain by other means.

It can be shown (Levy and Hockney, 1968) that the flow of electrons in a high magnetic field is exactly analogous to motion of vorticity in a two-dimensional incompressible and inviscid fluid. Figure 16 can then be regarded as a demonstration of the Kelvin–Helmholtz instability at the junction of two fluid streams with differing velocities. The particle model thus provides an alternative method for solving fluid problems involving vorticity, one in which the fluid is described by following the motion of a large number of individual rods of vorticity. The conservation of vorticity becomes the conservation of the number of rods (exactly conserved) and the streamfunction ψ is obtained from the vorticity ζ via Poisson's equation. Thus,

$$\nabla^2 \psi = \zeta(x, y),$$

and the velocity field is given by

$$V_x = -\partial \psi/\partial y, \qquad V_y = \partial \psi/\partial x.$$

Viewed in this way, Fig. 16 demonstrates the flow of energy from small to large wavelengths in two-dimensional turbulence—opposite to the direction observed in three-dimensional turbulence. We note that two-dimensional turbulence is difficult to set up in the laboratory, but is easily simulated exactly in a two-dimensional computer model. This type of approach has also been used by Abernathy and Kronauer (1962) in the study of the von Kármán vortex street.

The calculations were performed on an IBM 7090 with a 48 × 48 mesh in space. A timestep took 2.1 sec for 1000 rods of charge. This includes the generation of an output tape or rod positions for use in making a movie on a Stromberg Carlson 4020.

E. Galactic Simulations

An obvious analogy exists between the motion of ions and electrons in the electrostatic field of a fully ionized plasma and the motion of stars in the gravitational field of a galaxy. In both physical systems the effect of collisions is negligible so that the type of particle model described here is appropriate. To change a plasma model to a gravitational model, one need only change a sign in the potential calculation to make like particles attract instead of repel and to make the charge-to-mass ratio equal to the square root of the gravitational constant. In addition, the potential calculation must be modified to remove all boundaries.

1. *The Cylindrical Galaxy*

A two-dimensional plasma simulation, when converted to a galaxy model, gives a model of a galaxy of rodlike stars. Such models are not expected to be very realistic, except perhaps for cigar-shaped galaxies like NGC 2685, because most spiral galaxies are rather thin, disklike objects. However, many early experiments were performed with rod models since the existing technique developed for two-dimensional plasmas could be used (Hohl, 1967, 1968a,b; Hockney, 1967b, 1968c). The boundary conditions were adjusted by the method described in Section II,G.

One such experiment is shown in Fig. 17. A cylinder of stars of approximately uniform density is given an initial solid-body rotation equal to half that required to balance gravitational attraction against centrifugal force. The cylinder initially contracts to about half its initial radius and expands out again. During the expansion at $t = 0.5$, several condensations are apparent. The contraction and expansion continues with the condensations increasing in size. Barred structures occur quite frequently at $t = 1.3$, 1.8, and 2.2, for example and, at $t = 2.0$ a spiral structure is apparent. Finally after about three rotations, a hot structureless system is obtained.

Figure 18 shows comparisons between the structures seen in the computer simulation and some real galaxies. The similarities are obvious, but the computed spiral and barred structures are too short-lived to explain the frequent occurrence of such objects in the sky.

2. *The Thin-Disk Galaxy*

To improve the realism of galaxy simulation, calculations have been performed with a model of point stars moving in a plane. Miller and Prendergast (1968) have considered the motion of 120,000 point stars in a doubly periodic repeating system of galaxies. Hohl and Hockney (1969) have a model of an isolated system of 50,000–200,000 point stars (see Section V). In the latter case the fields are computed using the Fourier transform method of Section IV,B.

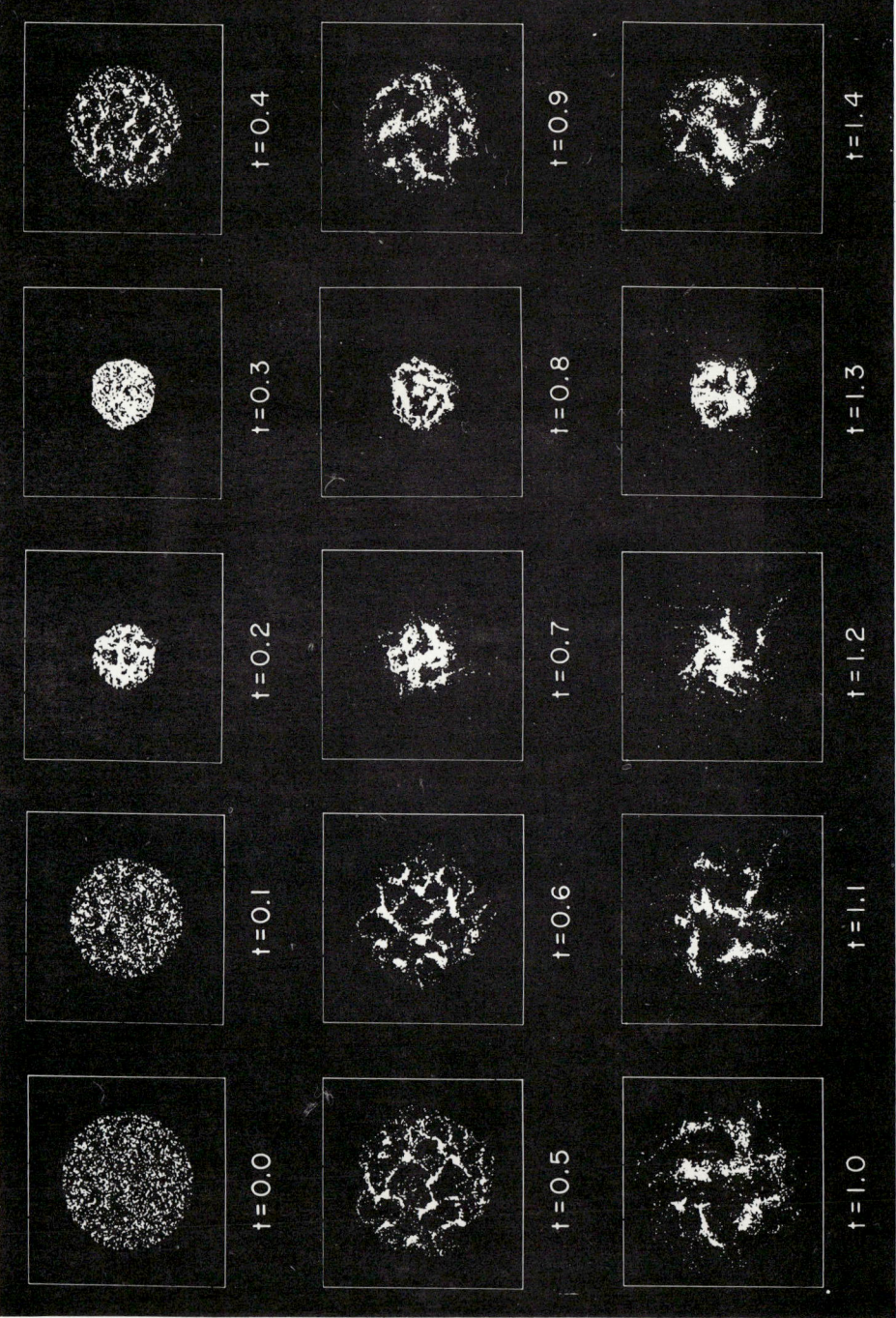

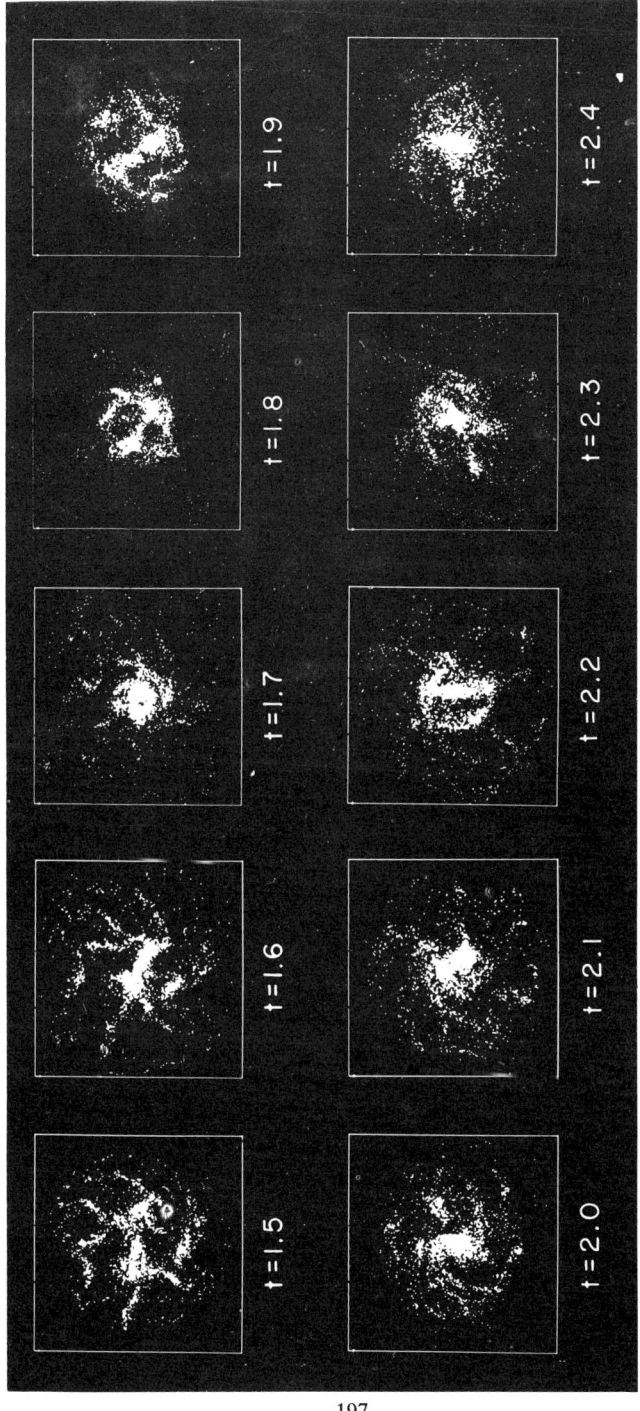

FIG. 17. The time development of a cylinder of rodlike stars which is initially given half the solid-body rotation required to balance centrifugal force and gravitational attraction. Time is in units of rotations. [Taken from R. W. Hockney, *Astrophys. J.* **150**, 797 (1967b), ©1967, University of Chicago Press.]

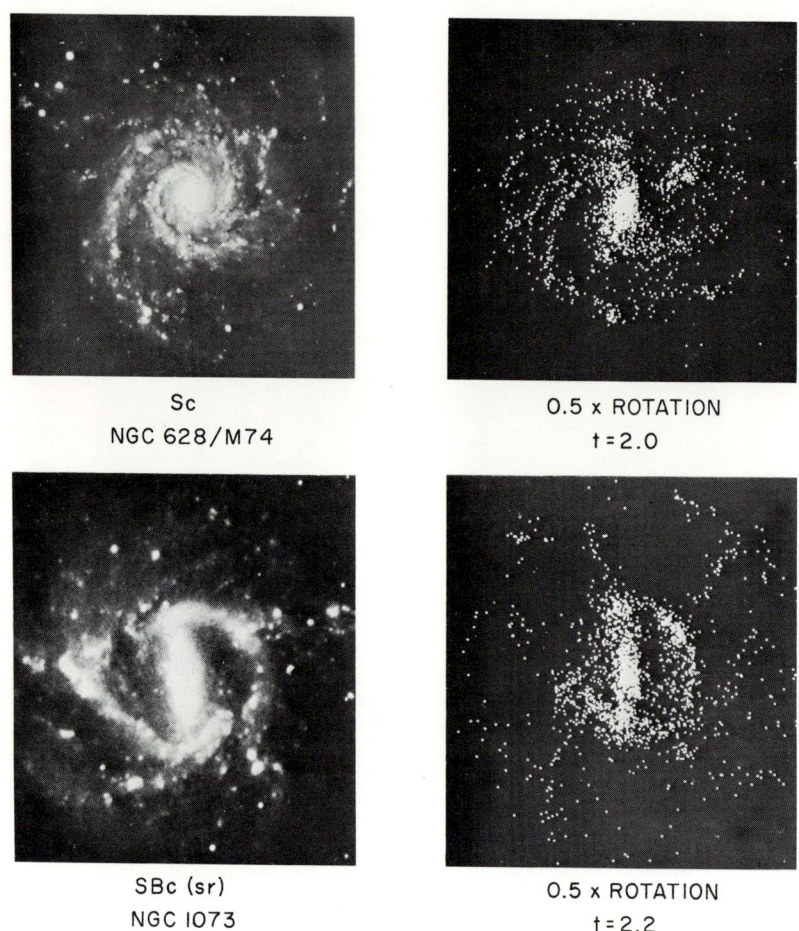

Fig. 18. Comparison of some of the structures computed in Fig. 17 with actual galaxies. Time is in units of rotations.

Figure 19 shows the breakup of a thin-disk galaxy. Initially the disk is given a solid-body rotation just sufficient to balance gravitational attraction, and there is no dispersion of velocity about this motion. The computer experiment shows that this system is violently unstable and that the disk breaks up into three or four subsystems in less than one rotation. This instability has been predicted by Toomre (1964) using a small-amplitude linear analysis. The contribution of the computer experiment is to show large amplitude nonlinear development of the system. After five rotations, the system is observed to form a single structureless condensation.

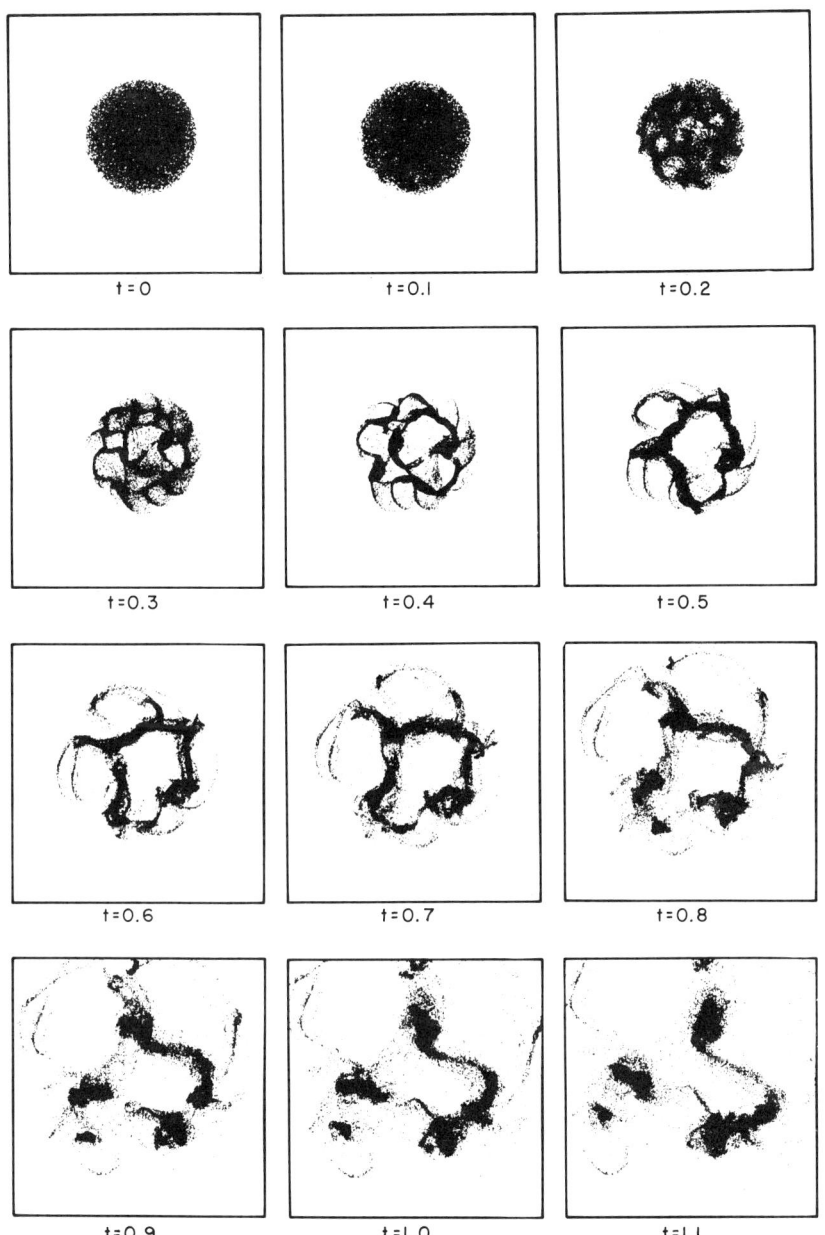

FIG. 19. The rapid breakup of a cold thin disk of 50,000 simulated point stars moving in a plane. The system is initially given a solid-body rotation sufficient to balance gravitational attraction. Time is in units of rotations.

```
CTHIS IS A PROGRAM TO TEST FOUR67 ON RANDOM VECTORS
C
      COMMON Z(1025),Y(1025),X(1025),X1(1025)
      DO 1 IQ=10,10,1
      NM=2**IQ
      FNM=FLOAT(NM)
      NM1=NM+1
      XNO=SQRT(2.0/FNM)
C
CMAKE A RANDOM ARRAY
C
      DO 2 KN=1,NM
    2 X(KN+1)=2.0*(RANF(0)-0.5 )
C
      X(1)=0.0
      X(NM1)=0.0
      IBC=1
C
CSETF67 MUST BE CALLED ONCE FOR A GIVEN IBC AND IQ
CTO PREPARE CERTAIN ARRAYS FOR USE BY FOUR67
      CALL SETF67(IBC,IQ)
      DO 3 I=1,NM1
    3 Z(I)=X(I)
      DO 17 I=1,NM1
   17 Y(I)=0.0
C
      CALL SECOND(T1)
C
CFOURIER ANALYSE THE INPUT ARRAY Z
      CALL FOUR67(IBC,IQ)
      CALL SECOND(T2)
C
CPUT IN NORMALISATION FACTOR AND TRANSFER RESULT TO INPUT ARRAY
      DO 4 I=1,NM1
    4 Z(I)=XNO*Y(I)
C
CFOURIER SYNTHESIS
      CALL FOUR67(IBC,IQ)
C
CPUT IN NORMALISATION FACTOR
      DO 5 I=1,NM1
    5 X1(I)=XNO*Y(I)
C
      PRINT 6,(IBC,IQ)
    6 FORMAT(//10X,'IBC=',I2,'   IQ=',I4)
C
CCOMPARE ORIGINAL ARRAY WITH THAT AFTER ANALYSIS AND SYNTHESIS.
CPRINT OUT MAXIMUM DIFFERENCE AND ITS POSITION
      CALL ERROR(NM,X,X1,T1,T2)
C
      X(1)=1.0
      X(NM1)=1.0
      DO 8 I=1,NM1
    8 Y(I)=0.0
      DO 9 I=1,NM1
    9 Z(I)=X(I)
C
      IBC=2
      CALL SETF67(IBC,IQ)
      CALL SECOND(T1)
      CALL FOUR67(IBC,IQ)
      CALL SECOND(T2)
C
      DO 10 I=1,NM1
   10 Z(I)=XNO*Y(I)
C
      CALL FOUR67(IBC,IQ)
C
      DO 11 I=1,NM1
   11 X1(I)=XNO*Y(I)
C
      PRINT 6,(IBC,IQ)
      CALL ERROR(NM,X,X1,T1,T2)
C
      IBC=3
      XN1=0.5*XNO
C
      X(1)=1.0
      X(NM1)=0.0
      CALL SETF67(IBC,IQ)
      DO 13 I=1,NM1
   13 Y(I)=0.0
      DO 14 I=1,NM1
   14 Z(I)=X(I)
      CALL SECOND(T1)
      CALL FOUR67(IBC, IQ)
      CALL SECOND(T2)
      DO 15 I=1,NM1
   15 Z(I)=XN1*Y(I)
      CALL FOUR67(IBC+1,IQ)
      DO 16 I=1,NM1
   16 X1(I)=XN1*Y(I)
      PRINT 6,(IBC,IQ)
    1 CALL ERROR(NM,X,X1,T1,T2)
      STOP
      END
```

```
      SUBROUTINE ERROR(N,X,X1,T1,T2)
C
CCOMPARES THE ARRAYS X AND X1 AND FINDS THE MAXIMUM
C DIFFERENCE AND ITS POSITION.
C
      DIMENSION X(1025),X1(1025)
C
      IMAX=0
      XMOX=0.0
      NN=N+1
C
      DO 1 I=1,NN
      IF (ABS(X1(I)-X(I)) .LE. ABS(XMOX)) GO TO 1
      XMOX=X1(I)-X(I)
      IMAX=I
    1 CONTINUE
C
      TIME=T2-T1
      PRINT 3,(IMAX,XMOX,TIME,N)
    3 FORMAT(1X,'I=',I4,4X,'MAX ERROR=',E12.4,4X,
     C'TIME=',F7.4,4X,'N=',I4)
C
      RETURN
      END
```

** CORRECT ANSWERS FROM THE TEST ROUTINE **

```
             IBC= 1    IQ=    8
I=  68       MAX ERROR= -0.5960E-05     TIME= 0.0625     N= 256

             IBC= 2    IQ=    8
I=  30       MAX ERROR= -0.5424E-05     TIME= 0.0664     N= 256

             IBC= 3    IQ=    8
I=   4       MAX ERROR=  0.5841E-05     TIME= 0.0352     N= 256

             IBC= 1    IQ=   10
I= 263       MAX ERROR=  0.7451E-05     TIME= 0.2969     N=1024

             IBC= 2    IQ=   10
I= 400       MAX ERROR= -0.7033E-05     TIME= 0.2930     N=1024

             IBC= 3    IQ=   10
I= 504       MAX ERROR= -0.7510E-05     TIME= 0.1758     N=1024
```

```
      SUBROUTINE SETF67(IBC1,IQ1)
C
CTHIS ROUTINE INITIALISES CERTAIN ARRAYS FOR USE BY FOUR67.
CIT MUST BE CALLED ONCE EVERY TIME IBC OR IQ CHANGES
C ARRAYS ARE DIMENSIONED FOR ANALYSIS OF 1024 POINTS MAXIMUM
C
      COMMON/F67COM/N2,INDEX(513),SI(513),N4,N3,N7,IP,ISL,I1,IBC
C
      IBC=IBC1
      IQ=IQ1
      IF (IBC .GE. 3) IQ=IQ-1
      N3=2**IQ
      N7=N3/2
      N5=N3/4
      I=1
      INDEX(I)=N5
      SI(I)=1.0/SQRT(2.0)
      K=I
      I=I+1
   11 IL=I
      IF (I .EQ. N7) GO TO 9
   10 K1=INDEX(K)/2
      INDEX(I)=K1
      SI(I)=DSIN(3.1415926535898*K1/N3)
      K1=N7-K1
      I=I+1
      INDEX(I)=K1
      SI(I)=DSIN(3.1415926535898*K1/N3)
      K=K+1
      I=I+1
      IF (K .NE. IL) GO TO 10
      GO TO 11
    9 RETURN
      END
```

FIG. 20. Test program for FOUR67 and answers. Subroutines ERROR and SETF67.

THE POTENTIAL CALCULATION AND SOME APPLICATIONS

```
C
C     SUBROUTINE FOUR67(IBC1,IQ1)
C
C                 * PROGRAM REQUIREMENTS *
C
C     INPUT PARAMETERS ARE IBC1 AND IQ1
C
C     SUBROUTINE SETF67 MUST BE CALLED ONCE EVERY TIME ANY OF THE PARAMETERS
C     TO FOUR67 CHANGE
C
C     INPUT VALUES MUST BE PLACED IN THE BLANK COMMON ARRAY Z BEFORE CALL
C     OF FOUR67
C
C     ANSWERS APPEAR IN THE BLANK COMMON ARRAY Y
C
C     COMMON Z(1025),Y(1025) DECLARATION MUST APPEAR IN THE PROGRAM THAT CALLS
C     FOUR67
C
C                 * MATHEMATICAL DESCRIPTION *
C
C     FOUR67(IBC,IQ) PERFORMS A FINITE FOURIER ANALYSIS OR SYNTHESIS ON THE COMMON
C                    INPUT ARRAY Z(I),I=1,...,N+1, AND PUTS THE RESULTS IN THE
C     COMMON OUTPUT ARRAY Y. THE TYPE OF ANALYSIS IS SELECTED BY IBC AND
C     THE NUMBER OF POINTS BY IQ.   N=2**IQ
C
C     IBC=1,   SINE  ANALYSIS OR SYNTHESIS ON THE INPUT VALUES Z(2),...,Z(N) IS
C              PERFORMED BY            CALL FOUR67(1,IQ)
C     AND YIELDS THE OUTPUT QUANTITIES
C              Y(K+1)=SUM S=1 TO N-1 OF SIN(PI*S*K/N)*Z(S+1),     1 .LE. K .LE. N-1
C              Y(1)=Y(N+1)=0
C     FOURIER ANALYSIS FOLLOWED BY FOURIER SYNTHESIS YIELDS N/2 TIMES THE ORIGINAL
C     VALUES
C
C     IBC=2,   COSINE ANALYSIS OR SYNTHESIS ON THE INPUT VALUES Z(1),...,Z(N+1) IS
C              PERFORMED BY            CALL FOUR67(2,IQ)
C     AND YIELDS THE OUTPUT VALUES
C              CY(K+1)=SUM S=0 TO N E(S,N)**2*COS(PI*S*K/N)*Z(S+1),  0 .LE. K .LE. N
C     WHERE            E(I,J)=1/SQRT(2)    IF I=0 OR I=J
C                            =1           OTHERWISE
C     ANALYSIS FOLLOWED BY SYNTHESIS YIELS N/2 TIMES THE ORIGINAL VALUES
C
C     IBC=3,   PERIODIC ANALYSIS ON THE INPUT VALUES Z(1),...,Z(N) IS PERFORMED BY
C                                      CALL FOUR67(3,IQ)
C     AND YIELDS THE HARMONIC AMPLITUDES
C              CY(K+1)=2*SUM S=0 TO N-1 E(K,N/2)*COS(2*PI*S*K/N)*Z(S+1),  0 .LE. K .LE.N/2
C                     =2*SUM S=0 TO N-1 SIN(2*PI*S*(K-N/2)/N)*Z(S+1),   N/2 .LT. K .LE. N-1
C              CY(N+1)=0
C
C     IBC=4,   PERIODIC SYNTHESIS OF THE INPUT VALUES Z(1),...,Z(N) IS A
C              DIFFERENT OPERATION FROM PERIODIC ANALYSIS AND IS PERFORMED BY
C                                      CALL FOUR67(4,IQ)
C     ACCORDING TO THE RELATIONS
C              Y(S+1)=2*SUM K=0 TO N/2 OF E(K,N/2)*COS(2*PI*S*K/N)*Z(K+1)+
C                      2*SUM K=N/2+1 TO N-1 OF SIN(2*PI*S*(K-N/2)/N)*Z(K+1),
C                                                  0 .LE. S .LE. N-1
C              Y(N+1)=0
C
C     EXAMPLES SEE THE PROGRAM FTEST FOR FOURIER ANALYSIS FOLLOWED BY
C              SYNTHESIS STARTING WITH RANDOM INPUT VECTORS.
C
C     TIMING ON THE CDC 6600 IN FORTRAN A 1024 POINT PERIODIC ANALYSIS OR
C     SYNTHESIS (IBC=3 OR 4, IQ=10) TAKES 1.25 F-1 SEC.  THIS TIME WAS
C     REDUCED BY A FACTOR 5.7 TO 2.2 E-2 SEC WHEN THE SUBROUTINES ZERO,
C     NEG,REVNEG,TFOLD,TFOLD1 AND KFOLD WERE WRITTEN IN CDC MACHINE CODE
C     (CALLED COMPASS). FOR IQ .GT. 4 THE COMPASS-CODED ROUTINE IS FITTED TO
C     WITHIN 3 PERCENT BY
C                             TIME=2*N*LOGBASE2(N)+500 MICROSECONDS.
C     THE SINE AND COSINE CASES(IBC=2,3)TAKE APPROXIMATELY TWICE THE TIME OF
C     THE PERIODIC CASE.
C
C     STORAGE- THIS ROUTINE IS DESIGNED FOR PROBLEMS WHERE SPEED IS MORE IMPORTANT
C              THAN STORAGE, AS FOR EXAMPLE IN THE SOLUTION OF PARTIAL DIFFERENTIAL
C     EQUATIONS BY PARTIAL FOURIER ANALYSIS(SEE JACM 12,95,1965).  STORAGE REQUIRED
C     IS APPROX 3*N.  FOR PROBLEMS IN WHICH STORAGE MUST BE KEPT TO A MINIMUM, AS
C     E.G. IN LONG TIME SERIES ANALYSIS, THE METHOD OF COOLEY-TUKEY(MATH. COMP.
C     19,297,1965) IS TO BE PREFERRED WITH A STORAGE REQUIREMENT OF N.
C
C     METHOD-  FOLDING THE INITIAL DATA VALUES TO MINIMISE ON MULTIPLICATIONS BY
C     A GENERALISATION OF THE METHODS GIVEN IN WHITTAKER AND ROBINSON*CALCULUS OF
C     OBSERVATIONS* (SEE HOCKNEY PHD THESIS STANFORD UNIVERSITY 1966), FOLLOWED BY
C     EVALUATION OF THE SUMS BY A RECURSIVE TECHNIQUE SIMILAR TO THAT USED BY
C     COOLEY-TUKEY(HOCKNEY UNPUBLISHED).
C
C     PROGRAMMED BY R.W.HOCKNEY JANUARY 1968.
C
        COMMON Z(1025),Y(1025)
        COMMON/F67COM/N7,INDEX(513),S1(513),N4,N3,N7,IP,ISL,L1,IBC
C
        IBC=IBC1
        IQ=IQ1
        A5=S1(1)
        N4=2**IQ
        N3=N4
C
        IF (IBC .NE. 3) GO TO 2
C
        Z(1)=Z(1)/2.0
        Z(N3+1)=Z(1)
        N2=N3
        CALL TFOLD(0,1,Z)
        N3=N3/2
        IQ=IQ-1
C
    2   IF (IBC .NE. 4) GO TO 4
C
        N3=N3/2
        IQ=IQ-1
C
    4   N5=N3/4
        N7=N3/2
        N11=3*N7
        N31=N3+1
C
        GO TO (6,12,18,24),IBC
```

```
C  *  IF IBC=1  *
    6   Z(N31)=0.0
        Z(1)=0.0
        N2=N3
C
        DO 8 I=2,IQ
        CALL TFOLD(1,1,Z)
        N2=N2/2
    8   C
        Y(N7+1)=Z(2)
        JF=N5
C
        DO 9 IP=2,IQ
        L1=N2+1
        CALL ZERO(L1)
        ISL=1
        CALL KFOLD
        I1=N5*JF+1
        I2=4*JF
        I3=L1+(N2/2-1)*I2
        CALL NEG(I1,I3,I2)
        N2=N2+N2
    9   JF=JF/2
C
        RETURN
C
C  *  IF IBC=2  *
   12   Z(1)=Z(1)/2.0
        Z(N31)=Z(N31)/2.0
        N2=N3
C
        DO 14 I=2,IQ
        CALL TFOLD(0,N31-N2,Z)
   14   N2=N2/2
        L1=N31-N2
        A=Z(L1)+Z(L1+1)
        Y(1)=A-Z(L1+1)
        Y(N31)=A-Z(L1+1)
        Y(N7+1)=Z(L1)-Z(L1+2)
C
        DO 15 IP=2,IQ
        ISL=N31-N2
        L1=ISL-N2
        CALL ZERO(ISL)
        CALL KFOLD
   15   N2=N2+N2
C
        CALL NEG(1,N31,2)
        RETURN
C
C  *  IF IBC=3  *
   18   N2=N3
        L2=N4
C
        DO 20 IP=2,IQ
        CALL TFOLD(0,1,Z)
        CALL TFOLD(1,L2-N2+1,Z)
   20   N2=N2/2
C
        L1=L2-N2+1
        A=Z(L1)+Z(L1+2)
        Y(N7+1)=2.0*(-Z(L1)+Z(L1+2))
        Y(1)=2.0*(A+Z(L1+1))
        Y(N31)=2.0*(A-Z(L1+1))
        Y(N11+1)=2.0*Z(2)
C
        DO 21 IP=2,IQ
        Z(N2+1)=2.0*Z(N2+1)
        ISL=N2+1
        CALL TFOLD1
        L1=L1-N2
        Z(L1)=-2.0*Z(L1)
        CALL KFOLD
   21   N2=N2+N2
        Y(1)=Y(1)*A5
        Y(N31)=Y(N31)*A5
        RETURN
C
C  *  IF IBC=4  *
   24   Z(1)=Z(1)*A5
        Z(N31)=Z(N31)*A5
C
        DO 26 IP=2,IQ
        CALL TFOLD(0,N31-N2,Z)
        CALL TFOLD(1,N31,Z)
   26   N2=N2/2
C
        L1=N31-N2
        A=Z(L1)+Z(L1+2)
        Y(1)=2.0*(A+Z(L1+1))
        Y(N31)=2.0*(A-Z(L1+1))
        Y(N7+1)=2.0*(A-Z(L1+1))
        Y(N11+1)=2.0*Z(N3+2)
C
        DO 27 IP=2,IQ
        ISL=N31-N2
        Z(ISL)=2.0*Z(ISL)
        CALL TFOLD1
        L1=L1-N2
        Z(L1)=-2.0*Z(L1)
        CALL KFOLD
   27   N2=N2+N2
C
        CALL REVNEG
        CALL NEG(2,N3,2)
        N2=N4
        CALL TFOLD(1,1,Y)
        Y(N4+1)=0.0
C
        RETURN
        END
```

FIG. 21. Subroutine FOUR67.

These calculations were performed on a CDC 6600 on a 64 × 64 mesh with 50,000 stars. The timestep without display was 5.6 sec. Some checks were made on a 128 × 128 mesh and with 200,000 stars.

More sophisticated galaxy simulations are underway taking into account the influence of stays lying outside the galactic disk. Also, Prendergast, (private communication 1969) simulates separately the gas and stellar components of the galaxy and includes the condensation of gas into stars.

Appendices

A. The Subroutine FOUR67

The FORTRAN IV code for the subroutine FOUR67 is given in Figs. 20–22. This includes a test program and answers reproduced directly from the printer output from the IBM 360/67 half-duplex machine. The subroutines RANF(0) and SECOND (T) must be supplied by the user. RANF(0) is a function producing a random real number in the range 0–1. SECOND(T) is a subroutine giving the central processor time in seconds as the output parameter T.

The code has also been run on the CDC 6600 computer. In this case the two appearances of the function DSIN in subroutine SETF67 should be changed to SIN.

B. The Subroutine POT1

The FORTRAN IV code for the subroutine POT1 is given in Figs. 23–26. These are reproduced directly from the printout of the IBM 360/67-2 half-duplex machine. The routines RANF(0) and SECOND(T) must be supplied by the user.

C. The Subroutine POT3

The FORTRAN IV code for the subroutine POT3 is given in Figs. 27 and 28. These are reproduced directly from the printout of the IBM 360/67-2 half-duplex machine. The routine SECOND(T) must be supplied by the user.

```
C                                          ... IN MACHINE CODE
      COMMON Z(1025),Y(1025)
      COMMON/F67COM/N2,INDEX(513),SI(513),N4,N3,N7,IP,ISL,L1,IBC
C
      JS1=N2
      I=1
      J5=ISL+N2
      IS1=ISL
      IC1=L1
      JS1=JS1/2
C
C     GO TO FIRST TIME IS LAST TIME
      IF (JS1 .EQ. 1) GO TO 404
C
C        FIRST TIME SN=CS
         SN=SI(I)
         IS1=IS1+JS1
         IC1=IC1+JS1
         J3=IS1+JS1
C
 302     IS0=IS1-JS1
         IC0=IC1-JS1
         ODD1=SN*(Z(IC1)-Z(IS1))
         ODD2=SN*(Z(IC1)+Z(IS1))
         Z(IC1)=Z(IC0)-ODD1
         Z(IC0)=Z(IC0)+ODD1
         Z(IS1)=-Z(IS0)+ODD2
         Z(IS0)=Z(IS0)+ODD2
         IS1=IS1+1
         IC1=IC1+1
         IF (IS1 .NE. J3) GO TO 302
C
         I=I+1
 301     IS1=ISL
         IC1=L1
         JS1=JS1/2
C
C        GO TO LAST TIME WITH K IN PAIRS
         IF (JS1 .EQ. 1) GO TO 304
C
C        TAKE K IN PAIRS INTERCHANGING SN AND CS
 300     SN=SI(I)
         I=I+1
         CS=SI(I)
         IS1=IS1+JS1
         IC1=IC1+JS1
         J3=IS1+JS1
C
 402     IS0=IS1-JS1
         IC0=IC1-JS1
         ODD1=CS*Z(IC1)-SN*Z(IS1)
         ODD2=SN*Z(IC1)+CS*Z(IS1)
         Z(IC1)=Z(IC0)-ODD1
         Z(IC0)=Z(IC0)+ODD1
         Z(IS1)=-Z(IS0)+ODD2
         Z(IS0)=Z(IS0)+ODD2
         IS1=IS1+1
         IC1=IC1+1
         IF (IS1 .NE. J3) GO TO 402
C
         IS1=IS1+JS1
         IC1=IC1+JS1
         J3=IS1+JS1
C
 502     IS0=IS1-JS1
         IC0=IC1-JS1
         ODD1=SN*Z(IC1)-CS*Z(IS1)
         ODD2=CS*Z(IC1)+SN*Z(IS1)
         Z(IC1)=Z(IC0)-ODD1
         Z(IC0)=Z(IC0)+ODD1
         Z(IS1)=-Z(IS0)+ODD2
         Z(IS0)=Z(IS0)+ODD2
         IS1=IS1+1
         IC1=IC1+1
         IF ( IS1 .NE. J3) GO TO 502
C
         I=I+1
         IF (IS1 .EQ. J5) GO TO 301
        GO TO 300
```

```
         SN=SI(I)
         IS0=IS1
         IS1=IS1+JS1
         IC0=IC1
         IC1=IC1+JS1
         ODD1=SN*(Z(IC1)-Z(IS1))
         Y(K1+1)=Z(IC0)+ODD1
         Y(N3-K1+1)=Z(IC0)-ODD1
         IF (IBC .LT. 3)GO TO 405
C
            ODD2=SN*(Z(IC1)+Z(IS1))
            Y(N3+K1+1)=Z(IS0)+ODD2
            Y(N4-K1+1)=-Z(IS0)+ODD2
C
 405     CONTINUE
         RETURN
C
C        LAST TIME TAKING K IN PAIRS
 304     K1=INDEX(I)
         SN=SI(I)
         I=I+1
         CS=SI(I)
         IS0=IS1
         IS1=IS1+JS1
         IC0=IC1
         IC1=IC1+JS1
         ODD1=CS*Z(IC1)-SN*Z(IS1)
         Y(K1+1)=Z(IC0)+ODD1
         Y(N3-K1+1)=Z(IC0)-ODD1
         IF (IBC .LT. 3) GO TO 305
C
            ODD2=SN*Z(IC1)+CS*Z(IS1)
            Y(N3+K1+1)=Z(IS0)+ODD2
            Y(N4-K1+1)=-Z(IS0)+ODD2
C
 305     IS1=IS1+1
         IC1=IC1+1
            K1=INDEX(I)
         IS0=IS1
         IS1=IS1+JS1
         IC0=IC1
         IC1=IC1+JS1
         ODD1=SN*Z(IC1)-CS*Z(IS1)
         Y(K1+1)=Z(IC0)+ODD1
         Y(N3-K1+1)=Z(IC0)-ODD1
C
         IF (IBC .LT. 3) GO TO 505
C
            ODD2=CS*Z(IC1)+SN*Z(IS1)
            Y(N3+K1+1)=Z(IS0)+ODD2
            Y(N4-K1+1)=-Z(IS0)+ODD2
C
 505     IS1=IS1+1
         IC1=IC1+1
         I=I+1
         IF (IS1 .NE. J5) GO TO 304
C
         RETURN
         END
```

```
      SUBROUTINE ZERO(L)
C
CTHIS ROUTINE SHOULD BE WRITTEN WITH CARE IN MACHINE CODE
C
      COMMON Z(1025),Y(1025)
      COMMON/F67COM/N2,INDEX(513),SI(513),N4,N3,N7,IP,ISL,L1,IBC
C
      DO 1 I=1,N2
 1          Z(L+I-1)=0.0
C
      RETURN
      END
```

```
C     ... SHOULD BE WRITTEN WITH CARE IN MACHINE CODE
      COMMON Z(1025),Y(1025)
      COMMON/F67COM/N2,INDEX(513),SI(513),N4,N3,N7,IP,ISL,L1,IBC
C
      DO 1 K=I1,I3,I2
 1          Y(K)=-Y(K)
C
      RETURN
      END
```

```
      SUBROUTINE REVNEG
C
CTHIS ROUTINE SHOULD BE WRITTEN WITH CARE IN MACHINE CODE
C
      COMMON Z(1025),Y(1025)
      COMMON/F67COM/N2,INDEX(513),SI(513),N4,N3,N7,IP,ISL,L1,IBC
C
      DO 1 I=1,N7
            J=N3+1+I
            K=N4+1-I
            A=Y(J)
            Y(J)=-Y(K)
 1          Y(K)=-A
C
      RETURN
      END
```

```
      SUBROUTINE TFOLD(IS,L,Z)
C
CTHIS ROUTINE FOLDS THE INPUT ARRAY Z.
CTHIS ROUTINE SHOULD BE WRITTEN WITH CARE IN MACHINE CODE
C
      DIMENSION Z(1025)
      COMMON/F67COM/N2,INDEX(513),SI(513),N4,N3,N7,IP,ISL,L1,IBC
C
      IH2=N2/2-1
C
      DO 1 I=IS,IH2
         I1=I+L
         I2=N2-I+L
         A=Z(I1)
         Z(I1)=A-Z(I2)
 1       Z(I2)=A+Z(I2)
C
      RETURN
      END
```

```
      SUBROUTINE TFOLD1
C
CTHIS ROUTINE FOLDS THE INPUT ARRAY Z.
CTHIS ROUTINE SHOULD BE WRITTEN WITH CARE IN MACHINE CODE
C
      COMMON Z(1025),Y(1025)
      COMMON/F67COM/N2,INDEX(513),SI(513),N4,N3,N7,IP,ISL,L1,IBC
C
      I1=N2-1
C
      DO 1 I=1,I1
            I1=ISL+I
            I2=L1-I
            A=Z(I1)
            Z(I1)=A+Z(I2)
 1          Z(I2)=A-Z(I2)
C
      RETURN
      END
```

FIG. 22. Subroutines KFOLD, ZERO, NEG, REVNEG, TFOLD, and TFOLD1.

```
C TESTS POT1 USING RANDOM INPUT
C
        COMMON Z(1025),Y(1025),AKX(1025),CORE(36000)
       ,COMMON/POTCOM/NX,NY,IMIN,IMAX,JMIN,JMAX,INC,
        CIR0,IBCX,IQX,IBCY,IQY,HX,HY,HXY2,PI,POTFAC
C
C GIVE VALUES TO THE SIX INPUT VARIABLES IQX,IQY,IBCX,IBCY,HX,HY
        DO 10   IQX=7,7
        DO 10 IBCX=1,3
        DO 10 IBCY=1,3
        IQY=IQX
        HX=1.0
        HY=2.0
C
C CALL THE SET UP ROUTINE FOR THESE VALUES,
C IR0,INC,POTFAC,HXY2 ARE CALCULATED
        CALL SETPT1
C
C ALLOCATE STORAGE IN THE ARRAY CORE().
C POT1 CALCULATES IN COPE(IR0) UPWARDS.
C EXACT ANSWER WILL BE IN CORE(IR01) UPWARDS.
        IR01=IR0+(IMAX-IMIN+3)*(JMAX-JMIN+3)
        I1=IMIN-1
        I2=IMAX+1
        J1=JMIN-1
        J2=JMAX+1
C
C INSERT RANDOM POTENTIAL, PHI1 SAY
        DO 1 I=I1,I2
        DO 1 J=J1,J2
        K=IR01+I+INC*J
        K1=IR0+I+INC*J
        CORE(K)=2.0*(RANF(0)-0.5)
 1      CORE(K1)=CORE(K)
C
C BORDER POTENTIAL ACCORDING TO BOUNDARY CONDITIONS
        CALL BORDER(IR01)
C
C ADJUST ZERO OF POTENTIAL WHEN IT IS ARBITRARY.
        IF ((IBCX .EQ. 3 .OR. IBCX .EQ. 2).AND.
       C(IBCY .EQ. 3 .OR. IBCY .EQ. 2)) GO TO 4
        GO TO 5
 4      S=0.0
        K=IR01+INC*JMIN
        I=K+IMIN
        X=CORE(I)
        IF (IBCX .EQ. 2) X=X/2.0
        S=S+X
        I=K+IMAX
        X=CORE(I)
        IF (IBCX .EQ. 2) X=X/2.0
        S=S+X
        I1=IMIN+1
        I2=IMAX-1
C
        DO 13 I=I1,I2
 13     S=S+CORE(K+I)
        IJ=NX
        IF (IBCY .NE. 2) GO TO 15
        K=IR01+INC*JMAX
        I=K+IMIN
        X=CORE(I)
        IF (IBCX .EQ. 2) X=X/2.0
        S=S+X
        I=K+IMAX
        X=CORE(I)
        IF (IBCX .EQ. 2) X=X/2.0
        S=S+X
        I1=IMIN+1
        I2=IMAX-1
C
        DO 16 I=I1,I2
 16     S=S+CORE(K+I)
        IJ=IJ+NX
 15     S=S/FLOAT(IJ)
        I1=IMIN-1
        I2=IMAX+1
        DO 7 I=I1,I2
        DO 7 J=J1,J2
        K=IR01+I+INC*J
        K1=IR0+I+INC*J
        CORE(K)=CORE(K)-S
 7      CORE(K1)=CORE(K)
C CALCULATE EXACT CHARGE CORRESPONDING TO POTENTIAL PHI1
 5      DO 2 I=IMIN,IMAX
        DO 2 J=JMIN,JMAX
        K=I+INC*J
        ICN1=IR01+K
        ICN=IR0+K
        ITP=ICN1+INC
        IBT=ICN1-INC
        ILT=ICN1-1
        IRT=ICN1+1
 2      CORE(ICN)= POTFAC*((CORE(ILT)+CORE(IRT)-2.0*CORE(ICN1))
       C           +HXY2*(CORE(ITP)+CORE(IBT)-2.0*CORE(ICN1)))
C
C USE POT1 TO GET POTENTIAL PHI2 FROM CHARGE
        CALL SECOND(T1)
        CALL POT1
        CALL SECOND(T2)
C
        TIME=T2-T1
        PRINT 50,(TIME,NX,NY)
 50     FORMAT(/,1X,'TIME=',F20.6,6X,'NX=',I3,6X,'NY=',I3)
C COMPARE PHI2 WITH EXACT ANSWER PHI1 AND
C PRINT OUT MAXIMUM DIFFERENCE.
        CALL BORDER(IR0)
        CALL ERROR(IR0,IR01)
C
 10     CONTINUE
C
        STOP
        END


        SUBROUTINE ERROR(IR0,IR01)
C
C FIND MAXIMUM DIFFERENCE AND POSITION
C
        COMMON Z(1025),Y(1025),AKX(1025),CORE(20000)
        COMMON/POTCOM/NX,NY,IMIN,IMAX,JMIN,JMAX,INC,
        CIR ,IBCX,IQX,IBCY,IQY,HX,HY,HXY2,PI,POTFAC
C
        XMAX=0.0
        IM=-999
        JM=-999
        I1=IMIN-1
        I2=IMAX+1
        J1=JMIN-1
        J2=JMAX+1
        DO 1 I=I1,I2
        DO 1 J=J1,J2
        K3=I+INC*J
        K1=IR0+K3
        K2=IR01+K3
        X1=CORE(K1)
        X2=CORE(K2)
        IF (ABS(X1-X2) .LE. ABS( XMAX)) GO TO 5
        XMAX=X1-X2
        IM=I
        JM=J
 5      CONTINUE
 1      CONTINUE
C
        PRINT 4,(XMAX,IM,JM,IBCX,IBCY)
 4      FORMAT(1X,'XMAX=',E12.4,3X,'IM=',I3,3X,'JM=',I3,3X,
       C        'IBCX=',I1,3X,'IBCY=',I1)
C
        RETURN
        END
```

** CORRECT ANSWERS FROM THE TEST ROUTINE **

```
TIME=   5.046875        NX=128          NY=128
XMAX=   0.8410E-04      IM= 67    JM= 56    IBCX=1    IBCY=1

TIME=   5.203125        NX=128          NY=128
XMAX= -0.2248E-03       IM= 69    JM=  0    IBCX=1    IBCY=2

TIME=   5.125000        NX=128          NY=128
XMAX= -0.1194E-03       IM= 69    JM= 44    IBCX=1    IBCY=3

TIME=   5.039062        NX=128          NY=128
XMAX= -0.1547E-03       IM=127    JM= 80    IBCX=2    IBCY=1

TIME=   5.187500        NX=128          NY=128
XMAX=   0.3542E-03      IM=128    JM=128    IBCX=2    IBCY=2

TIME=   5.097656        NX=128          NY=128
XMAX=   0.4261E-03      IM=126    JM= 72    IBCX=2    IBCY=3

TIME=   3.773437        NX=128          NY=128
XMAX=   0.1199E-03      IM= 59    JM= 42    IBCX=3    IBCY=1

TIME=   3.886719        NX=128          NY=128
XMAX= -0.1879E-03       IM=  9    JM=  6    IBCX=3    IBCY=2

TIME=   3.843750        NX=128          NY=128
XMAX= -0.3164E-03       IM= 95    JM= 68    IBCX=3    IBCY=3
```

FIG. 23. Test program for POT1 and answers. Subroutine ERROR.

THE POTENTIAL CALCULATION AND SOME APPLICATIONS

```
      SUBROUTINE POT1
C
C                   * PROGRAM REQUIREMENTS *
C
C REQUIRES SIX INPUT PARAMETERS WHICH ARE THE /POTCOM/ COMMON VARIABLES-
C                   IBCX,IQX,IBCY,IQY,HX,HY
C
C SUBROUTINE SETPT1 MUST BE CALLED ONCE EVERY TIME ANY OF THE PARAMETERS
C CHANGE.  SETPT1 CALCULATES NX,NY,POTFAC,IMIN,IMAX,JMIN,JMAX,IRO,INC,HXY2,
C AND FILLS AKX(I).
C
C BLANK AND /POTCOM/ COMMON DECLARATIONS MUST ALSO BE IN THE PROGRAM THAT
C CALLS POT1
C
C POT1 USES FOUR67, SETF67 AND THEIR DEPENDENT SUBROUTINES, ALL OF
C WHICH MUST BE LOADED INTO THE MACHINE.
C
C                   * MATHEMATICAL DESCRIPTION *
C
C OVERWRITES A CHARGE DISTRIBUTION WITH THE EQUIVALENT POTENTIAL DISTRIBUTION
C ON A RECTANGULAR FINITE DIFFERENCE MESH FOR 9 DIFFERENT BOUNDARY CONDITIONS
C SOLVES
C  (PHI(LEFT)+PHI(RIGHT)-2*PHI(CENTRE))+HXY2*(PHI(TOP)+PHI(BOTTOM)-2*PHI(CENTRE))
C                      =Q/POTFAC
C
C       HX=CONSTANT MESH DISTANCE IN X
C       HY=CONSTANT MESH DISTANCE IN Y
C       HXY2=HX**2/HY**2
C
C GIVEN Q FINDS PHI WITHIN SQRT(NO. OPS)*ROUNDING ERROR. PHI OVERWRITES Q.
C POTFAC IS A CONSTANT.  TO GET CORRECT POTENTIAL INSERT ACTUAL CHARGE *POTFAC.
C A SINGLE 1D ARRAY CORE(K) IS USED FOR THE MESH TO AVOID UNNECESSARY
C MULTIPLICATIONS WHEN ELEMENTS ARE REFERENCED.
C       (I,J) ELEMENT OF PHI OR Q IS FOUND IN
C                      CORE(IRO+I+INC*J)
C                IMIN-1 .LE. I .LE. IMAX+1
C                JMIN-1 .LE. J .LE. JMAX+1
C
C THE NUMBER OF POINTS IS SELECTED BY IQX AND IQY
C                NX=2**IQX         NY=2**IQY
C
C THE BOUNDARY CONDITIONS ARE SELECTED BY IBCX AND IBCY
C
C IBCX=1  POTENTIAL HAS GIVEN VALUES PLACED BEFORE ENTRY ON
C         PHI(0,J) AND PHI(NX,J)    JMIN .LE. J .LE. JMAX
C         IMIN=1    IMAX=NX-1
C
C IBCY=1  POTENTIAL HAS GIVEN VALUES PLACED BEFORE ENTRY ON
C         PHI(I,0) AND PHI(I,NY)    IMIN .LE. I .LE. IMAX
C         JMIN=1    JMAX=NY-1
C
C IBCX=2  POTENTIAL HAS ZERO FIELD AT I=0 AND I=NX
C         IMIN=0    IMAX=NX
C         PHI(IMIN-1,J)=PHI(IMIN+1,J)   JMIN .LE. J .LE. JMAX
C         PHI(IMAX+1,J)=PHI(IMAX-1,J)
C
C IBCY=2  POTENTIAL HAS ZERO FIELD AT J=0 AND J=NY
C         JMIN=0    JMAX=NY
C         PHI(I,JMIN-1)=PHI(I,JMIN+1)   IMIN .LE. I .LE. IMAX
C         PHI(I,JMAX+1)=PHI(I,JMAX-1)
C
C IBCX=3  POTENTIAL IS PERIODIC IN X
C         IMIN=0    IMAX=NX-1
C         PHI(IMIN-1,J)=PHI(IMAX,J)     IMIN .LE. I .LE. IMAX
C         PHI(IMIN,J)=PHI(IMAX+1,J)
C
C IBCY=3  POTENTIAL IS PERIODIC IN Y
C         JMIN=0    JMAX=NY-1
C         PHI(I,JMIN-1)=PHI(I,JMAX)     JMIN .LE. J .LE. JMAX
C         PHI(I,JMIN)=PHI(I,JMAX+1)
C
C ALL 9 COMBINATIONS OF BOUNDARY CONDITIONS ARE POSSIBLE.  THE ROUTINE
C FILLS IN THE ACTIVE POINTS DEFINED BY
C                IMIN .LE. I .LE. IMAX
C                JMIN .LE. J .LE. JMAX
C
C METHOD USES PARTIAL FOURIER ANALYSIS AND RECURSIVE CYCLIC REDUCTION AS GIVEN
C IN *A FAST DIRECT SOLUTION OF POISSONS EQUATION USING FOURIER ANALYSIS*
C                      (JACM 12,95,1965)
C
C NUMBER OF ARITHMETIC OPERATIONS IS 2.5*NX*NY*(LOG BASE 2(NY)+2.6) IF IBCX=3,
C IT IS ABOUT 50 P.C. MORE FOR IBCX=1 OR 2
C
C PROGRAMMED BY R.W.HOCKNEY FEB. 1968
C
      COMMON Z(1025),Y(1025),AKX(1025),CORE(20000)
      COMMON /POTCOM/ NX,NY,IMIN,IMAX,JMIN,JMAX,INC,
     C IRO,IBCX,IQX,IBCY,IQY,HX,HY,HXY2,PI,POTFAC
C
      IF (IBCX .NE. 1)GO TO 12
      K3=IRO+IMIN
      K4=IRO+IMAX
      J1=JMIN*INC
C
      DO 13 J=JMIN,JMAX
      K1=K3+J1
      K2=K4+J1
      CORE(K1)=CORE(K1)-POTFAC*CORE(K1-1)
      CORE(K2)=CORE(K2)-POTFAC*CORE(K2+1)
  13  J1=J1+INC
C
  12  CALL BORDER(IRO)
C
      J1=0
      IF (IBCY .EQ. 1) J1=2
      J2=NY-2
      IF (IBCY .EQ. 2) J2=NY
C
C NOW MODIFY R.H.S. ON EVEN LINES
      F=1.0/HXY2
      F1=R*R
      F2=2.0*R*(R+1)
C
      CALL RHSE(IBCX,F1,F2,R,J1,J2)
C
      IF (IBCY .NE. 1) GO TO 15
      K3=IRO+INC+J1
      K4=IRO+INC+J2
      K5=INC+INC
C
      DO 16 I=IMIN,IMAX
      K1=K3+I
      K2=K4+I
      CORE(K1)=CORE(K1)-POTFAC*CORE(K1-K5)
      CORE(K2)=CORE(K2)-POTFAC*CORE(K2+K5)
  16  CONTINUE
C
  15  CONTINUE
C
C NOW FOURIER ANALYSIS ON EVEN LINES
      K=IRO+INC+J1
C
      DO 4 J=J1,J2,2
         CALL FETCHX(K)
         CALL FOUR67(IBCX,IQX)
         CALL STOREX(K)
   4  K=K+INC+INC
C
C NOW SOLUTION IN Y BY CYCLIC REDUCTION
      DO 5 K=IMIN,IMAX
      A=AKX(K+1)
      L=IRO+K
      M=INC+INC
   5  CALL CRED(IBCX,L,M,A,IQY-1)
C
C NOW FOURIER SYNTHESIS ON EVEN LINES
C     GIVING SOLUTION ON EVEN LINES.
      IF (IBCX .EQ. 3) IBCX=4
C
      K=IRO+INC+J1
C
      DO 6 J=J1,J2,2
         CALL FETCHX(K)
         CALL FOUR67(IBCX,IQX)
         CALL STOREX(K)
   6  K=K+INC+INC
C
      IF (IBCX .EQ. 4) IBCX=3
C
C NOW MODIFY R.H.S. ON ODD LINES
      IF (IBCY .NE. 3) GO TO 18
C
      DO 19 I=IMIN,IMAX
      CORE(K+I)=CORE(IRO+I)
  19  CONTINUE
C
  18  F=1.0/POTFAC
      J2=NY-1
C
      CALL RHSO(F,HXY2,J2)
C
C NOW SOLUTION ON ODD LINES BY CYCLIC REDUCTION
      DO 7 J=1,J2,2
      L=IRO+INC*J
      A=2.0*(1+HXY2)
   7  CALL CRED(IBCX,L,1,A,IQX)
C
      RETURN
      END
```

FIG. 24. Subroutine POT1.

```
      SUBROUTINE SETPT1
C
CSETS CERTAIN ARRAYS AND CONSTANTS FOR USE BY POT1.
C MUST BE CALLED ONCE WHENEVER THE PARAMETERS TO POT1 CHANGE.
C
      COMMON Z(1025),Y(1025),AKX(1025),CORE(20000)
      COMMON/POTCOM/NX,NY,IMIN,IMAX,JMIN,JMAX,INC,IRO,IBCX,IQX,
     1IBCY,IQY,HX,HY,HXY2,PI,POTFAC
C
      CALL SETF67(IBCX,IQX)
C
      PI=3.1415926535898
      NX=2**IQX
      NY=2**IQY
      NX2=NX/2
      NY2=NY/2
      FNX2=FLOAT(NX2)
      FNY2=FLOAT(NY2)
C
C POTFAC IS FACTOR BY WHICH FINAL ANSWER MUST BE MULTIPLIED TO GET
C CORRECT RESULT. ALTERNATIVELY MULTIPLY INITIAL CHARGE OR POTFAC OR
C BETTER ABSORB IT IN SCALING OF CHARGE
      POTFAC=2.0/NX
      IF(IBCX .EQ. 3) POTFAC=POTFAC/4.0
C
C CALCULATE LIMITS OF ACTIVE MESH
C                      IMIN .LE. I .LE. IMAX
C                      JMIN .LE. J .LE. JMAX
      GO TO (5,7,9),IBCX
C
C     *  IF IBCX=1  *
    5       IMIN=1
            IMAX=NX-1
            GO TO 10
C
C     *  IF IBCX=2  *
    7       IMIN=0
            IMAX=NX
            GO TO 10
C
C     *  IF IBCX=3  *
    9       IMIN=0
            IMAX=NX-1
C
   10 GO TO (11,13,15),IBCY
C
C     *  IF IBCY=1  *
   11       JMIN=1
            JMAX=NY-1
            GO TO 16
C
C     *  IF IBCY=2  *
   13       JMIN=0
            JMAX=NY
            GO TO 16
C
C     *  IF IBCY=3  *
   15       JMIN=0
            JMAX=NY-1
C
C INC IS INTEGER TO BE ADDED TO GO FROM ROW TO ROW ON MESH
   16 INC=IMAX-IMIN+3
C
C IRO IS POINTER GIVING START OF PHI(I,J) IN ARRAY CORE.
C      PHI(I,J) IS IN CORE(IRO+J*INC+I)
      IRO=2+INC
C
      HXY2=(HX/HY)**2
      B=1.0/HXY2
      F1=(B+1)*(3.0*B+1)
      F2=B*B
      F3=4.0*B*(B+1)
C
C CALCULATE COEFFICIENTS IN THE HARMONIC EQUATIONS
      GO TO (18,18,19),IBCX
C
C     *  IBCX=1 OR 2  *
   18       F=PI/FLOAT(NX)
C
            DO 17 I=IMIN,IMAX
   17       AKX(I+1)=2.0*(F1-F3*COS(F*FLOAT(I))+F2*COS(F*FLOAT(I)*2.0))
            AKX(1)=2.0
            AKX(NX+1)=2.0*(F1+F3+F2)
            GO TO 21
C
C     *  IBCX=3  *
   19       I2=NX2-1
            F=2.0*PI/(FLOAT(NX))
C
            DO 20 I=1,I2
            X=2.0*(F1-F3*COS(F*FLOAT(I))+F2*COS(F*FLOAT(I)*2.0))
            AKX(I+1)=X
   20       AKX(I+NX2+1)=X
C
            AKX(1)=2.0
            AKX(NX2+1)=2.0*(F1+F3+F2)
C
   21 CONTINUE
      RETURN
      END
```

```
      SUBROUTINE CRED(IBC,L,M,A,IP1)
C
CRECURSIVE CYCLIC REDUCTION ROUTINE
CTHIS ROUTINE SHOULD BE WRITTEN WITH CARE IN MACHINE CODE
C
      COMMON Z(1025),Y(1025),AKX(1025),CORE(20000)
      COMMON/POTCOM/NX,NY,IMIN,IMAX,JMIN,JMAX,INC,
     1IRO,IBCX,IQX,IBCY,IQY,HX,HY,HXY2,PI,POTFAC
      DIMENSION BB(11)
C
      IP=IP1
      N2=M
      BB(1)=A
      B=A
      N4=0
      N=2**IP
      K=L+N*M
      IF (IBC .EQ. 1) IP=IP-1
C
      DO 2 N1=1,IP
            N4=N4+1
            N3=N2
            N2=N2+N2
            J1=N2+L
            J3=K-N3
            J2=K-N2
            IF (J1 .GT. J2) GO TO 21
C
            DO 1 J=J1,J2,N2
    1       CORE(J)=B*CORE(J)+CORE(J-N3)+CORE(J+N3)
C
   21       GO TO (3,4,6),IBC
C
C     *  IF IBC=3  *
    6            CORE(L)=B*CORE(L)+CORE(J3)+CORE(L+N3)
                 GO TO 3
C
C     *  IF IBC=2  *
    4            CORE(L)=B*CORE(L)+CORE(L+N3)+CORE(L+N3)
                 CORE(K)=B*CORE(K)+CORE(J3)+CORE(J3)
C
C     *  IF IBC=1  *
    3       B=B*B-2.0
            BB(N1+1)=B
            IF (B .LE. 1.0E14) GO TO 2
C
C SHORT CUT AND SOLVE BY DIVISION IF B LARGER THAN
C DESIRED ACCURACY.
            IF (J1 .GT. J2) GO TO 22
C
            DO 11 J=J1,J2,N2
   11       CORE(J)=-CORE(J)/B
C
   22       IF (IBC .EQ. 1) GO TO 12
C
            CORE(L)=-CORE(L)/B
            IF (IBC .NE. 3) GO TO 40
C
                 CORE(K)=CORE(L)
                 GO TO 12
C
   40       CORE(K)=-CORE(K)/B
            GO TO 12
C
    2 CONTINUE
C
   10 GO TO (16,20,18),IBC
C
C     *  IF IBC=1  *
   16       I=L+N*M/2
            CORE(I)=-CORE(I)/B
            GO TO 12
C
C     *  IF IBC=2  *
   20       AL1=0.0
            IF (B .NE. 2.0) AL1=(CORE(L)+CORE(K))/(2.0*(2.0-B))
            AL2=(CORE(K)-CORE(L))/(2.0*(2.0+B))
            CORE(L)=AL1+AL2
            CORE(K)=AL1-AL2
            GO TO 12
C
C     *  IF IBC=3  *
   18       IF (B .EQ. 2.0) CORE(L)=0.0
            IF(B .NE. 2.0) CORE(L)= CORE(L)/(2.0-B)
            CORE(K)=CORE(L)
C
   12 DO 13 NN=1,N4
            N1=N4-NN
            B=BB(N1+1)
            J2=K-N3
            J1=L+N3
            IF (IBC .NE. 1) GO TO 24
C
            CORE(J1)=(CORE(J1+N3)-CORE(J1))/B
            CORE(J2)=(CORE(J2-N3)-CORE(J2))/B
            J1=J1+N2
            J2=J2-N2
   24       IF (J1 .GT. J2) GO TO 25
C
            DO 14 J= J1,J2,N2
   14       CORE(J)=(CORE(J-N3)+CORE(J+N3)-CORE(J))/B
C
   25       N2=N3
   13       N3=N3/2
C
      RETURN
      END
```

FIG. 25. Subroutines SETPT1 and CRED.

THE POTENTIAL CALCULATION AND SOME APPLICATIONS 207

```
      SUBROUTINE RHSE(IRC,F1,F2,B,J1,J2)
C
CMODIFY RIGHT HAND SIDE ON EVEN LINES ROUTINE
CTHIS ROUTINE SHOULD BE WRITTEN WITH CARE IN MACHINE CODE
C
      COMMON Z(1025),Y(1025),AKX(1025),CORE(20000)
      COMMON/POTCOM/NX,NY,IMIN,IMAX,JMIN,JMAX,INC,
     CIRO,IRCX,IQX,IRCY,IQY,HX,HY,HXY2,PI,POTFAC
C
      L=IRC+INC*J1
C
      DO 10 J=J1,J2,2
      K=L+IMIN
      IF (IRC .EQ. 1) X=0.0
      IF (IRC .EQ. 2) X=CORE(K+1)
      IF (IRC .NE. 3) GO TO 3
      W=CORE(K-1+NX)
      A=CORE(K)
  3   X=-F1*(X+CORE(K+1))+F2*CORE(K)+B*(CORE(K+INC)+CORE(K-INC))
      I1=IMIN+1
      I2=IMAX-1
C
      DO 1 I=I1,I2
      K=L+I
      W=-F1*(CORE(K-1)+CORE(K+1))+F2*CORE(K)+
     C      B*(CORE(K+INC)+CORE(K-INC))
      CORE(K-1)=X
  1   X=W
C
      K=L+IMAX
      IF (IRC .EQ. 1) W=0.0
      IF (IRC .EQ. 2) W=CORE(K-1)
      IF (IRC .EQ. 3) W=A
      W=-F1*(CORE(K-1)+W)+F2*CORE(K)+B*(CORE(K+INC)+CORE(K-INC))
      CORE(K-1)=X
      CORE(K)=W
 10   L=L+INC+INC
C
      RETURN
      END
```

```
      SUBROUTINE RHSO(F1,F2,J2)
C
CMODIFY RIGHT HAND SIDE ON ODD LINES ROUTINE
CTHIS ROUTINE SHOULD BE WRITTEN WITH CARE IN MACHINE CODE
C
      COMMON Z(1025),Y(1025),AKX(1025),CORE(20000)
      COMMON/POTCOM/NX,NY,IMIN,IMAX,JMIN,JMAX,INC,
     CIRO,IRCX,IQX,IRCY,IQY,HX,HY,HXY2,PI,POTFAC
C
      L=IRO+INC
C
      DO 7 J=1,J2,2
      DO 8 I=1,IMAX
      K=L+I
  8   CORE(K)=F1*CORE(K)-F2*(CORE(K+INC)+CORE(K-INC))
  7   L=L+INC+INC
C
      RETURN
      END
```

```
      SUBROUTINE FETCHX(K)
C
C TRANSFERS DATA FROM ARRAY CORE TO ARRAY Z
C PRIOR TO FOURIER ANALYSIS.
CTHIS ROUTINE SHOULD BE WRITTEN WITH CARE IN MACHINE CODE
C
      COMMON Z(1025),Y(1025),AKX(1025),CORE(20000)
      COMMON/POTCOM/NX,NY,IMIN,IMAX,JMIN,JMAX,INC,
     CIRO,IRCX,IQX,IRCY,IQY,HX,HY,HXY2,PI,POTFAC
C
      DO 1 I=IMIN,IMAX
  1   Z(I+1)=CORE(K+I)
C
      RETURN
      END
```

```
      SUBROUTINE STOREX(K)
C
C TRANSFERS DATA FROM ARRAY Y TO ARRAY CORE
C AFTER FOURIER ANALYSIS.
CTHIS ROUTINE SHOULD BE WRITTEN WITH CARE IN MACHINE CODE
C
      COMMON Z(1025),Y(1025),AKX(1025),CORE(20000)
      COMMON/POTCOM/NX,NY,IMIN,IMAX,JMIN,JMAX,INC,
     CIRO,IRCX,IQX,IRCY,IQY,HX,HY,HXY2,PI,POTFAC
C
      DO 1 I=IMIN,IMAX
  1   CORE(K+I)=Y(I+1)
C
      RETURN
      END
```

```
      SUBROUTINE BORDER()
C
CBORDER THE ACTIVE POINTS ACCORDING TO
C THE BOUNDARY CONDITIONS.
C
      COMMON Z(1025),Y(1025),AKX(1025),CORE(20000)
      COMMON/POTCOM/NX,NY,IMIN,IMAX,JMIN,JMAX,INC,
     CIRO,IRCX,IQX,IRCY,IQY,HX,HY,HXY2,PI,POTFAC
C
      K3=   L+IMIN-1
      K4=   L+IMAX+1
C
      GO TO(10,6,9),IRCX
C
C   *  IF IRCX=2    *
  6      J1=JMIN*INC
C
      DO 8 J=JMIN,JMAX
      K1=K3+J1
      K2=K4+J1
      CORE(K1)=CORE(K1+2)
      CORE(K2)=CORE(K2-2)
  8      J1=J1+INC
      GO TO 10
C
C   *  IF IRCX=3    *
  9      J1=JMIN*INC
C
      DO 11 J=JMIN,JMAX
      K1=K3+J1
      K2=K4+J1
      CORE(K1)=CORE(K2-1)
      CORE(K2)=CORE(K1+1)
 11      J1=J1+INC
C
 10   K3=   L+INC*(JMIN-1)
      K4=   L+INC*(JMAX+1)
C
      GO TO(18,14,17),IRCY
C
C   *  IF IRCY=2    *
C
 14      DO 16 I=IMIN,IMAX
      K1=K3+I
      K2=K4+I
      K5=2*INC
      CORE(K1)=CORE(K1+K5)
 16   CORE(K2)=CORE(K2-K5)
C
      GO TO 18
C
C   *  IF IRCY=3    *
 17      DO 19 I=IMIN,IMAX
      K1=K3+I
      K2=K4+I
      CORE(K1)=CORE(K2-INC)
 19   CORE(K2)=CORE(K1+INC)
C
 18   RETURN
      END
```

FIG. 26. Subroutines RHSE, RHSO, FETCHX, STOREX, and BORDER.

```
C THIS IS THE TEST ROUTINE FOR POT3
C
      COMMON Z(1025),Y(1025),CORE(33000)
      COMMON/POTCOM/NX,NY,IMIN,IMAX,JMIN,JMAX,INC,IRO,IRCX,
     CIQX,IRCY,IQY,HX,HY,HXY2,PI,POTFAC,IRO1,INC1,ISMSQ
C
C SET THE FOUR PARAMETERS TO POT3
      IQX=7
      IQY=IQX
      HX=1.0
      HY=1.0
C
      NX=2**IQX
      NY=2**IQY
      NX2=NX/2
      NY2=NY/2
      NX4=NX/4
C
C CALL THE SETUP ROUTINE FOR THESE PARAMETERS
      CALL SETPT3
C
C INSERT TWO TEST CHARGES
      DO 1 ITEST=0,32,32
      DO 1 JTEST=3,10,7
      ITEST1=3
      JTEST1=5
C CLEAR THE Q ARRAY UP TO IMAX=NX-1, JMAX=NY-1
      DO 2 I=IMIN,IMAX
      DO 2 J=JMIN,JMAX
      K=IRO+INC*J+I
   2  CORE(K)=0.0
C
      K=IRO+INC*JTEST+ITEST
      CORE(K)=CORE(K)+1.0
      K=IRO+INC*JTEST1+ITEST1
      CORE(K)=CORE(K)+1.0
C
C CALL THE POTENTIAL SOLVER
      CALL SECOND(T1)
      CALL POT3
      CALL SECOND(T2)
      TIME=T2-T1
C COMPARE THE SOLUTION FROM POT3 WITH THAT BY DIRECT SUMMATION
      EMAX=0.0
      IM=999
      JM=999
C
      DO 3 I=IMIN,NX2
      DO 3 J=JMIN,NY2
      K=IRO+INC*J+I
      X=CORE(K)
      II=I-ITEST
      JJ=J-JTEST
      II1=I-ITEST1
      JJ1=J-JTEST1
      IF (II .NE. 0 .OR. JJ .NE. 0) GO TO 9
      Y0=1.0
      GO TO 11
C
   9  Y0=1.0/SQRT(FLOAT(II*II+JJ*JJ))
  11  IF (II1 .NE. 0 .OR. JJ1 .NE. 0) GO TO 19
      Y1=1.0
      GO TO 12
C
  19  Y1=1.0/SQRT(FLOAT(II1*II1+JJ1*JJ1))
  12  E=X-Y0-Y1
      IF (ABS(E) .LE. ABS(EMAX)) GO TO 6
      EMAX=E
      IM=I
      JM=J
C
   6  CONTINUE
   3  CONTINUE
C
C PRINTOUT TIME AND ERROR
      PRINT 5,(EMAX,NX,NY,TIME)
   5  FORMAT(//1X,'EMAX=',E13.4,6X,'NX=',I3,5X,'NY=',I3,5X,
     C       'TIME=',F8.3)
C
   1  CONTINUE
C
      STOP
      END
```

```
      SUBROUTINE SETPT3
C
C SETUP ROUTINE FOR POT3. MUST BE CALLED WHENEVER THE
C PARAMETERS TO POT3 CHANGE
C
      COMMON Z(1025),Y(1025),CORE(33000)
      COMMON/POTCOM/NX,NY,IMIN,IMAX,JMIN,JMAX,INC,IRO,IRCX,
     CIQX,IRCY,IQY,HX,HY,HXY2,PI,POTFAC,IRO1,INC1,ISMSQ
C
      PI=3.1415926535898
      NX=2**IQX
      NY=2**IQY
      NX2=NX/2
      NY2=NY/2
C
C SET RANGE OF INDICES
      IMIN=0
      IMAX=NX2
      JMIN=0
      JMAX=NY2
C
C SET INCREMENTS FROM ROW TO ROW
      INC1=NX2+1
      INC=INC1
C
C SET ORIGINS
      IRO1=1
      IRO=IRO1+(NX2+1)*(NY2+1)
C
C INSERT THE DESIRED INFLUENCE POTENTIAL,F.
C HERE IT IS THE R**-1 INTERACTION OF POINT CHARGES
      F=1.0/(NX*NX)
C
      DO 1 J=JMIN,NY2
      DO 1 I=IMIN,NX2
      K=IRO1+J*INC1+I
      IF (I+J) 2,3,2
   2  CORE(K)=F/SQRT(FLOAT(I*I+J*J))
      GO TO 1
   3  CORE(K)=F
   1  CONTINUE
C
      IRCX=2
      IRCY=2
      IQX=IQX-1
      IQY=IQY-1
C
C ISMSQ=1 IF THE PROBLEM IS SYMMETRIC IN X AND Y
      ISMSQ=0
      IF (IRCX .EQ. IRCY .AND. IQX .EQ. IQY) ISMSQ=1
      IF (ISMSQ .EQ. 1) CALL SETFA7(IRCX,IQX)
C
C FORM THE DOUBLE FOURIER TRANSFORM OF F
C ON THE SMALL MESH (I,J .LE. N/2)
      CALL FOURXY(IRO1,INC1)
C
      IRCX=3
      IRCY=3
      IQX=IQX+1
      IQY=IQY+1
      IMAX=NX-1
      JMAX=NY-1
      INC=NX
      ISMSQ=0
      IF (IRCX .EQ. IRCY .AND. IQX .EQ. IQY) ISMSQ=1
C
C CALL SETF67 FOR ANALYSIS ON LARGE MESH. (I,J .LE. N)
      IF (ISMSQ .EQ. 1) CALL SETF67(IRCX,IQX)
C
      RETURN
      END
```

```
      SUBROUTINE FETCHX(K)
C
C FETCHES A ROW OF VALUES FROM CORE IN PREPARATION
C FOR FOURIER ANALYSIS
C
      COMMON Z(1025),Y(1025),CORE(33000)
      COMMON/POTCOM/NX,NY,IMIN,IMAX,JMIN,JMAX,INC,IRO,IRCX,
     CIQX,IRCY,IQY,HX,HY,HXY2,PI,POTFAC,IRO1,INC1,ISMSQ
C
      DO 1 I=IMIN,IMAX
   1  Z(I+1)=CORE(K+I)
C
      RETURN
      END
```

** CORRECT ANSWERS FROM THE TEST ROUTINE **

EMAX= -0.9239E-05	NX=128	NY=128	TIME=	9.777
EMAX= -0.8285E-05	NX=128	NY=128	TIME=	9.777
EMAX= -0.6735E-05	NX=128	NY=128	TIME=	9.770
EMAX= -0.6735E-05	NX=128	NY=128	TIME=	9.777

FIG. 27. Test program for POT3 and answers. Subroutine SETPT3 and FETCHX.

Fig. 28. Subroutines POT3, FOURXY, FETCHY, STOREY, MLTFT3, and STOREX.

Acknowledgment

Most of this work was completed while the author held an NRC/NAS senior postdoctoral resident research associateship at the NASA Langley Research Center.

References

ABERNATHY, F., and KRONAUER, R. (1962). *J. Fluid Mech.* **13**, 1.
BIRDSALL, C. K., and FUSS, D. (1968). *Proc. APS Topical Conf. Numerical Simulation of Plasma*, Publ. LA-3990, p. D1-1. Los Alamos Sci. Lab., Los Alamos, New Mexico. Also in *J. Comp. Phys.* **3**, 494 (1969).
BIRDSALL, C. K., and KAMIMURA, T. (1966). Rept. PIPJ-54. Inst. of Plasma Phys., Nagoya Univ., Nagoya, Japan.
BIRDSALL, C. K., LANGDON, A. B., MCKEE, C. F., OKUDA, H., and WANG, D. (1968). *Proc. APS Topical Conf. Numerical Simulation of Plasma*, Publ. LA-3990, p. D2-1. Los Alamos. Sci Lab., Los Alamos, New Mexico.
BORIS, J., and ROBERTS, K. V. (1969). The optimization of particle calculations in 2 and 3 dimensions. *J. Comp. Phys.* (To appear).
BUNEMAN, O. (1968). FORTRAN program distributed at *APS Topical Conf. Numerical Simulation of Plasma*. Los Alamos, New Mexico. Also in SUIPR Rep. No. 294. Inst. for Plasma Res., Stanford Univ., Stanford, California, May 1969.
BUZBEE, B. L., GOLUB, G. H., and NIELSON, C. W. (1969). Tech. Rept. CS 128. Computer Science Dept., Stanford Univ., Stanford, California.
BYERS, J. A. (1966). *Phys. Fluids* **9**, 1038.
CHORIN, A. J. (1968). *Math. Comp.* **22**, 745.
COCHRAN, W. T., COOLEY, J. W., FAVIN, D. L., HELMS, H. D., KAENEL, R. A., LANG, W. W., MALING, G. C., NELSON, D. E., RADER, C. M., and WELCH, P. D. (1967). *IEEE Trans. Audio Electroacoustics* **AU-15**, 45.
COOLEY, J. W., and TUKEY, J. W. (1965). *Math. Comp.* **19**, 297.
COOLEY, J. W., LEWIS, P. A. W., and WELCH, P. D. (1967). The fast Fourier transform algorithm and its applications. *IBM Res. Rept.* RC 1743, Feb.
FORSYTHE, G. E., and WASOW, W. R. (1960). "Finite Difference Methods for Partial Differential Equations." John Wiley, New York.
FROMM, J. E. (1964). *Meth. Comp. Phys.* **3**, 354.
FROMM, J. E., and HARLOW, F. H. (1963). *Phys. Fluids* **6**, 975.
GENTLEMAN, W. M., and SANDE, G. (1966). Fast Fourier transforms—for fun and profit. *1966 Fall Joint Computer Conf. AFIPS Proc.* **29**, p. 563. Spartan, Washington, D.C.
GENTRY, R. A., HARLOW, F. H., and MARTIN, R. E. (1965). *Meth. Comp. Phys.* **4**, p. 211.
HIRSCH, R. L. (1967). *J. Appl. Phys.* **38**, 4522.
HOCKNEY, R. W. (1965). *J. Assoc. Comput. Mach.* **12**, 95.
HOCKNEY, R. W. (1966a). Tech. SUIPR Rep. No. 53. Inst. for Plasma Res., Stanford Univ., Stanford, California.
HOCKNEY, R. W. (1966b). *Phys. Fluids* **9**, 1826.
HOCKNEY, R. W. (1967a). Tech. SUIPR Rept. No. 202. Inst. for Plasma Res., Stanford Univ., Stanford, California.
HOCKNEY, R. W. (1967b). *Astrophys. J.* **150**, 797.
HOCKNEY, R. W. (1968a). *Phys. Fluids* **11**, 1381.
HOCKNEY, R. W. (1968b). *J. Appl. Phys.* **39**, 4166.

HOCKNEY, R. W. (1968c). *Publ. Astron. Soc. Pacific* **80**, 662.
HOCKNEY, R. W., and HOHL, F. (1969). Effects of velocity dispersion on the evolution of a disk of stars. *Astron. J.* **74**, 1102.
HOHL, F. (1967). *Symp. Computer Simulation of Plasmas and Many-Body Problems.* NASA Special Publ. SP-153, p. 323. Available from CFSTI, Springfield, Virginia.
HOHL, F. (1968a). NASA Tech. Note D-4646. Available from CFSTI, Springfield, Virginia.
HOHL, F. (1968b). *Bull. Astronom. Serie 3*, 3, Facsimile 2, p. 227.
HOHL, F., and HOCKNEY, R. W. (1969). A computer model of disks of stars. *J. Comp. Phys.* **4**, 306.
JANES, G. S., LEVY, R. H., BETHE, H. A., and FELD, B. T. (1966). *Phys. Rev.* **145**, 925.
KILLEEN, J., and ROMPEL, L. (1966). *J. Comp. Phys.* **1**, 29.
LEVY, R. H., and HOCKNEY, R. W. (1968). *Phys. Fluids* **11**, 766.
MILLER, R. H., and PRENDERGAST, K. H. (1968). *Astrophys. J.* **151**, 699.
PURI, S. (1966). *Phys. Fluids.* **9**, 1043.
RUNGE, C. (1903). *Z. Math. Phys.* **48**, 443.
SHAPIRO, V. D. (1965). *Soviet Phys.—JETP Letters* **2**, 10.
STURROCK, P. A. (1966). *Phys. Rev.* **141**, 186.
TOOMRE, A. (1964). *Astrophys. J.* **139**, 1217.
VARGA, R. S. (1926). "Matrix Iterative Analysis." Prentice Hall, Englewood Cliffs, New Jersey.
VERONIS, G. (1966). *Deep-Sea Res.* **13**, 31.
WADHWA, R. P., BUNEMAN, O., and BRAUCH, D. F. (1965). *AIAA J.* **3**, 107.
YU, S. P., KOOYERS, G. P., and BUNEMAN, O. (1965). *J. Appl. Phys.* **36**, 2550.

Multidimensional Plasma Simulation by the Particle-in-Cell Method*

R. L. MORSE

UNIVERSITY OF CALIFORNIA
LOS ALAMOS SCIENTIFIC LABORATORY
LOS ALAMOS, NEW MEXICO

I. Introduction. 213
II. Fluid PIC Simulation of Axisymmetric Plasma Guns 214
   A. Plasma Focus 216
   B. Continuous Flow Mode of a Coaxial Gun 218
III. Collisionless PIC 224
   A. The Two-Beam Instability 227
   B. Axisymmetric Plasmas Confined by a Variable Magnetic Field 233
   References 239

I. Introduction

THE PARTICLE-IN-CELL METHOD, or PIC, was originally developed by Frank Harlow and collaborators at Los Alamos in 1955 for doing multidimensional compressible fluid computations and is discussed in Volume 3 of this series in that context. The idea of PIC is that by combining the best Eulerian and Lagrangian features, the numerical instabilities and mass diffusion of the Eulerian method and the cell distortion difficulties of the Lagrangian method can be overcome. The region of interest is divided into regular Eulerian cells for purposes of computing field variables such as pressure and fluid velocity, but the material is transported from cell to cell in a Lagrangian fashion in the form of discrete simulation particles. These simulation particles, of which there are typically ten or more per cell, represent a fixed amount of mass and retain their identity throughout the computation. On each time step, a suitable conservative accounting of energy and momentum yields the internal, i.e., nonkinetic, energy in each cell. This internal energy, together with a directly computed mass density and a material equation of state, gives the pressure field which is then used to accelerate the fluid and obtain new cell velocities. These new cell velocities are then interpolated to particle positions and used to advance these positions in the cell grid, and so on. The material

---

* Work performed under the auspices of the United States Atomic Energy Commission.

equation of state is specified quite independently from the rest of the code. In particular, in the very simple and convenient axisymmetric plasma gun problem, the pressure from the single B_θ component of the magnetic field fits this scalar format without special modifications.

We shall briefly discuss two such plasma gun applications of fluid PIC and then proceed to develop the PIC method as it is used in collisionless plasma simulation. It may be useful to the reader to anticipate the following differences between the two areas of application. The velocity of a classical fluid is a single-valued function of position and is therefore a cell quantity in fluid PIC. By contrast, in a collisionless plasma there is a distribution of particle velocities at every point in space, and it is necessary to treat this microstructure in detail in order to obtain the important physical results. Accordingly, velocity becomes a particle quantity, and a simulation particle represents a number of real particles with the same electric charge, mass, position, and velocity. The cell quantities are then the electromagnetic fields and the summed particle densities and currents from which they are obtained. The macroscopic pressures employed in fluid PIC are available in principle from the distribution of particle velocities in each cell in collisionless PIC but are usually not computed.

II. Fluid PIC Simulation of Axisymmetric Plasma Guns

Because a two-dimensional treatment of an axisymmetric flow depends on the cylindrical coordinates r and z, a conventional rectangular cell grid in these coordinates is used, and the procedure only differs from a rectangular computation by corrections to the difference equations.

Because of the high densities and low temperatures encountered in plasma guns, and for additional reasons based on the small size of some charged particle gyro-radii, it is often reasonable to treat these gun plasmas as classical fluids. For parameters of interest, including time scale, classical resistive diffusion of the magnetic field through the plasma is negligible. There is always the possibility of some anomalous resistivity but comparisons with experiments indicate that the zero resistivity assumption made in these gun simulations is quite reasonable. Therefore, when there is magnetic flux frozen into the plasma, the ratio of flux to mass for a simulation particle is constant in time, and the equation of state combines the resulting magnetic pressure with the material equation of state which is usually a $\gamma = 5/3$ adiabatic law.

For the details of fluid PIC numerical analysis, the reader is referred to the article by Harlow in Vol. 3 of this series and to Amsden (1966). However, one point is worth discussing here, particularly because it is important in collisionless PIC. The author is aware that many people in the fluid dynamics and plasma physics communities know that, in practice, PIC codes contain some smoothing, but they are not sure about its form or degree. This smoothing is in the form of interpolations, and for fluid PIC this is done as follows. Suppose that a simulation particle is located at the dot in cell number 4, Fig. 1, so that the four nearest cell centers are numbers 1 through 4, indicated

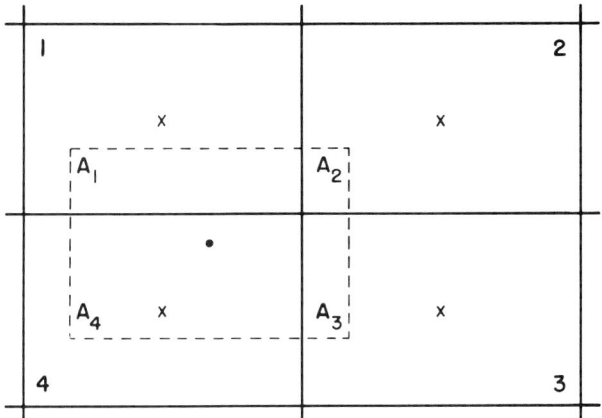

FIG. 1. Simulation of PIC smoothing techniques.

by crosses. Previous computations have assigned flow velocities to each of these cell centers, and now in order to move the particle we must assign it a velocity. For obvious physical reasons, this particle velocity should be a smooth, continuous function of position. A convenient, computationally fast, and the most commonly used prescription for the particle velocity is

$$\mathbf{V}_p = \frac{A_1 \mathbf{V}_1 + A_2 \mathbf{V}_2 + A_3 \mathbf{V}_3 + A_4 \mathbf{V}_4}{A_1 + A_2 + A_3 + A_4} \qquad (1)$$

where the $\mathbf{V}_i$'s are the cell center velocities and the A_i's are the respective cell overlap areas (Fig. 1) obtained by centering a cell-shaped figure (dashed lines) on the particle. This area weighting procedure is easily seen to be a bilinear interpolation and is readily generalized to one or three dimensions by using two or eight nearest cell centers, respectively. Especially in treating subsonic flow, it is sometimes also necessary to area weight particle contributions to cell quantities. With a limited number of simulation particles per cell, one particle crossing a cell boundary can cause a significant change in the pressure difference across the boundary and, if the particle is moving slowly, force itself back across the boundary thus setting up false oscillations. This particle quantity area weighting is done by assigning a particle's contribution to such cell quantities as density to the nearest cell centers in proportion to the A's.

A. Plasma Focus

Axisymmetric plasma guns are commonly operated in two different modes. In one mode, Fig. 2, the entire region in and around the gun is given a static filling of gas, usually deuterium. The electrical discharge starts at the rear of the cylindrical electrode, forms a bubble of heated gas as the magnetic piston pushes out in snow plow fashion, sweeps around the end of the electrode, and forms a small intense z-pinch, called a plasma focus, on the axis. Further descriptions of the system as well as references can be found in the excellent chapter by Roberts and Potter in this volume, or Butler et al. (1969). Figure 2 shows a corresponding pair of time sequences of fluid PIC particle plots and experimental photographs of this mode of gun operation (Butler et al., 1969). The usual outer cylindrical electrode was omitted in both the computations and the experiment because it was realized that, in this focus mode, the outer electrode only handicaps diagnostics and makes little contribution to performance.

In these computations, the plasma and magnetic field are not mixed. The magnetic field, B_θ, occupies the vacuum region inside the bubble and exerts a constant current $1/r^2$ pressure on the free boundary. The rest is a pure fluid computation. The uniform region outside the bubble is cold, The very sharp outer surface of the bubble is a shock which is stronger at smaller radius where it moves faster. The layer between the shock and the inner free boundary is the shock-heated plasma, which provides the illumination in the experimental photographs. As stated above, the PIC method handles such interfaces as this free boundary quite well (see Amsden, 1966, and its bibliography for further discussion of this point) and in particular avoids difficulties with the Courant condition which arise if the transition from finite to infinite sound velocity across this boundary is treated continuously. For an alternative treatment of this problem the reader is referred to the chapter by Roberts and Potter in this volume.

These PIC computations were the first full two-dimensional simulations of the material flow in the plasma focus, and, as the reader can see from Fig. 2. they give an adequate quantitative account of that flow, including the second bubble which occurs on axis at the tip of the focus itself. (Proceedings, 1967). The method could be extended to include other physical effects in the shocked layer that depend on density and temperature, since these are available on each time step. However, for two reasons, the method fails near the axis where the high temperature focus itself is formed. First, a cell grid which is convenient for treating the entire plasma flow is too coarse to resolve the focus. The thin stem seen on the axis in Fig. 2 is entirely inside

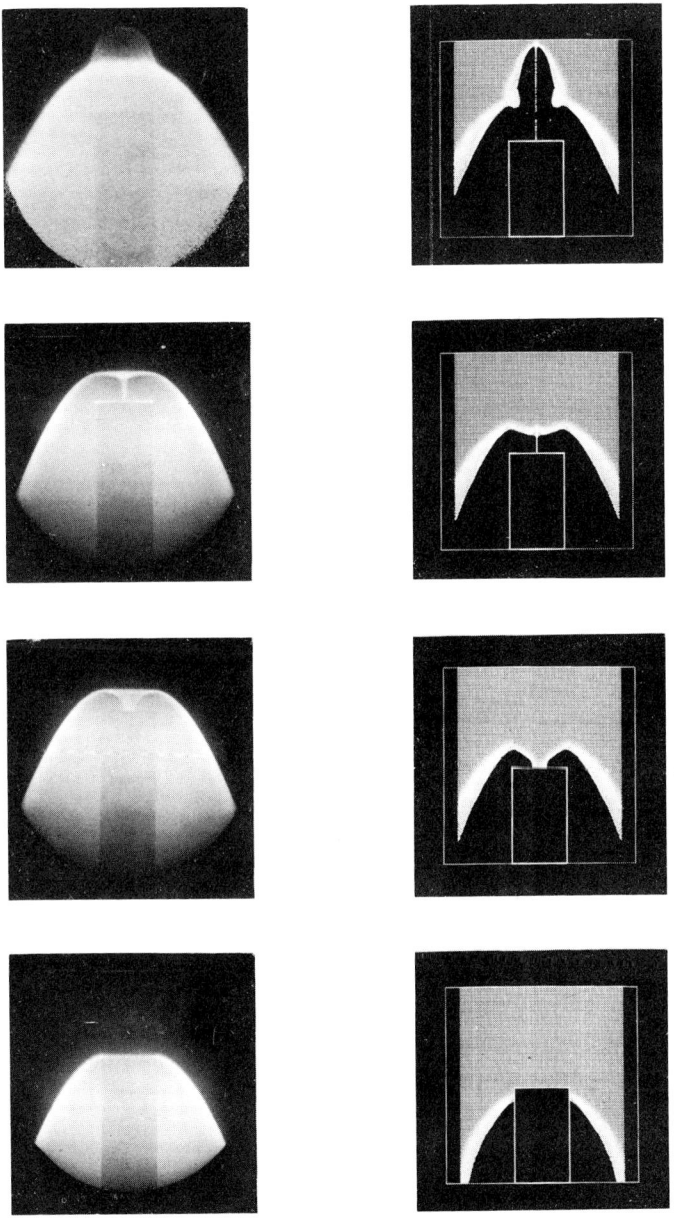

Fig. 2. Time sequences for the plasma focus mode.

the first row of cells. This difficulty could be overcome by using a finer grid in that region as done by Roberts and in the MHD treatment of the puff mode-continuous flow problem below. Second, however is the fact that the temperatures and magnetic field gradients in the focus that are predicted by fluid models seem not to be entirely consistent physically with fluid models motivated by either short mean free paths or small gyro-radii. At this time, the necessary collisionless methods, such as the collisionless PIC method discussed later in this chapter, are not sufficiently advanced nor are computers sufficiently large or fast to treat problems of the physical complexity of the focus problem, but progress is being made in that direction.

B. Continuous Flow Mode of a Coaxial Gun

In the second mode of operation, the plasma gun and the drift space into which it fires are first evacuated, and then a fast valve releases a puff of gas symmetrically around the inner electrode at a point approximately midway between the back and the tip. In this mode of operation, an outer, coaxial cylindrical electrode is necessary to restrict the expansion of the gas. A potential is then applied between the two electrodes, and the discharge develops in such a way that the gas becomes a plasma with a frozen-in magnetic field, B_θ, before a significant plasma flow has occurred. This is seen experimentally. The magnetic field pressure, which at this early time is considerably greater than the plasma pressure, must cause the plasma to expand out through the muzzle of the gun and into the drift space. This is a Marshall gun. If, in addition, the region between the electrodes is sufficiently long, then this burst of magnetized plasma may become a nearly continuous flow for a time. Fluid PIC computations have been done to study the gun operation and a conjecture by Morozov (1968) that continuous flow would produce very large densities and temperatures on axis in a so-called "continuous flow pinch" by adiabatic compression (Butler et al., 1968). In this application, the fluid approximation is a little weaker than for the plasma focus, and the initial distributions of density and magnetization can vary a lot and are usually not well known. The computations are, therefore, started from the following idealized initial conditions. The density is constant throughout the region between the coaxial electrodes and drops to zero at the muzzle. The ratio of B_θ flux to mass is also constant for all flux tubes, i.e., for all simulation particles. (This assures, by the way, that as long as the system is bounded radially, the Alfven velocity is likewise bounded, and this is very helpful.) This latter condition has been called isomagnetic by Morozov (1968) and together with the uniform initial density dictates that the initial B_θ has the vacuum form $B_\theta \sim 1/r$, which is consistent with the experimental method of initiation. Figure 3 shows a time sequence of particle plots starting with these

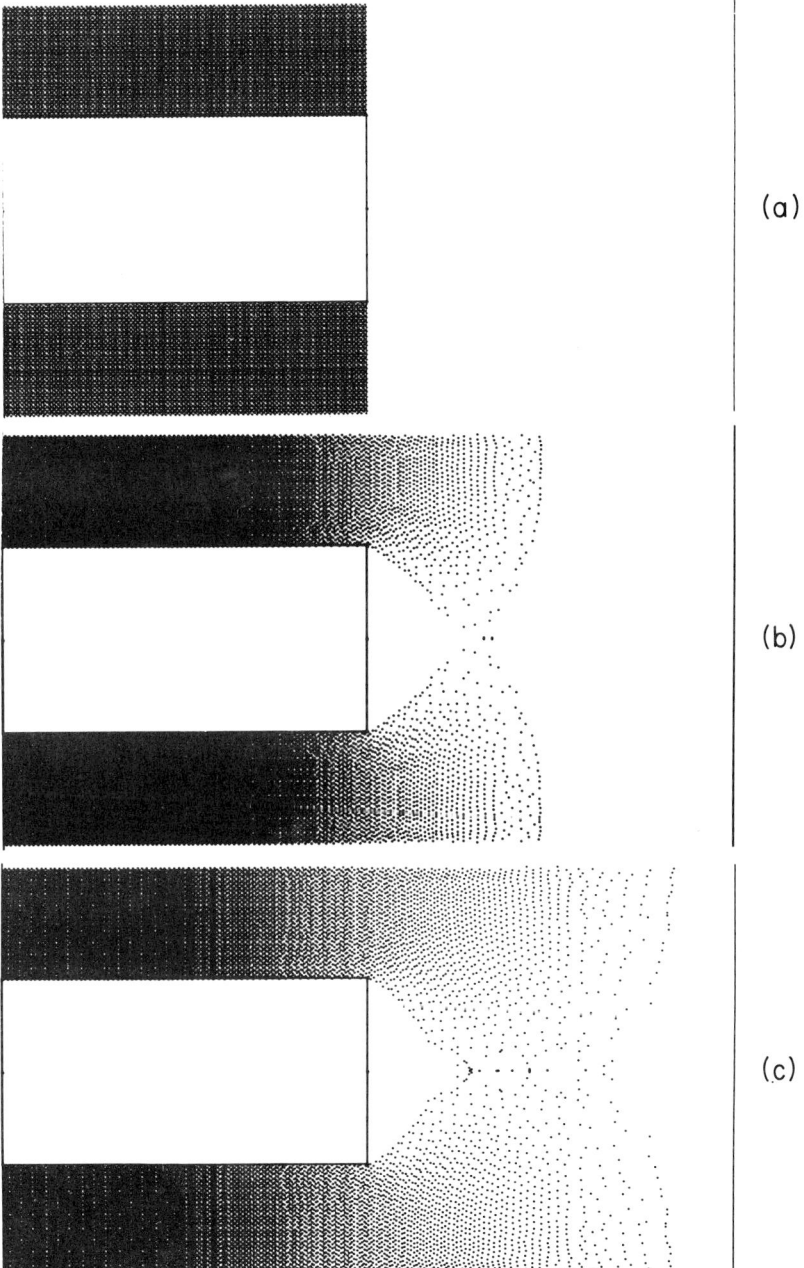

FIG. 3. (a), (b), and (c).

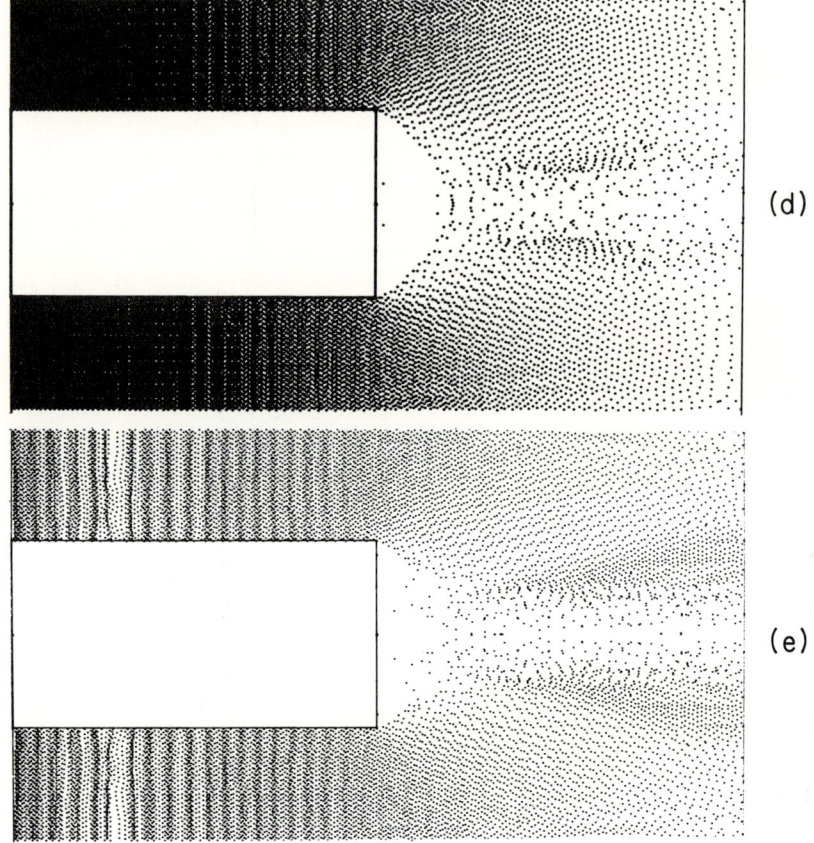

FIG. 3 (d) and (e). Time sequences for the continuous flow mode.

initial conditions, which are everywhere in equilibrium except along the vacuum–plasma interface at the gun muzzle. The basic equations of motion, before differencing, are

$$\rho \frac{du}{dt} = -\frac{\partial}{\partial r}\left(p + \frac{B_\theta{}^2}{8\pi}\right) - \frac{B_\theta{}^2}{4\pi r} \quad (2a)$$

$$\rho \frac{dv}{dt} = -\frac{\partial}{\partial z}\left(p + \frac{B_\theta{}^2}{8\pi}\right) \quad (2b)$$

and

$$\rho \frac{dI}{dt} = -\frac{p}{r}\frac{\partial}{\partial r}(ur) - p\frac{\partial v}{\partial z} \quad (2c)$$

where ρ, p, and I are the plasma density, pressure, and specific internal energy, respectively, and u and v are the r and z velocities. The last term in Eq. (2a) represents the constricting effect of field curvature which is responsible for both the sausage instabilities of z-pinches and the large adiabatic compressions predicted by Morozov. At first the plasma along the vacuum interface expands straight ahead into the drift space, while a rarefaction propagates back into the gun (Fig. 3), and then, only partly because of the constriction effect, the flow begins turning toward the axis. Up to the time when the flux first reaches the axis, the plasma is cold, having only received kinetic energy of ordered streaming from the expansion of the trapped B_θ. When the converging flow reaches the axis, it must produce a shock which converts some of the streaming energy into internal plasma energy. The computational grid contains sufficient cold, magnetized plasma to permit the development of a quasi-continuous flow in the muzzle region. The last frame in Fig. 3, which was taken somewhat later than the first four frames, shows this late time structure. The dominant feature of the flow is a standing shock shaped like a thin cone with its apex on axis about one inner electrode radius in front of the muzzle and its sides extending downstream and outward away from the gun. Figure 4 shows a set of stream vector plots that correspond in time to the particle plots of Fig. 3 and clearly show the refraction of the flow through this shock, which is essentially the same as the *wake shock* behind a blunt-ended projectile in supersonic flow. There is a near vacuum region bounded by the free surface on the inside of the flow extending from the corner of the inner electrode out to the apex of the shock. The shock itself is strongest near the apex and becomes progressively weaker further from the gun, which is why the specific internal energy (or temperature, I, Fig. 5) is higher near the axis where the more strongly shocked streamlines pass. The shock line in Fig. 5 was traced by hand from the last particle density plot in Fig. 3. The two profiles of I which are superimposed were plotted from listings of I, and the inner dashed line marks the division in a dual structure of the shocked region which is reflected in the steps in the I plots. The core is distinctly hotter than the outside. Corresponding to this hot core of the shocked region is a density dip there, which can be seen from the particle plot. Some care is required, however, in interpreting the particle plots near the axis from any such cylindrical PIC treatment, because a particle, which is really a ring encircling the axis, represents a constant amount of total mass, not mass per unit length, so a uniform density would be represented by a simulation particle density that increased linearly with radius from zero on axis. Hence, although there really is a density dip in the hot inner core of the shocked region, some of the apparent dip is due to this geometrical effect. In some fluid applications, this difficulty is eased by giving smaller masses to particles which are initially near the axis.

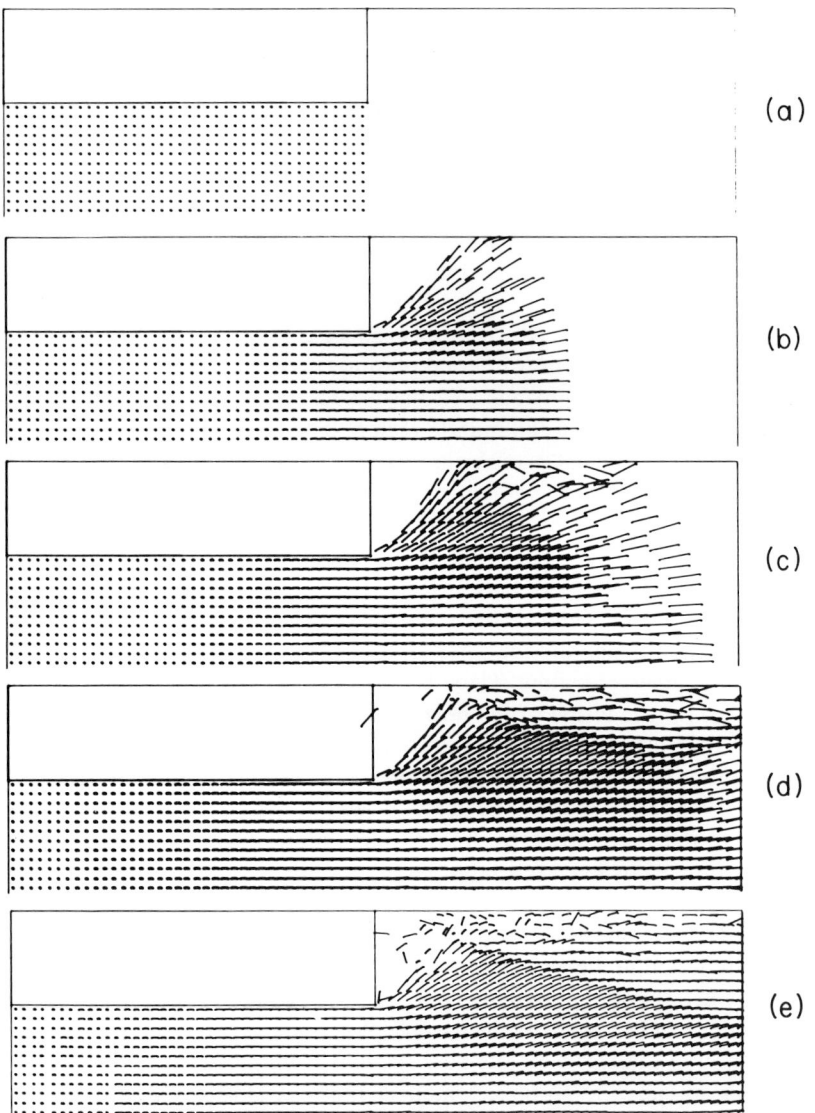

FIG. 4. Stream vector plots of time sequences in Fig. 3.

The physical conclusions from these computations are that the large compressions anticipated by Morozov are not possible with a blunt inner electrode because of entropy production by the wake shock, and the computed flow pattern, including the wake shock, is a qualitatively correct description of similar looking structures which have been seen experimentally in plasma guns by Marshall (1968) and Mawardi (1969).

This is an appropriate place for a few general remarks before going on to collisionless PIC.

Just inside the muzzle in the last particle plot in Fig. 3, the reader will note radial density striations. This is a reflection of the nonphysical oscillations (discussed above) which result from a failure to area weight particle quantities as well as cell quantities in the gun computations shown and would have been eliminated by such area weighting. In this case, however,

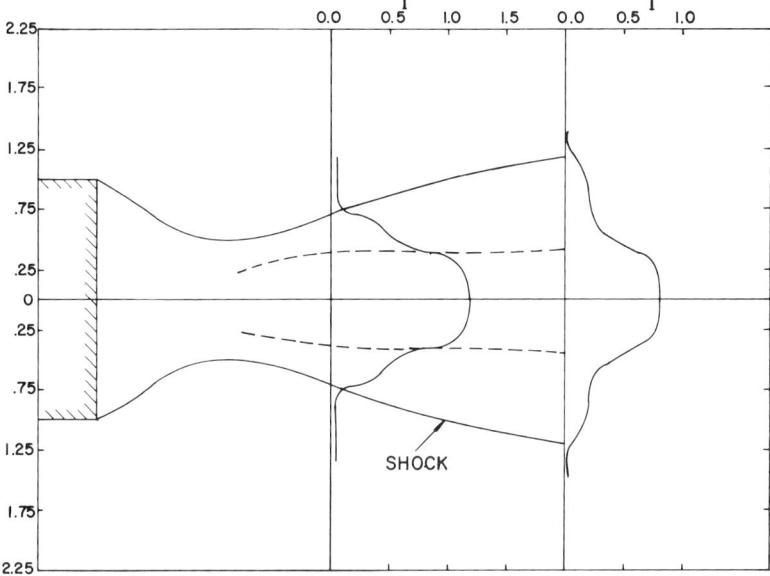

FIG. 5. Shock line of Fig. 3 with temperature (I) profiles.

these striations appeared to have no significant effect on the interesting parts of the flow. In the plasma focus computations where, likewise, only the cell quantities were area weighted, no such striations appeared. This is probably related to the fact that the flow velocity is everywhere zero or very fast relative to the cell grid.

For a given time step and cell size, Eulerian and Lagrangian codes are usually distinctly faster than PIC codes and hence more attractive when computer time is a limitation. However, PIC codes have the following compensating advantages. In addition to being free from Eulerian diffusion and Lagrangian Cell distortion, they are, in general, rather stable and require less special tinkering in changing from problem to problem. Using the cell size as a measure of resolution is a bit pessimistic, because, in some respects, the distribution of particles within a cell can give finer resolution. Finally, a direct plot of simulation particle positions gives a good visual indication of fluid or plasma density, one that is hard to match with an additional graphics package built into a code which computes density directly.

III. Collisionless PIC

According to the collisionless approximation to the behavior of a fully ionized, high-temperature plasma, the velocity and position distribution function of each charged particles species, $f_s(\mathbf{x}, \mathbf{v}, \mathbf{t})$, satisfies the collisionless Boltzmann equation with the Lorentz force,

$$\frac{\partial f_s}{\partial t} + \mathbf{v} \cdot \frac{\partial f_s}{\partial x} + \frac{q_s}{m_s}(\mathbf{E} + \mathbf{v} \times \mathbf{B}/c) \cdot \frac{\partial f_s}{\partial v} = 0 \qquad (3)$$

in which **E** and **B** are obtained from Maxwell's equations with the charge and current densities, ρ and **J**, given by the sums of the moments of the distribution functions.

$$\rho = \sum_s q_s \int d^3v\, f_s, \qquad \mathbf{J} = \sum_s q_s \int d^3v\, \mathbf{v} f_s \qquad (4)$$

Further approximations are made in practice to simplify calculations or to isolate particular effects. It is the purpose of collisionless PIC computations to obtain solutions of this system. In view of the fact that this description of a plasma, in which collisions, correlations, etc., are ignored, amounts to an incompressible flow of a fluid of density f in the phase space $(\mathbf{x}, \mathbf{v})$, the question may be raised: Why use a particle computing model at all? Why not use some conventional fluid model for computing the flow of f in phase space? Indeed, success has been achieved with problems reduced by symmetry to one dimension, i.e., the two-dimensional phase space (x, v_x) by Armstrong et al. (this volume) using a transformed Eulerian method, by Berk and Roberts (this volume) using the Lagrangian method (called "Water Bag"), and, in an heroic effort, Killeen and Rampel (1966) have treated some aspects of Astron behavior with a straight Eulerian method in the phase space of $(r, z, v_r, v_\theta, v_z)$. However, using an Eulerian or Lagrangian method with a formal grid extending over the full phase space has two important limitations. First, many important problems require phase spaces of more than two and up to six dimensions, and the storage and computing time required by the corresponding grids dictates that, if a better way could not be found, then for the time being, many, if not most, such problems simply could not be done. Second, the experience of the last few years in plasma simulation has taught that the nonlinear evolution of plasma instabilities usually involves a lot of sheared—sometimes vortex-like—flow in phase space, which requires a large amount of rezoning for Lagrangian grids and small cell size or smoothing for Eulerian grids. Hence, with increasing time, an increasing number of points are required to define the zone boundaries in the work of Berk and Roberts (this volume), and an increasing number of transform matrix elements are required in the work of Armstrong *et al.* (this volume).

In collisionless PIC, simulation particles are assigned time-varying velocities as well as positions which are computed and stored, and they move just as if they were real charged particles in the plasma. The electric and magnetic fields which accelerate these particles are computed and stored as a regular spatial Eulerian grid, but no velocity grid exists. In almost all applications, each simulation particle effectively represents a large number of real particles and is weighted accordingly in computing cell currents and charges. The author finds it useful, however, to think of the simulation particles in a cell not as a collection of super particles but as a Monte Carlo type representation of $f(\mathbf{v})$ in the cell. Whether or not a particle's contribution to cell charges and currents is apportioned to neighboring cells, according to an area weighting scheme (like Eq. 1 and Fig. 1) in obtaining this effective $f(\mathbf{v})$, depends on the application. The charges and currents obtained by these cell sums can then be thought of as the velocity integrals of Eq. (4) done by the Monte Carlo method, which has been shown to be especially effective for multiple quadratures (Kahn, 1965). By area weighting **E** and **B** and moving the simulation particles by time steps as if they were real particles, Eq. (3) is satisfied to within truncation errors. Numerical solutions to Maxwell's equations with ρ and J from Eq. (4) should then complete the loop and give the desired solutions to the complete collisionless system. But, in view of the particulate nature of the model, the question remains, do the simulation particles interact with one another or with the grid in a way that amounts to binary collisions, introducing a prohibitive amount of truncation error in the form of diffusion and field fluctuations. The answer, in general, is no. Most expectations seem to be too pessimistic in this regard. Understandably pseudocollisional effects in collisionless PIC come closest to being troublesome in applications where the full electrostatic behavior is included, in contrast to fully charge neutralized or quasi-neutral models. The most studied class of problems is that in which the heavy ions are treated as a uniformly distributed, fixed, positive background; the electrons are represented by simulation particles; and Poisson's equation is solved on each time step with the charge density obtained directly by subtracting the simulation particle density in each cell from the uniform positive background value. A worker in this area quickly discovers that area weighting of electron charges helps a lot. Failure to do so manifests itself as poor energy conservation—on the average an increase in total energy—and one possible reason is easily seen. If the electrostatic field on an electron is area weighted, but its contribution to adjacent cell charges is not, then the electron possesses a self-force, i.e., it interacts with the cell grid (for further discussion of related points, see the chapter by Lewis in this volume). A practical way of estimating the strength of the remaining collisional effects in the fully area-weighted scheme is to start a computing run with electrons which are spatially homogeneous and have a distribution of velocities which is stable but nonMaxwellian. Such runs have been done by the author's colleagues at Los Alamos, using the same numbers of particles, cell sizes, time steps, and length of runs used in studies of various velocity space instabilities, with the result that the observed thermalization was insignificant. That is, when the various parameters are chosen to satisfy other error criteria, which are discussed below, these conditions seem to be more than sufficient to suppress velocity diffusion.

Several other multidimensional methods have been proposed for simulation of collisionless plasma, which resemble PIC—most notably, N. Birdsall (this volume) has proposed a scheme called Cloud-in-Cell (CIC) in which the area weighting of a particle is regarded as giving it a finite extent, like a cloud. However, at this time it appears that the differences between collisionless PIC and these other methods are at most conceptual, i.e., related to the way the different authors view the approximations of the numerical model. In practice, all authors seem to be using almost exactly the same equations for production computations.

The same basic PIC format has been applied to a number of different collisionless plasma models. The main reason for different models is the multiplicity of time and length scales of the different physical phenomena in a collisionless plasma. The important length scales are the Debye length, magnetic gyro-radii of electrons and ions (which are very different because of the mass ratio), the electron and ion collisionless skin depths, c/ω_{pe} and c/ω_{pi} (which are also very different because the electron and ion plasma frequencies, ω_{pe} and ω_{pi}, contain the particle masses), and the dimensions of laboratory apparatus. Correspondingly, time scales range from the usually very short electron plasma period and electron gyro-period to the relatively long time required by a typical slow, heavy ion to traverse the apparatus. In discussing fluctuation problems above, we touched on the most microscopic class of problems, unstable plasma oscillations, for which the scales are the Debye length and the electron plasma period. In controlled fusion applications, it is not possible to compute on these scales and treat an entire experiment for the duration of an experimental cycle. Instead, a small piece of the plasma must be treated, using periodic boundary conditions, for the characteristic time of the microscopic phenomena and the result must be translated into transport coefficients for a more nearly continuum model of the entire plasma. At the opposite extreme are problems requiring a treatment of the entire plasma because, for example, a gross instability may break up the plasma into a few big lumps. In some such problems, the important collisionless physics is that of the ions, which exhibit persistent pressure anisotropies and have large gyro-radii, while the microscopic motion of the electrons may be ignored except in so far as they produce a fluid-like pressure which acts on the ions through some form of quasi-charge neutral, i.e., vanishing Debye length, approximation (Shonk and Morse, 1968).

We shall discuss an example of the first type, a small piece of plasma treated microscopically, and an example of the second type, a simulation of an entire plasma with a model which suppresses some of the most microscopic detail. In both cases, a bit more emphasis will be placed on useful numerical tricks than is usually done in plasma physics journal articles.

A. The Two-Beam Instability

In this section we discuss comparable one, two, and three-dimensional simulations of the electrostatic two-beam instability in collisionless plasma. The ions are treated as a uniform, fixed, positive background, and the initial electron distribution is spatially uniform with a velocity distribution consisting of two equal drifting Maxwellian beams.

$$f_0(\mathbf{v}) = (n_0/\pi^{3/2}v_0^3) \{\exp - [(v - u\hat{x})/v_0]^2 + \exp - [(\mathbf{v} + u\hat{x})\}]^2\} \tag{5}$$

No generality is lost by taking the x-axis parallel to the drift velocities, $\pm u$. A sufficiently large drift velocity, u, for a given thermal velocity, v_0, is known from linear theory to support the unstable growth of electrostatic modes for which the perturbed electrostatic potential has the form

$$\varphi \sim \exp i(\mathbf{k} \cdot \mathbf{x} - \omega t) \tag{6}$$

and when such modes are unstable, the largest growth rates, i.e. values of Im ω, belong to modes with pure k_x. These growth rates are largest for intermediate values of k and fall to zero for $k \to 0$ and above a finite cutoff value of k.

Because of simplicity and this fact that the fastest growing modes can be seen in the one-dimensional, (x, v_x), projection of the full three-dimensional problem, and also because of a limited class of physical experiments for which the 1-D description is sufficient, the 1-D problem has received a lot of study, including recently some full nonlinear simulations by Armstrong (this volume), Berk and Roberts (this volume) and Morse and Nielson (1968, 1969). (See also the sheet model work by Dawson in this volume). Some of the results of these 1-D simulations, including strong persistent single-mode structure, seem to conflict with basic assumptions of plasma turbulence theory, but it has also been widely suspected that these 1-D results are dominated by the symmetry of the restriction to x-dependence: hence the motivation to extend this work to two and three dimensions and to do it in such a way that the effect of the transitions can be clearly seen.

In order to do this, a particular three-dimensional $f_0(v_x, v_y, v_z)$, Eq. (5), and a particular periodicity length, L, are chosen. The three-dimensional simulation is done in a cube of length L with periodic boundary conditions on the electron motion and the electrostatic potential $\varphi(x, y, z)$ and starting with a spatially uniform electron distribution f_0. The two-dimensional simulation is done in an (x, y) square of length L with periodic boundary conditions and starting with the $f_0(v_x, v_y)$ velocity distribution obtained by integrating Eq. (1) over v_z. The one-dimensional simulation is done in x alone with periodicity length L and the $f_0(v_x)$ distribution obtained by integrating Eq. (1) over v_y and v_z.

The electrons are treated by collisionless PIC. On each time step electron positions are used to compute new area-weighted electron cell charges. These are subtracted from the background ion charge and the charge differences, ρ, for each are used in solving Poisson's equation,

$$\nabla^2 \varphi = -4\pi\rho \qquad (7)$$

on the grid of cell centers, subject to periodic boundary conditions. For problems of more than one dimension, the author's colleagues have used successive over-relaxation and a direct method (Buzbee et al., 1969) (in 1-D Poisson's equation is easy to solve exactly) and have found that, in spite of using a very tight convergence criterion, the relaxation results were inferior to results obtained from the direct method—total energy conservation was worse—in addition to taking more computimg time. The reason for this is not well understood at this time, but it seems to be a consequence of a requirement for greater accuracy in problems in which small relative charge separations are treated explicitly. By contrast, relaxation methods have worked quite well for computing **E** and **B** fields in quasi-neutral models and in the charge neutral finite β example below. From the new cell values of φ, new cell center values of the electric field, **E** are obtained by simple centered differencing.

The particle velocities and positions are kept in a table which is often stored on discs or external core and buffered into main memory in small blocks. When the computation comes to a particle, the indices of the nearest neighbor cells are determined, and their **E** field values are area-weighted to obtain the field at the particle position. (It should be called length, area, or volume weighting for the two, four, or, eight nearest neighbors in one, two, or three dimensions, respectively, but that is excessively wordy). Because of this procedure, the cell **E** fields must be randomly accessible unless the particle table can be continuously re-ordered in correspondence to particle position. If the particle positions used in solving Poisson's equation are, say, the $t = 0$ values, then the velocities stored with them are actually $t = -\Delta t/2$, where Δt is the time step, and the particle positions and velocities are advanced by the simple scheme

$$\mathbf{v}_{+1/2} = \mathbf{v}_{-1/2} + E_0 \Delta t, \qquad x_{+1} = x_0 + \mathbf{v}_{+1/2} \Delta t \qquad (8)$$

where $\mathbf{E}_0$ is the field at $t = 0$.

This system is time centered and is, moreover, time reversible, all of which happens so naturally for purely electrostatic problems that one may not think much about it. However, suppose that there were also a static magnetic field, **B**, present so that $\mathbf{E}_0$ were replaced by $\mathbf{E}_0 + \mathbf{v}_0 \times \mathbf{B}$. $\mathbf{v}_0$ is not immediately available, but a Runge–Kutta-like scheme which is consistent to second order in Δt results from substituting the first order estimate $\mathbf{v}_0 \simeq \mathbf{v}_{-1/2} + \mathbf{E}_0 \Delta t/2$.

It is possible to go even further by insisting that the difference scheme be reversible, i.e., $\mathbf{v}_0 = (\mathbf{v}_{+1/2} + \mathbf{v}_{-1/2})/2$, and still obtain a usable, explicit algebraic relation for $\mathbf{v}_{+1/2}$ in place of the first of Eqs. (8). In the plane perpendicular to **B** this results in

$$\mathbf{v}_{+1/2} = \mathbf{v}_{-1/2} + \frac{\Delta t}{1 + (\Delta t/2)^2 B^2} \left[\mathbf{E} + \mathbf{v}_{-1/2} \times \mathbf{B} + \frac{\Delta t}{2} (\mathbf{E} \times \mathbf{B} - \tfrac{1}{2} \mathbf{v}_{-1/2} B^2) \right] \qquad (8a)$$

If **B** is not static and must be determined self-consistently from the plasma current, the situation gets considerably worse. An implicit but nonreversible scheme has been used by Shonk and Morse (1968) for such a problem, but reversible schemes are difficult to devise short of going to the full electromagnetic wave equations.

The reason for this digression on time-centering is that in practice the particle transport must at least be time-centered to order $(\Delta t)^2$, and reversible schemes are enough better that they should always be used if possible. This has been borne out in two-dimensional simulations of electrostatic beam instabilities of the kind considered here, but with the addition of a static magnetic field normal to the direction of counter-streaming. This work by Nielson and Morse showed a steady increase in total energy when the $\mathbf{v} \times \mathbf{B}$

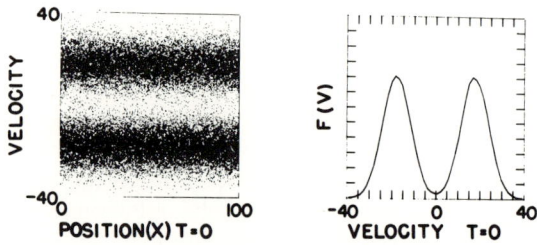

FIG. 6. Plots of (a) $f_0(v_x)$, and (b) initial (x, v_x) with $L = 100\,\lambda_D$.

term was not properly centered. (The author recalls that Oscar Buneman was the first to insist on reversibility in particle-type plasma simulation.)

Figure 6 shows (a) $f_0(v_x)$, and (b) an initial (x, v_x) phase space plot of a random subset of simulation particles for the two equal warm beam distribution, with $L = 100\lambda_D$. Figure 7 shows diagnostics from (a) 1-D, (b) 2-D, and (c) 3-D comparison runs of this case, which was done in 1-D by Morse and Nielson (1968, 1969) with greater L and showed formation, coalescing, and long-time persistence of BGK modes as seen here in Fig. 2. Each row in

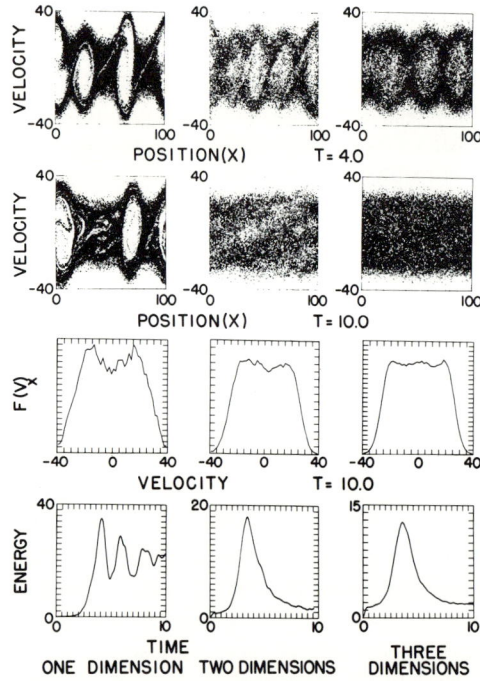

FIG. 7. Diagnostics of 1-D, 2-D, and 3-D comparison runs.

Fig. 7 shows two (x, v_x) phase plots, the first at field energy saturation time and the second at the final time of 10 plasma periods (*not* $10\omega_p^{-1}$), followed by $f(v_x)$ at final time and the time history, $\varepsilon(t)$ of the total electrostatic field energy per unit volume. In all three runs, the field energy first rises to the thermal level and then rises unstably until saturation, at first exponentially at the rate of the fastest linear mode and with most of the field energy in the corresponding $|E_\mathbf{k}|^2$ (Fourier mode energy plots were computed but are not shown here). This concentration of energy in the fastest growing modes is a natural consequence of growing a few e-folding times from a low, uniform, initial noise spectrum (Morse and Nielson, 1969). Extensive error checks which have been performed (Morse and Nielson, 1968, 1969) indicate that the number of simulation particles must be great enough to reduce the initial thermal level far below the maximum or saturation level of $\varepsilon(t)$ and correspondingly result in the preponderance of the energy ε appearing in the $|E_\mathbf{k}|^2$'s of these intermediate wavelength modes with the largest growth rates, in contrast with the $1/k^2$ thermal noise spectrum. If these criteria are not satisfied, then correct collisionless results do not simply sit on top of the thermal noise level but are instead destroyed by the noise. The height of the early thermal $\varepsilon(t)$ plateau increases in going from 1-D to 3-D here, because of an increasing need for economy in number of simulation particles; the 1-D run used 20,000 particles, which was more than enough; the 2-D run used 80,000; and the 3-D run used 332,750, which was just barely adequate. The number of simulation particles required could be reduced by reducing L, but because of the restriction on the number of unstable modes, the $L = 100\lambda_D$ used here is already a bit small. A time step of .04 plasma periods was used here as in Morse and Nielson (1968, 1969) for the reasons given in the error analysis there.

The 1-D, 2-D, and 3-D cell grids were 64, 64 × 64, and 32 × 32 × 32, respectively. The reader who wishes to do simulation work should note that the physical length, L, and the number of cells in L must be considered very carefully. If the object of the simulation is an understanding of plasma turbulence, then L should *at least* be large enough to contain several wavelengths of the linearly most unstable mode. The nonlinear behavior of one or two wavelengths may be interesting but tells little about turbulence. Using more cells both increases the density of Fourier modes in k-space, which is important in some turbulence applications, and provides shorter wavelength modes. In the latter connection, recent studies have shown that short wavelength modes with relatively small field energies, $|E_\mathbf{k}|^2$, are considerably more important in determining some nonlinear development than the relative energies might suggest.

The most obvious physical change occurs between 1-D and 2-D. In 1-D, the phase space eddies coalesce until one eddy remains in the length L and ε decreases after the overshoot to a level consistent with this stationary structure.

If L is greater, further coalescing occurs, and ε levels off at a correspondingly lower value, but one eddy remains, and ε does not go back down to the thermal level. In 2-D the eddies start to form as seen in Fig. 7b at saturation time but do not form completely and have virtually disappeared by the final time. Correspondingly, $\varepsilon(t)$ saturates at a lower level in 2-D than in 1-D (note the scale changes on the plots) and then falls quickly to about the initial thermal level. Note that saturation comes successively sooner in time in going from 1-D to 2-D to 3-D, presumably at least in part because of the successively higher initial noise levels. In 3-D, these changes from 1-D become more pronounced than in 2-D, enough so that quantitative comparisons with related experiments would require the 3-D results. The partially formed eddies are less distinct than in 2-D, and the saturation value of ε is still lower. The simulation particles shown in the (x, v_x) phase plots for 2-D and 3-D are taken from a slab restricted in y to reduce the effect of finite k_y modes in blurring the appearance of the eddies.

The final time $f(v_x)$ plots in Fig. 7 which are generated by a simple histogram procedure without any smoothing, are smoother for the higher dimensional runs because of the improved statistics. All three $f(v_x)$ curves are plotted on the same velocity scale of ± 40 Debye lengths per plasma period and show that the 2-D and 3-D curves are essentially unchanged from $f_0(v_x)$ in the tails, i.e., outside ± 30, while in 1-D the tails are broadened by the persistent large amplitude eddy structure. This same eddy structure gives the final time 1-D $f(v_x)$, a definite dip in the middle, while in the higher dimensional runs, which are spatially uniform by this time, $f(v_x)$ is essentially flat on top, especially in 3-D.

So far, nothing has been said about simulation particle initialization. In fluid PIC, the initial particle positions are usually placed on some kind of regular checkerboard pattern with the same periodicity as the grid and with density variations taken up by different particle masses. Initial velocities, when they are required, are cell quantities. By contrast, collisionless PIC simulation particles must have a continuous distribution of initial velocities and sometimes a variable initial density which is consistent with the velocity distribution according to some self-consistent, stationary solution to the collisionless equations. In almost all applications the velocity distributions used are Maxwellian, sometimes with different thermal spreads in different directions and sometimes with a spatially dependent mean drift velocity. Since the purpose of starting from such equilibria is usually the study of instabilities, the initial conditions should contain small departures or perturbations from the ideal equilibrium, preferably not orthogonal to any of the possible unstable modes. Also the continuous simulation particle mass spread of fluid PIC should be dropped in most applications because the high degree of intermingling of particles from different parts of the grid would make the visual interpretation of particle plots difficult. These needs are fulfilled by choosing random numbers for each velocity or coordinate of a particle and mapping then from the interval (0, 1) onto the range of velocities or coordinates through functions or tables. Maxwellian distributions are generated with a functional mapping involving logarithms, sines, and cosines. Where needed, the drift is computed as a function of position and added on, and anisotropy is obtained by multiplying different velocity components by an appropriate factor. It is also customary to cut off the high velocity tails at a few thermal units to eliminate a few energetic particles that would not interact properly with the grid. Spatial distributions when not uniform, as in rigid rotor distributions, for example, can be obtained from a random number weighting table that is generated by a separate initialization code. Random loading has several advantages. In addition to loading in a spectrum of initial perturbations, it avoids systematic errors caused by a particular checkerboard pattern, and it allows a check on sensitivity to initial conditions and other errors in the model through the simple expedient of picking another set of random numbers and running again.

Returning to explicit electrostatic problems like those considered above in which the ions are represented by a continuous background, there is an important exception to the initialization procedure described here. If initial electron positions are chosen randomly, the corresponding charge fluctuations cause unacceptably large initial **E** fields. Hence the electrons must be positioned uniformly and the perturbations left to the velocity initialization. Note that this does not apply to two species electrostatic problems in which electrons and ions are both treated as particles, because there one can simply position ions and electrons together in pairs to avoid initial charge density fluctuations. In either case, within about a plasma period the electrostatic field energy develops the thermal fluctuation level discussed above and seen in Fig. 8.

In order to suppress this fluctuation level and its interference with the desired physical results with fewer simulation particles, J. Byers has recently proposed a more uniform initial loading of velocities as well as coordinates, which is called "quiet start." It appears that this scheme can correctly represent some nonlinear effects before the initially uniform phase space loading becomes distorted and larger fluctuations develop.

B. Axisymmetric Plasmas Confined by a Variable Magnetic Field

As an example of the second type of simulation, which treats an entire confined plasma, and to show the reader that simulation can handle more than just electrostatic problems with static magnetic fields, we will now briefly discuss a very different collisionless model. The model is two-dimensional in the sense that all quantities depend on r and z but not on θ. Therefore, in the usual stability notation, only $m = 0$ modes can be seen. These include the rotational, tearing, mirror, and fire hose modes which linear theory predicts will grow unstably starting from finite β, collisionless and approximately z-independent equilibria of the Astron or θ-pinch types (by finite β it is meant that there is a magnetic field present which is not so strong that it cannot be distorted by available plasma pressure). The electromagnetic fields are entirely described by the θ component of the magnetic vector potential, $A_\theta(r, z, t)$, which means that the magnetic field components B_r and B_z and the inductive electric field E_θ are computed, but B_θ and all electrostatic fields are assumed to be zero. The basis for these assumptions, where applicable, is that cold electrons can move along magnetic field lines between maxima and minima of disturbances or by end shorting to exactly neutralize the plasma, and that these neutralizing currents are not significant compared to the usual diamagnetic θ current, J_θ. These approximations can be good or poor and must be considered separately with the applications. Only one particle species is explicitly considered. In the Astron context, they are considered the injected electrons. In the high temperature θ-pinch context, where electrons are found experimentally to be relatively cold, they are considered the hot ions. The current, J_θ, is computed directly from this one warm particle species, and A_θ is computed from J_θ. This procedure, while not exact because of the above approximations, is a Hamiltonian system and is exact when density and fields are stationary, with or without z-dependence. The inaccuracy of the model when these quantities are in flux depends on the rapidity of the time dependence as well as the particular application. At worst, this plasma model may be thought of as consisting of two species with equal particle mass but opposite charge. In that case, the simulations become exact calculations with an approximate model instead of the converse. The particles have all three velocities in addition to the two coordinates, so the phase space is five-dimensional. In most applications, the initial particle distribution is a Maxwellian rigid rotor independent of z. This class of rotating Maxwellian equilibria, which have $B_r = 0$, r-dependent density, and $B_z \neq 0$, are explained in detail in Proceedings (1967), Dickman et al. (1968. 1969), along with discussions of the dimensionless scaling used. The initial thermal spread in the z-direction is made larger or smaller than the perpendicular (i.e., r and θ) temperature to drive hose or mirror instabilities respectively. Working in scaled units, the current in a cell is given by the sum over particles in the cell

$$J_{\theta c} = Q \sum_{i=1}^{Nc} \frac{v_{\theta i}}{r_i} \qquad (9)$$

where N_c is the number of particles in the cell, Q reflects the number of real particles per simulation particle, and r_i is the particle radius. The $1/r_i$ is required by the fact that a simulation particle is a ring of constant total charge and therefore has more charge per unit length when at a smaller radius. v_θ for each particle is obtained directly from the conservation of its canonical angular momentum,

$$P_\theta = r(v_\theta + A_\theta) = \text{constant} \tag{10}$$

which is computed and stored initially. Then

$$J_{\theta c} = Q \sum_{i=1}^{Nc} \frac{1}{r_i} \left(\frac{P_{\theta i}}{r_i} - A_{\theta i} \right) \tag{11}$$

A great simplification in computing is achieved by making the statistical assumption that the particles in each cell are distributed uniformly over the cell in such a way that r_i's and $A_{\theta i}$'s in Eq. (11) may be replaced by the cell *center* values, r_c and $A_{\theta c}$. Then Eq. (3) becomes

$$J_{\theta c} = \frac{Q}{r_c} \left(\frac{1}{r_c} \sum_{i=1}^{Nc} P_{\theta i} - N_c A_{\theta c} \right) \tag{11a}$$

After the sums in Eq. (11a) are performed, A_θ is computed from the scaled field equation which is

$$\frac{\partial^2 A_\theta}{\partial z^2} + \frac{\partial}{\partial r} \left(\frac{1}{r} \frac{\partial}{\partial r} r A_\theta \right) = -J_\theta \tag{12}$$

When Eq. (11a) is substituted into the conventional second order differenced form of Eq. (12) and that is converted into successive over relaxation form, the resulting interative scheme for the cell center values of A_θ is

$$A_\theta(J, K) = \frac{W}{D(K) + [QGN(J, K)/r(K)]}$$

$$\times \left(G^2 A_\theta(J+1, K) + G^2 A_\theta(J-1, K) + B(K) A_\theta(J, K+1) \right.$$

$$+ C(K) A_\theta(J, K-1) + \frac{QG}{r^2(K)} \sum_{i=1}^{N(J, K)} P_i \right)$$

$$+ (1 - W) A_\theta(J, K)$$

$$B(K) = 1 + \frac{1}{2K-1}$$

$$C(K) = 1 - \frac{1}{2K-1}$$

$$D(K) = r\left[\frac{G^2+1}{2} + \frac{1}{(2K-1)^2}\right] \tag{13}$$

$$G = \Delta r/\Delta z$$

where J and K are r and z cell center indices, respectively, and new values are used on the right-hand side where available. Boundary conditions on A_θ are imposed during the relaxation. In practice, linear extrapolations from the last two time steps are used to obtain starting values of $A_\theta(J, K)$ for the iterative solution of Eq. (13). If the time step, Δt, is sufficiently small to give acceptable truncation errors in the rest of the problem, then these extrapolated values are excellent starting guesses. Any comparison of iterative methods with other methods such as Fourier transforms is incorrect if it does not consider this point. In practice, a convergence criterion of one part in 10^3 is achieved in 10 to 20 iterations with an SOR factor of $W \simeq 1.7$. When sufficient particles are used to hold statistical fluctuations to an acceptable level, these iterations take about 15% of the total computing time. After $A_\theta(J, K)$ is obtained, then B_r and B_z are computed from $\mathbf{B} = \nabla \times \mathbf{A}$ or

$$B_r = -\frac{\partial A_\theta}{\partial z}, \qquad B_z = \frac{1}{r}\frac{\partial}{\partial r}(rA_\theta) \tag{14}$$

by centered differences. Up to this point, the particle positions are known at the current time and the velocity components V_r and V_z are known at the last half time-step. Next the particles are transported with the equations of motion

$$\begin{aligned}
V_{\theta,1} &= P_\theta/r_0 - A_\theta \\
V_{r,+1/2} &= V_{r,-1/2} + [V_{\theta,0} B_z + (V_\theta^2{}_{,0}/r)]\,\Delta t \\
V_{z,+1/2} &= V_{r,-1/2} - V_\theta B_r \,\Delta t \\
r_{+1} &= r_0 + V_{r,+1/2}\,\Delta t \\
z_{+1} &= z_0 + V_{z,+1/2}\,\Delta t
\end{aligned} \tag{15}$$

Taken in this order, these equations are time centered and, in fact, reversible (a convenient result of the conservation of P_θ) and, therefore, give truncation errors of order $(\Delta t)^3$.

The values of A_θ, B_r, and B_z which appear in Eq. (15) are obtained for the position of every particle separately by area weighting between the four nearest cell centers. It should be noted that as long as $Q \ll 1$ it has not been found necessary to use area weighting to compute the sums in Eq. (13) for $J_{\theta c}$ and N_c.

Figure 8 shows a sequence of (r, z) particle plots from a fire hose instability run. The bottom edge is the cylindrical center axis, the top edge is an

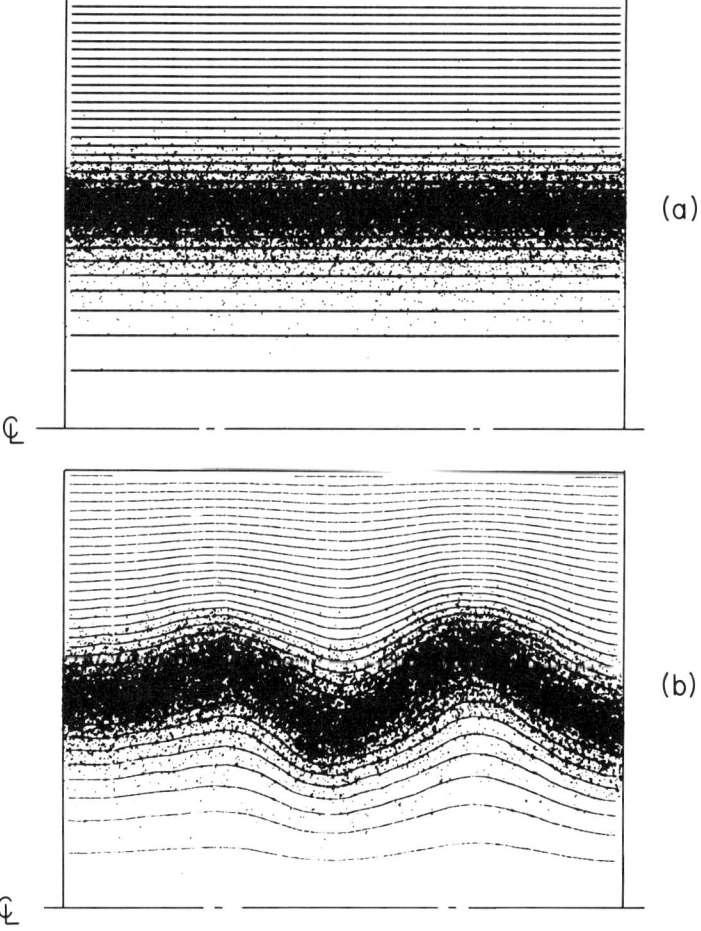

FIG. 8. (a), and (b).

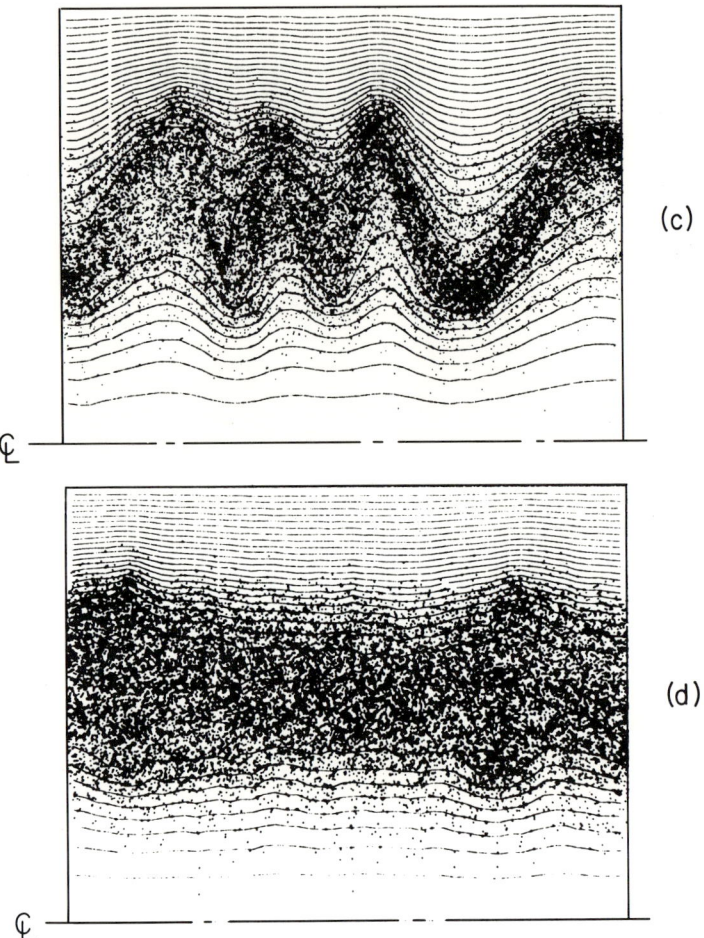

FIG. 8. (c), and (d). (r, z) particle plots from a fire hose instability run.

electrically conducting, i.e., $A_\theta = $ constant, boundary and reflective conditions are applied to both A_θ and particle motion at the ends. The superimposed lines are level contours of the flux function rA_θ, which are therefore magnetic field lines. The initial B_z field reverses between inside and outside of the plasma sheet, with a zero in the middle. The system is unstable because the initial z temperature, T_z, is twenty-five times the perpendicular temperature $T_\perp$. This run used 2×10^4 simulation particles and a cell grid 25 (in r) × 100 (in z). The time step was approximately 1/60 of a gyro-period of a particle in the vacuum magnetic field. The physical result of this was that the distortion of the plasma and field broke the z-symmetry and thereby caused T_z and $T_\perp$

to become more nearly equal. Subsequently, the plasma settled back to a z-independent sheet with a greater thickness in r than initially because of increased $T_\perp$. Applications of this model to mirror and tearing modes can be found in Dickman et al. (1968, 1969). An application to end loss from a θ-pinch can be found in Tuck (1968).

REFERENCES

AMSDEN, A. A. (1966). Los Alamos Report LA-3166.
BUTLER, T. D., COOK, J. L., MORSE, R. L. (1968). Paper 6 in Proc. APS Top. Conf. Numerical Simulation of Plasma (Sept., 1968). Available as Los Alamos Report LA-3990.
BUTLER, T. D., HENINS, I., JAHODA, F., MARSHALL, J., and MORSE, R. L. (1969). Phys. Fluids **12**, 1904.
BUZBEE, B. L., GOLUB, G. H., and NIELSON, C. W. (1969). Los Alamos Report LA-4141, LA-4288, and SIAM J. Numer. Anal. (to be published).
DICKMAN, D., MORSE, R. L., and NIELSON, C. W. (1968). Paper C2 in Proc. APS Top. Conf. Numerical Simulation of Plasma (Sept., 1968). Available as Los Alamos Report LA-3990.
DICKMAN, D., MORSE, R. L., and NIELSON, C. W. (1969). Phys. Fluids **12**, 1708.
KAHN, H. (1965). "Mathematical Methods for Digital Computers" (Rolsten, A., and Wilf, H. S., eds.). John Wiley, New York.
KILLEEN, J., and RAMPEL, S. J. (1966). J. Comp. Phys. **1**, 29.
MARSHALL, J. (1968). Private communication.
MAWARDI, O. (1969). Private communication.
MOROZOV, A. I. (1968). Soviet Physics- Tech. Phys. **12**, 1580.
MORSE, R. L. (1968). Los Alamos Report LA-3844-MS.
MORSE, R. L., and NIELSON, C. W., (1967). Paper A4 in Proc. APS Top. Conf. Numerical Simulation of Plasma (Sept., 1968).
MORSE, R L., and NIELSON, C. W. (1969). Phys. Fluids **12**, 2418; and Phys. Rev. Letters, **23**, 1087.
PROCEEDINGS (1967). Proc. APS Top. Conf. Pulsed, High-Density Plasmas (Sept., 1967). Available as Los Alamos Report LA-3770.
SHONK, C. R., and MORSE, R. L. (1968). Paper C3 in Proc. APS Top. Conf. Numerical Simulation of Plasma (Sept., 1968). Available as Los Alamos Report LA-3990.
TUCK, J. L. (1968). Paper K-5 in Third. Intern. Atomic Energy Agency Conf. Plasma Phys. and Controlled Nuclear Fusion Research, Novosibirsk, U.S.S.R (Aug., 1968).

Finite-Size Particle Physics Applied to Plasma Simulation

CHARLES K. BIRDSALL*, A. BRUCE LANGDON, H. OKUDA

ELECTRICAL ENGINEERING and COMPUTER SCIENCE DEPARTMENTS
UNIVERSITY OF CALIFORNIA,
BERKELEY, CALIFORNIA

I. Introduction 241
II. General Theory for a Model of Finite-Size Particles 243
   A. Small Amplitude Longitudinal Plasma Oscillations 244
   B. Potential Energy around a Shielded Test Cloud; Static Force 247
III. Scattering Cross Section 248
   A. Relation to Design of "Collisionless" Computer Simulations 250
IV. Fokker–Planck Drag and Diffusion Coefficients for a Cloud Plasma 252
V. The Effect of Using a Spatial Grid 254
VI. Historical Note 256
VII. Conclusions 257
   References 257

I. Introduction

PLASMA SIMULATION USING ION and electron particles is capable of reproducing all of the electric and magnetic interactions of real plasmas. A complete simulation, of course, would run into the obvious difficulty of processing anywhere near the number of ions and electrons in the plasma. Hence, one uses a reduced number of particles each with a larger charge; this results in increasing the fluctuations about the mean (say, of density, $\sim 1/\sqrt{n}$) or the particle noise (quite accurately called shot noise). Another difficulty is the nonphysical interaction of the particles with the spatial and temporal grids used for computing such quantities as densities, potentials, fields, and forces, which also results in an increase in noise (called grid noise). Both shot and grid noise can easily be so large as to mask the desired simulation.

Computationally, one can reduce the effects of shot or grid noise by increasing the number of particles or by using finer grids. These improvements have been made in one-dimensional simulations, are being pushed in two dimensions, and are presently impracticable in three. We are stuck with the physics of, and noise due to, too few particles and too coarse grids; hence, we must understand the physics and find suitable means for noise reduction.

* Also, Consultant, Lawrence Radiation Laboratory, Livermore, California

Physically, electrons and ions are point particles for most of plasma physics. Some interparticle interactions occur at short range in short times, producing effects at short wavelengths and high frequencies; fortunately, the details of such interactions are of relatively little interest in plasmas. The important effects are the *collective, long range, interactions* which produce wavelengths much larger than interparticle spacings and frequencies with periods much longer than particle crossing times. Such physics suggests introducing some form of *smoothing* of the forces at short range. The answers have been both numerical and physical, generally evolving (as given later in Section VI) into the concept of use of *finite size particles*. The physics of a plasma with these extended particles, or clouds, is the subject of this chapter; it is pertinent, as clouds in the form of slabs (1–D), rods (2–D) or cubes (3–D) are presently being used in plasma simulation in virtually all plasma laboratories.

The clouds are tenuous so that they may freely overlap and may have any convenient shape and density variation, such as uniform or Gaussian. Some properties of clouds can be noted before presenting the details of the theory. Suppose the density of a cloud, given by the shape factor, $S(x)$, is as shown in Fig. 1a for a cloud of uniform density with radius R. Let this cloud be a test particle at $x = 0$ in a two- or three-dimensional plasma of similar clouds. Then the potential near it will be as sketched in Fig. 1b, with no singularity at the origin, as would occur for a zero-size particle (ZSP, $R \to 0$). The force on a cloud at x due to the test particle is sketched in Fig. 1c, again without singularity. We see that not only are the divergences at short range removed as desired, but also that the potential and force at long range can be much reduced, the latter occurring for $R > \lambda_D$, the Debye length. Simple criteria for giving these advantages are: (i) the clouds should overlap many times, satisfied by making $N_c \gg 1$, where N_c is the number of clouds per cloud volume ($N_c = nR^3$); (ii) the radius R should be large enough to mask unwanted interactions at short range, but small enough to allow the interactions sought at long wavelengths; (iii) $2R \gtrsim \Delta x$ the cell size of a grid (if a grid is used), in order to reduce grid noise.

The initial finite-size-particle theories included some confirmations, for gridless systems (Dawson *et al.*, 1968) and gridded (Birdsall *et al.*, 1968). The concept of clouds is unifying between such systems and appears to be the simplest interpretation of other smoothed interactions. More recent theory for gridded systems (Langdon, 1969) has added support to this concept. One general conclusion is that those gridded systems which are good are very similar to gridless systems with an appropriately chosen interaction, which may then be regarded as Coulomb interactions among appropriately chosen clouds.

This chapter presents some theory for a gridless system and for gridded

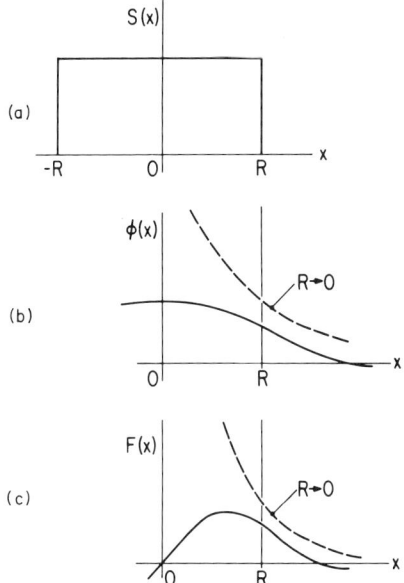

FIG. 1. (a) Shape factor, $S(x)$, giving the density variation of a cloud of uniform density of radius R, representing a slab in one dimension, cylindrical rod in two, or sphere in three. $S(\mathbf{x})$ need not be isotropic, but in what follows, it generally is.

(b) Sketch of potential $\phi(x)$, inside and outside the cloud of (a), compared with that for a point particle ($R = 0$). The cloud is among other clouds in a warm plasma so that there is shielding.

(c) Sketch of the force on a cloud at x due to a test cloud at 0. The potential and force, hence other properties (such as scattering cross sections) for other cloud shapes, such as Gaussian, $S(x) = \exp - x^2/2R^2$ are quite similar in character and magnitude, if appropriate changes are made in defining the cloud radius, e. g., $R_{\text{uniform}} \cong 2R_{\text{gaussian}}$.

systems, as sampled and condensed from Langdon and Birdsall, (1969), Okuda and Birdsall (1969), Wong and Birdsall (1969).

II. General Theory for a Model of Finite-Size Particles

The theory for interactions of a system of clouds can be obtained rather directly from the existing theory for point particle interactions. The charge density of a cloud whose center is at the origin is changed from $q\delta(\mathbf{x})$ to $qS(\mathbf{x})$ where q is the total charge. If $\mathbf{J}_p$ and ρ_p are the current and charge densities for a system of point particles, then the densities $\mathbf{J}_c$ and ρ_c, for a system of clouds whose centers coincide with the point particles, are

$$\begin{pmatrix} \rho_c(\mathbf{x}, t) \\ \mathbf{J}_c(\mathbf{x}, t) \end{pmatrix} = \int d\mathbf{x}' S(\mathbf{x} - \mathbf{x}') \begin{pmatrix} \rho_p(\mathbf{x}', t) \\ \mathbf{J}_p(\mathbf{x}', t) \end{pmatrix}. \tag{1}$$

These cloud densities are to be used in Maxwell's equations to find the fields **E** and **B**. The Lorentz force on a cloud with (center) position **x** and velocity **v** is then

$$\mathbf{F}(\mathbf{x}, \mathbf{v}, t) = q \int d\mathbf{x}' \, S(\mathbf{x}' - \mathbf{x}) \left(\mathbf{E}(\mathbf{x}', t) + \frac{1}{c} \mathbf{v} \times \mathbf{B}(\mathbf{x}', t) \right). \quad (2)$$

As these relations are convolutions, they take on a simple form when Fourier transformed:

$$\begin{pmatrix} \rho_c(\mathbf{k}, t) \\ \mathbf{J}_c(\mathbf{k}, t) \end{pmatrix} = S(\mathbf{k}) \begin{pmatrix} \rho_p(\mathbf{k}, t) \\ \mathbf{J}_p(\mathbf{k}, t) \end{pmatrix}, \quad (3)$$

$$\mathbf{F}(\mathbf{k}, \mathbf{v}, t) = qS(-\mathbf{k}) \left(\mathbf{E}(\mathbf{k}, t) + \frac{1}{c} \mathbf{v} \times \mathbf{B}(\mathbf{k}, t) \right), \quad (4)$$

where

$$S(\mathbf{k}) = \int d\mathbf{x} \, S(\mathbf{x}) \exp(-i\mathbf{k} \cdot \mathbf{x}). \quad (5)$$

One can now re-do most of plasma theory by the replacement of the charge q by $qS(k)$. For example, the dielectric tensor for a uniform Vlasov gas of clouds and, therefore, dispersion relations, are unchanged except that the plasma frequency squared, ω_p^2, must everywhere be multiplied by $S^2(k)$. However, some care must be used; for example, with a uniform imposed magnetic field, the correct k to use in the zero order cyclotron frequency, $\omega_{co} = qS(k)/mc$, is 0, so that ω_{co} is unchanged from the point particle value.

We now present two applications to make clearer the transition to cloud theory.

A. Small Amplitude Longitudinal Plasma Oscillations

The longitudinal dielectric function for a cloud plasma is

$$\varepsilon(\mathbf{k}, \omega) = 1 + S^2(k) \frac{\omega_p^2}{k^2} \int \mathbf{k} \cdot \frac{\partial f_0}{\partial \mathbf{v}} \frac{d\mathbf{v}}{\omega - \mathbf{k} \cdot \mathbf{v}}, \quad (6)$$

with the standard symbol definitions. Space-time dependence $\exp(i\mathbf{k} \cdot \mathbf{x} - i\omega t)$ is assumed, and the usual remarks about analyticity apply. For a Maxwellian velocity distribution with no drift and thermal velocity $v_t = [\frac{1}{3}(v^2)_{\text{average}}]^{1/2}$ the dielectric function becomes

$$\varepsilon(\mathbf{k}, \omega) = 1 - \frac{1}{2}\left(\frac{S\omega_p}{kv_t}\right)^2 Z'\left(\frac{\omega}{\sqrt{2}kv_t}\right), \tag{7}$$

where Z is the plasma dispersion function of Fried and Conte (1961).

The dispersion relation for longitudinal waves is $\varepsilon = 0$. Exact ω-k diagrams are given in Fig. 2 for small clouds ($R = 0.1\,\lambda_D$) and in Fig. 3 for **large**

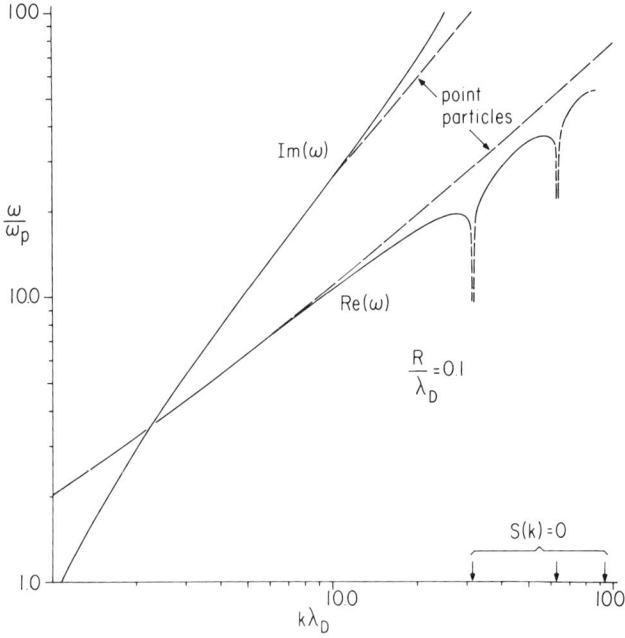

FIG. 2. Dispersion diagram, frequency, ω, versus wavenumber, k, for a uniform warm Maxwellian plasma of small uniform density clouds, $R = 0.1\,\lambda_D$. The agreement with point-particle plasmas is excellent, well into the region where damping dominates, with significant differences starting at about $kR = 1$. The singularities occur at very short wavelengths, where one, two, or three wavelengths fit into a cloud.

clouds ($R = 2\,\lambda_D$), both of uniform density. It is instructive to examine analytically where and why these differ from the point particle results, as are given in the following paragraphs.

When $kv_t/S\omega_p = k\lambda_D/S \ll 1$, we can use the large argument asymptotic expansion for Z' and find an approximate solution for ω which shows weak

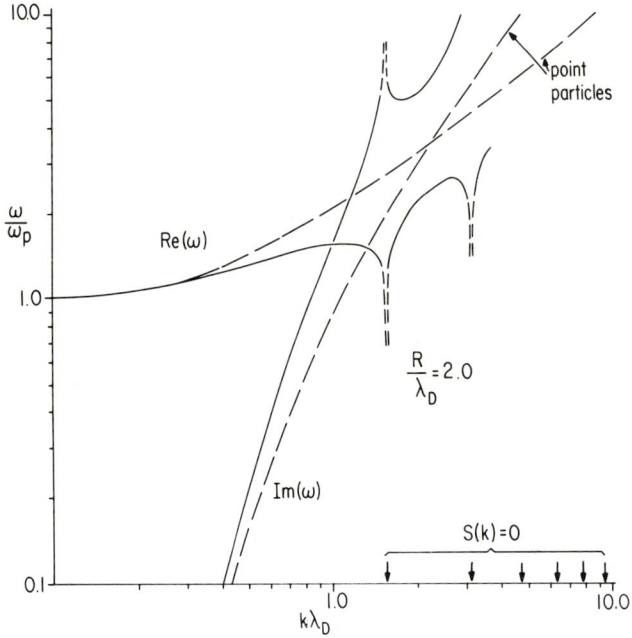

FIG. 3. Dispersion diagram like Fig, 2, but for thick clouds, $R = 2\,\lambda_D$. Again, differences show up past $kR \cong 1$, which now occurs at $k\lambda_D = 0.5$, indicating changes in the physics at long wavelengths from that of point particles and, hence, caution in using large radius clouds.

Landau damping of the oscillations (Jackson, 1960), as

$$(\text{Re } \omega)^2 \approx S^2(k)\omega_p^2 + 3k^2 v_t^2 \tag{8}$$

$$\text{Im } \omega \approx -\sqrt{\frac{\pi}{8}} S \omega_p \left(\frac{S}{k\lambda_D}\right)^3 \exp\left(-\frac{1}{2}\left(\frac{S}{k\lambda_D}\right)^2 - \frac{3}{2}\right) \tag{9}$$

With small clouds ($R < \lambda_D$) and weak damping, we have $kR < k\lambda_D \ll 1$, so that $S \approx 1$. Thus the weakly damped oscillations are little affected as we would hope and as confirmed by Fig. 2.

For large clouds ($R \gtrsim \lambda_D$) and weak damping, Re ω can be very different from the point-particle result when $kR \gtrsim 1$, as shown in Fig. 3.

When $k\lambda_D/S \gtrsim 1$, the oscillations are strongly damped. Thus, in a cloud plasma, the onset of damping as k increases occurs when $k\lambda_D \sim 1$ *or* when kR is large enough which can be seen in both figures. For some cloud shapes, such as those with uniform density ($S(k) = \sin kR/kR$), $S \to 0$ for finite k.

Where this happens, the asymptotic solutions for heavy damping show that Im $\omega \to -\infty$, Re $\omega \to 0$ as already shown in Figs. 2 and 3. Of course, when S is very small, the electric interaction is disabled, the clouds free-stream, and the time evolution will differ from $\exp(-i\omega t)$.

B. Potential Energy around a Shielded Test Cloud; Static Force

The potential around a test cloud with center position $\mathbf{x}_0 + \mathbf{v}_0 t$ moving in an otherwise-uniform stable Vlasov gas in steady-state is, in the linear approximation,

$$\phi(\mathbf{k}, t) = \frac{4\pi q S(k)}{k^2 \varepsilon(\mathbf{k}, \mathbf{k} \cdot \mathbf{v}_0)} \exp(i\mathbf{k} \cdot (\mathbf{x}_0 + \mathbf{v}_0 t)). \tag{10}$$

Let us fix the test cloud at the origin in a thermal plasma and look at the potential energy of a cloud, $V(\mathbf{k}) = qS(\mathbf{k}) \phi(\mathbf{k})$. We find

$$V(\mathbf{k}) = \frac{4\pi q^2 S^2(k)}{k^2 \varepsilon(\mathbf{k}, 0)} = \frac{4\pi q^2 S^2}{k^2 + S^2/\lambda_D^2}. \tag{11}$$

An example of $V(\mathbf{x})$ for uniform density clouds is given in Fig. 4.

In the small-cloud case, $R \ll \lambda_D$, we may replace S by 1 in the denominator,

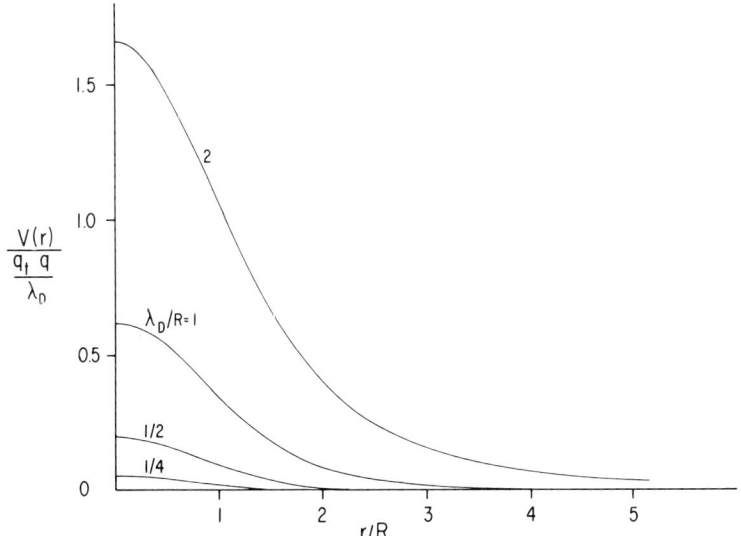

FIG. 4. Potential energy in the vicinity of a uniform density spherical test cloud of charge q_t in a warm plasma of similar clouds. Note the finite value of $V(0)$ and its rapid decay as R is increased.

since where S is significantly different from unity, $k^2 \gg S^2/\lambda_D^2$. Thus $V(\mathbf{x})$ is approximately the point particle result convolved twice with $S(\mathbf{x})$, and is therefore different from the point particle result only at distances $r \lesssim R$, where it is the unshielded potential energy of clouds instead of point particles. The maximum energy $V(\mathbf{x} = 0) \sim 4\pi q^2/R = (\theta/N_D)\lambda_D/R$, where $N_D \equiv n\lambda_D^3$, may become less than the thermal energy, θ, allowing the clouds to pass through each other easily and suppressing large-angle collisions.

For large clouds, $R > \lambda_D$, the potential is drastically different due to the fact that the plasma can maintain charge neutrality over distances $r > R$ and λ_D; the plasma neutralizing charge is inside the test cloud instead of outside as before. This shows up as follows: for $k < k_c$, $V(\mathbf{k})$ is close to $4\pi q^2 \lambda_D^2$, then drops to zero as $4\pi q^2 S^2/k^2$, when k is increased above k_c, where k_c is defined by $k_c^2 \lambda_D^2 = S^2(k_c)$. If S drops rapidly to zero for $k > R^{-1}$, then $k_c \sim R^{-1}$. A graph of $V(k)$ will be a peak of width $\sim R$. From this and the general properties of Fourier transforms, we know that $V(\mathbf{x})$ has a radius of about $k_c^{-1} \sim R$, and that there may be some oscillations in $V(\mathbf{x})$ due to the sharp cutoff of $V(\mathbf{k})$; these properties are seen in Fig. 4. Furthermore, since $\int d\mathbf{x}\, V(\mathbf{x}) = V(\mathbf{k} = 0) = 4\pi q^2 \lambda_D^2$ is unchanged while the radius is increased, it must be that $V(\mathbf{x} = 0)$ is decreased in magnitude, to $\sim 4\pi q^2 \lambda_D^2/R^3 \sim \theta/N_c$, where $N_c \equiv nR^3$ is a measure of the amount of overlapping of the clouds. For $N_c \gg 1$, large clouds readily pass through one another without large deflection. Therefore, N_c in a cloud plasma plays a role similar to that of N_D in a point-particle plasma.

The corresponding static force, $\mathbf{F} = -\nabla V$, is shown in Fig. 5. The maximum of $\mathbf{F}$ at $r \approx R$, as well as $\mathbf{F}$ for all r, drops off almost as fast as $(\lambda_D/R)^3$ in three dimensions, with decay approximately as $(\lambda_D/R)^2$ and (λ_D/R) in two and one dimensions. Hence, increasing R from zero rapidly decreases the force and scattering, as worked out in the next section.

III. Scattering Cross Section

In the previous sections, we used the Vlasov equation and ignored collisions. The justification for this neglect in a real plasma is that $N_D \gg 1$, a condition difficult to meet in two-dimensional simulation and economically impracticable in three-dimensional simulation. Hence, we must ask for the magnitude of collision frequency or cross section of clouds relative to that of points. We will first do this using the static force of the last section, in three dimensions, looking for the momentum transfer scattering cross section, σ, given by

$$\sigma = 2\pi \int (1 - \cos\theta) p\, dp, \tag{12}$$

where p is the impact parameter and θ is the angle of scatter.

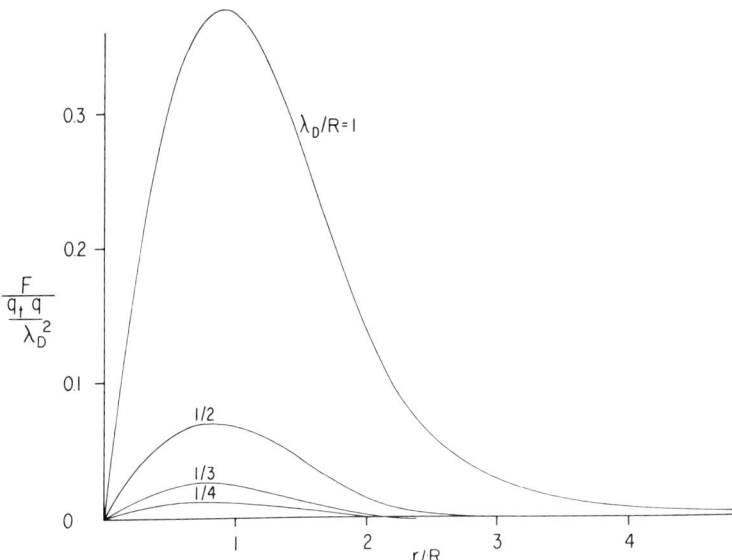

FIG. 5. Force F on a cloud at r in a warm plasma due to a uniform density spherical cloud at $r = 0$. The maximum value of F (and roughly the whole curve) decays roughly as $(\lambda_D/R)^3$, so that both short- and long-range interactions are rapidly reduced as R is increased. The curves for two and one dimensions are similar, with the power 3 changed to 2 and 1.

For a point-particle plasma, there is little difference between the transport coefficients and hence the scattering cross sections derived from the Coulomb force law plus Debye cutoff, or from the shielded Coulomb force law without cutoff. For the Coulomb $(1/r^2)$ force law, the scattering cross section is given by

$$\sigma_{\text{points}} = \frac{4\pi q^4}{(m_r v_r^2)^2} \ln\left[\frac{m_r v_r^2 \lambda_D}{q^2}\right] \approx \frac{4\pi q^4}{(m_r v_r^2)^2} \ln \Lambda = \frac{4\pi q^4}{(m_r v_r^2)^2} \ln 9N_D \quad (13)$$

where $\Lambda = m_r v_r^2 \lambda_D/q^2 = 9N_D$, and $m_r v_r^2$ was replaced by its average value $3kT_e$ which is valid for ion–electron and electron–electron collisions, m_r is the reduced mass; v_r is the relative velocity.

For cloud scattering, the potential energy is well behaved analytically, with no singularity, but is not a simple function of r; hence, the integration for σ was done numerically. The results are shown in Fig. 6, for clouds of uniform density.

The scattering cross section for clouds is much smaller than for points, if R/λ_D is sufficiently large. This last point is emphasized in Fig. 7, showing

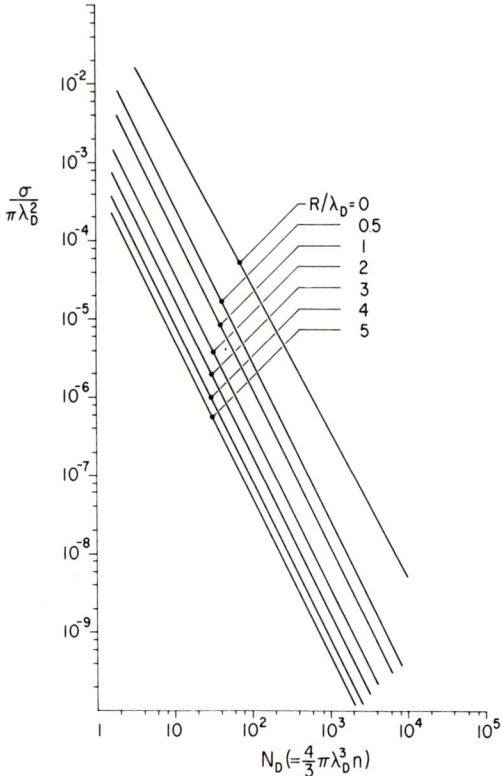

FIG. 6. Scattering cross section for collisions calculated from the static force in a warm plasma of spherical uniform density clouds, hence, valid primarily for clouds with velocity less than the thermal velocity. The point for simulation is that the increase in cross section that occurs as N_D is reduced from that of the real plasma to that practicable on the computer can be offset in part by increasing the radius R of the cloud.

$\sigma_{\text{clouds}}/\sigma_{\text{points}}$, with results also shown for two-dimensional uniform density clouds (versus line charges). The conversion to Gaussian clouds with $S(r) = \exp(-r^2/2R^2)$ is roughly $R_{\text{cloud}} = R_{\text{uniform}} \approx 2R_{\text{gaussian}}$.

A. Relation to Design of "Collisionless" Computer Simulations

Consider a two-dimensional plasma with size $100\lambda_D$ by $100\lambda_D$. The collision frequency for point (line) particles is

$$\nu = \overline{n v \sigma} \approx n v_t \sigma \approx \frac{\pi \omega_{\text{pe}}}{16 N_D}, \tag{14}$$

where $N_D = \pi n \lambda_D^2$. If we require that $v/\omega_{pe} \lesssim 1/1000$, then for point particles, we need $N_D \sim 200$, so that the total number of particles, N, is 600,000. If we ask $v/\omega_{pe} \lesssim 1/1000$ for a cloud plasma and use $N_D = 20$, then, using Fig. 7, we need $R/\lambda_D = 1.3$ and only 60,000 clouds; using $N_D = 2$, then we need $R/\lambda_D \sim 6$ and about 6000 clouds.

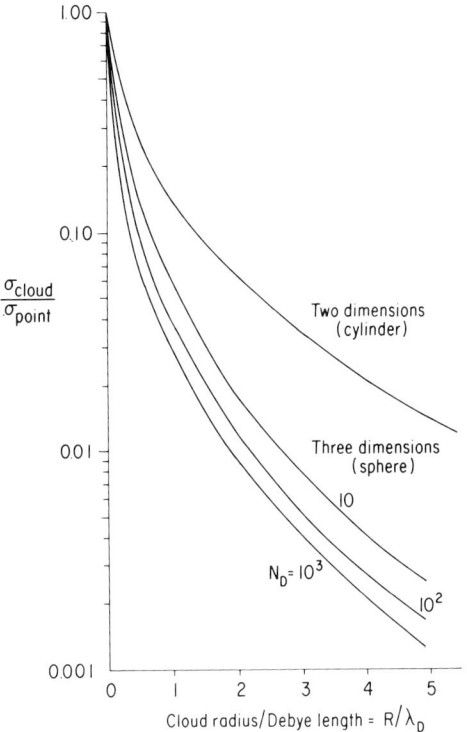

FIG. 7. Comparison of the cross section of clouds with those of points as a function of cloud radius, emphasizing the large reduction available for the initial increase in cloud radius beyond zero. Same model as in Fig. 6.

For a three-dimensional plasma with dimensions $100\lambda_D \times 100\lambda_D \times 100\lambda_D$, the collision frequency for point particles is

$$\frac{v}{\omega_p} \approx \frac{1}{27} \frac{1}{N_D} \ln(9N_D) \qquad (15)$$

If we require $v/\omega_{pe} < 1/1000$, then, for point particles, $N_D = 300$ and $N = 72$ million particles. For clouds, $v/\omega_{pe} \lesssim 1/1000$, using $N_D = 30$, requires $R/\lambda_D = 1.2$, $N = 7.2$ million; $N_D = 1$ requires $R/\lambda_D > 4$, $N = 240,000$.

These reductions by 10 and 100 in the number of particles required to reduce effects of collisions help make simulation of large size plasmas more practicable, where exact dynamics are used. An example of the usefulness of the reduction is a recent experiment by Morse and Nielson (1969). They used $N = 332{,}750$ clouds in a three-dimensional plasma, $100\lambda_D$ on a side, in a $32 \times 32 \times 32$ grid. These parameters make $n\lambda_D{}^3 \approx 0.3$, such that if the particles were points, they would not constitute a plasma. However, their particles may be viewed as clouds with $N_c \approx n(\Delta x)^3 \approx 10$, so that one may expect plasma-like behavior. Now applying Eq. (15) and Fig. 7, one finds $(\nu/\omega_p)_{\text{cloud}} \approx 1/240$. As their problem ran to $T \approx 30$ plasma periods, a time of $\nu T \approx 1$, collisional effects may not be wholly negligible. Furthermore, with $\lambda_D \approx 0.3\,\Delta x$, grid noise (Sec. V) may also play a role.

IV. Fokker–Planck Drag and Diffusion Coefficients for a Cloud Plasma

The previous results, using the static force, are applicable mostly to the plasma particles with $v < v_{\text{thermal}}$. We now improve the results by going to the kinetic equation of Balescu and Lenard, applicable to all v.

We consider first a three-dimensional, one-component, spatially-homogeneous plasma without macroscopic field. We single out a test cloud and find the evolution of the distribution function of the test cloud due to the collisions with the background plasma. We assume that the velocity distribution of the background plasma is Maxwellian and does not change with time due to the interaction with the test cloud. The Balescu–Lenard kinetic equation for a test cloud distribution function, $f(\mathbf{p}, t)$ can be written as

$$\frac{\partial f}{\partial t} = \frac{\partial}{\partial p_i}\left(D_{ij}\frac{\partial f}{\partial p_j}\right) + \frac{\partial}{\partial p_i}(A_i f), \qquad i, j = x, y, z, \qquad (16)$$

where the diffusion coefficients are,

$$D_{ij}(\mathbf{p}) = 2q^4 n \int \frac{|S(\mathbf{k})|^4 \, k_i k_j}{k^4 |\varepsilon(\mathbf{k}, \mathbf{k}\cdot\mathbf{v})|^2}\,\delta(\mathbf{k}\cdot\mathbf{v} - \mathbf{k}\cdot\mathbf{v}')F(\mathbf{p}')\,d\mathbf{k}\,d\mathbf{p}', \qquad (17)$$

and the drag coefficients are,

$$A_i(\mathbf{p}) = 2q^4 n \int \frac{|S(\mathbf{k})|^4 \, k_i k_j}{k^4 |\varepsilon(\mathbf{k}, \mathbf{k}\cdot\mathbf{v})|^2}\,\delta(\mathbf{k}\cdot\mathbf{v} - \mathbf{k}\cdot\mathbf{v}')\frac{\partial F(\mathbf{p}')}{\partial p_j'}\,d\mathbf{k}\,d\mathbf{p}', \qquad (18)$$

and the summation over repeated subscripts i, j is assumed. $F(\mathbf{p})$ is a three-dimensional Maxwell velocity distribution for the bulk of the plasma and is given by $F(p) = \exp(-p^2/2m^2 v_t^2)/(\sqrt{2\pi} m v_t)^3$, and $\varepsilon(\mathbf{k}, \mathbf{k}\cdot\mathbf{v})$ is the dielectric constant of the plasma, given earlier by Eq. 7.

The magnitudes of $A_\parallel$, $D_\parallel$, $D_\perp$ are governed mainly by N_D for point particles or R/λ_D for clouds. For small v/v_t ($v/v_t \leq 1$), $A \sim v/v_t$, which allows us to infer $A \sim \nu p$, where ν is a collision frequency for a Langevin-type equation, as implied in the earlier static force collision calculations. The ratio

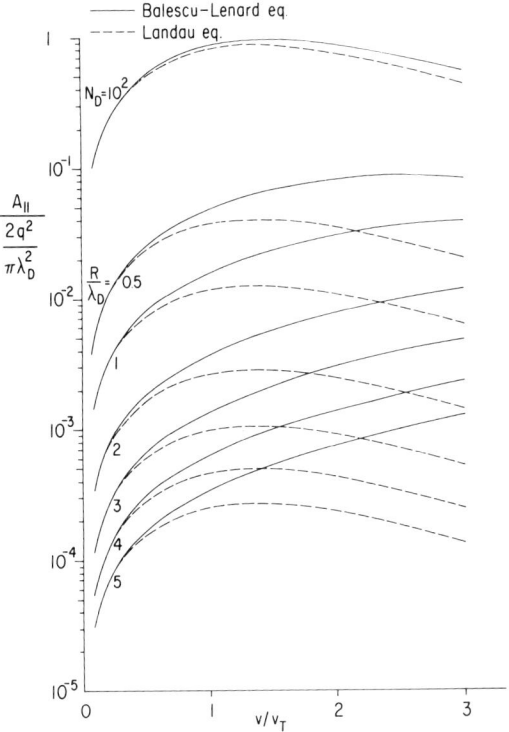

FIG. 8. Drag coefficient, $A_\parallel$, from kinetic equation, valid for all velocities, for Gaussian density spherical clouds as a function of the test cloud velocity. The $N_D = 10^2$ curve is for point particles. At low velocities, where $A_\parallel \sim v$, $A_\parallel$ may be considered proportional to a collision frequency and, hence, the cross sections given in Fig. 6; the reductions due to increase in R are roughly the same. At higher velocities, the reductions are not as large. $A_\perp = 0$. $\perp$ and $\parallel$ refer to directions relative to the velocity of the test cloud. $A_\parallel$ must vanish as $v \to \infty$, so that some maxima are located beyond $v = 3v_t$.

of cloud to point particle cross sections (Fig. 7) was found to be of the same order as the ratio of $A_\parallel$'s given here (Fig. 8). However, the reduction of $A_\parallel$ with the increase of cloud size also depends on the velocity of the cloud. For example, at $v/v_t = 0.5$, $A_\parallel (R/\lambda_D = 0, N_D = 10^2)/A_\parallel (R/\lambda_D = 5) \approx 5 \times 10^3$, while at $v/v_t = 3$, this ratio is about 2.5×10^2.

V. The Effect of Using a Spatial Grid

In most simulations, we set up a grid in x space, and define field quantities only at the grid points. However, the particle position still varies continuously. Various algorithms are used to relate field quantities defined only on the grid and particle quantities which are continuous. It is desirable to know what changes might be introduced in the physics due to the nonphysical grid.

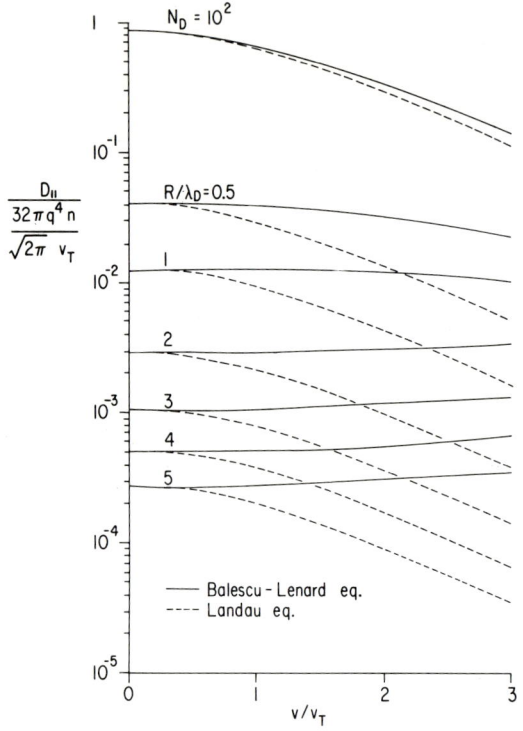

FIG. 9. Diffusion coefficient, $D_\parallel$, for the clouds described in Fig. 8. There is an appreciable decrease in diffusion as the cloud size is increased initially from zero, with some velocity dependence.

We will now discuss the algorithm used in CIC (Birdsall and Fuss, 1969) and plasma PIC (Morse and Nielson, 1968), in one dimension for the sake of clarity. In both methods, the charges may be viewed as clouds with elements of each charge found in more than one cell; each element of the cloud charge is assigned by linear interpolation to the nearest grid point, both in finding the source terms for the field equations and in finding particle forces from the fields. Let the equations for the fields be

$$\nabla^2 \phi = -4\pi\rho \to \phi_{i+1} - 2\phi_i + \phi_{i-1} = -4\pi\rho_i \Delta x^2,$$

$$E = -\nabla\phi \to E_i = -\frac{\phi_{i+1} - \phi_{i-1}}{2\Delta x},$$

where $E_i = E(i\Delta x)$, etc. The force on a cloud is the sum of the forces on all its elements associated with the several grid points.

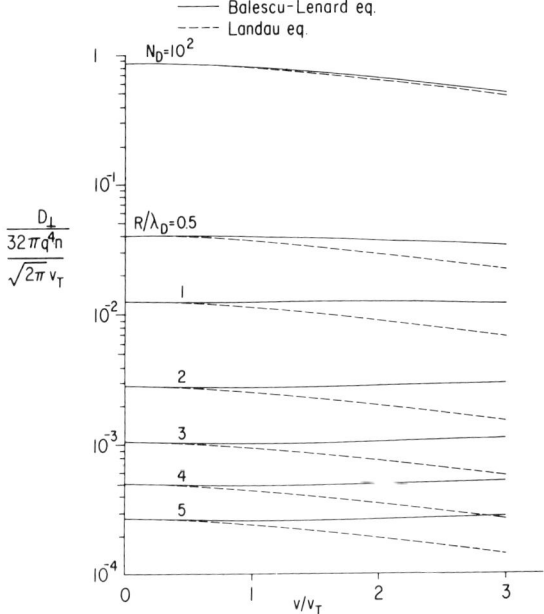

FIG. 10 Diffusion coefficient, $D_\perp$, for the clouds described in Fig. 8. Again, there is reduction, but roughly no velocity dependence.

Introduction of a grid presents a new problem. The interaction force of a particle at x_1 on a particle at x_2, $F(x_1, x_2)$, may depend not only on the separation of the particles but also, nonphysically, on their position in the grid. The nonphysical part can be visualized by doing two simple experiments with uniform density clouds. First, keep the charge at x_1 fixed and vary x_2; for $R = 0$ (NGP), F varies stepwise; for $2R > 0$ (CIC, PIC), F is continuous ($\partial F/\partial x_2$ varies stepwise). Second, keep the charge separation, $x \equiv x_2 - x_1$, constant and vary the mean position $\bar{x} \equiv (x_1 + x_2)/2$; for $R = 0$, F again varies stepwise; for $R > 0$, F again varies continuously and with much less fluctuation than for $R = 0$. Sketches of F may be constructed readily, or see Figs. 3 and 4 in Birdsall *et al.* (1968).

These experiments suggest separating the force into two parts, $F = \bar{F} + \delta F$, where $\bar{F}$ is the averaged part invariant under displacement,

$$\bar{F}(x_1, x_2) = \bar{F}(x_1 - x_2) = (1/\Delta x) \int_{\Delta x} F(\bar{x} - x/2, \bar{x} + x/2) \, d\bar{x},$$

and δF is the nonphysical force due to the grid.

If the effects of δF may be neglected, then the system can be analyzed by the methods discussed earlier. For example, in the dispersion relation one must multiply $(S^2)_{\text{gridless}}$ by $(\sin k\Delta x / k\Delta x)$; some early measurements on a cold plasma showed this effect (Birdsall *et al.*, 1968). Thus, one role of the grid is to smooth the interaction, which we have argued is beneficial.

A more detailed formulation of the grid force problem (Langdon, 1969) shows that the principal consequence of the grid force δF is that perturbations at wavevector k are coupled to perturbations at wavevectors differing from k by integer multiples of $2\pi/\Delta x$. This coupling is not important when $\lambda_D \gg \Delta x$.

VI. Historical Note

In early simulations with a grid, the methods used to relate particle quantities to grid quantities were chosen more or less on the basis of computational simplicity. For example, the density of particles at a grid point was taken to be the number of particles in the cell, divided by the cell volume, about that grid point; this was done in the fluids particle-in-cell method, PIC, by Harlow and Evans (1957) and Harlow (1957, 1964, p. 324). This nearest-grid-point assignment, NGP, applied to plasmas, achieved some smoothing such as eliminating forces between two charges of opposite sign in the same cell (Hockney, 1966), but made for a jump in density and force as a particle passed a cell-boundary. The next step was to weight the particle density and force by linear interpolation to the grid points nearest the particle, as done in the cloud-in-cell method, CIC (Birdsall and Fuss, 1969, which evolved from a suggestion by J. A. Byers, about 1964) and in an adaptation of the area weighting of velocities in PIC (Harlow, 1964, p. 329) to plasma density and force calculations by Morse and Nielson (1968). These interpolations removed the jump in density and force of NGP and lead to appreciable reduction in noise (Birdsall and Fuss, 1969).

Without a grid, parallel attempts at smoothing were made, for example, to reduce the error due to the jump in force when zero-size particles (ZSP) crossed. One choice was to assume that the charge density was uniform between charge coordinates (Hess, 1961); a related choice was the use of a force taper, saying that the simulation charge was a cylindrical cloud (Mihran and Yu, 1963). Dawson *et al.* (1968) attenuated the short wavelength components of a Fourier series expansion of the field. These choices allowed particles to slip past each other relatively smoothly.

All of these steps played a role in the evolution of the cloud concept and prompted the development of the physics of clouds presented here.

VII. Conclusions

We have examined several basic properties of a plasma consisting of finite-size particles (clouds) whose interactions are smooth at small separations. We found that, when the cloud size R is less than the Debye length, λ_D, longitudinal waves and Debye shielding are nearly the same as for a "real" plasma, while collisional phenomena (and short-wavelength fluctuations, given elsewhere) are much reduced. This observation is not unexpected and supports the trend towards use of simulation models having such "artificially" smoothed interactions. When the cloud size R is increased above the Debye length, λ_D, collisions and fluctuations rapidly disappear, but the plasma properties are much modified.

ACKNOWLEDGMENTS

Our group in Berkeley has had appreciable exchange with J. M. Dawson and his group at Princeton, for which we are most grateful. We have also worked closely and profitably with members of the plasma simulation group at Lawrence Radiation Lab. (Livermore), notably, J. A. Byers, H. Berk, and D. Fuss.

This work was supported in part by AEC Contract AT(11-1)-34, PA-128.

REFERENCES

BIRDSALL, C. K., and FUSS, D. (1969). *J. Comp. Phys.* **3**, 494.
BIRDSALL, C. K., LANGDON, A. B., MCKEE, C. F., OKUDA, H., and WONG, D. (1968). Paper D2, *Conf. Numerical Simulation Plasma.* Los Alamos Scientific Lab., LASL Report LA-3990. Abstracted in *Bull. Amer. Phys. Soc.* **13**, 1744.
DAWSON, J. M., HSI, C. G., and SHANNY, R. (1968). Paper A1, *Conf. Numerical Simulation Plasma.* Los Alamos Scientific Lab., LASL Report LA-3990. Abstracted in *Bull. Amer. Phys. Soc.* **13**, 1744.
FRIED, B. D., and CONTE, S. D. (1961). "The Plasma Dispersion Function." Academic Press, New York.
HARLOW, F. H. (1956-7). *J. Assoc. Comp. Mach.* **3-4**, 137.

HARLOW, F. H. (1964). In *Meth. Comp. Phys.* **3**, 319. Academic Press, New York.
HARLOW, F. H., and EVANS, W. M. (1957). Los Alamos Scientific Lab. Report LA-2139.
HESS, R. (1961). ASD Tech Report 61-15, Aero. Syst. Div. AF Syst. Comm. USAF Wright Patterson Air Force Base, Ohio.
HOCKNEY, R. W. (1966). *Phys. Fluids* **9**, 1826.
JACKSON, J. D. (1960). *J. Nucl. Energy (Part C)* **1**, 171.
LANGDON, A. B., (1969). Unpublished results.
LANGDON, A. B., and BIRDSALL, C. K. (1969). Unpublished results.
MIHRAN, T. G., and YU, S. P. (1963). *J. Appl. Phys.* **34**, 2976.
MORSE, R. L., and NIELSON, C. W. (1968). *Paper A4, Conf. Numerical Simulation Plasma.* Los Alamos Scientific Lab, LASL Report LA-3990. Abstracted in *Bull. Amer. Phys. Soc.* **13**, 1744.
MORSE, R. M., and NIELSON, C. W. (1969). *Phys. Rev. Letters* **23**, 19, 1087.
OKUDA, H., and BIRDSALL, C. K. (1969). Unpublished results.
WONG, D. P., and BIRDSALL, C. K. (1969). Unpublished results.

Finite-Difference Methods for Collisionless Plasma Models

JACK A. BYERS
LAWRENCE RADIATION LABORATORY, UNIVERSITY OF CALIFORNIA, LIVERMORE, CALIFORNIA

and

JOHN KILLEEN
LAWRENCE RADIATION LABORATORY, LIVERMORE, CALIFORNIA

and

DEPARTMENT OF APPLIED SCIENCE, UNIVERSITY OF CALIFORNIA, DAVIS, CALIFORNIA

I. Introduction 259
II. Numerical Solution of the Vlasov Equation 260
   A. One-Dimensional Models 260
   B. A Two-Dimensional Model 266
III. Low-Beta Plasma Models Using the Guilding-Center Drift Equations. 282
   A. A Linear Model 282
   B. A Two-Dimensional Nonlinear Model 290
   References 205

I. Introduction

IN OTHER ARTICLES OF this volume, finite-difference methods are described that are suitable for the mathematical models of plasmas which are collision dominated. In particular, the solution of the Boltzmann–Fokker–Planck equation and the fluid equations of magnetohydrodynamics are discussed in detail. In recent years most of the theoretical work particularly in controlled-fusion research, has been based on the collisionless plasma models. In this article we shall consider finite-difference methods that are applicable to some of these models.

Most numerical work on the Vlasov equation has used a Lagrangian representation, i.e., the trajectories of a large number of particles (sheets, rods, clouds, etc.) are computed and from these particle distributions, charge and current densities are calculated. In this work we shall consider the Eulerian form of the Vlasov equation in phase space. We shall give methods for the direct solution of the equations for the distribution functions. We first consider a two-dimensional phase space, and discuss a number of methods and examples. A problem in a four-dimensional phase space will then be described in detail.

In Section III we consider some problems using the guiding-center drift equations. Here again we consider the Eulerian representation for these models. The first example is a linear model used to study the stability of plasmas in mirror machines. The usual procedure in such problems is to obtain a dispersion relation and then try to solve it. In this example we consider an initial-value problem for the perturbed electric field and particle guiding-center densities. The resulting initial-value problem is solved by finite-difference methods which are described.

We then consider a two-dimensional nonlinear model in order to study plasma instabilities at large amplitudes. A two-fluid model is used and the Eulerian form of the equations is solved. An important part of this section is a survey of various difference approximations to the time derivatives in the equations for the particle densities.

II. Numerical Solution of the Vlasov Equation

A. ONE-DIMENSIONAL MODELS

1. Introduction

Consider the system of equations

$$\frac{\partial f_e}{\partial t} + v \frac{\partial f_e}{\partial x} - \frac{eE}{m} \frac{\partial f_e}{\partial v} = 0, \tag{1}$$

$$\frac{\partial f_i}{\partial t} + v \frac{\partial f_i}{\partial x} + \frac{eE}{M} \frac{\partial f_i}{\partial v} = 0, \tag{2}$$

$$dE/dx = 4\pi e \int_{-\infty}^{\infty} (f_i - f_e) \, dv, \tag{3}$$

where $f_e(x, v, t)$ and $f_i(x, v, t)$ are electron and ion distribution functions, m and M are the electron and ion masses, $-e$ and $+e$ ($Z = 1$) are the charges, and $E(x, t)$ is the electric field.

This system has probably received more attention than any other in plasma physics as far as computing is concerned. This is because of its straightforward, simple appearance and its importance to fundamental problems in plasma physics. This model is used in studies of instabilities such as the two-stream instability, in collisionless shocks, Landau damping, and other problems. It is called the "nonlinear Vlasov equation," which is a rather redundant name; it is obviously nonlinear since E is a function of f_e and f_i. However, a great deal of analytical effort has been devoted to the linearized Vlasov equation.

We can write either Eq. (1) or (2) as

$$\frac{\partial f}{\partial t} + v\frac{\partial f}{\partial x} + F\frac{\partial f}{\partial v} = 0. \tag{4}$$

Equation (4) can also be written

$$Df/Dt = 0, \tag{5}$$

where

$$\frac{D}{Dt} = \frac{\partial}{\partial t} + v\frac{\partial}{\partial x} + F\frac{\partial}{\partial v}.$$

We can refer to Eqs. (4) and (5) as the Eulerian and Lagrangian forms of the equation. Equation (5) implies that f remains constant along a trajectory which satisfies the equations

$$dx/dt = v, \tag{6}$$

$$dv/dt = F, \tag{7}$$

i.e., f_j is constant along a curve $x_j(t)$, $v_j(t)$ where $x_j(t)$ and $v_j(t)$ are solutions of Eqs. (6) and (7) with $x(0) = x_j$, $v(0) = v_j$. The various "sheet" models are based on Eqs. (5)–(7). Another method which is also based on Eqs. (5)–(7) is called the "water-bag" model. In this method step-function distributions are used, and the boundaries of a region in phase space of constant f are computed as a function of time by solving Eqs. (6) and (7) for a finite set of boundary points. At each time-step a new boundary curve is constructed from the discrete points.

A third method involves solving the Vlasov equation in the form given by Eq. (4) using a double expansion of $f(x, v, t)$ with orthogonal functions of x and v. The coefficients in the expansion are functions of time which satisfy an infinite set of ordinary differential equations. The series is truncated at some point and the resulting finite set of equations is solved numerically.

The above three methods are discussed in detail by other authors in this volume.

A fourth method involves solving the Eulerian form of the equation directly by finite-difference methods. We can write Eqs. (1) and (2) as the system

$$\frac{\partial f}{\partial t} + A \frac{\partial f}{\partial x} + B \frac{\partial f}{\partial v} = 0, \qquad (8)$$

where

$$f = \begin{bmatrix} f_e \\ f_i \end{bmatrix}, \quad A = \begin{bmatrix} v & 0 \\ 0 & v \end{bmatrix}, \quad B = \begin{bmatrix} F_e & 0 \\ 0 & F_i \end{bmatrix},$$

with $F_e = -(e/m)E$ and $F_i = (e/M)E$.

Equation (8) is a hyperbolic system written in advection form. We could also write the system as

$$\frac{\partial f}{\partial t} + \frac{\partial G}{\partial x} + \frac{\partial H}{\partial v} = 0, \qquad (9)$$

where

$$f = \begin{bmatrix} f_e \\ f_i \end{bmatrix}; \quad G = \begin{bmatrix} vf_e \\ vf_i \end{bmatrix}; \quad H = \begin{bmatrix} F_e f_e \\ F_i f_i \end{bmatrix}.$$

Equation (9) is a hyperbolic system written in conservation form. In the next section we shall discuss difference methods for hyperbolic systems of both forms.

2. *Difference Methods for Hyperbolic Systems*

We can write a hyperbolic system in the form

$$\frac{\partial U}{\partial t} + A \frac{\partial U}{\partial x} + V = 0 \qquad (10)$$

where U and V are m-dimensional column vectors and A is an $m \times m$ matrix. The system (10) is called hyperbolic if A has all real eigenvalues and m linearly independent eigenvectors. Since we are mainly interested in the advective terms, we shall consider the simpler system

$$\frac{\partial U}{\partial t} + A \frac{\partial U}{\partial x} = 0. \tag{11}$$

We consider a finite-difference grid with $x_j = j \Delta x$, $t_n = n \Delta t$ where j and n are integers and $U_j^n = U(x_j, t_n)$. The simplest difference approximation to Eq. (11) is

$$U_j^{n+1} = U_j^n - \frac{\Delta t}{2 \Delta x} A_j^n (U_{j+1}^n - U_{j-1}^n),$$

which is unstable (Richtmyer and Morton, 1967). A simple alternative which is stable is given by

$$U_j^{n+1} = \tfrac{1}{2}(U_{j+1}^n + U_{j-1}^n) - \frac{\Delta t}{2 \Delta x} A_j^n (U_{j+1}^n - U_{j-1}^n). \tag{12}$$

The stability condition is $|a \Delta t/\Delta x| < 1$ for all eigenvalues a of A. (The stability criteria given in this discussion are derived assuming that the coefficients are constant, so for our nonlinear equations they must be regarded as local conditions which must be tested numerically.) A better scheme is the so-called "upstream-downstream" difference equation which we give for the scalar equation

$$\frac{\partial u}{\partial t} + a \frac{\partial u}{\partial x} = 0. \tag{13}$$

The difference equations are

$$u_j^{n+1} = u_j^n - \frac{a_j^n \Delta t}{\Delta x} \begin{cases} u_{j+1}^n - u_j^n & \text{if } a_j^n < 0, \\ u_j^n - u_{j-1}^n & \text{if } a_j^n > 0. \end{cases} \tag{14}$$

The stability condition is again $|a \Delta t/\Delta x| < 1$. A scheme with higher order accuracy is the "leapfrog" difference equation

$$U_j^{n+1} = U_j^{n-1} - \frac{\Delta t}{\Delta x} A_j^n (U_{j+1}^n - U_{j-1}^n). \tag{15}$$

which has the same stability condition $|a \Delta t/\Delta x| < 1$, but has the disadvantage of being a three-time-level equation. Another equation which has second-order accuracy, but uses only two time levels, is based on the expansion

$$U_j^{n+1} = U_j^n + \Delta t \left(\frac{\partial U}{\partial t}\right)_j^n + \frac{(\Delta t)^2}{2}\left(\frac{\partial^2 U}{\partial t^2}\right)_j^n. \tag{16}$$

If A is assumed constant then we have the difference equation

$$U_j^{n+1} = U_j^n - \frac{\Delta t}{2\,\Delta x} A(U_{j+1}^n - U_{j-1}^n) + \frac{1}{2}\left(\frac{A\,\Delta t}{\Delta x}\right)^2 (U_{j+1}^n - 2U_j^n + U_{j-1}^n). \tag{17}$$

When A is not constant, Eq. (17) can become much more complicated. The condition is $|a\,\Delta t/\Delta x| < 1$.

It is sometimes possible to write the system (11) in conservation form

$$\partial U/\partial t + \partial F/\partial x = 0, \tag{18}$$

where F is an m-dimensional column vector. The second-order difference scheme for the system (18) can be written in a particularly simple form which is called the two-step Lax–Wendroff method. It is particularly convenient for generalization to two dimensions and has the advantage of conserving the quantity U. In the first step, Eq. (12) is used at the midpoints of the grid, i.e.,

$$U_{j+1/2}^{n+1/2} = \tfrac{1}{2}(U_{j+1}^n + U_j^n) - \frac{\Delta t}{2\Delta x}(F_{j+1}^n - F_j^n). \tag{19a}$$

The second step is the leapfrog equation

$$U_j^{n+1} = U_j^n - \frac{\Delta t}{\Delta x}(F_{j+1/2}^{n+1/2} - F_{j-1/2}^{n+1/2}). \tag{19b}$$

This system reduces to Eq. (17) when $\partial F/\partial x = A(\partial U/\partial x)$ and A is constant.

The difference schemes given by Eqs. (14) and (15) generalize to higher dimensions without difficulty in a straightforward way. The extension of the scheme (17) is not straightforward and can lead to an unstable method if it is not done correctly (Leith, 1965). If we merely add terms representing the derivatives in the other directions of the type given by Eq. (17), we obtain an unstable scheme. However, if a "splitting" technique is employed, the scheme is stable, i.e., for a two-dimensional problem we calculate advection in one direction, then, using the results of that cycle, calculate advection in the other direction. This technique will be discussed further in Section II,B.

3. Applications

Equation (9) is a hyperbolic system in conservation form and is well suited to the two-dimensional two-step Lax–Wendroff method. Let $x_i = i\,\Delta x$, $v_k = k\,\Delta v$, and $t_n = n\,\Delta t$. A unit cell in the finite-difference mesh has dimensions $2\,\Delta x$, $2\,\Delta v$, and $2\,\Delta t$. Provisional values at t_{n+1} are obtained from

$$f_{i,k}^{n+1} = \tfrac{1}{4}(f_{i+1,k}^n + f_{i-1,k}^n + f_{i,k+1}^n + f_{i,k-1}^n)$$
$$- \frac{\Delta t}{2\,\Delta x}(G_{i+1,k}^n - G_{i-1,k}^n) - \frac{\Delta t}{2\,\Delta v}(H_{i,k+1}^n - H_{i,k-1}^n), \quad (20)$$

then final values at t_{n+2} are obtained from

$$f_{i,k}^{n+2} = f_{i,k}^n - \frac{\Delta t}{\Delta x}(G_{i+1,k}^{n+1} - G_{i-1,k}^{n+1}) - \frac{\Delta t}{\Delta v}(H_{i,k+1}^{n+1} - H_{i,k-1}^{n+1}). \quad (21)$$

The electric field can be obtained by integrating Eq. (3) directly. For certain boundary conditions it is convenient to solve

$$d^2\phi/dx^2 = -\rho, \quad (22)$$

where $E = -d\phi/dx$ and ρ is the right-hand side of Eq. (3). The approximation to Eq. (22) is

$$\phi_{i+1}^n - 2\phi_i^n + \phi_{i-1}^n = -\Delta x \rho_i^n.$$

The above difference equations are being used in a code of John Clark, a graduate student in the Department of Applied Science, University of California at Davis to study plasma sheath problems. The mathematical model is the system of Eqs. (1)–(3) with appropriate boundary conditions. Results will appear as part of a Ph.D. thesis. The code has demonstrated excellent conservation properties in these problems.

Another one-dimensional model is the program RESIST (Killeen et al., 1966; Brettschneider and Weiss, 1968) which has been used to study the effect of resistors on the trapping of an electron layer in the Astron experiment. The mathematical model is the Vlasov equation for the electron distribution function in a $z - v_z$ phase space. The self-electric and self-magnetic fields are also calculated and included in the Vlasov equation. The difference method used for the Vlasov equation is the two-dimensional extension of the "upstream-downstream" scheme given by Eq. (14).

Another one-dimensional model is the program MINILAYER. This is a simplified version of the LAYER code (Killeen and Rompel, 1966). In

MINILAYER the Vlasov equation for the electron distribution function is solved in a $z - v_z$ phase space, whereas the LAYER code uses a four-dimensional phase space. The second-order difference scheme given by Eq. (17) is generalized to two dimensions using the splitting technique. We shall discuss the LAYER code in the next section.

In his investigation of the two-stream instability, Kellogg (1965) solved Eqs. (1)–(3) using the leapfrog difference shceme.

B. A Two-Dimensional Model

1. Introduction

Programs have been written to solve the Vlasov equation in two dimensions, i.e., a four dimensional phase space. Consider the equation

$$\frac{\partial f}{\partial t} + u \frac{\partial f}{\partial x} + v \frac{\partial f}{\partial y} + F_x \frac{\partial f}{\partial u} + F_y \frac{\partial f}{\partial v} = 0 \tag{23}$$

for both species and Poisson's equation

$$\partial^2 \phi / \partial x^2 + \partial^2 \phi / \partial y^2 = -\rho. \tag{24}$$

We can also write

$$Df/Dt = 0, \tag{25}$$

where

$$\frac{D}{Dt} = \frac{\partial}{\partial t} + u \frac{\partial}{\partial x} + v \frac{\partial}{\partial y} + F_x \frac{\partial}{\partial u} + F_y \frac{\partial}{\partial v}.$$

The characteristic equations are:

$$dx/dt = u, \quad dy/dt = v, \quad du/dt = F_x, \quad dv/dt = F_y. \tag{26}$$

The generalization of the sheet model to two dimensions is usually called the "rod" model. In some of these programs a time-independent magnetic field is included in the force terms. A fast method of solving Poisson's equation in difference form is an important feature of these programs.

Equation (23) can also be solved by finite-difference methods. The two-step method of Eqs. (20) and (21) can be generalized to four dimensions. A related problem in four dimensions is the self-consistent solution of the magnetic field in Astron which has been solved by finite-difference methods (Killeen and Rompel, 1966).

In the Lawrence Radiation Laboratory's controlled-fusion experiment, Astron, relativistic electrons are injected into a cylindrical region containing an applied magnetic field. The object is to form an *E*-layer—a cylindrical layer of electrons—so that the self-field exceeds the applied field. The resulting configuration is intended to be axially symmetric with no azimuthal component of the magnetic field.

The mathematical model for the buildup of the electron layer and the self-field is the time-dependent Vlasov equation coupled with Maxwell's equations. Field components B_r and B_z can be derived from a streamfunction $\psi(r, z, t)$. The canonical angular momentum, p_θ is a constant of the motion, and we assume that all electrons are injected with the same value of p_θ. Hence, we can consider an electron-distribution function f, defined in a four-dimensional phase space (r, z, p_r, p_z). In the present discussion we assume that the system is electrically neutral at every point. The ion distribution is not solved explicitly, but ions are assumed to be present, providing charge neutralization of the layer.

A new version of the code relaxing the constraint of neutrality is now being developed by Marcel Brettschneider. In this version the electric potential $\varphi(r, z, t)$ is also computed by finite-difference methods.

2. *Mathematical Model for the Formation of the E-Layer*

Transient radial and axial currents will exist in this model, but they are small compared to the azimuthal current. The radial and axial components of the magnetic vector potential are neglected in the present discussion. The addition of $A_z(r, z, t)$ to the model is included in the new version of the LAYER code.

We specify the magnetic field by the single component of the vector potential $A_\theta(r, z, t)$. The equation for A_θ is

$$\frac{1}{c^2}\frac{\partial^2 A_\theta}{\partial t^2} - \frac{\partial^2 A_\theta}{\partial z^2} - \frac{\partial}{\partial r}\left[\frac{1}{r}\frac{\partial}{\partial r}(rA_\theta)\right] = 4\pi j_\theta, \qquad (27)$$

and we have

$$B_r = -\frac{\partial A_\theta}{\partial z}, \qquad B_z = \frac{1}{r}\frac{\partial}{\partial r}(rA_\theta), \qquad E_\theta = -\frac{1}{c}\frac{\partial A_\theta}{\partial t}. \qquad (28)$$

We can write the canonical angular momentum as

$$p_\theta = m_0 \gamma r v_\theta + (e/c) r A_\theta,$$

where $\gamma = (1 - v^2/c^2)^{-1/2}$. It is convenient to introduce the function

$$\psi = (\gamma/c)rv_\theta \qquad (29)$$

so that

$$\psi = \frac{p_\theta}{m_0 c} - \frac{e}{m_0 c^2} rA_\theta, \qquad (30)$$

and since we are assuming that all the electrons have the same p_θ, we can use ψ in place of A_θ to determine the field. From Eqs. (27), (28), and (30), we have

$$\frac{1}{c^2}\frac{\partial^2 \psi}{\partial t^2} - \frac{\partial^2 \psi}{\partial z^2} - r\frac{\partial}{\partial r}\left[\frac{1}{r}\frac{\partial \psi}{\partial r}\right] = -\frac{4\pi e}{m_0 c^2} rj_\theta, \qquad (31)$$

$$B_r = \frac{m_0 c^2}{e}\frac{1}{r}\frac{\partial \psi}{\partial z}, \qquad B_z = -\frac{m_0 c^2}{e}\frac{1}{r}\frac{\partial \psi}{\partial r}. \qquad (32)$$

We introduce the dimensionless velcoity **u** defined by

$$\mathbf{u} = (\gamma/c)\mathbf{v}. \qquad (33)$$

The expression for γ becomes

$$\gamma = (1 + u_r^2 + u_\theta^2 + u_z^2)^{1/2},$$

and from Eq. (29) we have $\psi = ru_\theta$, hence,

$$\gamma = \{1 + u_r^2 + u_z^2 + (\psi^2/r^2)\}^{1/2}. \qquad (34)$$

Let $f(r, z, u_r, u_z, t)$ be the electron distribution function in phase space, such that $f(r, z, u_r, u_z, t)\, dr\, dz\, du_r\, du_z$ is the number of electrons in the element $dr\, dz\, du_r\, du_z$ at the point (r, z, u_r, u_z) at time t. The dimensions of f are the number of electrons per centimeters squared. The equation governing f is

$$\frac{\partial f}{\partial t} + \frac{\partial f}{\partial r}\frac{dr}{dt} + \frac{\partial f}{\partial z}\frac{dz}{dt} + \frac{\partial f}{\partial u_r}\frac{du_r}{dt} + \frac{\partial f}{\partial u_z}\frac{du_z}{dt} = S,$$

where S expresses the source of electrons injected into the phase space.

From Eq. (33) we have

$$dr/dt = (c/\gamma)u_r, \quad \text{and} \quad dz/dt = (c/\gamma)u_z. \tag{35}$$

We determine du_r/dt and du_z/dt from the relativistic equations of motion of the electrons. The radial and axial equations are

$$m_0(\gamma\ddot{r} + \dot{\gamma}\dot{r} - \gamma r\dot\theta^2) = (e/c)r\dot\theta B_z, \quad m_0(\gamma\ddot{z} + \dot{\gamma}\dot{z}) = -(e/c)r\dot\theta B_r.$$

From Eq. (35) we have

$$\ddot{r} = (c/\gamma)\dot{u}_r - (c/\gamma^2)\dot\gamma u_r, \quad \ddot{z} = (c/\gamma)\dot{u}_z - (c/\gamma^2)\dot\gamma u_z,$$

and using Eqs. (29) and (32), we have

$$\frac{du_r}{dt} = -\frac{c}{\gamma}\frac{\partial}{\partial r}\left(\frac{\psi^2}{2r^2}\right), \quad \frac{du_z}{dt} = -\frac{c}{\gamma}\frac{\partial}{\partial z}\left(\frac{\psi^2}{2r^2}\right). \tag{36}$$

The equation for f can now be written as

$$\frac{\gamma}{c}\frac{\partial f}{\partial t} + u_r\frac{\partial f}{\partial r} + u_z\frac{\partial f}{\partial z} - \frac{\partial}{\partial r}\left(\frac{\psi^2}{2r^2}\right)\frac{\partial f}{\partial u_r} - \frac{\partial}{\partial z}\left(\frac{\psi^2}{2r^2}\right)\frac{\partial f}{\partial u_z} = S\frac{\gamma}{c}. \tag{37}$$

The azimuthal current density j_θ is given by

$$j_\theta = \frac{e}{c}\frac{1}{2\pi r}\iint v_\theta f \, du_r \, du_z.$$

From Eq. (29) we have

$$j_\theta = \frac{e}{2\pi}\frac{\psi}{r^2}\iint \frac{f}{\gamma} du_r \, du_z.$$

Equation (31) becomes

$$\frac{1}{c^2}\frac{\partial^2\psi}{\partial t^2} - \frac{\partial^2\psi}{\partial z^2} - r\frac{\partial}{\partial r}\left[\frac{1}{r}\frac{\partial\psi}{\partial r}\right] = -r_e\frac{2\psi}{r}\iint\frac{f}{\gamma}du_r\,du_z, \tag{39}$$

where $r_e = e^2/m_0 c^2$. Equations (34), (37), and (39) are the self-consistent set of equations that describe the formation of the E-layer.

3. Dimensionless Equations, Boundary Conditions

It is useful in a numerical computation of this type to introduce an appropriate set of dimensionless variables. In place of ψ, given by Eq. (30), we see the variable $\bar{\mu}$ defined by $\bar{\mu} = \psi/(p_\theta/m_0 c)$. In order to evaluate p_θ we consider an equilibrium orbit in the vacuum field. At the midplane, $z = 0$, the end mirror fields are assumed to be negligible, i.e., the vacuum field at $z = 0$ is given by $A_\theta(r, 0) = \tfrac{1}{2} B_0 r$, where B_0 is a constant determined by the injection energy and radius and the desired pitch angle. For an equilibrium orbit at $z = 0$, we have from the radial equation of motion,

$$m_0 \gamma r_0 \dot\theta^2 = -(e/c) r_0 \dot\theta B_0,$$

where r_0 is the radius of the equilibrium orbit at $z = 0$. Hence,

$$p_\theta = -(e/c) B_0 r_0^2 + \tfrac{1}{2}(e/c) B_0 r_0^2 = -\tfrac{1}{2}(e/c) B_0 r_0^2,$$

and we have

$$\bar{\mu} = -\frac{2 m_0 c^2}{e B_0 r_0^2} \psi. \tag{40}$$

We introduce the following dimensionless variables:

$$R = r/r_0, \qquad Z = z/r_0, \qquad \tau = (ct)/r_0,$$

$$\bar{a}_\theta = A_\theta/(B_0 r_0), \qquad \bar{b}_r = B_r/B_0, \qquad \bar{b}_z = B_z/B_0.$$

From these definitions and Eqs. (30), (32), and (40), we have

$$\bar{\mu} = 1 + 2R\bar{a}_\theta, \qquad \bar{b}_r = -\frac{1}{2R}\frac{\partial \bar{\mu}}{\partial Z}, \qquad \bar{b}_z = \frac{1}{\partial R}\frac{\partial \bar{\mu}}{R}.$$

It is convenient to let $\bar{\mu} = \mu_c + \mu$, where μ_c represents the vacuum field and is created by external coils, and μ is the contribution due to the electron layer. The function μ_c satisfies the equation

$$\frac{\partial^2 \mu_c}{\partial \tau^2} - \frac{\partial^2 \mu_c}{\partial Z^2} - R\frac{\partial}{\partial R}\left(\frac{1}{R}\frac{\partial \mu_c}{\partial R}\right) = 0.$$

For the electron distribution function we use the dimensionless quantity ρ defined by

$$\rho = r_e r_0 f. \tag{41}$$

We introduce the parameter C_1 given by

$$C_1 = -\frac{eB_0 r_0}{2m_0 c^2} = -(2.93 + 10^{-4})B_0 r_0,$$

and define the function $P(R, Z, \tau)$ given by

$$P = \tfrac{1}{2} C_1^{\,2} (\mu^2/R^2). \tag{42}$$

This is the potential function for the electron motion, and the equations of motion in these variables become

$$\gamma(du_r/d\tau) = -\partial P/\partial R, \qquad \gamma(du_z/d\tau) = -\partial P/\partial Z.$$

We can now give the complete set of equations in dimensionless form. Equation (39) becomes

$$\frac{\partial^2 \mu}{\partial \tau^2} - \frac{\partial^2 \mu}{\partial Z^2} - R\frac{\partial}{\partial R}\left(\frac{1}{R}\frac{\partial \mu}{\partial R}\right) = -\frac{2\bar{\mu}}{R}\iint \frac{\rho}{\gamma}\, du_r\, du_z. \tag{43}$$

Equation (37) becomes

$$\frac{\partial \rho}{\partial \tau} + \frac{u_r}{\gamma}\frac{\partial \rho}{\partial R} + \frac{u_z}{\gamma}\frac{\partial \rho}{\partial Z} - \frac{P_r}{\gamma}\frac{\partial \rho}{\partial u_r} - \frac{P_z}{\gamma}\frac{\partial \rho}{\partial u_z} = \sigma, \tag{44}$$

where

$$\sigma = r_e r_0^{\,2} \frac{S}{c} = (2.82 \times 10^{-13}) r_0^{\,2} \frac{S}{c}, \tag{45}$$

$$P_r = \frac{\partial P}{\partial R} = C_1^{\,2}\left[\frac{2}{R}\bar{\mu}\bar{b}_z - \frac{1}{R^3}\bar{\mu}^2\right], \tag{46}$$

$$P_z = \frac{\partial P}{\partial Z} = C_1^2 \left[-\frac{2}{R} \bar{\mu} \bar{b}_r \right], \tag{47}$$

$$\bar{b}_r = b_{rc} - \frac{1}{2R} \frac{\partial \mu}{\partial Z}, \tag{48}$$

$$\bar{b}_z = b_{zc} + \frac{1}{2R} \frac{\partial \mu}{\partial R}, \tag{49}$$

$$\gamma = (1 + u_r^2 + u_z^2 + 2P)^{1/2}. \tag{50}$$

We wish to solve the initial-value problem given by Eqs. (43) and (44), together with Eqs. (45)–(50). At time $t = 0$, we have

$$\bar{\mu} = \mu_c = 1 + 2Ra_{\theta c}.$$

Hence, the initial condition for Eq. (43) is

$$\mu(R, Z, 0) = 0.$$

We solve the equation on the domain

$$0 \leq R \leq R_{\max}, \qquad -l^* \leq Z \leq l^*,$$

where $l^* = l/r_0$ and $R_{\max}$ is chosen sufficiently large so that the effect of the electron layer can be neglected. The boundary conditions are those of conducting walls, given by

$$\mu(R_{\max}, Z, \tau) = 0, \qquad \mu(R, -l^*, \tau) = 0, \qquad \mu(R, l^*, \tau) = 0.$$

The initial condition for Eq. (44) is

$$\rho(R, Z, u_r, u_z, 0) = 0.$$

We solve the equation on the domain

$$R_1 \leq R \leq R_2, \qquad -l^* \leq Z \leq l^*,$$

$$-(u_r)_{\max} \leq u_r \leq (u_r)_{\max}, \qquad -(u_z)_{\max} \leq u_z \leq (u_z)_{\max},$$

where R_1 and R_2 are the radii of the inner and outer material walls of the cylindrical region where the electron layer is formed. The velocity space, i.e., $(u_r)_{\max}$ and $(u_z)_{\max}$ is taken large enough to accommodate all but the high velocity tail of the electron distribution function which is small because electrons of too high a velocity would leave the system.

The boundary conditions for Eq. (44) in velocity space are that $\rho = 0$ for $u_z > (u_z)_{max}$, $u_z < -(u_z)_{max}$, $u_r > (u_r)_{max}$, or $u_r < -(u_r)_{max}$. In configuration space we use the following conditions. At $Z = l^*$ for $u_z < 0$, we take $\rho = 0$ for all R except the injection point; for $u_z > 0$ we can compute ρ and also a flux of particles leaving at $Z = l^*$. At $Z = -l^*$ for $u_z > 0$, we take $\rho = 0$ for all R; for $u_z < 0$ we can compute ρ and the flux of particles leaving at $Z = -l^*$. At $R = R_2$ for $u_r < 0$, we take $\rho = 0$ for all Z; for $u_r > 0$ we can compute ρ and the flux of particles leaving at $R = R_2$. At $R = R_1$ for $u_r > 0$, we take $\rho = 0$ for all Z; for $u_r < 0$ we can compute ρ and the flux of particles leaving at $R = R_1$.

4. Finite-Difference Methods

We subdivide the phase space into the finite-difference mesh given by $Z_i = imh$, $R_j = jh$, $(u_z)_k = kh^*$, $(u_r)_l = lh^*$, where i, j, k, l, m are integers. We have $-I \leq i \leq I$, $0 \leq j \leq J$, $-K \leq k \leq K$, $-L \leq l \leq L$, where $Imh = l^*$, $Jh = R_{max}$, $Kh^* = (u_z)_{max}$, $Lh^* = (u_r)_{max}$. Let $\tau_n = n\,\Delta\tau$, with $n = 0, 1, 2, 3, \ldots$, and introduce the notation $\mu_{i,j}^n = \mu(R_j, Z_i, \tau_n)$, and $\rho_{i,j,k,l}^n = \rho(R_j, Z_i, u_{rl}, u_{zk}, \tau_n)$.

The simplest method for solving Eq. (43) is an explicit difference scheme. For stability reasons it is convenient to use half-time-steps for this equation. We have

$$\frac{\mu_{i,j}^{n+1/2} - 2\mu_{i,j}^n + \mu_{i,j}^{n-1/2}}{(\Delta\tau/2)^2} = \frac{\mu_{i+1,j}^n - 2\mu_{i,j}^n + \mu_{i-1,j}^n}{m^2 h^2} + \bar{I}_{i,j}^n$$

$$+ \frac{2j}{h^2}\left[\frac{\mu_{i,j+1}^n - \mu_{i,j}^n}{2j+1} - \frac{\mu_{i,j}^n - \mu_{i,j-1}^n}{2j-1}\right],$$

$$\frac{\mu_{i,j}^{n+1} - 2\mu_{i,j}^{n+1/2} + \mu_{i,j}^n}{(\Delta\tau/2)^2} = \frac{\mu_{i+1,j}^{n+1/2} - 2\mu_{i,j}^{n+1/2} + \mu_{i-1,j}^{n+1/2}}{m^2 h^2} + \bar{I}_{i,j}^{n+1/2} \qquad (51)$$

$$+ \frac{2j}{h^2}\left[\frac{\mu_{i,j+1}^{n+1/2} - \mu_{i,j}^{n+1/2}}{2j+1} - \frac{\mu_{i,j}^{n+1/2} - \mu_{i,j-1}^{n+1/2}}{2j-1}\right],$$

where

$$\bar{I}_{i,j}^n = -2\frac{\bar{\mu}_{i,j}^n}{jh}(h^*)^2 \sum_{k=-K}^{K}{}' \sum_{l=-L}^{L} \frac{\rho_{i,j,k,l}^n}{\gamma_{i,j,k,l}^n} \qquad (52)$$

$$\gamma_{i,j,k,l}^n = [1 + (kh^*)^2 + (lh^*)^2 + C_1^{\,2}(jh)^{-2}(\bar{\mu}_{i,j}^n)^2]^{1/2}. \qquad (53)$$

The expression for $\bar{I}_{i,j}^{n+1/2}$ uses the same sum over k and l but replaces $\bar{\mu}_{i,j}^n$ by $\bar{\mu}_{i,j}^{n+1/2}$.

Another version of the code solves Eq. (43) by the alternating-direction implicit (ADI) method. This method takes longer to compute, but it has the virtue that it can also be used to solve the field equations with the time derivative absent. The details of the application of the ADI method to this problem are given in Killeen and Rompel (1966).

At the end of a full-time-step the magnetic field is calculated at each point in the (r, z) domain. From Eqs. (48) and (49) we have

$$(\bar{b}_r)_{i,j}^n = (b_{rc})_{i,j} - (4jmh^2)^{-1}[\mu_{i+1,j}^n - \mu_{i-1,j}^n], \tag{54}$$

$$(\bar{b}_z)_{i,j}^n = (b_{zc})_{i,j} + (4jh^2)^{-1}[\mu_{i,j+1}^n - \mu_{i,j-1}^n]. \tag{55}$$

The vacuum-field expressions b_{rc} and b_{zc} are given and will be discussed later. The above field components, $\bar{b}_r$ and $\bar{b}_z$, are printed and plotted output; in addition they are used to compute P_r and P_z which are needed in the solution of Eq. (44). From Eqs. (46) and (47) we have

$$(P_r)_{i,j}^n = C_1^2[2(jh)^{-1}\bar{\mu}_{i,j}^n(\bar{b}_z)_{i,j}^n - (jh)^{-3}(\bar{\mu}_{i,j}^n)^2], \tag{56}$$

$$(P_z)_{i,j}^n = -C_1^2[2(jh)^{-1}\bar{\mu}_{i,j}^n(\bar{b}_r)_{i,j}^n], \tag{57}$$

where $\bar{\mu}_{i,j}^n = (\mu_c)_{i,j} + \mu_{i,j}^n$.

In the new code the electric potential $\varphi(r, z, t)$ and the axial component of the vector potential $A_z(r, z, t)$ are also solved by the finite-difference method. In the explicit version their difference equations are similar to Eq. (51). There is also a version of the new code which solves the three field equations by the ADI method.

We shall now consider solution of Eq. (44) by finite-difference methods. It is an example of a hyperbolic partial differential equation, hence the difference methods discussed in Section II,A,2 are applicable. The "upstream-downstream" scheme given by Eq. (14) can be generalized to four dimensions, and the stability conditions are given by

$$\left|\frac{kh^* \Delta\tau}{m\gamma h}\right| \leq 1, \quad \left|\frac{lh^* \Delta\tau}{\gamma h}\right| \leq 1, \quad \left|\frac{P_z \Delta\tau}{\gamma h^*}\right| \leq 1, \quad \left|\frac{P_r \Delta\tau}{\gamma h^*}\right| \leq 1. \tag{58}$$

The first version of the LAYER code employed this scheme and an explicit approximation of Eq. (43). Unfortunately the above scheme introduces an artificial diffusion which spoils the result after a short time.

We can consider a space and time centered three-level approximation of the "leapfrog" type given by Eq. (15). The extension to more than one dimension is again immediate, leading to the stability condition Eq. (58). The second version of LAYER used this scheme. Considerable computation has been done with this method leading to fairly satisfactory results, but with the crude mesh employed in this problem it is still not accurate enough for extremely long running times. Furthermore, it has the disadvantage of being a three-level formula, and when the time-step must be decreased for stability reasons, it is quite awkward.

The third version of LAYER uses a three-point approximation to the advective term of the type given by Eq. (17). It is accurate to second order, and has the convenience of being a two-level formula. The extension to more than one dimension is not straightforward and can lead to an unstable method if not done correctly (Leith, 1965). We can write the one-dimensional approximation of Eq. (17) in matrix form as $\rho^{n+1} = (I + A)\rho^n$. If we consider a two-dimensional equation and take the approximation given by the equation $\rho^{n+1} = (I + A + B)\rho^n$, the scheme is unstable. However, if we use the operator equation $\rho^{n+1} = (I + A)(I + B)\rho^n$, the scheme is stable. This is the scheme that is used in the third version of LAYER. The difference equation can be represented by

$$\rho^{n+1} = (I + A)(I + B)(I + C)(I + D)\rho^n.$$

The computational process involved in a single time-step is divided into four cycles. In the first cycle advection in the Z-direction is calculated, then in the R-direction using the results of the first cycle, then in the u_z-direction using the results of the second cycle, and, finally, in the u_r-direction using the results of the third cycle. The actual difference equations for Eq. (44) are given in Eqs. (59a)–(59d); the fractional time notation is used as a convenient labeling of the cycles and does not represent fractional time-steps:

$$\rho_{i,j,k,l}^{n+1/4} = \rho_{i,j,k,l}^n + \tfrac{1}{4}\sigma_{i,j,k,l}\Delta\tau - \left(\frac{kh^*\Delta\tau}{2mh\gamma_{i,j,k,l}^n}\right)(\rho_{i+1,j,k,l}^n - \rho_{i-1,j,k,l}^n)$$
$$+ \left(\frac{kh^*\Delta\tau}{mh}\right)^2 \frac{1}{\gamma_{i,j,k,l}^n}\left(\frac{\rho_{i+1,j,k,l}^n - \rho_{i,j,k,l}^n}{\gamma_{i+1,j,k,l}^n + \gamma_{i,j,k,l}^n} - \frac{\rho_{i,j,k,l}^n - \rho_{i-1,j,k,l}^n}{\gamma_{i,j,k,l}^n + \gamma_{1-i,j,k,l}^n}\right),$$
(59a)

$$\rho_{i,j,k,l}^{n+1/2} = \rho_{i,j,k,l}^{n+1/4} + \tfrac{1}{4}\sigma_{i,j,k,l}\Delta\tau - \left(\frac{lh^*\Delta\tau}{2h\gamma_{i,j,k,l}^n}\right)(\rho_{i,j+1,k,l}^{n+1/4} - \rho_{i,j-1,j,l}^{n+1/4})$$
$$+ \left(\frac{lh^*\Delta\tau}{h}\right)^2 \frac{1}{\gamma_{i,j,k,l}^n}\left(\frac{\rho_{i,j+1,k,l}^{n+1/4} - \rho_{i,j,k,l}^{n+1/4}}{\gamma_{i,j+1,k,l}^n + \gamma_{i,j,k,l}^n} - \frac{\rho_{i,j,k,l}^{n+1/4} - \rho_{i,j-1,k,l}^{n+1/4}}{\gamma_{i,j,k,l}^n + \gamma_{i,j-1,k,l}^n}\right),$$
(59b)

$$\rho_{i,j,k,l}^{n+3/4} = \rho_{i,j,k,l}^{n+1/2} + \tfrac{1}{4}\sigma_{i,j,k,l}\Delta\tau + \left(\frac{(P_z)_{i,j}^n \Delta\tau}{2h^*\gamma_{i,j,k,l}^n}\right)(\rho_{i,j,k+1,l}^{n+1/2} - \rho_{i,j,k-1,l}^{n+1/2})$$

$$+ \left[\frac{(P_z)_{i,j}^n \Delta\tau}{h^*}\right]^2 \frac{1}{\gamma_{i,j,k,l}^n}\left(\frac{\rho_{i,j,k+1,l}^{n+1/2} - \rho_{i,j,k,l}^{u+1/2}}{\gamma_{i,j,k+1,l}^n + \gamma_{i,j,k,l}^n} - \frac{\rho_{i,j,k,l}^{n+1/2} - \rho_{i,j,k-1,l}^{n+1/2}}{\gamma_{i,j,k,l}^n + \gamma_{i,j,k-1,l}^n}\right),$$

(59c)

$$\rho_{i,j,k,l}^{n+1} = \rho_{i,j,k,l}^{n+3/4} + \tfrac{1}{4}\sigma_{i,j,k,l}\Delta\tau + \left(\frac{(P_r)_{i,j}^n \Delta\tau}{2h^*\gamma_{i,j,k,l}^n}\right)(\rho_{i,j,k,l+1}^{n+3/4} - \rho_{i,j,k,l-1}^{n+3/4})$$

$$+ \left[\frac{(P_r)_{i,j}^n \Delta\tau}{h^*}\right]^2 \frac{1}{\gamma_{i,j,k,l}^n}\left(\frac{\rho_{i,j,k,l+1}^{n+3/4} - \rho_{i,j,k,l}^{n+3/4}}{\gamma_{i,j,k,l+1}^n + \gamma_{i,j,k,l}^n} - \frac{\rho_{i,j,k,l}^{n+3/4} - \rho_{i,j,k,l-1}^{n+3/4}}{\gamma_{i,j,k,l}^n + \gamma_{i,j,k,l-1}^n}\right).$$

(59d)

The stability conditions for this finite-difference method are given by Eq. (58).

Since the finite-difference mesh of the four-dimensional phase space consists of such a large number of points, only a part of it can be in the core storage at any one time; the rest of it is on discs. The ρ's of four i strips and the γ's of four i strips are in core storage, i.e., for a fixed value of i: $\gamma_{i,j,k,l}^n$, $\rho_{i,j,k,l}^n$, $\rho_{i-1,j,k,l}^n$, $\gamma_{i-1,j,k,l}^n$, $\rho_{i+1,j,k,l}^n$, etc., for all j, k, l are used to compute $\rho_{i,j,k,l}^{n+1/4}$ all j, k, l. The $\rho_{i,j,k,l}^{n+1/2}$ all j, k, l, are then computed and stored on top of the $\rho_{i-1,j,k,l}^n$ which is no longer needed; then the $\rho_{i,j,k,l}^{n+3/4}$ are computed and stored on top of the $\rho_{i,j,k,l}^{n+1/4}$; and finally the $\rho_{i,j,k,l}^{n+1}$ are computed and stored on top of the $\rho_{i,j,k,l}^{n+1/2}$. Before passing on to the next value of i the contributions to the various integrals such as $\bar{I}$ and the conservation checks are added in. When the ρ cycles are completed for all values of i, the μ equation can be solved, completing the self-consistent solution for that time-step.

We must consider the boundary conditions for the ρ equation and the conservation of particles. Particles can be lost at the physical boundaries $Z = l^*$, $Z = -l^*$, $R = R_1$, and $R = R_2$. Numerically they can also be lost at the boundaries of the velocity domain.

For $i = I(Z = +l^*)$, for $k \geq 0$, instead of Eq. (59a) we use

$$\rho_{I,j,k,l}^{n+1/4} = \rho_{I,j,k,l}^n - \left(\frac{kh^*\Delta\tau}{mh\gamma_{I,j,k,l}^n}\right)(\rho_{I,j,k,l}^n - \rho_{I-1,j,k,l}^n), \tag{60}$$

and then use Eqs. (59b)–(59d) to compute $\rho_{I,j,k,l}^{n+1}$, $k \geq 0$. In this equation we have assumed $\sigma_{I,j,k,l} = 0$ for $k \geq 0$. At $i = I$, for $k < 0$, we are injecting particles. In this case Eq. (59a) becomes

$$\rho_{I,j,k,l}^{n+1/4} = \rho_{I,j,k,l}^{n} + \tfrac{1}{4}\sigma_{I,j,k,l}\Delta\tau + \left(\frac{kh^*\Delta\tau}{2mh\gamma_{I,j,k,l}^{n}}\right)\rho_{I-1,j,k,l}^{n}$$
$$+ \left(\frac{kh^*\Delta\tau}{mh}\right)^2 \frac{1}{\gamma_{I,j,k,l}^{n}}\left(\frac{-\rho_{I,j,k,l}^{n}}{2\gamma_{I,j,k,l}^{n}} - \frac{\rho_{I,j,k,l}^{n} - \rho_{I-1,j,k,l}^{n}}{\gamma_{I,j,k,l}^{n} + \gamma_{I-1,j,k,l}^{n}}\right). \tag{61}$$

We then use Eqs. (59b)–(59d) to compute $\rho_{I,j,k,l}^{n+1}$, $k < 0$. We also wish to compute the flux of particles lost at $Z = l^*$. For $k > 0$, $\rho_{I,j,k,l}^{n+1}$ is added to the sum

$$M_I^{n+1} = h^{*3}h\,\Delta\tau \sum_{m=1}^{n+1}\sum_{k=1}^{K}\sum_{l=-L}^{L}\sum_{j=1}^{J} k\frac{\rho_{I,j,k,l}^{m}}{\gamma_{I,j,k,l}^{m}}. \tag{62}$$

For $i = -I$ ($Z = -l^*$), for $k \le 0$, instead of Eq. (59a) we use

$$\rho_{-I,j,k,l}^{n+1/4} = \rho_{-I,j,k,l}^{n} - \left(\frac{kh^*\Delta\tau}{mh\gamma_{-I,j,k,l}^{n}}\right)(\rho_{-I+1,j,k,l}^{n} - \rho_{-I,j,k,l}^{n}), \tag{63}$$

and then use Eqs. (59b)–(59d) to compute $\rho_{-I,j,k,l}^{n+1}$, $k \le 0$. Since there are no particles injected at that end for $k > 0$, we set $\rho_{-I,j,k,l}^{n+1} = 0$. At $i = -I$, for $k < 0$, we compute the sum

$$M_{-I}^{n+1} = h^{*3}h\,\Delta\tau \sum_{m=1}^{n+1}\sum_{k=-1}^{-K}\sum_{l=-L}^{L}\sum_{j=1}^{J} |k|\frac{\rho_{-I,j,k,l}^{m}}{\gamma_{-I,j,k,l}^{m}}. \tag{64}$$

At the inner radial boundary for Eq. (44), $R = R_1$, we let $R_1 = j_{\min}h$ and at the outer boundary we let $R_2 = J_\rho h$. At $j = J_\rho$, for $l < 0$, we set $\rho_{i,J_\rho,k,l}^{n+1} = 0$ for all i, k, n. For $l \ge 0$ we compute ρ at $j = J_\rho$. In order to do this we first compute $\rho_{i,J_\rho,k,l}^{n+1/4}$ using Eq. (59a). Instead of Eq. (59b) we use

$$\rho_{i,J_\rho,k,l}^{n+1/2} = \rho_{i,J_\rho,k,l}^{n+1/4} - \left(\frac{lh^*\Delta\tau}{h\gamma_{i,J_\rho,k,l}^{n}}\right)(\rho_{i,J_\rho,k,l}^{n+1/4} - \rho_{i,J_\rho-1,k,l}^{n+1/4}). \tag{65}$$

We then compute $\rho_{i,J,k,l}^{n+1}$ ($l \ge 0$) using Eqs. (59c) and (59d). It is added to the sum of particles lost at $R = R_2$,

$$Q_{J_\rho}^{n+1} = h^{*3}(mh)\,\Delta\tau \sum_{m'=1}^{n+1}\sum_{k=-K}^{K}\sum_{l=1}^{L}\sum_{i=-I}^{I} l\frac{\rho_{i,J_\rho,k,l}^{m'}}{\gamma_{i,J_\rho,k,l}^{m'}}, \tag{66}$$

($mh = \Delta Z$ and m' is a summation index).

At $j = j_{\min}$, for $l > 0$, we set $\rho^n_{i, j_{\min}, k, l} = 0$ for all i, k, n. For $l \leq 0$ we first compute $\rho^{n+1/4}_{i, j_{\min}, k, l}$, using Eq. (59a). Instead of Eq. (59b) we use

$$\rho^{n+1/2}_{i, j_{\min}, k, l} = \rho^{n+1/4}_{i, j_{\min}, k, l} - \left(\frac{lh^* \Delta\tau}{h\gamma^n_{i, j_{\min}, k, l}}\right)(\rho^{n+1/4}_{i, j_{\min}+1, k, l} - \rho^{n+1/4}_{i, j_{\min}, k, l}). \quad (67)$$

We then compute $\rho^{n+1}_{i, j_{\min}, k, l}$ ($l \leq 0$) using Eqs. (59c) and (59d). It is added to the sum of particles lost at $R = R_1$,

$$Q^{n+1}_{j_{\min}} = h^{*3}(mh) \Delta\tau \sum_{m'=1}^{n+1} \sum_{k=-K}^{K} \sum_{l=-1}^{-L} \sum_{i=-I}^{I} |l| \frac{\rho^{m'}_{i, j_{\min}, k, l}}{\gamma^{m'}_{i, j_{\min}, k, l}}. \quad (68)$$

Along the boundaries in velocity space $k = \pm K$ and $l = \pm L$, we compute ρ from the regular Eqs. (59a)–(59d). In order to do this we set.

$$\rho^n_{i, j, K+1, l} = \rho^n_{i, j, -K-1, l} = 0$$

for all i, j, l, n when using Eq. (59c), and

$$\rho^n_{i, j, k, L+1} = \rho^n_{i, j, k, -L-1} = 0$$

for all i, j, k, n when using Eq. (59d). In order to justify the above procedure we must take Kh^* and Lh^* sufficiently large.

In addition to the sums M and Q of particles lost at the material boundaries, a sum of particles injected and a sum of particles in the mesh are computed.

We can give the total number of particles injected into the system at time t by the expression $\Delta u_r \, \Delta u_z \, \Delta r \, \Delta z \int_0^t S \, dt'$ where $\Delta u_r \, \Delta u_z \, \Delta r \, \Delta z$ is the element of phase space used for injection. If we inject the particles into one cell, we compute the dimensionless quantity

$$N^{n+1} = h^{*2} h^2 m \sum_{m'=1}^{n+1} \sigma^{m'} \Delta\tau_{m'}. \quad (69)$$

The total number of particles in the system at time $t = t_{n+1}$ is proportional to

$$SUM^{n+1} = h^{*2} h^2 m \sum_{i=-I}^{I} \sum_{j=1}^{J} \sum_{k=-K}^{K} \sum_{l=-L}^{L} \rho^{n+1}_{i, j, k, l}. \quad (70)$$

We should then have

$$SUM^{n+1} + M^{n+1} + Q^{n+1} = N^{n+1} \quad (71)$$

for conservation of particles, where M and Q are the total number of particles lost through the physical boundaries and are defined in Eqs. (62), (64), (66), and (68).

We define the energy in the electromagnetic field by the expression

$$\frac{1}{8\pi} \int_0^{2\pi} d\theta \int_{-l}^{+l} dz \int_0^{r_{max}} r \, dr [B^2 + E^2].$$

If we divide the above expression by the constant $r_0^3 B_0^2/4$ we obtain the quantity

$$F(t) = \int_{-l*}^{l} dZ \int_0^{R_{max}} R \, dR [\bar{b}_r^2 + \bar{b}_z^2 + \bar{e}_\theta^2]$$

where

$$\bar{e}_\theta = E_\theta/B_0 = -\frac{1}{2R} \frac{\partial \bar{\mu}}{\partial \tau}.$$

A finite-difference approximation to this integral is

$$F^{n+1} = h^3 m \sum_{i=-I}^{I} \sum_{j=0}^{J} j\{[(\bar{b}_r)_{i,j}^{n+1}]^2 + [(\bar{b}_z)_{i,j}^{n+1}]^2 + [(\bar{e}_\theta)_{i,j}^{n+1}]^2\}. \quad (72)$$

The energy of injected particles can be defined by

$$m_0 c^2 \, \Delta u_r \, \Delta u_z \, \Delta r \, \Delta z \int_0^t \gamma S \, dt'.$$

If we divide the above by $r_0^3 B_0^2/4$ and use the mode of injection described we have

$$T^{n+1} = C_1^{-2} h^{*2} h^2 m \sum_{m'=1}^{n+1} \gamma_{inj}^{m'} \sigma^{m'} \Delta \tau_{m'} \quad (73)$$

where $\gamma_{inj}^{m'}$ is the γ of the element into which the particles are injected. The energy of particles in the system is given by

$$m_0 c^2 \iiiint \gamma f \, dr \, dz \, du_r \, du_z.$$

Again, dividing by $r_0^3 B_0^2/4$, we can compute the dimensionless quantity

$$E^{n+1} = C_1^{-2} h^{*2} h^2 m \sum_{i=-I}^{I} \sum_{j=1}^{J} \sum_{k=-K}^{K} \sum_{l=-L}^{L} \gamma_{i,j,k,l}^{n+1} \rho_{i,j,k,l}^{n+1}. \qquad (74)$$

The conservation check is then

$$F^{n+1} - F^0 + E^{n+1} = T^{n+1}. \qquad (75)$$

5. Applications

There are two optional forms of the applied magnetic field available in the LAYER code. One form is given by

$$a_{\theta c} = A_1 R + A_2 I_1(\lambda R) \cos \lambda Z, \qquad (76a)$$

$$b_{rc} = \lambda A_2 I_1(\lambda R) \sin \lambda Z, \qquad (76b)$$

$$b_{zc} = 2A_1 + \lambda A_2 I_0(\lambda R) \cos \lambda Z, \qquad (76c)$$

where I_0 and I_1 are modified Bessel functions of the first kind and λ, A_1, A_2 are given constants.

Another form is

$$a_{\theta c} = R/2 + (\alpha/\lambda) J_1(\lambda R) e^{-\lambda l^*} \cosh \lambda Z, \qquad (77a)$$

$$b_{rc} = -\alpha J_1(\lambda R) e^{-\lambda l^*} \sinh \lambda Z, \qquad (77b)$$

$$b_{zc} = 1 + \alpha J_0(\lambda R) e^{-\lambda l^*} \cosh \lambda Z, \qquad (77c)$$

where J_0 and J_1 are Bessel functions of the first kind and λ, α are given constants. An advantage of the above expression is that if λ satisfies the equation

$$\lambda J_0(\lambda) = J_1(\lambda)$$

then $P_r = 0$ at $R = 1$ for all Z. Hence, if we inject at $R = 1$ with $u_r = 0$, the particles will not spread radially in the early formation of the electron layer. Of course as the self-field develops P_r will no longer be zero at $R = 1$ and the layer will spread radially. We determine α by the desired pitch angle in the midplane. Consider an equilibrium particle orbit, $R \equiv 1$, with velocity components in the midplane $Z = 0$ given by

$$(\dot{R}, R\dot{\theta}, \dot{Z}) = (0, v \sin \delta, v \cos \delta),$$

then for such an orbit to be reflected at $Z = l^*$ requires

$$\alpha = -2\lambda(\csc \delta + 1)/J_1(\lambda).$$

The constant B_0 defined earlier can be given by

$$B_0 = -\frac{m_0 c^2 \gamma \beta}{e r_0} \sin \delta$$

where β and γ are determined by the injection energy. With B_0 and r_0 we can determine the parameter C_1, e.g., for $r_0 = 30$ cm and $B_0 = 600$ G we have $C_1 = -5.27$.

Many cases have been run with the program for a variety of injection conditions and several versions of the applied magnetic field for both long and short E-layers. Earlier calculations were usually done with the applied field described by Eq. (77). Some of these results are shown in Killeen and Rompel (1966).

More recent cases have used the applied field described by Eq. (76) with A_1, A_2 given, but different for $Z > 0$ and $Z < 0$. The reason for this choice is to obtain a strong magnetic mirror field at $Z = -l^*$ with injection at $Z = +l^*$. We show the field lines for a solution which reached field reversal in Fig. 1.

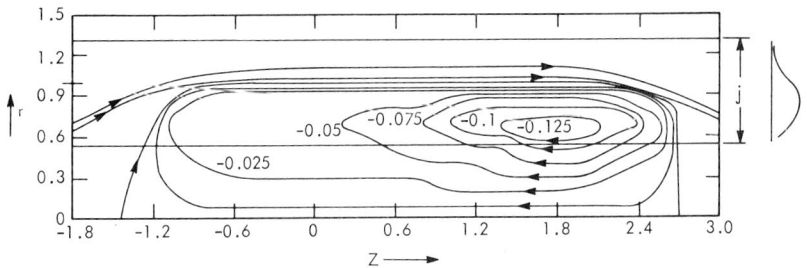

FIG. 1. Magnetic field lines for a reversed-field solution obtained with the LAYER code.

For the case shown in Fig. 1 the Z domain is $-3 \le Z \le 3$ with the unit of length $r_0 = 30$ cm. The R domain is $0 \le R \le 2$ with $R_1 = 0.5$ and $R_2 = 1.5$. The velocity domain is $-10 \le u_z \le 10$ and $-5 \le u_r \le 5$. The finite difference grid used was $\Delta R = h = 0.1$, $\Delta Z = 2h = 0.2$, $\Delta u_r = \Delta u_z = h^* = 1.0$.

The source of electrons is described by the function σ in Eq. (45). We have injected at one point in phase space; i.e., at the point $Z = 3$, $R = 1$, $u_z = -1$, $u_r = 0$, an amount $\sigma \Delta \tau$ is added every time-step. If 1000 A of electrons are injected into a volume of phase space $\Delta R \Delta Z \Delta u_r \Delta u_z = (0.1)(0.2)(30)^2$ cm^2, then we obtain from Eq. (45) a value of $\sigma = 3.0$. The usual procedure is to solve the buildup problem defined by Eqs. (43) and (44) until a steady-state solution is obtained that balances the source and particle losses. We can then double σ and continue the solution until a new steady-state is reached, and so on. The result shown in Fig. 1 was obtained with $\sigma = 12.0$. It should be pointed out that the trapping effect of resistive wires was not included in the model although they are included in the new version of the LAYER code.

III. Low-Beta Plasma Models Using the Guiding-Center Drift Equations

A. A Linear Model

1. *Basic Equations*

We consider the gross stability problem for a finite inhomogeneous plasma which is collisionless and has a low β. The theoretical treatment includes the stabilizing effects resulting from the finite size of the ion orbits in addition to several new features not included in previous work. The effects of a zero-order electric field and unequal ion and electron densities are investigated. Both the electric field and the magnetic field have been assumed to be arbitrary functions of the spatial coordinate r. These features are added in an attempt to explain experimental phenomena observed in the ALICE neutral injection experiment (Futch *et al.*, 1966).

We write the equations in cylindrical geometry adopting the approach used by Kuo *et al.* (1964) which takes into account the cylindrical plasma shape together with the boundary conditions at the metal walls. In general, it is not possible to obtain analytical solutions to the resulting differential equation; therefore, the basic equations are solved numerically by finite-difference methods. Several limiting cases for which it has been possible to obtain analytical solutions are in agreement with the numerical calculations.

We consider a two-dimensional, two-fluid mathematical model. The perturbed variables are all functions of the cylindrical coordinates r and φ and the time t. The unperturbed plasma density, the magnetic field, and the zero-order electric field are functions of r only.

The equation for the perturbed electrostatic potential ψ is given by

$$\nabla^2 \psi = -4\pi e c \left[\frac{2}{\pi} \int_{r-a}^{r+a} \frac{n_+(R, \varphi, t) R \, dR}{[4R^2 r^2 - (R^2 + r^2 - a^2)^2]^{1/2}} - n_-(r, \varphi, t) \right] \quad (78)$$

where n_+ and n_- are the perturbed guiding-center densities of the ions and electrons, e is the electronic change, c is the velocity of light, and a is the ion gyroradius. Equation (78) was obtained by substituting for the ion density in Poisson's equation the expression

$$\frac{2}{\pi} \int_{r-a}^{r+a} \frac{n_+(R, \varphi, t) R \, dR}{[4R^2 r^2 - (R^2 + r^2 - a^2)^2]^{1/2}},$$

which is an exact expression for the particle density in terms of the density of guiding centers (Futch et al., 1962). For the electrons, we assume that the particle density equals the density of guiding centers.

Since the magnetic field and the zero-order electric field, $\mathbf{E}_0$, are functions of r only, and $\mathbf{E}_0$ is in the r-direction, the r components of the zero-order drift velocities are zero. The linearized continuity equations for the densities of guiding centers become

$$\partial n_+/\partial t + (\mathbf{V}_+ \cdot \nabla) n_+ + (\mathbf{v}_+ \cdot \nabla) N_+ + N_+ \operatorname{div} \mathbf{v}_+ = 0, \qquad (79)$$

$$\partial n_-/\partial t + (\mathbf{V}_- \cdot \nabla) n_- + (\mathbf{v}_- \cdot \nabla) N_- + N_- \operatorname{div} \mathbf{v}_- = 0, \qquad (80)$$

where $N_+(r)$ and $N_-(r)$ are the unperturbed ion and electron guiding-center densities, $\mathbf{V}_+$ and $\mathbf{V}_-$ are the zero-order drift velocities of the ions and electrons due to both the magnetic field gradient and $\mathbf{E}_0 \times \mathbf{B}/B^2$, and $\mathbf{v}_+$, $\mathbf{v}_-$ are the perturbed drift velocities. The latter are given by

$$\mathbf{v}_+ = \frac{\mathbf{E}_1 \times \mathbf{B}}{B^2} + \frac{a^2}{4} \frac{\nabla^2 \mathbf{E}_1 \times \mathbf{B}}{B^2} \qquad (81)$$

$$\mathbf{v}_- = \frac{\mathbf{E}_1 \times \mathbf{B}}{B^2}, \qquad (82)$$

where

$$\mathbf{E}_1 = -\nabla \psi, \qquad \mathbf{B} = B_r(r)\mathbf{r}_0 + B_\varphi(r)\boldsymbol{\varphi}_0 + B_z(r)\mathbf{z}_0$$

$$B^2 = B_r{}^2 + B_\varphi{}^2 + B_z{}^2.$$

In Eq. (81) we have used,

$$\langle \mathbf{E}_1 \rangle = \mathbf{E}_1 + \frac{a^2}{4} \nabla^2 \mathbf{E}_1, \qquad (83)$$

an average taken around the ion orbit, which is an expansion to second-order in a, the ion gyroradius. This averaging process is not necessary in the equation for the perturbed electron velocity since the gyroradius of the electrons is assumed to be negligible. In Eqs. (81) and (82) we have also neglected the drift velocity terms $(\partial/\partial t + \mathbf{V}_{\pm} \cdot \nabla) \mathbf{E}_1/B\omega_c$, which for typical magnetic mirror fields are small compared with the correction terms arising from the finite orbit size of the ions.

We assume that the perturbed electrostatic potential and the perturbed ion and electron densities are of the following form:

$$\psi(r, \phi, t) = \psi(r, t)e^{im\phi}, \quad n_+(r, \phi, t) = n_+(r, t)e^{im\phi},$$

$$n_-(r, \phi, t) = n_-(r, t)e^{im\phi}.$$

Equation (78) becomes

$$\nabla^2 \psi = \frac{\partial^2 \psi}{\partial r^2} + \frac{1}{r} \frac{\partial \psi}{\partial r} - \frac{m^2}{r^2} \psi$$

$$= -4\pi ec \left[\frac{2}{\pi} \int_{r-a}^{r+a} \frac{n_+(R, t) R \, dR}{[4R^2 r^2 - (R^2 + r^2 - a^2)^2]^{1/2}} - n_-(r, t) \right]. \quad (84)$$

Although magnetic and electric fields of the type we are considering give rise to perturbed drift velocities having components in the z-direction, the z components of the velocities do not enter into the equations. From Eq. (81) we can give the r component and the divergence of the ion drift velocity

$$v_{+r} = -\frac{im}{r} \frac{B_z}{B^2} \left[\psi + \frac{a^2}{4} \nabla^2 \psi \right] e^{im\phi}, \quad (85)$$

$$\operatorname{div} \mathbf{v}_+ = -\frac{im}{r} \frac{d}{dr} \left(\frac{B_z}{B^2} \right) \left[\psi + \frac{a^2}{4} \nabla^2 \psi \right] e^{im\phi}. \quad (86)$$

The zero-order ion drift velocity is given by $\mathbf{V}_+ = \boldsymbol{\phi}_0 V_+(r)$, where

$$V_+(r) = r(\Omega_M + \Omega_E). \quad (87)$$

The ions are assumed to have no energy spread, i.e., the distribution function for the ions is a δ-function. The gradient B precessional frequency of the ion is given by

$$\Omega_M = \frac{cT}{er} \frac{B_z}{B^3} \frac{dB}{dr}, \quad (88)$$

where T is the ion energy. The electric precessional frequency due to the zero-order electric field is given by

$$\Omega_E = -\frac{4\pi ec(1-\Gamma)}{r^2 B} \int_0^r \eta_+(r') r' \, dr', \tag{89}$$

where $\eta_+(r)$ is the unperturbed ion density. In Eq. (89) we have assumed that both $\eta_+(r)$ and $\eta_-(r)$ have the same spatial dependence, i.e., $\eta_-(r) = \Gamma \eta_+(r)$, where Γ is a constant. Using Eqs. (85)–(89), Eq. (79) becomes

$$\frac{\partial n_+}{\partial t} + iGn_+ + iH\left[\psi + \frac{a^2}{4}\nabla^2\psi\right] = 0 \tag{90}$$

where

$$G(r) = \frac{m}{r} V_+(r) = m(\Omega_M + \Omega_E), \qquad H(r) = -\frac{m}{r}\left[\frac{B_z}{B^2}\frac{dN_+}{dr} + N_+ \frac{d}{dr}\left(\frac{B_z}{B^2}\right)\right].$$

In solving Eq. (90) we substitute for $\nabla^2 \psi$ from the equation

$$\nabla^2 \psi = -4\pi ec\left[n_+ - n_- + \frac{a^2}{4}\nabla^2 n_+\right].$$

This equation is obtained by substituting for the ion density in Poisson's equation the expression $n_+ + (a^2/4)\nabla^2 n_+$, which is an expansion accurate to second order in a, the ion gyroradius. Equation (90) can now be written as

$$\frac{\partial n_+}{\partial t} + iGn_+ + iH\left[\psi - \pi eca^2\left(n_+ - n_- + \frac{a^2}{4}\nabla^2 n_+\right)\right] = 0. \tag{91}$$

The advantage of Eq. (91) is that it is in the form of a diffusion equation in $n_+(r,t)$ and we can use an implicit difference scheme for its solution.

In a similar manner we have that Eq. (80) becomes

$$\frac{\partial n_-}{\partial t} + iPn_- + iQ\psi = 0 \tag{92}$$

where

$$P(r) = \frac{m}{r} V_-(r) = m\Omega_E, \qquad Q(r) = -\frac{m}{r}\left[\frac{B_z}{B^2}\frac{dN_-}{dr} + N_- \frac{d}{dr}\left(\frac{B_z}{B^2}\right)\right].$$

Equations (84), (91), and (92) are the basic equations of our model. They are a set of partial differential equations for the complex dependent variables ψ, n_+, and n_-. If we let

$$\psi = V + iW, \quad n_+ = \rho + i\gamma, \quad n_- = \theta + i\delta, \qquad (93)$$

and equate real and imaginary parts of the equations, then we obtain the following set of real equations:

$$\frac{\partial^2 V}{\partial r^2} + \frac{1}{r}\frac{\partial V}{\partial r} - \frac{m^2}{r^2}V$$
$$= -4\pi ec\left[\frac{2}{\pi}\int_{r-a}^{r+a}\frac{\rho(R,t)R\,dR}{[4R^2r^2-(R^2+r^2-a^2)^2]^{1/2}} - \theta(r,t)\right], \qquad (94)$$

$$\frac{\partial^2 W}{\partial r^2} + \frac{1}{r}\frac{\partial W}{\partial r} - \frac{m^2}{r^2}W$$
$$= -4\pi ec\left[\frac{2}{\pi}\int_{r-a}^{r+a}\frac{\gamma(R,t)R\,dR}{[4R^2r^2-(R^2+r^2-a^2)^2]^{1/2}} - \delta(r,t)\right], \qquad (95)$$

$$\frac{\partial \rho}{\partial t} = G\gamma + HW - \pi eca^2 H\left[\gamma - \delta + \frac{a^2}{4}\left(\frac{\partial^2 \gamma}{\partial r^2} + \frac{1}{r}\frac{\partial \gamma}{\partial r} - \frac{m^2}{r^2}\gamma\right)\right], \qquad (96)$$

$$\frac{\partial \gamma}{\partial t} = -G\rho - HV + \pi eca^2 H\left[\rho - \theta + \frac{a^2}{4}\left(\frac{\partial^2 \rho}{\partial r^2} + \frac{1}{r}\frac{\partial \rho}{\partial r} - \frac{m^2}{r^2}\rho\right)\right], \qquad (97)$$

$$\frac{\partial \theta}{\partial t} = P\delta + QW, \qquad (98)$$

$$\frac{\partial \delta}{\partial t} = -P\theta - QV. \qquad (99)$$

We wish to solve Eqs. (94)–(99) subject to the following initial conditions: at $t = 0$, the real parts of the perturbed densities of the electrons and the ions are assumed to have the form

$$\rho(r) = \theta(r) = (r_0^2 - r^2)/r_0^2 \quad \text{for} \quad r < r_0,$$
$$= 0 \quad \text{for} \quad r > r_0,$$

where $r_0 = r_{\max} - a$, and a is the gyroradius of the ions. The boundary conditions at $r = 0$ are given by

$$\frac{dV}{dr} = \frac{dW}{dr} = \frac{d\rho}{dr} = \frac{d\gamma}{dr} = \frac{d\theta}{dr} = \frac{d\delta}{dr} = 0.$$

The boundary conditions at $r = r_{\max}$ are given by

$$V = W = \rho = \gamma = \theta = \delta = 0.$$

2. Difference Methods

We wish to solve the initial-value problem specified by Eqs. (94)–(99) on the domain

$$0 \leq r \leq r_{\max}, \qquad t \geq 0.$$

On this domain, consider the finite-difference mesh given by

$$r_j = j\,\Delta r, \qquad j = 0, 1, 2, 3, \ldots, J;$$

where $r_J = r_{\max} = J\,\Delta r$, and $t_n = n\,\Delta t$, $n = 0, 1, 2, 3, \ldots$. We use the standard notation, i.e.,

$$V_j^n = V(r_j, t_n), \quad \text{etc.}$$

and the following difference approximations:

$$\left(\frac{\partial V}{\partial r}\right)_j^n = \frac{V_{j+1}^n - V_{j-1}^n}{2\Delta r}, \qquad \left(\frac{\partial^2 V}{\partial r^2}\right)_j^n = \frac{V_{j+1}^n - 2V_j^n + V_{j-1}^n}{(\Delta r)^2}.$$

The difference approximations to Eqs. (94) and (95) can be written

$$-a_j V_{j+1}^{n+1} + b_j V_j^{n+1} - c_j V_{j-1}^{n+1} = d_j^{n+1}, \tag{100}$$

$$-a_j W_{j+1}^{n+1} + b_j W_n^{n+1} - c_j W_{j-1}^{n+1} = k_j^{n+1}, \tag{101}$$

where

$$-a_j = \frac{1}{(\Delta r)^2} + \frac{1}{2r_j\,\Delta r}, \qquad b_j = -\frac{2}{(\Delta r)^2} - \frac{m^2}{r_j^2}, \qquad -c_j = \frac{1}{(\Delta r)^2} - \frac{1}{2r_j\,\Delta r},$$

$$d_j^{n+1} = k\left[\frac{2}{\pi}\left(\int_{r-\bar{a}}^{r+\bar{a}} \frac{\rho(R) R\,dR}{[4R^2 r^2 - (R^2 + r^2 - \bar{a}^2)^2]^{1/2}}\right)_j^{n+1} - \theta_j^{n+1}\right],$$

$$k_j^{n+1} = k\left[\frac{2}{\pi}\left(\int_{r-\bar{a}}^{r+\bar{a}} \frac{\gamma(R) R\,dR}{[4R^2 r^2 - (R^2 + r^2 - \bar{a}^2)]^{1/2}}\right)_j^{n+1} - \delta_j^{n+1}\right],$$

where $k = -4\pi ec$, and $\bar{a}$ is the ion gyroradius. The integrals above are evaluated numerically at r_j using ρ_j^{n+1} and γ_j^{n+1}, $j = 0, 1, 2, \ldots, J$. The integrands are singular at the endpoints, but integrable. In the neighborhood of the endpoints the mean value theorem is used, and in the remaining interval $r - \bar{a} + \Delta \leq R \leq r + \bar{a} - \Delta$, the trapezoidal rule is used. To maintain accuracy, at least 10 points are used in the integration, so $\bar{a}$ spans at least 5 points, r_j. For small r, where the range is less than 10 r_j points, interpolation is required.

The difference approximation to Eq. (96) is given by the following implicit difference equation:

$$\frac{\rho_j^{n+1} - \rho_j^n}{\Delta t} = \tfrac{1}{2} G_j(\gamma_j^{n+1} + \gamma_j^n) + H_j W_j^n$$

$$+ \tfrac{1}{8} k \bar{a}_j^2 H_j \left[\gamma_j^{n+1} - \delta_j^{n+1} + \frac{\bar{a}_j^2}{4} (-a_j \gamma_{j+1}^{n+1} + b_j \gamma_j^{n+1} - c_j \gamma_{j-1}^{n+1}) \right]$$

$$+ \tfrac{1}{8} k \bar{a}_j^2 H_j \left[\gamma_j^n - \delta_j^n + \frac{\bar{a}_j^2}{4} (-a_j \gamma_{j+1}^n - b_j \gamma_j^n - c_j \gamma_{j-1}^n) \right].$$

Similarly, Eq. (97) is approximated by

$$\frac{\gamma_j^{n+1} - \gamma_j^n}{\Delta t} = -\tfrac{1}{2} G_j(\rho_j^{n+1} + \rho_j^n) - H_j V_j^n$$

$$- \tfrac{1}{8} k \bar{a}_j^2 H_j \left[\rho_j^{n+1} - \theta_j^{n+1} + \frac{\bar{a}_j^2}{4} (-a_j \rho_{j+1}^{n+1} + b_j \rho_j^{n+1} - c_j \rho_{j-1}^{n+1}) \right]$$

$$- \tfrac{1}{8} k \bar{a}_j^2 H_j \left[\rho_j^n - \theta_j^n + \frac{\bar{a}_j^2}{4} (-a_j \rho_{j+1}^n + b_j \rho_j^n - c_j \rho_{j-1}^n) \right].$$

The above implicit difference equations can be written as the following set of linear algebraic equations:

$$A_j \gamma_{j+1}^{n+1} + \rho_j^{n+1} - B_j \gamma_j^{n+1} + C_j \gamma_{j-1}^{n+1} = D_j^n, \tag{102}$$

$$-A_j \rho_{j+1}^{n+1} + B_j \rho_j^{n+1} + \gamma_j^{n+1} - C_j \rho_{j-1}^{n+1} = K_j^n, \tag{103}$$

where

$A_j = \tfrac{1}{32} k \bar{a}_j^4 H_j a_j \Delta t,$

$B_j = \tfrac{1}{2} G_j \Delta t + \tfrac{1}{8} k \bar{a}_j^2 H_j \Delta t + \tfrac{1}{32} k \bar{a}_j^2 H_j b_j \Delta t,$

$C_j = \tfrac{1}{32} k \bar{a}_j^4 H_j c_j \Delta t,$

$D_j^n = -A_j \gamma_{j+1}^n + \rho_j^n + B_j \gamma_j^n - C_j \gamma_{j-1}^n + H_j W_j^n \Delta t - \tfrac{1}{8} k \bar{a}_j^2 \Delta t (\delta_j^n + \delta_j^{n+1}),$

$K_j^n = A_j \rho_{j+1}^n - B_j \rho_j^n + \gamma_j^n + C_j \rho_{j-1}^n - H_j V_j^n \Delta t + \tfrac{1}{8} k \bar{a}_j^2 \Delta t (\theta_j^n + \theta_j^{n+1}).$

Equations (98) and (99) contain only derivatives with respect to the time and we approximate them by the equations

$$\theta_j^{n+1} = \theta_j^{n-1} + 2\Delta t(P_j \delta_j^n + Q_j W_j^n), \qquad (104)$$

$$\delta_j^{n+1} = \delta_j^{n-1} - 2\Delta t(P_j \theta_j^n + Q_j V_j^n). \qquad (105)$$

We can consider the solution of the system of Eqs. (100)–(105). At a given time-step, quantities with superscript n or $n-1$ are known and the quantities with superscript $n+1$ are the unknowns. The first step is to compute θ_j^{n+1} and δ_j^{n+1}, for all j, from Eqs. (104) and (105). The next step is to compute ρ_j^{n+1} and γ_j^{n+1}, for all j. In order to solve the systems of equations given by (102) and (103), we write them as the single system

$$-\bar{A}_j \bar{V}_{j+1}^{n+1} + \bar{B}_j \bar{V}_j^{n+1} - \bar{C}_j \bar{V}_{j-1}^{n+1} = \bar{\phi}_j^n \qquad (106)$$

where

$$\bar{V}_j^{n+1} = \begin{bmatrix} \rho_j^{n+1} \\ \gamma_j^{n+1} \end{bmatrix}, \qquad \bar{\phi}_j^n = \begin{bmatrix} D_j^n \\ K_j^n \end{bmatrix},$$

and

$$-\bar{A}_j = \begin{bmatrix} 0 & A_j \\ -A_j & 0 \end{bmatrix}, \qquad \bar{B}_j = \begin{bmatrix} 1 & -B_j \\ B_j & 0 \end{bmatrix}, \qquad -\bar{C}_j = \begin{bmatrix} 0 & C_j \\ -C_j & 0 \end{bmatrix}.$$

In order to solve the system (106), we use the algorithm

$$\bar{V}_j^{n+1} = \bar{E}_j \bar{V}_{j+1}^{n+1} + \bar{f}_j^{n+1}, \qquad j = 0, 1, 2, \ldots, J-1$$

where the matrices $\bar{E}_j$ and vectors $\bar{f}_j^{n+1}$ are determined from the recurrence relations

$$\bar{E}_j = (\bar{B}_j - \bar{C}_j \bar{E}_{j-1})^{-1} \bar{A}_j, \qquad \bar{f}_j^{n+1} = (\bar{B}_j - \bar{C}_j \bar{E}_{j-1})^{-1} (\bar{\phi}_j^n + \bar{C}_j \bar{f}_{j-1}^{n+1}).$$

The boundary conditions at $r = 0$ give

$$\bar{E}_0 = \begin{bmatrix} 1 & 0 \\ 0 & 1 \end{bmatrix}, \qquad \text{and} \qquad \bar{f}_0^{n+1} = \begin{bmatrix} 0 \\ 0 \end{bmatrix}.$$

The computation consists of a double sweep. On the first sweep the above coefficients are evaluated and on the reverse sweep the $\bar{V}_j^{n+1}$ are evaluated starting with $\bar{V}_J^{n+1}$, which is given by $\rho(r_{\max}, t)$ and $\gamma(r_{\max}, t)$. The third step in the computation cycle is to evaluate V_j^{n+1} and W_j^{n+1} for all j. The method of solution of (100) and (101) is the same as that just described for Eqs. (102) and (103).

This mathematical model and the computational methods described have been used to explain several phenomena observed in plasmas produced by neutral-atom injection into magnetic mirror fields. Some results have been published (Futch et al., 1966) which explain the effects of a large potential on the cooperative behavior of a low-density plasma, and verify the finite orbit stabilization of a plasma under conditions which have been observed experimentally. The stability of plasmas in positive-gradient (minimum-B) mirror fields can also be studied with this program.

B. A Two-Dimensional Nonlinear Model

1. Basic Equations

Plasma instabilities at large amplitudes are obtained by computer calculation of the two-dimensional motion of an ion fluid and an electron fluid. The two charge fluids move with guiding-center velocities in applied magnetic and gravitational fields, with self-electric field due to net charge or charge separation. The two fluids are tenuous, coexist in the same space, and are subject to similar forces. The relatively light electrons are not allowed to undergo the forces that are proportional to mass; hence, there is a difference in fluid velocities. The difference causes charge separation, hence an electric field $\mathbf{E}$. This field in turn acts with the magnetic field $\mathbf{B}$ to produce oscillatory or exponentially growing motion starting from small perturbations. One objective of the program is to determine the final state of (known) instabilities when the plasma is excited initially at small amplitudes.

The plasma is neutral or nearly so and is immersed in a constant, uniform magnetic field $\mathbf{B}$ and external force field $\mathbf{g}$: The velocities of the two fluids are obtained from guiding-center theory (Northrop, 1963) Each fluid obeys an equation of continuity. The net charge density $e(n_i - n_e)$ is used in Poisson's equation to obtain the potential φ. The new electric field changes the velocities the fluid divergence, and hence, the densities.

Plasma interchange is considered as meaning cooperative, charged particle motion, perpendicular to the magnetic field $\mathbf{B}$. The ratio of the plasma pressure to the magnetic field pressure is so low that changes in the value of $\mathbf{B}$ due to the plasma currents can be ignored. The strong magnetic field is also justification for the two-dimensionality. The effects of $\mathbf{B}$-field curvature are simulated by a uniform gravitational field $\mathbf{g}(\perp \mathbf{B})$. The guiding-center drift description of a plasma is known to be valid for many low-frequency phenomena (Chandrasekhar, 1960). The effects of finite size of gyro orbits can be included in the drift description as correction factors (Rosenbluth and Simon, 1965). The physical theory and numerical results have been reported elsewhere (Byers, 1966, 1967b).

The independent variables are x, y, and t. The region is bounded at $y = 0$, $y = h$ by conducting walls at zero potential, $\varphi = 0$; in x, the model is assumed to be periodic with period $L = 48\,\Delta x$. The dependent variables are: the electron and ion number densities n_e, n_i; the potential (due solely to net charge or charge separation $n_i - n_e$); the corresponding electric field $\mathbf{E} = -\nabla\varphi$; and the electron and ion fluid guiding-center velocities $\mathbf{v}_e$ and $\mathbf{v}_i$. The following are the governing equations:

$$\nabla^2 \varphi = -e(n_i - n_e)/\varepsilon_0, \tag{107}$$

$$\mathbf{E} = -\nabla\varphi, \tag{108}$$

$$\mathbf{v}_e = \mathbf{E} \times \mathbf{B}/B^2, \tag{109}$$

$$\mathbf{v}_i = \mathbf{E} \times \mathbf{B}/B^2 + m/e(\mathbf{g} \times \mathbf{B}/B^2) + m/eB^2 \frac{d\mathbf{E}}{dt}, \tag{110}$$

$$\partial n_i/\partial t = -\nabla \cdot (n_i \mathbf{v}_i). \tag{111}$$

$$\partial n_e/\partial t = -\nabla \cdot (n_e \mathbf{v}_e). \tag{112}$$

In difference form the solutions will be obtained at the points $x_i = i\,\Delta x$, $i = 1, 2, \ldots, 48$, $y_j = j\,\Delta y$, $j = 1, 2, \ldots, 48$, and at times $t_n = n\,\Delta t$, $n = 1, 2, 3, \ldots$.

The general program proceeds as follows: Initially, densities n_i and n_e are given. From these, the potential φ, electric field $\mathbf{E}$, and hence, guiding-center velocities are found, all at one time level. The calculations involving the differencing of $\partial/\partial t$ require storage at more than one time level. The new values of the densities n_i and n_e at the new time level are obtained from difference solutions of the equations of continuity.

We are describing a plasma where the cooperative motion of both charge species is a slow $\mathbf{E} \times \mathbf{B}/B^2$ drift of guiding centers across the externally imposed magnetic field. This guiding-center drift description of charged-particle motion demands only that all frequencies are small compared to the ion gyrofrequency,

$$\omega \ll \omega_{ci},$$

and that all macroscopic lengths be much larger than the ion gyroradius,

$$L \gg a_i.$$

These requirements impose a restriction on the maximum allowable net charge density:

$$|n_i - n_e| m_i/(\varepsilon_0 B^2) \ll 1$$

Note that $K = n_i m_i/(\varepsilon_0 B^2)$ can still be much larger than unity if $|n_i - n_e|$ is sufficiently small. K is a critical parameter and is a measure of the effectiveness of the response of the plasma to changes in the electric field.

The assumption that the magnetic field **B** is a constant in time requires that all plasma currents be sufficiently low. This essentially is the "low-beta" approximation and is a restriction on the magnitude of "thermal" velocities, or simply that the plasma thermal energy density be much less than the magnet magnetic energy density.

Readers familiar with incompressible, hydrodynamic models will recognize the close relationship with this plasma model. In one limit where we follow only a single charge species with $\mathbf{v}_E = \mathbf{E} \times \mathbf{B}/B^2$, this plasma model is exactly analogous to those hydrodynamic models where the charge density plays the role of the vorticity (the component perpendicular to the plane of motion), and the electrostatic potential plays the role of the streamfunction. The new feature in this plasma model is the presence of two oppositely charged fluids where the net charge density is obtained from the difference between the densities of those fluids. The significance of this is that when the two charge fluids have approximately equal densities, even small relative velocities are important because they can cause separation and, hence, lead to changes in the electric field. This is the reason that the last two terms in the ion velocity are important (similar terms are ignored for the electrons because of the large mass ratio). The $m_i/eB^2 \mathbf{g} \times \mathbf{B}$ term leads to charge separation and is the reason for the existence of flutes (Rayleigh–Taylor modes) in the plasma (Rosenbluth and Longmire, 1957). The last term, $m_i/eB^2\, d\mathbf{E}/dt$, known as the polarization drift, also leads to charge separation and is the reason for the existance of the low-frequency plasma dielectric constant $\varepsilon_0(1 + K)$ where

$$K = n_i m_i/(\varepsilon_0 B^2).$$

It is this polarization drift which leads to strong computational instability when using the usual procedure for time differencing (the leapfrog or midpoint scheme). We shall deal with alternative time-differencing methods that retain some of the desirable qualities of the leapfrog scheme, and which eliminate the computational instability due to the polarization drift.

2. Spatial Finite-Differencing Procedures

The spatial-differencing procedures used on this model are well-known, ordinary space-centered, fluid-conserving schemes, which are discussed in Section II.

The method used for solving the five-point finite difference form of Poisson's equation is simliar to that of Hockney (1966), which is a fast, direct solution that proceeds by Fourier analysis of the charge density along each row, solving for the potential Fourier amplitudes, and finally synthesizing the actual potentials at each grid point by summing the Fourier terms along each row. The method appears to be considerably faster than any known relaxation method. Knowledge of the Fourier mode amplitudes for the charge density and electrostatic potential can also be a useful diagnostic.

During the integration of the equation of continuity, fluid conservation is obtained by using a space-centered difference analog of $\nabla \cdot (nv)$ which, in the simplest two point form in one dimension, is

$$[(nv)_{j+1} - (nv)_{j-1}]/(2 \Delta x). \tag{113}$$

With the interpretation of $n_j = \int_{-\Delta x/2}^{+\Delta x/2} n \, dx = N_j$, the total fluid in the cell of dimension Δx centered about the grid point j, it is clear that the flux in the total fluid for cells $j + 2$ and $j - 2$ will include contributions that exactly cancel the flux in total fluid for cell j, as given by Eq. (113). This scheme has the somewhat unpleasant aspect that adjacent cells are uncoupled. (Even-numbered cells cancel the fluid flux in other even-numbered cells, and odd numbered cells cancel the fluid flux in other odd-numbered cells.) In one particular model it is known that this property is the cause of a nonlinear computational instability at short wavelengths (Phillips, 1959). (Lilly 1965) shows that this particular instability can be avoided by using certain spatial-differencing schemes. Many other spatial-differencing schemes are possible. It is known that nonlinear fluid calculations frequently encounter serious computational stability problems (evidenced by large amounts of spurious energy appearing in short wavelengths) due to the spatially differenced terms. In many models artificial damping is included to control short wavelengths. One such method is the particular finite-difference scheme given by Eq. (17). In that scheme the amplification factor obtained from carrying out the stability analysis has the form

$$|\lambda| = 1 - O(k \Delta x)^4.$$

The minus sign means that the finite-difference scheme will tend to damp waves, and the $(k\,\Delta x)^4$-dependence means that the short wavelengths will be affected most strongly.

Short run calculations, as are appropriate for some simple single "events," may not be plagued by such problems. That is, the complete calculation may be of sufficiently short duration that errors in short wavelengths do not have enough time to build up to dangerous levels. Several successful, short-run calculations (Byers, 1966, 1967b) were made with the present model with little or no evidence of short wavelength problems. Other calculations with the present model, applied to more complicated situations with a requirement for somewhat longer computer runs, presented computational stability problems of exactly this nature. Completely successful runs require some form of control on short wavelengths.

The finite orbit corrections to the guiding-center drift equations can be expressed with a simple addition to the ion equation of continuity. This additional term involves the spatial operators ∇ and ∇^2. These spatially differenced terms complicate the short wavelength problem mentioned above, but nothing fundamentally new is added to the spatial-differencing problem.

3. *Time-Differencing Procedures; Use of Composite Schemes*

We consider numerical instability of finite-difference equations which are analogs of the equation

$$\partial u/\partial t = F(u, t), \qquad (114)$$

which is the general form of the continuity equations. Truncation error is measured by comparing Eq. (114) with a Taylor series expansion of the finite-difference form of Eq. (114); the net error that results from the cumulative addition of a single time-step truncation error must remain small. Practically all nonlinear fluid calculations are restricted by computer storage limitations to time-difference schemes that use information at two time levels to predict the new values. There are still a large number of schemes in this class, however, and they differ widely in their accuracy and stability properties. The "best" choice of scheme usually depends on the particular type of solution expected.

We examine the stability (cumulative truncation error) of several schemes used to solve the oscillator equation,

$$du/dt = i\omega u. \qquad (115)$$

Lilly (1965) and Kurihara (1965) present comparative list of several schemes as applied to Eq. (115). In this section we construct and analyze composite schemes that retain some of the desirable properties of several schemes. The analytic solution of Eq. (115) is, of course,

$$u(t) = u_0 \exp(i\omega t).$$

The finite-difference solution of Eq. (115) should correspond as closely as possible to the constant amplitude oscillation of the analytic solution. We have obtained composite-difference schemes that maintain a nearly constant amplitude and tolerable errors in phase.

A second problem is to eliminate or damp the extraneous computational modes that always occur when the difference scheme is of higher order than the differential equation. Under certain conditions, our equations are subject to a particularly strong instability due to growing computational modes. In the next section this problem is discussed. The damping of computational modes is a requirement on any composite scheme we derive.

The leapfrog (LF) scheme applied to the general equation, Eq. (114), is with time levels indicated by superscripts,

$$(u^1 - u^{-1})/(2\,\Delta t) = F^0,$$

where the truncation error is $\sim \partial^3 u/\partial t^3$. To obtain the solution of a finite-difference equation, we follow the conventional technique (Richtmyer and Morton, 1967), which represents the difference solution of $u(n\,\Delta t)$ as

$$u^n = \lambda^n u^0,$$

where the λ's are called the amplification factors. Thus, for LF applied to Eq. (115), we have

$$u^1 - u^{-1} = 2ibu^0$$

with $b = \omega\,\Delta t$; the characteristic equation is

$$\lambda = ib \pm (1 - b^2)^{1/2},$$

and λ_+ corresponds to the correct mode and λ_- corresponds to an extraneous computational mode. Note that $|\lambda_\pm| = 1$ if $b^2 \leq 1$. The correct mode therefore shows no error in the amplitude of the wave. The computational mode in this case does not grow or damp. Unfortunately, LF is subject to a strong computational instability when applied to our equations and must be rejected.

The Adams–Bashforth (AB) scheme as applied to Eq. (114) is

$$(u^1 - u^0)/\Delta t = \tfrac{3}{2}F^0 - \tfrac{1}{2}F^{-1},$$

where the truncation error is again $\sim \partial^3 u/\partial t^3$. For AB applied to Eq. (115) we have

$$u^1 - u^0 = \tfrac{3}{2}ibu^0 - \tfrac{1}{2}ibu^{-1},$$

which results in the characteristic equation

$$\lambda^2 - \lambda(1 + \tfrac{3}{2}ib) + \tfrac{1}{2}ib = 0.$$

When $b \ll 1$, this yields

$$|\lambda_+| = 1 + 0(b^4) + \ldots,$$

i.e., a small amplification of the correct mode, and

$$|\lambda_-| = b/2 \ll 1,$$

i.e., a large damping of the computational mode. The amplification of the correct mode may not be tolerable for long time observation.

Composite schemes, which use various combinations of single-step schemes for successive time-steps, have been tested with respect to Eq. (115). The object was to obtain partial cancellation of truncation errors and damping of computational modes. The net effect is more subtle, however, than simply adding errors of opposite "sign." For example, as applied to Eq. (115), LF (no growth) + AB (slow growth) gives net slow damping.

Details of the analysis of stability of composite schemes may be found in Byers (1967a). Many different composite schemes were analyzed and a few superior schemes discovered. As an example of the improvement obtainable we we compare the AB scheme and the composite scheme LF AB AB, i.e., the scheme which uses LF for the 1st, 4th, etc., time-steps and uses AB for the 2nd, 3rd, 5th, 6th, etc., time-steps. We compare the $|\text{amplitude}|^2 = R^2$ at time $\omega t = 50.0$, i.e., after approximately eight full cycles of the wave. If $b = 0.2$, R^2 for AB at this time is 1.24, while R^2 for the composite scheme at this time is 0.99. Thus we see that the AB scheme will increase the energy in the wave by 24%, while the composite scheme will decrease the energy in the wave by only 1%.

There may appear to be undue emphasis on the simple equation, Eq. (115), as our numerical procedure does not actually involve integration of this equation. But since we expect many oscillating or wave-type solutions, the above analysis and our problem should agree, at least qualitatively. Several schemes have been tried in our program when the linear analysis predicts a simple oscillating solution. LF-dominated schemes were unstable due to growing computational modes, as will be discussed in the next section. Other schemes were stable to computational modes, and in all cases there was good quantitative agreement between the predictions of the analysis and the actual results obtained. (Most of these schemes were tested before their analysis was attempted; the relatively large damping and amplification led to the analysis.)

4. *Time-Differencing Instability Due to Computational Modes*

It is well known that LF is computationally unstable when used with the equation

$$\partial u/\partial t = -\omega u.$$

The characteristic equation for the LF scheme is

$$\lambda^2 + 2b\lambda - 1 = 0 \quad \text{where} \quad b = \omega \, \Delta t.$$

This yields

$$\lambda_\pm = -b \pm (1 + b^2)^{1/2}.$$

Note that $|\lambda_-| > 1$; therefore, the computational mode grows and quickly dominates the solution. Contrast this with the AB scheme where the characteristic equation is

$$\lambda^2 - \lambda(1 - \tfrac{3}{2}b) - \tfrac{1}{2}b = 0,$$

or

$$\lambda_\pm = \tfrac{1}{2}(1 - \tfrac{3}{2}b) \pm \tfrac{1}{2}(1 - b + \tfrac{9}{4}b^2)^{1/2},$$

and note that $|\lambda_-| \ll 1$ for small b. This means that the AB scheme will cause a large damping of the computational mode.

Our equations are subject to a dangerous instability due to growing computational modes when the LF scheme or an LF-dominated composite scheme is used. A complete stability analysis of the entire problem using the technique described by Richtmyer and Morton (1967) is easily formulated but is not easily solved. The best that can be done in most complicated systems is to isolate each part and to determine the subsystem stability conditions. The hope is, of course, that the sum of such separate stability conditions will also be sufficient for stability for the actual system. This is the procedure we followed. [It is worth pointing out, however, that Kasahara (1965) found an example where just this subsystem procedure was found to fail.] The term that produces instability in the plasma problem is the polarization drift in the ion velocity. Accordingly, we ignore other terms and examine the subsystem that is a reasonable approximation of the actual system.

Writing the charge densities as

$$\rho_i = en_i, \qquad \rho_e = -en_e, \qquad \rho = \rho_i + \rho_e = e(n_i - n_e), \tag{116}$$

we obtain from Eqs. (111), (112), and (116) an equation for the net charge density,

$$\partial \rho/\partial t = -e\nabla \cdot (n_i \mathbf{v}_i - n_e \mathbf{v}_e). \tag{117}$$

For illustration, net flux will be taken as due to velocity difference which allows us to use

$$n_i \approx n_e = n.$$

The difference $v_i - v_e$ comes from $\mathbf{v}_g (\sim m\mathbf{g} \times \mathbf{B})$ and $\mathbf{v}_P (\sim m\, d\mathbf{E}/dt)$. Since the troublesome part is $\partial \mathbf{E}/\partial t$ in $\partial \mathbf{E}/dt$, we will use $\mathbf{v}_p \sim m\, \partial \mathbf{E}/\partial t$ and ignore $\mathbf{v}_g$. (The common drift $\mathbf{v}_E \gg \mathbf{v}_P$.) Thus, approximately,

$$\frac{\partial \rho}{\partial t} = -\nabla \cdot \left(\frac{nm_i}{B^2} \frac{\partial \mathbf{E}}{\partial t} \right) + \cdots. \tag{118}$$

Replacing ρ with $-\varepsilon_0 \nabla^2 \phi$ and $\mathbf{E} = -\nabla \phi$, and expanding the divergence, we obtain an equation in n and ϕ

$$\frac{\partial}{\partial t}(\nabla^2 \phi) = -\frac{nm}{\varepsilon_0 B^2}\left[\frac{\partial}{\partial t}(\nabla \phi)^2\right] - \frac{m}{\varepsilon_0 B^2}\left[\frac{\partial}{\partial t}(\nabla \phi) \cdot \nabla n\right] + \cdots. \tag{119}$$

In solving, we estimate the r.h.s. from past and present times and the value obtained is used to predict new values; the details depend on the differencing scheme used, as will be shown. The two $\partial(\nabla^2\phi)/\partial t$ terms are not combined; as in our two-fluid model this equation is not solved explicitly.

For simplicity, let n be taken as a zero-order variable and let the variations of ϕ be along only one coordinate, $x = j\,\Delta x$. Let $\nabla \phi$ be given by the two-point expression $(\phi_{j+1} - \phi_{j-1})/(2\,\Delta x)$ and $\nabla^2 \phi$ by the three-point expression $(\phi_{j+1} - 2\phi_j + \phi_{j-1})/\Delta x^2$. Let ϕ be given by a Fourier expansion,

$$\phi(x) = \phi(j\,\Delta x) = \sum_k \phi^k \exp(ikj\,\Delta x). \tag{120}$$

Thus, Eq. (119) is, for a given k,

$$\frac{\partial \phi^k}{\partial t} = \frac{nm}{\varepsilon_0 B^2}\left\{-1 + \left(\frac{i\,\nabla n}{kn}\right)\left(\frac{\sin k\,\Delta x}{k\,\Delta x}\right)\left[\frac{k\,\Delta x/2}{\sin(k\,\Delta x/2)}\right]^2\right\}\frac{\partial \phi^k}{\partial t} + \cdots, \quad (121)$$

or

$$\frac{\partial \phi^k}{\partial t} = (-K + iKD)\frac{\partial \phi^k}{\partial t} + \cdots \quad (122)$$

where

$$D = \left(\frac{\nabla n}{kn}\right)\left(\frac{\sin k\,\Delta x}{k\,\Delta x}\right)\left[\frac{k\,\Delta x/2}{\sin(k\,\Delta x/2)}\right]^2.$$

The r.h.s. may use present and past times; the l.h.s. may use past, present, and future times.

LF differencing gives (dropping the Fourier index k)

$$\phi^1 - \phi^{-1} = (-2K + 2iKD)(\phi^0 - \phi^{-1}),$$

which uses past and present times on the r.h.s. and past and future on the l.h.s. Let

$$S = -2K + 2iKD,$$

then the characteristic equation is

$$\lambda^2 - S\lambda - (1 - S) = 0.$$

The desired solution is

$$\lambda_+ - 1,$$

and the undesired computational mode solution is

$$\lambda_- = -1 + S \quad \text{with} \quad |\lambda_-|^2 = 1 + 4K + 4K^2 + 4K^2 D^2 > 1.$$

Strict inequality holds as $K = n_i m_i/\varepsilon_0 B^2 > 0$. Hence this mode is unconditionally unstable.

AB differencing gives

$$\phi^1 - \phi^0 = \tfrac{1}{2}S[\tfrac{3}{2}(\phi^0 - \phi^{-1}) - \tfrac{1}{2}(\phi^{-1} - \phi^{-2})]$$

with the characteristic equation

$$\lambda^3 - \lambda^2(1 + \tfrac{3}{4}S) + \lambda S - \tfrac{1}{4}S = 0.$$

The desired solution is

$$\lambda = 1.$$

and there are two computational modes obtained from

$$\lambda^2 - \tfrac{3}{4}\lambda S + \tfrac{1}{4}S = 0.$$

For negligible D, marginal stability $|\lambda| = 1$ holds for one of these modes for $K = 0.5$; for the other, $|\lambda| = 0.25$, and hence is damped.

Composite schemes not dominated by LF are stable for $K < 1$. In general, schemes which are composed of a larger fraction of LF are harder to stabilize, i.e., the larger the percentage of LF, the lower the marginal stability value of K. LF-dominated schemes are unstable unless $K \ll 1$.

There should be some mention made about the possible magnitudes of the coefficient D defined in Eq. (122). The trignometric function varies from 1.0 to 0.0 as $k \, \Delta x$ increases from 0 to π where $\lambda = 2 \, \Delta x$ is as short as can be "seen" on the spatial grid. The $\nabla n/kn$ term is roughly $1/k\delta$, where δ is the thickness of the boundary layer. The difficulty arises here at small k, long wavelength. If taken at face value, it means that even the AB scheme would be unstable due to some long wavelength effect of the polarization drift on the electrostatic field. The source of the trouble is the difference analog of the Laplacian operator ∇^2. Similar problems with this term have appeared in previous stability analyses (Charney et al., 1950), where it was remarked that long wavelength phenomena are not expected to cause trouble. In practice, we have found no instability not predictable on the assumption that $D < 1$.

Unless $K \ll 1$, there is an additional damping of the physical mode caused by the inaccuracy of our finite-difference form for $\partial \phi/\partial t$ at $t = 0$; $(\phi^0 - \phi^{-1})/\Delta t$ has an error term $\sim \partial^2 \phi/\partial t^2$. The damping, of course, is reduced as $\omega \, \Delta t$ is reduced but is quite large at $\omega \, \Delta t = 0.3$ if $K \sim 1$. A more accurate finite-difference expression is

$$\frac{1}{\Delta t}(\tfrac{3}{2}\phi^0 - 2\phi^{-1} + \tfrac{1}{2}\phi^{-2}),$$

but the use of more time-steps also introduces more computational modes which may result in more stringent stability conditions. For example, with the use of this more accurate expression for $\partial \phi/\partial t$, the LF scheme is more strongly unstable, and the AB scheme allows a K only one-half as large as previously for marginal stability.

Thus, by restricting K to <1, various difference schemes that are stable to the polarization term can be devised. This is not an entirely satisfactory situation however, because it would be desirable to have K range over values from $\ll 1$ to $\gg 1$. In the next section the changes in the model necessary for $K > 1$ are described.

5. Round-Off Errors; One-Fluid Model

In the last section we showed that the source of the computational mode difficulty in our two-fluid model is the ion polarization velocity; $\mathbf{v}_P = m_i/(B^2 e)(d\mathbf{E}/dt)$ which represents the response of the plasma to changes in $\mathbf{E}$. The higher the value of $K = n_i m_i/\varepsilon_0 B^2$, the more effective the plasma is in responding to changes in $\mathbf{E}$. As K is increased to large values, the resulting net charge separation becomes very small, $|n_i - n_e| \ll n_i$. Even if the two-fluid model were computationally stable, there would be increased round-off errors as $K \gg 1$, due to taking the difference of nearly equal values.

To surmount both the round-off error and the computational instability inherent in the two fluid model, we change the program from two-fluid to one-fluid. Instead of following the electron fluid and ion fluid separately, we follow a neutral fluid ($n = n_i \approx n_e$) and a charged fluid ($n_c = n_i - n_e$) with E/B drifts only; the remaining ion drifts, v_g, v_p, are used only to cause charge separation. (These approximations imply that $v_E \gg v_g$, which usually is a good assumption when $K > 1$.)

The change in the computational stability criterion can be calculated. Equation (118) (corrected for the terms omitted in the previous discussion) in the one-fluid model is now solved explicitly so we can combine $\nabla^2 \phi$ terms, changing Eq. (119) to

$$\frac{\partial}{\partial t}(\nabla^2 \phi) = \left(1 + \frac{nm}{\varepsilon_0 B^2}\right)^{-1} \left(-\frac{m}{\varepsilon_0 B^2}\right) \left[\frac{\partial}{\partial t}(\nabla \phi) \cdot \nabla n\right] + \cdots. \qquad (123)$$

Equation (122) becomes

$$\frac{\partial \phi}{\partial t} = i \frac{K}{1+K} D\left(\frac{\partial \phi}{\partial t}\right) = iD'\left(\frac{\partial \phi}{\partial t}\right) + \cdots. \qquad (124)$$

The stability condition for the AB scheme is now that $D' < 1/2$, and is satisfied (if D itself is sufficiently small) whatever the value of K. This behavior is typical of many composite schemes. LF is still unstable (although not as strongly), but the LF-dominated schemes may not be.

In the range, $K < 1$, the one-fluid model can provide a check against the round-off error in the two fluid model. Some runs have been made with both the one-fluid model and the two-fluid model where the behavior was expected to be one-fluid in nature (E/B drift dominating). No essential differences were found, so we feel confident that round-off error in the two-fluid model is not serious.

6. Applications

As diagnostic computer output, the electric, kinetic, and gravitational energies are followed in time, and the total energy, of course, is to be conserved. Energy plots are frequently a good early indicator of computational trouble.

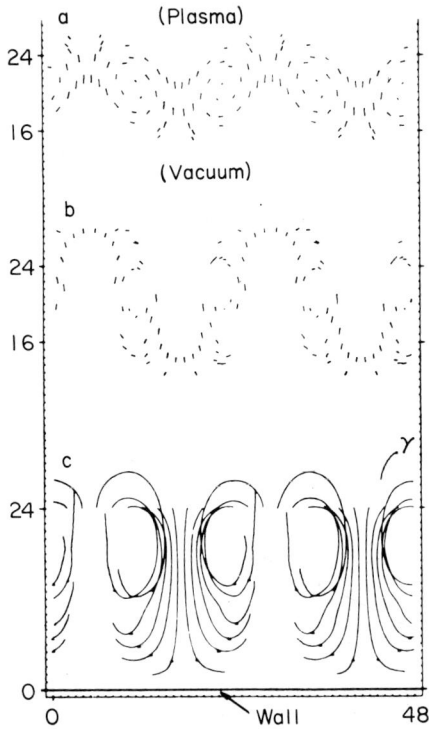

FIG. 2. Rayliegh–Taylor instability growth. Marker particle positions and velocity vectors are shown at two intermediate times: (a) $t = 7.200$; (b) $t = 9.350$; (c) shows the trajectories for the entire run, ending at $t = 12.975$ for those particles initially on line $y = 24\ \Delta x$. The small triangles mark the positions at $t = 11.775$. $t = 7.200$ corresponds to approximately 5 e-folding times of the linear theory. γ is the last part of a trajectory for a particle initially on the bottom row at $(x, y) = (48\ \Delta x, 16\ \Delta x)$. Boundary initially extends from $y \approx 15\ \Delta x$ ($n = 0$ for $y < 15\ \Delta x$) to $y \approx 25\ \Delta x$ ($n = n_{\max}$ for $y > 25\ \Delta x$).

The time behavior of spatial Fourier modes (we have periodicity in x) is available for more detailed understanding and for developing nonlinear theory. The Fourier amplitudes for $\rho = e(n_i - n_e)$ and ϕ $[\rho^k(y)$ and $\phi^k(y)]$ are obtained in each time-step as part of the potential solution. Hence, no additional computation is required.

The primary initial objective has been to obtain growth to large amplitude of various boundary layer instabilities. It was especially desirable to distinguish instabilities that saturated, i.e., with plasma spatially confined, from those that pumped plasma to the wall or were nonconfined. Initial results showed that the Rayleigh–Taylor growth was nonconfined but that the Kelvin–Helmholtz growth was confined—both for low densities, $K \ll 1$ (Byers, 1966). The development was followed with plots of marker particles, which are

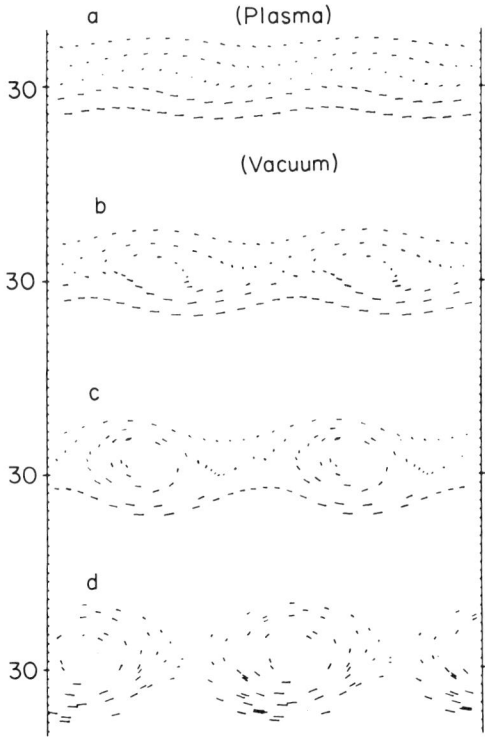

FIG. 3. Kelvin–Helmholtz instability growth. Marker particle positions and velocity vectors are shown at four different times: (a) 15 Δt; (b) 30 Δt, (3) 60 Δt; (d) 120 Δt. The center of the boundary layer is at $y = 30$ as marked. Conducting wall is at $y = 0$. $\Delta t \approx 0.5\,\Delta x/V_{\max}$.

points with forward-pointing "tails" giving velocity vectors. Snapshots and time exposures or trajectory plots were obtained. The marker particles are fictitious particles inserted (usually uniformly) in the plasma and followed with local E/B velocity. Results are given in Byers (1966, 1967a,b). We show some typical snapshots and exposure plots showing ion and electron trajectories for selected marker particles in Figs. 2, 3, and 4.

FIG. 4. A two-fluid flute. Full-time history trajectories are shown for selected ion and electron marker particles. The ions are not maked differently than the electrons, but they can be clearly distinguished by the large g/ω_{ci} streaming of the ions in the negative x-direction. During the time of this run, the ions were able to stream slightly more than the total length of the system, which is two wavelengths. The y-motion of both ions and electrons is caused by the E/B drift velocity. The small triangles show the initial positions of the marker particles. The center of the boundary layer is at $y = 20$ as marked. The instability can be seen to grow almost out to the wall (at $y = 0$) and then reduce somewhat, at which time the calculation was stopped.

Acknowledgments

In the application of the methods described in this article to problems of fusion research, John Killeen wishes to acknowledge the collaboration of Mrs. Shirley Rompel, Dr. Archer H. Futch, Jr., and Mr. Robert P. Freis.

Both authors with to thank Miss Margaret R. Thomas for careful preparation of the typed manuscript.

This work was performed under the auspices of the U.S. Atomic Energy Commission.

REFERENCES

BRETTSCHNEIDER, M., and WEISS, P. B. (1968). *Bull. Am. Phys. Soc.* **13**, 1532.
BYERS, J. .A (1966). *Phys. Fluids.* **9**, 1038.
BYERS, J. A. (1967a). *J. Comp. Phys.* **1**, 496.
BYERS, J. A. (1967b). *Phys. Fluids* **10**, 2235.
CHANDRASEKHAR, S. (1960). "Plasma Physics." Univ. of Chicago Press, Chicago, Illinois.
CHARNEY, J. G., FJORTOFT, R., and VON NEUMANN, J. (1950). *Tellus* **2**, 237.
FUTCH, A. H. JR., HECKROTTE, W., DAMN, C. C., KILLEEN, J., and MISH, L. E. (1962). *Phys. Fluids* **5**, 1277.
FUTCH, A. H., JR., DAMM, C. C., FOOTE, J. H., FREIS, R., GORDON, F. J., HUNT, A. H., KILLEEN, J., MOSES, K. G., POST, R. F., and STEINHAUS, J. F. (1966). *In* "Plasma Physics and Controlled Nuclear Fusion Research," Vol. II, p. 3. IAEA, Vienna.
HOCKNEY, R. W. (1966) *Phys. Fluids* **9**, 1826.
KASAHARA, T. (1965). *Monthly Weather Rev.* **93**, 27.
KELLOGG, P. J. (1965). *Phys. Fluids* **8**, 102.
KILLEEN, J., and ROMPEL, S. L. (1966). *J. Comp. Phys.* **1**, 29.
KILLEEN, J., NEIL, V. K., and HECKROTTE, W. (1966). In " Plasma Physics and Controlled Nuclear Fusion Research," Vol. II, p. 227. IAEA, Vienna.
KUO, L. C., MURPHY, E. G., PETRAVIC, M., and SWEETMAN, D. R. (1964). *Phys. Fluids* **7**, 988.
KURIHARA, A. (1965). *Monthly Weather Rev.* **93**, 33.
LEITH, C. E. (1965). *Meth. Comp. Phys.* **4**, 1.
LILLY, D. K. (1965). *Monthly Weather Rev.* **93**, 11.
NORTHROP, T. G. (1963). "The Adiabatic Motion of Charged Particles." Wiley (Interscience) New York.
PHILLIPS, N. A. (1959). *In* "The Atmosphere and Sea in Motion," pp. 501–504. Rockefeller Inst. Press in association with Oxford Univ. Press, New York.
RICHTYMER, R. D., and MORTON, K. W. (1967). "Difference Methods for Initial Value Problems," Wiley (Interscience), New York.
ROSENBLUTH, M. N., and LONGMIRE, C. L. (1957). *Ann. Phys.* **1**, 120.
ROSENBLUTH, M. N., and SIMON, A. (1965). *Phys. Fluids* **8**. 1300.

Application of Hamilton's Principle to the Numerical Analysis of Vlasov Plasmas†

H. Ralph Lewis

UNIVERSITY OF CALIFORNIA
LOS ALAMOS SCIENTIFIC LABORATORY
LOS ALAMOS, NEW MEXICO

I. Introduction.... 307
II. Lagrangian Description of the Physical System 311
    A. The Physical System 311
    B. Derivation of the Exact Equations from Hamilton's Principle 314
    C. Discussion of the Restrictions on Variations of the Vector Potential 318
III. Derivation of Approximation Schemes from Hamilton's Principle 320
    A. Lagrangian Formulation 320
    B. Hamiltonian Formulation and Energy Theorem 322
IV. Specialization to a Finite Number of Particles 325
    A. One-Dimensional Electrostatic Case 326
    B. Two-Dimensional Electrostatic Case 328
V. Application to the Cold Two-Stream Instability with a Continuum of Particles 332
Appendix A. Gradients with Respect to Position and Velocity 335
Appendix B. Formulas for L and H in the General Case 337
References 338

I. Introduction

THE PROBLEM OF OBTAINING useful numerical descriptions of the behavior of high-temperature plasmas is currently of intense interest, for example in the field of controlled-thermonuclear-fusion research.[1] For sufficiently high temperatures, it is appropriate to use the Vlasov approximation, in which the particles can be represented by time-dependent distribution functions, one for each particle species. These distribution functions are functions of position and velocity in a single-particle phase space, and they satisfy collisionless Boltzmann equations in which the electromagnetic field due to the particles is approximated by the so-called "self-consistent" field. A completely equivalent

---

† Work performed under the auspices of the United States Atomic Energy Commission.

[1] A recent survey of activity in this area can be found in the proceedings of an APS Topical Conference (Proceedings, 1968).

way to represent the particle motion is to specify the trajectories of the points in the single-particle phase space for each species. The trajectories, which are the characteristic curves of the Boltzmann equations, are the solutions of the single-particle equations of motion that are satisfied for each particle when the electromagnetic field due to the particles is replaced by the "self-consistent" field. This latter method of describing the particle motion, that of specifying particle trajectories instead of distribution functions, is being used with increasing favor, especially for numerical work.

In this chapter, we present a general method for deriving numerical approximation schemes within the framework of the trajectory approach, a method based on an exact Lagrangian description of plasmas in the Vlasov limit. The functions to be determined in this Lagrangian formulation are the scalar and vector potentials, $\phi(\mathbf{r}, t)$ and $\mathbf{A}(\mathbf{r}, t)$, as functions of position $\mathbf{r}$ and time t, and functions $\mathbf{R}_k(\mathbf{r}', \mathbf{v}', t)$ that describe the particle trajectories as functions of initial conditions and time.[2] The vectors $\mathbf{r} = \mathbf{R}_k(\mathbf{r}', \mathbf{v}', t)$ and $\mathbf{v} = \dot{\mathbf{R}}_k(\mathbf{r}', \mathbf{v}', t)$, where the dot denotes differentiation with respect to t, are the position and velocity vectors, respectively, of that particle of species k whose initial position and velocity vectors were, respectively, $\mathbf{r}'$ and $\mathbf{v}'$. We consider arbitrary approximations of these functions that can be represented in terms of time-dependent parameters. For example, $\phi(\mathbf{r}, t)$ could be approximated by its time-dependent values at the points of a finite spatial mesh together with a method for interpolating between the mesh points. A more general possibility, which includes this as a special case, would be to approximate $\phi(\mathbf{r}, t)$ by a sum of linearly independent functions of position with time-dependent coefficients. The dependence of the approximation to $\phi(\mathbf{r}, t)$ on the time-dependent parameters could also be highly nonlinear. In general, we allow any approximations of $\phi(\mathbf{r}, t)$, $\mathbf{A}(\mathbf{r}, t)$, and $\mathbf{R}_k(\mathbf{r}', \mathbf{v}', t)$ of the form

$$\phi(\mathbf{r}, t) \cong \Phi[\mathbf{r}, t, \{\alpha_n(t)\}],$$

$$\mathbf{A}(\mathbf{r}, t) \cong \mathscr{A}[\mathbf{r}, t, \{\beta_m(t)\}], \quad (1)$$

and

$$\mathbf{R}_k(\mathbf{r}', \mathbf{v}', t) \cong \mathscr{R}_k[\mathbf{r}', \mathbf{v}', t, \{\gamma_{kl}(t)\}],$$

where Φ, $\mathscr{A}$, and $\mathscr{R}_k$ are arbitrary specified functions, and the dependence on t of the sets of parameters $\alpha_n(t)$, $\beta_m(t)$, and $\gamma_{kl}(t)$ is to be determined.

Once specific functions Φ, $\mathscr{A}$, and $\mathscr{R}_k$ have been chosen, we must still choose a principle that determines the time dependence of the parameters. By using different principles, it is nearly always possible to derive infinitely many different systems of equations for the time-dependent parameters starting from the exact equations of motion. The crux of our approach is to

---

[2] A somewhat different approach, in which the electromagnetic potentials are eliminated at the outset by neglecting retardation effects, has been used by Mjolsness (1970).

use Hamilton's variational principle to choose one of these systems of equations. The system of equations implied by Hamilton's principle is unique and is obtained by substituting Eqs. (1) into the exact Lagrangian and then satisfying the variational principle exactly for those variations of ϕ, **A**, and $\mathbf{R}_k$ allowed by the approximation. The only difference between deriving the exact equations and deriving the equations for the time-dependent parameters is that the variations are carried out within a restricted class of functions in the latter case. These equations for the time-dependent parameters should be optimal in some useful sense.

An important consequence of the variational method of deriving equations for the time-dependent parameters is that there is an exact energy theorem for these equations no matter what choice of Φ, $\mathscr{A}$, and $\mathscr{R}_k$ is made. As an example, if there is no *explicit* time dependence of these functions, and if the physical system is energy-conserving, then the equations for the time-dependent parameters also conserve energy exactly.

Because of the complexity of the behavior of Vlasov plasmas, the great freedom allowed in the choice of Φ, $\mathscr{A}$, and $\mathscr{R}_k$ is highly desirable. These functions can be chosen so as to take account of knowledge or intuition concerning the behavior of the plasma for the problem at hand, and they can be modified as the knowledge or intuition improves. For each choice, the variational principle implies a unique system of equations for the time-dependent parameters. Furthermore, the variational principle can be adapted to include the imposition of auxiliary approximations that are appropriate to a given physical problem. The great generality inherent in the variational approach should be advantageous in obtaining numerical solutions to the problems encountered in experimental research.

The simplest application of Hamilton's principle is to approximate the continuum of particles envisioned in the Vlasov limit by a finite number of particles and the potentials by some class of continuous functions. Some approximation schemes that are obtained in this way are closely related to numerical methods currently in use. For example, if magnetic effects are ignored, and if a piecewise bilinear approximation is used for the scalar potential, then a finite-difference formula for the scalar potential is obtained that includes the "area-weighting" procedure used in particle-in-cell (PIC or CIC) calculations (Morse and Nielson, 1968; Birdsall and Fuss, 1968, 1969). Hamilton's principle prescribes a specific difference scheme for Poisson's equation in this representation, and a specific way of calculating the electric field, such that energy conservation is preserved. The variational approach with a finite number of particles is directly applicable in three dimensions with the full Maxwell equations and external fields, so that a class of schemes can be derived which are energy-conserving generalizations of the particle-in-cell method.

Hamilton's principle can also be applied to cases in which a *continuum* of particles is represented approximately in terms of a finite number of parameters. A particular instance of this, in which the cold two-stream instability is considered, is under investigation by the author (Lewis and Melendez, 1968), and it appears that some quasi-analytical understanding of the asymptotic state of the cold two-stream instability may emerge from this work. Probably the most attractive long-range aspect of the variational method is the possiblity of learning how to describe a continuum of particles usefully in terms of a small number of parameters.

Hamilton's principle is relevant to numerical analyses of Vlasov plasmas when the particles are represented by their trajectories—for a finite number of particles and for continua. To place the method in perspective further, we compare it briefly to methods that involve time-dependent distribution functions. A major difficulty that is encountered in numerical analyses of Vlasov plasmas when the particles are represented by time-dependent distribution functions is that the distribution functions for initially unstable plasmas tend to become ever more convoluted in phase space as time goes on. This effect is the most severe limitation of the applicability of a method involving time-dependent distribution functions, be it a finite-difference scheme for the Boltzmann equation, an expansion method (Armstrong *et al.*, 1970), or the "water-bag" model (Berk and Roberts, 1970). (The "water-bag" model uses time-dependent distribution functions, even though the motion of boundaries in phase space is calculated by means of particle equations of motion.) The observation that representing the particles by their trajectories is quite different in *detail* from using time-dependent distribution functions, and that it may allow useful numerical approximations for longer times, is an important reason for pursuing various trajectory approaches.

There is a superficial similarity of the variational formulation to those methods that represent a time-dependent distribution function as a linear combination of a finite number of basis functions of position and velocity with time-dependent coefficients. The similarity is simply the common use of of parametrization in terms of time-dependent quantities. However, the similarity ends there. In the variational formulation, we do not parametrize time-dependent distribution functions; we parametrize the solution of the particle equations of motion as a function of initial conditions and time. The two procedures are equivalent only if each is carried out exactly.

In Section II, we present the Lagrangian description of Vlasov plasmas in detail. The formulation includes the possibility of nonelectromagnetic potentials that can be velocity-dependent. It also includes the description of material media that exhibit a certain type of nonlinear polarizability or magnetizability. Although no specific application to plasma physics involving nonlinear material media is proposed, there may be useful applications to the numerical study of nonlinear optical phenomena. The derivation of approximation schemes from Hamilton's principle is discussed in Section III. Both Lagrangian and Hamiltonian formulations are presented, and the energy theorem is derived. In Section IV, we specialize the method to the consideration of a finite number of particles, and thereby obtain classes of energy-conserving generalizations of the particle-in-cell method. The application of the variational method to the cold two-stream instability with a continuum of particles is described in Section V.

II. Lagrangian Description of the Physical System

A. The Physical System

We consider a plasma consisting of N species of particles and denote the mass and charge of particles of species k by M_k and Q_k, respectively. The single-particle distribution function for particles of species k in the phase space of position vector $\mathbf{r}$ and velocity $\mathbf{v}$ is denoted by $f_k(\mathbf{r}, \mathbf{v}, t)$ and normalized to the total number of particles of species k. The particles move in the "self-consistent" electromagnetic field and, possibly, in generalized nonelectromagnetic potentials that we denote by $U_k(\mathbf{r}, \mathbf{v}, t)$ for species k. We also allow the possibility of external (prescribed) charge and current densities $\rho_0(\mathbf{r}, t)$ and $\mathbf{j}_0(\mathbf{r}, t)$. The total charge and current densities, $\rho(\mathbf{r}, t)$ and $\mathbf{j}(\mathbf{r}, t)$, are

$$\rho(\mathbf{r}, t) = \rho_0(\mathbf{r}, t) + \sum_{k=1}^{N} Q_k \int d^3v\, f_k(\mathbf{r}, \mathbf{v}, t) \tag{2a}$$

and

$$\mathbf{j}(\mathbf{r}, t) = \mathbf{j}_0(\mathbf{r}, t) + \sum_{k=1}^{N} Q_k \int d^3v\, \mathbf{v} f_k(\mathbf{r}, \mathbf{v}, t). \tag{2b}$$

The force $\mathbf{F}_k(\mathbf{r}, \mathbf{v}, t)$ on a particle of species k whose position and velocity vectors at time t are $\mathbf{r}$ and $\mathbf{v}$ is the Lorentz force plus the force derived from the generalized potential $U_k(\mathbf{r}, \mathbf{v}, t)$:

$$\mathbf{F}_k(\mathbf{r}, \mathbf{v}, t) = Q_k\left[\mathbf{E}(\mathbf{r}, t) + \frac{1}{c} \mathbf{v} \times \mathbf{B}(\mathbf{r}, t)\right]$$
$$- \nabla_\mathbf{r} U_k(\mathbf{r}, \mathbf{v}, t) + \frac{d}{dt} \nabla_\mathbf{v} U_k(\mathbf{r}, \mathbf{v}, t), \tag{3}$$

where $\mathbf{E}$ is the electric field, $\mathbf{B}$ is the magnetic field, and c is the speed of light. The precise meaning of gradients with respect to **r** and **v** acting on a function of **r** and **v** is explained in Appendix A. We denote the position vector of a particle of species k whose initial position and velocity vectors are **r**′ and **v**′, respectively, by $\mathbf{R}_k(\mathbf{r}', \mathbf{v}', t)$. For conciseness of notation, we shall frequently omit the arguments of this function. It satisfies the usual nonrelativistic equation of motion,

$$M_k \ddot{\mathbf{R}}_k = \mathbf{F}_k(\mathbf{R}_k, \dot{\mathbf{R}}_k, t), \tag{4}$$

with the initial conditions

$$\mathbf{R}_k(\mathbf{r}', \mathbf{v}', 0) = \mathbf{r}', \tag{5a}$$

and

$$\dot{\mathbf{R}}_k(\mathbf{r}', \mathbf{v}', 0) = \mathbf{v}'. \tag{5b}$$

A dot always denotes differentiation with respect to t:

$$\dot{\mathbf{R}}_k(\mathbf{r}', \mathbf{v}', t) \equiv \frac{\partial}{\partial t} \mathbf{R}_k(\mathbf{r}', \mathbf{v}', t).$$

If there is a continuum of initial positions and velocities, then the equation of motion for $\mathbf{R}_k(\mathbf{r}', \mathbf{v}', t)$ implies a collisionless Boltzmann equation for $f_k(\mathbf{r}, \mathbf{v}, t)$:

$$\frac{\partial f_k}{\partial t} + \mathbf{v} \cdot \nabla_\mathbf{r} f_k + \frac{1}{M_k} \mathbf{F}_k(\mathbf{r}, \mathbf{v}, t) \cdot \nabla_\mathbf{v} f_k = 0. \tag{6}$$

Equation (6) is equivalent to Eq. (4) since the solutions of Eq. (4) are the characteristic curves of Eq. (6). If we write the inverse of the equations

$$\mathbf{r} = \mathbf{R}_k(\mathbf{r}', \mathbf{v}', t), \tag{7a}$$

and

$$\mathbf{v} = \dot{\mathbf{R}}_k(\mathbf{r}', \mathbf{v}', t), \tag{7b}$$

as

$$\mathbf{r}' = \mathbf{G}_k(\mathbf{r}, \mathbf{v}, t). \tag{8a}$$

and

$$\mathbf{v}' = \mathbf{P}_k(\mathbf{r}, \mathbf{v}, t), \tag{8b}$$

then $f_k(\mathbf{r}, \mathbf{v}, t)$ can be expressed as

$$f_k(\mathbf{r}, \mathbf{v}, t) = f_k[\mathbf{G}_k(\mathbf{r}, \mathbf{v}, t), \mathbf{P}_k(\mathbf{r}, \mathbf{v}, t), 0]. \tag{9}$$

The approximation of describing plasmas in terms of continuum single-particle distribution functions in this way is known as the Vlasov approximation.

In our description of the electromagnetic field, we shall allow a certain class of material media that exhibit nonlinear polarizability and magnetizability. It happens to be easy to do so within the variational formulation, and it may be useful for some problems of *nonlinear optics*. It may also find application in problems of plasma physics, although no specific application is proposed here. In order to allow polarizable and magnetizable media, we take Maxwell's equations in the form

$$\nabla \cdot \mathbf{B} = 0, \tag{10a}$$

$$\nabla \times \mathbf{E} = -\frac{1}{c}\dot{\mathbf{B}}, \tag{10b}$$

$$\nabla \cdot \mathbf{D} = 4\pi\rho, \tag{11a}$$

$$\nabla \times \mathbf{H} = \frac{4\pi}{c}\mathbf{j} + \frac{1}{c}\dot{\mathbf{D}}. \tag{11b}$$

The vectors $\mathbf{D}$ and $\mathbf{H}$ that we shall allow are those that are derivable from scalar functions $\psi(\mathbf{E}, \mathbf{r}, t)$ and $\chi(\mathbf{B}, \mathbf{r}, t)$ by means of the formulas

$$\mathbf{D}(\mathbf{r}, t) = 4\pi \nabla_{\mathbf{E}}\psi(\mathbf{E}, \mathbf{r}, t) \tag{12a}$$

and

$$\mathbf{H}(\mathbf{r}, t) = 4\pi \nabla_{\mathbf{B}}\chi(\mathbf{B}, \mathbf{r}, t). \tag{12b}$$

The vectors $\mathbf{D}$ and $\mathbf{H}$ depend on $\mathbf{r}$ and t implicitly through the dependence of $\mathbf{E}$ and $\mathbf{B}$ on $\mathbf{r}$ and t. In addition to this implicit dependence, explicit dependence on $\mathbf{r}$ and t is also allowed. As a result, ψ and χ may be useful in describing situations in which the nature and distribution of polarizable and magnetizable material media change spatially and temporally. Normally, in regions where particles are allowed, we would take

$$\psi = \frac{1}{8\pi}E^2 \quad \text{and} \quad \chi = \frac{1}{8\pi}B^2, \tag{13}$$

so that **D** and **H** are related to **E** and **B** by

$$\mathbf{D} = \mathbf{E} \quad \text{and} \quad \mathbf{H} = \mathbf{B}. \tag{14}$$

In any event, we introduce scalar and vector potentials $\phi(\mathbf{r}, t)$ and $\mathbf{A}(\mathbf{r}, t)$ in the standard way by the relations

$$\mathbf{E} = -\nabla\phi - \frac{1}{c}\dot{\mathbf{A}}, \tag{15a}$$

and

$$\mathbf{B} = \nabla \times \mathbf{A}. \tag{15b}$$

Then Eqs. (10) are satisfied automatically.

B. Derivation of the Exact Equations from Hamilton's Principle

For a finite number of point particles that interact via the electromagnetic field, there is an exact Lagrangian for describing both the particles and the field (Goldstein, 1950). The Lagrangian that we use is a particular continuum approximation to the Lagrangian for point particles, extended to include the possibility of nonlinear material media and generalized nonelectromagnetic potentials (Lewis, 1967, 1970.) The relevance to Vlasov plasmas of this continuum approximation to the Lagrangian was first pointed out by Low (1958) and Sturrock (1958) in connection with linearized analyses.

The Lagrangian is

$$L = \sum_{k=1}^{N} \int d^3r' \, d^3v' \, f_k(\mathbf{r}', \mathbf{v}', 0) \Big\{ \frac{1}{2} M_k \dot{\mathbf{R}}_k^2 - U_k(\mathbf{R}_k, \dot{\mathbf{R}}_k, t)$$

$$- Q_k \phi(\mathbf{R}_k, t) + \frac{1}{c} Q_k \dot{\mathbf{R}}_k \cdot \mathbf{A}(\mathbf{R}_k, t) \Big\}$$

$$+ \int_V d^3r \Big\{ \psi(\mathbf{E}, \mathbf{r}, t) - \chi(\mathbf{B}, \mathbf{r}, t)$$

$$- \rho_0(\mathbf{r}, t)\phi(\mathbf{r}, t) + \frac{1}{c} \mathbf{j}_0(\mathbf{r}, t) \cdot \mathbf{A}(\mathbf{r}, t) \Big\}. \tag{16}$$

For conciseness, we have simply written $\mathbf{R}_k$ instead of $\mathbf{R}_k(\mathbf{r}', \mathbf{v}', t)$ in this formula. Whenever the arguments of $\mathbf{R}_k$ are omitted, they are to be understood in this way. The integration over $\mathbf{r}'$ and $\mathbf{v}'$ extends over the full range of these variables. The integration over **r** extends over a volume V on whose boundaries appropriate boundary conditions on the electromagnetic field have been prescribed. The volume V must contain all of the particles during the time of interest; that is, it must contain the vectors $\mathbf{R}_k(\mathbf{r}', \mathbf{v}', t)$ for all values of $\mathbf{r}'$ and $\mathbf{v}'$ during that time. However, if we are dealing with a system that is spatially infinite and periodic, we may modify Eq. (16) by allowing the integrations over $\mathbf{r}'$ and $\mathbf{r}$ to extend only over one periodicity cell. The integral over a periodicity cell does not depend on the choice of cell, so that integration over one cell instead of the full region only changes the Lagrangian by an unimportant numerical factor. The vectors **E** and **B** are to be expressed in terms of ϕ and **A** by Eqs. (15).

The exact equations for the physical system can be derived from Hamilton's principle,

$$\delta \int_{t_1}^{t_2} L \, dt = 0, \tag{17}$$

where the functions to be varied independently are ϕ, **A**, and $\mathbf{R}_k$, and where t_1 and t_2 are two arbitrary times. In this section, we shall derive the exact equations from Eq. (17) and, in so doing, determine what restrictions must be placed on the variations of ϕ, **A**, and $\mathbf{R}_k$.

The variation of the integral of the Lagrangian with respect to $\mathbf{R}_k$ is

$$\begin{aligned}
\delta_{\mathbf{R}_k} \int_{t_1}^{t_2} L \, dt &= \int_{t_1}^{t_2} dt \int d^3\mathbf{r}' \, d^3\mathbf{v}' \, f_k(\mathbf{r}', \mathbf{v}', 0) \Big\{ \Big[-\nabla_{\mathbf{R}_k} U_k(\mathbf{R}_k, \dot{\mathbf{R}}_k, t) \\
&\quad - Q_k \nabla_{\mathbf{R}_k} \phi(\mathbf{R}_k, t) + \frac{1}{c} Q_k (\nabla_{\mathbf{R}_k} \mathbf{A}(\mathbf{R}_k, t)) \cdot \dot{\mathbf{R}}_k \Big] \cdot \delta \mathbf{R}_k \\
&\quad + \Big[M_k \dot{\mathbf{R}}_k - \nabla_{\dot{\mathbf{R}}_k} U_k(\mathbf{R}_k, \dot{\mathbf{R}}_k, t) + \frac{1}{c} Q_k \mathbf{A}(\mathbf{R}_k, t) \Big] \cdot \delta \dot{\mathbf{R}}_k \Big\} \\
&= \int_{t_1}^{t_2} dt \int d^3\mathbf{r}' \, d^3\mathbf{v}' \, f_k(\mathbf{r}', \mathbf{v}', 0) \Big\{ - M_k \ddot{\mathbf{R}}_k - \nabla_{\mathbf{R}_k} U_k(\mathbf{R}_k, \dot{\mathbf{R}}_k, t) \\
&\quad + \frac{d}{dt} \nabla_{\dot{\mathbf{R}}_k} U_k(\mathbf{R}_k, \dot{\mathbf{R}}_k, t) - Q_k \nabla_{\mathbf{R}_k} \phi(\mathbf{R}_k, t) - \frac{1}{c} Q_k \dot{\mathbf{A}}(\mathbf{R}_k, t) \\
&\quad + \frac{1}{c} Q_k \Big[(\nabla_{\mathbf{R}_k} \mathbf{A}(\mathbf{R}_k, t)) \cdot \dot{\mathbf{R}}_k - \dot{\mathbf{R}}_k \cdot \nabla_{\mathbf{R}_k} \mathbf{A}(\mathbf{R}_k, t) \Big] \Big\} \cdot \delta \mathbf{R}_k \\
&\quad + \Big\{ \Big[M_k \dot{\mathbf{R}}_k - \nabla_{\dot{\mathbf{R}}_k} U_k(\mathbf{R}_k, \dot{\mathbf{R}}_k, t) + \frac{1}{c} Q_k \mathbf{A}(\mathbf{R}_k, t) \Big] \cdot \delta \mathbf{R}_k \Big\} \Big|_{t_1}^{t_2}, \tag{18}
\end{aligned}$$

where, as before, the dot denotes partial differentiation with respect to t:

$\dot{\mathbf{A}}(\mathbf{r}, t) \equiv (\partial/\partial t) \mathbf{A}(\mathbf{r}, t)$. We now restrict the variations of $\mathbf{R}_k$ by requiring that they vanish for $t = t_1$ and $t = t_2$:

$$\delta \mathbf{R}_k(\mathbf{r}', \mathbf{v}', t_1) = \delta \mathbf{R}_k(\mathbf{r}', \mathbf{v}', t_2) = 0. \tag{19}$$

This means that $\mathbf{R}_k$ is varied only among those functions that coincide with the desired solution for $\mathbf{R}_k$ at times t_1 and t_2. As a result of this restriction, the part of Eq. (18) that is simply evaluated at the limits t_1 and t_2 vanishes:

$$\left\{ \left[M_k \dot{\mathbf{R}}_k - \nabla_{\dot{\mathbf{R}}_k} U_k(\mathbf{R}_k, \dot{\mathbf{R}}_k, t) + \frac{1}{c} Q_k \mathbf{A}(\mathbf{R}_k, t) \right] \cdot \delta \mathbf{R}_k \right\} \Big|_{t_1}^{t_2} = 0. \tag{20}$$

Since the right-hand side of Eq. (18) must vanish for arbitrary $\delta \mathbf{R}_k$ satisfying Eq. (19), the integrand itself must vanish. As a result of the vector identity

$$(\nabla_{\mathbf{R}_k} \mathbf{A}(\mathbf{R}_k, t)) \cdot \dot{\mathbf{R}}_k - \dot{\mathbf{R}}_k \cdot \nabla_{\mathbf{R}_k} \mathbf{A}(\mathbf{R}_k, t) = \dot{\mathbf{R}}_k \times (\nabla_{\mathbf{R}_k} \times \mathbf{A}(\mathbf{R}_k, t)), \tag{21}$$

the equation obtained by setting the integrand of Eq. (18) equal to zero is precisely the particle equation of motion, Eq. (4).

The variation of the integral of the Lagrangian with respect to ϕ is

$$\delta_\phi \int_{t_1}^{t_2} L \, dt = -\sum_{k=1}^{N} \int_{t_1}^{t_2} dt \int d^3\mathbf{r}' \, d^3\mathbf{v}' \, f_k(\mathbf{r}', \mathbf{v}', 0) Q_k \, \delta\phi(\mathbf{R}_k, t)$$

$$+ \int_{t_1}^{t_2} dt \int_V d^3\mathbf{r} \{ -[\nabla_\mathbf{E} \psi(\mathbf{E}, \mathbf{r}, t)] \cdot \delta[\nabla\phi(\mathbf{r}, t)] - \rho_0(\mathbf{r}, t) \, \delta\phi(\mathbf{r}, t) \}. \tag{22}$$

In the kth term of the summation in Eq. (22), we change the variables of integration from $\mathbf{r}'$ and $\mathbf{v}'$ to $\mathbf{r}$ and $\mathbf{v}$ as defined by Eqs. (7) and (8). It can be shown that the Jacobian of this transformation is unity. We also use the identity given by Eq. (9). Then the variation with respect to ϕ can be written as

$$\delta_\phi \int_{t_1}^{t_2} L \, dt = \int_{t_1}^{t_2} dt \int_V d^3\mathbf{r} \left\{ - \left[\sum_{k=1}^{N} Q_k \int d^3\mathbf{v} \, f_k(\mathbf{r}, \mathbf{v}, t) \right] \delta\phi(\mathbf{r}, t) \right.$$

$$\left. - \frac{1}{4\pi} \mathbf{D}(\mathbf{r}, t) \cdot \delta[\nabla\phi(\mathbf{r}, t)] - \rho_0(\mathbf{r}, t) \, \delta\phi(\mathbf{r}, t) \right\}$$

$$= \int_{t_1}^{t_2} dt \int_V d^3\mathbf{r} \left\{ -\rho(\mathbf{r}, t) + \frac{1}{4\pi} \nabla \cdot \mathbf{D}(\mathbf{r}, t) \right\} \delta\phi(\mathbf{r}, t)$$

$$- \frac{1}{4\pi} \int_{t_1}^{t_2} dt \int_{\text{boundary of } V} d\mathbf{S} \cdot [\delta\phi(\mathbf{r}, t) \mathbf{D}(\mathbf{r}, t)]. \tag{23}$$

We now impose the boundary condition

$$\int_{\text{boundary of } V} d\mathbf{S} \cdot [\delta\phi(\mathbf{r}, t)\mathbf{D}(\mathbf{r}, t)] = 0. \tag{24}$$

One way of satisfying this boundary condition is to prescribe the values of $\phi(\mathbf{r}, t)$ on the boundary of V so that $\delta\phi(\mathbf{r}, t)$ vanishes there. Since the right-hand side of Eq. (23) must vanish for arbitrary $\delta\phi$ satisfying Eq. (24), the integrand of the volume integral must vanish. The equation so obtained is one of the required Maxwell equations, Eq. (11a).

The variation of the integral of the Lagrangian with respect to $\mathbf{A}$ is

$$\delta_{\mathbf{A}} \int_{t_1}^{t_2} L \, dt = \sum_{k=1}^{N} \int_{t_1}^{t_2} dt \int d^3\mathbf{r}' \, d^3\mathbf{v}' \, f_k(\mathbf{r}', \mathbf{v}', 0) \frac{1}{c} Q_k \dot{\mathbf{R}}_k \cdot \delta\mathbf{A}(\mathbf{R}_k, t)$$

$$+ \int_{t_1}^{t_2} dt \int_V d^3\mathbf{r} \left\{ -\frac{1}{c} [\nabla_{\mathbf{E}} \psi(\mathbf{E}, \mathbf{r}, t)] \cdot \delta[\dot{\mathbf{A}}(\mathbf{r}, t)] \right.$$

$$\left. - [\nabla_{\mathbf{B}} \chi(\mathbf{B}, \mathbf{r}, t)] \cdot \delta[\nabla \times \mathbf{A}(\mathbf{r}, t)] + \frac{1}{c} \mathbf{j}_0(\mathbf{r}, t) \cdot \delta\mathbf{A}(\mathbf{r}, t) \right\}. \tag{25}$$

We transform the integrals in the summation in Eq. (25) in the same way in which the integrals in the summation in Eq. (22) were transformed. Then the variation with respect to $\mathbf{A}$ can be written as

$$\delta_{\mathbf{A}} \int_{t_1}^{t_2} L \, dt = \int_{t_1}^{t_2} dt \int_V d^3\mathbf{r} \left\{ \frac{1}{c} \left[\sum_{k=1}^{N} Q_k \int d^3\mathbf{v} \, \mathbf{v} f_k(\mathbf{r}, \mathbf{v}, t) \right] \cdot \delta\mathbf{A}(\mathbf{r}, t) \right.$$

$$- \frac{1}{4\pi c} \mathbf{D}(\mathbf{r}, t) \cdot \delta[\dot{\mathbf{A}}(\mathbf{r}, t)] - \frac{1}{4\pi} \mathbf{H}(\mathbf{r}, t) \cdot \delta[\nabla \times \mathbf{A}(\mathbf{r}, t)]$$

$$\left. + \frac{1}{c} \mathbf{j}_0(\mathbf{r}, t) \cdot \delta\mathbf{A}(\mathbf{r}, t) \right\}$$

$$= \int_{t_1}^{t_2} dt \int_V d^3\mathbf{r} \left\{ \frac{1}{c} \mathbf{j}(\mathbf{r}, t) + \frac{1}{4\pi c} \dot{\mathbf{D}}(\mathbf{r}, t) - \frac{1}{4\pi} \nabla \times \mathbf{H}(\mathbf{r}, t) \right\} \cdot \delta\mathbf{A}(\mathbf{r}, t)$$

$$- \frac{1}{4\pi c} \int_V d^3\mathbf{r} \left\{ \mathbf{D}(\mathbf{r}, t) \cdot \delta\mathbf{A}(\mathbf{r}, t) \Big|_{t_1}^{t_2} \right\}$$

$$- \frac{1}{4\pi} \int_{t_1}^{t_2} dt \int_{\text{boundary of } V} d\mathbf{S} \cdot [\delta\mathbf{A}(\mathbf{r}, t) \times \mathbf{H}(\mathbf{r}, t)]. \tag{26}$$

We now restrict the variation of the component of $\delta\mathbf{A}$ along $\mathbf{D}$ by requiring that it vanish for $t = t_1$ and $t = t_2$:

$$\mathbf{D}(\mathbf{r}, t_1) \cdot \delta\mathbf{A}(\mathbf{r}, t_1) = \mathbf{D}(\mathbf{r}, t_2) \cdot \delta\mathbf{A}(\mathbf{r}, t_2) = 0. \tag{27}$$

This means that $\mathbf{A}$ is varied only among those functions whose components along $\mathbf{D}$ coincide with the component along $\mathbf{D}$ of the desired solution for $\mathbf{A}$ at times t_1 and t_2. As a result of this restriction, the next to last term in Eq. (26) vanishes:

$$\mathbf{D}(\mathbf{r}, t) \cdot \delta\mathbf{A}(\mathbf{r}, t) \Big|_{t_1}^{t_2} = 0. \tag{28}$$

We also impose the boundary condition

$$\int_{\text{boundary of } V} d\mathbf{S} \cdot [\delta\mathbf{A}(\mathbf{r}, t) \times \mathbf{H}(\mathbf{r}, t)] = 0, \tag{29}$$

so that the last term of Eq. (26) vanishes too. One way of satisfying this boundary condition is to prescribe the values of $\mathbf{A}(\mathbf{r}, t)$ on the boundary of V so that $\delta\mathbf{A}(\mathbf{r}, t)$ vanishes there. However, it is clearly not necessary to restrict $\delta\mathbf{A}$ so severely. Since the right-hand side of Eq. (26) must vanish for arbitrary $\delta\mathbf{A}$ satisfying Eqs. (27) and (29), the integrand of the volume integral must vanish. The equation so obtained is the other required Maxwell equation, Eq. (11b).

In summary, Hamilton's principle, Eq. (17), leads to the correct equations for the physical system provided that the variations are restricted to satisfy Eqs. (19), (24), (27), and (29).

C. Discussion of the Restrictions on Variations of the Vector Potential

For the approximation schemes that we shall consider, it will be necessary to restrict all components of the variations of $\mathbf{A}(\mathbf{r}, t)$ to vanish at times t_1 and t_2. This is a much more severe restriction than Eq. (27), which was the only restriction on $\delta\mathbf{A}$ required for deriving the exact equations from Hamilton's principle. In this section, we show that the requirement of gauge invariance for the electromagnetic field allows us to restrict the variations of $\mathbf{A}(\mathbf{r}, t)$ to vanish at times t_1 and t_2 without loss of generality for the electromagnetic field.

First we note that the electromagnetic potentials are only needed for computing the electric and magnetic fields. When the potentials are varied in the integral of the Lagrangian, they only need be varied within a class of functions from which all allowable electric and magnetic fields can be derived and which satisfy the boundary and initial conditions that we deduced in the previous section. There are many such classes of functions, and they are related by gauge transformations.

The variations of **E** and **B** induced by variations of ϕ and **A** are:

$$\delta \mathbf{E}(\mathbf{r}, t) = -\delta \nabla \phi(\mathbf{r}, t) - \frac{1}{c} \delta \left(\frac{\partial}{\partial t} \mathbf{A}(\mathbf{r}, t) \right)$$

$$= -\nabla \delta \phi(\mathbf{r}, t) - \frac{1}{c} \frac{\partial}{\partial t} \delta \mathbf{A}(\mathbf{r}, t), \tag{30a}$$

$$\delta \mathbf{B}(\mathbf{r}, t) = \delta(\nabla \times \mathbf{A}(\mathbf{r}, t)) = \nabla \times \delta \mathbf{A}(\mathbf{r}, t). \tag{30b}$$

The initial conditions that are required for $\mathbf{B}(\mathbf{r}, t)$ to be unique are equivalent to fixing $\mathbf{B}(\mathbf{r}, t)$ at times t_1 and t_2. Therefore, we only need consider variations such that $\delta \mathbf{B}(\mathbf{r}, t_1)$ and $\delta \mathbf{B}(\mathbf{r}, t_2)$ vanish, in which case Eq. (30b) implies that $\delta \mathbf{A}(\mathbf{r}, t_1)$ and $\delta \mathbf{A}(\mathbf{r}, t_2)$ are the gradients of scalar functions. We now introduce a scalar function $\eta(\mathbf{r}, t)$ to make a gauge transformation to new variations of the potentials, denoting the new variations by primes:

$$[\delta \phi(\mathbf{r}, t)]' = \delta \phi(\mathbf{r}, t) - \frac{1}{c} \frac{\partial}{\partial t} \eta(\mathbf{r}, t),$$

$$[\delta \mathbf{A}(\mathbf{r}, t)]' = \delta \mathbf{A}(\mathbf{r}, t) + \nabla \eta(\mathbf{r}, t).$$

The variations of $\mathbf{E}(\mathbf{r}, t)$ and $\mathbf{B}(\mathbf{r}, t)$ are left unchanged by this transformation. Since $\delta \mathbf{A}(\mathbf{r}, t_1)$ and $\delta \mathbf{A}(\mathbf{r}, t_2)$ are gradients of scalar functions, we can make $[\delta \mathbf{A}(\mathbf{r}, t_1)]'$ and $[\delta \mathbf{A}(\mathbf{r}, t_2)]'$ vanish by choosing $\eta(\mathbf{r}, t)$ to satisfy

$$\nabla \eta(\mathbf{r}, t_1) = -\delta \mathbf{A}(\mathbf{r}, t_1) \quad \text{and} \quad \nabla \eta(\mathbf{r}, t_2) = -\delta \mathbf{A}(\mathbf{r}, t_2).$$

Therefore, when applying Hamilton's principle we may replace Eq. (27) by the more convenient condition

$$\delta \mathbf{A}(\mathbf{r}, t_1) = \delta \mathbf{A}(\mathbf{r}, t_2) = 0. \tag{31}$$

Henceforth, we shall always use Eq. (31) instead of Eq. (27).

III. Derivation of Approximation Schemes from Hamilton's Principle

A. LAGRANGIAN FORMULATION

The first step in using Hamilton's principle to derive an approximation scheme for the functions ϕ, $\mathbf{A}$, and $\mathbf{R}_k$ is to choose a specific type of approximation of those functions. We consider those approximations that can be represented in terms of a set of time-dependent parameters whose time dependence is to be found. That is, we consider any approximations of $\phi(\mathbf{r}, t)$, $\mathbf{A}(\mathbf{r}, t)$, and $\mathbf{R}_k(\mathbf{r}', \mathbf{v}', t)$ of the form

$$\phi(\mathbf{r}, t) \cong \Phi[\mathbf{r}, t, \{\alpha_n(t)\}], \tag{32a}$$

$$\mathbf{A}(\mathbf{r}, t) \cong \mathscr{A}[\mathbf{r}, t, \{\beta_m(t)\}], \tag{32b}$$

and

$$\mathbf{R}_k(\mathbf{r}', \mathbf{v}', t) \cong \mathscr{R}_k[\mathbf{r}', \mathbf{v}', t, \{\gamma_{kl}(t)\}], \tag{32c}$$

where Φ, $\mathscr{A}$, and $\mathscr{R}_k$ are specified functions of their arguments, and the dependence on t of the sets of parameters $\alpha_n(t)$, $\beta_m(t)$, and $\gamma_{kl}(t)$ is to be determined. The functions Φ, $\mathscr{A}$, and $\mathscr{R}_k$, and the initial conditions on $\alpha_n(t)$, $\beta_m(t)$, and $\gamma_{kl}(t)$, must be chosen to satisfy the boundary and initial conditions on the potentials and trajectories appropriate to the problem at hand. The crux of our method of deriving approximation schemes is to use Hamilton's principle to determine a unique set of equations for the time-dependent parameters. Before proceeding to apply Hamilton's principle, we illustrate the choice of functions Φ, $\mathscr{A}$, and $\mathscr{R}_k$ by an example. The *simplest* example is to choose Φ, $\mathscr{A}$, and $\mathscr{R}_k$ without *explicit* time dependence as linear combinations of a finite number of linearly independent basis functions with time-dependent coefficients:

$$\Phi[\mathbf{r}, t, \{\alpha_n(t)\}] = \sum_{n=1}^{N_1} \alpha_n(t)\Phi_n(\mathbf{r}), \tag{33a}$$

$$\mathscr{A}[\mathbf{r}, t, \{\beta_m(t)\}] = \sum_{m=1}^{N_2} \beta_m(t)\mathscr{A}_m(\mathbf{r}), \tag{33b}$$

$$\mathscr{R}_k[\mathbf{r}', \mathbf{v}', t, \{\gamma_{kl}(t)\}] = \sum_{l=1}^{N_3} \gamma_{kl}(t)\mathscr{R}_{kl}(\mathbf{r}', \mathbf{v}'). \tag{33c}$$

This particular choice, in which a finite number of parameters enter linearly, is often convenient. However, it is a very special choice, and the functions can be chosen such that the parameters enter in a highly nonlinear way. The reason for the generality of Eqs. (32) is to allow the type of approximation used for a given problem to be chosen both on the basis of convenience and on the basis of knowledge or intuition about the behavior of the physical system. Indeed, if the exact solution can be represented by Φ, $\mathscr{A}$, and $\mathscr{R}_k$, then there is no approximation involved.

Once specific functions Φ, $\mathscr{A}$, and $\mathscr{R}_k$ have been chosen, we use them in the Lagrangian, Eq. (16), in place of the general functions ϕ, $\mathbf{A}$, and $\mathbf{R}_k$. The quantities that we allow to vary in applying Hamilton's principle are the time-dependent parameters $\alpha_n(t)$, $\beta_m(t)$, and $\gamma_{kl}(t)$. The possible variations of Φ, $\mathscr{A}$, and $\mathscr{R}_k$ are:

$$\delta\Phi[\mathbf{r}, t, \{\alpha_n(t)\}] = \sum_{n=1}^{N_1} \frac{\partial \Phi}{\partial \alpha_n} \delta\alpha_n, \tag{34a}$$

$$\delta\mathscr{A}[\mathbf{r}, t, \{\beta_m(t)\}] = \sum_{m=1}^{N_2} \frac{\partial \mathscr{A}}{\partial \beta_m} \delta\beta_m, \tag{34b}$$

$$\delta\mathscr{R}_k[\mathbf{r}', \mathbf{v}', t, \{\gamma_{kl}(t)\}] = \sum_{l=1}^{N_3} \frac{\partial \mathscr{R}_k}{\partial \gamma_{kl}} \delta\gamma_{kl}. \tag{34c}$$

In order that the variations of Φ, $\mathscr{A}$, and $\mathscr{R}_k$ corresponding to varying each of the parameters separately be linearly independent, the three sets of functions $\partial\Phi/\partial\alpha_n$, $\partial\mathscr{A}/\partial\beta_m$, and $\partial\mathscr{R}_k/\partial\gamma_{kl}$ must be linearly independent sets for all t. As a result of this linear independence, the restrictions that must be placed on the variations of $\beta_m(t)$ and $\gamma_{kl}(t)$ at times t_1 and t_2 to satisfy the restrictions on $\delta\mathbf{R}_k$ and $\delta\mathbf{A}$ at those times, Eqs. (19) and (31), are

$$\delta\beta_m(t_1) = \delta\beta_m(t_2) = 0, \tag{35a}$$

and

$$\delta\gamma_{kl}(t_1) = \delta\gamma_{kl}(t_2) = 0. \tag{35b}$$

Satisfaction of the remaining conditions that are required for applying Hamilton's principle, Eqs. (5), (24), and (29), is ensured because the boundary and initial conditions on the potentials and trajectories are satisfied by Eqs. (32).

The only difference between using Hamilton's principle to derive the exact equations for the physical system and using it to derive equations for the time-dependent parameters is that the variations in the latter case are within the *restricted* classes of functions represented by Φ, $\mathscr{A}$, and $\mathscr{R}_k$. Because of the requirements expressed by Eqs. (35), the equations obtained from the variational principle for the time-dependent parameters are the usual Euler–Lagrange equations that correspond to considering L to be a function of generalized coordinates α_n, β_m, and γ_{kl}, generalized velocities $\dot\beta_m$ and $\dot\gamma_{kl}$, and possibly t. The quantity $\dot\alpha_n$ does not appear because $\dot\phi$ does not appear in the exact Lagrangian. The Euler–Lagrange equations are:

$$\frac{d}{dt}\left(\frac{\partial L}{\partial \dot\gamma_{kl}}\right) - \frac{\partial L}{\partial \gamma_{kl}} = 0, \tag{36a}$$

$$\frac{d}{dt}\left(\frac{\partial L}{\partial \dot\beta_m}\right) - \frac{\partial L}{\partial \beta_m} = 0, \tag{36b}$$

$$\frac{\partial L}{\partial \alpha_n} = 0. \tag{36c}$$

These are the approximation equations implied by Hamilton's principle. It should be noticed that Eq. (36c) is not a differential equation. It can always be solved in principle for $\alpha_n(t)$ in terms of the other variables, and the result substituted into Eqs. (36a) and (36b).

B. Hamiltonian Formulation and Energy Theorem

The energy theorem that was mentioned in the Introduction as an important consequence of the variational approach can be demonstrated by going to a Hamiltonian formulation. Such a formulation can also be useful for numerical work by providing a natural system of first-order differential equations to replace the Euler–Lagrange equations, Eqs. (36).

We define generalized momenta σ_m and τ_{kl} corresponding to the generalized velocities $\dot\beta_m$ and $\dot\gamma_{kl}$ by

$$\sigma_m = \frac{\partial L}{\partial \dot\beta_m} \tag{37a}$$

and

$$\tau_{kl} = \frac{\partial L}{\partial \dot\gamma_{kl}}. \tag{37b}$$

In terms of them, we define a Hamiltonian function H by

$$H = \sum_m \dot{\beta}_m \sigma_m + \sum_{k,l} \dot{\gamma}_{kl} \tau_{kl} - L, \qquad (38)$$

where H is to be considered a function of the α_n, β_m, γ_{kl}, σ_m, τ_{kl}, and possibly t. This Hamiltonian is somewhat different in kind than that for a usual mechanical system in that momenta conjugate to the α_n do not occur. This is because the $\dot{\alpha}_n$ do not occur in L. Nevertheless, by using Eqs. (36)–(38), it is easy to verify the following Hamiltonian equations of motion:

$$\dot{\gamma}_{kl} = \frac{\partial H}{\partial \tau_{kl}}, \qquad (39a)$$

$$\dot{\tau}_{kl} = -\frac{\partial H}{\partial \gamma_{kl}}, \qquad (39b)$$

$$\dot{\beta}_m = \frac{\partial H}{\partial \sigma_m}, \qquad (39c)$$

$$\dot{\sigma}_m = -\frac{\partial H}{\partial \beta_m}, \qquad (39d)$$

$$\frac{\partial H}{\partial \alpha_n} = 0. \qquad (39e)$$

As was the case for the last Euler–Lagrange equation, Eq. (36c), the last Hamiltonian equation, Eq. (39e), is not a differential equation, and it can always be solved in principle for $\alpha_n(t)$ in terms of the other variables.

The Hamiltonian equations imply

$$\frac{dH}{dt} = \frac{\partial H}{\partial t}. \qquad (40)$$

This equation is a statement of the energy theorem. It applies for *arbitrary* choice of the functions Φ, $\mathscr{A}$, and $\mathscr{R}_k$ in Eqs. (32). An important special case is that in which none of the functions Φ, $\mathscr{A}$, and $\mathscr{R}_k$ have *explicit* time dependence. Then Eq. (40) is of the same form as the analogous relation for the exact physical system because the right-hand side can only be nonzero as a result of explicit time dependence in the prescribed functions $\rho_0(\mathbf{r}, t)$, $\mathbf{j}_0(\mathbf{r}, t)$, and $U(\mathbf{r}, \mathbf{v}, t)$. If, in addition, ρ_0, $\mathbf{j}_0$, and U_k are not explicitly time-dependent, so that the exact physical system is energy conserving, then Eq. (40) reduces to

$$\frac{dH}{dt} = 0. \tag{41}$$

This shows that the approximation scheme is energy conserving in this case just as the exact physical system is.

We conclude this section by giving the formulas for L and H appropriate to the case in which there are no material media present and none of the functions Φ, $\mathscr{A}$, and $\mathscr{R}_k$ have *explicit* time dependence. The formulas appropriate to the general case are given in Appendix B.

Since there are no material media present, $\psi(\mathbf{E}, \mathbf{r}, t)$ and $\chi(\mathbf{B}, \mathbf{r}, t)$ have the simple forms given by Eqs. (13), so that $\mathbf{D}$ and $\mathbf{H}$ are related to $\mathbf{E}$ and $\mathbf{B}$ as given by Eqs. (14): $\mathbf{D} = \mathbf{E}$ and $\mathbf{H} = \mathbf{B}$. In the formulas, we shall write $\Phi[\mathbf{r}, t, \{\alpha_n(t)\}]$, $\mathscr{A}[\mathbf{r}, t, \{\beta_m(t)\}]$, and $\mathscr{R}_k[\mathbf{r}', \mathbf{v}', t, \{\gamma_{kl}(t)\}]$ as $\Phi[\mathbf{r}, \{\alpha_n(t)\}]$, $\mathscr{A}[\mathbf{r}, \{\beta_m(t)\}]$, and $\mathscr{R}_k[\mathbf{r}', \mathbf{v}', \{\gamma_{kl}(t)\}]$, in recognition of the fact that the functions do not have explicit time dependence. The formula for L that we obtain by substituting these functions into Eq. (16) is

$$\begin{aligned}L = \sum_{k=1}^{N} \int d^3\mathbf{r}'\, d^3\mathbf{v}'\, f_k(\mathbf{r}', \mathbf{v}', 0) \Bigg\{ &\frac{1}{2} M_k \Bigg[\sum_l \dot{\gamma}_{kl} \frac{\partial \mathscr{R}_k}{\partial \gamma_{kl}} \Bigg]^2 \\ &- U_k\Bigg(\mathscr{R}_k(\mathbf{r}', \mathbf{v}', \{\gamma_{kl}\}), \sum_l \dot{\gamma}_{kl} \frac{\partial \mathscr{R}_k}{\partial \gamma_{kl}}, t\Bigg) \\ &- Q_k \Phi(\mathscr{R}_k(\mathbf{r}', \mathbf{v}', \{\gamma_{kl}\}), \{\alpha_n\}) \\ &+ \frac{1}{c} Q_k \Bigg[\sum_l \dot{\gamma}_{kl} \frac{\partial \mathscr{R}_k}{\partial \gamma_{kl}} \Bigg] \cdot \mathscr{A}(\mathscr{R}_k(\mathbf{r}', \mathbf{v}', \{\gamma_{kl}\}), \{\beta_m\}) \Bigg\} \\ + \int_V d^3\mathbf{r} \Bigg\{ &\frac{1}{8\pi}\Bigg[-\nabla\Phi(\mathbf{r}, \{\alpha_n\}) - \frac{1}{c}\sum_m \dot{\beta}_m \frac{\partial \mathscr{A}}{\partial \beta_m} \Bigg]^2 \\ &- \frac{1}{8\pi} [\nabla \times \mathscr{A}(\mathbf{r}, \{\beta_m\})]^2 - \rho_0(\mathbf{r}, t)\Phi(\mathbf{r}, \{\alpha_n\}) \\ &+ \frac{1}{c}\mathbf{j}(\mathbf{r}, t) \cdot \mathscr{A}(\mathbf{r}, \{\beta_m\}) \Bigg\}. \end{aligned} \tag{42}$$

The generalized momenta defined by Eqs. (37) are:

$$\sigma_m = \frac{1}{4\pi c} \int_V d^3\mathbf{r}\, \frac{\partial \mathscr{A}}{\partial \beta_m} \cdot \Bigg[\nabla\Phi(\mathbf{r}, \{\alpha_n\}) + \frac{1}{c}\sum_i \dot{\beta}_i \frac{\partial \mathscr{A}}{\partial \beta_i} \Bigg], \tag{43a}$$

$$\tau_{kl} = \int d^3\mathbf{r}' \, d^3\mathbf{v}' \, f_k(\mathbf{r}', \mathbf{v}', 0) \frac{\partial \mathscr{R}_k}{\partial \gamma_{kl}} \cdot \left\{ M_k \sum_i \dot{\gamma}_{ki} \frac{\partial \mathscr{R}_k}{\partial \gamma_{ki}} \right.$$

$$- \left. \nabla_{\mathbf{v}} U_k(\mathscr{R}_k(\mathbf{r}', \mathbf{v}', \{\gamma_{kj}\}), \mathbf{v}, t) \right|_{\mathbf{v} = \sum_i \dot{\gamma}_{ki}(\partial \mathscr{R}_k/\partial \gamma_{ki})}$$

$$+ \left. \frac{1}{c} Q_k \mathscr{A}(\mathscr{R}_k(\mathbf{r}', \mathbf{v}', \{\gamma_{jk}\}), \{\beta_m\}) \right\}. \tag{43b}$$

Equation (43a) gives a linear relation between the generalized momentum σ_m and the set of generalized velocities $\dot{\beta}_i$. If $U_k(\mathbf{r}, \mathbf{v}, t)$ vanishes, or if its dependence on $\mathbf{v}$ is simply v^2, then Eq. (43b) gives a linear relation between the generalized momentum τ_{kl} and the set of generalized velocities $\dot{\gamma}_{ki}$. Without any restriction on the functional form of $U_k(\mathbf{r}, \mathbf{v}, t)$, the Hamiltonian defined by Eq. (38) is

$$H = \sum_{k=1}^{N} \int d^3\mathbf{r}' \, d^3\mathbf{v}' \, f_k(\mathbf{r}', \mathbf{v}', 0) \left\{ \frac{1}{2} M_k \left[\sum_l \dot{\gamma}_{kl} \frac{\partial \mathscr{R}_k}{\partial \gamma_{kl}} \right]^2 \right.$$

$$+ U_k\left(\mathscr{R}_k(\mathbf{r}', \mathbf{v}', \{\gamma_{kl}\}), \sum_l \dot{\gamma}_{kl} \frac{\partial \mathscr{R}_k}{\partial \gamma_{kl}}, t\right)$$

$$- \left[\sum_l \dot{\gamma}_{kl} \frac{\partial \mathscr{R}_k}{\partial \gamma_{kl}} \right] \cdot \nabla_{\mathbf{v}} U_k(\mathscr{R}_k(\mathbf{r}', \mathbf{v}', \{\gamma_{kl}\}), \mathbf{v}, t) \bigg|_{\mathbf{v} = \sum_l \dot{\gamma}_{kl}(\partial \mathscr{R}_k/\partial \gamma_{kl})}$$

$$+ \left. Q_k \Phi(\mathscr{R}_k(\mathbf{r}', \mathbf{v}', \{\gamma_{kl}\}), \{\alpha_n\}) \right\}$$

$$+ \int_V d^3\mathbf{r} \left\{ -\frac{1}{8\pi} [\nabla \Phi(\mathbf{r}, \{\alpha_n\})]^2 + \frac{1}{8\pi} \left[\frac{1}{c} \sum_m \dot{\beta}_m \frac{\partial \mathscr{A}}{\partial \beta_m} \right]^2 \right.$$

$$+ \frac{1}{8\pi} [\nabla \times \mathscr{A}(\mathbf{r}, \{\beta_m\})]^2 + \rho_0(\mathbf{r}, t) \Phi(\mathbf{r}, \{\alpha_n\})$$

$$\left. -\frac{1}{c} \mathbf{j}_0(\mathbf{r}, t) \cdot \mathscr{A}(\mathbf{r}, \{\beta_m\}) \right\}, \tag{44}$$

where the generalized velocities are to be expressed in terms of the generalized coordinates and momenta by means of Eqs. (43).

IV. Specialization to a Finite Number of Particles

The variational approach is easily applicable to numerical simulation of plasmas by a finite number of point particles, and the simplest applications with a finite numer of particles are closely related to methods currently in use (Morse and Nielson, 1968; Birdsall and Fuss, 1968, 1969). When a finite number of point particles are treated, the variational method provides specific approximation schemes for the potentials and a specific way of calculating the fields that appear in the particle equations of motion. In this section we consider two special cases: a one-dimensional electrostatic case and a two-dimensional electrostatic case.

A. One-Dimensional Electrostatic Case

We specialize to the simple case of one spatial dimension, x, with periodic boundary conditions at $x = 0$ and $x = \lambda$, and we consider a single species of particles in the presence of a fixed, uniform, neutralizing background charge density ρ_0. Because there is only one dimension, we can set the vector potential identically equal to zero. The initial distribution function is a sum of δ-functions,

$$f(x', v', 0) = \sum_{i=1}^{N_3} \delta(x' - x_i)\delta(v' - v_i), \tag{45}$$

where x_i and v_i are the initial position and velocity of the ith particle, respectively, and N_3 is the number of particles. There is only one function $\mathscr{R}_k$; we denote its x component by ξ, and choose ξ and Φ as

$$\Phi[x, t, \{\alpha_n(t)\}] = \sum_{n=1}^{N_1} \alpha_n(t)\Phi_n(x), \tag{46a}$$

and

$$\xi[x', v', t, \{\gamma_l(t)\}] = \sum_{l=1}^{N_3} \gamma_l(t)X_l(x', v'), \tag{46b}$$

which are of the special form given by Eqs. (33). The $\Phi_n(x)$ must satisfy the boundary conditions at $x = 0$ and $x = \lambda$. Because of the singular initial distribution function, it is convenient to choose the X_l as

$$X_l(x', v') = \begin{cases} 1, & \text{if } x' = x_l \text{ and } v' = v_l, \\ 0, & \text{otherwise}, \end{cases} \tag{47}$$

in which case the initial conditions on $\gamma_l(t)$ are

$$\gamma_l(0) = x_l \quad \text{and} \quad \dot{\gamma}_l(0) = v_l. \tag{48}$$

Clearly, $\gamma_l(t)$ is the x coordinate of the lth particle at time t. Substituting into the Lagrangian given by Eq. (42) we obtain

$$\begin{aligned} L = & \int_0^\lambda dx' \int dv' \sum_{i=1}^{N_3} \delta(x' - x_i) \, \delta(v' - v_i) \Bigg\{ \frac{1}{2} M \Bigg[\sum_{l=1}^{N_3} \dot{\gamma}_l X_l(x', v') \Bigg]^2 \\ & - Q \sum_{n=1}^{N_1} \alpha_n \Phi_n \Bigg(\sum_{l=1}^{N_3} \gamma_l X_l(x', v') \Bigg) \Bigg\} \\ & + \int_0^\lambda dx \Bigg\{ \frac{1}{8\pi} \Bigg[\sum_{n=1}^{N_1} \alpha_n \Phi_n'(x) \Bigg]^2 - \rho_0 \sum_{n=1}^{N_1} \alpha_n \Phi_n(x) \Bigg\} \\ = & \sum_{l=1}^{N_3} \Bigg\{ \frac{1}{2} M \dot{\gamma}_l^2 - Q \sum_{n=1}^{N_1} \alpha_n \Phi_n(\gamma_l) \Bigg\} \\ & + \int_0^\lambda dx \Bigg\{ \frac{1}{8\pi} \Bigg[\sum_{n=1}^{N_1} \alpha_n \Phi_n'(x) \Bigg]^2 - \rho_0 \sum_{n=1}^{N_1} \alpha_n \Phi_n(x) \Bigg\}, \end{aligned} \quad (49)$$

where

$$\Phi_n'(x) \equiv \frac{d}{dx} \Phi_n(x).$$

The Euler–Lagrange equations for this Lagrangian, Eqs. (36a) and (36c), are:

$$M \ddot{\gamma}_l = -Q \sum_{i=1}^{N_1} \alpha_i(t) \Phi_i'(\gamma_l), \quad (50a)$$

$$\frac{1}{4\pi} \sum_{i=1}^{N_1} \alpha_i \int_0^\lambda dx \, \Phi_i'(x) \Phi_n'(x) = \rho_0 \int_0^\lambda dx \, \Phi_n(x) + Q \sum_{l=1}^{N_3} \Phi_n(\gamma_l). \quad (50b)$$

Equation (50a) is the usual equation of motion for the lth particle, and Eq. (50b) is a definite approximation scheme for solving Poisson's equation. As a consequence of Eq. (41), the equations are energy-conserving.

A simple special case of Eqs. (50) is closely related to the numerical simulation method used by Morse and Nielson (1968). The variational approach has provided an energy-conserving version of their method, as well as a wide variety of energy-conserving generalizations. The energy-conserving version of the method used by Morse and Nielson is obtained by taking a piecewise linear approximation for the scalar potential. We set the scalar potential equal to zero at the endpoints $x = 0$ and $x = \lambda$, and use a local basis for periodic, piecewise linear functions that vanish at the endpoints. The local basis functions are the functions $g_n(x)$ defined by

$$g_n(x) = \begin{cases} \dfrac{1}{\Delta}[x - (n-1)\Delta], & \text{if } (n-1)\Delta \le x \le n\Delta, \\ \dfrac{1}{\Delta}[(n+1)\Delta - x], & \text{if } n\Delta \le x \le (n+1)\Delta, \\ 0, & \text{otherwise}, \end{cases} \qquad (51)$$

where $\Delta = \lambda/(N_1 + 1)$. If we take the functions $\Phi_n(x)$ to be these piecewise linear functions $g_n(x)$, then $\alpha_n(t)$ is the value of the potential at $x = n\Delta$; and the integrals occurring in Eq. (50b) are:

$$\int_0^\lambda dx\, \Phi_n(x) = \Delta, \qquad (52a)$$

$$\int_0^\lambda dx\, \Phi_i'(x)\Phi_n'(x) = \begin{cases} \dfrac{2}{\Delta}, & \text{if } i = n, \\ -\dfrac{1}{\Delta}, & \text{if } |i - n| = 1, \\ 0, & \text{otherwise}. \end{cases} \qquad (52b)$$

The matrix defined by Eq. (52b) represents the usual central-difference approximation for the second derivative. As a consequence of these formulas, Eq. (50b) is identical to the formula for Poisson's equation used by Morse and Nielson. Their scheme differs only in that they use a piecewise linear approximation for the derivatives $\Phi_i'(\gamma_l)$ in the equation of motion, Eq. (50a); because of that difference, their scheme is not energy conserving.

B. Two-Dimensional Electrostatic Case

Our second example with a finite number of point particles is the same as that considered in the previous section, except that we now allow two spatial dimensions, with cartesian coordinates x and y, and we take periodic boundary conditions on the edge of a square whose side is of length λ. As before, there is one species in the presence of a fixed, uniform neutralizing background charge density ρ_0, and we ignore the vector potential. The initial distribution function is

$$f(\mathbf{r}', \mathbf{v}', 0) = \sum_{i=1}^{N_3} \delta(\mathbf{r}' - \mathbf{r}_i)\, \delta(\mathbf{v}' - \mathbf{v}_i), \qquad (53)$$

where $\mathbf{r}_i$ and $\mathbf{v}_i$ are the initial position and velocity vectors of the ith particle, respectively, and N_3 is the number of particles. There is only one function $\mathcal{R}_k$; we denote it by $\mathcal{R}$, and choose $\mathcal{R}$ and Φ as

$$\Phi[\mathbf{r}, t, \{\alpha_{nm}(t)\}] = \sum_{n=1}^{N_1} \sum_{m=1}^{N_1} \alpha_{nm}(t)\Phi_{nm}(x, y), \tag{54a}$$

and

$$\mathcal{R}[\mathbf{r}', \mathbf{v}', t, \{\gamma_{lx}(t), \gamma_{ly}(t)\}] = \sum_{l=1}^{N_3} \{\gamma_{lx}(t)\mathcal{R}_{lx}(\mathbf{r}', \mathbf{v}') + \gamma_{ly}(t)\mathcal{R}_{ly}(\mathbf{r}', \mathbf{v}')\}, \tag{54b}$$

which are of the special form given by Eqs. (33). On the edge of the square we set the scalar potential equal to zero. To achieve this, we require that the $\Phi_{nm}(x, y)$ vanish on the edge of the square. The basis functions $\mathcal{R}_{lx}$ and $\mathcal{R}_{ly}$ are defined by

$$\mathcal{R}_{lx}(\mathbf{r}', \mathbf{v}') = \begin{cases} \hat{\imath}, & \text{if } \mathbf{r}' = \mathbf{r}_l \text{ and } \mathbf{v}' = \mathbf{v}_l, \\ 0, & \text{otherwise,} \end{cases} \tag{55a}$$

and

$$\mathcal{R}_{ly}(\mathbf{r}', \mathbf{v}') = \begin{cases} \hat{\jmath}, & \text{if } \mathbf{r}' = \mathbf{r}_l \text{ and } \mathbf{v}' = \mathbf{v}_l, \\ 0, & \text{otherwise,} \end{cases} \tag{55b}$$

where $\hat{\imath}$ and $\hat{\jmath}$ are unit vectors in the directions of increasing x and y, respectively. The initial conditions on $\gamma_{lx}(t)$ and $\gamma_{ly}(t)$ are

$$\gamma_{lx}(0)\hat{\imath} + \gamma_{ly}(0)\hat{\jmath} = \mathbf{r}_l \tag{56a}$$

and

$$\dot{\gamma}_{lx}(0)\hat{\imath} + \dot{\gamma}_{ly}(0)\hat{\jmath} = \mathbf{v}_l. \tag{56b}$$

Clearly, $\gamma_{lx}(t)\hat{\imath} + \gamma_{ly}(t)\hat{\jmath}$ is the position vector of the lth particle at time t. Substituting into the Lagrangian given by Eq. (42), we obtain

$$L = \sum_{l=1}^{N_3} \left\{ \frac{1}{2} M[\dot{\gamma}_{lx}^2 + \dot{\gamma}_{ly}^2] - Q \sum_{n=1}^{N_1} \sum_{m=1}^{N_1} \alpha_{nm} \Phi_{nm}(\gamma_{lx}, \gamma_{ly}) \right\}$$

$$+ \int_0^\lambda dx \int_0^\lambda dy \left\{ \frac{1}{8\pi} \left[\sum_{n=1}^{N_1} \sum_{m=1}^{N_1} \alpha_{nm} \nabla\Phi_{nm}(x, y) \right]^2 \right.$$

$$\left. - \rho_0 \sum_{n=1}^{N_1} \sum_{m=1}^{N_1} \alpha_{nm} \Phi_{nm}(x, y) \right\}. \tag{57}$$

We now introduce the notation

$$\Phi_{nm,x}(x, y) = \frac{\partial}{\partial x} \Phi_{nm}(x, y), \qquad \Phi_{nm,y}(x, y) = \frac{\partial}{\partial y} \Phi_{nm}(x, y), \tag{58}$$

so that

$$\nabla \Phi_{nm}(x, y) = \hat{\imath}\Phi_{nm,x}(x, y) + \hat{\jmath}\Phi_{nm,y}(x, y).$$

In terms of this notation, the Euler–Lagrange equations, Eqs. (36a) and (36c), are:

$$M\ddot{y}_{lx} = -Q \sum_{n=1}^{N_1} \sum_{m=1}^{N_1} \alpha_{nm}(t) \Phi_{nm,x}(\gamma_{lx}, \gamma_{ly}), \tag{59a}$$

$$M\ddot{y}_{ly} = -Q \sum_{n=1}^{N_1} \sum_{m=1}^{N_1} \alpha_{nm}(t) \Phi_{nm,y}(\gamma_{lx}, \gamma_{ly}), \tag{59b}$$

$$\frac{1}{4\pi} \sum_{i=1}^{N_1} \sum_{j=1}^{N_1} \alpha_{ij} \int_0^\lambda dx \int_0^\lambda dy [\Phi_{ij,x}(x, y)\Phi_{nm,x}(x, y) + \Phi_{ij,y}(x, y)\Phi_{nm,y}(x, y)]$$

$$= \rho_0 \int_0^\lambda dx \int_0^\lambda dy\, \Phi_{nm}(x, y) + Q \sum_{l=1}^{N_1} \Phi_{nm}(\gamma_{lx}, \gamma_{ly}). \tag{60}$$

Equations (59) are the usual equations of motion for the *l*th particle, and Eq. (60) is a definite approximation scheme for solving Poisson's equation. Again, *the equations are energy conserving.*

A simple special case of Eqs. (59) and (60) is closely related to the method used by Morse and Nielson (1968) and to one of the procedures of Birdsall and Fuss (1968, 1969). As in the one-dimensional case, the variational approach has provided an energy-conserving version of their method, as well as a wide variety of energy-conserving generalizations. The energy-conserving version of their method is obtained by taking a piecewise bilinear approximation for the scalar potential. A local basis for periodic, piecewise bilinear functions that vanish on the edge of the square is conveniently expressed in terms of the functions g_n defined by Eq. (51). The local basis functions are the products $g_n(x)g_m(y)$. Correspondingly, we now choose $\Phi_{nm}(x, y)$ as

$$\Phi_{nm}(x, y) = g_n(x)g_m(y). \tag{61}$$

With the notation $g_n'(x) = (d/dx)g_n(x)$, Eqs. (59) and (60) can now be written as:

$$M\ddot{\gamma}_{lx} = -Q\sum_{n=1}^{N_1}\sum_{m=1}^{N_1} \alpha_{nm}(t)g_n'(\gamma_{lx})g_m(\gamma_{ly}), \qquad (62a)$$

$$M\ddot{\gamma}_{ly} = -Q\sum_{n=1}^{N_1}\sum_{m=1}^{N_1} \alpha_{nm}(t)g_n(\gamma_{lx})g_m'(\gamma_{ly}), \qquad (62b)$$

$$\frac{1}{4\pi}\sum_{i=1}^{N_1}\sum_{j=1}^{N_1}\alpha_{ij}\int_0^\lambda dx\int_0^\lambda dy[g_i'(x)g_n'(x)g_j(y)g_m(y) + g_i(x)g_n(x)g_j'(y)g_m'(y)]$$

$$= \rho_0\int_0^\lambda dx\int_0^\lambda dy\, g_n(x)g_m(y) + Q\sum_{l=1}^{N_3} g_n(\gamma_{lx})g_m(\gamma_{ly}). \qquad (63)$$

The integrals occurring in Eq. (63) are:

$$\int_0^\lambda dx\, g_n(x) = \Delta, \qquad (64a)$$

$$\int_0^\lambda dx\, g_n(x)g_m(x) = \frac{2}{3}\Delta\, \delta_{nm} + \frac{1}{6}\Delta(\delta_{n,m+1} + \delta_{n+1,m}), \qquad (64b)$$

$$\int_0^\lambda dx\, g_n'(x)g_m'(x) = \frac{2}{\Delta}\delta_{nm} - \frac{1}{\Delta}(\delta_{n,m+1} + \delta_{n+1,m}). \qquad (64c)$$

Therefore, Eq. (63), the approximation scheme for solving Poisson's equation, can be written as

$$\frac{1}{4\pi}\sum_{i=1}^{N_1}\sum_{j=1}^{N_1}\alpha_{ij}\left[3\delta_{in}\delta_{jm} - \frac{1}{3}(\delta_{in} + \delta_{i+1,n} + \delta_{i,n+1})(\delta_{jm} + \delta_{j+1,m} + \delta_{j,m+1})\right]$$

$$= \rho_0\Delta^2 + Q\sum_{l=1}^{N_3} g_n(\gamma_{lx})g_m(\gamma_{ly}). \qquad (65)$$

The last term on the right-hand side of this equation corresponds precisely to the "area-weighting" procedure used by Morse and Nielson and by Birdsall and Fuss for computing the charge in their approximation scheme for Poisson's equation. The left-hand side of Eq. (65) corresponds to a nine-point difference approximation for the two-dimensional Laplacian whose matrix is

$$\begin{pmatrix} -\frac{1}{3} & -\frac{1}{3} & -\frac{1}{3} \\ -\frac{1}{3} & \frac{8}{3} & -\frac{1}{3} \\ -\frac{1}{3} & -\frac{1}{3} & -\frac{1}{3} \end{pmatrix}.$$

V. Application to the Cold Two-Stream Instability with a Continuum of Particles

In this section, we use the variational method to derive an approximation scheme for a problem in which a continuum of particles is considered instead of a finite number of particles (Lewis, 1967; Lewis and Melendez, 1968). As we have seen in Section II, it is the continuum approximation that leads to the Vlasov formulation of plasmas, in which the particles can be represented by single-particle distribution functions satisfying collisionless Boltzmann equations. One of the most attractive aspects of the variational approach to numerical approximations is the possibility of learning how to describe a continuum of particles effectively in terms of a small number of parameters. The example presented here is a first step in that direction, and it is under active investigation by Lewis and Melendez.

We consider a single-species plasma in one spatial dimension, x, in the presence of a fixed, uniform neutralizing background charge density ρ_0, and we impose periodic boundary conditions at $x = 0$ and $x = \lambda$. Because there is only one dimension, we set the vector potential identically equal to zero. Initially, the particles form two possibly distorted "streams" in the phase space of position and velocity. The initial distribution function is

$$f(x', v', 0) = \sum_{i=1}^{2} f_i(x') \delta[v' - g_i(x')], \tag{66}$$

where

$$g_1(x') = -V + A_1 \sin \frac{2\pi m}{\lambda} x' + B_1 \cos \frac{2\pi m}{\lambda} x', \tag{67a}$$

$$g_2(x') = V + A_2 \sin \frac{2\pi m}{\lambda} x' + B_2 \cos \frac{2\pi m}{\lambda} x', \tag{67b}$$

and

$$f_i(x') = \frac{n_0}{2} + C_i \sin \frac{2\pi m}{\lambda} x' + D_i \cos \frac{2\pi m}{\lambda} x'. \tag{68}$$

The quantity m is an integer, V is a speed, n_0 is the initial average spatial density, and the numbers A_i, B_i, C_i, and D_i are constants that determine the deviation of the initial distribution function from equilibrium. The background charge density is expressed in terms of n_0 and Q by

$$\rho_0 = -n_0 Q. \tag{69}$$

There is only one function $\mathscr{R}_k$, whose x component we denote by ξ. We choose ξ and Φ in a form that is a slight generalization of Eqs. (33):

$$\Phi[x, t, \{\alpha_n(t)\}] = \alpha_0(t) + \sum_{n=1}^{N_1} \frac{1}{n}\sqrt{\frac{2\lambda}{\pi}} \left\{\alpha_{(2n)}(t) \sin \frac{2\pi n}{\lambda} x \right.$$

$$\left. + \alpha_{(2n-1)}(t) \cos \frac{2\pi n}{\lambda} x \right\}, \tag{70a}$$

$$\xi[x', v', t, \{\gamma_{l1}^{(i)}(t), \gamma_{l2}^{(i)}(t)\}] = x' + \sum_{i=1}^{2} \varepsilon_i(x', v') \left\{ \gamma_{02}^{(i)}(t) + \sum_{l=1}^{N_3} \left[\gamma_{l1}^{(i)}(t) \sin \frac{2\pi l}{\lambda} x' \right.\right.$$

$$\left.\left. + \gamma_{l2}^{(i)}(t) \cos \frac{2\pi l}{\lambda} x' \right] \right\}, \tag{70b}$$

where

$$\varepsilon_i(x', v') = \begin{cases} g_i(x'), & \text{if } v' = g_i(x'), \\ 0, & \text{otherwise.} \end{cases} \tag{71}$$

The initial conditions on $\gamma_{l1}^{(i)}(t)$ and $\gamma_{l2}^{(i)}(t)$ are:

$$\gamma_{l1}^{(i)}(0) = \gamma_{l2}^{(i)}(0) = 0, \tag{72a}$$

$$\dot{\gamma}_{l1}^{(i)}(0) = \dot{\gamma}_{l2}^{(i)}(0) = 0, \quad \text{if } l \neq 0, \tag{72b}$$

$$\dot{\gamma}_{02}^{(i)}(0) = 1. \tag{72c}$$

Substituting into the Lagrangian given by Eq. (42), we obtain

$$L = \frac{1}{2} M \sum_{i=1}^{2} \int_0^\lambda dx'\, f_i(x') g_i^2(x') \left\{ \dot{\gamma}_{02}^{(i)} \right.$$

$$\left. + \sum_{l=1}^{N_3} \left[\dot{\gamma}_{l1}^{(i)} \sin \frac{2\pi l}{\lambda} x' + \dot{\gamma}_{l2}^{(i)} \cos \frac{2\pi l}{\lambda} x' \right] \right\}^2$$

$$- Q \sum_{i=1}^{2} \sum_{n=1}^{N_1} \frac{1}{n}\sqrt{\frac{2\lambda}{\pi}} \int_0^\lambda dx'\, f_i(x') \left\{ \alpha_{(2n)} \sin\left[\frac{2\pi n}{\lambda} \xi(x', g_i(x'), \gamma)\right] \right.$$

$$\left. + \alpha_{(2n-1)} \cos\left[\frac{2\pi n}{\lambda} \xi(x', g_i(x'), \gamma)\right] \right\}$$

$$+ \frac{1}{2} \sum_{n=1}^{N_1} [\alpha_{(2n)}^2 + \alpha_{(2n-1)}^2], \tag{73}$$

where we have used the abbreviation

$$\xi(x', v', \gamma) = \xi[x', v', t, \{\gamma_{11}^{(i)}(t), \gamma_{12}^{(i)}(t)\}]. \tag{74}$$

The Euler–Lagrange equations for this Lagrangian, Eqs. (36a) and (36c), are:

$$\alpha_{(2n)} = Q \frac{1}{n} \sqrt{\frac{2\lambda}{\pi}} \sum_{i=1}^{2} \int_0^\lambda dx' f_i(x') \sin\left[\frac{2\pi n}{\lambda} \xi(x', g_i(x'), \gamma)\right] \tag{75a}$$

$$\alpha_{(2n-1)} = Q \frac{1}{n} \sqrt{\frac{2\lambda}{\pi}} \sum_{i=1}^{2} \int_0^\lambda dx' f_i(x') \cos\left[\frac{2\pi n}{\lambda} \xi(x', g_i(x'), \gamma)\right], \tag{75b}$$

$$M \int_0^\lambda dx' f_i(x') g_i^2(x') \left\{ \ddot{y}_{02}^{(i)} + \sum_{l=1}^{N_3} \left[\ddot{y}_{11}^{(i)} \sin \frac{2\pi l}{\lambda} x' + \ddot{y}_{12}^{(i)} \cos \frac{2\pi l}{\lambda} x' \right] \right\}$$

$$= -Q \sqrt{\frac{8\pi}{\lambda}} \sum_{n=1}^{N_1} \int_0^\lambda dx' f_i(x') g_i(x') \left\{ \alpha_{(2n)} \cos\left[\frac{2\pi n}{\lambda} \xi(x', g_i(x'), \gamma)\right] \right.$$

$$\left. - \alpha_{(2n-1)} \sin\left[\frac{2\pi n}{\lambda} \xi(x', g_i(x'), \gamma)\right] \right\}, \tag{75c}$$

$$M \int_0^\lambda dx' f_i(x') g_i^2(x') \sin \frac{2\pi k}{\lambda} x' \left\{ \ddot{y}_{02}^{(i)} + \sum_{l=1}^{N_3} \left[\ddot{y}_{11}^{(i)} \sin \frac{2\pi l}{\lambda} x' + \ddot{y}_{12}^{(i)} \cos \frac{2\pi l}{\lambda} x' \right] \right\}$$

$$= -Q \sqrt{\frac{8\pi}{\lambda}} \sum_{n=1}^{N_1} \int_0^\lambda dx' f_i(x') g_i(x') \sin \frac{2\pi k}{\lambda} x' \left\{ \alpha_{(2n)} \cos\left[\frac{2\pi n}{\lambda} \xi(x', g_i(x'), \gamma)\right] \right.$$

$$\left. - \alpha_{(2n-1)} \sin\left[\frac{2\pi n}{\lambda} \xi(x', g_i(x'), \gamma)\right] \right\}, \tag{75d}$$

$$M \int_0^\lambda dx' f_i(x') g_i^2(x') \cos \frac{2\pi k}{\lambda} x' \left\{ \ddot{y}_{02}^{(i)} + \sum_{l=1}^{N_3} \left[\ddot{y}_{11}^{(i)} \sin \frac{2\pi l}{\lambda} x' + \ddot{y}_{12}^{(i)} \cos \frac{2\pi l}{\lambda} x' \right] \right\}$$

$$= -Q \sqrt{\frac{8\pi}{\lambda}} \sum_{n=1}^{N_1} \int_0^\lambda dx' f_i(x') g_i(x') \cos \frac{2\pi k}{\lambda} x' \left\{ \alpha_{(2n)} \cos\left[\frac{2\pi n}{\lambda} \xi(x', g_i(x'), \gamma)\right] \right.$$

$$\left. - \alpha_{(2n-1)} \sin\left[\frac{2\pi n}{\lambda} \xi(x', g_i(x'), \gamma)\right] \right\}. \tag{75e}$$

These equations are energy conserving.

Results obtained so far from numerical integration of Eqs. (75) with unstable initial distribution functions indicate that certain quantities that can be derived from the solutions are insensitive to the number of basis functions ($m = 1$, $N_1 \leq 5$, $N_3 \leq 5$). In particular, the peak value of the electric energy, the time of occurrence of this peak value, the average value of the electric energy at long times, and the velocity distribution at long times have been insensitive to the number of basis functions.

The integrals in Eqs. (75c)–(75e) that multiply $\ddot{\gamma}_{02}^{(i)}$, $\ddot{\gamma}_{11}^{(i)}$, and $\ddot{\gamma}_{12}^{(i)}$ do not involve t, and they need be evaluated only once. The other integrals in Eqs. (75) involve $\xi(x', g_i(x'), \gamma)$, and therefore depend on t through the dependence of $\gamma_{02}^{(i)}$, $\gamma_{11}^{(i)}$, and $\gamma_{12}^{(i)}$ on t. All of the integrals that involve $\xi(x', g_i(x'), \gamma)$ can be expressed as linear combinations of integrals of the form

$$I(s; \{a_k, b_k\}) = \frac{1}{2\pi} \int_0^{2\pi} d\theta \exp\left\{i\left[s\theta + \sum_{k=1}^M (a_k \cos k\theta + b_k \sin k\theta)\right]\right\}, \quad (76)$$

where s and M are integers, and the a_k and b_k are linear combinations of the $\gamma_{02}^{(i)}$, $\gamma_{11}^{(i)}$, and $\gamma_{12}^{(i)}$. Integrals of this form cannot generally be performed analytically, and their numerical evaluation has been a major problem in obtaining numerical solutions of Eqs. (75). Because of this, a special technique was developed for evaluating the integrals accurately and efficiently (Thomas *et al.*, (1970). The integrals become ever more difficult to evaluate as the a_k and b_k increase in magnitude, because the integrands are more highly oscillatory. Results for unstable initial distribution functions indicate that the solutions of Eqs. (75) finally lead to such large values of the a_k and b_k that the integrals can be evaluated accurately by the method of stationary phase. This possibility of asymptotic evaluation of the integrals may lead to some quasi-analytical understanding of the long-time behavior of the two-stream instability.

Appendix A. Gradients with Respect to Position and Velocity

The operators $\nabla_\mathbf{r}$ and $\nabla_\mathbf{\dot{r}}$ applied to a function $U(\mathbf{r}, \mathbf{\dot{r}})$, where $\mathbf{\dot{r}} \equiv d\mathbf{r}/dt$, are defined with respect to the variation of $U(\mathbf{r}, \mathbf{\dot{r}})$ induced by a variation $\delta\mathbf{r}$ and an associated variation $\delta\mathbf{\dot{r}} \equiv (d/dt) \delta\mathbf{r}$. By saying that U is a function of $\mathbf{r}$ and $\mathbf{\dot{r}}$, we mean that it is a function of three independent coordinates of $\mathbf{r}$ and, in addition, a function of three variables that determine $\mathbf{\dot{r}}$ for fixed $\mathbf{r}$. Let us suppose that the latter three variables are the components of $\mathbf{\dot{r}}$ in the coordinate system chosen for $\mathbf{r}$. The dependence of U on $\mathbf{\dot{r}}$ can always be expressed in terms of these variables. Define the coordinate system for $\mathbf{r}$ by unit vectors $\hat{e}_j(\mathbf{r})$, and denote the coordinates of $\mathbf{r}$ in this system by x_j. The function $U(\mathbf{r}, \mathbf{\dot{r}})$ is considered to be an explicit function of the variables x_j and $\hat{e}_j \cdot \mathbf{\dot{r}}$.

The derivative of **r** with respect to x_j is expressed as usual in terms of a function $h_j(\mathbf{r})$ by

$$\frac{\partial \mathbf{r}}{\partial x_j} = h_j(\mathbf{r})\hat{e}_j. \tag{A1}$$

The variation of $U(\mathbf{r}, \dot{\mathbf{r}})$ induced by variations $\delta\mathbf{r}$ and $\delta\dot{\mathbf{r}}$ is

$$\begin{aligned}
\delta U &= \sum_{j=1}^{3} \left\{ \delta x_j \frac{\partial U}{\partial x_j} + \delta(\hat{e}_j \cdot \dot{\mathbf{r}}) \frac{\partial U}{\partial(\hat{e}_j \cdot \dot{\mathbf{r}})} \right\} \\
&= \sum_{j=1}^{3} \left\{ (h_j \, \delta x_j)\left(\frac{1}{h_j} \frac{\partial U}{\partial x_j}\right) + [\delta\mathbf{r} \cdot (\nabla\hat{e}_j) \cdot \dot{\mathbf{r}} + \hat{e}_j \cdot \delta\dot{\mathbf{r}}] \frac{\partial U}{\partial(\hat{e}_j \cdot \dot{\mathbf{r}})} \right\} \\
&= \delta\mathbf{r} \cdot \sum_{j=1}^{3} \left\{ \frac{1}{h_j} \frac{\partial U}{\partial x_j} \hat{e}_j + \frac{\partial U}{\partial(\hat{e}_j \cdot \dot{\mathbf{r}})} (\nabla\hat{e}_j) \cdot \dot{\mathbf{r}} \right\} \\
&\quad + \delta\dot{\mathbf{r}} \cdot \sum_{j=1}^{3} \frac{\partial U}{\partial(\hat{e}_j \cdot \dot{\mathbf{r}})} \hat{e}_j. \tag{A2}
\end{aligned}$$

The operators $\nabla_\mathbf{r}$ and $\nabla_{\dot{\mathbf{r}}}$ are defined by

$$\delta U = \delta\mathbf{r} \cdot \nabla_\mathbf{r} U + \delta\dot{\mathbf{r}} \cdot \nabla_{\dot{\mathbf{r}}} U, \tag{A3}$$

where

$$\nabla_\mathbf{r} U = \sum_{j=1}^{3} \left\{ \frac{1}{h_j} \frac{\partial U}{\partial x_j} \hat{e}_j + \frac{\partial U}{\partial(\hat{e}_j \cdot \dot{\mathbf{r}})} (\nabla\hat{e}_j) \cdot \dot{\mathbf{r}} \right\} \tag{A4}$$

and

$$\nabla_{\dot{\mathbf{r}}} U = \sum_{j=1}^{3} \frac{\partial U}{\partial(\hat{e}_j \cdot \dot{\mathbf{r}})} \hat{e}_j. \tag{A5}$$

Thus we see that $\nabla_\mathbf{r} U$ is the usual gradient with respect to the position vector where the *vector* $\dot{\mathbf{r}}$ is held fixed. Also, $\nabla_{\dot{\mathbf{r}}}$ can be represented as

$$\nabla_{\dot{\mathbf{r}}} = \sum_{j=1}^{3} \hat{e}_j \frac{1}{h_j} \frac{\partial}{\partial \dot{x}_j}, \tag{A6}$$

where the differentiations with respect to the $\dot{x}_j$ are performed holding the vector **r** fixed.

Appendix B. Formulas for L and H in the General Case

The formula for L that we obtain by substituting $\Phi[\mathbf{r}, t, \{\alpha_n(t)\}]$, $\mathscr{A}[\mathbf{r}, t, \{\beta_m(t)\}]$, and $\mathscr{R}_k[\mathbf{r}', \mathbf{v}', t, \{\gamma_{kl}(t)\}]$ into Eq. (16) is

$$L = \sum_{k=1}^{N} \int d^3\mathbf{r}'\, d^3\mathbf{v}'\, f_k(\mathbf{v}', \mathbf{v}', 0) \left\{ \frac{1}{2} M_k \left[\frac{\partial \mathscr{R}_k}{\partial t} + \sum_l \dot{\gamma}_{kl} \frac{\partial \mathscr{R}_k}{\partial \gamma_{kl}} \right]^2 \right.$$

$$- U_k\!\left(\mathscr{R}_k(\mathbf{r}', \mathbf{v}', t, \{\gamma_{kl}\}), \frac{\partial \mathscr{R}_k}{\partial t} + \sum_l \dot{\gamma}_{kl} \frac{\partial \mathscr{R}_k}{\partial \gamma_{kl}}, t \right)$$

$$- Q_k \Phi(\mathscr{R}_k(\mathbf{r}', \mathbf{v}', t, \{\gamma_{kl}\}), t, \{\alpha_n\})$$

$$+ \frac{1}{c} Q_k \left[\frac{\partial \mathscr{R}_k}{\partial t} + \sum_l \dot{\gamma}_{kl} \frac{\partial \mathscr{R}_k}{\partial \gamma_{kl}} \right] \cdot \mathscr{A}(\mathscr{R}_k(\mathbf{r}', \mathbf{v}', t, \{\gamma_{kl}\}), t, \{\beta_m\}) \bigg\}$$

$$+ \int_V d^3\mathbf{r} \left\{ \psi\!\left(-\nabla\Phi(\mathbf{r}, t, \{\alpha_n\}) - \frac{1}{c}\frac{\partial \mathscr{A}}{\partial t} - \frac{1}{c}\sum_m \dot{\beta}_m \frac{\partial \mathscr{A}}{\partial \beta_m}, \mathbf{r}, t \right) \right.$$

$$- \chi(\nabla \times \mathscr{A}(\mathbf{r}, t, \{\beta_m\}), \mathbf{r}, t) - \rho_0(\mathbf{r}, t)\Phi(\mathbf{r}, t, \{\alpha_n\})$$

$$+ \frac{1}{c}\mathbf{j}_0(\mathbf{r}, t) \cdot \mathscr{A}(\mathbf{r}, t, \{\beta_m\}) \bigg\}. \tag{B1}$$

The generalized momenta defined by Eqs. (37) are:

$$\sigma_m = -\frac{1}{c}\int_V d^3\mathbf{r}\, \frac{\partial \mathscr{A}}{\partial \beta_m} \cdot \nabla_{\mathbf{E}} \psi(\mathbf{E}, \mathbf{r}, t) \bigg|_{\mathbf{E} = -\nabla\Phi(\mathbf{r},\{\alpha_n\}) - (1/c)(\partial\mathscr{A}/\partial t) - (1/c)\sum_i \dot{\beta}_i(\partial\mathscr{A}/\partial\beta_i)} \tag{B2a}$$

$$\tau_{kl} = \int d^3\mathbf{r}'\, d^3\mathbf{v}'\, f_k(\mathbf{r}', \mathbf{v}', 0) \frac{\partial \mathscr{R}_k}{\partial \gamma_{kl}} \cdot \left\{ M_k \left[\frac{\partial \mathscr{R}_k}{\partial t} + \sum_i \dot{\gamma}_{ki} \frac{\partial \mathscr{R}_k}{\partial \gamma_{ki}} \right] \right.$$

$$- \nabla_{\mathbf{v}} U_k(\mathscr{R}_k(\mathbf{r}', \mathbf{v}', t, \{\gamma_{kj}\}), \mathbf{v}, t) \bigg|_{\mathbf{v} = (\partial\mathscr{R}_k/\partial t) + \sum_i \dot{\gamma}_{ki}(\partial\mathscr{R}_k/\partial\gamma_{ki})}$$

$$+ \frac{1}{c} Q_k \mathscr{A}(\mathscr{R}_k(\mathbf{r}', \mathbf{v}', t, \{\gamma_{kj}\}), t, \{\beta_m\}) \bigg\}. \tag{B2b}$$

The Hamiltonian defined by Eq. (38) is

$$H = \sum_{k=1}^{N} \int d^3\mathbf{r}'\, d^3\mathbf{v}'\, f_k(\mathbf{r}', \mathbf{v}', 0) \left\{ \frac{1}{2} M_k \left[\frac{\partial \mathscr{R}_k}{\partial t} + \sum_l \dot{\gamma}_{kl} \frac{\partial \mathscr{R}_k}{\partial \gamma_{kl}} \right]^2 \right.$$

$$- M_k \frac{\partial \mathscr{R}_k}{\partial t} \cdot \left[\frac{\partial \mathscr{R}_k}{\partial t} + \sum_l \dot{\gamma}_{kl} \frac{\partial \mathscr{R}_k}{\partial \gamma_{kl}} \right]$$

$$+ U_k\left(\mathscr{R}_k(\mathbf{r}', \mathbf{v}', t, \{\gamma_{kl}\}), \frac{\partial \mathscr{R}_k}{\partial t} + \sum_l \dot{\gamma}_{kl} \frac{\partial \mathscr{R}_k}{\partial \gamma_{kl}}, t\right)$$

$$- \left[\sum_l \dot{\gamma}_{kl} \frac{\partial \mathscr{R}_k}{\partial \gamma_{kl}}\right] \cdot \nabla_{\mathbf{v}} U_k(\mathscr{R}_k(\mathbf{r}', \mathbf{v}', t, \{\gamma_{kl}\}), \mathbf{v}, t)\bigg|_{\mathbf{v} = (\partial \mathscr{R}_k/\partial t) + \sum_l \dot{\gamma}_{kl} (\partial \mathscr{R}_k/\partial \gamma_{kl})}$$

$$+ Q_k \Phi(\mathscr{R}_k(\mathbf{r}', \mathbf{v}', t, \{\gamma_{kl}\}), t, \{\alpha_n\})$$

$$- \frac{1}{c} Q_k \frac{\partial \mathscr{R}_k}{\partial t} \cdot \mathscr{A}(\mathscr{R}_k(\mathbf{r}', \mathbf{v}', t, \{\gamma_{kl}\}), t, \{\beta_m\})\bigg\}$$

$$+ \int_V d^3\mathbf{r} \bigg\{-\frac{1}{c}\left[\sum_m \dot{\beta}_m \frac{\partial \mathscr{A}}{\partial \beta_m}\right]$$

$$\cdot \nabla_{\mathbf{E}} \psi(\mathbf{E}, \mathbf{r}, t)\bigg|_{\mathbf{E} = -\nabla\Phi(\mathbf{r}, t, \{\alpha_n\}) - (1/c)(\partial \mathscr{A}/\partial t) - (1/c)\sum_m \dot{\beta}_m (\partial \mathscr{A}/\partial \beta_m)}$$

$$- \psi\left(-\nabla\Phi(\mathbf{r}, t, \{\alpha_n\}) - \frac{1}{c}\frac{\partial \mathscr{A}}{\partial t} - \frac{1}{c}\sum_m \dot{\beta}_m \frac{\partial \mathscr{A}}{\partial \beta_m}, \mathbf{r}, t\right)$$

$$+ \chi(\nabla \times \mathscr{A}(\mathbf{r}, t, \{\beta_m\}), \mathbf{r}, t) + \rho_0(\mathbf{r}, t)\Phi(\mathbf{r}, t, \{\alpha_n\})$$

$$- \frac{1}{c}\mathbf{j}_0(\mathbf{r}, t) \cdot \mathscr{A}(\mathbf{r}, t, \{\beta_m\})\bigg\}. \tag{B3}$$

References

Armstrong, T. P., Harding, R. C., Knorr, G., and Montgomery, D. (1970). This volume.
Berk, H. L., and Roberts, K. V. (1970). This volume.
Birdsall, C. K., and Fuss, D. (1968). Paper D1 *in* Proceedings (1968).
Birdsall, C. K., and Fuss, D. (1969). *J. Computational Phys.* **3**, 494.
Goldstein, H. (1950). "Classical Mechanics." Addison-Wesley, Reading, Massachusetts.
Lewis, H. R. (1967). "Hamilton's Principle and Numerical Solution of the Vlasov Equations." Los Alamos Scientific Laboratory Report LA-3803.
Lewis, H. R., and Melendez, K. J. (1968). Paper B1 *in* Proceedings (1968).
Lewis, H. R. (1970). "Energy-Conserving Numerical Approximations for Vlasov Plasmas" (to be published in *J. Computational Phys.*).
Low, F. E. (1958). *Proc. Roy. Soc.* (*London*) **A248**, 282.
Mjolsness, R. C. (1970). "Variational Solution of the Vlasov Equation" (to be published).
Morse, R. L., and Nielson, C. W. (1968). Paper A4 *in* Proceedings (1968).
Proceedings (1968). *Proc. APS Topical Conf. Numerical Simulation of Plasma, Sept. 18-20, 1968.* Los Alamos Scientific Laboratory Report LA-3990.
Sturrock, P. A. (1958). *Ann. Phys.* **4**, 306.
Thomas, J. D., Lewis, H. R., and Melendez, K. J. (1970). "An Efficient Method for Computing a Class of Definite Integrals" (to be published).

Magnetohydrodynamic Calculations

Keith V. Roberts
CULHAM LABORATORY, ABINGDON, BERKSHIRE, ENGLAND

and
D. E. Potter
IMPERIAL COLLEGE, LONDON, ENGLAND

I. Introduction 340
   A. One-Dimensional Calculations 340
   B. Two-Dimensional Calculations 343
   C. R-Codes and I-Codes 344
   D. Three-Dimensional Calculations. 345
II. Magnetohydrodynamic Models. 345
   A. Incompressible Magnetohydrodynamics 347
   B. Boussinesq Approximation 348
   C. Compressible Magnetohydrodynamics with Constant Transport Coefficients 349
   D. Two-Fluid Magnetohydrodynamics with Variable Coefficients. 349
   E. Neutral and Impurity Components 354
   F. Boundary Conditions 357
III. Difference Methods. 360
   A. Preliminary Remarks 360
   B. Mathematical Nature of the Equations. 361
   C. Explicit and Implicit Schemes. 362
   D. The Tridiagonal Method in One Dimension 364
   E. Hain's Implicit Method 365
   F. Eulerian and Lagrangian Coordinates 367
   G. Explicit Schemes 370
   H. The Treatment of Diffusion Terms 375
   I. Special Difference Methods. 378
   J. Vector Difference Notation. 384
IV. One-Dimensional Codes. 387
   A. The Hain–Roberts Code 387
   B. Boundary Conditions at the Wall 389
   C. Extension of the Code 391
V. Two-Dimensional Codes 392
   A. Previously Reported Codes. 392
   B. The Focus Code 394
VI. Calculations on the Plasma Focus Experiment 398
   A. General Description 398
   B. Run-Down Stage 401
   C. Collapse Stage 401
   D. Dense Pinch Stage. 404
   E. Discussion of the Results. 413

VII. A Three-Dimensional Code 414
    A. Choice of Language and Machine 414
    B. Physical Equations 415
    C. Boundary Conditions 415
    D. Leapfrog Difference Scheme 415
VIII. Concluding Remarks 416
    References 417

I. Introduction

COMPUTER SIMULATION OF THE behavior of conducting fluids or plasmas in magnetic fields is of interest in astrophysical situations, and also in geophysics, space physics, and controlled thermonuclear research. Most of the phenomena are two- or three-dimensional, and many of them are nonlinear. This makes analytic calculations difficult, and it is often equally difficult to make controlled experimental measurements, either because the physical processes are beyond our reach (interstellar gas clouds, solar surface physics, earth's dynamo problem), or because the insertion of a probe into a plasma can damage both the plasma and the probe. One may therefore expect that large-scale computer simulation will be of considerable help in elucidating the basic processes of magnetohydrodynamics (MHD), and in building up our visual intuition with the help of graphical display techniques. This contrasts with the situation in ordinary fluid dynamics, where the equations are simpler and better defined, and where many of the phenomena were familiar from daily observation before the analytical development of the subject began.

On the other hand it must be recognized that MHD is, in a sense, an "open-ended" theory. The MHD model of a plasma is only a model, and the simplest set of equations must often be supplemented by extra terms involving finite Larmor radius, anisotropic heat conduction, ionization and recombination of neutrals, emission and diffusion of radiation, and so on, if any accurate comparison with experiment is to be achieved. Often the model itself breaks down, and it is necessary to use the more complete Vlasov or Fokker–Planck equations. Fine-scale turbulence may arise, either throughout the plasma or in local regions, and should then be simulated by empirical diffusion coefficients. The full elucidation of the subject by means of observations, experiments, analytic theory, and computer simulation may be expected to take a considerable time. Meanwhile, both the computational physics and the numerical analysis offer interesting fields for research.

A. ONE-DIMENSIONAL CALCULATIONS

In one space dimension, realistic calculations on the dynamics of cylindrical plasma devices have been routine at several laboratories for about a decade

(Hain et al., 1960; Hain, 1961; Hain and Kolb, 1962; Fisser and Schluter, 1962; Niblett and Fisher, 1962; Oliphant, 1963; Duchs and Griem, 1966), and good agreement with experiment has been obtained, especially for the θ-pinch (Hain and Kolb, 1962; Niblett and Fisher, 1962; Fisser and Schluter, 1962; Ribe et al., 1963, Duchs and Griem, 1966; Bodin et al., 1968; Beach et al., 1969) and for the fast stabilized z-pinch (Ashby et al., 1961; Paul et al., 1965, 1967). Most of the calculations have assumed that the plasma is fully ionized, although a number of simple partially ionized models have been developed (Roberts, 1963; Duchs, 1963) and the excitation and ionization of impurities have also been followed (Kolb and McWhirter, 1964). Numerical calculations on MHD shocks have been carried out by a number of workers (Auer et al., 1961; Morton, 1962, 1964; Chu, 1965; Chu and Taussig, 1967). A comprehensive review of plasma shocks and references is given by Chu and Gross (1968), while the lectures by Killeen (1968) may be consulted for a review of plasma calculations in general.

There are two main numerical problems in one-dimensional MHD; the advection of magnetic field and plasma variables by the moving fluid, and the high Alfven wave speed which occurs in regions of low plasma density. An advective term $\mathbf{v} \cdot \nabla f$ occurs in each equation, and truncation errors which arise from the numerical treatment of this term can lead to an unacceptable diffusion and dispersion of the variable f if an Eulerian scheme is employed. Although Eulerian schemes of improved accuracy are available (Roberts and Weiss, 1966), the simplest solution for one-dimensional problems is to use a Lagrangian mesh moving with the plasma, since this avoids the advective term altogether. The implicit Eulerian code developed by Hain et al. (1960) was later converted to Lagrangian form by D. L. Fisher (unpublished), and an explicit Lagrangian code has been described by Oliphant (1963).

The maximum timestep Δt that can be used in an explicit calculation is restricted by a Courant–Friedrichs–Lewy condition (Richtmyer and Morton, 1967) of the form $C_A \Delta t/\Delta x < 1$, where Δx is the spacestep, $C_A \sim B/\rho^{1/2}$, B is the magnetic field strength, and ρ is the density. If ρ is small in some local region, or if the duration of the numerical experiment is long compared to the bounce time of the plasma, an explicit calculation may require an excessive amount of computer time, and Hain therefore developed a powerful implicit method in which this restriction does not occur (Hain et al., 1960). This method is currently being extended to two- and three-dimensional problems (Hain, 1967b) and will be described in Section III.

In many ways these one-dimensional MHD calculations seem easier now than they did in 1959. At that time the thin-skin stabilized pinch was popular (Rosenbluth, 1958), and the original code was designed to deal with large changes in the dependent variables over narrow radial intervals, especially near the plasma boundary which was calculated to be very sharp. Mesh points were arranged to move themselves automatically to the thin regions where they were most needed (Hain *et al.*, 1960). Nowadays one is more interested in the behavior of diffuse stabilized pinches such as the experiment of Ohkawa *et al.* (1963), Zeta (Robinson and King, 1968), or the new high-β toroidal experiment which is being constructed at Culham, in which the physical quantities vary more smoothly and are therefore easier to represent on a discrete mesh. There is evidence from theta-pinch experiments (Bodin *et al.*, 1968) to show that regions of strong magnetic field gradients (high current density) broaden themselves automatically due to an enhanced resistivity caused by microinstabilities (Sagdeev, 1965; Sagdeev and Galeev, 1966), which switches itself off again when the current density has decreased. By including this effect in the code, McCartan obtained good agreement with experiment (Beach *et al.*, 1969; Bodin and Newton, 1969), and at the same time the numerical functions and the plasma boundaries became smoother and easier to handle.

Future MHD calculations will probably include a variety of enhanced transport coefficients of this general type, simulating physical diffusion processes caused by a local plasma turbulence whose level is determined by the parameters of the main solution. It is interesting that a parallel development is occurring in numerical hydrodynamics, where the Navier–Stokes equations for incompressible flow at high Reynolds numbers lead to strong velocity gradients, culminating in fluid turbulence which cannot be represented adequately on a finite mesh. The influence of this turbulence on the mean flow can be simulated by a set of eddy diffusion coefficients, determined in a self-consistent manner by turbulence transport equations which are to be solved numerically in conjunction with the modified Navier–Stokes equations describing the mean flow (Harlow and Nakayama, 1967, 1968; Amsden and Harlow, 1968; Harlow, 1968).

One major physical problem remains. If the particle collision times are long, the MHD equations may not correctly represent the internal structure of shocks, and may then give a wrong result for the division of shock heating between the electron and ion temperatures T_e, T_i. This error will then affect the main flow behind the shock. To solve this problem it will be necessary to obtain a valid model for the structure of a collisionless shock, either from experiment or from analytical or numerical calculations, and to match this on to the main MHD solution, e.g., by shock-fitting or by choosing an appropriate set of enhanced transport coefficients.

This problem does not occur in ordinary compressible hydrodynamics. The viscous fluid equations do indeed break down within strong shocks, but the three conservation laws for mass, momentum, and energy (Rankine–Hugoniot relations) are sufficient to determine the jump conditions across the shock for the three variables: ρ (density), v (velocity), and T (temperature). The main flow is independent of the internal shock structure, and therefore it is possible to compute right through the shock, using an artificially enhanced viscosity to broaden the numerical solution (von Neumann and Richtmyer, 1949; Richtmyer and Morton, 1967). In MHD there are four conservation laws for mass, momentum, flux, and energy, but five variables, ρ, v, B, T_e, and T_i, and therefore the solution is indeterminate. An artificial viscosity is frequently used, but care should be used in interpreting the results.

B. Two-Dimensional Calculations

Until recently only a limited amount of work had been done in two dimensions (Roberts *et al.*, 1963; Roberts and Weiss, 1966; Weiss, 1966; Duchs, 1968a,b; Hain, 1967a,b; Hertweck and Schneider, 1967), since for several reasons the numerical difficulties seemed quite formidable:

(1) If the anomalous numerical diffusion due to inaccurate treatment of the advective term is avoided by using a moving Lagrangian mesh, it becomes difficult to express the complicated MHD equations in difference form and expensive to solve them, and it is also impracticable to use the Hain implicit scheme. An Eulerian scheme is therefore indicated, except for calculations in which the mesh distortion is not too severe.

(2) The vacuum fields (B_r, B_θ, B_z) outside the moving plasma boundary $r_0 = r_0(z, t)$ of an axial discharge no longer have the simple form $B_\theta \sim 1/r$, $B_z = $ constant, $B_r = 0$, which holds for one-dimensional cylindrical geometry, and in general it is necessary to solve Laplace's equation in an awkwardly shaped and changing region at each timestep.

(3) In most cases, the concentration of mesh points into regions of rapid variation is incompatible with an Eulerian grid.

(4) Because the electron heat conductivity is markedly anisotropic (perhaps 10^3 times larger along the field than across it), it is clear that the usual difference schemes for solving the field equations will not work, and that the field lines themselves should be used as coordinates (Hertweck and Schneider, 1967). On the other hand, the topology of the field lines may be complex and constantly changing in a general problem.

Fortunately, attention has recently been diverted from these difficulties by the plasma focus experiment, to be discussed in Sections V and VI (Filippov *et al.*, 1962; Filippov and Filippova, 1966; Mather, 1965; Mather *et al.*, 1967; Coudeville *et al.*, 1967; Long *et al.*, 1967; Patou *et al.*, 1967; Meskan *et al.*, 1967; Bottoms *et al.*, 1968; Peacock *et al.*, 1968; Butler *et al.*, 1968). This is a cylindrical plasma apparatus in which the interesting phenomena occur in the (r, z) plane provided that axial symmetry is maintained, while the magnetic field is only in the θ-direction. All transport coefficients are therefore isotropic, while the vacuum field has a simple $1/r$ dependence and presents no problems. The physical processes to be studied are supersonic so that an explicit method can be used, and consist mainly of a shock which collapses on to a known small region on the axis (focus), followed by axial flow. Diffusion is of lesser interest so that an Eulerian mesh can justifiably be employed, and at least two reasonably accurate explicit Eulerian schemes are now available, the Lax–Wendroff method (Richtmyer and Morton, 1967) and the leapfrog scheme (Roberts and Weiss, 1966; Roberts, 1967). The code to be discussed in this paper (Morgan *et al.*, 1969) uses a modified Lax–Wendroff method, and switches in a local fine-scale mesh when the focus is about to occur.

Since there is now extensive work on the plasma focus in several countries, with a number of different experimental devices and computer programs, it should be possible to make a thorough study of MHD in this type of geometry, and then extend the computational techniques to other two- and three-dimensional situations. For example, it has turned out to be rather straightforward after all to add B_r and B_z fields to the focus code, since although Laplace's equation must be solved in the vacuum at each step by the successive over-relaxation (SOR) method, the difference scheme for this is so simple that it can be iterated, many times, in less computer time than it takes to solve the complicated explicit plasma equations. The problem of anisotropic electron thermal conductivity has however not yet been solved.

C. R-Codes and I-Codes

There are two main approaches to computational MHD. In the first approach, already discussed in this introduction, one tries to simulate a *real* experiment as accurately as possible, and in plasma physics this usually means struggling with ill-defined boundary conditions and a host of different terms in the equations. This type of computer program will be called an "R-code." The second approach is similar to that often adopted in applied mathematics; one chooses the simplest *ideal* geometry, equations, and boundary conditions that will lead to interesting results, and then explores their consequences: for example, a rectangular region with a rectangular Eulerian mesh; uniform isotropic resistivity, heat conduction, and viscosity; and either periodic boundary conditions or rigid, perfectly conducting, thermally insulating walls. Such a computer program will be called an "I-code."

A certain amount of work has been done along this second line, and one field of interest is two-dimensional incompressible MHD. With motion only in the (x, y) plane there are two Poisson equations to be solved, one for the hydrodynamic streamfunction ψ_z in terms of the vorticity ζ_z, and the other for the vector potential A_z in terms of the current j_z. If the geometry is simple enough one can use the Hockney Poisson-solver (Hockney, 1965, 1968), or one of the other fast Fourier transform packages that are now available in many subroutine libraries. This type of I-code can be used to study nonlinear stability, convection, and turbulence at low magnetic Reynolds numbers.

D. THREE-DIMENSIONAL CALCULATIONS

Using I-codes it is now practicable to study an important class of compressible three-dimensional MHD problems, of interest in astrophysics and elsewhere. Machines such as the IBM 360/91 and CDC 7600 are certainly fast enough to solve these problems on a (64 × 64 × 64) mesh, and the main requirement is a large fast backing-store to hold the $2M$ words of data. (2.5×10^5 mesh points with eight variables ρ, **v**, T, **B**, or say $\sim 10^8$ bits altogether.) The Illiac 4 computer (Barnes et al., 1968; Kuck, 1968) will be faster and has a backing store of 10^9 bits with a data transfer rate of 10^9 bits/second, more than adequate for the purpose. In the meantime, these codes can be developed and tested on much less powerful machines, using fewer grid points (Section VII).

II. Magnetohydrodynamic Models

This section discusses some possible sets of partial differential equations and boundary conditions. The discussion is intended to be suggestive rather than complete, but should provide a basis for the construction of a variety of R-codes and I-codes. A convenient starting point is the set of equations for an isotropic compressible conducting fluid given by Jeffrey (1966), which can be specialized to simpler cases which are easier to solve on the computer (for example, constant transport coefficients and incompressible flow), or generalized to include a variety of physical effects which are important in real plasmas. Programming can be simplified by choosing the units in such a way that factors 4π, c (velocity of light), k (Boltzmann constant) do not appear. Then material pressure is related to density and temperature by $p = \rho T$, while the magnetic pressure is $B^2/2$.

The equations in Eulerian conservative form are:

$$\frac{\partial \rho}{\partial t} = -\text{div}(\rho \mathbf{v}) \quad \text{(mass)}, \tag{1}$$

$$\frac{\partial}{\partial t}(\rho v_i) = -\frac{\partial P_{ij}}{\partial x_j} \qquad \text{(momentum)}, \tag{2}$$

$$\frac{\partial \mathbf{B}}{\partial t} = -\text{curl } \mathbf{E} \qquad \text{(magnetic field)}, \tag{3}$$

$$\frac{\partial U}{\partial t} = -\text{div } \mathbf{g} \qquad \text{(total energy)}, \tag{4}$$

so that in three dimensions there are eight main dependent variables altogether. The density is denoted by ρ and the velocity by $\mathbf{v}$. The total momentum tensor is

$$P_{ij} = P_{ij}^0 - V_{ij},$$

where

$$P_{ij}^0 = p\delta_{ij} + \rho v_i v_j + \tfrac{1}{2}(B^2)\,\delta_{ij} - B_i B_j, \tag{5}$$

and the viscous stress tensor is

$$V_{ij} = \mu\left(\frac{\partial v_i}{\partial x_j} + \frac{\partial v_j}{\partial x_i} - \tfrac{2}{3}\delta_{ij}\,\text{div }\mathbf{v}\right) + \lambda\,\delta_{ij}\,\text{div }\mathbf{v}, \tag{6}$$

with μ the coefficient of dynamic or shear viscosity, and λ the coefficient of bulk viscosity. The total energy is

$$U = \tfrac{1}{2}\rho v^2 + \tfrac{1}{2}B^2 + e\rho. \tag{7}$$

Normally the internal energy per unit mass e and the pressure p are defined by

$$e = T/(\gamma - 1), \qquad p = \rho T, \tag{8}$$

where T is the temperature and $\gamma = 5/3$ is the ratio of specific heats. The electric field is given by the simplest version of Ohm's law for a moving material,

$$\mathbf{E} + \mathbf{v} \times \mathbf{B} = \eta \mathbf{j}, \tag{9}$$

where $\mathbf{j} = \text{curl }\mathbf{B}$ is the current and η is the electrical resistivity. The energy flux vector is

$$\mathbf{g} = \mathbf{v}\,[\tfrac{1}{2}\rho v^2 + e\rho + p] - V_{ij} v_i \mathbf{e}_j + \mathbf{E} \times \mathbf{B} - \kappa\,\text{grad }T, \tag{10}$$

where **e** is a unit vector and κ is the thermal conductivity. There are six terms altogether, representing the transport of kinetic and thermal energy, the work done by the material pressure and viscous stresses, the Poynting vector, and thermal conduction.

Since Eqs. (1)–(4) are in conservative form they can readily be solved by a conservative difference method, for example, by a generalization of the Lax–Wendroff scheme used in hydrodynamics (Richtmyer and Morton, 1967). Exact conservation of mass, momentum, magnetic flux, and total energy can then be guaranteed automatically, because each term on the right-hand side of a difference equation occurs twice, representing first the flow out of one mesh cell, and then the flow into the adjacent cell. Some difficulty may however be foreseen if the three terms in Eq. (7) have widely different magnitudes; for example in a low-β configuration (β is the ratio of material to magnetic pressure), small errors in calculating the magnetic field might become amplified and appear as anomalous heating or cooling of the plasma. It may therefore be preferable to use a nonconservative difference scheme based on the thermal energy equation:

$$\frac{\partial(\rho e)}{\partial t} = -\text{div}(\rho e \mathbf{v}) - p\,\text{div}\,\mathbf{v} + V_{ij}\frac{\partial v_i}{\partial x_j} + \eta j^2 + \text{div}(\kappa\,\text{grad}\,T). \quad (11)$$

In this formulation all the heating terms appear explicitly, and one advantage is that the first four terms on the right-hand side involve only first-order derivatives, evaluated at the center of the mesh cell, so that they are easy to calculate. (In Eq. (4) the quantities **j** and V_{ij} must be evaluated on the faces of the cell.)

We now define three sets of equations, to be referred to as (A, B, C), which describe the behavior of idealized incompressible and compressible fluids with constant transport coefficients. By choosing a rectangular Cartesian mesh with simple boundary conditions, it should be possible to use these equations to study magnetohydrodynamic processes in three dimensions on the largest existing computers (Section VII).

A. Incompressible Magnetohydrodynamics

The equation of motion for an incompressible fluid with constant density and viscosity is

$$\rho(\partial \mathbf{v}/\partial t + \mathbf{v} \cdot \nabla \mathbf{v}) = -\text{grad}\,p + \mathbf{j} \times \mathbf{B} + \mu \nabla^2 \mathbf{v}. \quad (12)$$

There are two principal methods for solving this numerically. The first method (A1) is to eliminate the pressure by taking the curl of the equation of motion

$$\partial \zeta/\partial t = \mathrm{curl}(\mathbf{v} \times \boldsymbol{\zeta}) + v \nabla^2 \boldsymbol{\zeta} + \rho^{-1} \mathrm{curl}(\mathbf{j} \times \mathbf{B}), \tag{13}$$

where $\boldsymbol{\zeta} = \mathrm{curl}\,\mathbf{v}$ is the vorticity and $v = \mu/\rho$ is the kinematic viscosity. The corresponding equation for the magnetic field is

$$\partial \mathbf{B}/\partial t = \mathrm{curl}(\mathbf{v} \times \mathbf{B}) + \eta \nabla^2 \mathbf{B}, \tag{14}$$

where the resistivity η is also assumed constant. The velocity is obtained from a streamfunction $\boldsymbol{\psi}$, which is calculated from the vorticity by solving Poisson's equation:

$$\mathbf{v} = \mathrm{curl}\,\boldsymbol{\psi}, \qquad \nabla^2 \boldsymbol{\psi} = -\boldsymbol{\zeta}. \tag{15}$$

The incompressibility of the fluid is taken into account by solving Eq. (15) implicitly. Since both $\boldsymbol{\zeta}$ and $\mathbf{j}$ propagate with the Alfven speed (Jeffrey, 1966, Chapter 1), there will be a Courant–Friedrichs–Lewy condition on the timestep if Eqs. (13) and (14) are solved explicitly.

The second method (A2) is to take the divergence of the equation of motion (12), thus obtaining a Poisson equation for the pressure. It seems logical to combine the fluid and magnetic pressures, obtaining

$$\nabla^2 \left(p + \frac{B^2}{2} \right) = -\rho \frac{\partial v_i}{\partial x_j} \frac{\partial v_j}{\partial x_i} + \frac{\partial B_i}{\partial x_j} \frac{\partial B_j}{\partial x_i}. \tag{16}$$

When the total pressure has been calculated it is inserted in Eq. (12) which is solved in the usual way.

B. Boussinesq Approximation

An interesting extension is to allow for slight changes in fluid density by adding a buoyancy term $\rho \mathbf{g}$ to the right-hand side of Eq. (12). The corresponding additions to Eqs. (13) and (16) are $\mathrm{grad}\,\rho \times \mathbf{g}$ and $\mathrm{div}(\rho \mathbf{g})$, respectively (B1, B2). If the density changes are due to thermal expansion with coefficient α, then

$$\mathrm{grad}\,\rho = -\alpha\,\mathrm{grad}\,T, \tag{17}$$

and the temperature equation is

$$\rho/(\gamma - 1)(\partial T/\partial t + \mathbf{v}\cdot\nabla T) = \mu \zeta^2 + \eta j^2 + \kappa \nabla^2 T, \tag{18}$$

if the thermal conductivity is also assumed constant.

C. Compressible Magnetohydrodynamics with Constant Transport Coefficients

For a compressible fluid with constant transport coefficients there are eight equations (C), namely Eq. (1), the equation of motion

$$\frac{\partial(\rho v_i)}{\partial t} = -\frac{\partial P^0_{ij}}{\partial x_j} + \mu \nabla^2 v_i + \left(\lambda + \frac{\mu}{3}\right)\frac{\partial}{\partial x_i} \text{div } \mathbf{v}, \qquad (19)$$

the field equation (14), and the thermal energy equation

$$\frac{\partial(\rho e)}{\partial t} = -\text{div}(\rho e \mathbf{v}) - p \,\text{div } \mathbf{v} + \mu(\text{curl } \mathbf{v})^2$$
$$+ \left(\lambda + \frac{\mu}{3}\right)(\text{div } \mathbf{v})^2 + \eta \mathbf{j}^2 + \kappa \nabla^2 T. \qquad (20)$$

D. Two-Fluid Magnetohydrodynamics with Variable Coefficients

To extend magnetohydrodynamic calculations from the idealized study of particular physical phenomena (I-codes) to the description of real experimental devices (R-codes) it is necessary to consider models involving several fluids (electrons, ions, neutrals) and to take into account the variation of transport coefficients with density, temperature, magnetic field, and direction.

1. *Isotropic Transport Coefficients*

A useful model for many devices (z-pinches, dense plasma focus) is a fully ionized plasma with separate electron and ion energies and isotropic transport coefficients. The introduction of a separate electron temperature necessarily leads to terms involving equipartition of energy and Joule heating, and it is as well to include bremsstrahlung radiation. It is assumed that the plasma is collision dominated,

$$\omega_{ce} \tau_{ei} \ll 1,$$

where $\omega_{ce} = (eB)/(m_e c)$ is the electron cyclotron frequency and τ_{ei} is the electron–ion collision time. In three dimensions there are nine equations, namely Eqs. (1)–(4), and the electron energy equation:

$$\frac{\partial}{\partial t}(\rho e_e) = -p_e \,\text{div } \mathbf{v} - \text{div}(\rho e_e \mathbf{v} + \kappa_e \,\text{grad } T_e)$$
$$+ \eta \mathbf{j}^2 - \rho \frac{(e_e - e_i)}{\tau_{eq}} - C_{rad}\rho^2 T_e^{1/2}. \qquad (21)$$

The electron thermal energy loss terms, to the ions (equipartition time τ_{eq}), and through bremsstrahlung radiation (constant C_{rad}) are included explicitly. The equation of state relates e_e to T_e,

$$e_e = T_e/(\gamma - 1).$$

As discussed previously, it may be preferable to use the ion energy equation rather than the equation for the conservation of total energy,

$$\frac{\partial}{\partial t}(\rho e_i) = -p_i(\text{div } \mathbf{v}) - \text{div}(\rho e_i \mathbf{v} + \kappa_i \text{ grad } T_i)$$

$$+ \rho \frac{(e_e - e_i)}{\tau_{eq}} + V_{ij}\frac{\partial v_i}{\partial x_j}. \quad (22)$$

If not, it will be necessary to include a bremsstrahlung term in Eq. (4).

For this collision-dominated case the transport coefficients given by Spitzer (1956) are appropriate:

resistivity, $\quad\quad\quad\quad \eta = \dfrac{m_e}{ne^2} v_{ei};\quad\quad\quad\quad (23)$

electron heat conductivity, $\quad\quad \kappa_e = \dfrac{5nk^2 T_e}{m_e v_{ei}};\quad\quad\quad\quad (24)$

ion heat conductivity, $\quad\quad \kappa_i = \dfrac{5nk^2 T_i}{m_i v_{ii}};\quad\quad\quad\quad (25)$

ion viscosity, $\quad\quad \mu = \dfrac{5nk^2 T_i}{m_i v_{ii}};\quad\quad\quad\quad (26)$

equipartition time, $\quad\quad \tau_{eq} = \dfrac{m_i}{2m_e}\dfrac{1}{v_{ei}},\quad\quad\quad\quad (27)$

where $n = n_e = n_i$ is the electron number density for a fully ionized hydrogen-like plasma, m_i is the ion mass, m_e the electron mass, e the electron charge, k is Boltzmann's constant, and v_{ii} is the ion–ion collision frequency.

The collision frequencies v are proportional to $T^{-3/2}$ and involve the logarithm of the collision parameter Λ. Since $\ln \Lambda$ is a slowly varying function it is frequently not justifiable to invoke a logarithmic function at each space timestep throughout the calculation. Useful variable transport coefficients then reduce to $\eta = c_1/T_e^{3/2}$, $\kappa_e = c_2 T_e^{5/2}$, $\kappa_i = c_3 T_i^{5/2}$, $\mu = c_4 T_i^{5/2}$, $\tau_{eq} = c_5 T_e^{3/2} \rho^{-1}$ where c_1, c_2, c_3, c_4, c_5, are constants which of course depend on the choice of units (Section II,A).

The transport terms outlined here all take the entropy-producing form div(κ grad ϕ) and may readily be included in conservative difference formulations by using either the implicit Crank–Nicholson scheme, or the explicit scheme with forward time difference (Richtmyer and Morton, 1967, Chapter 8).

2. Anisotropic Ion Pressure

As the magnetic field increases it is appropriate to consider an intermediate situation, in which collisions remain important but the transport processes become anisotropic. The ion pressure may also be anisotropic, $p_\parallel \neq p_\perp$ where $p_\parallel$ represents the component parallel to the local magnetic field, and $p_\perp$ is the perpendicular component. (Normally it is not necessary to introduce two separate electron pressures.) Although there is no good reason to expect the ion velocity distribution to be a double Maxwellian in this case, it is often convenient to think of two ion temperatures defined by $p_\parallel = \rho T_\parallel$, $p_\perp = \rho T_\perp$.

A consistent set of equations may be constructed, which reduces to the Chew–Goldberger–Low limit for strong magnetic fields (Chew et al., 1956). In addition to the equations of continuity (1), momentum (2), magnetic field (3), and electron energy (21), we introduce an equation for the parallel ion pressure:

$$\frac{\partial p_\parallel}{\partial t} + (\mathbf{v} \cdot \mathbf{\nabla}) p_\parallel + (\mathbf{\nabla} \cdot \mathbf{v}) p_\parallel + 2 p_\parallel \mathbf{\nabla}_\parallel \cdot \mathbf{v}_\parallel$$
$$- V_{i\parallel} \mathbf{\nabla}_\parallel \cdot \mathbf{v}_i + \mathbf{\nabla} \cdot \mathbf{q}_{i1} = (p_\perp - p_\parallel)/\tau_{ii} + (p_e - p_\parallel)/\tau_{eq}. \quad (28)$$

Rather than using an equation for the perpendicular ion pressure $p_\perp$, it is preferable to use the equation for the total ion energy.

$$\frac{\partial}{\partial t}(\rho e_i) = -p_\perp(\mathbf{\nabla}_\perp \cdot \mathbf{v}) - \mathbf{\nabla} \cdot (\rho e_i \mathbf{v}) - p_\parallel \mathbf{\nabla}_\parallel \cdot \mathbf{v}_\parallel + V_{ij} \frac{\partial}{\partial x_j} \mathbf{v}_i + \mathbf{\nabla} \cdot \mathbf{q}_{i2}$$
$$+ \rho\{(e_e - e_i)/\tau_{eq}\}. \quad (29)$$

Here $\mathbf{\nabla}_\parallel$ is the gradient operator parallel to the field, $\mathbf{\nabla}_\perp$ is the gradient operator perpendicular to the field, and τ_{ii} is the ion–ion collision time. $\mathbf{q}_{i1}$ and $\mathbf{q}_{i2}$ are the appropriate components of the ion heat flux tensor. A one-dimensional θ-pinch code with separate $T_{i\parallel}$ and $T_{i\perp}$ was developed by Fisher (unpublished).

3. Generalized Transport Coefficients

The transport terms $\mathbf{j}$, $\mathbf{q}_e$, $\mathbf{q}_i$, and $\mathbf{V}$ are no longer simply related to the "apparent" force terms $\mathbf{E} + \mathbf{v} \times \mathbf{B}$, ∇T_e, ∇T_i, and $\partial v_i/\partial x_j$. If the first moment of Boltzmann's equation is taken for the electron fluid, and if electron inertia is ignored, the generalized Ohm's law is obtained:

$$\mathbf{E} = -\mathbf{v} \times \mathbf{B} + \eta \mathbf{j} + \frac{m_i}{e} \frac{\mathbf{j} \times \mathbf{B}}{\rho} - \frac{m_i}{e} \frac{\nabla p_e}{\rho}. \tag{30}$$

The electron and ion heat conductivities now have the tensor form

$$\mathbf{q}_e = \underline{\underline{\kappa_e}} \cdot \nabla T_e, \tag{31}$$

$$\mathbf{q}_i = \underline{\underline{\kappa_i}} \cdot \nabla T_i, \tag{32}$$

which more explicitly may be written as:

$$\mathbf{q}_{e\perp} = -\frac{\kappa_e}{1 + \beta_e^2} \nabla T_e - \frac{\kappa_e \beta_e}{1 + \beta_e^2} \times \nabla T_e, \tag{33}$$

$$\mathbf{q}_{e\parallel} = -\kappa_{e\parallel} \nabla T_e, \tag{34}$$

$$\mathbf{q}_{i\perp} = -\frac{\kappa_{i\perp}}{1 + \beta_i^2} \nabla_\perp T_{i\perp} + \frac{\kappa_{i\perp} \beta_i}{1 + \beta_i^2} \times \nabla T_{i\perp}, \tag{35}$$

$$\mathbf{q}_{i\parallel} = -\kappa_{i\parallel} \nabla T_{i\parallel}, \tag{36}$$

where $\beta_i = \omega_{ci} \tau_{ii}$ and $\beta_e = \omega_{ce} \tau_{ie}$, with $\omega_c = eB/mc$.

The traceless stress tensor V_{ij} may be related to the Navier–Stokes viscous tensor $\underline{\underline{U}}$,

$$\underline{\underline{U}} = \widetilde{\nabla \mathbf{v}} + \nabla \mathbf{v} - \tfrac{2}{3} \delta_{ij} (\nabla \cdot \mathbf{v}) \tag{37}$$

where $\widetilde{\nabla \mathbf{v}}$ is the transpose of $\nabla \mathbf{v}$. Choosing local coordinates $\hat{\mathbf{e}}_1$, $\hat{\mathbf{e}}_2$, $\hat{\mathbf{e}}_3$ where $\hat{\mathbf{e}}_3 = \mathbf{B}/|B|$, V_{ij} is related to $\underline{\underline{U}}$ as shown by Chapman and Cowling (1960) or

Kaufman (1960).

$$V_{11} = \frac{2\mu_0}{1+4\beta_i^2} \{U_{11} + 2\beta_i U_{12} + 2\beta_i^2(U_{11} + U_{22})\}, \quad (38)$$

$$V_{22} = \frac{2\mu_0}{1+4\beta_i^2} \{U_{22} - 2\beta_i U_{12} + 2\beta_i^2(U_{11} + U_{22})\}, \quad (39)$$

$$V_{33} = 2\mu_\parallel U_{33}, \quad (40)$$

$$V_{12} = \frac{2\mu_0}{1+4\beta_i^2} \{U_{12} - \beta_i(U_{11} - U_{22})\}, \quad (41)$$

$$V_{13} = \frac{2\mu^2}{1+\beta_i^2} \{U_{13} + \beta_i U_{23}\}, \quad (42)$$

$$V_{23} = \frac{2\mu}{1+\beta_i^2} \{U_{23} - \beta_i U_{13}\}, \quad (43)$$

and κ_e, κ_i, and μ are related to the electron and ion temperatures as before.

It is noteworthy that when $\beta_i \to 0$ and $\beta_e \to 0$, this system of equations reduces to the collision-dominated case, while if $\beta \to \infty$, the Chew–Goldberger–Low form is obtained. The momentum equation is affected by separate parallel and perpendicular ion energies through the stress tensor terms $(\partial/\partial x_i)V_{ij}$. The advantage of field lines as local coordinates (Hertweck and Schneider, 1967) can readily be seen here, since the transport tensors then reduce to diagonal form in the collisionless limit.

Equations (30) and (31) are not entirely consistent, since according to Onsager (1931) the flux terms **j** and **q**$_e$ should be linearly related to the force terms **D** and ∇T_e where

$$\mathbf{D} = \mathbf{E} + \mathbf{v} \times \mathbf{B} + \frac{m}{e}\frac{\nabla p_e}{\rho}.$$

Therefore,

$$\mathbf{j} = \underline{\underline{\sigma}} \cdot \mathbf{D} + \underline{\underline{\tau}} \cdot \nabla T_e, \quad (44)$$

$$\mathbf{q}_e = -\underline{\underline{\mu}} \cdot \mathbf{D} - \underline{\underline{\kappa}} \cdot \nabla T_e. \quad (45)$$

The terms $\mu \cdot \mathbf{\underline{\underline{D}}}$ and $\tau \cdot \nabla T_e$ are the so-called thermoelectric terms. As above, in terms of local coordinates $\hat{\mathbf{e}}_1, \hat{\mathbf{e}}_2, \hat{\mathbf{e}}_3$,

$$\sigma_\| = \sigma_0 T_e^{3/2}, \qquad \sigma_\perp = \frac{\sigma_0 T_e^{3/2}}{1+\beta_e^2}\begin{bmatrix} 1 & \beta \\ -\beta & 1 \end{bmatrix}, \qquad (46)$$

$$\tau_\| = 0, \qquad \tau_\perp = \frac{\tau_0 T_e^{3/2}}{1+\beta_e^2}\begin{bmatrix} 1 & \beta \\ -\beta & 1 \end{bmatrix}, \qquad (47)$$

$$\kappa_{e\|} = \kappa_0 T_e^{5/2}, \qquad \kappa_{e\perp} = \frac{\kappa_0 T_e^{5/2}}{1+\beta_e^2}\begin{bmatrix} 1 & \beta \\ -\beta & 1 \end{bmatrix}, \qquad (48)$$

$$\mu_\| = 0, \qquad \mu_\perp = \frac{\mu_0 T_e^{5/2}}{1+\beta_e^2}\begin{bmatrix} 1 & \beta \\ -\beta & 1 \end{bmatrix}. \qquad (49)$$

The variation in $\ln \Lambda$ has again been ignored, and $\sigma_0, \tau_0, \kappa_0, \mu_0$ are assumed constant. Accurate values of constants of the order of 1 appearing with β_e and β_i in Eqs. (33)–(36) and (38)–(49) have been tabulated by Shkarofsky *et al.* (1963).

E. Neutral and Impurity Components

1. *Partially Ionized Plasmas*

A detailed description of the variety of atomic, molecular, and ionic states in low temperature plasmas can lead to unmanageable complexity in the fluid equations. Some of the essential effects of partial ionization on plasma dynamics can however be obtained with a simple three-component fluid: ions, electrons, and hydrogen-like neutrals.

(a) *Equal Ion and Neutral Temperatures, No Slip.* As a first approximation, equal ion and neutral temperatures may be assumed, and the ions and neutrals dynamically "tied together" so that no ion slip is allowed. To the equations (C) for $\rho, \mathbf{v}, \mathbf{B}, e_e$, and e_i, an equation for the electron density is added (Appleton and Bray, 1964)

$$\partial n_e/\partial t + \nabla \cdot (n_e \mathbf{v}) = S n_n n_e - \alpha n_i n_e. \qquad (50)$$

This is essentially a conservation equation where n_n, n_i are the neutral and ion densities respectively, and the right-hand side represents the production of electrons through chemical reactions. α is the collisional-radiative recombination coefficient, and S is the collisional-radiative ionization coefficient.

α and S have been determined by a number of authors (Hinnov and Hirschberg, 1962; Makin and Keck, 1963) for a variety of plasma parameters. For the two cases of high electron density and low temperature (three-body electron–ion recombination dominant), and low density plasma (radiative recombination dominant), α takes the forms

$$\alpha = 2.3 \times 10^{-8} n_e T_e^{-9/2} \quad \text{cm}^3 \text{ sec}^{-1}, \tag{51}$$

$$\alpha = 4.1 \times 10^{-10} T_e^{-3/4} \quad \text{cm}^3 \text{ sec}^{-1}, \tag{52}$$

respectively, and the equilibrium condition provides S,

$$\frac{\alpha}{S} = n_e \left(\frac{h^2}{2\pi m_e k T_e}\right)^{3/2} \exp\left(\frac{I_1}{kT_e}\right) \tag{53}$$

where I_1 is the ionization energy.

(b) *Equal Ion and Neutral Temperatures, Slip Allowed.* A dynamic model may be constructed by permitting finite ion slip but equating the ion and neutral temperatures. It is convenient to use the equations for total plasma momentum,

$$\rho \mathbf{v} = n_e m_e \mathbf{v}_e + n_i m_i \mathbf{v}_i + n_n m_n \mathbf{v}_n,$$

and neutral momentum $\rho_n v_n$,

$$\frac{\partial}{\partial t}(\rho \mathbf{v}) + \nabla \cdot (\rho \mathbf{v}\mathbf{v} + \underline{\underline{P^1}}) - \mathbf{j} \times \mathbf{B} = 0, \tag{54}$$

$$\frac{\partial}{\partial t}(\rho_n v_n) + \nabla \cdot (\rho_n \mathbf{v}_n \mathbf{v}_n + p_n) = (\alpha n_i^2 \mathbf{v}_i - S n_i n_n \mathbf{v}_n) m_n$$
$$+ \nu_{ia} \rho_n (\mathbf{v}_i - \mathbf{v}_n), \tag{55}$$

where $\underline{\underline{P^1}}$ is the total plasma pressure tensor, and ν_{ia} is the ion-neutral collision frequency. Ohm's law must now be modified to include the effects of collisions between the electron and neutral fluids:

$$\mathbf{E} + \mathbf{v} \times \mathbf{B} = \eta^1 \mathbf{j} + \eta_{ea}(\mathbf{v}_n - \mathbf{v}_i) + \frac{m}{e\rho}(\mathbf{j} \times \mathbf{B} - \nabla p_e), \tag{56}$$

η^1 is the modified resistivity, incorporating the electron-neutral collision frequency v_{ea},

$$\eta^1 = \eta_{ei} + \eta_{ea}, \tag{57}$$

$$v_{ea} = n_n \sigma_{en} \left(\frac{8kT_e}{\pi m_e}\right)^{1/2}, \tag{58}$$

where σ_{en} is the electron-neutral cross section.

(c) *Separate Ion and Neutral Temperature.* A final model is the three-fluid model with separate ion and neutral temperatures. An equation for the thermal energy of the neutrals must now be included:

$$\frac{\partial}{\partial t}(\rho_n e_n) = -p_n(\nabla \cdot v_n) - \nabla \cdot (\rho_n e_n \mathbf{v}_n) + \rho_n \frac{e_i - e_n}{\tau_{in}}$$
$$+ e_n m_n n_e(n_i \alpha - n_n S), \tag{59}$$

e_n is the internal energy per unit mass of the neutrals and τ_{in} is the equipartition time due to elastic ion-neutral collisions. The last term in Eq. (59) is the thermal energy gain from the neutral fluid due to "chemical reactions."

In each of the three models described above the electron energy equation (21) is modified by the occurrence of "chemical" reactions. If I_1 is the ionization energy, Appleton and Bray (1964) have shown that for optically thin plasmas, an additional term Q_e can be added to the right-hand side of Eq. (21):

$$Q_e = I_1(Sn_n n_e - \alpha n_i n_e) - Q_{rad}, \tag{60}$$

where Q_{rad} is the radiation per unit volume lost in inelastic collisions. Elastic exchange of energy between electrons and neutrals may also be included in the appropriate equations, if required. A one-dimensional partially ionized code essentially equivalent to case (c) was written by Mrs. J. Taylor and one of the authors (KVR), and a similar code was developed by Duchs (Roberts, 1963; Duchs, 1963; Duchs and Griem, 1966).

2. *Impurity Calculations*

A small percentage of impurity ions can have a profound effect in cooling laboratory plasmas (Knorr, 1958). Such an energy loss mechanism may be included at minimum expense of complexity to the MHD equations by an explicit treatment. Radiation loss due to bremsstrahlung has been included in the electron energy equation (21); the effect of impurities is to add a term $-Q_{imp}$ to the right-hand side of Eq. (21).

Impurity atoms are assumed to be tied to the ion flow, as determined by the MHD equations. At the completion of each timestep it remains to calculate the local power loss due to impurities with the values of electron density and temperature provided by the code. The energy loss mechanism is due to electron-impurity atom interaction in which two processes are considered:

ionization by electron collision,

$$N(Z, z, g) + e \to N(Z, z + 1, g) + e + e, \tag{61}$$

and radiative recombination,

$$N(Z, z, g) + e \to N(Z, z - 1, g) + h_\nu, \tag{62}$$

where $N(Z, z, g)$ is an ion of atomic number Z and ionic charge z.

Local thermodynamic equilibrium and hence the steady state ionization equations should not be assumed since typical characteristic relaxation times for these processes to achieve an equilibrium may be greater than the lifetime of the plasma. Time-dependent equations from the corona model are used (Hobbs et al., 1961),

$$\frac{dN_k}{dt} = \sum_i \alpha_{ik} N_i. \tag{63}$$

Here N_k is the number of impurity atoms (ions) in state k and a variety of atomic processes are included each of rate $\alpha_{ik}(n_e, T_e)$.

F. Boundary Conditions

1. *I-Codes*

In studying idealized physical phenomena it is appropriate to choose the simplest mathematical boundary conditions consistent with the problem. The mesh domain may usually be bounded by rigid impermeable walls, geometrical singularities or symmetry planes. Another possibility is to impose periodic boundary conditions.

The treatment of symmetry planes is straightforward, since an additional mesh plane may be included in the calculation on which the physical variables are merely reproduced. This is also true for periodic boundary conditions, in an explicit calculation.

Singularities in the geometry of the problem, for example, $r = 0$ in cylindrical and spherical systems, may often be most conveniently handled by applying exact integral conservation laws to the local mesh volume surrounding the singularity, e.g., for the density at the origin of a one-dimensional cylindrical system

$$\frac{\partial}{\partial t}(\pi(\Delta r)^2 \rho(0)) = -2\pi \, \Delta r \rho(\Delta r) v_r(\Delta r),$$

where $\rho(0)$ is assumed to represent the average density over a cylinder of radius Δr, while for the azimuthal magnetic field, $B_\theta(0) = 0$ and

$$\frac{\partial}{\partial t}(2 \, \Delta r B_\theta(\Delta r)) = E_z(2 \, \Delta r) - E_z(0).$$

The electric field $E_z(0)$ to be inserted in Faraday's law may be related to the current by $E_z(0) = \eta(0)j_z(0)$. Since $(\partial j_z/\partial r)_0 = 0$ we assume that j_z is uniform over the cylinder of radius Δr, so that the total current within this cylinder is $J = \pi(\Delta r)^2 j_z(0)$. This determines $B_\theta(\Delta r)$ in the usual way, and we find

$$E_z(0) = 2\eta B_\theta(\Delta r)/\Delta r.$$

A numerical problem arises with an explicit scheme, however, if one of the mesh intervals becomes very small in the neighborhood of the singularity [for example, the interval $r \, \Delta\theta$ near the origin of the (r, θ)-plane], and special methods must be employed if Δt is not to become unacceptably small because of the Courant–Friedrichs–Lewy condition.

At an impermeable wall $v_\perp$ is taken to be zero, while two extreme conditions are available for $v_\|$: either the plasma is allowed to flow without hindrance adjacent to the wall (free slip), or else it is tied to the wall ($v_\| = 0$, no slip). In the free-slip case an exact integral conservation law may again be applied to the half-cell just inside the wall in order to calculate $v_\|$ (Fig. 1).

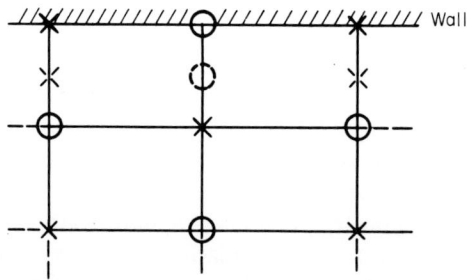

FIG. 1. Wall box. Only a half-box of area $2\Delta^2$ is available near a wall. To retain the conservation laws, those variables which are not identically zero at the wall are assumed to be displaced inwards by a distance $\Delta/2$ (dashed circle), and similarly for the parallel fluxes.

Some of the variables such as $v_\parallel$ are then effectively centered a distance $\Delta/2$ from the wall, and it may be appropriate to take account of this when calculating normal derivatives.

For the magnetic field equations we assume either that the walls are perfectly conducting, $E_\parallel = 0$, or else that they are perfectly conducting walls covered by a thin insulating layer, $j_\perp = 0$, so that interchange motions can take place at the boundary (Roberts and Taylor, 1965). This prevents any penetration of the changing magnetic field beyond the region of calculation. In the case of the energy equations, the walls may be treated as constant heat sinks, $T_e = T_i$ = constant.

2. *R-Codes*

Greater complexity is demanded in studying real experimental devices. The MHD model assumed for the problem may well break down at a wall, and ideally a separate set of equations (consistent with the physical wall conditions and including neutrals and the work function of the material) should be solved to provide boundary conditions for the main calculation. Such a method is in general too complicated and has not been attempted; the best approach is to apply problem-oriented heuristic boundary conditions, some of which are mentioned elsewhere in this paper. Four typical situations may be mentioned.

(a) The simplest case is that of a confined plasma which is kept away from the wall by a magnetic field whose lines of force close within the plasma, as in the toroidal pinch. Here the wall is unlikely to be important, once the discharge has moved inwards, although it may have a critical effect which is difficult to calculate in the early stages. For a Tokomak or Stellarator, it may be necessary to study the boundary conditions at the divertor or aperture limiter rather carefully.

(b) In a θ-pinch, the lines of force leave the plasma at the ends of the coil and pass through the insulating tube wall, so that the plasma is coupled to a region whose properties are difficult to define. The main problems are concerned with the electric field E_z at this part of the wall, which may propagate a rotational Alfven wave back into the plasma, and with the thermal coupling between the electron temperature and the wall. This is an interesting two-dimensional problem which has not yet been tackled adequately.

(c) A closer coupling between the plasma and the wall occurs in the plasma focus apparatus, where flow occurs in the (r, z)-plane along a coaxial duct between the two cylindrical electrodes, with the magnetic field only in the θ-direction. Hydrodynamic boundary layers of some complexity may be expected to occur at the electrode surfaces. In contrast to the corresponding situation in ordinary fluid theory, we do not yet know what boundary conditions to impose.

(d) Finally, one may mention the stabilized linear z-pinch, where the field lines emerge from the two electrodes into the plasma, causing strong cooling and contamination by metal impurities.

3. *Electrical Circuit*

The magnetic and electric fields on the boundary of the region of calculation may be coupled to one or more electrical circuits, with lumped capacitance C, resistance R, and inductance L. Although the details depend on the problem, symmetry usually enables each circuit current I to be related to a tangential magnetic field on the boundary, and the effective voltage V_p across the plasma to a tangential electric field. In the simplest case, we then have to solve the circuit equations

$$C\frac{dV_c}{dt} = -I, \qquad L\frac{dI}{dt} = V_c - V_p - RI, \qquad (64)$$

where V_c is the voltage on the capacitor. If the plasma equations are being solved by the leapfrog method, it may be convenient to use a similar method for the circuit,

$$\frac{C}{2\,\Delta t}(V_c^{n+1} - V_c^{n-1}) = -I^n,$$

$$\frac{L}{2\,\Delta t}(I^{n+1} - I^{n-1}) = V_c^n - V_p^n - RI^n, \qquad (65)$$

although this difference scheme introduces a weak computational instability which may have to be removed by filtering.

III. Difference Methods

A. Preliminary Remarks

Solution of the MHD equations in two and three dimensions presents a number of formidable and partially unsolved problems, whose origins may be grouped under the headings: anisotropy, magnetic configuration, high propagation speeds, advection.

The equations are anisotropic because diffusion and wave propagation processes depend on the local direction of the magnetic field. For example, electron temperature, fluid motion, and torsional oscillations can all be "piped" along curved field lines. Most of the standard finite difference methods have been established for the nearly isotropic case, and may therefore break down. One would like to use the field lines themselves as coordinates, but they often have a complicated topology which changes with time because resistive diffusion causes the lines to "cut and rejoin."

Since the Alfven propagation speed $c_A = B/\rho^{1/2}$ becomes large in regions of low density and strong magnetic field, explicit methods can lead to severe restrictions on the timestep, and one would prefer to use an implicit technique. On the other hand, it has not been mathematically established that the usual alternating-direction and fractional-step implicit methods (Richtmyer and Morton, 1967, Chap. 8) will work in the strongly anisotropic case, and on physical grounds it seems rather doubtful.

Since many of the physical quantities are advected with the plasma it would be natural to use Lagrangian coordinates, thus avoiding fictitious numerical diffusion altogether (Roberts and Weiss, 1966), but this is impracticable unless the fluid motion is rather simple because the mesh becomes too distorted. Eulerian schemes of higher order accuracy in the advective term must therefore usually be employed. Short-wavelength ripples propagating with a slightly incorrect velocity (numerical dispersion) may then cause variables to take nonphysical values; for example, the density or temperature may become negative. This must be prevented by ad hoc checks.

No single difference scheme will yet handle the general MHD problem in more than one dimension, and only a limited number of cases can yet be tackled at all. Rather than a complete account of MHD difference methods, this section will therefore contain a number of prescriptions and suggestions. Three schemes will be emphasized: Hain implicit scheme, leapfrog explicit scheme, Lax–Wendroff explicit scheme.

A Lagrangian version of the Hain implicit method provides a general solution to the one-dimensional problem, and it is currently being extended to two and three dimensions, although it is not yet clear how well it will handle the anisotropic case. The leapfrog scheme (Section VII) is appropriate for I-codes in which the transport coefficients are isotropic and constant, and provides a fairly general solution to this type of problem. It uses the Dufort–Frankel method for the diffusion terms (Richtmyer and Morton, 1967, Chap. 8), but since this becomes awkward when the diffusion coefficients are no longer constant in space and time it seems preferable to use the Lax–Wendroff method for R-codes.

B. Mathematical Nature of the Equations

The sets of partial differential equations defined in Section II, which describe increasingly complex MHD models, involve four basic kinds of physical process:

(a) elliptic,
(b) hyperbolic,
(c) parabolic,
(d) local.

Elliptic processes represent the instantaneous transmission of pressure (in an incompressible fluid, Section II, A and B), or magnetic stress (in the vacuum region surrounding a confined plasma), and do not occur within a real plasma. Local processes include equipartition of energy, momentum exchange between ions and neutrals, ionization, etc., and are not difficult to handle. For mathematical purposes therefore, most of our models are of mixed hyperbolic and parabolic type. The hyperbolic terms represent MHD waves which can evidently be quite complex in the general case of a nonlinear, anisotropic, inhomogeneous fluid which is in motion, while the parabolic terms represent diffusion processes which may also be strongly anisotropic, since they depend on the direction of the magnetic field.

Such a system may be described by a vector equation

$$d\mathbf{u}/dt = L\mathbf{u}, \tag{66}$$

where $\mathbf{u} = \mathbf{u}(x, y, z, t)$, and L is a differential operator containing terms of first (hyperbolic) and second (parabolic) order in the space derivatives. In MHD the system is nonlinear so that $L = L(\mathbf{u})$. A difference formulation of Eq. (66) is obtained by replacing the continuous spacetime (x, y, z, t) by a discrete lattice (x_i, y_j, z_k, t^n) where $t^n = \sum_{m=1}^{n} \Delta t_m$, and the differential operator L by a difference operator L^*.

C. Explicit and Implicit Schemes

The difference between explicit and implicit schemes may best be seen by examining the simplest case of formulas employing only two time levels, which are obtained by integrating Eq. (66) over the interval (t^n, t^{n+1}),

$$\int_{t^n}^{t^{n+1}} \frac{du}{dt} dt = \int_{t^n}^{t^{n+1}} L\mathbf{u}\, dt, \tag{67}$$

in the approximate form

$$\mathbf{u}_{ijk}^{n+1} - \mathbf{u}_{ijk}^{n} = \varepsilon\, \Delta t L^{*n+1}\mathbf{u}_{ijk}^{n+1} + (1-\varepsilon)\, \Delta t L^{*n}\mathbf{u}_{ijk}^{n}, \tag{68}$$

where $0 \leq \varepsilon < 1$. (The asterisk will subsequently be omitted.)

1. Explicit Scheme

If $\varepsilon = 0$ the system of difference equations (68) is said to be explicit and may be solved immediately, since $\mathbf{u}_{ijk}^{n+1}$ is the only unknown. However, an explicit scheme will not be numerically stable unless it satisfies stability conditions of the general form (constants of order 1 are omitted),

$$\Delta t \lesssim \Delta/c \tag{69}$$

for the hyperbolic terms (where Δ represents a space step and c is a wave or fluid velocity), and

$$\Delta t \lesssim \Delta^2/\sigma \tag{70}$$

for the parabolic term (where σ is a diffusion coefficient). Physically these conditions simply state that the difference solution, which can propagate information across the mesh at a maximum rate of one space-step Δ during each timestep Δt, must be able to keep up with all the propagation speeds of the differential system, including waves, fluid motion, and diffusion. Equations (69) and (70) are local conditions, and the most unfavorable case must necessarily be taken.

It is characteristic of compressible MHD that very large changes in the plasma parameters can occur between different regions of the domain of calculation, for example, in the density ρ, temperature T, and magnetic field B. In particular, the Alfven velocity $c_A = B/\rho^{1/2}$ may vary by several orders of magnitude. An explicit scheme can thus demand a vanishingly small timestep, if there are regions of high magnetic field and low density. This may be contrasted with the usual situation in hydrodynamics where the characteristic velocity is the sound speed, proportional to $T^{1/2}$ and independent of ρ, so that much smaller variations occur. Except for problems involving a slow passage through a succession of near-equilibrium states (as in stellar evolution), an explicit scheme is usually quite acceptable in hydrodynamics. Another awkward feature of two- or three-dimensional MHD is the high electron thermal conductivity along the magnetic field lines.

2. Implicit Schemes

If $\varepsilon \neq 0$ the system (68) is implicit, and the solution of Eq. (66), a time integration problem, has now been reduced to the solution of a set of simultaneous algebraic equations at each timestep n. In principle then, $\mathbf{u}_{ijk}^n$ may be solved for all ijk. Such an implicit scheme may be chosen to be always numerically stable, so that Δt is restricted only by considerations of accuracy. The scheme will only be useful, however, if there is some algorithm which enables the equations to be solved efficiently.

D. The Tridiagonal Method in One Dimension

The set of simultaneous algebraic equations (68) may be written

$$(I - \varepsilon \,\Delta t L^{n+1})\mathbf{u}_{ijk}^{n+1} = (I + (1 - \varepsilon) \,\Delta t L^{n})\mathbf{u}_{ijk}^{n}, \tag{71}$$

where the right-hand side is a known quantity, and I is the identity operator, or, say,

$$S^{n+1}\mathbf{u}_{ijk}^{n+1} = T^{n}\mathbf{u}_{ijk}^{n}. \tag{72}$$

In the special case of a one-dimensional linear equation in one dependent variable, the matrix S^{n+1} reduces to a tridiagonal form and may be inverted readily (Richtmyer and Morton, 1967, Chap. 8) by a simple recursive technique. If L_+ and L_- are ladder operators, such that

$$L_+ u_j = u_{j+1}, \qquad L_- u_j = u_{j-1},$$

then since S is tridiagonal, it may be written as

$$(AL_+ + B + CL_-)u = w, \tag{73}$$

where A, B, C are diagonal and $w = w(t^n)$ is known. It is convenient to split the double recursion in Eq. (73) into two stages by defining a diagonal matrix X and a vector y by

$$L_+ u = Xu + y, \tag{74}$$

so that

$$(AL_+ - AX + O)u = Ay,$$

and subtracting from Eq. (73),

$$(B + AX)u = -CL_- u + w - Ay,$$

or

$$u = -(B + AX)^{-1} CL_- u + (B + AX)^{-1}(w - Ay). \tag{75}$$

A, B, C, X are diagonal; therefore if Eq. (75) is compared with Eq. (74).

$$X_j = -C_j/(B_j + A_j X_{j+1}), \qquad y_j = (w_j - A_j y_{j+1})/(B_j + A_j X_{j+1}), \tag{76}$$

when the double subscripts have been dropped on the diagonal matrices. The pair of recursive relations (76) and (74) are employed respectively in turn. The right boundary condition determines X_J, while the left boundary condition determines u_1. The method is rapid since it involves few multiplications at each point. However in general the problem is nonlinear, $S = S(u^{n+1})$, and an iteration must be used to obtain a self-consistent solution.

E. Hain's Implicit Method

1. *One Dimension*

The one-dimensional MHD equations can be solved implicitly by reducing them all to the tridiagonal form studied in Section III,D (Hain *et al.*, 1960). We shall present it here in a modified, slightly more accurate version which is not necessarily the one that would be used in practice, and assume that a Lagrangian mesh is employed so that advection can be ignored. It is sufficient to consider the simple equations:

$$\rho \frac{dv}{dt} = -B \frac{\partial B}{\partial x}, \tag{77}$$

$$\frac{d\rho}{dt} = -\rho \frac{\partial v}{\partial x}, \tag{78}$$

$$\frac{dB}{dt} = -B \frac{\partial v}{\partial x} + \eta \frac{\partial^2 B}{\partial x^2}. \tag{79}$$

Since these equations are nonlinear, they must be iterated, so we suppose that $\mathbf{u}^n$, $\mathbf{u}^{n+1,p}$ are known (where p represents the iteration parameter), and that $\mathbf{u}^{n+1,p+1}$ is to be determined. The essence of the method is to solve Eq. (71) formally and substitute into Eq. (77), obtaining an equation of parabolic type which we solve by the tridiagonal method, with $\varepsilon = \frac{1}{2}$ so that the space derivatives are centered in time. A bar will denote an average of (n), $(n+1, p)$, while a tilde will denote an average of (n), $(n+1, p+1)$. Then

$$B^{n+1, p+1} = B^n - \bar{B} \Delta t \left(\frac{\partial \tilde{v}}{\partial x}\right) + \eta \Delta t \left(\frac{\partial^2 \bar{B}}{\partial x^2}\right),$$

or

$$\tilde{B} = B^n - \frac{\bar{B} \Delta t}{2} \left(\frac{\partial \tilde{v}}{\partial x}\right) + \eta \frac{\Delta t}{2} \left(\frac{\partial^2 \bar{B}}{\partial x^2}\right),$$

or combining the first and third terms on the right-hand side, say,

$$\tilde{B} = \hat{B} - \frac{\bar{B}\,\Delta t}{2}\left(\frac{\partial \tilde{v}}{\partial x}\right). \tag{80}$$

Differentiating Eq. (80) and substituting it into Eq. (77) we have the required parabolic equation

$$\bar{\rho}\frac{d\tilde{v}}{dt} = -\bar{B}\frac{\partial \hat{B}}{\partial x} + \frac{\bar{B}\,\Delta t}{2}\frac{\partial}{\partial x}\left(\bar{B}\frac{\partial \tilde{v}}{\partial x}\right). \tag{81}$$

Stability analysis shows that the amplification factor has modulus unity, and that the diffusion term in Eq. (81) just cancels an instability arising from the explicit formulation of the magnetic pressure gradient in the first term of the equation.

It is convenient in practice to define the velocity at integral space points, and all other variables at half-integral space points, so that the first derivatives are centered properly in space. The magnetic field equation (79) is solved by using the known quantity $\partial \tilde{v}/\partial x$ in the second term, while the continuity equation (77) is solved according to

$$\rho^{n+1,\,p+1} = \rho^n\left\{\left(1 - \frac{\partial \tilde{v}}{\partial x}\frac{\Delta t}{2}\right)\bigg/\left(1 + \frac{\partial \tilde{v}}{\partial x}\frac{\Delta t}{2}\right)\right\}. \tag{82}$$

The timestep is constantly adjusted so that no variable changes too much in one timestep, subject to the overall requirement

$$\frac{\partial \tilde{v}}{\partial x}\frac{\Delta t}{2} \ll 1,$$

which is implied by Eq. (82) and by the other adiabatic compression terms. Usually only two or three iterations are needed. The electron and ion pressure equations are solved in a similar form to Eq. (80) and the derivatives included in Eq. (81), and if the field equations for B_θ, B_z are coupled by anisotropic resistivity these equations are solved together in (2×2)-matrix form.

2. Two and Three Dimensions

Hain (1967b) has generalized his method to two space dimensions, and more recently to three dimensions (unpublished). Consider the simple set of hydrodynamic equations:

$$\frac{d\rho}{dt} = -\rho \nabla \cdot \mathbf{v}, \tag{83}$$

$$\rho \frac{dv_x}{dt} = -\frac{\partial p}{\partial x}, \tag{84}$$

$$\rho \frac{dv_y}{\partial t} = -\frac{\partial p}{\partial y}, \tag{85}$$

$$\frac{dp}{dt} = -\gamma p \nabla \cdot \mathbf{v}. \tag{86}$$

Eq. (86) is solved in the form

$$\tilde{p} = p^n - \frac{\gamma \Delta t}{2} \bar{p} \nabla \cdot \mathbf{v} \tag{87}$$

by analogy with Eq. (80) and substituted into Eqs. (84) and (85), giving

$$\bar{\rho} \frac{d\tilde{v}_x}{dt} = -\frac{\partial p^n}{\partial x} + \frac{\gamma \bar{p} \Delta t}{2} \left(\frac{\partial^2 \tilde{v}_x}{\partial x^2} + \frac{\partial^2 \tilde{v}_y}{\partial x \partial y} \right), \tag{88}$$

$$\bar{\rho} \frac{d\tilde{v}_y}{dt} = -\frac{\partial p^n}{\partial y} + \frac{\gamma \bar{p} \Delta t}{2} \left(\frac{\partial^2 \tilde{v}_x}{\partial x \partial y} + \frac{\partial^2 \tilde{v}_y}{\partial y^2} \right), \tag{89}$$

so that the terms in $\partial^2/\partial x^2$, $\partial^2/\partial y^2$ are solved by the tridiagonal method, and the mixed derivatives by iteration. Equations (83) and (86) are solved by formulas analogous to Eq. (82). The velocity components are defined on staggered space meshes, so that if ρ, p are at the points (i,j), v_x is at $(i + \frac{1}{2}, j)$ and v_y at $(i, j + \frac{1}{2})$.

F. Eulerian and Lagrangian Coordinates

One of the major problems in MHD calculations arises from the dominance of the advective term $\mathbf{v} \cdot \nabla f$ which occurs in each equation. This represents the transport of physical variables such as density, temperature, magnetic field, and velocity from point to point by the bulk motion of the fluid, leaving their values unchanged. Superimposed on this advection are other kinematic effects of the bulk motion such as adiabatic compression (div **v**), and rotation [for example, the term $(\mathbf{B} \cdot \nabla)\mathbf{v}$ in the field equation], as well as diffusive processes which may be physically smaller but are nevertheless important to calculate accurately. Clearly a Lagrangian formulation using a mesh which moves with the fluid can transform away the bulk motion altogether, allowing the remaining terms to be treated more accurately, and in one dimension this approach has proved successful.

In two or three dimensions a Lagrangian mesh is considerably more difficult, since it immediately becomes nonorthogonal and may eventually become excessively distorted. Pseudo-Lagrangian formulations have been developed for specific problems by Hain (1967a) and Hertweck and Schneider (1967), but a fixed Eulerian mesh is normally used in practice, and this requires careful treatment of the advective term if physical diffusion is not to be masked by numerical effects.

1. *Accurate Treatment of the Advective Term*

The numerical accuracy of various treatments of the advective term has been examined by Roberts and Weiss (1966). Consider the equation

$$\frac{\partial f}{\partial t} + v \frac{\partial f}{\partial x} = 0. \tag{90}$$

The method ascribed to Lelevier (Richtmyer and Morton, 1967, Chap. 12) uses a forward or backward space difference for the derivative $\partial f/\partial x$, according to whether $v < 0$ or $v > 0$, respectively. This difference is uncentered and therefore represents a combination of derivatives,

$$\frac{\partial f}{\partial x} \mp \frac{\Delta x}{2} \frac{\partial^2 f}{\partial x^2},$$

so that Eq. (90) is replaced by

$$\frac{\partial f}{\partial t} + v \frac{\partial f}{\partial x} = \frac{|v| \Delta x}{2} \frac{\partial^2 f}{\partial x^2}, \tag{91}$$

where the right-hand side corresponds to a diffusion or damping process.

Numerical diffusion may be eliminated quite simply by centering both derivatives properly, and several schemes are available for doing this. Those that we shall discuss in this paper employ three time levels, so that Eq. (90) is solved in the form

$$f_j^{n+1} - f_j^{n-1} = -\frac{v \Delta t}{\Delta x}(f_{j+1}^n - f_{j-1}^n). \tag{92}$$

Although diffusion has been eliminated, numerical *dispersion* still occurs so that modes of short-wavelength travel with a velocity which is different from the correct speed v. Difference schemes of higher-order accuracy have therefore been developed by Roberts and Weiss (1966) to reduce this effect, although it cannot be removed completely.

2. *Elimination of Nonphysical Values*

One advantage of the Lelevier scheme is that a function which is everywhere positive, such as the density or temperature, remains positive throughout the calculation. This is because the prescription amounts to a linear interpolation between the two values $f_j^n, f_{j\pm1}^n$. Alternatively we may say that although numerical dispersion occurs, the short-wavelength modes are so heavily damped that they die away before they can propagate very far, and so never cause any ripples in the solution.

When the damping is removed the short wavelengths can propagate freely, and since they have a speed which is different from the physical speed v of the long-wavelength modes (and possibly also a different direction), they may travel into "quiet" regions of the calculation where their amplitude is large enough to give an obviously wrong result. In particular, the density or temperature may become negative, which has serious effects in a nonlinear calculation. The Lax–Wendroff method introduces a numerical fourth-order diffusion term which has a mitigating effect (Richtmyer and Morton, 1967, Chap. 12), but it provides no guarantee that nonphysical values cannot occur.

This possibility has been recognized for some time and prevented by ad hoc methods (Roberts *et al.*, 1963), but recently Hain (private communication) has defined a more elegant prescription. Consider only the advective term in a three-dimensional calculation, then if

$$f_{\max} = \max(f_{ijk}^{n-1}, f_{i\pm1, j\pm1, k\pm1}^n),$$

$$f_{\min} = \min(f_{ijk}^{n-1}, f_{i\pm1, j\pm1, k\pm1}^n),$$

the new value f_{ijk}^{n+1} is to be replaced by

$$f^* = \max(f_{\min}, \min(f_{\max}, f_{ijk}^{n+1})). \tag{93}$$

This simply states that the new value f^* must not lie outside the range of the seven known values which have been used to compute it. The prescription prevents spurious maxima and minima from arising, but it will cause some erosion of true maxima and minima as they move across the mesh. Other terms, such as compression, are to be left unchanged. We estimate that if

Eq. (93) is coded with maximum efficiency, it might add 30% to the computing time for an I-code such as that described in Section VII.

3. *Pseudo-Lagrangian Methods*

An experiment such as the 8-meter θ-pinch (Bodin *et al.*, 1968; Beach *et al.*, 1969) produces a long thin column of plasma, whose length is several hundred times its diameter, enclosed within an almost-parallel magnetic field. The plasma is nearly in equilibrium against radial displacements, while flow along the field lines occurs at speeds of sonic order. Diffusion and heat conduction take place very slowly across the field, but heat conduction along the field may be very rapid. The topology of the field lines remains invariant.

This type of problem is best solved by constructing a coordinate mesh based on the field lines themselves, and two-dimensional codes have been written by Hain (1967a) and Hertweck and Schneider (1967). An explicit method can be used for the flow along the field, and an implicit method for the transverse motion (since the transverse spacestep is much smaller). Hain chooses the field lines as one set of coordinate curves, and reconstructs a new orthogonal set of curves at each timestep. The transverse motion is therefore treated by a Lagrangian method (diffusion being neglected), but the longitudinal flow is pseudo-Eulerian because otherwise velocity shear ($\partial v_z/\partial r \neq 0$) would distort the mesh. Another possibility is to use a nonorthogonal mesh in which the field lines form one set of coordinate curves, and the lines $z = k\,\Delta z$, the other (fixed) set.

G. Explicit Schemes

Provided that the Alfven speed is nowhere too large and the physical duration of the calculation not too long, explicit schemes may be preferred on grounds of simplicity.

1. *Conservative Methods*

The conservative MHD equations (1)–(4) may be written generally in an $(N + 1)$-dimensional rectangular space–time as:

$$\partial \mathbf{u}/\partial t + \nabla \cdot \underline{\underline{F}} = 0, \tag{94}$$

where, for example, **u** is the eight-component vector

$$\mathbf{u} = (\rho, \rho\mathbf{v}, \mathbf{B}, U),$$

in a one-fluid system with equal electron and ion temperatures and $\underline{\underline{F}} = \underline{\underline{F}}(u)$.

Integrating Eq. (94) over a space–time region R bounded by two planes $t = t^n$, $t = t^{n+1}$ and the time-like surface S, we obtain the integral conservation law

$$\int \mathbf{u}(t^{n+1}) \, dv - \int \mathbf{u}(t^n) \, dv = -\int dt \oint_S \underline{\underline{F}} \cdot d\mathbf{s}. \tag{95}$$

A conservative difference scheme is formulated by dividing R into a set of rectangular boxes whose space-like faces have volume Δv, and representing Eq. (94) in the form

$$(\mathbf{u}^{n+1} - \mathbf{u}^n) \, \Delta v = \sum_{\alpha=1}^{2N} F_\alpha \, \Delta t, \tag{96}$$

where each term on the right-hand side represents a flux through one of the $2N(N-1)$-dimensional time-like faces. Since each face internal to the region R is shared by two boxes with oppositely directed normals, when Eq. (96) is summed over R, the contributions from the internal faces cancel in pairs, leaving only the contribution from the unpaired faces which make up the boundary S. Therefore, the difference scheme provides an exact integral conservation law equivalent to Eq. (95). One advantage of this type of scheme is that each flux need be calculated only once, and can then be preserved until it is used the second time.

2. An Unstable Scheme

A straightforward explicit scheme is illustrated in Fig. 2, for the two-dimensional case. (The points at which the flux is evaluated will be denoted by N, E, S, W and the central point by C. Corner points can be denoted by NE, SW, etc., and more distant points by FN (far north), FE, etc. In three dimensions, two further points U (upper), L (lower) are added.

If the fluxes are evaluated at time t^n at the points N, E, S, W, then the scheme (96) is unstable. The simplest way to see this is to notice that the time difference is uncentered, and really represents the combination of derivatives

$$\frac{\partial}{\partial t} + \frac{\Delta t}{2} \frac{\partial^2}{\partial t^2}.$$

Therefore, to a first approximation, each occurrence of ω in the true dispersion relation [we assume a variation $\exp(i\omega t)$] is replaced by

$$\omega + i \frac{\Delta t}{2} \omega^2,$$

and so the frequency of each root ω_0 is modified to

$$\omega_0 - i\frac{\Delta t}{2}\omega_0{}^2$$

giving real growth rate $\lambda = \Delta t\,\omega_0{}^2/2$.

Another interesting feature of the scheme is that it really describes four uncoupled meshes, labeled 1–4 in Fig. 2. The conserved quantity flows from

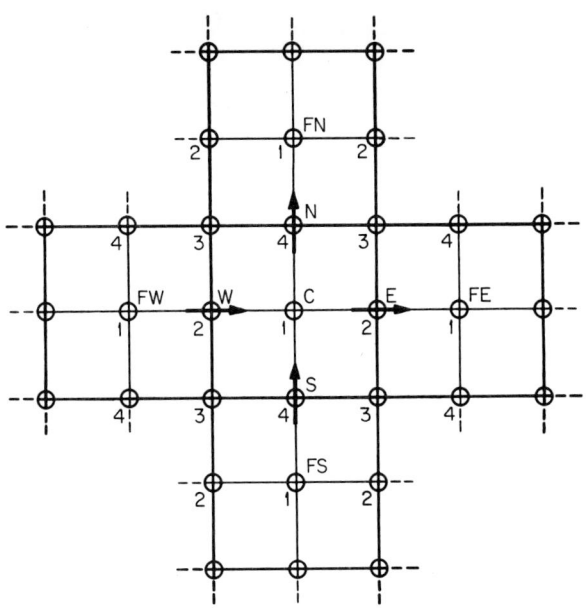

FIG. 2. An unstable scheme. The box area $4\Delta^2$ centered at C is coupled by fluxes through the sides N, E, S, W to four boxes centred at FN, FE, FS, FW. Each of the meshes 1, 2, 3, 4 is decoupled from the others and obeys a separate conservation law.

the boxes centered at FN, FE, FS, FW into the box centered at C, but there are three other sets of boxes which obey separate conservation laws. In three dimensions, there would be eight sets altogether.

3. *The Lax Scheme*

A stable scheme can be achieved by replacing u^n in Eq. (96) by the spatial average at the points where the flux is evaluated (Lax, 1954). This introduces a numerical diffusion, and the scheme really represents an approximation to the differential equation

$$\frac{\partial \mathbf{u}}{\partial t} + \nabla \cdot \underline{\underline{F}} = \frac{\Delta^2}{2N\,\Delta t} \nabla^2 \mathbf{u} - \frac{\Delta t}{2} \frac{\partial^2 \mathbf{u}}{\partial t^2}, \qquad (97)$$

where Δ is the spacestep. If c is the maximum propagation velocity,

$$\frac{\partial^2 \mathbf{u}}{\partial t^2} \leqslant c^2 \, \nabla^2 \mathbf{u},$$

and the scheme should be stable if the condition

$$\Delta t < \Delta/c\sqrt{N}$$

is satisfied.

This scheme is conservative but the flow is now quite complicated, because the term $\nabla \cdot \underline{\underline{F}}$ couples the box C to the boxes FN, FE, FS, FW as before, while the term $\nabla^2 u$ now couples C to boxes N, E, S, W (Fig. 3). All four meshes are therefore linked together and the scheme is free from spurious computational modes caused by the meshes becoming out of step.

4. *The Two-Step Lax–Wendroff Scheme*

If the Lax scheme is to be stable it must in practice contain second-order diffusion, since the first term on the right-hand side of Eq. (97) must always exceed the second by a finite amount. We can however avoid both of these error terms by using schemes which employ three time levels, so that Eq. (96) is replaced by

$$(\mathbf{u}^{n+1} - \mathbf{u}^{n-1})\,\Delta v = 2 \sum_{\alpha=1}^{2N} \underline{\underline{F}}_\alpha(t^n)\,\Delta t, \qquad (98)$$

which allows both space and time derivatives to be properly centered.

The two-step Lax–Wendroff method (Lax and Wendroff, 1960; Richtmyer, 1962; Richtmyer and Morton, 1967, Chap. 13) is of that type and uses the "sodium chloride" lattice illustrated in Fig. 4. The circle points are defined at even times $2m\,\Delta t$, and the cross points at odd times $(2m+1)\,\Delta t$. At the beginning t^{2m} of the double timestep, variables are defined only at the circle points. The Lax method is first used to construct auxiliary variables at the cross points at the intermediate time t^{2m+1}, and then these values are used to define fluxes which are employed in Eq. (98) to step on the main variables

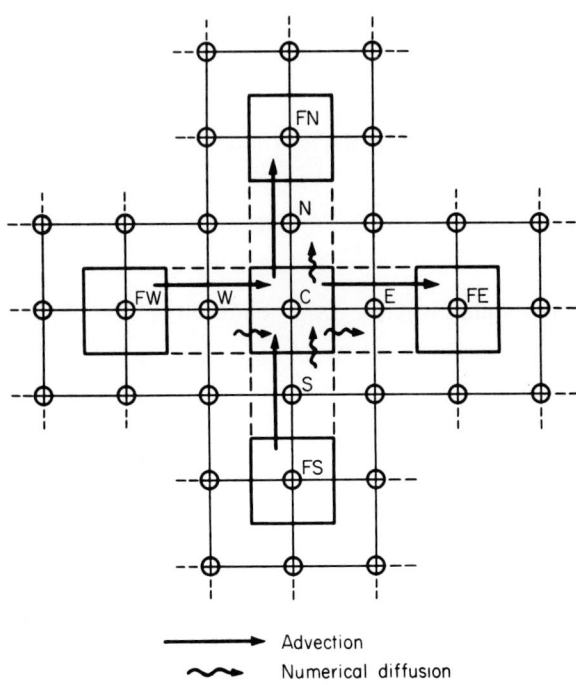

FIG. 3. Lax scheme. This scheme can be thought of in terms of boxes of area Δ^2, centered at the mesh points. The advection term couples the boxes marked by heavy lines, while the numerical diffusion couples the dashed boxes at N, E, S, W to C and so links the four meshes together.

from t^{2m} to t^{2m+2}. The auxiliary variables are discarded after they have been used.

Accuracy and stability of the scheme may be analyzed for the simple advective equation

$$\frac{\partial u}{\partial t} + A \frac{\partial u}{\partial x} + B \frac{\partial u}{\partial y} = 0, \tag{99}$$

where A and B are constants. We choose a mode $\exp(i\mathbf{k} \cdot \mathbf{x})$ with $\lambda = k_x \Delta x$, $\mu = k_y \Delta y$, and set $\alpha = A \Delta t/\Delta x$, $\beta = B \Delta t/\Delta y$. Then the auxiliary variable w satisfies

$$w = \{\tfrac{1}{2}(\cos \lambda + \cos \mu) - i(\alpha \sin \lambda + \beta \sin \mu)\} u, \tag{100}$$

while if G^2 is the amplification factor for the double step,

$$(G^2 - 1)u = -2i(\alpha \sin \lambda + \beta \sin \mu)w, \tag{101}$$

so that

$$G^2 = 1 - 2(\alpha \sin \lambda + \beta \sin \mu)^2 - i(\alpha \sin \lambda + \beta \sin \mu)(\cos \lambda + \cos \mu), \tag{102}$$

or approximately,

$$|G^2|^2 \simeq 1 - 2(\alpha\lambda + \beta\mu)^2(\lambda^2 + \mu^2 - 2(\alpha\lambda + \beta\mu)^2). \tag{103}$$

The scheme is therefore stable provided that Δt satisfies a Courant–Friedrichs–Lewy condition, and gives a small but useful fourth-order damping for all modes for which $\alpha\lambda + \beta\mu \neq 0$.

It is however clear from Fig. 4 that the two-dimensional scheme has two uncoupled meshes (labeled 1 and 3 in Fig. 4), while a three-dimensional scheme has four uncoupled meshes. These must be linked together in some way if unwanted computational modes are to be avoided.

5. *The Leapfrog Scheme*

An alternative method is the leapfrog scheme, which uses the same space-time lattice but treats the circle and cross points on an equal footing, each set defining the fluxes for the other. The amplification factor for Eq. (99) is then given by

$$G^2 - 1 = -2i(\alpha \sin \lambda + \beta \sin \mu)G, \tag{104}$$

and has modulus unity provided that

$$(\alpha \sin \lambda + \beta \sin \mu)^2 \leqslant 1. \tag{105}$$

There are now 2^N uncoupled meshes in N dimensions (Roberts, 1967).

H. The Treatment of Diffusion Terms

Apart from the continuity equation (1), all the main MHD equations contain diffusion terms which represent the production of entropy. These can be expressed in conservative form, e.g.,

$$\partial u/\partial t - \nabla(\eta \nabla u) = 0, \tag{106}$$

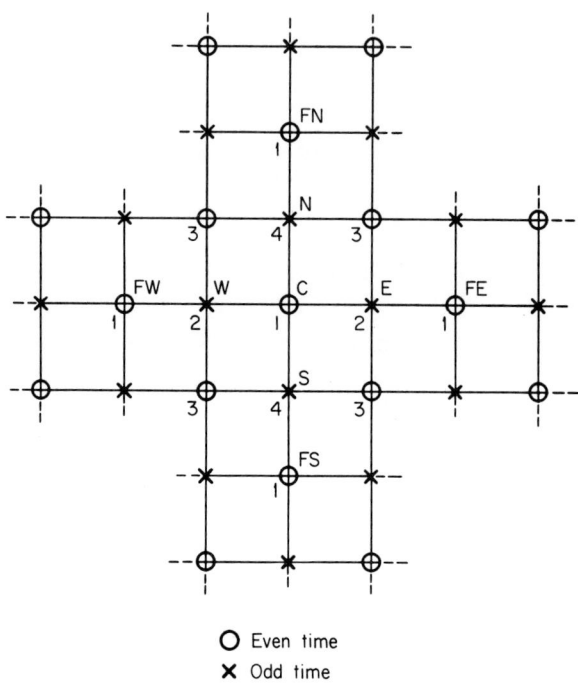

Fig. 4. Lax–Wendroff and Leapfrog mesh. The same "NaCl" mesh is used for both schemes, with all variables defined at the circle points at even times, and at the cross points at odd times. With the Lax–Wendroff scheme the cross points hold auxiliary variables which are discarded at the end of each double step.

and in a practical numerical scheme can if desired be used to link the various meshes together, so removing the computational modes without introducing any extra damping of the physical modes (Roberts and Weiss, 1966).

The numerical solution of the simple diffusion equation (106) has been widely investigated and is discussed, for example, by Richtmyer and Morton (1967), Chap. 8. If the MHD equations are solved implicitly the Crank–Nicholson scheme can be used. For the explicit three-level methods discussed in Section III,F, two main choices are available: the explicit scheme with forward time difference, and the Dufort–Frankel scheme.

1. *The Explicit Scheme with Forward Time Difference*

In a one-dimensional scheme with two time levels, Eq. (106) can be solved in the form

$$u_j^{n+1} - u_j^n = \frac{\Delta t}{(\Delta x)^2} \{\eta_{j+1/2}^n(u_{j+1}^n - u_j^n) - \eta_{j-1/2}^n(u_j^n - u_{j-1}^n)\}, \quad (107)$$

which is conservative, and stable for $\eta \Delta t/(\Delta x)^2 \leq \frac{1}{2}$ in the case of constant η.

When the Lax–Wendroff method is used to solve the two-dimensional MHD equations, a natural arrangement is to ignore the diffusion terms in constructing the auxiliary variables at the cross points at time t^{2m+1} (Fig. 4), and only to bring them in at the second step when the physical variables are recomputed at time t^{2m+2}. The points N, E, S, W can then be used to evaluate the diffusion coefficients, and the points C, FN, FE, FS, FW for the derivatives (Fig. 4). This arrangement has been used for the focus code (Sections V and VI), and applies equally well in three dimensions.

Although a second-order method is being used for the advective terms while a first-order method is suggested for the diffusion terms, the scheme is consistent provided that the diffusion is sufficiently small. This is true for the focus experiment because the magnetic field is transverse to the plane of calculation, so that all the transport coefficients are isotropic and limited by cyclotron orbiting effects. It is not so clear how to treat a problem in which the enhanced transport of heat *along* the field lines must be taken into account, since both explicit and Eulerian methods seem to fail.

The method that we have described does not couple the meshes 1 and 3 of Fig. 4 but is presented here because some ad hoc filtering technique can be applied periodically to remove the unwanted modes. If one prefers to use the physical diffusion for this purpose, the derivatives might be evaluated from the four corner points $NE-NW$ at time t^{2m} (Fig. 5). We then get a complicated conservation scheme in which the dynamical terms couple the boxes centered on C, $FN-FW$, while the diffusion terms couple the boxes centered on C, $NE-NW$ (Fig. 5). The diffusion coefficients must be evaluated at the four points MNE (mid-northeast)–MNW, presumably by averaging the points N, E, S, W in pairs. It is still necessary to make some ad hoc arrangement for the density.

2. The Dufort–Frankel Scheme

If the leapfrog scheme is used for the dynamical terms, it is natural to choose the Dufort–Frankel scheme for the diffusion, since this couples all the meshes together (Roberts and Weiss, 1966; Roberts, 1967).

In Fig. 4, the points N, E, S, W at time t^{2m+1} are used to express the derivatives, together with the average of the values at C at t^{2m} and t^{2m+2}. It is awkward to retain exact conservation if the transport coefficients are functions of space and time, and the leapfrog method probably only has an

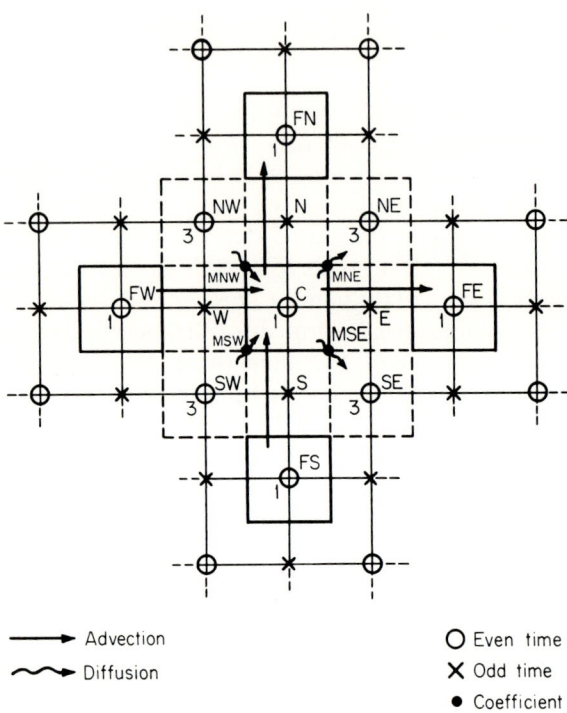

Fig. 5. Coupled Lax–Wendroff scheme. To prevent decoupling of the meshes 1 and 3, the diffusion term can be "angled" so that the box C is coupled to those at the corner points NE, SE, SW, NW.

advantage over the Lax–Wendroff method in the constant-coefficient case. The Dufort–Frankel scheme is stable for all Δt, but is inaccurate unless $\eta\, \Delta t/(\Delta x)^2$ is sufficiently small.

I. Special Difference Methods

1. *The Outer Vacuum Region*

During a pinch discharge, the plasma is pushed away from the walls by the rising magnetic field, and the main plasma is therefore usually surrounded by a region of low density whose physical properties cannot readily be computed from the MHD equations. Most Lagrangian difference schemes predict that the layer of plasma particles initially in contact with the wall will move inward leaving a vacuum behind, but this result should not entirely be trusted since the exact mathematical solutions of the MHD differential equations possess unacceptable singularities at the plasma boundary which are removed by the finite difference mesh. See for example, Rosenbluth and Kaufmann (1958), who studied the case $T_e = T_i$ and found that the temperature became singular. Physically, this occurs because the electrical conductivity σ is independent of density, so that the Joule heating σE^2 is shared among fewer and fewer particles as $\rho \to 0$. Furthermore, σ rises as T increases, thus increasing the heating still further, while the transverse heat conductivity falls so that the heat cannot easily escape. The singularity becomes sharper if $T_e \neq T_i$. In reality, however, the MHD model breaks down at the plasma boundary, and the paradox should presumably be resolved by introducing a set of enhanced transport coefficients which will smooth out the density variation and remove the other singularities.

In a real experiment the density is likely to be low outside the main discharge but can hardly be zero, since some charged particles must escape into the outer region due to various nonclassical processes, while neutral particles will be emitted from the walls and some will subsequently be ionized. Since the Alfven speed is high this region will be in near equilibrium, $\nabla p \simeq \mathbf{j} \times \mathbf{B}$, which in turn implies $j_\perp \simeq 0$ since p is negligible. The region may be a good electrical conductor for weak longitudinal currents, but strong currents should lead to anomalous field diffusion which will tend to restore a vacuum field configuration. In the absence of any definite experimental evidence, the most satisfactory prescription is to treat the outer region as a vacuum,

$$\sigma = 0 \quad \text{for} \quad \rho < \rho_{\min}, \tag{108}$$

where $\rho_{\min}$ is an arbitrary minimum density. In one-dimensional cylindrical geometry this simply requires $B_r = 0$, $B_\theta \sim 1/r$, $B_z = $ constant, while in two-dimensional axial geometry,

$$B_r = -\frac{\partial A_\theta}{\partial z}, \qquad B_\theta \sim \frac{1}{r}, \qquad B_z = \frac{1}{r}\frac{\partial}{\partial r}(rA_\theta), \tag{109}$$

where $\nabla^2 A_\theta = 0$. The vacuum region therefore presents no problem for the plasma focus device which has only a B_θ field, but for a general axial system it is necessary to solve Laplace's equation at every timestep in a region of awkward and changing geometry, between the plasma boundary and the outer conductors, which in some devices may extend to infinity. In three dimensions the vector equation $\nabla^2 \mathbf{A} = 0$ must be solved, with $\mathbf{B} = $ curl $\mathbf{A}$.

2. Solution by Successive Overrelaxation

Hain (1967b) has suggested the use of Green's functions, but an iterative solution of Laplace's equation can in practice be made sufficiently fast not to dominate the total time required for the calculation. The successive overrelaxation (SOR) method (Young, 1962) solves the scalar equation on a rectangular mesh in two dimensions by the algorithm

$$u_{i,j}^{p+1} = \frac{\omega}{4}\{u_{i-1,j}^{p+1} + u_{i,j-1}^{p+1} + u_{i+1,j}^{p} + u_{i,j+1}^{p}\} - (\omega - 1)u_{i,j}^{p} \quad (110)$$

where the mesh spacings have been assumed equal. The parameter ω is chosen to maximize the rate of convergence. If the numbers of mesh points in each direction are (M, N), the optimum value is approximately

$$\omega_b = \frac{2}{1 + \pi[(2M^2)^{-1} + (2N^2)^{-1}]^{1/2}}, \quad (111)$$

and the spectral radius (damping factor for the most persistent mode) is

$$\lambda = \omega_b - 1 \simeq 1 - 2\pi[(2M^2)^{-1} + (2N^2)^{-1}]^{1/2}. \quad (112)$$

The difference scheme (110) has obvious simplicity and elegance from a programming point of view, since the scanning of the space mesh involves the old iteration value (p) at the points ahead, and the new iteration value $(p + 1)$ at the points behind which have just been recalculated.

In a practical code the vector potential A^{n+1} is calculated by the Lax–Wendroff method wherever $\rho \geqslant \rho_{min}$, and then the solution in the vacuum region R where $\rho < \rho_{min}$ is obtained by the SOR method. The value A^{n+1} on the borders of R are used as boundary conditions, and the old values A^n are used to start the iteration ($p = 0$). The fact that R continually changes its shape is not important.

It has been pointed out by Garabedian (1956) and Young (1962) that Eq. (110) really represents the damped hyperbolic equation

$$\frac{\partial u}{\partial t} = \frac{\omega}{2 - \omega} \frac{\Delta^2}{2 \Delta t} \frac{\partial}{\partial x_i}\left(\frac{\partial u}{\partial x_i} - \frac{\Delta t}{\Delta x_i} \frac{\partial u}{\partial t}\right), \quad (113)$$

where Δt is a fictitious timestep and $\Delta x = \Delta y = \Delta$. Both Eq. (113) and the difference scheme Eq. (110) are in conservative form and must therefore represent the flux of a conserved quantity (namely, the residual error) from place to place on the mesh. If the last term in Eq. (113) is omitted the equation is parabolic, and the error can only diffuse to the boundary in a time $t \propto N^2$. By making the equation hyperbolic, the error can be made to travel as a wave in a time $t \propto N$. The net error (lowest eigenmode) can only disappear at the boundary, although errors of opposite sign can cancel one another out within R, which explains why the higher order modes decay more quickly.

Since we are effectively computing the vacuum field by an explicit method which allows the error to propagate only of order one mesh interval during each iteration step, a considerable number of iterations will be required, but Eq. (110) is so much simpler than the plasma equations that this should not occupy a major part of the calculation time. If necessary it would be quite straightforward to code Eq. (110) in assembly language.

3. *The Solution of Poisson's Equation*

The incompressible MHD equations (A) and (B) of Section II require the solution of Poisson's equation (15) for the vorticity ζ. In two dimensions, set (A) can be written as

$$\frac{\partial \zeta}{\partial t} = \frac{\partial(\psi, \zeta)}{\partial(x, y)} + \nu \nabla^2 \zeta + \frac{1}{\rho} \nabla \cdot (\mathbf{B} j), \tag{114}$$

$$\frac{\partial A}{\partial t} = -\nabla \cdot (\mathbf{v} A) + \eta \nabla^2 A, \tag{115}$$

$$\nabla^2 \psi = -\zeta, \tag{116}$$

where

$$(v_x, v_y) = \left(\frac{\partial \psi}{\partial y}, -\frac{\partial \psi}{\partial x}\right), \quad \nabla \cdot \mathbf{v} = 0,$$

$$(B_x, B_y) = \left(\frac{\partial A}{\partial y}, -\frac{\partial A}{\partial x}\right), \quad \nabla \cdot \mathbf{B} = 0, \tag{117}$$

$$j = \frac{\partial B_y}{\partial x} - \frac{\partial B_x}{\partial y} = -\nabla^2 A.$$

It is convenient to use a leapfrog scheme (Fig. 6) with $(\zeta, \psi, \mathbf{B})$ defined at the circle points and $(A, \mathbf{v})$ at the cross points at even times, and conversely at odd times. The main dependent variables are the two scalars ζ (vorticity) and A (magnetic streamfunction, or z-component of the vector potential).

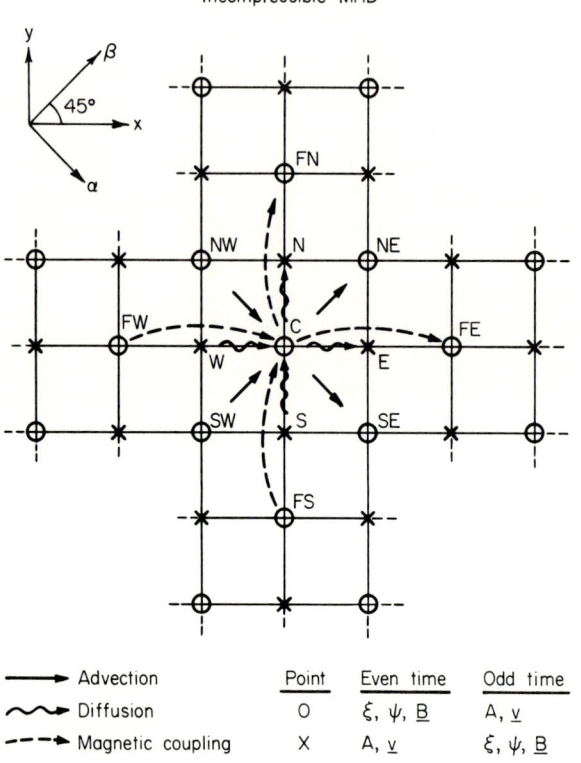

Fig. 6. Incompressible MHD. This scheme uses an NaCl mesh similar to that of Fig. 4, but the magnetic streamfunction A and velocity $\mathbf{v}$ are staggered with respect to the other variables. Each of the main terms couples a different combination of mesh boxes, and the Jacobian is evaluated in angled coordinates α, β.

If ζ is known at time t^n we construct the fluid streamfunction ψ by solving Poisson's equation, and then obtain $\mathbf{v}$ by differencing. If A is known, $\mathbf{B}$ is obtained by differencing. The only awkward quantity is the current j, which is required at the same point as $\mathbf{B}$ and can be constructed by differencing it in the two diagonal directions (Fig. 6):

$$j = \frac{\partial B_\beta}{\partial \alpha} - \frac{\partial B_\alpha}{\partial \beta}. \tag{118}$$

The accuracy and speed of the calculations are mainly limited by the need to solve Poisson's equation at every timestep, but several methods are available for rectangular regions, based on fast Fourier analysis and synthesis (Hockney 1965, 1968; Boris and Roberts, 1969). Peckover (unpublished) has developed a version of the Hockney Poisson-solver which is suitable for the mesh shown in Fig. 6, and used it to solve two-dimensional MHD convection problems.

Equation (114) represents the transfer of vorticity by advection, diffusion and magnetic forces. It can be solved in conservative form by using the Dufort–Frankel method for the diffusion term. The exchange of vorticity is somewhat complicated since the first term on the right-hand side couples point N to the corner points NE–NW, the second to the points N–W, and the third to the points FN–FW. Provided that the Dufort–Frankel method is used for Eq. (115), all the submeshes are properly coupled together.

4. *The Fractional-Step Method*

Because the realistic MHD equations describe a large number of semi-independent physical effects, the operator L of Eq. (66) may often be expressed as the sum of number of terms

$$L = \sum_{r=1}^{R} L_r. \tag{119}$$

The formal solution of Eq. (66) to second order is

$$u^{n+1} = \left(I - \frac{\Delta t}{2} L\right)^{-1} \left(I + \frac{\Delta t}{2} L\right) u^n. \tag{120}$$

The idea of the fractional-step method (Bagrinovskii and Godunov, 1957; Yanenko, 1964; Richtmyer and Morton, 1967) is to solve the various terms in succession,

$$\tilde{u}^{n+r/R} = \left(I - \frac{\Delta t}{2} L_r\right)^{-1} \left(I + \frac{\Delta t}{2} L_r\right) \tilde{u}^{n+(r-1)/R}, \tag{121}$$

where $\tilde{u}^n = u^n$. If all the operators commute with one another the accuracy may readily be analyzed,

$$\tilde{u}^{n+1} - \tilde{u}^n - \Delta t L \frac{\tilde{u}^{n+1} + \tilde{u}^n}{2}$$

$$= \frac{-(\Delta t)^2}{4} (L_1 L_2 + L_1 L_3 + \cdots + L_{R-1} L_R)(\tilde{u}^{n+1} - \tilde{u}^n) + O[(\Delta t)^3], \tag{122}$$

so that $\tilde{u}^{n+1}$ differs from u^{n+1} to second order in Δt.

Provided that this decrease of accuracy is acceptable, the fractional-step method enables a large program to be built up from a number of separate packages or modules, each representing a small part of the total physics, thus making it easier to organize and to modify.

J. Vector Difference Notation

In formulating difference schemes for complicated sets of coupled partial differential equations it is convenient to be able to write down vector difference formulas in a concise symbolic form which avoids the explicit mention of point values such as u_{ijk}^n, or vector components such as v_x. The scheme described here extends the ordinary notation of vector analysis (grad, div, curl, ∇^2), which is intended for continuous functions $u(x, y, z, t)$, to functions which are defined only at points of a discrete lattice. The notation is meant to be mnemonic, and in most cases the difference operators are formed from the corresponding differential operators by adding an extra "d":

Discrete lattice	Continuous function
gradd	grad
dotd	d/dt
curld	curl
deld	∇
divd	div

1. Basic Lattice Operators

For simplicity we consider only a regular cartesian lattice, with points defined at some or all of the locations $(j\,\Delta x + k\,\Delta y + l\,\Delta z + n\,\Delta t)$ where (j, k, l, n) are integers. The translation operators through distances $(\Delta x, \Delta y, \Delta z, \Delta t)$ are then denoted by

$$(E_x, E_y, E_z, E_t), \qquad (123)$$

respectively, and the differential operators $(d/dx, d/dy, d/dz, d/dt)$ by

$$(D_x, D_y, D_z, D_t). \qquad (124)$$

Evidently the operators (123) and (124) are related; for example, $E_x = \exp(\Delta x\, D_x)$. Applying this operator relation to a function $f(x)$ gives Taylor's series

$$f(\Delta x) \equiv E_x f(0) = \left[1 + \Delta x \frac{d}{dx} + \frac{(\Delta x)^2}{2!} \frac{d^2}{dx^2} + \frac{(\Delta x)^3}{3!} \frac{d^3}{dx} + \cdots\right] f(0).$$

2. *The Operators* deld *and* dotd

We shall mainly be concerned with the leapfrog or staggered mesh, on which functions are only defined at points for which $(j + k + l + n)$ is an odd integer. Then the time-difference operator can be expressed in the centered form

$$\text{dotd} \equiv (E - E^{-1})/2\,\Delta t, \tag{125}$$

while the vector space-difference operator has the components

$$\text{deld} \equiv ((E_x - E_x^{-1})/2\,\Delta x,\ (E_y - E_y^{-1})/2\,\Delta y,\ (E_z - E_z^{-1})/2\,\Delta z). \tag{126}$$

These equations can be written symbolically as

$$\text{dotd} \equiv \sinh(\Delta t\, D_t)/\Delta t, \tag{127}$$

and so on, but from the point of view of linear stability analysis it is more illuminating to write

$$\text{dotd} \equiv i \sin(\hat{w}\,\Delta t)/\Delta t, \tag{128}$$

$$(\text{deld})_x \equiv i \sin(\hat{k}_x\,\Delta x)/\Delta x, \tag{129}$$

where the operators $(d/dt, d/d\mathbf{x})$ are now denoted by $(i\hat{w}, -i\hat{\mathbf{k}})$, corresponding to the usual Fourier expansion

$$\exp(iwt - i\mathbf{k} \cdot \mathbf{x}). \tag{130}$$

3. *The Operators* divd, curld, *and* gradd

The difference analogs of the usual vector operators div, curl, grad may be defined symbolically by

$$\text{divd}\,\mathbf{A} \equiv \text{deld} \cdot \mathbf{A}, \tag{131}$$

$$\text{curld}\,\mathbf{A} \equiv \text{deld} \times \mathbf{A}, \tag{132}$$

$$\text{gradd}\,\phi \equiv \text{deld}\,\phi, \tag{133}$$

where **A** is any vector and ϕ is any scalar, defined at appropriate points of the lattice.

To see the compression in notation achieved by this means, one may consider the usual difference expression of the *first* component of

$$\text{curld}(\mathbf{v} \times \mathbf{B}), \tag{134}$$

which involves 118 symbols in addition to brackets, commas, and addition, subtraction, and division operators (Table I). A tensor divergence can be handled in the same way.

TABLE I

Expanded First Component of curld($\mathbf{v} \times \mathbf{B}$)

$$[(v_{x,i,j+1,k}^n B_{y,i,j+1,k}^n - v_{y,i,j+1,k}^n B_{x,i,j+1,k}^n)$$
$$- (v_{x,i,j-1,k}^n B_{y,i,j-1,k}^n - v_{y,i,j-1,k}^n B_{x,i,j-1,k}^n)]/2\,\Delta y$$
$$- [(v_{z,i,j,k+1}^n B_{x,i,j,k+1}^n - v_{x,i,j,k+1}^n B_{z,i,j,k+1}^n)$$
$$- (v_{z,i,j,k-1}^n B_{x,i,j,k-1}^n - v_{x,i,j,k-1}^n B_{z,i,j,k-1}^n)]/2\,\Delta z$$

4. *The Dufort–Frankel Operator* dufd

Many difference schemes use the Dufort–Frankel operator which is an approximation to ∇^2 defined by:

$$\text{dufd} \equiv (E_x + E_x^{-1} - (E_t + E_t^{-1}))/\Delta x^2$$

$$+ (E_y + E_y^{-1} - (E_t + E_t^{-1}))/\Delta y^2$$

$$+ (E_z + E_z^{-1} - (E_t + E_t^{-1}))/\Delta z^2. \tag{135}$$

Since

$$(E_x^{1/2} - E_x^{-1/2})^2 = E_x + E_x^{-1} - 2 \tag{136}$$

and

$$E_x^{1/2} - E_x^{-1/2} = 2i \sin \hat{k}_x \frac{\Delta x}{2}, \tag{137}$$

we have

$$\text{dufd} \equiv -\left[\frac{\sin^2 \hat{k}_x \frac{\Delta x}{2}}{\left(\frac{\Delta x}{2}\right)^2} + (\text{etc.}) + (\text{etc.})\right]$$

$$+ \left(\frac{\Delta t^2}{\Delta x^2} + \frac{\Delta t^2}{\Delta y^2} + \frac{\Delta t^2}{\Delta z^2}\right) \frac{\sin^2 \hat{w} \frac{\Delta t}{2}}{\left(\frac{\Delta t}{2}\right)^2}. \tag{138}$$

The second term represents an inaccuracy, in the sense that the correct limit is only reached if $\Delta t/\Delta x \to 0$ as $\Delta x \to 0$. Expanding the first term in powers of k^2, and using the approximation $i\omega = \eta k^2$ in the second term, we find that the error introduced by the second term is less than that in the first provided that $\eta \, \Delta t/\Delta^2 < 1/6\sqrt{3}$ (assuming $\Delta x = \Delta y = \Delta z = \Delta$).

5. *The Averaging Operators* savd *and* tavd

If variables are not available at the points where they are needed, it may be necessary to use a space or time average. We define:

$$\text{savd} \equiv \tfrac{1}{6}(E_x + E_x^{-1} + E_y + E_y^{-1} + E_z + E_z^{-1}), \tag{139}$$

$$\text{tavd} \equiv \tfrac{1}{2}(E_t + E_t^{-1}). \tag{140}$$

A three-dimensional difference scheme which uses this notation is discussed in Section VII.

IV. One-Dimensional Codes

A. THE HAIN-ROBERTS CODE

One of the earliest codes was constructed by Hain *et al.* (1960). Cylindrical geometry is used so that all functions depend only on r and not on (θ, z), and the azimuthal velocity v_θ is restricted to zero. (This is a consistent but not a necessary assumption.) The simplest version of the Hain-Roberts code assumes a fully ionized two-component plasma, with variables $\rho, v_r, T_e, T_i, B_r, B_\theta$. It uses a compressible fluid model with realistic transport coefficients, including the effect of the magnetic field on the transverse electron and ion thermal conductivities, and the difference between the parallel and perpendicular electrical conductivities. Hall effect, finite electron inertia, finite ion Larmor radius, and thermoelectric effects are omitted, and an artificial von Neumann viscosity is used for the ions (unless the physical value is sufficiently large).

The code solves the six coupled equations for mass conservation (1), radial momentum (2), electron energy (21), ion energy (22), and axial and azimuthal magnetic fields (3). The implicit Eulerian version uses the mesh shown in Fig. 7, with the velocity defined at the circle points, and all other

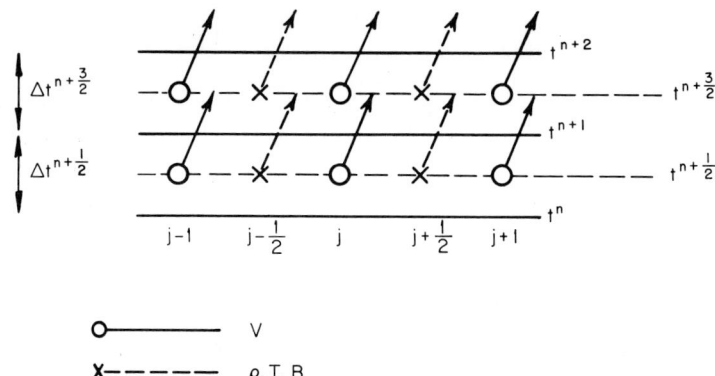

FIG. 7. Pseudo-Lagrangian difference scheme. In the implicit scheme used for the Eulerian one-dimensional MHD code the velocity v is centered at integral space points (circles and solid lines), and all other variables (ρ, T, **B**) at half-integral points (crosses and dashed lines). The equations are solved in Lagrangian form and transferred back to the original mesh by fourth-order interpolation at the end of each step. To obtain a fully Lagrangian scheme the interpolation routine is dropped and the points themselves are moved.

variables at the cross points. The advective term is omitted from every equation so that within each timestep the problem is solved in Lagrangian form, except that a single set of mesh coordinates is used at the intermediate time $t^{n+1/2} = t^n + \frac{1}{2}\Delta t^{n+1/2}$. At the end of the step the mesh displacement

$$\Delta \bar{r}_j^{n+1} = v_j^{n+1}(\Delta t^{n+1/2} + \Delta t^{n+3/2})/2 \tag{141}$$

is calculated, and then the function values at the displaced points are transformed back to the original mesh by four-point Lagrangian interpolation

$$f(x) = \sum_{i=1}^{4} a_i f(x_i), \tag{142}$$

where

$$a_i = \frac{(x-x_2)(x-x_3)(x-x_4)}{(x_1-x_2)(x_1-x_3)(x_1-x_4)}, \quad (143)$$

etc., and $x_2 \leqslant x \leqslant x_3$. This minimizes numerical diffusion (the one-sided Lelevier method corresponds to two-point interpolation), and also avoids a limitation on the timestep of the form $|v|\,\Delta t/\Delta r < 1$ if the mesh spacing is small. Checks of the type described in Section II,E are used to prevent nonphysical values from arising.

The mesh is automatically adjusted to obtain the greatest resolution in regions where the state of the plasma or magnetic field varies rapidly, using a weight function of the form

$$w(r) = \sum_\alpha \frac{a_\alpha(du_\alpha/dr)}{|u_\alpha| + b_\alpha}, \quad (144)$$

where $\Delta r \sim w^{-1}$, α runs over the physical variables, and a_α, b_α are control constants which can be chosen by the user to make the run go properly. In practice, a considerable amount of smoothing is applied to Eq. (143) to prevent sudden spatial variations in Δr.

This separation of the advective terms is a special case of the fractional-step method described in Section III,I, and certain other terms are also handled on their own. Although the method works quite well and should be better than most Eulerian schemes, interpolation errors can be avoided altogether by using a moving Lagrangian mesh. The original code enables this to be done quite simply by incrementing the coordinates according to Eq. (140) and bypassing the interpolation procedure, except when the mesh has to be redistributed. For θ-pinch problems in which the outer region can be treated as a vacuum and the mesh allowed to move in from the wall, this modification has been made by D. L. Fisher (unpublished). The implicit method of solution developed by Hain has been discussed in Section III,E.

B. Boundary Conditions at the Wall

1. *Inward Motion*

The Eulerian versions of the code use an assumption due to Colgate *et al.* (1958), by which conducting "pressureless plasma" is allowed to flow in from the wall at approximately the velocity of the field lines $(\mathbf{E} \times \mathbf{B})/B^2$, so that a vacuum is never created. For inward motion the wall density ρ_J is therefore allowed to decrease smoothly according to

$$\rho_J^{n+1} - \rho_{\min} = \exp(-|v_w|\,\Delta t/\lambda)(\rho_J{}^n - \rho_{\min}), \qquad (145)$$

where v_w is the normal velocity at the wall, λ is a characteristic length, and $\rho_{\min}$ is a suitable minimum density, say $R/50$, $\rho_0/100$, respectively, where R is the wall radius and ρ_0 is the initial density. This prescription works quite well in practice provided that it is understood that λ and $\rho_{\min}$ are entirely arbitrary. But the sharpness of the computed plasma boundary is usually determined by this arbitrary length λ if the Spitzer resistivity is used, and therefore it is physically more satisfactory if the boundary is widened by an enhanced resistive diffusion, as McCartan has assumed (Bodin et al., 1968; Beach et al., 1969, Bodin and Newton, 1969).

If the outer region contains low density plasma, small-amplitude compression waves will travel to and fro at the Alfven speed $\sim B/(\rho_{\min})^{1/2}$ and these are seen in the calculations. They are not seen in the actual experiments, either because $\rho_{\min}$ is low enough for approximate pressure balance to be maintained or because the waves are smoothed out by random three-dimensional density fluctuations, and it is therefore preferable to assume that the region is a true vacuum and to use a Lagrangian mesh.

If an Eulerian mesh is used it is necessary to maintain the correct momentum balance at the wall. Physically one assumes that plasma is created with zero velocity, and that it is accelerated to the wall velocity v_w by a magnetic pressure jump $\Delta(B^2/2)$ across a thin layer, equivalent to a small wall current ΔB. This can be arranged quite conveniently by using the one-sided Lelevier method for the advective term in the equation of motion for the point $J - \tfrac{1}{2}$, which in a simplified form can be written

$$\rho\frac{\partial v}{\partial t} = -\left[\rho v\frac{\partial v}{\partial x} + \frac{\partial p}{\partial x}\right], \qquad (146)$$

where p is the total pressure, and assuming that $v_{J+1/2} = 0$ so that

$$\bar{\rho}_{J-1/2}(v_{J-1/2}^{n+1} - v_{J-1/2}^n) = -(\Delta \bar{p}_{J-1/2} - \bar{\rho}_{J-1/2}\bar{v}_{J-1/2}^2)\,\Delta t/\Delta, \qquad (147)$$

where the bar denotes a time average and ρ is also averaged over the points $J, J-1$. When the velocity becomes stationary it automatically satisfies the correct pressure balance condition $\Delta p = \rho v_w{}^2$. Since there is a stability or convergence condition of the form $|v_w|\,\Delta t/\Delta x \lesssim 1$ it is necessary to prevent the mesh spacing at the wall from becoming too narrow.

A satisfactory prescription for the wall temperature $T_{J+1/2}$ is

$$T_{J+1/2} = \max(T_0, T_{J-1/2}/(1 + \Delta/\lambda)), \tag{148}$$

where T_0 is a suitable minimum temperature such as 2 eV, and λ^{-1} is a maximum logarithmic slope. The magnetic field at the wall may either be a prescribed function of time (which is appropriate for many θ-pinch problems), or may be determined by a circuit calculation.

2. *Outward Motion*

If the plasma is moving towards the wall it can simply be allowed to pile up, in which case we assume $v_{J+1/2} = 0$ and solve the equations for the outer cells in the usual way. Alternatively it can be allowed to flow freely into the wall and disappear. Here the most convenient prescription seems to be to use the Lelevier method for the advective term in Eq. (146),

$$(\partial v/\partial x)_{J-1/2} \simeq (v_{J-1/2} - v_{J-3/2})/\Delta,$$

and to retain only the advective term in the density equation

$$\partial \rho/\partial t + \mathbf{v} \cdot \nabla \rho = 0,$$

again using the Lelevier method with $v \approx v_{J-1/2}$. Temperature and magnetic field are determined as before.

C. Extension of the Code

The essential method of the Hain–Roberts code has been developed and extended at a number of laboratories. At Culham, D. L. Fisher has written a version which can be used to study the axial flow in a long θ-pinch, taking into account a variable area $A(z)$ which is determined by the radial pressure balance. The physics has also been broadened to describe a full three-fluid model (Section II,F) which includes equations for the neutral density, momentum, and temperature. For fully ionized θ-pinch problems, separate parallel and perpendicular ion temperatures are allowed for. The Kolb and McWhirter (1964) model has been incorporated in the code, using five impurities: carbon, nitrogen, oxygen, silicon, and neon. A Lagrangian version has been described by Oliphant (1963), and a three-fluid model by Duchs (1963).

V. Two-Dimensional Codes

A wide variety of interesting plasma phenomena and experimental devices are two dimensional or quasi-two dimensional, and if the problem is strongly time dependent the complexity of the MHD equations excludes the possibility of an analytic approach. The study of the (r, z) plane in axial devices such as the plasma focus or the θ- or z-pinch is probably the simplest step in the direction of real numerical fusion experiments, and the same geometry applies in principle to the minor cross section of a toroidal device with axial symmetry such as Tokomak (Artsimovich *et al.*, 1968) or the toroidal stabilized pinch, although the boundary conditions are more complicated because the cross section is usually circular.

As a further step forward, it may not be too difficult to include a slowly varying third dimension. Problems in MHD power generation and accelerators are essentially two-dimensional, and of particular interest in this field are the nonlinear aspects of electrothermal and magnetosonic instabilities (Velikhov and Dykhne, 1963) which corrupt the flow and lower the efficiency of the system by increasing the impedance.

A rough estimate of the time required for a realistic two-dimensional MHD calculation can be given. A typical space mesh of 64×64 points gives reasonable resolution, and the number of timesteps in an explicit calculation may be of order 300. Thus, the calculation domain includes about 10^6 space-time points, while a fairly complete MHD description requires $\sim 10^3$ arithmetic operations for an efficiently written explicit code. On present-day machines with an instruction time ~ 1 μsec, a useful MHD calculation can therefore be performed in some 20 minutes, so that sophisticated time-dependent MHD models in two space dimensions are more than practicable.

An I-code may be designed to include only those physical effects which are relevant to a specific problem (for example, the two-dimensional MHD convection problem studied by Weiss, 1966), and results may then be obtained with minimum programming effort. But in most cases a numerical experiment requires a fairly complete description of the physics to simulate a real process or apparatus. Such an R-code becomes a major project, and to justify the effort one should attempt to treat the general case so that the program can be used for a range of different problems. A variety of initial and boundary conditions must therefore be allowed for.

A. Previously Reported Codes

An early two-dimensional MHD code was constructed by Roberts *et al.* (1963) to describe the (r, z) plane of an axial device, using the six dependent variables ρ, T, B_r, B_z, v_r, v_z. Azimuthal magnetic field B_θ and velocity v_θ are assumed to be zero so that j_θ is the only current component. The equations are Eqs. (1), (2), (3), (11) with the resistivity $\eta = \eta(T)$, $T_e = T_i$, scalar pressure, and $\mu = \kappa = \lambda = 0$. Such a model might for example be used to simulate short linear θ-pinches, conical θ-pinch guns, cusp devices, and multistage compressional mirror machines.

In a real apparatus of this type the magnetic field lines are closed, since they emerge from the containing tube outside the two ends of the coil and return through the vacuum. Plasma can escape along the lines of force to the insulating tube wall, or into partially ionized gas at the ends. The real boundary conditions are therefore awkward, and to simplify the program the calculation assumes periodic geometry, with a continuous conducting wall at radius $r = r_w(z)$, and $dr_w/dz = 0$, $B_z = 0$ at the two ends $z = (0, L)$. At the plane $z = L$ the plasma is allowed to flow out freely, using the prescription discussed in Section IV,B,2, which should be satisfactory provided that most of the pressure drop $\Delta(\rho T)$ along the field lines occurs within the region of calculation. The plane $z = 0$ may either be treated in the same way, or it may be a symmetry plane. The conducting wall $r = r_w(z)$ is allowed to emit low-density plasma as described in Section IV,B,1 so that an Eulerian mesh can be used. To enable the wall to have any shape (provided that the angle is not too steep), a nonorthogonal mesh is employed:

$$r_{j,k} = (j/J) r_w(z_k), \qquad z_k = k\, \Delta z.$$

The magnetic field at the wall satisfies $B_\perp = 0$ and is determined by a circuit calculation.

The code uses an explicit difference scheme which has since been superseded, but the angled-derivative method employed for the advective terms may be of interest (Roberts and Weiss, 1966); in one dimension:

$$u_j^{n+1} - u_j^n - \frac{v\,\Delta t}{2\Delta}\{(u_{j+1}^n + u_j^{n+1}) - (u_j^n + u_{j-1}^{n+1})\},$$

which is stable for $v\,\Delta t/\Delta < 1$.

An explicit code which solves the equation

$$\partial \mathbf{B}/\partial t = \operatorname{curl}(\mathbf{v} \times \mathbf{B}) + \eta\, \nabla^2 \mathbf{B}$$

for a prescribed velocity field has been written by Weiss (1966), and used to study the expulsion of magnetic flux by eddies in a two-dimensional incompressible fluid with finite resistivity. The fluid equations are decoupled from the field equations so that the treatment is entirely kinematic and the advective term is treated by the fourth-order method of Roberts and Weiss (1966).

The interesting methods developed by Hertweck and Schneider (1967) and Hain (1967a), which employ the field lines as coordinates, have been briefly mentioned in Section III,F. The (r, θ) plane has been considered by Duchs (1968a,b) in a study of Hall rotation, using the fluid model of Section II, with the generalized Ohm's law Eq. (30). The success with which the Lax–Wendroff method has recently been applied in hydrodynamics has encouraged its application to MHD. Freeman and Lane (1968) have used this method for the (r, z) plane in the case $B_\theta = 0$ (j_θ currents only). The two-fluid model of Section II,D is chosen with variable collision-dominated coefficients for the resistivity, electron and ion thermal conductivity, and for the electron–ion equipartition coefficient. Diffusion coefficients are treated numerically by the Dufort–Frankel scheme for the main mesh, and by a modification of this scheme for the auxiliary mesh.

Artificial diffusion is imposed on the variables, following the method of Lapidus (1967). The code has initially been applied to a θ-pinch, but end-losses are not taken into account because periodic boundary conditions are assumed at the ends. Large Alfven velocities in the outer region are prevented by allowing it to fill with low-density plasma, using the method of Hain *et al.* (1960) described above and in Section IV,B.

B. The Focus Code

The authors have developed a two-dimensional code, first reported by Peacock (1968), for studying motions in the (r, z) plane of an axially symmetric device when $v_\theta = 0$ and only a magnetic field B_θ is present. This work was stimulated in the first instance by the recent widespread experimental studies of the dense plasma focus (Filippov *et al.*, 1962; Filippov and Filippova, 1966; Mather, 1965, 1966; Bottoms *et al.*, 1968) which is a high-density pinch produced by the collapse of an (r, z) current sheet on to the axis at the end of a plasma gun. This effect is of particular interest because of the high temperatures which are measured, $T_e \simeq 2$ keV (Peacock *et al.*, 1968), and the anomalously long duration of the pinch.

1. *Physical Model*

The model assumes a two-fluid fully ionized plasma, with the equations of continuity (1), radial and axial momentum (2), azimuthal magnetic field (3), electron energy (21), and total energy (4). The electric field in Faraday's law (3) is defined by the generalized Ohm's law (30), including the Hall effect and the electron pressure gradient field. An attempt has been made to cover the general case, so far as the transport terms are concerned, and finite $\omega_{ce}\tau_{ei}$ and $\omega_{ci}\tau_{ii}$ have been allowed for. This is certainly necessary for the plasma focus, since although the density is high the very large electron and ion temperatures ensure that $\omega_{ce}\tau_{ei} \gg 1$ and $\omega_{ci}\tau_{ii} \sim 1$. Without the inclusion of cyclotron orbit effects the electron heat conductivity ($\propto T_e^{5/2}$ in the collision-dominated limit) would certainly be quite wrong. Equations (33), (35), and (37) have therefore been used to describe electron heat conduction, ion heat conduction and the stress tensor respectively, although the latter has been modified. In the collisionless limit the ion pressure should of course be described by separate $P_{i\|}$, $P_{i\perp}$ satisfying Eqs. (28) and (29), but the model of a magnetic field perpendicular to the calculation plane is a particularly straightforward one to treat, since the field reduces to a scalar. The stress tensor is diagonal in the calculation plane, and the parallel pressure is confined to the θ-direction and would appear not to have a dominant physical part to play in the plasma focus. An isotropic ion temperature has therefore been assumed, and in order to be consistent the $(\omega_{ci}\tau_{ii})^2$ terms in the numerator of the stress tensor have not been included. This is equivalent to the assumption that the equipartition time between $T_{i\|}$, $T_{i\perp}$ is small.

2. *Numerical Scheme*

Because flow occurs at sonic speeds an explicit method is appropriate, and the accuracy and simplicity of the two-step Lax–Wendroff scheme suggested its use. The Dufort–Frankel scheme for the diffusion terms is awkward when the transport coefficients are functions of space and time, and therefore the alternative conservative scheme, the leapfrog method (Section VII) is less convenient here. Diffusion has been treated by the forward time-difference method described in Section III,H,1. The complex transport terms are evaluated only once during the double timestep, and thus the computing time required does not dominate the rest of the calculation.

3. *Equipartition*

A problem arises in the electron energy equation, where nonconservative terms necessarily appear, and in particular the ion–electron equipartition term may be large. An explicit treatment of this term can lead to instability if the equipartition time is less than Δt, as reported by Freeman and Lane (1968). In the Hain–Roberts code this difficulty is avoided by a separate exact solution of the equipartition equation using exponential functions, in the spirit of the fractional-step method, but it is perhaps undesirable to call the exponential routine too frequently in a two-dimensional program. In the focus code the equipartition term is included implicitly and an iteration is used to obtain a self-consistent solution since the electron–ion equipartition time is a function of temperature, $\tau_{eq} = \tau_{eq}(T_e)$. In each step of the Lax–Wendroff method, the equipartition term is time-centered using the time average

$$\frac{p_i^{n+1/2} - p_e^{n+1/2}}{\tau_{eq}} = \frac{1}{2}\frac{p_i^n - p_e^n}{\tau_{eq}^n} + \frac{1}{2}\frac{p_i^{n+1} - p_e^{n+1}}{\tau_{eq}^{n+1}}. \tag{149}$$

The first term in Eq. (149) is included in the explicit Lax–Wendroff scheme to give the values $p_e'^{n+1}$ and $p_i'^{n+1}$ as determined from the total energy equation and electron pressure equation.

The final values $p_e'^{n+1}$ and $p_i'^{n+1}$ are obtained from the formulas

$$p_e^{n+1} = \frac{1+\varepsilon}{1+2\varepsilon} p_e'^{n+1} + \frac{\varepsilon}{1+2\varepsilon} p_i'^{n+1}, \tag{150}$$

$$p_i^{n+1} = \frac{1+\varepsilon}{1+2\varepsilon} p_e'^{n+1} + \frac{\varepsilon}{1+2\varepsilon} p_i'^{n+1}, \tag{151}$$

where $\varepsilon = \Delta t/2\tau_{eq}$. Since $\tau_{eq} = \tau_{eq}(T_e)$, Eq. (150) is solved by an iteration using successively improved values for $\varepsilon = \varepsilon(T_e)$. The iteration is always convergent and is rapid if $\varepsilon \leftrightarrow \frac{1}{2}$. This ensures unconditional stability in the solution of the equipartition term. A similar solution in which the iteration is avoided, $\varepsilon = \varepsilon(T_e'^{n+1})$, has been used by Freeman and Lane (1968).

4. Boundaries

Fixed boundaries are treated by conserving the dependent variable identically in the mesh volume adjacent to the boundary. Hence, on the axis, for example, the local mesh volume is a cylinder of volume $V = 2\pi(\Delta r)^2 \Delta z$ where Δr is the radial mesh step and Δz the axial mesh step (Fig. 8). The difference formulas are reconstructed to conserve the dependent variables in

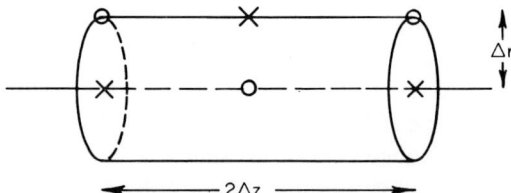

FIG. 8. Axial box. Near the axis the mesh box is a cylinder of volume $2\pi(\Delta r)^2 \Delta z$. Variables which are not identically zero on the axis represent averages over the volume of the box, and the fluxes represent averages over the two discs at the ends and the cylindrical boundary.

V identically, except for B_θ flux which can disappear at the axis when the resistivity is finite.

Surrounding wall boundaries are treated in a similar way. Thermal energy is removed from the plasma by cold electrodes, and hence following Hain et al. (1960), the electron and ion temperatures were initially set to some constant low value on the electrodes (typically, $T_e = T_i = 2$ eV). This assumption is not entirely satisfactory, however, since if a volume of plasma remains near an electrode its density will continue to rise until it reaches an extreme value at which pressure balance is achieved with the much hotter plasma in the interior. This is probably a gross overestimate of the effect of a cold electrode. Treating the boundary value temperatures as constant will remain a reasonable approximation only so long as a typical boundary layer thickness λ exceeds the mesh spacing Δ.

It has been found preferable to calculate electron and ion temperatures on the electrodes from the conservation equations, and to permit finite heat loss ΔQ from the adjacent mesh volume according to the formula

$$\Delta Q \propto \Delta t T^{5/2}(T \sim T_0).$$

The constant is calculated by assuming some typical thickness λ for the boundary layer.

This problem is characteristic of the channel flow which occurs in the first stage of the plasma focus experiment, and also in MHD ducts, but it did not arise for the one or two-dimensional pinch calculations in which plasma was pushed away from the wall at the beginning of the discharge. A similar problem will however appear in two-dimensional calculations on stabilized z-pinches, where the end electrodes are always in contact with the plasma.

5. *Low-Density Region*

The problem of a very large Alfven velocity in the low-density region behind the main plasma is circumvented by modifying the electromagnetic calculation wherever the density ρ falls below some minimum density ρ_{min}. Because $j_\perp$ is proportional to the pressure gradient $\nabla p \simeq 0$, while $j_\parallel$ is strictly zero, this region behaves like an insulator. We therefore combine the inductance of the region with that of the external circuit, with which it is electrically in series, and share the total magnetic flux between them to give a current I. Then B_θ is determined on the mesh by $B_\theta \propto I/r$. The current is calculated at each main and auxiliary step.

This modified magnetic field can be used in the plasma equation of motion. Evidently it provides a zero force wherever $\rho < \rho_{min}$, so that waves travel only at the sonic speed which is independent of ρ, and the Courant–Friedrichs–Lewy condition does not restrict the timestep. The incorrect treatment of the plasma variables in the outer region does not seriously affect the main body of the plasma, since their influence is very small, and there is no difficulty in treating a moving plasma boundary with a complicated reentrant shape, even if it divides into several portions. (A special treatment would be needed if the *outer region* consisted of several disconnected parts, but this has not been observed.)

6. *Extension of the Code*

The code has recently been extended by one of the authors (D.E.P.) and M. L. Watkins to include B_r and B_z fields and an azimuthal velocity V_θ. Since $\mathbf{V} \cdot \mathbf{B} = 0$ it seems appropriate to use the magnetic vector potential A_θ, rather than separate equations for the two field components. This satisfies the equation

$$\partial A_\theta/\partial t + \mathbf{v} \cdot \nabla A_\theta = \eta \, \nabla^2 A_\theta - (m/e\rho)(\mathbf{j} \times \mathbf{B})_\theta. \tag{152}$$

There is no contribution from the ∇p_e term in Eq. (30) since there is no variation in the θ-direction. One of the major problems is now the solution of the vacuum fields which is performed by the SOR method (Section III,H).

Freeman (private communication) has used the magnetic vector potential rather than separate equations for B_r and B_z, while Olman and Freeman are developing a code which is similar to the Focus code described here.

VI. Calculations on the Plasma Focus Experiment

A. General Description

The dense plasma focus formed by the two-dimensional collapse of a fast axisymmetric current sheet has recently been investigated experimentally by a number of authors (Filippov *et al.*, 1962; Filippov and Filippova, 1966; Mather, 1965; Long *et al.*, 1967; Peacock *et al.*, 1968; Coudeville *et al.*, 1967; Bottoms *et al.*, 1968; Butler *et al.*, 1968). Figure 9 indicates the apparatus. A current is passed between two cylindrical electrodes, producing a field $B_\theta \sim 1/r$ which drives the plasma along the annular space between them (run-down stage). When the shock reaches the end of the central rod, the pressure of the plasma and the pressure and tension in the lines of force cause it to converge towards the axis (collapse stage), producing a localized region of high density and pressure (plasma focus).

Interest has been generated by the remarkably high thermal energy densities which occur, and electron densities $n_e \sim 2 \times 10^{19}$ cm^{-3} and electron temperatures $T_e \sim 2$ keV have been reported. The focus stage is characterized

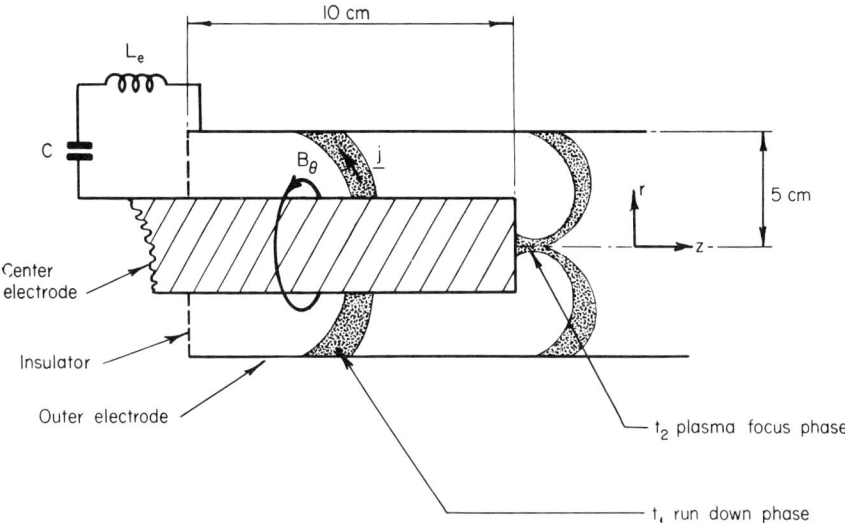

FIG. 9. Plasma focus experiment. An electric field is applied between two coaxial electrodes. A shock moves down the annular space between the electrodes (time t_1) and collapses to the axis (time t_2).

by a large neutron yield $\sim 10^{11}$, produced in a time of order 100 nsec. X-ray emission occurs from two sources: hard X-rays by electron bombardment of the anode, and soft X-rays from within the dense plasma region.

Experiment has indicated the occurrence of two apparently contradictory mechanisms, since the soft X-ray emission and apparent long lifetime of the focus stage suggest a thermal plasma, while the hard X-rays and angular anisotropy in the leading (in time) edge of the neutron pulse suggest a beam interaction.

The two-dimensional magnetohydrodynamic code described in Section V has been applied to the plasma focus in an attempt to elucidate the following features of the experiment: the dynamics of the run-down and collapse stages; the heating mechanism in the dense pinch; the exceptionally long apparent lifetime of the pinch, when hydromagnetic unstable modes would be expected to break it up in times of 15 nsec, and the gross question of how well the plasma focus can be described by a thermal fluid model.

Table II shows the geometry and initial conditions corresponding to the results which will be discussed in this paper. Each timestep of the calculation takes 4 sec on an IBM 360/65, and approximately 500 timesteps are needed altogether.

The plasma focus is particularly amenable to a two-dimensional numerical study. The symmetry of the problem removes several obstacles usually

TABLE II

GEOMETRY AND INITIAL CONDITIONS FOR THE PLASMA FOCUS

Radius of inner electrode	$r_1 = 2.5$ cm
Radius of outer electrode	$r_2 = 5.0$ cm
Length of inner electrode	$l = 10.0$ cm
Capacitance of external condenser	$C = 40$ μfarad
Voltage on condenser	$V = 40$ kV
External inductance	$L_e = 15$ nH
Ambient filling density	$n_e = 4.5 \times 10^{16}$ cm^{-3}
Gas	Deuterium
Initial temperature	$T_e = T_i = 2$ eV
Number of mesh points	2025

encountered in multidimensional MHD codes, while the abrupt change in scale lengths and times introduces fresh points of interest. On the one hand, with the assumption of azimuthal symmetry the magnetic field is perpendicular to the plane of interest and the calculation is then executed in an isotropic two-dimensional space. Mathematically this means that the Eulerian coordinates in the $(r - z)$-plane are the "natural coordinates" of the system, and transport terms are consequently at their simplest. Thus we can include cyclotron-orbiting effects, which limit diffusion in the $(r - z)$-plane, without the otherwise necessary transformation to field lines as local coordinates to determine transport along field lines. A reasonably satisfactory treatment of transport processes can thus be incorporated.

On the other hand, the unique characteristic of the dense plasma focus—the rapid switch from one geometrical and time scale to a considerably smaller space–time scale—demands particular treatment. Practical considerations of machine space and time exclude the continual use of a sufficiently small mesh through the entire calculation to resolve the final dense stage. The alternative device of concentrating points into rapidly varying regions, as employed in one dimension (Hain et al., 1960), is not feasible in two dimensions: the difference mesh becomes complex and unmanageable. To overcome this, therefore, a dual calculation has been performed. The entire calculation is executed on an Eulerian gross mesh with a spatial resolution ~0.15 cm. In the dense pinch stage a fine-scale subordinate mesh is switched in. The boundary conditions for the minor mesh are the time-dependent values supplied by interpolation from the major mesh. The spatial resolution on the minor mesh is ~0.02 cm.

The dense plasma focus illustrates a number of features in the application of a difference model to MHD which have been discussed elsewhere (Section III, A) in this paper. The density in the domain of calculation varies by five to six orders of magnitude (Mather et al., 1967), and one therefore needs the special treatment of the near-vacuum region behind the current sheet desscribed in Section III,I. Particularly in the dense focus stage diffusive processes are important (ion viscosity and ion heat conduction are large due to very high ion temperatures $T_i \sim 2$ keV, and the resistive electric field is finite, due to the very small scale lengths). Thus, while on a short time scale, the "hyperbolic terms" may be dominant in "driving" the focus, the long-time behavior depends crucially on diffusive processes. In contrast to the difference methods described in this paper, Butler *et al.* (1969) have applied the particle-in-cell method (Butler and Cook, 1968) to obtain good agreement with experiment in describing the motion of the shock in, and at the end of, the coaxial gun, while Dyachenko and Imshennik (1969), have reported good qualitative agreement with experiment through the application of a particle method for solving the one fluid hydromagnetic equations with ion viscosity.

B. Run-Down Stage

The motion of the current sheet between the electrodes is well understood and can be grossly described by a steady-state snowplow analytic model. The magnetic pressure in the vacuum falls off as $1/r^2$, so that the current sheet takes up a characteristic parabolic form [Fig. 10(I)]. This in turn produces an outward component of the mass flow [Fig. 10(II)].

Figure 11 shows the equilibrium structure at a point during the rundown stage ($t = 0.4025$ μsec), when the total current has become nearly constant (Fig. 18). The existence of a steady state ensures that the current sheet retains no "memory" of the insulator at $z = 0$, in contrast to the conventional z-pinch in which the shape of the outer wall determines that of the ingoing shock. The configuration of the insulator would therefore appear to be immaterial for a fully ionized model, although in a partially ionized model it would evidently affect the quantity of un-ionized gas left behind.

The cold electrodes remove thermal energy by heat conduction, and in order to maintain pressure balance a buildup of mass occurs at the electrodes [Fig. 11(a)]. In the center of the current sheet a peak electron temperature $T_e = 50$ eV and ion temperature $T_i = 120$ eV are found, the ions being heated by adiabatic compression and viscous heating, with a shock velocity $v_s \simeq 17$ cm/μsec.

C. Collapse Stage

When the current sheet reaches the end of the central electrode the plasma is free to move inwards and is initially cooled by adiabatic expansion. The

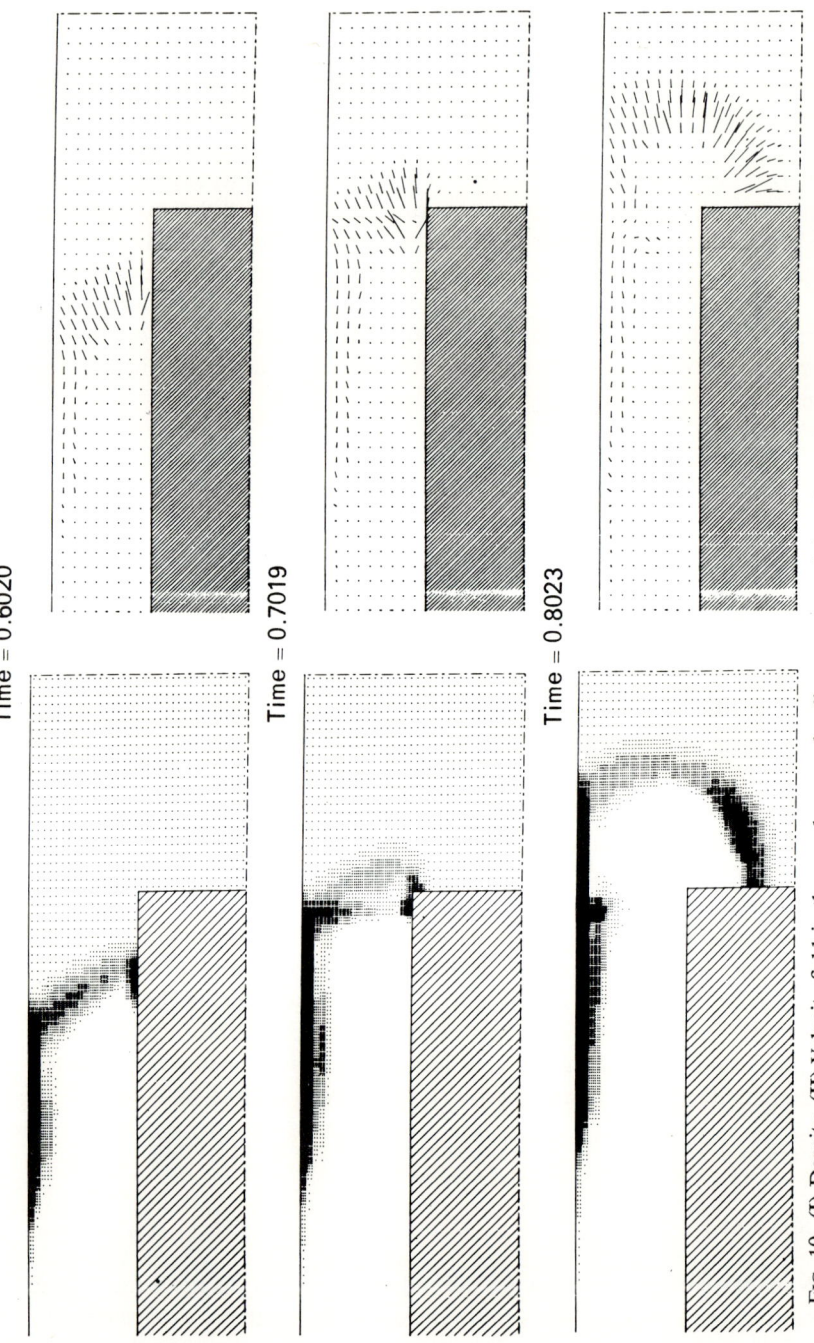

FIG. 10. (I) Density. (II) Velocity field in the run-down and collapse stages of the plasma focus. The shock structure in the steady-state run-down stage has a parabolic form with mass collection on the inner and outer electrodes. Equilibrium is obtained by momentum flow to the outer electrode (II).

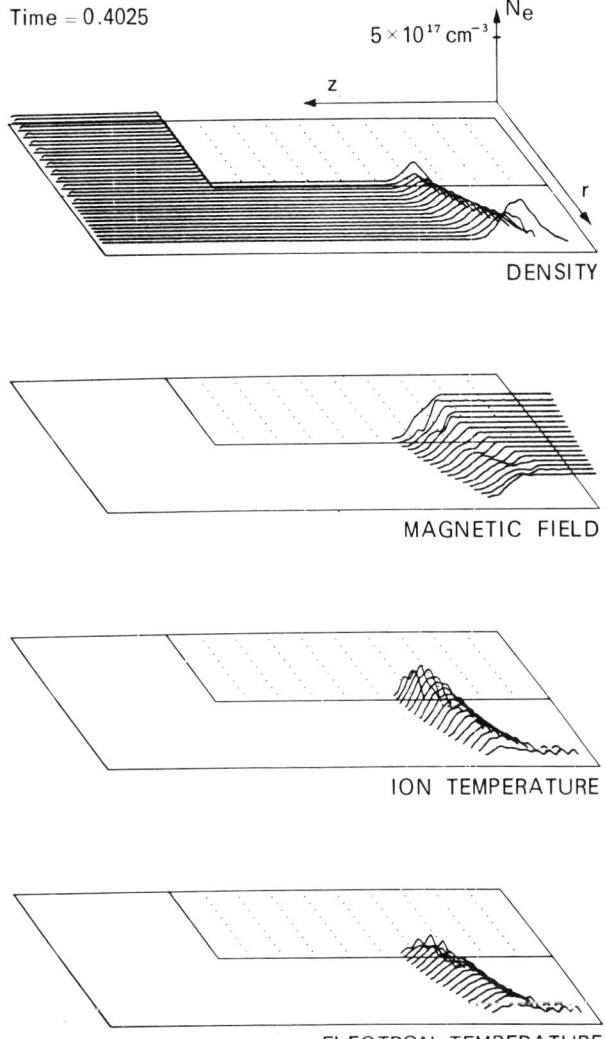

FIG. 11. Steady-state run-down stage. The diagrams represent the magnitudes of the dependent variables (a) ρ, (b) B_θ, (c) T_i, (d) T_e, at a time when the current has nearly reached its maximum value ($t = 0.4025$ μsec). In (c) and (d) the cooling on the electrodes can be seen with a corresponding increase in the density (a).

current sheet is accelerated to the axis by the magnetic pressure and tension in the field lines, which become larger as the radius decreases.

In the outer region, mass flow in the outward direction continues during the collapse stage [Fig. 10(f)], and is an important mechanism for the removal of plasma. It is calculated that less than 10% of the plasma initially beyond the end of the central electrode is actually transported into the dense pinch region. The relatively small amount of mass collected permits the attainment of high thermal energies by adiabatic compression. Typical collapse velocities of $v_s \simeq 30$ cm/μsec and temperatures $T_e \simeq 100$ eV and $T_i \simeq 250$ eV are found.

The cold end-face of the central electrode removes thermal energy by electron heat conduction from the adjacent plasma (note that B_θ vanishes at the axis). A density buildup therefore occurs in this region [Fig. 12(I)], which has important consequences for the structure of the ultimate axial pinch.

D. Dense Pinch Stage

The time-dependent density and flow behavior are shown in Fig. 12 at the end of the collapse stage, and throughout the subsequent pinch. (The scales have been increased from those of Fig. 10.) The collapse on to the axis depends strongly on z, and the pressure largely releases itself by an axial emission of plasma,

$$\delta(\rho v_z) = \int_t^{t+\Delta t} \frac{dp}{dz} dt \ .$$

Thus the characteristic radial bounce of a z-pinch is largely avoided [Fig. 12(II,c)], although some outward motion occurs.

The formation of the focus can thus be described in terms of the motion of a moving "magnetic funnel" or cone. The cone travels rapidly in the z-direction while its apex half-angle θ increases in time. A dense z-pinch is left on the axis.

It can be seen from Fig. 13(c) that the pinch is maintained by plasma trapped at the central electrode. As remarked in Section VI,C, thermal energy is removed from the plasma by conduction to the electrode during the collapse stage, and the density increases in order to maintain pressure balance. Because of the low electron temperature in this region the electrical resistivity is fairly high, so that the magnetic field penetrates the plasma and a radial near-equilibrium is attained. This magnetic trap near the central electrode acts as a source for the flow through the constricted z-pinch.

Short-wavelength hydromagnetic instabilities are stabilized by the large ion viscosity, arising from the high ion temperature. Figures 12(d) and 13(d) demonstrate the partial breakup of the pinch due to a long wavelength $m = 0$ mode after a time ~ 40 nsec. Radial flow occurs [Fig. 12(d)] and the density falls [Fig. 13(d)]. This instability is seen more clearly in Fig. 17 on the fine-scale mesh. The nonlinear behavior of the instability is interesting, however,

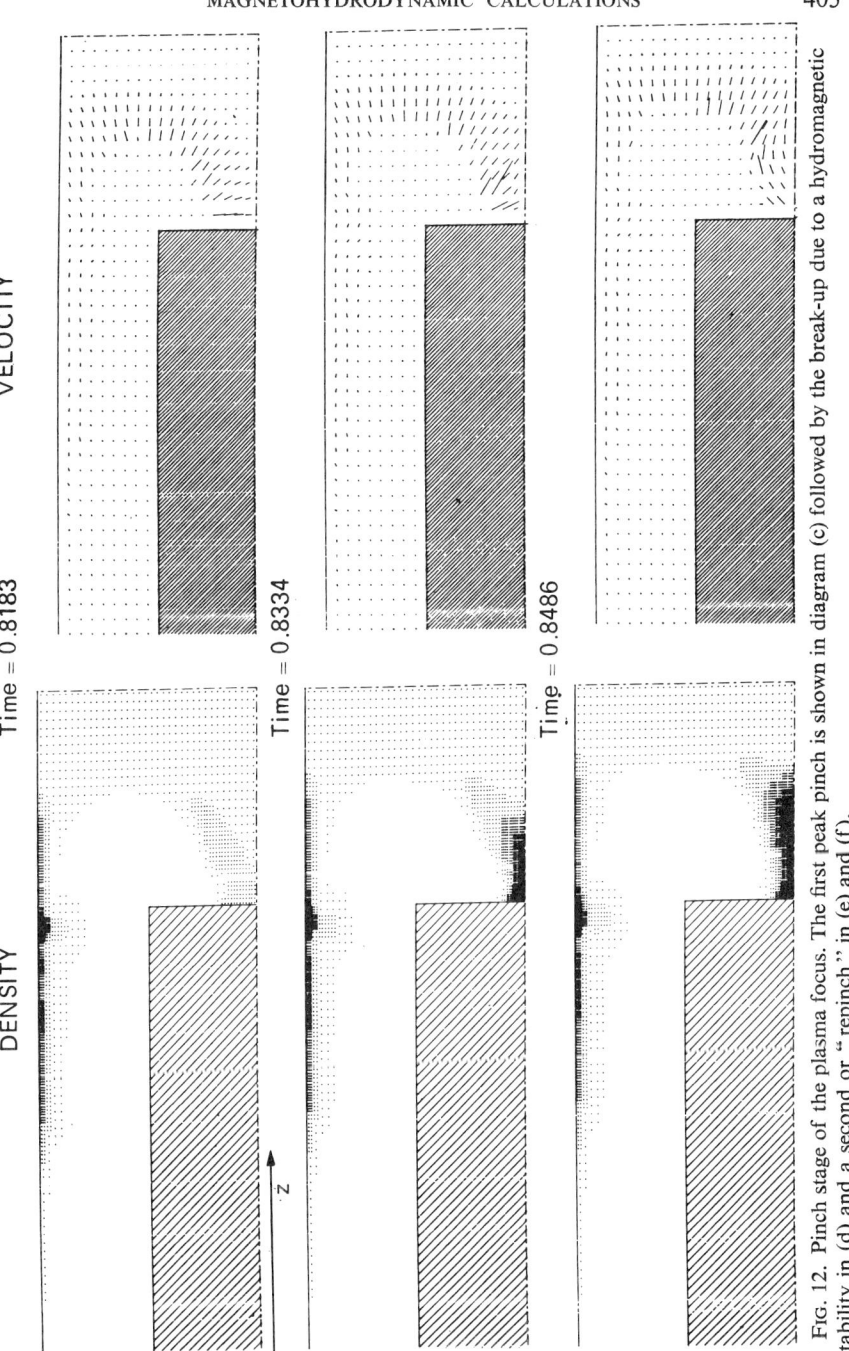

FIG. 12. Pinch stage of the plasma focus. The first peak pinch is shown in diagram (c) followed by the break-up due to a hydromagnetic instability in (d) and a second or "repinch" in (e) and (f).

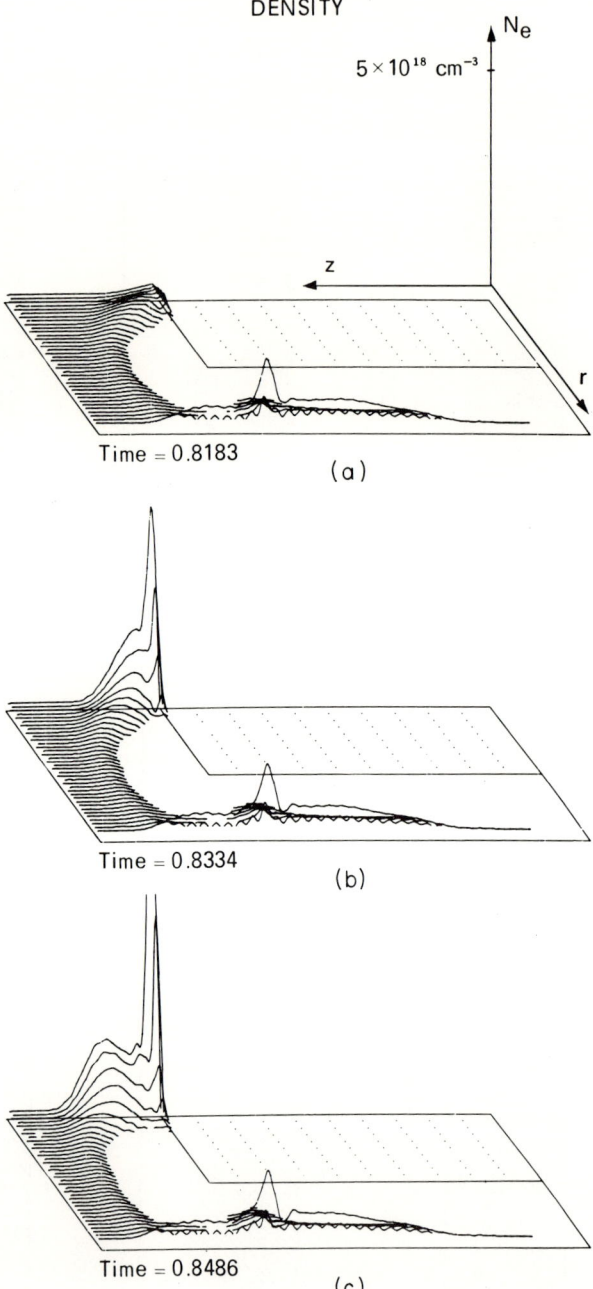

Time = 0.8183 (a)

Time = 0.8334 (b)

Time = 0.8486 (c)

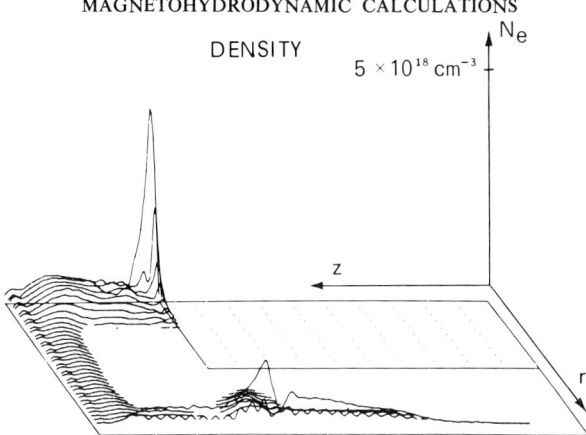

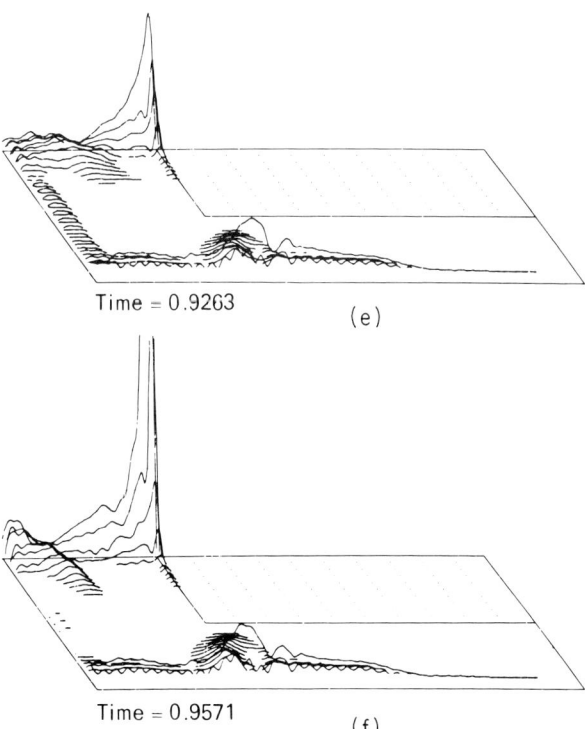

Fig. 13. Plasma density. (a), (b), (c) show the rise in the plasma density on the axis in the initial plasma focus pinch. A long-wavelength instability causes the break-up in (d), followed by the subsequent repinch (e) and (f).

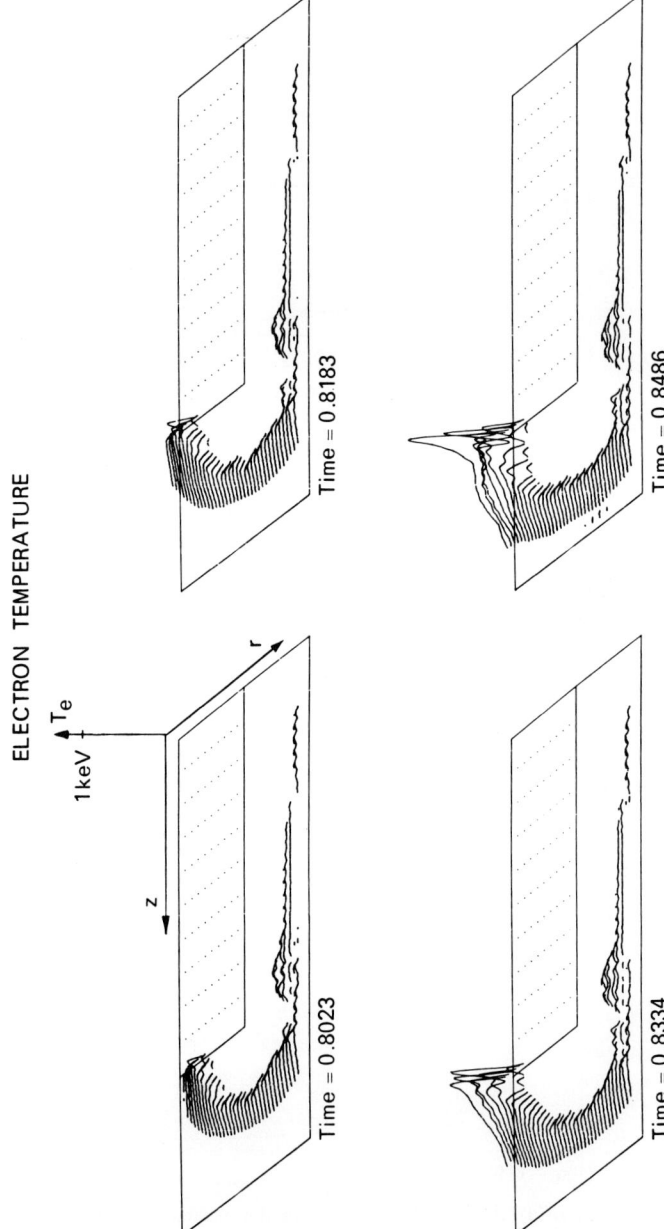

FIG. 14. Electron temperature. The diagrams show the rise in electron temperature in the initial formation of the plasma focus on the axis.

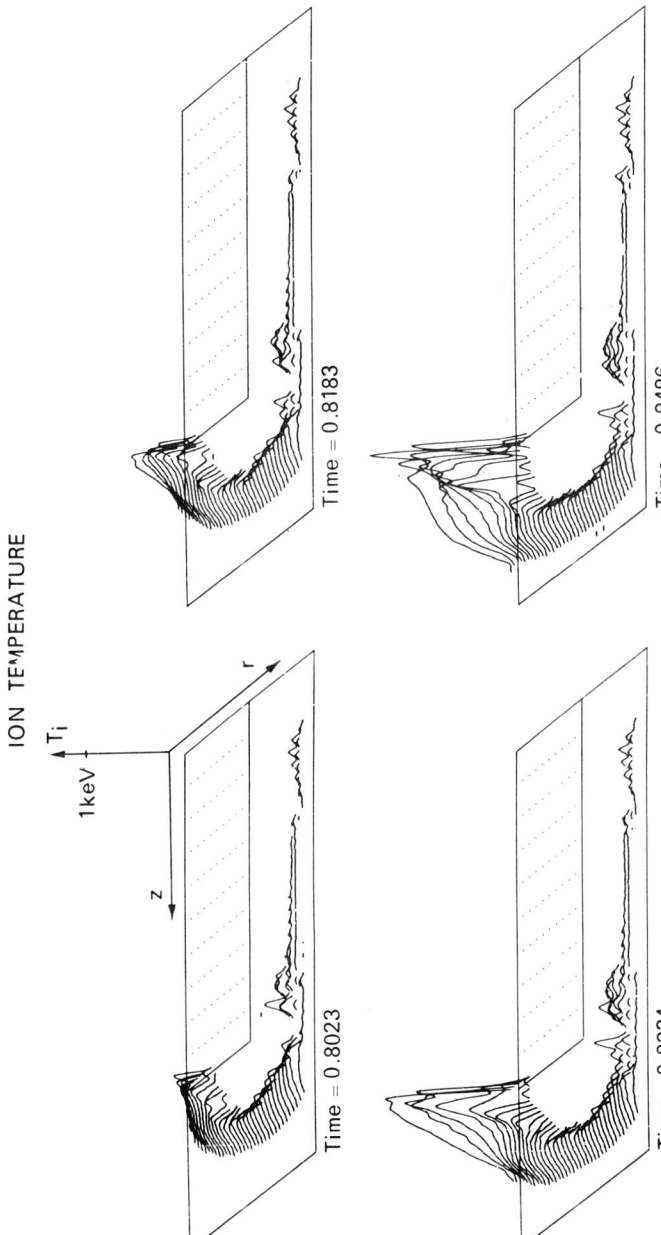

FIG. 15. Ion temperature. The diagrams show the rise in the ion temperature in the initial formation of the plasma focus on the axis. Heating is due mainly to adiabatic compression.

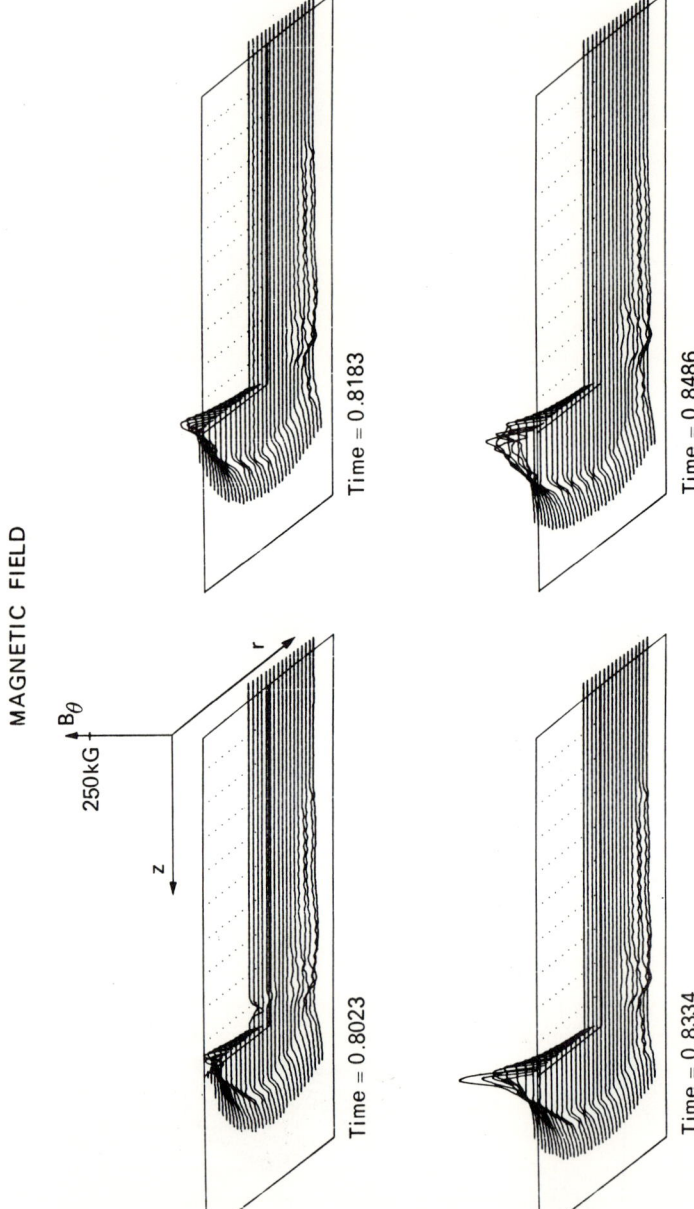

FIG. 16. Azimuthal magnetic field. The diagrams show the rise in magnetic field (producing the plasma focus compression) as the current sheet reaches the axis. The curvature of the compressing "magnetic funnel," which is a strong function of z, can be observed.

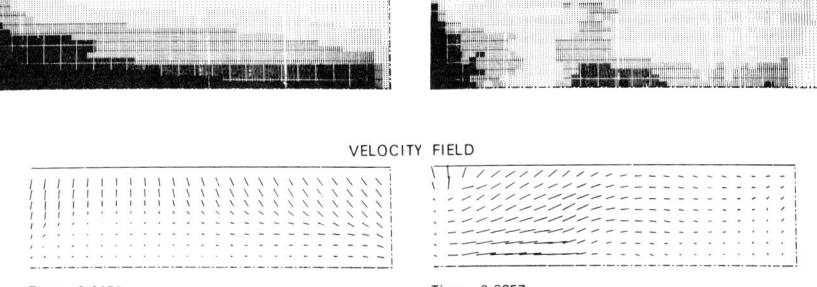

FIG. 17. $m = 0$ instability. The diagrams represent the density and velocity fields in the pinch of the plasma focus obtained from a fine-scale mesh situated in the dense-pinch region. The region shown has dimensions $r = 0.3$ cm, $z = 1.0$ cm. A short-wavelength instability is shown for the case where the viscosity coefficient has been reduced by a factor 10.

since the growth is eventually halted by the field [Fig. 13(e)] and a second or repinch occurs [Figs. 12(e), (f) and 13(f)]. This manifests itself in the inductance [Fig. 18(b)] and current [Fig. 18(a)] curves, and a number of authors

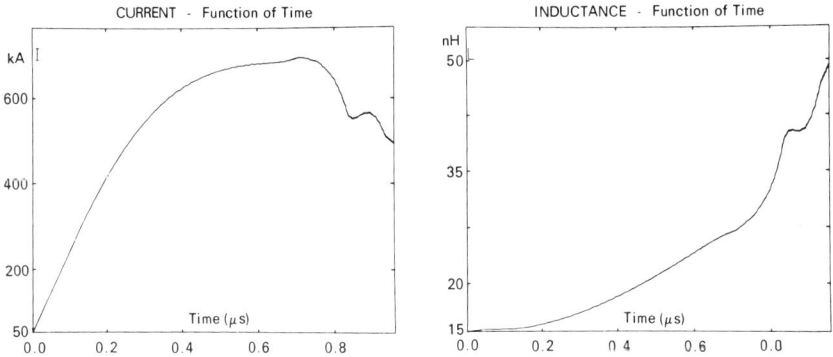

FIG. 18. Circuit current and inductance. The sharp drop in the current from $t = 0.73$ μsec is characteristic of the plasma focus formation on the axis. The slight rise in the current at $t = 0.83$ μsec is caused by the temporary break-up of the pinch due to an $m = 0$ instability.

have obtained experimental evidence consistent with such an effect (Butler et al., 1968). Experimental curves (Peacock, private communication) of the current, tube voltage, and neutron production are reproduced in Figs. 19, 20, and 21, respectively, and show the double voltage and neutron peaks. The measured current curve (Fig. 19) may be compared with the calculated

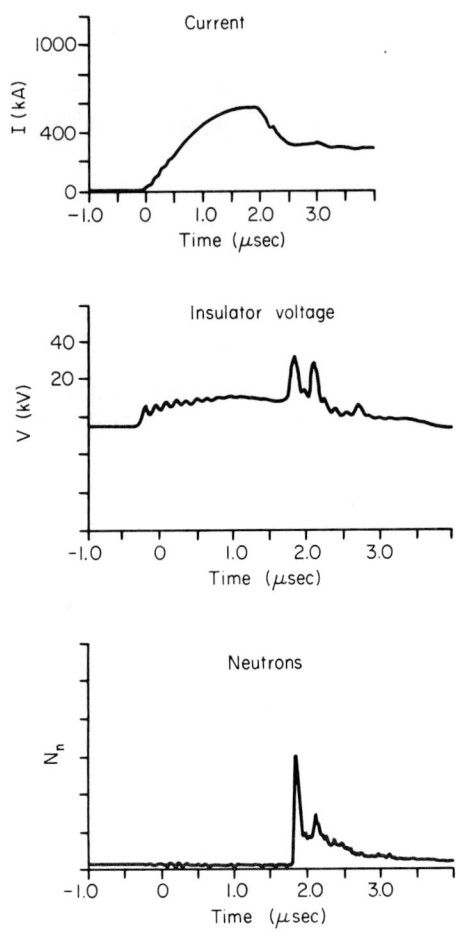

FIG. 19. Experimental curves: (a) current, (b) tube voltage, (c) neutron production in the plasma focus. The current curve (a) illustrates the interruption in the fall of the current at the focus stage (cf. Fig. 18) with corresponding double voltage and neutron spikes. (The time scale is greater as the electrode length was 18 cm, c.f. Table II, N. J. Peacock, unpublished.)

Fig. 18(a). The interruption in the sharp fall of current (due to rapidly increasing inductance from field near the axis) is demonstrated in both curves.

The characteristic plasma parameters in the focus are found on the major mesh to be $T_e \sim 1$ keV, $T_i \sim 2$ keV, $n_e \sim 4 \times 10^{18}$ cm^{-3}. These values compare qualitatively with the experimental results. The density, however, is somewhat too small, since it is found that the pinch collapses to a radius smaller than the radial spatial mesh step $\Delta r = 0.139$ cm. The more accurate calculation on the minor mesh gives a characteristic electron density $n_e \sim 10^{19}$ cm^{-3} with a minimum $r \sim 0.06$ cm.

The duration of the pinch including the partial breakup and repinch is typically 200 nsec.

E. DISCUSSION OF THE RESULTS

The two-dimensional numerical fluid model gives qualitative agreement with experimental observations. To reasonable agreement the high kinetic energy densities are explicable through a magnetohydrodynamic adiabatically compressed plasma. The long lifetime of the plasma focus is due to two effects: ion viscous stabilization of the fast short-wavelength modes, with repinching of the long-wavelength slower $m = 0$ instability, and sustainment by axial plasma flow. The 200-nsec lifetime of the focus is a sustainment time rather than a containment time. An analysis of the neutron production has not yet been carried out, although it is clear that the parameters given by the code within the pinch will give rise to a thermal neutron flux, produced by a source moving with a center of mass velocity of 40 cm/μsec.

Larger electron densities $n_e \sim 2 \times 10^{19}$ cm^{-3} and electron temperatures $T_e \sim 2$keV have been observed experimentally. In addition, analyses of the neutron flux (Bottoms et al., 1968) suggest a larger anisotropy in the neutron energy distribution, and a center of mass velocity of 100 cm/μsec has been inferred. It is therefore worth considering the sufficiency of both the MHD model and the difference scheme.

The parameters of the plasma focus suggest a regime for the ion fluid which is intermediate between the collision-dominated and collisionless regimes, with $\omega_{ci} \tau_{ii} \sim 10$. (The electron fluid is essentially collisionless.) Since the ion–ion collision time $\tau_{ii} \sim 30$ nsec is of the same order as the macroscopic time scale of the plasma focus, the conditions for the fluid approximation are only partially fulfilled. In addition, the ion Larmor radius a_i is of the same order as the scale length (radius ~ 0.06 cm) and hence, the Chew–Goldberger–Low condition $\varepsilon = a_i/L \ll 1$ is not rigorously obeyed. However, since these conditions are not violated by an order of magnitude or more, we would expect the fluid model to give qualitative agreement.

The finite scale of the major mesh in the difference model is more serious however. The superposition of a fine-scale mesh provides valuable information, although it is not entirely satisfactory since the boundary functions are imposed from the major mesh which inherently disallows short-wavelength modes. For short-time scales however, during the initial formation of the pinch, the fine-scale mesh proves adequate, before the effects of the axial boundaries influence the central pinch region. A detailed analysis of the neutron pulse as provided by the numerical modes will in addition give greater comparison with experiment.

VII. A Three-Dimensional Code

There are many physical situations in which three-dimensional MHD calculations would be of interest. In thermonuclear fusion research one would like to be able to calculate the maximum plasma pressure in three-dimensional devices such as Stellarators or mirror magnetic wells and to follow the onset of three-dimensional instabilities in two-dimensional devices such as Tokomaks or pinches. In geophysics, Cowling's theorem (Cowling, 1934; Hide and Roberts, 1961) shows that only three-dimensional motions in the core are capable of generating the earth's magnetic field. Other three-dimensional problems occur in space physics, solar physics, and astrophysics.

A useful two-dimensional MHD calculation can be performed on a 64×64 mesh with a medium-speed machine such as the IBM 7090 or the Culham ICL KDF9 computer, taking about 10–15 sec/timestep, and therefore one would expect to be able to do three-dimensional calculations on a ($64 \times 64 \times 64$) mesh with one of the large new machines such as the CDC 7600 or IBM 360/91, which are of order 64 times as fast (Boris and Roberts, 1969). The backing store requirements are however quite severe, since eight dependent variables must be stored at 256 K mesh points.

This section discusses a simple explicit three-dimensional MHD code which is being developed by Dr. J. P. Boris and one of the authors (K.V.R.), explaining the reasons for some of the decisions which have been taken.

A. Choice of Language and Machine

A rough working rule for the KDF9 is that each Usercode (assembly language instruction costs about \$10 to write, and that 10^7 instructions can be executed for the same cost. Since Usercode is considerably more expensive to write than FORTRAN or ALGOL but runs 2–4 times faster, it is logical to write those instructions that are to be executed more than 10^7 times in Usercode, and the remainder in higher-level language. On one of the fast new computers 10^8 is probably a better criterion. With a three-dimensional computation on a ($64 \times 64 \times 64$) mesh, 10^8 executions correspond to only 400 timesteps and the inner loop of the program should almost certainly be in assembly language, but a two-dimensional calculation should probably be in higher-level language, and a one-dimensional calculation certainly so.

Another interesting point is that by reducing the number of mesh points in each direction by a factor α, much slower computers or coding techniques can be employed because the calculation proceeds α^4 times faster. For example, a (16 × 16 × 16) calculation in FORTRAN on the KDF9 should run at the same physical speed as a (64 × 64 × 64) calculation in assembly language on the IBM 360/91, and it can be accommodated in the 32 K core if two numbers are packed into each 48-bit word. This enables programs to be tested on medium-speed machines and transferred to the large fast machines for production runs.

B. Physical Equations

The simplest set of equations is the set (C) of Section II, namely equations (1), (14), (19), and (20) with the momentum tensor defined by Eqs. (5) and (6). The program can be made much faster and easier to code in assembly language if the transport coefficients are constant, and the diffusion terms then take the form $\nabla^2 f$ which allows a straightforward Dufort–Frankel scheme to be used. For similar reasons, the calculation should use a cubic lattice in a rectangular box, and should be explicit.

C. Boundary Conditions

The boundaries can either be periodic, or rigid conducting walls ($v_\perp = E_\parallel = 0$). In the second case, either the free-slip (zero stress) or no-slip ($v_\parallel = 0$) boundary condition can be used. The walls can be either thermally insulating (zero heat flux), or at constant temperature. All these conditions are easy to apply. An interesting variant is to anchor flux tubes to one of the boundaries, which is then made to move in a prescribed way, thus simulating the twisting of ropes of flux in the sun's chromosphere by motions in the photosphere. A gravitational term can readily be added to Eq. (19).

D. Leapfrog Difference Scheme

The simplest difference scheme seems to be the leapfrog method, in which all variables ρ, **v**, **B**, T are defined at the same points on a cubic lattice of the NaCl type (Fig. 4) with the Na atoms corresponding to even times $2n\,\Delta t$, and the Cl atoms to odd times $(2n + 1)\,\Delta t$. In the symbolic notation defined in Section III,J the equations then become:

$$\operatorname{dotd}(\rho) = -\operatorname{divd}(\rho \mathbf{v}), \tag{153}$$

$$\operatorname{dotd}(\rho v_i) = \operatorname{deld}_j(P^0_{ij}) + \mu\,\operatorname{dufd}(v_i) + \Gamma_i, \tag{154}$$

$$\operatorname{dotd}(\mathbf{B}) = \operatorname{curld}(\mathbf{v} \times \mathbf{B}) + \eta\,\operatorname{dufd}(\mathbf{B}), \tag{155}$$

$$\text{dotd}(\rho e) = -\text{divd}(\rho e\mathbf{v}) - \text{avd}(p)\,\text{divd}(\mathbf{v}) + \mu(\text{curld}(\mathbf{v}))^2$$
$$+ (\lambda + \mu/3)(\text{divd }\mathbf{v})^2 + \eta(\text{curld}(\mathbf{B}))^2 + \kappa\,\text{dufd}(T), \qquad (156)$$

where Γ_i represents the viscous term $(\lambda + \mu/3)(\partial/\partial x_i)\,\text{div }\mathbf{v}$ of Eq. (19).

It is clear that all the terms except Γ_i and the coefficient avd(p) in Eq. (156) are neatly centered. The first derivatives divd, deld, curld on the right-hand side involve only the variables at the face centers (*FC*) at the mid-time, while the Laplacians can be evaluated by the Dufort–Frankel method, so tying the eight spatial meshes together. The coefficient avd(p) can either be evaluated as a space average, or implicitly as a time average.

The difficulty in evaluating Γ_i is that div $\mathbf{v}$ is not properly centered at the points *FC*. It would be possible to use a formula based on the 12 nearest neighbors of *FC* which are located at the same time (i.e., the midpoints of the edges of the cube centered at *FC*), but this would be time-consuming. Boris has suggested breaking Γ_i into two kinds of term, e.g., $\partial^2 \mathbf{v}_x/\partial x^2$ and $\partial^2 v / \partial x\, \partial y$. The first would be evaluated by the Dufort–Frankel scheme, and the second by using the four corner points of the xy-plane through the center of the main cube, two of which are located at the old time, and two at the new time. This procedure introduces small errors which could be removed by alternating the direction of scan.

This leapfrog difference scheme is presented here because it seems to be the simplest that can be devised. In particular, the tensor divergence in Eq. (19) appears to be preferable to terms such as $(\mathbf{v} \cdot \nabla)\mathbf{v}$ or $\mathbf{j} \times \mathbf{B}$, and there is some advantage in using $\mathbf{B}$ rather than the vector potential $\mathbf{A}$. The scheme has been programmed in FORTRAN and is currently being tested but some points remain to be decided, for example, an artificial viscosity for treating shocks, and the filtering of computational density modes which might arise from the absence of a diffusion term in Eq. (1).

VIII. Concluding Remarks

We have discussed MHD computer calculations in one, two, and three dimensions. Realistic fully ionized codes have been constructed for one-dimensional cylindrical problems and good agreement with experiment has been obtained, first for the basic dynamics of the discharge, and more recently for the diffusion of plasma across the magnetic field. In order to explain the early stages of the θ-pinch discharge it has been necessary to include an enhanced resistivity in the code, but a detailed comparison between calculation and experiment shows that the diffusion later becomes classical (Beach *et al.*, 1969).

Two-dimensional calculations have been carried out for several years but only recently have the results been compared quantitatively with experiment. Calculations on the plasma focus device are especially straightforward because the field B_θ is a scalar and has the simple variation $B_\theta \sim 1/r$ in the vacuum region, and the initial comparison with experiment is encouraging. The main difficulty in generalizing to arbitrary cylindrical geometry with fields (B_r, B_θ, B_z) lies in the strongly anisotropic thermal conductivity.

Three-dimensional calculations have only recently been attempted. Existing and projected machines are fast enough to perform the necessary computations in the CPU, and the chief problem will be to achieve a sufficiently rapid data flow (several million words per step), between the core store and a massive fast backing store. This is partly a question of machine configuration, since most large installations do not yet have the necessary storage devices, and partly a question of efficient software engineering. In the meantime, programs can be developed and tested on much smaller and slower machines by using fewer mesh points. Finally, another interesting problem is that of displaying the results.

References

AMSDEN, A. A., and HARLOW, F. H. (1968). Transport of turbulence in numerical fluid dynamics. Los Alamos Sci. Lab. Preprint LA-DC-9497.

APPLETON, J. P., and BRAY, K. N. C. (1964). *J. Fluid Mech.* **20**, 659.

ARTSIMOVICH, L. A., BOBROVSKII, G. A., GORBUNOV, E. P., IVANOV, D. P., KIRILLOV, V. D., KUZNETSOV, Z. I., MIRNOV, S. V., RAZUMOVA, K. A., STRELKOV, V. D., and SHCHEGLOV, D. A. (1968). Experimental investigations on the Tokomaks TM-3 and T-3. *Third IAEA Conf. Plasma Phys. and Controlled Nucl. Fusion Res. Novosibirsk, Aug. 1968*. Paper CN-24/B-1. (In Russian.) Culham Lab. Transl. CTO/536.

ASHBY, D. E., ROBERTS, K. V., and ROBERTS, S. J. (1961). *J. Nucl. Energy, Part C*, **3**, 1962.

AUER, P. L., HURWITZ, H., Jr., and KILB, R. W. (1961). *Phys. Fluids* **4**, 1105.

BAGRINOVSKII, K. A., and GODUNOV, S. K. (1957). *Dokl. Akad. Nauk USSR* **115**, 431.

BARNES, G. H., BROWN, R. M., KATO, M., KUCK, D. J., SLOTNICK, D. L., and STOKES, R. A. (1968). *IEEE Trans. Computers* **C-17**, 746.

BEACH, A. D., BODIN, H. A. B., BUNTING, C. A., DANCY, D. J., HEYWOOD, G. C. H., KENWARD, M. R., MCCARTAN, J., NEWTON, A. A., PASCO, I. K., PEACOCK, R., WATSON, J. L. (1969). Temperature and density measurements in the midplane of a long theta pinch. (To be published in *Nucl. Fusion*.)

BODIN, H. A. B., and NEWTON, A. A. (1969). A study of the diffusion of high-β plasma in a theta pinch. Culham Lab. Rept. CLM-P 185.

BODIN, H. A. B., MCCARTAN, J., NEWTON, A. A., and WOLF, G. H. (1968). Diffusion and stability of high-β plasma in an 8-metre theta pinch. *Third IAEA Conf. Plasma Phys. and Controlled Nucl. Fusion Res., Novosibirsk, Aug. 1968*. Paper CN-24/K-1.

BORIS, J. P., and ROBERTS, K. V. (1969). The optimization of particle calculations in 2 and 3 dimensions. (To be published in *J. Comp. Phys.*)

Bottoms, P. J., Carpenter, J. P, Mather, J. W., Ware, K. D., and Williams, A. H (1968). *Third IAEA Conf. Plasma Phys. and Controlled Nucl. Fusion Res., Novosibirsk, Aug. 1968.* Paper CN-24/G-5.

Butler, T. D. and Cook, J. L. (1968) *Phys. Fluids* **11**, 2286.

Butler, T. D., Henins, I., Jahoda, F. C., Marshall, J., and Morse, R. L. (1968). Coaxial snowplow discharge. Los Alamos Sci. Lab. Preprint LA-DC-9003.

Chapman, S., and Cowling, T. G. (1960). "The Mathematical Theory of Non-Uniform Gases," 2nd ed. Cambridge Univ. Press, London and New York.

Chew, G. F., Goldberger, M. L., and Low, F. E. (1956). *Proc. Roy. Soc.* **A236**, 12.

Chu, C. K. (1965). *Proc. Symp. Appl. Math.* **18**, 1.

Chu, C. K., and Gross, R. A. (1968). Shock waves in plasma physics. (To be published in *Advan. Plasma Phys.*, **2**.)

Chu, C. K., and Taussig, R. T. (1967). *Phys. Fluids* **10**, 249.

Colgate, S. A., Ferguson, J. P., and Furth, H. P. (1958). External conductivity theory of stabilized pinch formation. Lawrence Rad. Lab. Rept. UCRL-5086.

Coudeville, A., Jolas, A., and Watteau, J. P. (1967). Production of neutrons by a non-cylindrical Z-pinch. *APS Topical Conf. Pulsed High-Density Plasmas, Los Alamos, Sept. 1967.* Los Alamos Sci. Lab. Rept. LA-3770, Paper C3.

Cowling, T. G. (1934). *Monthly Notices Roy. Astron. Soc.* **94**, 39.

Duchs, D. (1963). Three-fluid model for a partially ionized plasma in θ-pinch discharges. *Sixth Intern. Conf. Ionization Phenomena in Gases, Paris, July 1963*, Vol. 2, p. 567.

Duchs, D. (1968a). Zweidimensionale theta-pinch-Dynamik bei transversalen Magnetfeldern. Inst. Plasmaphysik, Garching Rept. IPP 1/81.

Duchs, D. (1968b). *Phys. Fluids.* **11**, 2010.

Duchs, D., and Griem, H. R. (1966). *Phys. Fluids.* **9**, 1099.

Dyachenko, V. F. and Imshennik, V. S. (1969). *Zhurnal Eksperimentalnoi i Teoreticheskoi Fisiki* **56** (5), 1766. Transl. in CTO/639 (Culham Translations Office).

Filippov, N. V., and Filippova, T. I. (1966). Phenomena associated with the build-up of a non-cylindrical focused Z-pinch. *Second IAEA Conf. on Plasma Phys. and Controlled Nucl. Fusion Res. Culham, Sept. 1965*, Vol. 2, 405. IAEA, Vienna. (In Russian.) Transl. in AEC-tr-6760 (TID-4500), p. 270.

Filippov, N. V., Filippova, T. I., and Vinogradov, V. P. (1962). *Nucl. Fusion Suppl.*, 2, 577.

Fisser, H., and Schluter, J. (1962). *Nucl. Fusion Suppl.* **2**, 571.

Freeman, J. R., and Lane, F. O. (1968). Initial results from a two-dimensional Lax-Wendroff hydromagnetic code. *APS Topical Conf. Numerical Simulation of Plasma, Los Alamos, Sept. 1968.* Los Alamos Sci. Lab. Rept. LA-3990, Paper C7.

Garabedian, P. R. (1956). *Math. Tables and Other Aids to Computation* **10**, 183.

Hain, K. (1961). Pinch collapse. AERE Harwell Rept. AERE-R-3383.

Hain, K. (1967a). Numerical solution for 1.5-dimensional time-dependent problems. *Symp. Computer Simulation of Plasma and Many-Body Problems, Williamsburg, April, 1967.* NASA Rept. SP-153, p.237.

Hain, K. (1967b). Numerical calculations in magnetohydrodynamics. *APS Topical Conf. Pulsed High-Density Plasmas, Los Alamos, Sept. 1967.* Los Alamos Sci. Lab. Rept. LA-3770, Paper F1.

Hain, K., and Kolb, A. C. (1962). *Nucl. Fusion Suppl.*, Pt. 2, 561.

Hain, K., Hain, G., Roberts, K. V., Roberts, S. J., and Köppendorfer, W. (1960). *Z. Naturforsch.* **15a**(12), 1039.

Harlow, F. H. (1968). Transport of anisotropic or low-intensity turbulence. Los Alamos Sci. Lab. Rept. LA-3947.

Harlow, F. H., and Nakayama, P. I. (1967). *Phys. Fluids* **10**, 2323.

HARLOW, F. H., and NAKAYAMA, P. I. (1968). Transport of turbulence energy decay rate. Los Alamos Sci. Lab. Rept. LA-3854.
HERTWECK, F., and SCHNEIDER, W. (1967). *Second European Conf. Nucl. Fusion and Plasma Phys.*, Stockholm.
HIDE, R., and ROBERTS, P. H. (1961). The origin of the main geomagnetic field. *In* " Physics and Chemistry of the Earth " (L. H. Ahrens *et al.*, eds.), Vol. 4. Pergamon Press, Oxford.
HINNOV, E., and HIRSCHBERG, J. G. (1962), *Phys. Rev.* **125**, 795.
HOBBS, G. D., MCWHIRTER, R. W. P., GRIFFIN, W. G., and JONES, T. J. L. (1961). The temporal variation of line radiation from impurities in zeta. *Fifth Intern. Conf. Ionization Phenomena in Gases, Munich, Aug. 1961*, Vol. 2, p. 1965. North Holland, Amsterdam.
HOCKNEY, R. W. (1965). *J. Assoc. Comput. Mach.* **12**, 95.
HOCKNEY, R. W. (1968). The potential calculation. *APS Topical Conf. Numerical Simulation of Plasma, Los Alamos, Sept. 1968*. Los Alamos Sci. Lab. Rept. LA-3990, Paper D6.
JEFFREY, A. (1966). " Magnetohydrodynamics." Wiley (Interscience), New York.
KAUFMANN, A. N. (1960). *Phys. Fluids* **3**, 610.
KILLEEN, J. (1968). Computational problems in plasma physics and controlled thermonuclear research. Rept. UCRL-71205, Lawrence Rad. Lab., Livermore, California.
KNORR, G. (1958). *Z. Naturforsch.* **13A**, 941.
KOLB, A. C., and MCWHIRTER, R. W. P. (1964). *Phys. Fluids.* **7**, 519.
KUCK, D. J. (1968). *IEEE Trans. Computers*, **C17**, 758.
LAPIDUS, A. (1967). *J. Comp. Phys.* **2**, 154.
LAX, P. D. (1954). *Comm. Pure Appl. Math.* **7**, 159.
LAX, P. D., and WENDROFF, B. (1960). *Comm. Pure Appl. Math.* **13**, 217.
LONG, J. W., PEACOCK, N. J., WILCOCK, P. D., and SPEER, R. J. (1967). The formation and break-up of the pinch in plasma focus. *APS Topical Conf. Pulsed High-Density Plasmas, Los Alamos, Sept. 1967*. Los Alamos Sci. Lab. Rept. LA-3770, Paper C5.
MAKIN, B., and KECK, J. C. (1963). *Phys. Rev. Letters* **11**, 281.
MATHER, J. W. (1965). *Phys. Fluids* **8**, 366.
MATHER, J. W. (1966). High density deuterium plasma. *Second IAEA Conf. Plasma Phys. and Controlled Nucl. Fusion Res., Culham, Sept. 1965*, Vol. 2, p. 389. IAEA, Vienna.
MATHER, J. W., BOTTOMS, P. J., and WILLIAMS, A. H. (1967). Some characteristics of the dense plasma focus. *APS Topical Conf. Pulsed High-Density Plasma, Los Alamos, Sept. 1967*. Los Alamos Sci. Lab. Rept. LA-3770, Paper C1.
MESKAN, D. A., VAN PAASSEN, H. L., and COMISAR, G. G. (1967). Neutron and X-ray production in a focused Z-pinch. *APS Topical Conf. Pulsed High-Density Plasmas, Los Alamos, Sept. 1967*. Los Alamos Sci. Lab. Rept. LA-3770, Paper C6.
MORGAN, P. D., PEACOCK, N. J., and POTTER, D. E. (1969). Comparison of a two-dimensional magnetohydrodynamic numerical model with the dense plasma focus experiment. *Third European Conf. Plasma Phys. and Controlled Fusion, Utrecht, June 1969*.
MORTON, K. W. (1962). *J. Fluid Mech.* **14**, 369.
MORTON, K. W. (1964). *Phys. Fluids* **7**, 1800.
NIBLETT, G. B. F., and FISHER, D. L. (1962). Numerical calculations on reversed field heating in the thetatron. Culham Lab. Rept. CLM-R-19.
OHKAWA, T., FORSEN, H. K., SCHUPP, A. A., and KERST, D. W. (1963). *Phys. Fluids* **6**, 846.
OLIPHANT, T. A. (1963). Numerical studies of the theta pinch. Los Alamos Sci. Lab. Rept. LAMS-2944.
ONZAGER, L. (1931). *Phys. Rev.* **37**, 405.
PATOU, C., SIMMONET, A., and WATTEAU, J. P. (1967). Dynamics and neutron emission of a plasma focus experiment. *APS Topical Conf. Pulsed High-Density Plasmas, Los Alamos, Sept. 1967*. Los Alamos Sci. Lab. Rept. LA-3770, Paper C2.

PAUL, J. W. M., PARKINSON, M. J., SHEFFIELD, J., and HOLMES, L. S. (1965). *Nature* **208**, 133.

PAUL, J. W. M., GOLDENBAUM, G. C., IIYOSHI, A., HOLMES, L. S., and HARDCASTLE, R. A. (1967). *Nature* **216**, 363.

PEACOCK, N. J., WILCOCK, P. D., SPEER, R. J., and MORGAN, P. D. (1968). Properties of the dense plasma produced in plasma focus. *Third IAEA Conf. Plasma Phys. and Controlled Nucl. Fusion Res., Novosibirsk, Aug. 1968*, Paper CN-24/G-4.

RIBE, F. L., GILMER, R. M., HOYT, H. C., HAIN, G., and HAIN, K. (1963). Comparison of computed and measured behaviour of fast θ pinches. Los Alamos Sci. Lab. Rept. LAMS-2911.

RICHTMYER, R. D. (1962). A survey of difference methods for non-steady fluid dynamics. NCAR Tech. Note 63-2, Natl. Center for Atmos. Res., Boulder, Colorado.

RICHTMYER, R. D., and MORTON, K. W. (1967). "Difference Methods for Initial Value Problems." Wiley (Interscience), New York.

ROBERTS, K. V. (1963). *J. Nucl. Energy, Pt. C*, **5**, 365.

ROBERTS, K. V. (1967). Magnetohydrodynamic plasma calculations *Symp. on Computer Simulation of Plasma and Many-Body Problems, Williamsburg, April 1967*. NASA SP-153, p. 163.

ROBERTS, K. V., and TAYLOR, J. B. (1965). *Phys. Fluids* **8**, 315.

ROBERTS, K. V., and WEISS, N. O. (1966). *Math. Comp.* **20**, 272.

ROBERTS, K. V., HERTWECK, F., and ROBERTS, S. J. (1963). Thetatron: A two-dimensional magnetohydrodynamic computer program. Culham Lab. Rept. CLM-R-29.

ROBINSON, D. C., and KING, R. E. (1968). Factors in influencing the period of impower stability in zeta. *Third IAEA Conf. Plasma Phys. and Controlled Nucl. Fusion Res., Novosibirsk, Aug. 1968*, Paper CN-24/B-8.

ROSENBLUTH, M. N. (1958). Stability and heating in the pinch effect. *Second Intern. Conf. Atomic Energy, Geneva, 1958*, Vol. 31, p. 85.

ROSENBLUTH, M. N., and KAUFMANN, A. N. (1958). *Phys. Rev.* **109**, 1.

SAGDEEV, R. A. (1965). *Proc. Symp. Appl. Math.* **18**, 281.

SAGDEEV, R. Z., and GALEEV, A. A. (1966). Rept. IC/66/64, IAEA, Trieste.

SHKARAFSKY, I. P., BERNSTEIN, I. B., and ROBINSON, B. B. (1963). *Phys. Fluids* **6**, 40.

SPITZER, L. (1956). "Physics of Fully Ionized Gases." Wiley (Interscience), New York.

VELIKHOV, E. P., and DYKHNE, A. M. (1963). Plasma turbulence due to the ionization instability in a strong magnetic field. *Sixth Intern. Conf. Ionization Phenomena in Gases, Paris, July 1963*, Vol. 4, p. 511.

VON NEUMANN, J., and RICHTMYER, R. D. (1949). *J. Appl. Phys.* **21**, 232.

WEISS, N. O. (1966). *Proc. Roy. Soc.* **A293**, 310.

YANENKO, N. N. (1964). On a weak approximation of systems of differential equations. *Sibirsk. Mat. Zh.* **5**, 1430.

YOUNG, D. M. (1962). The numerical solution of elliptic and parabolic differential equations. In "A Survey of Numerical Analysis" (J. Todd, ed.), Chap. 11. McGraw Hill, New York.

The Solution of the Fokker–Planck Equation for a Mirror-Confined Plasma

JOHN KILLEEN

LAWRENCE RADIATION LABORATORY, LIVERMORE, CALIFORNIA
and
DEPARTMENT OF APPLIED SCIENCE, UNIVERSITY OF CALIFORNIA, DAVIS, CALIFORNIA

AND

KENNETH D. MARX

SANDIA LABORATORY, LIVERMORE, CALIFORNIA
and
DEPARTMENT OF APPLIED SCIENCE, UNIVERSITY OF CALIFORNIA, DAVIS, CALIFORNIA

I. Introduction	422
A. Motivation	422
B. Previous Calculations and Scope of the Present Work	422
II. Mathematical Formulation Which Describes the Collisional Behavior of a Plasma	424
A. Fokker–Planck Equation	424
B. Plasmas in Mirror-Confinement Systems	425
III. One-Dimensional (Isotropic or Pseudoisotropic) Problems	429
A. Introduction	429
B. The Fokker–Planck Equations for Ions and Electrons	430
C. The Case of One Species Assumed to Be Maxwellian	434
D. Source and Loss Terms	435
E. The Difference Equations and Method of Solution	438
IV. Two-Dimensional (Nonisotropic) Problems	441
A. Boundary Conditions and Independent Variables in Velocity Space	441
B. The Ion Fokker–Planck Operator	443
C. The Source Term	444
D. Difference Methods	444
E. Applications for Single Species of Particle	449
F. Method of Treating the Electron Distribution	456
G. Addition of the Ambipolar Potential and Second Particle Species to the Fokker–Planck Equation	459
H. Solutions of the Ion Fokker–Planck Equation with Maxwellian Electrons and Ambipolar Potential Included	461
V. Nonisotropic Problems with Spatial Dependence of the Magnetic Field	467
A. Method of Solution of the Problem with Spatial Dependence	467
B. Results of Calculations with Spatial Dependence	477
Appendix A. Transformation of the Fokker–Planck Equation to (v, θ) Coordinates and Specialization to a Two-Component Plasma	481

Appendix B. Derivation of "Simpson's Rule" Quadrature Formula for Unequal
    Intervals 484
Appendix C. Other Methods of Calculating g 485
Appendix D. Solution of the Difference Equations. 486
References 489

I. Introduction

A. Motivation

VARIOUS MIRROR-CONFINEMENT SCHEMES for a plasma have been proposed in the search for a solution to the problem of harnessing controlled fusion as a source of power. One problem that must always be considered in such schemes is the calculation of the rate of loss of particles out of the ends of the device due just to the effects of collisions. As is well known, there is a certain region of velocity space, i.e., the "loss cone," in which charged particles cannot be contained in a mirror device, or "open-ended" system. A particle that is contained can be scattered by interparticle collisions into the loss cone, where it will be immediately lost.

A calculation of loss rates due to collisions alone gives a lower limit on the particle loss rate, and hence an upper limit on the particle density that can be achieved in the system for a given input current. Instabilities, charge exchange, the effect of impurities, and any other deleterious effects will then be superposed to enhance losses further and thereby reduce the density.

A second factor to be considered is the effect of the detailed shapes of the particle distribution functions on the loss-cone instability (Post and Rosenbluth, 1965, 1966). This instability is inherent to open-ended systems because of the departure from thermodynamic equilibrium necessitated by the existence of the loss cone in velocity space. Post and Rosenbluth (1966) have shown that the severity of this instability is critically dependent on the shape of the distribution function. In particular, the more sharply peaked the distribution in velocity space, the greater will be the growth rate.

B. Previous Calculations and Scope of the Present Work

Detailed calculations of loss rates have been made by several authors. The work of Roberts and Carr (1960) and Bing and Roberts (1961) consists of a solution of the complete Fokker–Planck equation for ions only, ignoring the effects of the electrons, electrostatic ambipolar potential, and spatial inhomogenities except for the existence of a loss cone. They have also investigated the adequacy of an approximation to the Fokker–Planck equation in which the solution is assumed to be approximately separable.

BenDaniel and Allis (1962) extended the work of Roberts and Carr, particularly in the area of approximating the solution by a separated solution. They also made some progress toward approximate solutions in the case where spatial inhomogeneities exist.

Killeen and Futch (1968) and Fowler and Rankin (1966) have solved the Fokker–Planck equations for both ions and electrons, assuming that the evolution of the distribution functions can be described by the equations for isotropic distributions, with certain factors included to take the presence of the loss cone into account. This assumption and the ensuing approximations are directly related to the assumption of separability. Fowler and Rankin have included the effect of the ambipolar potential. Killeen and Futch also do this, and they include the effect of charge exchange as well in a time-dependent calculation of a plasma formed by neutral injection.

In this paper we first describe the mathematical model of a plasma confined by magnetic mirrors. The Fokker–Planck equation is given, and the boundary conditions for a plasma with a loss cone in velocity space are described.

In Section III we consider the time dependent solution of the Fokker–Planck equations for both electrons and ions in the case where the distribution functions are assumed to be isotropic in velocity space. The presence of a loss cone is approximated by a loss term in each of the equations, and the effect of the ambipolar potential is included in this term. A source of particles appropriate to neutral injection experiments is included, and the effect of charge-exchange loss is included in the ion equation.

In Section IV we solve the complete Fokker–Planck equation for the ions, including the collisional effects of the electrons on the ions. We make a somewhat weaker assumption on the electron distribution, namely that the electron distribution in velocity space can be approximately described by a Maxwellian with a hole cut out of it in the region where electron confinement is impossible. This assumption would be weak, indeed, were it not for the fact that the effect of the ambipolar potential is always included in our calculations whenever electron effects are included. Because of this, and because the ambipolar potential is expected to be somewhat greater than the average electron energy, previously obtained results (Killeen and Futch, 1968) indicate that the assumption is rather good. It is made to avoid increased complexity in numerical techniques and to shorten computer time.

Finally, in Section V, we extend the calculations to include the addition of one space variable, namely a coordinate along magnetic field lines. Ion distributions, electron densities and temperatures, and the ambipolar potential are simultaneously calculated as a function of this coordinate. We still neglect any effects due to gradients perpendicular to field lines.

Our model of a mirror machine is the classical one consisting of two identical coils spaced some distance apart. For simplicity, the calculations can be thought of as pertaining to the distributions on the axis of this axially symmetric configuration. We also assume mirror symmetry about the midplane of the device. However, the results should apply to field lines off the axis and to devices with asymmetric mirrors, as well as field lines in more sophisticated geometries, e.g., minimum-B fields.

II. Mathematical Formulation Which Describes the Collisional Behavior of a Plasma

A. Fokker–Planck Equation

The usual transport equation for particles in a plasma is

$$\frac{\partial f_a}{\partial t} + \mathbf{v} \cdot \frac{\partial f_a}{\partial \mathbf{r}} + \frac{\mathbf{F}}{m} \cdot \frac{\partial f_a}{\partial \mathbf{v}} = \left(\frac{\partial f_a}{\partial t}\right)_c + S_a, \tag{1}$$

where $f_a(\mathbf{r}, \mathbf{v}, t)$ is the distribution function for particles of species a in six-dimensional phase space. $(\partial f_a/\partial t)_c$ is a term describing collisional effects; $S_a(\mathbf{r}, \mathbf{v}, t)$ describes a particle source if applicable. $\mathbf{F}$ is the force on a particle.

The left side of Eq. (1) is df_a/dt, the time derivative of f as seen by a particle in its orbit. We shall refer to this concept when describing the solution of a version of Eq. (1) with a spatial dependence. For the present, note that if spatial gradients are absent, and if the force arises only from a magnetic field about which f possesses azimuthal symmetry, then the left side is just $\partial f_a/\partial t$, so Eq. (1) becomes

$$\frac{\partial f_a}{\partial t} = \left(\frac{\partial f_a}{\partial t}\right)_c + S_a. \tag{2}$$

The collision operator most often applied in plasma theory is the Fokker–Planck operator. It is given by Rosenbluth et al. (1957) or Montgomery and Tidman (1964),

$$\frac{1}{\Gamma_a}\left(\frac{\partial f_a}{\partial t}\right)_c = -\frac{\partial}{\partial \mathbf{v}} \cdot \left(f_a \frac{\partial h_a}{\partial \mathbf{v}}\right) + \frac{1}{2}\frac{\partial^2}{\partial \mathbf{v}\, \partial \mathbf{v}} : \left(f_a \frac{\partial^2 g_a}{\partial \mathbf{v}\, \partial \mathbf{v}}\right), \tag{3}$$

where

$$h_a(\mathbf{v}) = \sum_b \frac{m_a + m_b}{m_b} \left(\frac{Z_b}{Z_a}\right)^2 \int d\mathbf{v}' f_b(\mathbf{v}')/|\mathbf{v} - \mathbf{v}'|,$$

$$g_a(\mathbf{v}) = \sum_b \left(\frac{Z_b}{Z_a}\right)^2 \int d\mathbf{v}' f_b(\mathbf{v}')|\mathbf{v} - \mathbf{v}'|,$$

$$\Gamma_a = \frac{4\pi Z_a^4 e^4}{m_a^2} \log_e D_a, \quad D_a = \frac{3KT_a}{2Z_a^2 e^2}\left(\frac{KT_e}{\pi N_e e^2}\right)^{1/2} = \frac{2E_a \lambda_D}{Z_a^2 e^2}.$$

T_e and N_e refer to electron temperature and density, and λ_D is the electron Debye length:

$$\lambda_D = \left(\frac{KT_e}{4\pi N_e e^2}\right)^{1/2}.$$

The normalization of f_a is such that particle density is

$$N_a = \int d\mathbf{v}\, f_a(\mathbf{v}).$$

We shall henceforth assume $(\partial f_a/\partial t)_c$ in Eqs. (1) and (2) to be given by Eq. (3), and we shall refer to either of these equations as the Fokker–Planck equation.

In Sections III and IV, all the terms in Eq. (3) that evolve under appropriate choices of coordinate systems and symmetry conditions will be given. Note that, in general, Eq. (2) is a parabolic partial differential equation in time and velocity space. The numerical techniques applicable to this equation are therefore those which are used in diffusion and heat conduction problems. Furthermore, the left side of Eq. (1) will be treated in such a way that the same statement holds for spatially dependent problems.

It can be shown that, in the absence of sources and losses, the number of particles, as well as total momentum and energy, are conserved within the formalism of the Fokker–Planck equation. Furthermore, under the same conditions, in a homogeneous system with no forces, the distribution functions will approach Maxwellians. These properties can provide convenient checks on the accuracy of numerical solutions.

B. Plasmas in Mirror-Confinement Systems

Since the majority of examples discussed here are devoted to the problem of plasma confinement within systems of magnetic mirrors, in this section we consider the mathematical description of such systems. We employ the usual spherical polar coordinate system in velocity space, with the pole in the direction of the component of velocity along the magnetic field, which is taken to be in the z-direction of a Cartesian system. Two assumptions are made concerning the particle distributions:

(1) The distribution is azimuthally symmetric in velocity space.
(2) The distribution has reflection symmetry about the midplane in configuration space and velocity space.

These assumptions are convenient for numerical computation, but they are actually not at all stringent from a physical standpoint. The first is well known, and is made in virtually all work done in the field. The second is also seen to be valid if one recognizes that, in all cases of interest, the particle transit time is much shorter than a typical collision time. Thus, a particle which appears at a point in velocity space will appear at very nearly the mirror image of the point after it undergoes reflection and travels back in the opposite direction (ignoring a difference in the azimuthal angle, or phase of the gyrating velocity vector).

We assume that the magnetic moment of a gyrating particle is adiabatically conserved. Because of this, we shall henceforth find it convenient to consider only the motion of the particle guiding centers whenever we have occasion to deal with single-particle motion or orbits in phase space. The letter z will be used to denote distance along field lines. Restricting our discussion to symmetric mirror machines, we choose $z = 0$ as the center of the mirror device, and $z = \pm L$ as the value of z at the mirrors. When convenient, quantities at $z = 0$ and $z = L$ will be denoted by subscripts 0 and m, respectively.

The loss-cone angle is given (Spitzer, 1962) by

$$\sin^2 \theta_{LC} = 1/R_m, \qquad (4)$$

where $R_m = B_m/B(z)$; B_m is the magnetic field at the mirror, and $B(z)$ is the magnetic field at the interior point being considered. The orientation of the loss cone in velocity space is displayed in Fig. 1. A particle whose angle in velocity space is less than θ_{LC} will be immediately lost from the mirror system. θ_{LC} is independent of velocity as well as particle mass and charge. Equation (4) is derived under the assumption that no electrostatic potential exists, and θ_{LC} is the actual loss angle only under that condition.

However, because the scattering rate of electrons will be greater than that of ions because of their greater mobility, more electrons than ions will start to leak out of the ends of the device, and an ambipolar potential will start to build up, being greatest at the center and decreasing towards the ends.

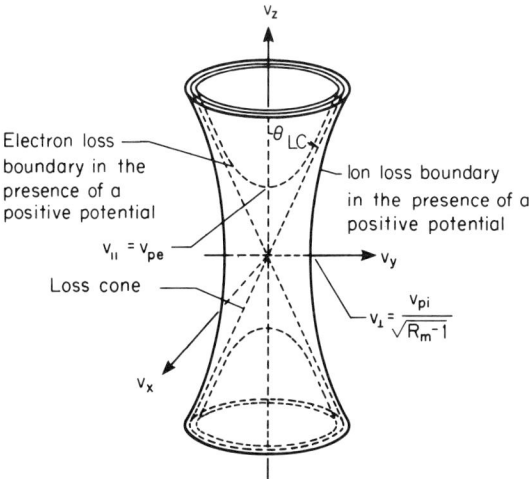

FIG. 1. Loss cone and electron and ion loss boundaries.

The fact that this potential is established leads to a fundamental change in the loss characteristics for the two types of particles. Assume for the moment that magnetic field and potential have a "square-well" z-dependence. The loss regions are then defined by a loss angle which is a function of speed and charge (Kaufman, 1956; Post, 1961; BenDaniel, 1961; Yushmanov, 1966). If $Z_a e$ is charge and Φ is electrostatic potential, the loss angle is given by

$$\sin^2 \theta_L = (1 \pm v_{pa}^2/v^2)/R_m, \qquad (5)$$

where

$$v_{pa}^2 = |(2Z_a e/m_a)[\Phi(z) - \Phi_m]|,$$

the ambiguous sign is to be chosen as that of the particle charge, and $\Phi(z) - \Phi_m$ is the potential difference between the interior point being considered and the mirrors. Equation (5) approaches Eq. (4) asymptotically as $v \to \infty$. For ions, the right-hand side of Eq. (5) can exceed unity; no ion in such a velocity regime can be contained. Conversely, for electrons, this term can be less than zero; all electrons at such velocities will be trapped. These regions are shown in Fig. 1. The loss region for ions is transformed from a cone into a hyperboloid of one sheet. Its minimum radius occurs at $\theta = \pi/2$, and is equal to the minimum ion velocity possible for confinement, given by

$$v_{mi}^2 = v_{pi}^2/(R_m - 1).$$

(It may appear that any ion with zero parallel velocity would be contained at the point $z = 0$, where the electric field is zero, but this is a point of unstable equilibrium for particles with $v < v_{\text{mi}}$, except in the case of trapping due to peculiar field configurations, as discussed in the next section. If the potential and magnetic field comprise a "square well," the equilibrium is metastable.) The electron loss region is transformed into a hyperboloid of two sheets. The minimum electron speed at which an electron may be lost (if its angle is just $\theta = 0$) is given by

$$v_{\text{me}}^2 = v_{\text{pe}}^2.$$

Consider now the variation of loss regions along magnetic field lines. We limit our discussion to the region $0 \leq z \leq L$, recalling that the configuration is symmetric about $z = 0$. In the absence of an ambipolar potential, the behavior of the loss region as a function of z is very simple. The loss-cone angle increases as the local mirror ratio decreases, approaching $\theta_{\text{LC}} = \pi/2$ at the mirrors. In the presence of the potential, the behavior of the electron loss region is also quite easy to express. Assume $\Phi(z)$ to be monotonically decreasing. Then v_{me}^2 decreases monotonically to zero, and we see that the cup-shaped loss regions broaden and elongate with increasing z. The ion picture is complicated in the presence of the potential, however. Let subscript 0 refer to quantities at $z = 0$, and subscripts $\perp$ and $\parallel$ refer to directions perpendicular and parallel to magnetic field, respectively. Yushmanov (1966) writes a potential function for the parallel component of ion motion. It is equivalent to

$$V = Ze\Phi + \mu_{\text{m}} B, \tag{6}$$

where $\mu_{\text{m}} = mv_{\perp 0}^2/2B_0$ is the magnetic moment. With this definition of V, the equation for ion motion is

$$m(dv_{\parallel}/dt) = -dV/dz.$$

Yushmanov demonstrates the trapping of slow ions, a possibility that could not be predicted from consideration of only the difference in potential between the points $z = 0$ and $z = L$. Such a situation is indicated by a possible $V(z)$ shown in Fig. 2. We have included the effects of Yushmanov trapping in some of our calculations. Other effects related to the functional shape of $\Phi(z)$ are possible, of course, but do not appear to be of importance; hence they have been ignored.

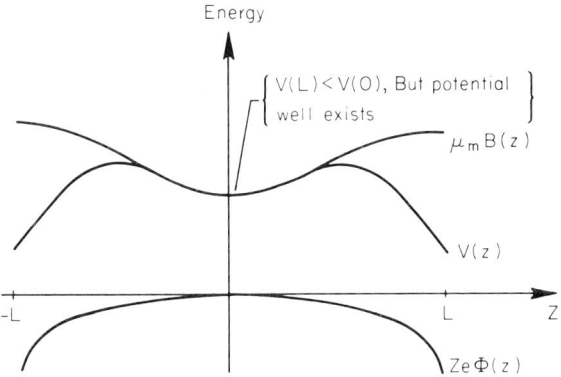

FIG. 2. Configuration giving rise to Yushmanov trapping.

III. One-Dimensional (Isotropic or Pseudoisotropic) Problems

A. INTRODUCTION

Calculations performed in two-dimensional velocity space for the ion distribution function indicate that approximate results can be obtained by separating the distribution function into a product of two terms (Bing and Roberts, 1961; BenDaniel and Allis, 1962). The first term is a function of v and t, and the second term is a function of θ only. The equation for the function of θ is a Legendre differential equation on the domain $-\theta_c \leq \theta \leq \theta_c$, where θ_c defines the magnetic mirror loss cone. The equation for $f(v, t)$ must be solved numerically, and it is given in Eq. (12) of this paper for each species. The boundary condition on the distribution function in such a loss-cone problem is $f(v, \theta_c, t) = 0$ for all v and t for each species, which implies $f = 0$ at $v = 0$ in the separated solution. In those problems where we assume that the distribution functions are isotropic, we take a symmetry condition at $v = 0$, i.e., $\partial f/\partial v = 0$ for all t.

In the equations for ions and electrons we include source terms which are appropriate for the neutral injection experiments such as ALICE (Futch et al., 1966) or PHOENIX (Bernstein et al., 1966). We also include the loss of both species by scattering into the velocity-space loss cone of the magnetic mirror configuration, and the hot ions can be lost by charge exchange with the background gas.

A plasma potential is computed at each time step of the calculation by requiring charge neutrality. A critical velocity $v_c(t)$ is determined such that electrons with $v < v_c$ are not lost and those with $v > v_c$ can be lost by scattering into the loss cone. At each time step, the electron density is compared to the ion density and the velocity v_c modified accordingly. The plasma potential is obtained from $e\varphi = \frac{1}{2}mv_c^2$.

We have coupled nonlinear partial differential equations for the functions $f_e(v, t)$ and $f_i(v, t)$. We solve the equations numerically using finite difference methods. The equations are not linearized, i.e., the coefficients which involve moments of the distribution functions are computed at each time step. An implicit difference scheme is used, i.e., the velocity derivatives are replaced by difference quotients taken at the new time step, while the coefficients are evaluated using the distribution function of the previous time step, and extrapolated. The scheme is stable numerically in practice, with no restriction on the time step.

B. The Fokker–Planck Equations for Ions and Electrons

We assume that the distribution functions are isotropic in velocity space, i.e., functions depend only on v, the magnitude of the velocity, and t, the time. Under this assumption the Fokker–Planck equation becomes

$$\Gamma_a^{-1} \frac{\partial f_a}{\partial t} = \frac{\partial^2 f_a}{\partial v^2}\left[\frac{1}{2}\frac{\partial^2 g}{\partial v^2}\right] + \frac{\partial f_a}{\partial v}\left[-\frac{\partial h_a}{\partial v} - \frac{1}{v^2}\frac{\partial g}{\partial v} + \frac{2}{v}\frac{\partial^2 g}{\partial v^2} + \frac{\partial^3 g}{\partial v^3}\right]$$
$$+ f_a\left[-\frac{2}{v}\frac{\partial h_a}{\partial v} - \frac{\partial^2 h_a}{\partial v^2} + \frac{2}{v}\frac{\partial^3 g}{\partial v^3} + \frac{1}{2}\frac{\partial^4 g}{\partial v^4}\right]. \quad (7)$$

The function $f_a(v, t)$ is the distribution function for particles of type a. The functions $h_a(v, t)$ and $g(v, t)$ are defined by the equations

$$h_a(v, t) = 4\pi \sum_b \frac{m_a + m_b}{m_b}\left[\int_0^v f_b(v', t)\frac{v'^2}{v} dv' + \int_v^\infty f_b(v', t)v' dv'\right], \quad (8)$$

$$g(v, t) = 4\pi \sum_b \left[\int_0^v f_b(v' t)v\left(1 + \frac{1}{3}\frac{v'^2}{v^2}\right)v'^2 dv'\right.$$
$$\left. + \int_v^\infty f_b(v', t)\left(1 + \frac{1}{3}\frac{v^2}{v'^2}\right)v'^3 dv'\right]. \quad (9)$$

The summations are taken over all the species of particles being considered, including type a.

The number density of particles of type a is given by

$$n_a(t) = 4\pi \int_0^\infty f_a(v, t)v^2 dv. \quad (10)$$

In Eq. (7), there are no source or loss terms, i.e., $dn_a/dt = 0$. We can consider the loss of particles by Coulomb scattering. The loss rate for such a process has been given by Chandrasekhar (1942) and can be written as

$$dn_a/dt = -(4\pi)^2 \int_0^\infty f_a(v, t) v^2 \left[\sum_b \int_0^\infty k_a(v, v') f_b(v', t) v'^2 \, dv' \right] dv, \quad (11)$$

where

$$k_a(v, v') = p_a(v) \Gamma_a \lambda_{ab} \frac{1}{v^3} \begin{cases} 1 - \dfrac{1}{3} \dfrac{v'^2}{v^2}, & v \geq v', \\ \dfrac{2}{3} \dfrac{v}{v'}, & v \leq v', \end{cases}$$

with λ_{ab} a separation constant which can be specified, and $p_a(v)$ is the probability that particles of type a and velocity v will be lost. We shall discuss the form of $p_a(v)$ that we use later. We can also add a source term, $s_a(v, t)$, to Eq. (7). The details of this term will be given in Section D.

If we use Eqs. (8) and (9) to evaluate the coefficients of Eq. (7), and also include the source and loss terms discussed above, then the equation for $f_a(v, t)$ becomes

$$(4\pi\Gamma_a)^{-1} \frac{\partial f_a}{\partial t} = \frac{\partial^2 f_a}{\partial v^2} \left\{ \sum_b \left[\frac{1}{3v^3} \int_0^v f_b(v', t) v'^4 \, dv' + \frac{1}{3} \int_v^\infty f_b(v', t) v' \, dv' \right] \right\}$$

$$+ \frac{\partial f_a}{\partial v} \left\{ \frac{1}{v} \sum_b \left[\frac{m_a}{m_b} \frac{1}{v} \int_0^v f_b(v', t) v'^2 \, dv' - \frac{1}{3v^3} \int_0^v f_b(v', t) v'^4 \, dv' \right. \right.$$

$$\left. \left. + \frac{2}{3} \int_v^\infty f_b(v', t) v' \, dv' \right] \right\} + f_a \left(\sum_b \frac{m_a}{m_b} f_b \right) \quad (12)$$

$$- f_a \left\{ \frac{p_a(v)}{v^3} \sum_b \lambda_{ab} \left[\int_0^v f_b(v', t) v'^2 \, dv' \right. \right.$$

$$\left. \left. - \frac{1}{3v^2} \int_0^v f_b(v', t) v'^4 \, dv' + \frac{2v}{3} \int_v^\infty f_b(v', t) v' \, dv' \right] \right\} + s_a(v, t).$$

The term for charge-exchange loss must be added to Eq. (12) for ions. The term $s_a(v, t)$ represents the source of injected particles.

We consider electrons and ions of $Z = 1$. We introduce the dimensionless variable $x = v/v_0$, where v_0 is a constant and is a characteristic velocity.

Let $f = (4\pi v_0^3/K_e)f_e$, where K_e is determined from the equation

$$n_e(0) = K_e \int_0^\infty f(x, 0)x^2 \, dx,$$

i.e., the constant is determined by the initial conditions with $n_e(0)$ equal to the initial electron density. Similarly, we let $g = (4\pi v_0^3/K_i)f_i$, where

$$n_i(0) = K_i \int_0^\infty g(x, 0)x^2 \, dx.$$

We introduce the dimensionless variable τ, where $\tau = (\tfrac{1}{2}\Gamma_e K_e/v_0^3)t$. Let $\mu = m_e/m_i$ and $K = K_i/K_e$. We define functionals

$$M(f) = \int_x^\infty f(y, \tau)y \, dy, \tag{13}$$

$$N(f) = \int_0^x f(y, \tau)y^2 \, dy, \tag{14}$$

$$E(f) = \int_0^x f(y, \tau)y^4 \, dy. \tag{15}$$

In terms of these new variables, the equation for the electron-distribution function becomes

$$\frac{\partial f}{\partial \tau} = A \frac{\partial^2 f}{\partial x^2} + B \frac{\partial f}{\partial x} + Cf + D, \tag{16}$$

where

$$A = \frac{2}{3}\left\{\left[\frac{1}{x^3} E(f) + M(f)\right] + K\left[\frac{1}{x^3} E(g) + M(g)\right]\right\},$$

$$B = \frac{4}{3x}\left\{\left[\frac{3}{2x} N(f) - \frac{1}{2x^3} E(f) + M(f)\right]\right.$$
$$\left. + K\left[\mu \frac{3}{2x} N(g) - \frac{1}{2x^3} E(g) + M(g)\right]\right\},$$

$$C = 2(f + K\mu g) - p_e(x)\frac{4}{3x^2}\left\{\lambda_{ee}\left[\frac{3}{2x} N(f) - \frac{1}{2x^3} E(f) + M(f)\right]\right.$$
$$\left. + K\lambda_{ei}\left[\frac{3}{2x} N(g) - \frac{1}{2x^3} E(g) + M(g)\right]\right\}.$$

The term $D(x, \tau)$ describes the time-dependent source of electrons. The equation for the ion-distribution function becomes

$$\frac{\partial g}{\partial \tau} = F \frac{\partial^2 g}{\partial x^2} + G \frac{\partial g}{\partial x} + Hg + L, \qquad (17)$$

where

$$F = \frac{2}{3}\mu^2 \left\{ \left[\frac{1}{x^3} E(f) + M(f)\right] + K\left[\frac{1}{x^3} E(g) + M(g)\right] \right\},$$

$$G = \frac{4}{3x}\mu^2 \left\{ \left[\frac{1}{\mu}\frac{3}{2x} N(f) - \frac{1}{2x^3} E(f) + M(f)\right] \right.$$
$$\left. + K\left[\frac{3}{2x} N(g) - \frac{1}{2x^3} E(g) + M(g)\right] \right\},$$

$$H = 2\mu^2 \left(\frac{1}{\mu} f + Kg\right) - H_1(x, \tau)$$
$$- \mu^2 p_i(x) \frac{8}{3x^2} \left\{ \lambda_{ie} \left[\frac{3}{2x} N(f) - \frac{1}{2x^3} E(f) + M(f)\right] \right.$$
$$\left. + K\lambda_{ii} \left[\frac{3}{2x} N(g) - \frac{1}{2x^3} E(g) + M(g)\right] \right\}.$$

The term $H_1(x, \tau)$ contains the charge-exchange loss term, and $L(x, \tau)$ describes the time-dependent source of ions.

At any time step we can determine the number density and average energy of each type of particle. Let $I_2^-(\tau)$ and $I_4^-(\tau)$ be the second and fourth moments of the electron distribution function, i.e.,

$$I_2^-(\tau) = \int_0^\infty f(x, \tau) x^2 \, dx, \qquad (18)$$

$$I_4^-(\tau) = \int_0^\infty f(x, \tau) x^4 \, dx. \qquad (19)$$

The number density of electrons is given by

$$n_e(\tau) = K_e I_2^-(\tau), \qquad (20)$$

and the mean electron energy is given by

$$E_e(\tau) = \tfrac{3}{2}kT_e = \tfrac{1}{2}m_e v_0^2 \frac{I_4^-(\tau)}{I_2^-(\tau)}. \tag{21}$$

Let

$$I_2^+(\tau) = \int_0^\infty g(x,\tau)x^2\,dx, \tag{22}$$

$$I_4^+(\tau) = \int_0^\infty g(x,\tau)x^4\,dx. \tag{23}$$

The number density of ions is given by

$$n_i(\tau) = K_i I_2^+(\tau), \tag{24}$$

and the mean ion energy is given by

$$E_i(\tau) = \tfrac{3}{2}kT_i = \tfrac{1}{2}m_i v_0^2 \frac{I_4^+(\tau)}{I_2^+(\tau)}. \tag{25}$$

C. The Case of One Species Assumed to Be Maxwellian

In a two-species model of the type just described we can sometimes assume that the distribution function of one of them is of a particular form. In this case only one partial differential equation need be solved, and the problem of the very different time scales of ions and electrons is avoided.
Let

$$g(x,\tau) = a(\tau)e^{-b(\tau)x^2}$$

then

$$M(g) = \frac{a}{2b}e^{-bx^2},$$

$$N(g) = -\frac{a}{2b}xe^{-bx^2} + \frac{a}{2b}\int_0^x e^{-by^2}\,dy,$$

$$E(g) = -\frac{ax}{2b}\left(x^2 + \frac{3}{2b}\right)e^{-bx^2} + \frac{3a}{4b^2}\int_0^x e^{-by^2}\,dy.$$

The above functionals, which appear in the coefficients A, B, and C of Eq. (16), can easily be evaluated using standard exponential and error function routines. The functions $a(\tau)$ and $b(\tau)$ are calculated from the density and average energy of the second species.

The above procedure was used to calculate the energy transfer from hot ions to cold electrons in a plasma (Killeen et al., 1962). In that work the ions were kept at a fixed temperature and the electron equation solved numerically.

In the present version of the isotropic code (Killeen and Futch, 1968) both Eqs. (16) and (17) are solved simultaneously. Because the difference scheme is stable the time step can be increased by several orders of magnitude during the calculation. Hence the problem of different time scales for electron and ion relaxation is not a serious one in the isotropic calculations.

D. Source and Loss Terms

In this section we shall describe the form of the source and loss terms that appear in Eqs. (16) and (17). The mechanisms for trapping the neutral-atom beam are the Lorentz ionization of excited hydrogen atoms and ionization of the neutral beam atoms by collisions with background gas molecules and with previously trapped ions and electrons. The growth rates of electrons and ions are given by the equations (Futch et al., 1962)

$$\frac{dn_e}{dt} = \frac{If^*}{V} + n_i\left[\frac{IL}{V}\left(\overline{\frac{\sigma_t^i v_r}{v_0}}\right) + \sigma_i^i v n_0\right] + n_e\left[\frac{IL}{V}\left(\overline{\frac{\sigma_t^e v_r}{v_0}}\right) + \sigma_i^e v n_0\right], \quad (26)$$

$$\frac{dn_i}{dt} = \frac{If^*}{V} + n_i\left[\frac{IL}{V}\left(\overline{\frac{\sigma_t^i v_r}{v_0}}\right)\right] + n_e\left[\frac{IL}{V}\left(\overline{\frac{\sigma_t^e v_r}{v_0}}\right)\right], \quad (27)$$

where I is the injected neutral beam current, V is the plasma volume, f^* is the fraction of the neutral beam ionized by the Lorentz force, L is the path length of the neutral beam through the plasma, v_r is the relative velocity between interacting particles, and v_0 is the characteristic velocity defined earlier, which is determined by the beam velocity. The cross sections for ionization of the beam atoms by collisions with hot ions and electrons are σ_t^i and σ_t^e. Cross sections for ionization of the background gas by hot ions and electrons are σ_i^i and σ_i^e, and n_0 is the background gas density. In a magnetic mirror field, the cold ions (produced by charge-exchange collisions and by ionization of the background gas) may be neglected since they are rapidly scattered into the mirror escape cone and lost from the system, hence these terms are omitted from the above ion equation.

We assume that the injected electrons and ions have a velocity distribution defined by $S_e(x)$ and $S_i(x)$. Let

$$N(S_e) = \int_0^\infty S_e(x)x^2\, dx, \qquad N(S_i) = \int_0^\infty S_i(x)x^2\, dx.$$

Hence, in Eq. (16) we have

$$D(x,\tau) = S_e(x)\left(\frac{t}{\tau}\right)\frac{1}{K_e N(S_e)}\left(\frac{dn_e}{dt}\right), \tag{28}$$

and in Eq. (17) we have

$$L(x,\tau) = S_i(x)\left(\frac{t}{\tau}\right)\frac{1}{K_i N(S_i)}\left(\frac{dn_i}{dt}\right). \tag{29}$$

In the calculations we keep $n_e(\tau) = n_i(\tau)$ by adjusting the plasma potential, so we can write Eqs. (28) and (29) as

$$D(x,\tau) = S_e(x)[l_0 + l_1 n_i(\tau)], \tag{30}$$

$$L(x,\tau) = S_i(x)[p_0 + p_1 n_i(\tau)], \tag{31}$$

where

$$l_0 = \left(\frac{2v_0^3}{\Gamma_e K_e}\right)\frac{1}{K_e N(S_e)}\frac{If^*}{V},$$

$$l_1 = \left(\frac{2v_0^3}{\Gamma_e K_e}\right)\frac{1}{K_e N(S_e)}\left[\frac{IL}{V}\left(\frac{\overline{\sigma_t^i v_r}}{v_0} + \frac{\overline{\sigma_t^e v_r}}{v_0}\right) + n_0 v(\sigma_i^{\,i} + \sigma_i^{\,e})\right],$$

$$p_0 = \left(\frac{2v_0^3}{\Gamma_e K_e}\right)\frac{1}{K_i N(S_i)}\frac{If^*}{V},$$

$$p_1 = \left(\frac{2v_0^3}{\Gamma_e K_e}\right)\frac{1}{K_i N(S_i)}\left[\frac{IL}{V}\left(\frac{\overline{\sigma_t^i v_r}}{v_0} + \frac{\overline{\sigma_t^e v_r}}{v_0}\right)\right],$$

and $n_i(\tau)$ is given by Eq. (24).

We can include up to ten sources of the type given by Eq. (31), corresponding to multiple ion beam injection at different energies. In the above discussion of source terms the (σv) terms were treated as constants; however, the cross sections have a velocity dependence determined by experimental measurements. We have polynomial descriptions for these functions so the terms

$\sigma v n(\tau)$ can be replaced by integrals involving the distribution functions. This is illustrated in the next paragraph on charge-exchange loss.

In Eq. (17) the charge-exchange loss term is $-H_1(x)g(x, \tau)$, where

$$H_1(x) = (t/\tau)n_0 \, v\sigma_{cx}(v) = (t/\tau)n_0 \, v_0 \, x\sigma_{cx}(x) \tag{32}$$

and $\sigma_{cx}(v)$ is the charge-exchange cross section. We have fit the experimental cross section σ_{cx} with a fifth-degree polynomial, so we write

$$H_1(x) = x[H_{a1} + H_{b1}x + H_{c1}x^2 + H_{d1}x^3 + H_{e1}x^4 + H_{h1}x^5], \tag{33}$$

where the coefficients are constants, including the constant factor, $(t/\tau)n_0 v_0$, which is an input parameter of the problem.

We shall now give the terms $p_e(x)$ and $p_i(x)$, which appear in Eqs. (16) and (17), and are the probabilities that electrons and ions of velocity $v_0 x$ are scattered into the loss cone of the magnetic mirror machine. In the case of no plasma potential these terms are equal and are given by Simon (1955). With a potential we follow the derivation by Kaufman (1956) of the critical pitch angles in velocity space for the loss of ions and electrons. We denote the value of the magnetic field in the midplane by B_0, and the value at the mirror by B_{max}. We consider a plasma potential which has value φ in the midplane and goes to zero at the mirror. Let W be the kinetic energy of a particle; then the total energy $H = W \pm e\varphi$ is a constant of the charged particle motion. We also assume that the magnetic moment $\lambda = W_\perp/B$ is a constant of the motion, where $W_\perp = \tfrac{1}{2}mv_\perp^2$ and $v_\perp$ is the component of velocity perpendicular to the magnetic field. The pitch angle in the midplane, α, is defined by

$$\sin^2 \alpha = \frac{W_\perp(\text{at } B_0)}{W(\text{at } B_0)} = \frac{\lambda B_0}{W(\text{at } B_0)} = \frac{B_0}{W(\text{at } B_0)} \frac{W_\perp(\text{at } B_{max})}{B_{max}}.$$

We define the critical pitch angle by the condition that $v_\parallel = 0$ at B_{max}, and since $\varphi = 0$ at B_{max} we have

$$W_\perp(\text{at } B_{max}) = H = W(\text{at } B_0) \pm e\varphi.$$

The critical pitch angle is then given by

$$\sin^2 \alpha_c^\pm = \frac{B_0}{B_{max}} \left(1 \pm \frac{e\varphi}{W(\text{at } B_0)}\right). \tag{34}$$

Electrons with energy $|W| < |e\varphi|$ are not lost, and electrons with $|W| > |e\varphi|$

are lost with probability $p_e = 1 - \cos \alpha_c$. Let the mirror ratio be given by $R = B_{max}/B_0$, then we have

$$p_e(v) = \begin{cases} \left\{1 - \left\{1 - \frac{1}{R}\left(1 - \frac{v_c^2}{v^2}\right)\right\}^{1/2}\right., & v \geq v_c, \\ 0, & v \leq v_c, \end{cases} \tag{35}$$

The above expression is also used in the steady-state treatment of Fowler and Rankin (1966).

The plasma potential is given by

$$e\varphi = \tfrac{1}{2} m_e v_c^2. \tag{36}$$

The procedure for determining v_c is the following: At every time step, $n_e(\tau)$ and $n_i(\tau)$ are computed from Eqs. (20) and (24), and the difference $n_i(\tau) - n_e(\tau)$ is also computed. During the buildup of plasma, electrons tend to be lost faster than ions. Since we wish to keep $n_e(\tau) = n_i(\tau)$, the above difference is compared to a preassigned small number. If the difference exceeds this number, then v_c is increased by an amount Δv_c in order to decrease the electron loss rate and the time step is repeated. This process is repeated until $n_i(\tau) - n_e(\tau)$ is sufficiently small, and the calculation continues. As the plasma builds up and the electron energy increases, the plasma potential also increases.

The term $p_e(x)$ is then

$$p_e(x) = \begin{cases} \left\{1 - \left\{1 - \frac{1}{R}\left(1 - \frac{x_c^2}{x^2}\right)\right\}^{1/2}\right., & x \geq x_c, \\ 0, & x \leq x_c, \end{cases} \tag{37}$$

where $v_0 x_c = v_c$. The term $p_i(x)$ which appears in Eq. (17) is then

$$p_i(x) = 1 - \left\{1 - \frac{1}{R}\left(1 + \frac{e\varphi}{\tfrac{1}{2}m_i v_0^2 x^2}\right)\right\}^{1/2}. \tag{38}$$

If the above square root becomes imaginary then $p_i(x)$ is equal to a given constant.

E. The Difference Equations and Method of Solution

We wish to solve the two nonlinear differential Eqs. (16) and (17) on the domain $0 \leq x \leq \infty$, $\tau \geq 0$, with the boundary conditions $f \to 0$, $g \to 0$ as

$x \to \infty$, and $\partial f/\partial x = \partial g/\partial x = 0$ at $x = 0$ for $\tau > 0$, or in the separated solution case we have $f = g = 0$ at $x = 0$. The initial distribution $f(x, 0)$ and $g(x, 0)$ are given.

For the numerical solution we choose a domain $0 \leq x \leq x_J$, where x_J is specified for each problem and is taken large enough to include the high velocity tail of the electron distribution. As the electrons increase in temperature, the distribution spreads out; thus the choice of x_J determines when the calculation must be stopped in order to preserve accuracy. At $x = x_J$, we take the boundary condition $f = g = 0$.

In the domain $0 \leq x \leq x_J$, $\tau \geq 0$, consider the finite-difference mesh defined by $x_j = j\,\Delta x$, $j = 0, 1, 2, \ldots, J$; $\tau^n = n\,\Delta \tau$, $n = 0, 1, 2, \ldots$. Let $f_j^n = f(x_j, \tau^n)$ and $g_j^n = g(x_j, \tau^n)$; $A_j^n = A(f_j^n, g_j^n, x_j, \tau^n)$, $B_j^n = B(f_j^n, g_j^n, x_j, \tau^n)$, etc. We define the first and second difference approximations by

$$(\delta f)_j^n = (f_{j+1}^n - f_{j-1}^n)/2\,\Delta x, \qquad (\delta^2 f)_j^n = (f_{j+1}^n - 2f_j^n + f_{j-1}^n)/(\Delta x)^2.$$

We approximate Eqs. (16) and (17) by the following implicit difference equations

$$(f_j^{n+1} - f_j^n)/\Delta \tau = \rho[A_j^{n+1}(\delta^2 f)_j^{n+1} + B_j^{n+1}(\delta f)_j^{n+1} + C_j^{n+1} f_j^{n+1} + D_j^{n+1}]$$
$$+ (1 - \rho)[A_j^n(\delta^2 f)_j^n + B_j^n(\delta f)_j^n + C_j^n f_j^n + D_j^n],$$

$$(g_j^{n+1} - g_j^n)/\Delta \tau = \rho[F_j^{n+1}(\delta^2 g)_j^{n+1} + G_j^{n+1}(\delta g)_j^{n+1} + H_j^{n+1} g_j^{n+1} + L_j^{n+1}]$$
$$+ (1 - \rho)[F_j^n(\delta^2 g)_j^n + G_j^n(\delta g)_j^n + H_j^n g_j^n + L_j^n],$$

where $\tfrac{1}{2} \leq \rho \leq 1$. We wish to solve these equations for the unknowns f_j^{n+1} and g_j^{n+1}, $j = 0, 1, 2, \ldots, J$.

We write the above difference equations as a set of simultaneous algebraic equations:

$$\alpha_j^{n+1} f_{j+1}^{n+1} - (1 + \beta_j^{n+1}) f_j^{n+1} + \gamma_j^{n+1} f_{j-1}^{n+1} = \psi_j^n, \tag{39}$$

$$\zeta_j^{n+1} g_{j+1}^{n+1} - (1 + \eta_j^{n+1}) g_j^{n+1} + \theta_j^{n+1} g_{j-1}^{n+1} = \varphi_j^n, \tag{40}$$

for $j = 1, 2, \ldots, J - 1$. The coefficients are defined by

$$\alpha_j^n = \rho \frac{\Delta \tau}{\Delta x}\left[\frac{A_j^n}{\Delta x} + \tfrac{1}{2} B_j^n\right], \qquad \beta_j^n = \rho\,\Delta \tau \left[\frac{2 A_j^n}{(\Delta x)^2} - C_j^n\right],$$

$$\gamma_j^n = \rho \frac{\Delta \tau}{\Delta x}\left[\frac{A_j^n}{\Delta x} - \tfrac{1}{2} B_j^n\right],$$

$$\psi_j^n = -\frac{1-\rho}{\rho}\alpha_j^n f_{j+1}^n - \left(1 - \frac{1-\rho}{\rho}\beta_j^n\right)f_j^n - \frac{1-\rho}{\rho}\gamma_j^n f_{j-1}^n$$
$$- \rho\,\Delta\tau D_j^{n+1} - (1-\rho)\,\Delta\tau D_j^n,$$

$$\zeta_j^n = \rho\frac{\Delta\tau}{\Delta x}\left[\frac{F_j^n}{\Delta x} + \tfrac{1}{2}G_j^n\right], \qquad \eta_j = \rho\,\Delta\tau\left[\frac{2F_j^n}{(\Delta x)^2} - H_j^n\right],$$

$$\theta_j^n = \rho\frac{\Delta\tau}{\Delta x}\left[\frac{F_j^n}{\Delta x} - \tfrac{1}{2}G_j^n\right],$$

$$\varphi_j^n = -\frac{1-\rho}{\rho}\zeta_j^n g_{j+1}^n - \left(1 - \frac{1-\rho}{\rho}\eta_j^n\right)g_j^n - \frac{1-\rho}{\rho}\theta_j^n g_{j-1}^n$$
$$- \rho\,\Delta\tau L_j^{n+1} - (1-\rho)\,\Delta\tau L_j^n.$$

In Eqs. (39) and (40) we have the unknowns f_j^{n+1}, g_j^{n+1}, $j = 1, \ldots, J-1$ on the left-hand side of the equation, and the known quantities on the right-hand side. We are interested in solving these equations for the interior points $j = 1, \ldots, J-1$, since the boundary conditions at $x = 0$ and $x = x_J$ determine the solutions for $j = 0$ and $j = J$. Consequently, we do not have to worry about singularities at $x = 0$ in the coefficients. The system given by Eqs. (39) and (40) is nonlinear in the unknowns f_j^{n+1}, g_j^{n+1}. If we extrapolate the coefficients α_j^{n+1}, β_j^{n+1}, etc., from their values at the previous times τ^n, τ^{n-1}, then Eqs. (39) and (40) become a linear algebraic system in the unknowns f_j^{n+1}, g_j^{n+1}. The procedure is to extrapolate the coefficients and solve the linear system, then compute the coefficients α_j^{n+1}, β_j^{n+1}, etc., with the new values of f_j^{n+1}, g_j^{n+1}. This procedure works very well since the coefficients change in a very smooth manner with time.

We shall now give the method of solving the linearized equations. In Eq. (39) let

$$f_{j-1}^{n+1} = e_{j-1}^{n+1} f_j^{n+1} + d_{j-1}^{n+1}, \tag{41}$$

where e, d are to be determined. Then Eq. (39) becomes

$$\alpha_j^{n+1} f_{j+1}^{n+1} - (1 + \beta_j^{n+1}) f_j^{n+1} + \gamma_j^{n+1} e_{j-1}^{n+1} f_j^{n+1} + \gamma_j^{n+1} d_{j-1}^{n+1} = \psi_j^n,$$

or

$$f_j^{n+1} = \frac{\alpha_j^{n+1} f_{j+1}^{n+1} + \gamma_j^{n+1} d_{j-1}^{n+1} - \psi_j^n}{1 + \beta_j^{n+1} - \gamma_j^{n+1} e_{j-1}^{n+1}}.$$

From Eq. (41) we can define

$$e_j^{n+1} = \frac{\alpha_j^{n+1}}{1 + \beta_j^{n+1} - \gamma_j^{n+1} e_{j-1}^{n+1}}, \qquad d_j^{n+1} = \frac{\gamma_j^{n+1} d_{j-1}^{n+1} - \psi_j^n}{1 + \beta_j^{n+1} - \gamma_j^{n+1} e_{j-1}^{n+1}}, \qquad (42)$$

$$j = 1, \ldots, J - 1.$$

In Eq. (40) let

$$g_{j-1}^{n+1} = a_{j-1}^{n+1} g_j^{n+1} + b_{j-1}^{n+1}, \qquad (43)$$

then

$$a_j^{n+1} = \frac{\zeta_j^{n+1}}{1 + \eta_j^{n+1} - \theta_j^{n+1} a_{j-1}^{n+1}}, \qquad b_j^{n+1} = \frac{\theta_j^{n+1} b_{j-1}^{n+1} - \varphi_j^n}{1 + \eta_j^{n+1} - \theta_j^{n+1} a_{j-1}^{n+1}}, \qquad (44)$$

$$j = 1, 2, \ldots, J - 1.$$

From the boundary conditions at $z = 0$ we take $f_0^{n+1} = f_1^{n+1}$, $g_0^{n+1} = g_1^{n+1}$, so we have $e_0^{n+1} = 1$, $d_0^{n+1} = 0$, $a_0^{n+1} = 1$, $b_0^{n+1} = 0$ for all n. The computation procedure is to calculate e_j^{n+1}, d_j^{n+1}, a_j^{n+1}, b_j^{n+1}, $j = 1, \ldots, J - 1$, from the recursion formulas (42) and (44); set $f_J^{n+1} = 0$, $g_J^{n+1} = 0$, and then calculate f_j^{n+1}, g_j^{n+1}, $j = 0, 1, 2, \ldots, J - 1$ from Eqs. (41) and (43).

At each time step we compute the number density and average energy of the electrons and ions as given by Eqs. (20), (21), (24), and (25). If Eqs. (16) and (17) arc solved without source and loss terms, for an arbitrary initial distribution function the above integrals should all be constant and provide computational checks for the program. We find that the best results are obtained when the parameter ρ that appears in the difference equations is set equal to 1.

IV. Two-Dimensional (Nonisotropic) Problems

A. Boundary Conditions and Independent Variables in Velocity Space

We now consider problems in which the assumption of isotropic or pseudo-isotropic ion distributions is removed. The only restrictions that we wish to place on the ion distribution are those mentioned in Section II concerning azimuthal symmetry and reflection symmetry about the midplane. The two possible pairs of independent variables which are then most suitable are v and θ, or v and μ, where $\mu = \cos \theta$. For regions of velocity space in which a loss angle is assumed to exist, there is little difference in the two choices. One then demands that the distribution function vanish at $\theta = \theta_L$ or $\mu = \cos\theta_L$ (BenDaniel and Allis, 1962). Indeed, if the mirror ratio is small, the problem is restricted to values of θ relatively near $\pi/2$, and then $\cos\theta \approx \pi/2 - \theta$. So the two coordinates differ only by a transformation which is approximately linear.

However, in problems where one wants to observe the relaxation of a distribution in the absence of a loss cone or other constraints, then the problem must be solved over all of velocity space. Furthermore, in the presence of the ambipolar potential, the electron distribution extends to $\theta = 0$ and $\theta = \pi$ at low velocities. In these cases, there is no clear-cut boundary condition which can be applied to the distribution function at $\mu = \pm 1$ in (v, μ) space. In (v, θ) space, however, the following conditions must hold:

$$f(0, \theta) \text{ must be the same for all } \theta, \tag{45}$$

$$\partial f/\partial v(0, \pi/2) = 0, \tag{46}$$

$$\partial f/\partial \theta(v, 0) = \partial f/\partial v(v, \pi) = 0. \tag{47}$$

The first is true because $v = 0$ corresponds to the same point (the origin) for all θ. The last two conditions are a result of the requirement that the distribution be azimuthally symmetric. Using the transformation from Cartesian to polar coordinates, it can be shown that

$$\frac{\partial f}{\partial v} = \frac{\partial f}{\partial v_x} v \sin\theta \cos\phi + \frac{\partial f}{\partial v_y} \sin\theta \sin\phi + \frac{\partial f}{\partial v_z} \cos\theta, \tag{48}$$

$$\frac{\partial f}{\partial \theta} = \frac{\partial f}{\partial v_x} v \cos\theta \cos\phi + \frac{\partial f}{\partial v_y} v \cos\theta \sin\phi - \frac{\partial f}{\partial v_z} v \sin\theta. \tag{49}$$

Approaching the v_z-axis, which is the axis of symmetry, we must have $\partial f/\partial v_x = \partial f/\partial v_y = 0$, for to do otherwise would either violate the symmetry conditions or lead to a discontinuity in $\partial f/\partial v_x$ or $\partial f/\partial v_y$, which is nonphysical. Under this restriction, Eqs. (48) and (49) lead directly to the conditions given by Eqs. (46) and (47).

Equations (45) and (46) are valid in (v, μ) space, but Eq. (47) is not, because

$$\frac{\partial f}{\partial \mu} = -\frac{1}{\sin\theta} \frac{\partial f}{\partial \theta},$$

and this leads to an indeterminacy in $\partial f/\partial \mu$. In order to avoid restriction to loss-angle boundary conditions, we therefore choose to solve the problem in (v, θ) space.

B. THE ION FOKKER–PLANCK OPERATOR

The transformation of Eq. (3) to polar coordinates and its subsequent specialization to a two-component system is outlined in Appendix A. The resulting form of the Fokker–Planck equation given by Eq. (3) is:

$$\frac{1}{\Gamma_i}\frac{\partial f_i}{\partial t} = \frac{1}{2}\frac{\partial^2 g_i}{\partial v^2}\frac{\partial^2 f_i}{\partial v^2} + \left[\frac{1}{v^2}\frac{\partial^2 g_i}{\partial v\,\partial\theta} - \frac{1}{v^3}\frac{\partial g_i}{\partial\theta}\right]\frac{\partial^2 f_i}{\partial f\,\partial\theta}$$

$$+ \frac{1}{2}\left[\frac{1}{v^4}\frac{\partial^2 g_i}{\partial\theta^2} + \frac{1}{v^3}\frac{\partial g_i}{\partial v}\right]\frac{\partial^2 f_i}{\partial\theta^2}$$

$$+ \left[\frac{1}{2v^3}\frac{\partial^2 g_i}{\partial\theta^2} + \frac{\cot\theta}{2v^3}\frac{\partial g_i}{\partial\theta} + \frac{1}{v^2}\frac{\partial g_i}{\partial v}\right]\frac{\partial f_i}{\partial v}$$

$$+ \left[\frac{1}{v^4\sin^2\theta}\left(1 - \frac{\cos^2\theta}{2}\right)\frac{\partial g_i}{\partial\theta} - \frac{1}{v^3}\frac{\partial^2 g_i}{\partial v\,\partial\theta} + \frac{\cot\theta}{2v^3}\frac{\partial g_i}{\partial v}\right]\frac{\partial f_i}{\partial\theta}$$

$$+ \frac{\partial C}{\partial v}\frac{\partial f_i}{\partial v} + \frac{1}{v^2}\frac{\partial C}{\partial\theta}\frac{\partial f_i}{\partial\theta}$$

$$+ 4\pi\left(\frac{\gamma f_e}{Z^2} + f_i\right)f_i + \frac{S}{\Gamma_i}, \tag{50}$$

where $\gamma = m_i/m_e$, and

$$C(v,\theta) = \frac{(1-\gamma)}{Z^2}\int_0^\infty v'^2\,dv'\int_0^\pi \sin\theta'\,d\theta'\,f_e(v',\theta')\Lambda(v',\theta';v,\theta),$$

$$g_i(v,\theta) = \int_0^\infty v'^2\,dv'\int_0^\pi \sin\theta'\,d\theta'\left[\frac{f_e(v',\theta')}{Z^2} + f_i(v',\theta')\right]\Omega(v',\theta';v,\theta),$$

where Λ and Ω are defined in terms of the complete elliptic integrals K and E as follows:

$$\Lambda = (4/q)K(p/q), \qquad \Omega = 4qE(p/q),$$

where

$$p = (4vv' \sin \theta \sin \theta')^{1/2},$$
$$q = [v^2 + v'^2 - 2vv'(\cos \theta \cos \theta' - \sin \theta \sin \theta')]^{1/2}.$$

C. The Source Term

Since some of the problems which we solve that involve a source are modeled after injection experiments such as ALICE (Futch, et al., 1966), in what follows we assume that the input current is of a nature appropriate to such experiments. We place no restriction on the shape of the source in velocity space, i.e., the functional dependence of S on v and θ, but we assume that the total input current, defined by

$$I = \int S(\mathbf{v}) \, d\mathbf{v}, \qquad (51)$$

is given by

$$I = I_0 + I'n.$$

The second term on the right permits one to include an increasing collisional ionization with increasing density. Upon introduction of spatial dependence into the problem, a functional dependence of I_0 and I' on the space coordinate will be defined.

D. Difference Methods

In this section, the subscript denoting particle species will be dropped to avoid confusion.

1. The Difference Mesh

Figure 3 gives a schematic illustration of the mesh used in differencing the nonisotropic Fokker–Planck operator. The subscripts i and j are used to denote different θ values and v values, respectively. The superscript n is used to denote different discrete points in time, when necessary, We then identify functions in velocity space by $f(v_j, \theta_i, t^n)$ by $f_{i,j}^n$, etc.

We include the capability of varying the mesh spacing in both the v and θ meshes. This is done for several reasons. First, since the distribution functions

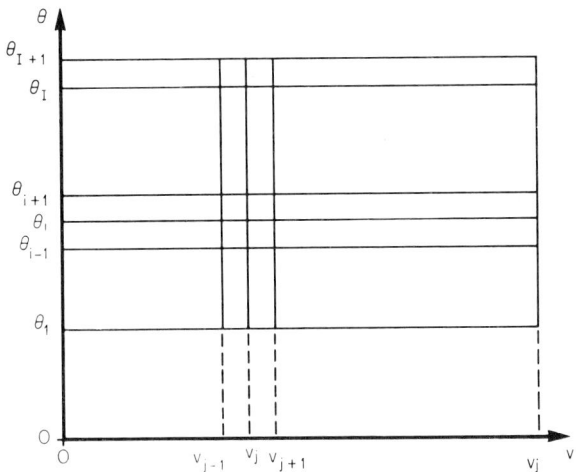

FIG. 3. Difference mesh in velocity space: $\theta_1 = \theta_{LC}$, $\theta_I = \pi/2$, $v_1 = 0$.

are found to decay rapidly at larger velocities (e.g., the Maxwellian "tail"), the larger values of v are not as important, and a wider v-spacing is justified in such regions. This is especially true if cold electrons are included in the calculation, since the ensuing cooling effect virtually eliminates high-energy ions. Also, in the presence of an ambipolar potential, the ion distribution must be zero up to a certain minimum velocity, and it is clearly not efficient to waste a dense mesh spacing in the low velocity regions where the potential will eventually eliminate the distribution function. For these reasons, the best v-spacing is one which increases with increasing v in problems in which no potential is assumed present, but one in which the v-spacing is most dense in the middle and increases at both large and small v if a potential does exist.

A variable θ-spacing is convenient if one wishes to use certain quadrature formulas which involve unequal spacing to calculate integrals over θ. For example, Gaussian quadrature has been employed in a code written to solve problems in the complete velocity space. Apart from the convenience and accuracy of Gaussian quadrature, it was felt that the use of this particular spacing rather than equal spacing improved the accuracy of the solution of the difference equation for the following reason: The boundary condition at $\theta = 0$ is then $\partial f / \partial \theta = 0$, and if one approximates this condition by $f^n_{2,j} = f^n_{1,j}$, it is more accurate to have $\theta_2 - \theta_1$ relatively small. Gaussian quadrature places just such a requirement on this first spacing. However, if a loss angle exists, the boundary condition at $\theta = \theta_{LC}$ is $f(v, \theta_{LC}) = 0$, and no advantage seems to be gained by using a variable spacing in this case. Therefore, in such problems an equal θ-spacing is employed.

The quadrature formula sometimes used for integrals over θ and the one always used for integrals over v is Simpson's rule. A generalization of Simpson's rule for unequal mesh spacing is required for integrals over v. It is given in Appendix B. In Fig. 3 note that one mesh point in θ is included beyond $\theta = \pi/2$. This is necessary in treating the boundary condition at $\theta = \pi/2$ as being the symmetry condition $f(v, \theta) = f(v, \pi - \theta)$; the reason for this will be given in Appendix D.

The distribution is truncated at some value of v, denoted by v_J, at which it must be established that the distribution function is so small as to be negligible. Since the mechanics of Coulomb collisions cause less energetic particles to be lost more rapidly, it is important to occasionally check this approximation in problems in which cooling due to less energetic species is not sufficient to prevent a large increase in average ion energy. If this occurs, an artificial ion loss that may not be negligible will appear at the truncation velocity.

2. Calculation of the Coefficients in the Fokker–Planck Operator

Equation (50) shows that the coefficients of the partial differential equation to be solved involve derivatives of the function $g(v, \theta)$. We shall describe a procedure for evaluating these coefficients that is essentially the same as that of Roberts and Carr (1960), except that we allow for a variable mesh spacing.

In evaluating $g(v, \theta)$, it is important to note that since g involves an integral of the distribution function over velocity space, g is relatively insensitive to changes in the shape of the distribution. For this reason, it is not necessary to recalculate g at each time step. The frequency of recalculation depends on the rapidity of the change of shape of f. Empirically, we find that if one uses a time step that is near the limit of computational stability it is necessary to recalculate g only every 25–100 time steps.

In calculating g, one first prepares a set of integration coefficients $a_{iji'j'}$ such that $g(v_j, \theta_i)$ can be approximated by

$$g_{ij} = \sum_{i'=1}^{I} \sum_{j'=1}^{J} a_{iji'j'} f_{i'j'}.$$

These coefficients involve the complete elliptic integral E, for which an approximation is obtained from Hastings (1955). They also involve the various functions of v_j, $v_{j'}$, θ_i, $\theta_{i'}$, indicated in Eq. (50), as well as the coefficients for the particular quadrature formulas used in the velocity space mesh. Because the total number of $a_{iji'j'}$ exceeds 300,000, it is necessary to put them on magnetic tape or discs and buffer them into the computer memory in small blocks during the computation of g.

The derivatives of g are calculated by straightforward differencing as follows:

$$\frac{\partial g}{\partial v} \to (g_{i,j+1} - g_{i,j-1})/2\,\Delta v_j,$$

$$\frac{\partial^2 g}{\partial v^2} \to \frac{(g_{i,j+1} - g_{i,j})/\Delta v_{j+\frac{1}{2}} - (g_{i,j} - g_{i,j-1})/\Delta v_{j-\frac{1}{2}}}{\Delta v_j},$$

$$\frac{\partial g}{\partial \theta} \to (g_{i+1,j} - g_{i-1,j})/2\,\Delta \theta_i \qquad (52)$$

$$\frac{\partial^2 g}{\partial \theta^2} \to \frac{(g_{i+1,j} - g_{i,j})/\Delta \theta_{i+\frac{1}{2}} - (g_{i,j} - g_{i-1,j})/\Delta \theta_{i-\frac{1}{2}}}{\Delta \theta_i},$$

$$\frac{\partial^2 g}{\partial v\,\partial \theta} \to \frac{(g_{i+1,j+1} - g_{i-1,j+1})/2\,\Delta \theta_i - (g_{i+1,j-1} - g_{i-1,j-1})/2\,\Delta \theta_i}{2\,\Delta v_j},$$

where we define

$$\Delta v_{j+\frac{1}{2}} = v_{j+1} - v_j, \qquad \Delta v_{j-\frac{1}{2}} = v_j - v_{j-1}, \qquad \Delta v_j = \tfrac{1}{2}(v_{j+1} - v_{j-1}),$$

and similar forms for the $\Delta\theta$'s.

It is important to note that, although g is insensitive to the shape of f, it is directly proportional to the total density. Therefore, the magnitude of the coefficients in Eq. (50) is changed each time step proportionally to the change in the magnitude of n. Although the factor $\log D_i$ is very insensitive to small changes in density and temperature, it is a simple matter to calculate it at each time step to maintain whatever accuracy and consistency may be involved. Other methods of computing g are discussed in Appendix C.

3. *Difference Equations and Their Solutions*

Equation (50) now assumes the form

$$\frac{\partial f}{\partial t} = a_1 \frac{\partial^2 f}{\partial v^2} + a_2 \frac{\partial^2 f}{\partial v\,\partial \theta} + a_3 \frac{\partial^2 f}{\partial \theta^2} + b_1 \frac{\partial f}{\partial v} + b_2 \frac{\partial f}{\partial \theta} + cf + S. \qquad (53)$$

This is a parabolic equation with two space dimensions. ("Space dimensions" refers to the analogy to the heat conduction equation.) The Peaceman and Rachford (1955) alternating-direction implicit (ADI) method is a finite-difference scheme particularly adaptable to this type of equation. The term involving the mixed second derivative can be handled explicitly in the straightforward manner indicated by Eqs. (52), but it seems to be a primary factor in contributing to numerical instability when the time step is increased. It is difficult to analyze the stability of the solution to the difference scheme with the mixed derivative term present, and we forgo any such attempt. However, one has the intuitive feeling that if some degree of implicitness can be introduced into the computation of this term, numerical stability might be enhanced. It is possible to do this, and it is found that stability is improved in the case of problems involving the complete velocity space. In fact, the time step can be increased by a factor of 10 or more. However, the improvement is not as striking, if it exists at all, in the case when loss-cone boundary conditions are imposed.

We now write the difference equations in their final form. In the ADI method, particular attention is given to the point in time at which the differences are formed. A single time step is cut in half, i.e., let $t^{n+\frac{1}{2}} = t^n + \Delta t/2$ and $t^{n+1} = t^{n+\frac{1}{2}} + \Delta t/2 = t^n + \Delta t$. We have

$$\frac{f_{i,j}^{n+\frac{1}{2}} - f_{i,j}^n}{\Delta t/2} = a_{1i,j} \left[\frac{(f_{i,j+1}^{n+\frac{1}{2}} - f_{i,j}^{n+\frac{1}{2}})/\Delta v_{j+\frac{1}{2}} - (f_{i,j}^{n+\frac{1}{2}} - f_{i,j-1}^{n+\frac{1}{2}})\Delta v_{j-\frac{1}{2}}}{\Delta v_j} \right]$$

$$+ \frac{a_{2i,j}}{2} \left[\frac{f_{i,j+1}^{n+\frac{1}{2}} - f_{i,j-1}^{n+\frac{1}{2}} - f_{i-1,j+1}^{n+\frac{1}{2}} + f_{i-1,j-1}^{n+\frac{1}{2}}}{2\,\Delta v_j\,\Delta\theta_{i-\frac{1}{2}}} \right]$$

$$+ \frac{a_{2i,j}}{2} \left[\frac{f_{i+1,j+1}^n - f_{i+1,j-1}^n - f_{i,j+1}^n + f_{i,j-1}^n}{2\,\Delta v_j\,\Delta\theta_{i+\frac{1}{2}}} \right]$$

$$+ a_{3i,j} \left[\frac{(f_{i+1,j}^n - f_{i,j}^n)\Delta\theta_{i+\frac{1}{2}} - (f_{i,j}^n - f_{i-1,j}^n)/\Delta\theta_{i-\frac{1}{2}}}{\Delta\theta_i} \right]$$

$$+ b_{1i,j} \left[\frac{f_{i,j+1}^{n+\frac{1}{2}} - f_{i,j-1}^{n+\frac{1}{2}}}{2\,\Delta v_j} \right] + b_{2i,j} \left[\frac{f_{i+1,j}^n - f_{i-1,j}^n}{2\,\Delta\theta_i} \right]$$

$$+ \frac{c_{i,j}}{2} f_{i,j}^{n+\frac{1}{2}} + \frac{c_{i,j}}{2} f_{i,j}^n + S_{i,j}, \qquad (54)$$

$$\frac{f_{i,j}^{n+1} - f_{i,j}^{n+\frac{1}{2}}}{\Delta t/2} = a_{1i,j} \left[\frac{(f_{i,j+1}^{n+\frac{1}{2}} - f_{i,j}^{n+\frac{1}{2}})/\Delta v_{j+\frac{1}{2}} - (f_{i,j}^{n+\frac{1}{2}} - f_{i,j-1}^{n+\frac{1}{2}})/\Delta v_{j-\frac{1}{2}}}{\Delta v_j} \right]$$

$$+ \frac{a_{2i,j}}{2} \left[\frac{f_{i,j+1}^{n+1} - f_{i-1,j}^{n+1} - f_{i+1,j-1}^{n+1} + f_{i-1,j-1}^{n+1}}{2\,\Delta v_{j-\frac{1}{2}}\,\Delta\theta_i} \right]$$

$$+ \frac{a_{2i,j}}{2} \left[\frac{f_{i+1,j+1}^{n+\frac{1}{2}} - f_{i-1,j+1}^{n+\frac{1}{2}} - f_{i+1,j}^{n+\frac{1}{2}} + f_{i-1,j}^{n+\frac{1}{2}}}{2\,\Delta v_{j+\frac{1}{2}}\,\Delta\theta_i} \right]$$

$$+ a_{3i,j} \left[\frac{(f_{i+1,j}^{n+1} - f_{i,j}^{n+1})/\Delta\theta_{i+\frac{1}{2}} - (f_{i,j}^{n+1} - f_{i-1,j}^{n+1})/\Delta\theta_{i-\frac{1}{2}}}{\Delta\theta_i} \right]$$

$$+ b_{1i,j} \left[\frac{f_{i,j+1}^{n+\frac{1}{2}} - f_{i,j-1}^{n+\frac{1}{2}}}{2\,\Delta v_j} \right] + b_{2i,j} \left[\frac{f_{i+1,j}^{n+1} - f_{i-1,j}^{n+1}}{2\,\Delta\theta_i} \right]$$

$$+ \frac{c_{i,j}}{2} f_{i,j}^{n+1} + \frac{c_{i,j}}{2} f_{i,j}^{n+\frac{1}{2}} + S_{i,j}. \qquad (55)$$

The essence of the method is that the differencing is done implicitly in one direction (the v-direction) and explicitly in the other on the first half time step, and the situation is reversed on the second half time step. (The coefficients a_1, a_2, etc., as well as S, should all have a superscript n in both equations, but it has been deleted for clarity.) A standard technique is available for solving Eqs. (54) and (55). The details are presented in Appendix D.

It should be pointed out that the reason for using the ADI method is to gain an advantage over a completely explicit differencing scheme in terms of the maximum time step that can be achieved while maintaining numerical stability. In heat conduction problems with constant coefficients in cartesian coordinates, this method can be shown to be unconditionally stable. It is empirically found that this is not the case in the present problem. However, investigation of predicted stability conditions for explicit differencing schemes leads one to believe that the ADI method affords a considerable improvement.

This completes a discussion of the method of relaxing the nonisotropic Fokker–Planck equation in the absence of electrons and ambipolar potential. As we shall see, introduction of the electrons will, under the assumptions that will be made, affect the ion equation only through the addition of some relatively simple terms to the coefficients of the differential equation. Furthermore, introduction of the potential will affect it only by requiring that the boundaries of the ion distribution be varied in a somewhat complicated fashion. The form of the right-hand side of Eq. (1) is not altered at all when a spatial dependence is introduced. Therefore, the preceding discussion is essentially a complete analysis of the method of calculation of df/dt for all the problems that we shall consider. In anticipation of some calculations discussed in Section IV,H,2, we also point out that the preceding development applies equally well to a description of the self-collisions of electrons.

E. APPLICATIONS FOR SINGLE SPECIES OF PARTICLE

1. *Relaxation of an Arbitrary Distribution Function to a Maxwellian*

Solving for the relaxation of an anisotropic distribution allows one to observe the approach to isotropy, as well as the approach to thermal equilibrium. Figures 4 and 5 show plots of the distribution function at various times during such a calculation. In this example, protons were assumed to be initially distributed according to

$$f(v, \theta) = N \exp\{-(v - 1)^2 - (\theta - \pi/2)^2\}$$

where v is in units of 1.702×10^8 cm/sec, which corresponds to 15 kV protons, and N is a normalization constant adjusted to give a density of 5×10^{11} cm^{-3}.

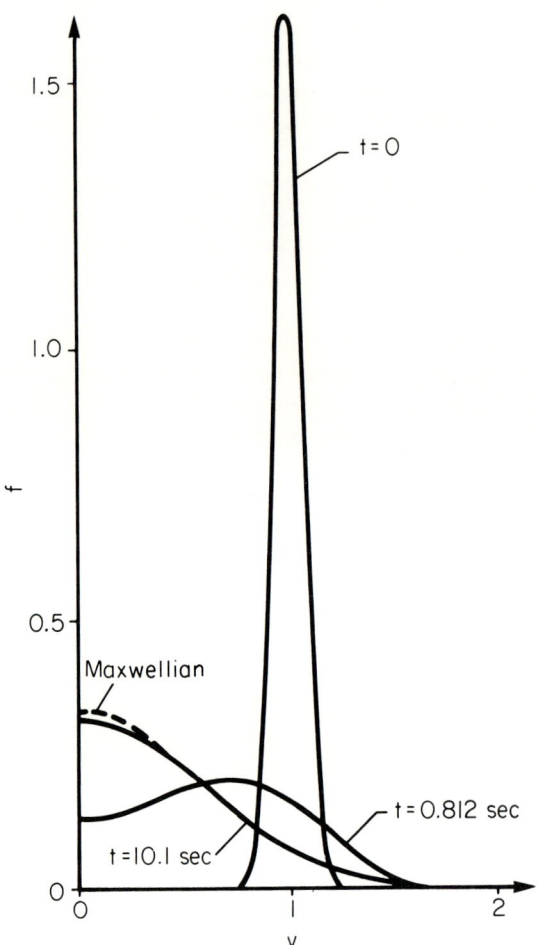

Fig. 4. Relaxation to a Maxwellian: f vs v at $\theta = \pi/2$; $f(t=0) \sim \exp(-100(v-1)^2 - 10(\theta - \pi/2)^2)$, $n = 5 \times 10^{11}$ cm^{-3}, $\langle E \rangle = 15.37$ kV.

The dashed line in Fig. 4 shows a Maxwellian of the same density and average energy.

In this problem, particles and energy should both be conserved. It is of interest to relate some of the effects of varying the computational techniques on the constancy of these quantities. The data shown was taken from a run in which, at early times, when the distribution changes most rapidly, the time step was 4.06 msec in real time, and the coefficients of the differential equation were recomputed every five time steps. Under these conditions, the number of particles remained constant to within 2.6%, and the energy remained constant

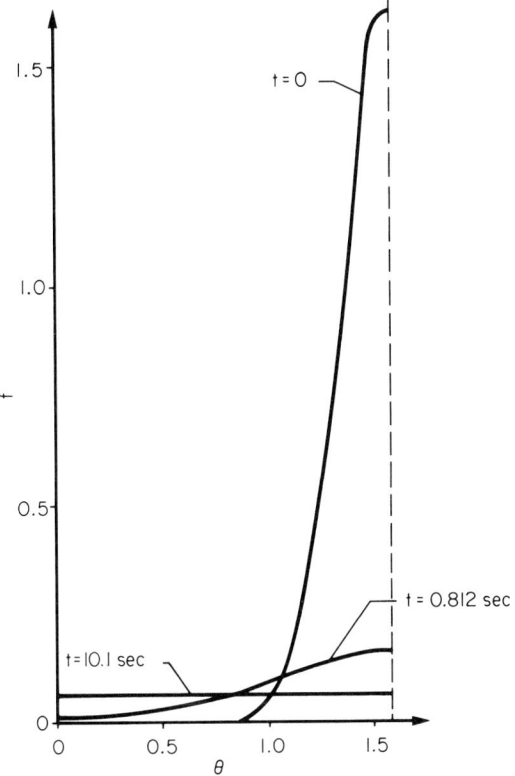

FIG. 5. Same problem as in Fig. 4, but f vs θ at $v = 1$.

to within 1.2%. When the time step remained the same, but the coefficients were calculated only every 50 time steps, these figures increased to 3.5% and 1.6%. And when, in addition to computing the coefficients only every 50 time steps, the time step was increased by a factor of 5, the inaccuracies were 7% in the density and 9.6% in the energy. Such figures present guidelines for estimation of accuracy in problems in which the loss cone is assumed existent, in which case there are no conserved quantities against which to check the accuracy of the code.

2. ALICE *Buildup Problems*

Now consider a problem involving a particle source; namely, that of simulating conditions in the ALICE experiment (Futch *et al.*, 1966), a neutral injection experiment with a mirror ratio of 2. The results of two different runs are shown in Fig. 6. In the first, the proton source was centered around 15 kV, with an energy spread of roughly one-fourth the total energy. The

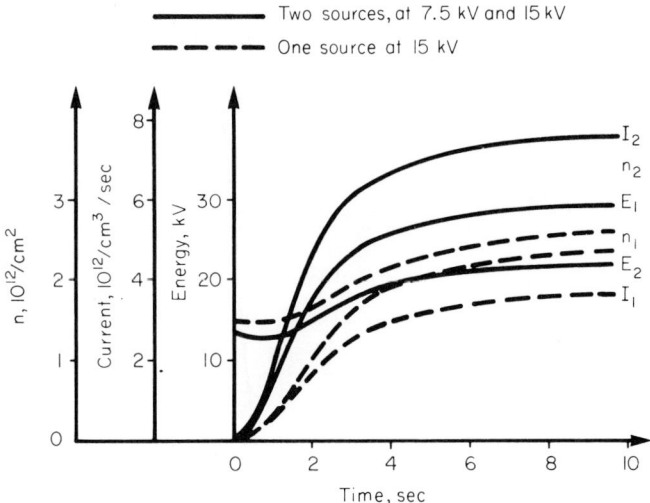

FIG. 6. ALICE buildup simulation including only ion–ion collisions; mirror ratio equals 2.

θ-dependence was arbitrarily chosen as a Gaussian function sharply peaked about $\theta = \pi/2$. The resulting shape for the source was defined as

$$S_1(v, \theta) = \begin{cases} 0, & v < (0.935), \\ \exp\{-10(\theta - \pi/2)^2\}, & 0.935 \leqslant v \leqslant 1.061, \\ 0, & 1.061 < v. \end{cases}$$

The total magnitude of the source was adjusted so that the total current was

$$I_1 = I_{01} + I_1'n,$$

where

$I_{01} = 1.6 \times 10^{-8}$ A/cm³ $= 9.99 \times 10^{10}$ particles/cm³/sec,

$I_1' = 2.4 \times 10^{-19}$ A $= 1.498$ particles/sec.

In the second run, two sources were included. The first was identical to that just described. The shape of the second was defined in exactly the same way, except that it was centered at 7.5 kV, and its total current was given by

$$I_2 = I_{02} + I_2'n,$$

where

$$I_{02} = 3.2 \times 10^{-9} \text{ A/cm}^3 = 1.997 \times 10^{10} \text{ particles/cm}^3/\text{sec},$$
$$I_2' = 1.7 \times 10^{-19} \text{ A} = 1.061 \text{ particles/sec}.$$

The parameters for the two sources were taken from realistic source structures in the ALICE experiment. Figure 6 shows the density, average energy, and current for the two runs. Figures 7 and 8 show the distribution function in the

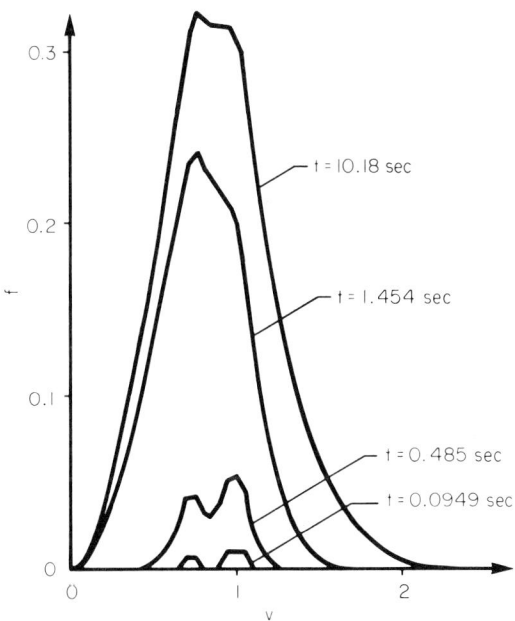

FIG. 7. Distribution function in two-source problem of Fig. 6; f vs v at $\theta = \pi/2$.

second run as a function of velocity and of θ. The data of Fig. 6 shows much higher densities than those experimentally observed. This is to be expected, since the effects of electrons and ambipolar potential have not been included at this stage.

3. *End-Loss Calculations in the Absence of a Source—2X Experiment*

As an example of the calculation of the decay of particle density due to end losses, consider an attempted simulation of conditions in the $2X$ device, an experiment with a mirror ratio of 1.33 (Coensgen *et al.*, 1967). In this experiment, a deuterium density of 2×10^{13} particles/cm^3 is observed 300 μsec after the start of the experiment; the calculation starts at this point. The energy spectrum of the distribution is measured at $\theta = \pi/2$, and we use this measured

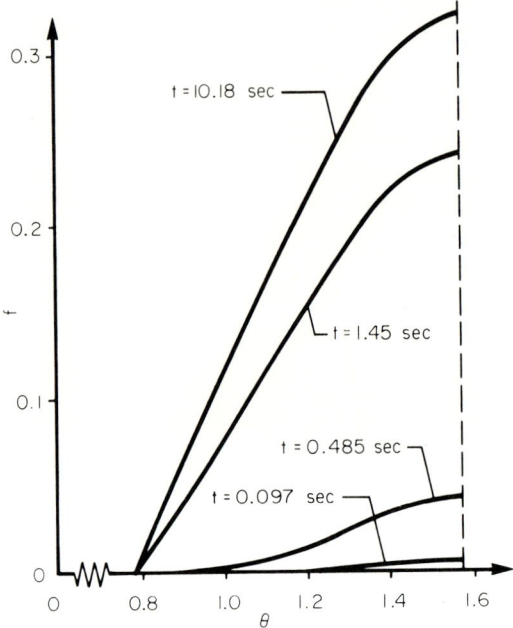

FIG. 8. Distribution function in two-source problem of Fig. 6; f vs θ at $v = 0.746$.

spectrum to obtain the functional dependence of the initial distribution on velocity. The problem is then solved using different initial functional dependences on θ, to determine the effect of various θ-dependences on the loss rates. Figure 9 is a plot of f vs v for a run in which the θ-dependence was a sharply peaked Gaussian. The data at 300 μsec is the initial, experimentally observed spectrum. Figure 10 shows f vs θ for the same run. Figure 11 shows density vs time for three different runs made with different initial θ-dependences:

(1) $f \sim \exp\{-100(\theta - \pi/2)^2\}$ (peaked I.C.),
(2) $f \sim 1 - \cos^2 \theta / \cos^2 \theta_{LC}$ ("normal mode" I.C.),
(3) $f \sim \begin{cases} 1, & |\pi/2 - \theta| < |\pi/2 - \theta_{LC}| \\ 0, & |\pi/2 - \theta| > |\pi/2 - \theta_{LC}| \end{cases}$ ("isotropic" I.C.).

One naturally expects these three configurations to be in the order of increasing initial loss rate, since the number of particles near the loss cone increases from (1) to (3), and this is borne out in Fig. 11.

It should be mentioned that the loss rates shown in Fig. 11 are all less than those experimentally observed. Again, this was to be expected, for the same reasons given in the case of the ALICE buildup calculations. These calculations are similar to those performed by Roberts and Carr (1960). In cases where results could be compared, the agreement in values of density and energy are within 5%.

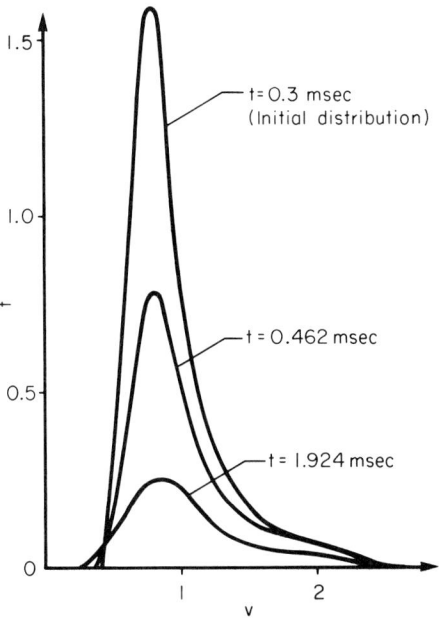

FIG. 9. Distribution function in $2X$ simulation including only ion–ion collisions; f vs v at $\theta = \pi/2$; mirror ratio equals 1.33.

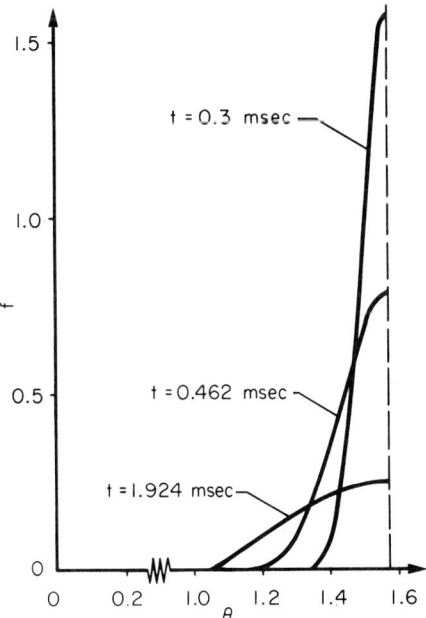

FIG. 10. Distribution function in $2X$ simulation; f vs θ at $v = 0.795$.

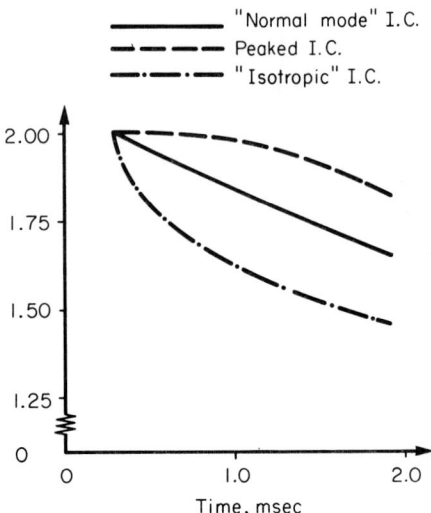

FIG. 11. Densities in $2X$ simulations for three different initial conditions; mirror ratio equals 1.33.

F. Method of Treating the Electron Distribution

We now consider the introduction of a distribution of electrons into the calculation. There are two formidable obstacles to a simultaneous solution of the Fokker–Planck equation for both ions and electrons, especially in problems with space dependence. The first is that the electron distribution varies on a much faster time scale than does the ion distribution. Therefore, it would be necessary to solve the equation using a much smaller time step than is necessary for the ion equation, and the calculation, which is long enough for ions alone, would require large amounts of computer time.

The second obstacle becomes apparent upon consideration of Eq. (50). When a second species is present, the function $C(v, \theta)$ must be calculated, and unless the distribution is isotropic, it involves the complete elliptic integral K. This function has a singularity when its argument is unity, which, in our problem, occurs at points where $\mathbf{v} = \mathbf{v}'$. Although this singularity is of course integrable, the calculation of $C(v, \theta)$ would be more difficult than the calculation of $g(v, \theta)$, which must be done in any case.

For these reasons it is desirable to make some simplifying assumptions concerning the electron distribution. Previous calculations (Killeen and Futch, 1968) indicate that at times long compared to electron relaxation times, but short on the ion time scale, the electron distribution is approximately Maxwellian, provided that an ambipolar potential exists at an energy somewhat above the average electron energy. Such a potential enables the low-energy electrons to be trapped, and the only appreciable deviation from a Maxwellian distribution that need be considered is a "hole" cut out of the tail of the distribution where the loss region for electrons appears.

Since these conditions are precisely those that we expect to prevail, we make the assumption that the electron distribution is given by

$$f_e(v) = \begin{cases} \dfrac{n_e \exp(-v^2/2v_e{}^3)}{2^{3/2} v_e{}^3}, & \text{if } v < v_{pe} \text{ or } v > v_{pe}, \\ & \text{but } \theta_L \leq \theta \leq \pi - \theta_L, \\ 0, & \text{if } v > v_{pe}, \text{ and} \\ & |\pi/2 - \theta| > \pi/2 - \theta_L, \end{cases} \quad (56)$$

where v_{pe} and θ_L are defined by Eq. (5). This is identical to the assumption made by Post (1961) and BenDaniel (1961) in their investigation of the ambipolar potential.

The two parameters n_e and v_e which characterize the electron distribution are functions of the time, which must be determined. The loss rate for particles with an isotropic distribution is given by Eq. (11). If we use the Maxwellian distribution given by Eq. (56) we can write the collisional electron loss rate as

$$\left(\frac{dn_e}{dt}\right)_c = \left(\frac{dn_e}{dt}\right)_{ce} + \left(\frac{dn_e}{dt}\right)_{ci},$$

where

$$\left(\frac{dn_e}{dt}\right)_{ce} = -\frac{4\,\Gamma_e n_e{}^2}{\pi\, v_e{}^3} \int_0^\infty \frac{dw}{w} \left[\frac{e^{-w^2/2}}{w} + \left(1 - \frac{1}{w^2}\right) \right.$$

$$\left. \cdot \left(\frac{\pi}{2}\right)^{1/2} \operatorname{erf}\!\left(\frac{w}{\sqrt{2}}\right) \right] e^{-w^2/2} p(w), \quad (57)$$

and

$$\left(\frac{dn_e}{dt}\right)_{ci} = -\left(\frac{2}{\pi}\right)^{1/2} \frac{Z^2 \Gamma_e n_e n_i}{v_e{}^3} \int_0^\infty \frac{dw}{w} \left(1 - \frac{m_e E_i}{m_i E_e w^2}\right) e^{-w^2/2} p(w), \quad (58)$$

with

$$p(w) = \begin{cases} \left\{ 1 - \left[1 - \dfrac{1}{R_m}\left(1 - \dfrac{w_p{}^2}{w^2}\right)\right]^{1/2}\right\}, & w \geq w_p \\ 0, & w < w_p \end{cases} \quad w_p = v_{pe}/v_e.$$

[erf(x) is the error function, erf(x) $=(2/\sqrt{\pi})\int_0^x e^{-t^2}\,dt$.] The equation for $n_e(t)$ is then

$$\frac{dn_e}{dt} = \left(\frac{dn_e}{dt}\right)_c + \left(\frac{dn_e}{dt}\right)_s \tag{59}$$

where $(dn_e/dt)_s$ is the electron source term which is given by Eq. (26).

It is simpler to deal with v_e^2 than v_e, because v_e^2 is proportional to electron energy. Ignoring the absence of particles in the loss region, the average electron energy is

$$E_e = \tfrac{3}{2} m_e v_e^2, \quad \text{where} \quad v_e = (kT_e/m_e)^{1/2}.$$

The electron energy is determined by the following three influences:

(1) ion–electron interactions.
(2) electron end losses.
(3) injection of electrons at some characteristic energy.

Let E_i and E_{es} be average ion energy and average electron source energy. Then define

$$v_i^2 = 2E_i/3m_i \quad \text{and} \quad v_{es}^2 = 2E_{es}/3m_e.$$

The parameter (Marx, 1968) characterizing the average energy of electrons undergoing loss through the mirrors is

$$v_{ec}^2 = \left(-\tfrac{1}{3}v_e^2\left\{\left[\frac{d}{dt}(n_e\langle w^2\rangle)\right]_{ce} + \left[\frac{d}{dt}(n_i\langle w^2\rangle)\right]_{ci}\right\}\right)\bigg/\left(\frac{dn_e}{dt}\right)_c,$$

where

$$\left[\frac{d}{dt}(n_e\langle w^2\rangle)\right]_{ce} = \frac{4}{\pi}\frac{\Gamma_e n_e^2}{v_e^3}\int_0^\infty w\,dw$$

$$\cdot\left[\frac{e^{-w^2/2}}{w} + \left(1 - \frac{1}{w^2}\right)\left(\frac{\pi}{2}\right)^{1/2}\mathrm{erf}\left(\frac{w}{\sqrt{2}}\right)\right]e^{-w^2/2}p(w),$$

$$\left[\frac{d}{dt}(n_e\langle w^2\rangle)\right]_{ci} = \sqrt{\frac{2}{\pi}}\,Z^2\,\frac{\Gamma_e n_e n_i}{v_e^3}\int_0^\infty w\,dw$$

$$\cdot\left(1 - \frac{m_e E_i}{m_i E_e w^2}\right)e^{-w^2/2}p(w).$$

The equation for v_e^2 is then

$$\frac{dv_e^2}{dt} = \left(\frac{dv_e^2}{dt}\right)_i + \frac{v_{ec}^2 - v_e^2}{n_e}\left(\frac{dn_e}{dt}\right)_c + \frac{v_{es}^2 - v_e^2}{n_e}\left(\frac{dn_e}{dt}\right)_s \qquad (60)$$

where

$$\left(\frac{dv_e^2}{dt}\right)_i = \frac{2\sqrt{2}}{3\sqrt{\pi}} Z^2 n_e \Gamma_e \left(v_i^2 - \frac{m_e}{m_i} v_e^2\right)(v_i^2 + v_e^2)^{3/2}.$$

This last is just the heating formula given in Spitzer (1962).

We now have two ordinary differential equations, Eqs. (59) and (60), which must be solved for the quantities n_e and v_e^2. This has been accomplished through application of a second-order Runge–Kutta method. The integrals in Eqs. (57) and (58) can be evaluated by Weddle's rule. An approximation for the error function is obtained from Hastings (1955).

G. Addition of the Ambipolar Potential and Second Particle Species to the Fokker–Planck Equation

1. *Method of Including the Effects of the Potential*

Before we discuss some results of the solution of the electron equations and their accuracy, it is necessary to describe the changes in the method of solution of the Fokker–Planck equation when the effects of the ambipolar potential and a second particle species are brought to bear on the particle distribution of interest.

The boundary in velocity space at which the distribution function must vanish is defined by Eq. (5) for any particle species and electrostatic potential. This boundary condition is approximated as follows: For a given j (point on the v mesh) find the value of i, call it i_0 such that θ_{i_0} is nearest $\theta_L(v_j)$ where the latter is evaluated from Eq. (5). The points $i_0(j), j$ in the velocity space mesh, then form a discrete set of points that approximate the loss boundary. When solving the difference equations, the arrays $E_{i,j}$ and $F_{i,j}$ defined in Appendix D are adjusted so that $f_{i_0(j),j}$ and all $f_{i,j}$ within the loss region are zero.

We have noted in Section II,B that the boundary conditions for a given sign of the potential vary considerably for species of different charge sign, or, equivalently, for different signs of the potential for a given species. When $\Phi(z) - \Phi(L)$ is positive, as it is in all situations considered here, the ion-loss boundary starts at $\theta = \pi/2$ at some v and asymptotically approaches θ_{LC}

as $v \to \infty$. Therefore, the ion boundary condition $f(v, \theta_L) = 0$ maintains the same form as $\Phi(z) - \Phi(L)$ increases from 0 to a finite positive value as time evolves. The electron boundary, on the other hand, starts at $\theta = 0$ at $v = v_{pe}$ and asymptotically approaches θ_{LC} from the opposite direction. The electron boundary conditions, then, are modified for $v < v_{pe}$, and are just those given by Eqs. (45)–(47) as being appropriate for problems in the complete velocity space. The arrays $E_{i,j}$ and $F_{i,j}$ defined in Appendix D must therefore be adjusted accordingly when solving the Fokker–Planck equation for electrons as described in Section IV,H,2.

2. Addition of a Second (Maxwellian) Particle Species

As noted in Section IV,F, the presence of a second particle species would be difficult to handle in the Fokker–Planck equation in general. However, the necessary coefficients are much easier to compute if the distribution of the other species is assumed to be isotropic. Under the additional assumption that the other species is Maxwellian, the coefficients can be evaluated in terms of exponentials and error functions.

We shall start from Eqs. (50), which are written for the ion Fokker–Planck equation with electrons present. Let

$$g^e(\mathbf{v}) = (Z^2)^{-1} \int d\mathbf{v}'\, f_e(\mathbf{v}') |\mathbf{v} - \mathbf{v}'|, \qquad g^i(\mathbf{v}) = \int d\mathbf{v}\, f_i(\mathbf{v}') |\mathbf{v} - \mathbf{v}'|,$$

so that

$$g_i(\mathbf{v}) = g^e(\mathbf{v}) + g^i(\mathbf{v}).$$

(Note that superscripts are used in the above equations to distinguish between the total g and the contributions from each species). If we have

$$f_e(v) = \frac{n_e \exp(-v^2/2v_e^2)}{(2\pi)^{3/2} v_e^3},$$

then

$$C(v) = \frac{4\pi}{Z^2}(1-\gamma) \int_0^v f_e(v') \frac{v'^2}{v}\, dv' + \int_v^\infty f_e(v') v'\, dv'$$

$$= \frac{1}{Z^2}(1-\gamma) \frac{n_e}{v} \operatorname{erf}(v/\sqrt{2}\,v_e),$$

and

$$g^e(v) = \frac{4\pi}{Z^2}\left[\int_0^v f_e(v')v\left(1 + \frac{1}{3}\frac{v'^2}{v^2}\right)v'^2\,dv' + \int_v^\infty f_e(v')\left(1 + \frac{1}{3}\frac{v^2}{v'^2}\right)v'^3\,dv'\right]$$

$$= \frac{n_e}{Z^2}\left[\left(\frac{2}{\pi}\right)^{1/2} v_e \exp(-v^2/2v_e^2) + v\,\mathrm{erf}(v/\sqrt{2}\,v_e) + \frac{v_e^2}{v}\,\mathrm{erf}(v/\sqrt{2}\,v_e)\right].$$

Since f_e, and therefore C and g_e, is independent of θ, inspection of Eq. (50) shows that we need the following three terms in addition to f_e:

$$\frac{\partial C}{\partial v} = \frac{n_e}{Z^2}(1-\gamma)\left[\left(\frac{2}{\pi}\right)^{1/2}\frac{\exp(-v^2/2v_e^2)}{vv_e} - \frac{1}{v^2}\,\mathrm{erf}(v/\sqrt{2}\,v_e)\right],$$

$$\frac{\partial g^e}{\partial v} = \frac{n_e}{Z^2}\left[\frac{v_e}{v}\left(\frac{2}{\pi}\right)^{1/2}\exp(-v^2/2v_e^2) + \left(1 - \frac{v_e^2}{v^2}\right)\mathrm{erf}(v/\sqrt{2}\,v_e)\right],$$

$$\frac{\partial^2 g^e}{\partial v^2} = \frac{n_e}{Z^2}\left[-2\frac{v_e}{v^2}\left(\frac{2}{\pi}\right)^{1/2}\exp(-v^2/2v_e^2) + 2\frac{v_e^2}{v^3}\,\mathrm{erf}(v/\sqrt{2}\,v_e)\right].$$

The necessary additions to the coefficients of the difference equation can easily be computed from the above equations at each time step for each value of j in the velocity mesh.

The error function is evaluated by an approximate formula from Hastings (1955), except when its argument is small. Note that all three of these equations involve a term like

$$G(x) = (2/\pi)^{1/2} e^{-x^2/2} - x^{-1}\,\mathrm{erf}(x/\sqrt{2}).$$

When x is small, the two terms on the right are nearly equal, and Hastings' approximation is not sufficiently accurate to permit accurate evaluation of their difference. In this case, one uses the first three terms of the Taylor expansion of $G(x)$, viz.,

$$G(x) = \left(\frac{2}{\pi}\right)^{1/2}\left[-\frac{x^2}{3} + \frac{x^4}{10} - \frac{x^6}{56}\right].$$

H. Solutions of the Ion Fokker–Planck Equation with Maxwellian Electrons and Ambipolar Potential Included

1. Procedure. Difficulties

We list here the sequence of calculations observed in each time step when solving simultaneously for the ion distribution function, the electron density and temperature, and the potential. It is very similar to that employed in Section III.

(a) The ion Fokker–Planck equation is advanced, using the electron density and temperature to obtain electron–ion collisional effects. The ambipolar potential is used to establish boundary conditions on the ions. The ion density and energy are calculated.

(b) The electron equations are solved, using the ion density and energy from the previous time step along with the ambipolar potential to determine the electron losses.

(c) The new electron density is compared to the ion density, and the change in electrons is compared to the change in ions. Since charge neutrality is to be maintained, if the electron density is less than the ion density, *and* the electron change is less than the ion change, the ambipolar potential is increased by a small amount and step (b) is repeated. This cycling is continued until either of the two conditions

$$n_e \geq n_i, \qquad \Delta n_e \geq \Delta n_i$$

is obtained.

On the other hand, if the ion density is less than the electron density, and the ion change is less than the change in electrons, the potential is decreased and step (b) is repeated, this cycling continuing until either

$$n_e \leq n_i \quad \text{or} \quad \Delta n_e \leq \Delta n_i.$$

The requirement on the change in densities keeps the electron density from getting too far ahead of the ion density, and vice versa. This could happen due to discrepancies in rates that might otherwise build up.

Several numerical difficulties present themselves when solving problems of this nature. At first, instead of step (c) in the form given above, an iterative procedure was employed to try to find the ambipolar potential with more precision. In other words, at each time step, Φ was given a series of positive or negative corrections, progressively smaller in magnitude, until $n_e = n_i$ to within some predetermined accuracy. It was found that this led to extremely erratic behavior, i.e., large positive and negative fluctuations in densities and potential. A close examination of the origin of this behavior showed that because the ion-loss boundary must make descrete jumps along the velocity space mesh, the accuracy of the losses in a single time step is not sufficient to determine the potential with such precision. Therefore, one can really not do better than to simply increase or decrease the potential and then wait for the densities to catch up with each other, even though this may take several time steps. Once one is resigned to this fact, it is found that the smaller the jumps in Φ that are allowed, the better the results. If ΔΦ is too large, the electron density tends to jump ahead of the ion density, etc., and again very erratic variations in the densities and the potential result. We shall discuss these difficulties again in connection with the solution of the spatially dependent problem, where they are even more severe.

2. *Results of Buildup Calculations. Adjustment of Electron Rates for Accuracy*

Figure 12 shows results of this scheme when applied to a buildup problem

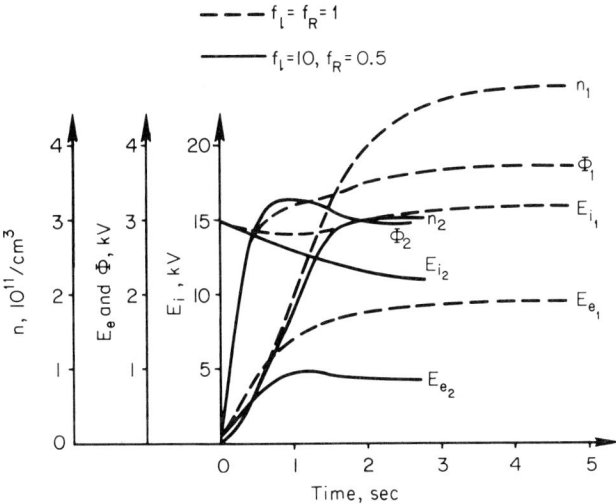

FIG. 12. Buildup problems with electrons and potential included, illustrating adjustment of factors in electron equations; mirror ratio equals 2.

with ion parameters similar to those described in Section IV,E,2. The total input current is the same as that given, but the shape of the source is now

$$S(v, \theta) \sim \exp\{-100(v-1)^2 - 10(\theta - \pi/2)^2\}.$$

The dashed lines in Fig. 12 show the results obtained using the electron equations as given in Section IV,F. After this run was made, a version of the code designed to solve the complete Fokker–Planck code for electrons with a Maxwellian ion background was set up. Inputs to this program were obtained from the steady-state data of the ion buildup problem; the potential was set at 3.75 kV and was not varied; the Maxwellian ion temperature was maintained at 15.8 kV; the input particle current was the same function of density, and the electron source energy was 0.1 kV. The steady-state values of the electron density and temperature were then found. A comparison of these results with those obtained from the ordinary differential equation used in the buildup problem is given in Table I. The error in the density is 35%, and

TABLE I

COMPARISON OF ELECTRON FOKKER–PLANCK CALCULATION WITH APPROXIMATE CALCULATION

	$n_e(10^{11}\text{ cm}^{-3})$	E_e (kV)
Electron Fokker–Planck equation	3.59	1.17
Buildup problem	4.84	1.90

the error in the energy is 62%. It is clear that this error is a result of inaccuracy in the terms $(dn_e/dt)_c$ in Eq. (57) and (58) and the term $(dv_e^2/dt)_i$ in Eq. (60). In particular, the electron heating rate due to electron–ion interactions appears to be too great. This seems to be in agreement with results obtained from the investigation of this effect by Killeen et al. (1962). The situation can be remedied by multiplying these two functions by constant factors, i.e., redefine the rates as

$$(dn_e/dt)_c = f_I(dn_e/dt)'_c, \qquad (dv_e^2/dt)_i = f_R(dv_e^2/dt)'_i,$$

where the primed quantities are the old rates defined in Eqs. (57), (58), and (60). The constant factors are determined empirically from a separate solution of the electron equations. It was found in this particular case that best agreement was obtained when

$$f_I = 10, \qquad f_R = 0.5.$$

That the largest deviation from unity occurs in f_I is somewhat surprising in view of the fact that the greatest discrepancy was originally in the energy rather than density. However, it is found that a slight change in f_R has a profound effect on the loss rate. Decreasing f_R reduces the loss rate if $E_i > E_e$, since the hotter the electrons are, the more rapidly they are lost. This necessitates a large increase in f_I to bring the loss rate back up.

The electron Fokker–Planck equation was solved again, with new inputs from the steady-state solution to the buildup problem. Table II exhibits the results. We see that much better agreement is obtained.

This introduction of constant factors in the electron equations enables one to ensure that they are adequately representing the more accurate Fokker–Planck equation. In particular, in buildup problems such as this, where

TABLE II

COMPARISON OF ELECTRON FOKKER–PLANCK CALCULATION WITH
APPROXIMATE CALCULATION WHEN $f_I = 10, f_R = 0.50$

	$n_e (10^{11}$ cm$^{-3})$	E_e (kV)
Electron Fokker–Planck equation	3.00	0.867
Buildup problem	3.02	0.887

steady-state solutions are sought, one could obtain as close agreement as desired by iterating on f_I and f_R over several different runs of the program.

The solid lines in Fig. 12 show the results of the buildup calculation when these new empirical factors are introduced. The steady-state electron energy is reduced as expected, and the potential is thereby lowered. The combination of these two effects reduces the ion energy, and the steady-state density is less than before, even though the potential is not as great.

Some profiles of the ion distribution function for the latter run discussed above are shown in Fig. 13. Note that the steady-state distribution is rather

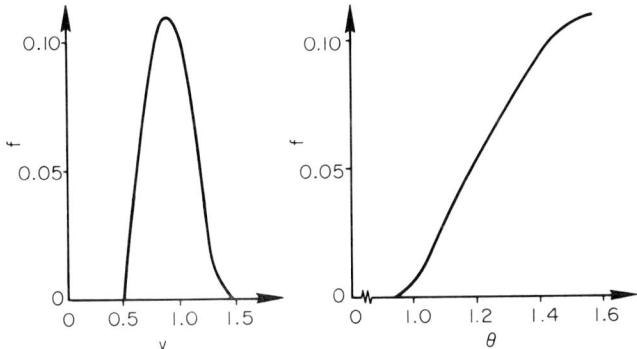

FIG. 13. Steady-state distribution function in second problem of Fig. 12; f vs v at $\theta = \pi/2$ and f vs θ at $v = 0.782$.

sharply peaked along the velocity coordinate. This fact is of importance in determining the effects of the loss-cone instability Post and Rosenbluth 1965, 1966. The shape of the source, which is sharply peaked, is sketched in the graph, but the shape of the source is found to have relatively little influence on the shape of the steady-state distribution. The real reason for the sharp peaking is that the cold electrons cool the ions and prevent them from spreading into the higher energy regions. The presence of the ambipolar potential places a lower bound on the ion energy, so the two effects cause the ion distribution to be squeezed into a relatively narrow energy range. Comparison of Figs. 6 and 12 show the large reduction in steady-state density brought about by electron and ambipolar effects.

3. *End-Loss Calculations*

The techniques outlined in Section IV,H,1 have also been successfully applied to calculations of end losses in the absence of a source, e.g., simulation of $2X$ experiments. Results of such a run are given in Figs. 14 and 15. This

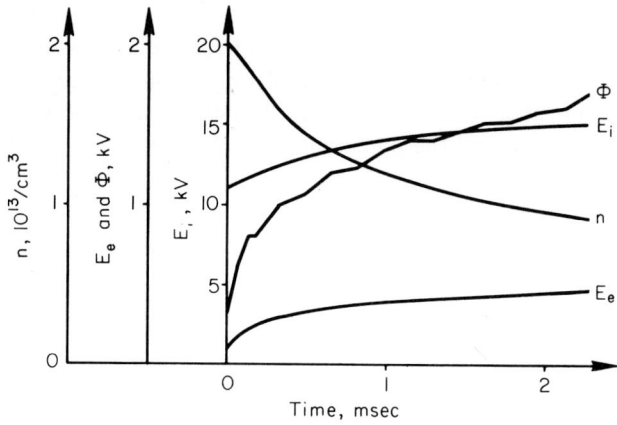

FIG. 14. Time evolution of $2X$ simulation with electron and ambipolar effects included; mirror ratio equals 1.33.

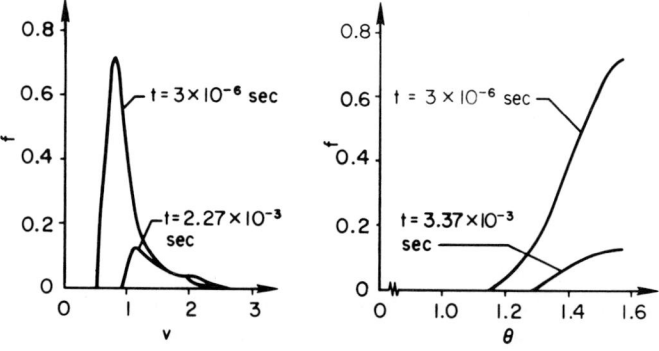

FIG. 15. Distribution functions in $2X$ problem of Fig. 14; f vs v at $\theta = \pi/2$, f vs θ at $v = 0.795$ (upper curve), and $v = 1.15$ (lower curve).

problem was set up to correspond to the calculations discussed in Section IV,E,3 and illustrated in Fig. 11. The initial distribution in velocity approximately corresponds to an experimentally measured distribution, and the initial angular distribution is sharply peaked. The mirror ratio is 1.33.

The addition of the ambipolar potential and electron cooling effects increases the loss rate considerably. It is found that it is difficult to match numerically the ion and electron loss rates in this type of calculation, and that the potential tends to increase monotonically, but irregularly, as the computation progresses. This behavior is exhibited in Fig. 14.

V. Nonisotropic Problems with Spatial Dependence of the Magnetic Field

A. METHOD OF SOLUTION OF THE PROBLEM WITH SPATIAL DEPENDENCE

1. *Departure from Conventional Difference Techniques. Integration along Orbits*

We now return to consideration of Eq. (1) in order to discuss spatially varying distributions in mirror systems. Thus, our attention will be focused on the second and third terms on the left-hand side. Since the right-hand side is treated via difference techniques, it would be convenient to devise some differencing scheme to account for these new terms. Unfortunately, this cannot be done in any practical way; the basic reason for this is that the particle transit time between reflections is much smaller than the relaxation times effected by collisions. Since there is a limit to the size of the time step that can be used in order to insure reasonable accuracy in the term $\mathbf{v} \cdot (\partial f/\partial \mathbf{r})$, an enormous number of time steps would be required to complete a problem. Furthermore, such a procedure would provide more information than is actually of interest. The approach that is used takes advantage of the widely disparate time scales by evaluating changes in f via an integration of the time rate of change in f along orbits in phase space. Equation (1) is an expression of this rate of change, i.e., we can write it as

$$df/dt = (\partial f/\partial t)_c + S,$$

where d/dt, the total derivative, represents the derivative as seen by an orbiting particle.

In Marx (1968) it is shown that the rate of change of particles can be expressed as

$$\frac{\partial f}{\partial t}(v_0, \theta_0, 0) \equiv \frac{\oint_{\text{orbit}} dz \, \frac{B(z)v_0 \cos \theta_0}{B(0)v \cos \theta} \frac{df}{dt}(v, \theta, z)}{\oint_{\text{orbit}} dz \, \frac{B(z)v_0 \cos \theta_0}{B(0)v \cos \theta}} \tag{61}$$

where the guiding-center orbits are defined by the equations for conservation of energy and magnetic moment:

$$\tfrac{1}{2}mv_0^2 + Ze\Phi_0 = \tfrac{1}{2}mv^2 + Ze\Phi(z), \qquad \frac{\tfrac{1}{2}mv_0^2 \sin^2 \theta_0}{B(0)} = \frac{\tfrac{1}{2}mv^2 \sin^2 \theta}{B(z)}. \tag{62}$$

Equation (61), an approximate formula, is sufficiently accurate to describe collision processes in many mirror-confinement systems. Note that Eq. (61) defines the distribution at $z = 0$. One of the underlying assumptions in its derivation is that the distribution is quasistationary; i.e., at any given time it is an approximate solution to the time-independent Vlasov equation. Thus, the distribution function is constant along a guiding center orbit, and

$$f(v, \theta, z) = f(v_0, \theta_0, 0), \tag{63}$$

where v, θ, v_0, θ_0 are related by Eqs. (62). Note that this precludes consideration of any particles whose orbits do not pass through the plane $z = 0$. While probably not impossible, such situations are unimportant.

The content of Eq. (61) can be clarified by considering a "tube" in phase space made up of neighboring orbits, as shown in Fig. 16. Let Δn be the

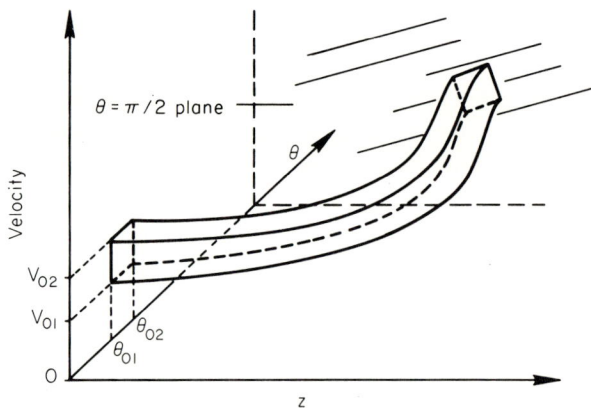

FIG. 16. Tube in phase space defined by guiding center orbits. Note that figure shows only $\tfrac{1}{4}$ of a complete orbit.

number of particles in the tube and let ΔV be its volume. Then

$$\frac{\partial f}{\partial t} = \lim_{\substack{v_{02} - v_{01} \to 0 \\ \theta_{02} - \theta_{01} \to 0 \\ \Delta t \to 0}} \frac{\Delta n / \Delta t}{\Delta V}. \tag{64}$$

The numerator and denominator in (61) correspond to those in (64).

2. Spatial Dependence of Electron Distribution and Ambipolar Potential

Just as in the case of the ion distribution, the electron distribution must be an approximate solution of the Vlasov equation. However, we retain the assumption made in Section IV,F that the electron distribution is a Maxwellian with particles in the loss region absent. The rates of change of density and temperature at each point along the field lines are assumed to obey the same equations derived in Section IV,F. The mirror ratio and potential difference required for solution of these equations are, of course, the local values calculated at each value of z.

Previously, it was deemed sufficiently accurate to assume the electron distribution to be a Maxwellian without directly accounting for the absence of particles in the loss region. The loss region entered the problem only via the calculation of the particle loss rate in a probabilistic manner. However, when considering the spatial variation of the electron density and the potential, it is necessary to be very careful to accurately take into account the absence of particles in the loss region. In keeping with Eq. (56), assume

$$f_e(v, \theta, z) = \begin{cases} \dfrac{n_e(0) \exp\{-(v^2 + v_{\Phi e}^2)/2v_e^2\}}{(2\pi)^{3/2} v_e^3 D_2}, & \text{if } v < v_{pe} \text{ or } v > v_{pe}, \\ & \text{but } \theta_L \leq \theta \leq \pi - \theta_L, \\ 0, & \text{if } v > v_{pe} \text{ and} \\ & |\pi/2 - \theta| > \pi/2 - \theta_L, \end{cases} \quad (65)$$

where

$$v_{\Phi e}^2 = |(2/m_e)e\Phi(z)|.$$

This is precisely the form of the electron distribution chosen by BenDaniel (1961). Note the presence of a normalization constant D_2 in Eq. (65) so that the calculated density of particles at the midplane can be exactly equal to $n_e(0)$; i.e., the normalization used in conjunction with Eq. (56) is only approximately valid. BenDaniel (1961) makes the following definitions:

$$\gamma = \frac{-e\Phi(L)}{m_e v_e^2}, \qquad \eta(z) = \frac{-e\Phi(z)}{m_e v_e^2}, \qquad R(z) = \frac{B(z)}{B(0)}.$$

He then shows that the density is given in terms of the density at $z = 0$ by the formula

$$n_e(z)/n_e(0) = e^{-\eta} F_2(z)/D_2,$$

where

$$F_2(z) = 2\pi \left(\frac{2v_e^2}{m_e}\right)^{3/2} \left\{ E_1(\gamma - \eta)^{1/2} \right.$$
$$\left. + \left(1 - \frac{R}{R_m}\right)^{1/2} e^{-(\gamma-\eta)} E_T\left[\left(\frac{\gamma-\eta}{1 - R/R_m}\right)^{1/2}\right] \right\},$$

and the normalization constant is $D_2 = F_2(0)$, with E_1 and E_T being defined as

$$E_1(x) = \int_0^x \exp(-x^2)\,dx, \qquad E_T(x) = \exp(x^2)[\sqrt{\pi}/2 - E_1(x)].$$

Now if one assumes Eq. (65) to be correct and knows $\Phi(L)$ and $n_i(z)$, then the condition of charge neutrality, $n_e(z) = n_i(z)$, is sufficient to determine $\Phi(z)$. BenDaniel (1961) gives an iterative procedure for calculating $\Phi(z)$. In the next section we describe the manner in which these considerations are included in a numerical procedure for solving the spatially dependent problem.

3. Numerical Procedure

We first describe the choice of a mesh in z-space. Although no differencing in z is done, the ion and electron equations must be solved at a number of discrete points along the field lines. In what follows, the magnetic field is assumed to be given by

$$B(z)/B(0) = P - Q \cos(\pi z/L), \tag{66}$$

where P and Q are simply adjusted to yield the proper mirror ratio, with the condition that the right-hand side be unity at $z = 0$. Since only the ratios of magnetic fields appear in any of the equations, the actual magnitude of the field is of no consequence, and one can deal only with this normalized function.

Figure 17 is a plot of the loss-cone angle vs z with no potential present. The magnetic field is given by Eq. (66) for a mirror ratio of 2. Superimposed on this graph are lines corresponding to the θ-mesh employed in the Fokker–Planck calculation. It is tempting to use some of the points of intersection of these mesh lines with the loss-cone curve as points on the z-mesh. The reason for this is that because of limitations on computer memory and speed, the same θ-mesh must be used for all z, and it seems most natural to be able to impose the boundary condition $f = 0$ at an exact loss angle. (In the presence of a potential, of course, the loss angle is modified, so the value of this contrivance then becomes debatable.)

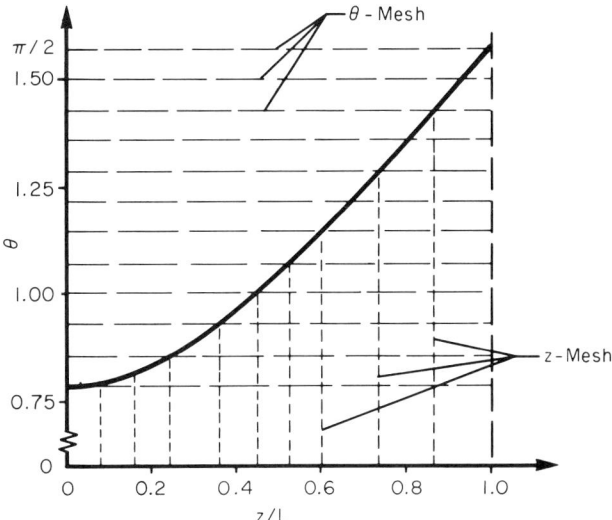

FIG. 17. Loss-cone angle vs position for mirror ratio equal to 2; θ- and z-meshes.

From Fig. 17, however, we see that the first intersection occurs at $z/L \approx 0.25$. Thus, it is clear that some mesh points in z must be placed off the intersections in order to obtain a reasonable mesh density at small values of z, where the greatest particle densities are expected. The z-values for a mesh of 11 points are shown in Fig. 17, wherein two points are chosen between $z/L = 0$ and $z/L = 0.25$, and the rest are chosen at intersections. Note that the spacing is such that it increases at large z, where the particle densities are small.

We now briefly mention the definition of the particle sources as a function of z. The parameters I_0 and I' which define the ion source [see Eq. (51)] are given a functional z-dependence, and the Fokker–Planck equation is solved accordingly. For the purposes of calculation, however, the electron source is given the same functional dependence on z as the electron particle density, with the amplitude adjusted so that input charge currents are equal and opposite. The reason for this choice of z-dependence of the electron current is that the electron collision time is much shorter than that of the ions. Because of this, the electron distribution relaxes sufficiently fast that it is deemed more realistic from the standpoint of numerical solution of the electron equations to assume that the electron source assumes the form of the instantaneous equilibrium solution to the Vlasov equation for the electrons.

Let the z-mesh points be denoted by the subscripts l, and

$$f(v_j, \theta_i, z_l, t^n) = f^n_{i,j,l},$$

etc. To solve for the ion distribution, one develops an approximate solution to Eq. (61). First, the distribution function is evaluated at a z-point from its value on the corresponding orbit at $z = 0$. In this process, as in all such calculations involving points in phase space not lying precisely on a mesh point, a linear interpolation formula can be used:
Let

$$f_j(\theta) = f_{i,j} + (f_{i+1,j} - f_{i,j})(\theta - \theta_i)/(\theta_{i+1} - \theta_i),$$

where $\theta_i \leq \theta \leq \theta_{i+1}$. Then we approximate f by

$$f(v, \theta) = f_j(\theta) + [f_{j+1}(\theta) - f_j(\theta)](v - v_j)/(v_{j+1} - v_j),$$

where $v_j \leq v \leq v_{j+1}$. In cases where an approximation for a function at a value of z not on a z-mesh point is required, this formula is extended in a similar fashion.

Once $f(v, \theta)$ is evaluated for all (v_j, θ_i), the Fokker–Planck operator is relaxed and the change in f over one time step is calculated from $\Delta f_{i,j}^n = f_{i,j}^{n+1} - f_{i,j}^n$. After this procedure is followed at all z_l, one then evaluates the new distribution at $z = 0$ by a numerical evaluation of the integrals indicated in Eq. (61), i.e.,

$$f_{i,j,0}^{n+1} = f_{i,j,0}^n + \frac{\oint_{\text{orbit}} dz \, \frac{B(z)v_0 \cos \theta_0}{B(0)v \cos \theta} \Delta f_{i,j}^n(z)}{\oint_{\text{orbit}} dz \, \frac{B(z)v_0 \cos \theta_0}{B(0)v \cos \theta}}. \tag{67}$$

In performing the integrations in Eq. (67), one progresses from z_l to z_{l+1} until the point is reached at which the turning point occurs. At this point $\cos \theta = 0$, and a singularity occurs in the integrand. We denote this point by z^*. As long as z^* does not lie between z_l and z_{l+1}, one breaks up the interval into two equal parts and evaluates the integrals by Simpson's rule, using interpolatory formulas for Δf^n as indicated above. When $z_l < z^* < z_{l+1}$, however, the integrals require special consideration because of the singularity. We wish to investigate the behavior of $\cos \theta$ in the neighborhood of z^*. We use the equation

$$v^2(z) = v_0^2 + v_\Phi^2(z), \quad \frac{v^2(z) \sin^2 \theta(z)}{B(z)} = \frac{v_0^2 \sin^2 \theta_0}{B(0)},$$

where $v_\Phi^2(z) = -(2/m)Ze\Phi(z)$. B and v_Φ^2 can be approximated in the neighborhood of z^* by

$$B(z) = B(z^*) + \frac{dB}{dz}(z^*)(z - z^*), \qquad v_\Phi^2(z) = v_\Phi^2(z^*) + \frac{dv_\Phi^2}{dz}(z^*)(z - z^*).$$

We use the condition $\sin^2 \theta(z^*) = 1$ so that

$$\frac{v^2(z^*)}{B(z^*)} = \frac{v_0^2 \sin^2 \theta_0}{B(0)}. \tag{68}$$

Then to first order

$$\cos^2 \theta = \left\{ \left[\frac{-dv^2(z^*)/dz}{v^2(z^*)} + \frac{dB(z^*)/dz}{B(z^*)} \right] (-z + z^*) \right\}^{-1}.$$

Thus, $\cos \theta$ is proportional to $(z^* - z)^{-1/2}$ near $z = z^*$. We assume that we are dealing with a simple singularity, i.e., that

$$\frac{v^2(z^*)}{B(z^*)} \frac{dB(z^*)}{dz} - \frac{dv_\Phi^2(z^*)}{dz} \neq 0. \tag{69}$$

Noting that $\mu_m = v^2(z^*)/B(z^*)$, from Eq. (6), it is clear that if the left-hand side of Eq. (69) were zero, z^* would be an extremum point of the potential V. This would mean that z^* is not a true turning point, but a point of unstable equilibrium for the guiding center. As will be seen, one is not required to evaluate variables precisely at the turning points. Therefore, negligible error is incurred if one always assumes that the turning point for an orbit lies just inside such a point, if this situation occurs in the numerical computation.

The improper integrals are evaluated in the following way. First, solve for z^* by interpolating to evaluate $v_\Phi^2(z)$, setting $\sin^2 (z^*) = 1$, and applying Newton's method to Eq. (68). Then write the integration within the z-increment that contains z^* in the form

$$I = \int_z^{z^*} \frac{dz}{(z^* - z)^{1/2}} \frac{\alpha(z)(z^* - z)^{1/2}}{\cos \theta(z)},$$

where $\alpha(z)$ represents the nonsingular portion of the integrand.

$$\alpha(z)(z^* - z)^{1/2} \cos \theta(z)$$

is a well-behaved function, and by a change of variables to $\rho = (z^* - z)/$

$(z^* - z_l)$, we have

$$I = \int_0^1 \frac{d\rho}{\sqrt{\rho}} \beta(\rho),$$

where $\beta(\rho)$ is a well-behaved function. This integral can then be approximated by an integration formula of the form (Krylov, 1962, p. 120)

$$I = \sum_{K=1}^N a_K \beta(\rho_K),$$

where ρ_K is never zero. Thus, evaluation of the limit of $\beta(\rho)$ as $\rho \to 0$ is unnecessary.

The requirement of charge neutrality plays a large part in the numerical solution of the spatially dependent problem, just as in the case of its counterpart in the problem without spatial dependence. With a view to this, one defines the total number of particles per unit area and its time derivative for use in describing the numerical procedure:

$$N_a = \int_{-L}^L dz\, n_a(z)$$

$$= 2\pi \int_{-L}^L dz \int_0^\infty v^2\, dv \int_0^\pi \sin\theta\, d\theta\, f_a(v, \theta, z), \tag{70}$$

$$\frac{dN_a}{dt} = \int_{-L}^L dz\, \frac{dN_a(z)}{dt}$$

$$= 2\pi \int_{-L}^L dz \int_0^\infty v^2\, dv \int_0^\pi \sin\theta\, d\theta\, \frac{\partial f_a}{\partial t}(v, \theta, z).$$

The numerical sequence is:

(1) The ion Fokker–Planck equation is solved at each mesh point in z, using the old values of the potential. In this way, $\Delta f^n_{i,j,l}$ is obtained, and the new ion distribution is obtained via Eq. (67).

(2) The electron equation is solved at each mesh point in z, and the new electron densities are integrated over z to obtain the total number of electrons (per unit area).

(3) This number is compared to the total number of ions, and the changes in total number of ions and electrons are also compared. Just as in the problem without space dependence, if both the total number of electrons and the change in total electrons are less than the corresponding ion quantities, the potential at $z = L$ is increased in magnitude by some predetermined increment, and Φ_l is increased proportionally, so as to maintain the same

functional dependence of Φ on z. In other words,

$$\Phi_l^{n+1} \to (\Phi_L^{n+1}/\Phi_L^n)\Phi_l^n. \tag{71}$$

The electron equations are then solved again, and the cycle is repeated until either

$$N_e \geq N_i \quad \text{or} \quad dN_e/dt \geq dN_i/dt.$$

Conversely, if the number of electrons and the change in electrons is greater than that of the ions, the potential at $z = L$ is decreased until either

$$N_e \leq N_i \quad \text{or} \quad dN_e/dt \leq dN_i/dt.$$

(4) The functional dependence of Φ on z is then recomputed as outlined in Section V,A,2. Φ_L is maintained at the value computed in step (3) above. Rather than requiring the total number of electrons to be equal to the total number of ions, the electron densities are set equal to the ion densities multiplied by the ratio of total electrons to total ions.

This scheme has yielded good results. Again, the requirement on the rate of change in total electrons as well as the total itself prevents erratic fluctuations due to large differences in rates that can occur before the total number of particles equalize. However, when comparing rates in this fashion, it is necessary to be extremely careful that no artificial gains or losses in particles occur because of the way the distribution functions are evaluated. Checks against the occurrence of this sort of error are made by calculating the total number of particles and the changes in the totals in different ways. The total number of ions is given by Eq. (70). Another way of computing the same number is by use of the formula

$$N_i = 2\pi \int_0^\infty v_0^2 \, dv_0 \int_0^\pi \sin\theta_0 \, d\theta_0 \oint_{\text{orbit}} dz \, \frac{B(z)v_0 \cos\theta_0 \, f(v,\theta,z)}{B(0)v \cos\theta}.$$

We use three different numerical formulas to calculate dN_i/dt. They are:

$$\frac{dN_i}{dt} = 2\pi \int_{-L}^{L} dz \int_0^\infty v^2 \, dv \int_0^\pi \sin\theta \, d\theta \left(\frac{f_b^{n+1} - f^n}{\Delta t}\right), \tag{72}$$

$$\frac{dN_i}{dt} = 2\pi \int_0^\infty v_0^2 \, dv_0 \int_0^\pi \sin\theta \, d\theta_0 \oint_{\text{orbit}} dz \, \frac{B(z)v_0 \cos\theta_0}{B(0)v \cos\theta} \left(\frac{f_b^{n+1} - f^n}{\Delta t}\right) \tag{73}$$

$$\frac{dN_i}{dt} = 2\pi \int_{-L}^{L} dz \int_0^\infty v^2 \, dv \int_0^\pi \sin\theta \, d\theta \left(\frac{f^{n+1} - f^n}{\Delta t}\right). \tag{74}$$

In these equations we have used the subscript b to denote the value of the distribution function obtained *after* the Fokker–Planck operator has been relaxed, but *before* Eq. (67) has been applied to determine the new values of the distribution function. These three formulas should yield the same result, but because of numerical inaccuracies they do not do so, especially at densities near steady state, where the changes in the total number of particles per time step are but a small fraction of the total density. In such situations, the interpolatory procedures used in calculating the distribution functions at values of z not equal to zero can lead to relatively large inaccuracies in dN_i/dt. Equation (72) should give the best approximation, so one renormalizes the distribution function so as to obtain agreement between Eq. (74) and (72). Equation (73) usually agrees quite well with Eq. (72) (to within 10–15% at worst), until the distribution is very near its steady-state value, at which time the relative accuracy of the two calculations diminishes because the change per time step is very small.

It is found that, under straightforward application of step (4) in the previous computational sequence, the values of the potential near the mirrors are prone to oscillate. This is due to the fact that the ion density in these regions is very sensitive to rather small changes in the distribution in the center of the mirror machine. One effective technique for eliminating these oscillations is to limit the change in the potential at one time step to just a fraction of the change required to equalize the electron and ion densities. Specifically, if the change in Φ should be $\Delta\Phi$ in order to obtain $n_e = n_i$, the potential is varied according to

$$\Phi_l^{n+1} = \Phi_l^n + v\,\Delta\Phi$$

where v is a positive constant less than unity. This has the effect of artificially "damping" the oscillations of the potential. If v is properly chosen, the calculation proceeds very smoothly. Empirically, it is found that a good choice is $v = 0.1$.

Another numerical difficulty that crops up is the inability to define the distribution function accurately at large values of z, especially when the potential builds up to an appreciable fraction of the ion energy. We use Eq. (63) to evaluate the distribution at $z \ne 0$. Since the particles whose orbits pass near the mirrors have values of v_0 and θ_0 very near the loss boundary at $z = 0$, straightforward application of Eq. (63) would require very accurate values of the distribution function at those points in velocity space. However, the loss boundary is approximated by a sawtooth-shaped boundary on the difference mesh and accuracy is a practical impossibility in this case. Therefore, the distribution at $z = 0$ is approximated by a fit to a smooth function, and Eq. (63) is applied to this function to evaluate the distribution at large z. The function used is

$$f^*(v, \theta, 0) = \begin{cases} a_0 + a_2(v - v_p)^2, & v \leq v_p, \\ a_0 \exp[-(v - v_p)^2/2\xi_0^2], & v \geq v_p, \end{cases}$$

where a_0 is equal to the maximum value of $f(v, \theta, 0)$ at $\theta = \theta_0$, v_p is the value of v at that maximum, a_2 is a constant adjusted to give $f^* = 0$ at the loss boundary at $\theta = \theta_0$, and ξ_0 is a constant that gives the distribution the proper value of $\langle (v - v_p)^2 \rangle$ for $v \geq v_p$.

This approximation compares favorably with the correct distribution function in cases where it is possible to apply Eq. (63) directly to the distribution at $z = 0$.

B. Results of Calculations with Spatial Dependence

1. Buildup Calculations

a. Comparison with Square-Well Calculations. In the interest of brevity, we shall henceforth refer to calculations without spatial dependence as "square-well" calculations; spatially dependent calculations will be denoted as "z-dependent." The functional dependence of the magnetic field will be assumed to be that given by Eq. (66). Thus, the z-dependence could be called a "cosine-well."

In comparing z-dependent calculations with those for a square well, one sets the input current per unit area per unit machine length, I_T, equal to the same constant value in all cases [$I' = 0$ in Eq. (51)]. The total current in the square-well case is simply equal to the current per unit volume; i.e., the well lengths can be normalized to unity. Note that the machine length in the z-dependent calculation is $2L$, since $z = \pm L$ at the mirrors. In Fig. 18 the results of two different z-dependent calculations made on this basis are compared with the results of the square-well run of Fig. 12. The source is a sharply peaked function in velocity space, $S \sim \exp[-100(v-1)^2 - 10(\theta - \pi/2)^2]$. The current has a Gaussian z-dependence $I = I_0 e^{-\alpha z^2}$. The total current is chosen equal to the steady-state current of the square well calculation: $I_T = 5.53 \times 10^{11}$ particles/sec/cm²/cm length. In run 1, $\alpha = 10$; in run 2, $\alpha = 40$. Steady-state values are given in Table III.

Note that although the particle density at $z = 0$ is substantially increased in the z-dependent calculation, the total particle loss rate increases. This leads to some 30–40% fewer particles per unit area that are trapped at steady-state. This phenomenon is easily explained on physical grounds (Marx, 1968).

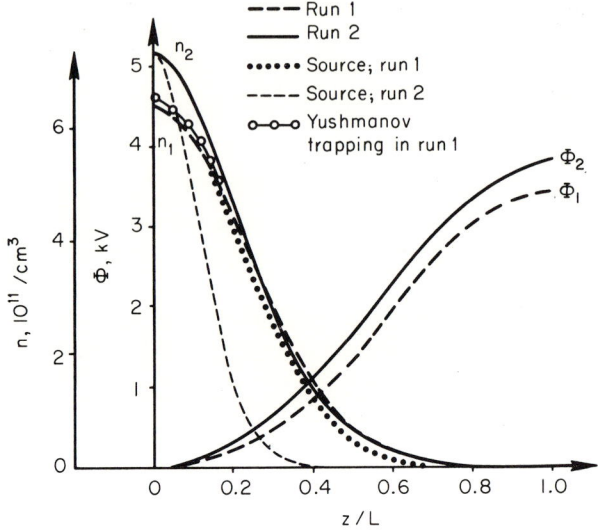

FIG. 18. Examples of spatially dependent calculations with two different sources, and with Yushmanov trapping included; Mirror ratio equals 2. The corresponding square-well values are $n = 3.05 \times 10^{11}$ cm^{-2}/cm length, $\Phi(L) = 2.98$ kV.

TABLE III

COMPARISON OF STEADY-STATE VALUES FOR z-DEPENDENT CALCULATIONS WITH CORRESPONDING SQUARE-WELL RESULTS

Run	$n(0)$ (10^{11} cm^{-3})	n_T(10^{11} cm^{-2}/cm length)	$\Phi(L)$ (kV)
1	6.39	1.865	3.41
2	7.35	1.970	3.80
Square well	3.05	3.05	2.98

b. Yushmanov Trapping. The effect of Yushmanov trapping is included in these problems by merely calculating the loss boundaries based on the maximum value of the longitudinal potential defined by Eq. (6) instead of the value at $z = L$. $V(L)$ was used in runs 1 and 2, discussed above, but it may not be the maximum.

The density profile from a calculation identical to run 1 except that Yushmanov trapping was included is shown by a dashed line in Fig. 18. The effects are seen to be extremely slight, increasing the density at $z = 0$ by about 2.5%. This means that the more accurate calculation extends the boundaries to include regions of velocity space only slightly removed from the boundaries calculated from the potential at $z = L$.

c. *Effect of Different Mirror Ratios.* The effect of the mirror ratio on buildup problems is exhibited in runs 3 and 4, shown in Fig. 19. These runs

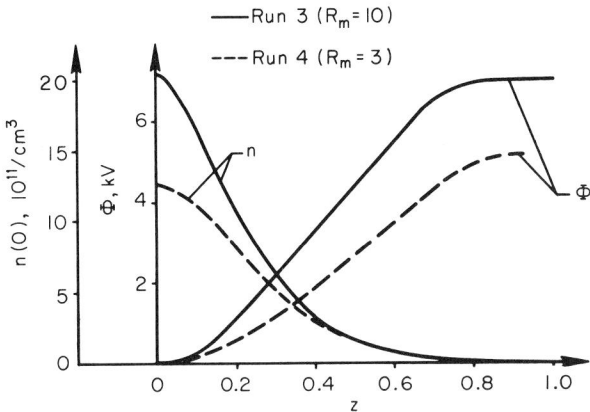

FIG. 19. Steady-state spatial variations in runs 3 and 4; $f_l = f_R = 1$.

coincide with run 1 of Fig. 18 in total current and z-dependence of the current. However, now $m_i = 2$ amu to correspond approximately to a deuterium plasma, and the factors f_l and f_R involving the electron loss and heating rates are equal to unity. (See Section IV,H,2.) The mirror ratios in run 3 and run 4 are 3 and 10, respectively.

We see that the density at the midplane is considerably increased in run 4, as is the number of total particles contained. We expect that the squares of the densities at the midplane ought to scale as the logarithm of the mirror ratio; see, e.g., Marx (1968). In fact,

$$(n_3/n_4)^2 = (20.4/12.6)^2 = 2.62, \quad \log 10/\log 3 = 2.3/1.098 = 2.38,$$

indicating a difference of about 10%.

Another effect of the higher mirror ratio is to cause the density profile to be more sharply peaked in z. This is evident in Fig. 19, and is due to the fact that the guiding center orbits turn in more sharply towards the plane $\theta = \pi/2$ for higher mirror ratios, thereby reducing the relative number of particles that reach a given value of z.

As mentioned above, the factors f_l and f_R were set equal to unity in runs 3 and 4. To illustrate the effect of varying these parameters, we present in Fig. 20 the results of run 4 with those of an identical calculation made with $f_l = 10$ and $f_R = 0.5$. These were the corrected values for $R_m = 2$ obtained in the procedure described in Section IV,H,2. As indicated by these results, the density

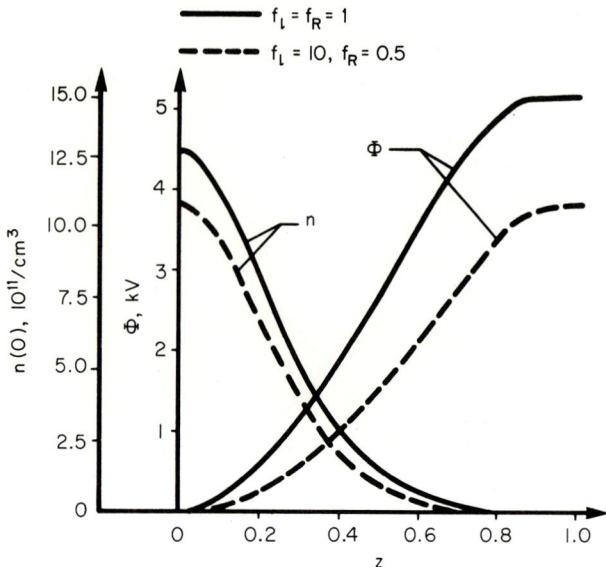

FIG. 20. Run 4 with varying parameters in electron equation; mirror ratio equals 3.

and potential are somewhat greater when $f_l = f_R = 1$, the larger deviation being that of the potential.

2. *Calculation of End Losses Only*

Calculations of end losses in the absence of a source can also be made with z-dependence taken into account. They proceed along the lines of the square-well problems described in Section IV,H,3, the techniques of Section V,A being applied. The energy dependence of a distribution measured in a $2X$ experiment was used, along with a moderately peaked θ-dependence. Figure 21 gives results from calculations at a mirror ratio of 1.33.

The only appreciable difference manifested by the z-dependence was a very rapid initial decrease in the density at the midplane at early times. This was found to be due, not to an anomalously rapid loss of particles from the mirror system, but to a redistribution of particles along the z-axis that is effected by the rapid buildup of the ambipolar potential. To illustrate, Fig. 22 shows the distribution function and the potential as a function of z at two different times for the run depicted in Fig. 21. The quantity n_T, the total number of particles per unit area per length of the mirror system, is given for comparison. While n_T decreases by only 5%, $n(0)$ decreases by 20%.

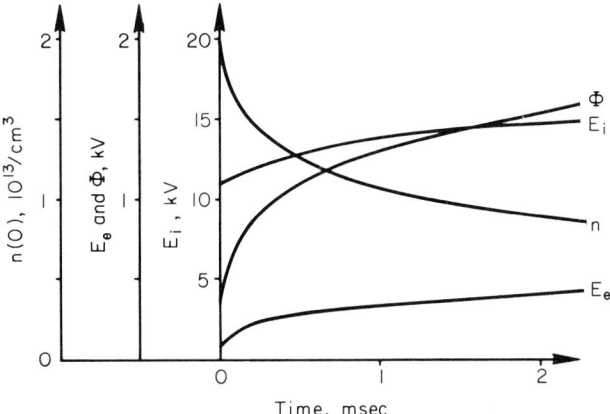

FIG. 21. Time evolution of $2X$ simulation with spatial dependence. Mirror ratio equals 1.33. (Φ does not advance smoothly as shown; see Section IV,H,3.)

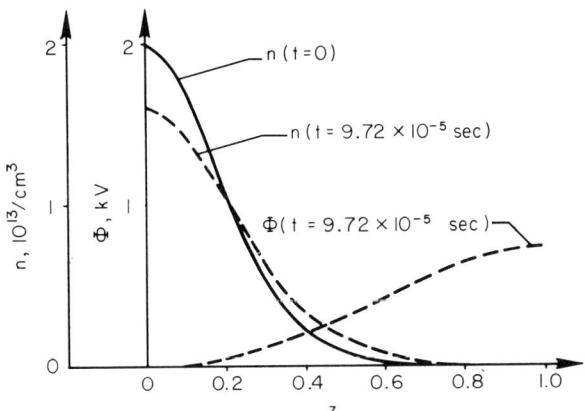

FIG. 22. Spatial variation in problem in Fig. 21. Two different points in time are shown, illustrating redistribution of particles due to buildup of potential: $n_T(t=0) = 4.69 \times 10^{12}$ cm^{-2}/cm length, n_T ($t = 9.72 \times 10^{-5}$ sec) $= 4.45 \times 10^{12}$ cm^{-2}/cm length, $\Phi(t=0) = 0$.

Appendix A. Transformation of the Fokker-Planck Equation to (v, θ) Coordinates and Specialization to a Two-Component Plasma

Equation (3) is of the form

$$\frac{1}{\Gamma_a}\left(\frac{\partial f_a}{\partial t}\right)_c = -\nabla \cdot (f_a \nabla h_a) + \tfrac{1}{2}\nabla\nabla : (f_a \nabla\nabla g_a),$$

where $\nabla\nabla g$ implies the second-rank tensor covariant derivative, the colon (:) implies the operation of contraction performed twice (double dot product), etc. Expanding the derivatives, we have

$$\frac{1}{\Gamma_a}\left(\frac{\partial f_a}{\partial t}\right)_c = (\tfrac{1}{2}\nabla^4 g_a - \nabla^2 h_a)f_a + [\nabla(\nabla^2 g_a) - \nabla h_a] \cdot \nabla f_a + \tfrac{1}{2}(\nabla\nabla g_a):(\nabla\nabla f_a) \tag{A1}$$

where $\nabla^4 = \nabla\nabla : \nabla\nabla g_a = \nabla^2(\nabla^2 g_a)$. We have the following identities:

$$\nabla^2(|\mathbf{v} - \mathbf{v}'|)^{-1} = -4\pi\delta(\mathbf{v} - \mathbf{v}'), \qquad \nabla^2(|\mathbf{v} - \mathbf{v}'|) = 2/|\mathbf{v} - \mathbf{v}'|,$$

where $\delta(\mathbf{v})$ is the Dirac delta function in three-dimensional space.

Application of these formulas to expressions defining h_a and g_a for a two-component plasma of ions and electrons yields, for the quantities of concern in the ion equation,

$$\nabla^2 h_i = -4\pi\left[\frac{(1+\gamma)}{Z^2} f_e - 2f_i\right], \qquad \nabla^4 g_i = \frac{2f_e}{Z^2} + 2f_i,$$

$$\nabla^2 g_i = \frac{2}{Z^2}\int\frac{d\mathbf{v}' f_e(\mathbf{v}')}{|\mathbf{v}-\mathbf{v}'|} + 2\int\frac{d\mathbf{v}' f_i(\mathbf{v}')}{|\mathbf{v}-\mathbf{v}'|}.$$

Thus,

$$\tfrac{1}{2}\nabla^4 g_i - \nabla^2 h_i = \frac{\gamma f_e}{Z^2} + f_i.$$

We define $C(\mathbf{v})$ by

$$C = \nabla^2 g_i - h_i;$$

then

$$C = \frac{1-\gamma}{Z^2}\int\frac{d\mathbf{v}' f_e(\mathbf{v}')}{|\mathbf{v}-\mathbf{v}'|}.$$

This is the function C appearing in Eq. (50).

Equation (A1) for the ions can now be written

$$\frac{1}{\Gamma_i}\left(\frac{\partial f_i}{\partial t}\right)_c = \tfrac{1}{2}(\nabla\nabla g_i):(\nabla\nabla f_i) + \nabla C \cdot \nabla f_i + 4\pi\left(\frac{\gamma f_e}{Z^2} + f_i\right)f_i.$$

The last term on the right is already in the form indicated in Eq. (50). The second term is identical to the terms in Eq. (50) that involve the function C, as can be seen by carrying out the transformation to polar coordinates. It remains to transform the first term; as this transformation is not readily available in most standard tensor calculus references, we shall outline the details.

The covariant components of the metric tensor for our polar coordinate system are:

$$a_{ij} = \begin{bmatrix} 1 & 0 & 0 \\ 0 & v^2 & 0 \\ 0 & 0 & v^2 \sin^2 \theta \end{bmatrix}.$$

Its contravariant components are:

$$a^{ij} = \begin{bmatrix} 1 & 0 & 0 \\ 0 & 1/v^2 & 0 \\ 0 & 0 & 1/v^2 \sin^2 \theta \end{bmatrix}.$$

The nonzero Christoffel symbols of the second kind are:

$$\begin{Bmatrix} 1 \\ 22 \end{Bmatrix} = -v, \quad \begin{Bmatrix} 2 \\ 21 \end{Bmatrix} = \begin{Bmatrix} 2 \\ 12 \end{Bmatrix} = \frac{1}{v}, \quad \begin{Bmatrix} 1 \\ 33 \end{Bmatrix} = -v \sin^2 \theta,$$

$$\begin{Bmatrix} 2 \\ 33 \end{Bmatrix} = -\sin \theta \cos \theta, \quad \begin{Bmatrix} 3 \\ 31 \end{Bmatrix} = \begin{Bmatrix} 3 \\ 13 \end{Bmatrix} = \frac{1}{v}, \quad \begin{Bmatrix} 3 \\ 32 \end{Bmatrix} = \begin{Bmatrix} 3 \\ 23 \end{Bmatrix} = \cot \theta.$$

By definition, under the usual summation convention,

$$f_{,ij} \equiv \frac{\partial f_{,j}}{\partial x^i} - \begin{Bmatrix} q \\ ij \end{Bmatrix} f_{,q};$$

whence, remembering that $\partial f/\partial \varphi = 0$, we have

$$f_{,ij} = \begin{bmatrix} \dfrac{\partial^2 f}{\partial v^2} & \dfrac{\partial^2 f}{\partial v \, \partial \theta} - \dfrac{1}{v} \dfrac{\partial f}{\partial \theta} & 0 \\[6pt] \dfrac{\partial^2 f}{\partial v \, \partial \theta} - \dfrac{1}{v} \dfrac{\partial f}{\partial \theta} & \dfrac{\partial^2 f}{\partial \theta^2} + v \dfrac{\partial f}{\partial v} & 0 \\[6pt] 0 & 0 & v \sin^2 \theta \dfrac{\partial f}{\partial v} + \sin \theta \cos \theta \dfrac{\partial f}{\partial \theta} \end{bmatrix}$$

with a similar expression for $\nabla\nabla g = g_{,ij}$. By definition,

$$\tfrac{1}{2}\nabla\nabla g : \nabla\nabla f \equiv \tfrac{1}{2} a^{ik} a^{jl} g_{,kl} f_{,ij}.$$

Carrying out the indicated summation and simplifying yields

$$\begin{aligned}
\tfrac{1}{2}\nabla\nabla g : \nabla\nabla f =\ & \frac{1}{2}\frac{\partial^2 g}{\partial v^2}\frac{\partial^2 f}{\partial v^2} + \left(\frac{1}{v^2}\frac{\partial^2 g}{\partial v\,\partial\theta} - \frac{1}{v^3}\frac{\partial g}{\partial\theta}\right)\frac{\partial^2 f}{\partial v\,\partial\theta} \\
& + \left(\frac{1}{2v^4}\frac{\partial^2 g}{\partial\theta^2} + \frac{1}{2v^3}\frac{\partial g}{\partial\theta}\right)\frac{\partial^2 f}{\partial\theta^2} \\
& + \left(\frac{1}{2v^3}\frac{\partial^2 g}{\partial\theta^2} + \frac{1}{v^2}\frac{\partial g}{\partial v} + \frac{1}{2v^3}\cot\theta\,\frac{\partial g}{\partial\theta}\right)\frac{\partial f}{\partial v} \\
& + \left[\frac{1}{v^4\sin\theta}\left(1 - \frac{\cos^2\theta}{2}\right)\frac{\partial g}{\partial\theta} - \frac{1}{v^3}\frac{\partial^2 g}{\partial v\,\partial\theta} + \frac{\cot\theta}{2v^3}\frac{\partial g}{\partial v}\right]\frac{\partial f}{\partial\theta}
\end{aligned}$$

in congruence with the corresponding term in Eq. (50).

Appendix B. Derivation of "Simpson's Rule" Quadrature Formula for Unequal Intervals

We require a three-point quadrature formula for use in approximating various integrals in phase space, where the mesh spacing may contain unequal intervals. Assume that three mesh points are given by $x = -h_-$, 0, and $+h_+$, and that the three corresponding values of the function to be integrated are f_-, f_0, and f_+. The quadratic passing through the three points is given by

$$f^* = a_0 + a_1 x + a_2 x^2,$$

where

$$a_0 = f_0,$$

$$a_1 = \frac{h_-^2 f_+ + (h_+^2 - h_-^2) f_0 - h_+^2 f_-}{h_-^2 h_+ + h_+^2 h_-},$$

$$a_2 = \frac{h_- f_+ - (h_+ + h_-) f_0 + h_+ f_-}{h_+ h_- (h_+ + h_-)},$$

Then, if $I \equiv \int_{-h_-}^{h_+} f^* \, dx$, we have

$$I = \left[\frac{2h_+^3 - h_-^3 + 3h_+^2 h_-}{6h_+(h_+ + h_-)}\right] f_+ + \left[\frac{h_+^3 + h_-^3 + 3h_+ h_-(h_+ + h_-)}{6h_+ h_-}\right] f_0$$
$$+ \left[\frac{2h_-^3 - h_+^3 + 3h_-^2 h_+}{6h_-(h_+ + h_-)}\right] f_-.$$

This formula reduces to Simpson's rule if $h_+ = h_-$. Its repeated application permits approximation of an integral over any odd number of mesh points, just as in the case of Simpson's rule.

Appendix C. Other Methods of Calculating g

The first method makes use of the fact that h and g obey the following Poisson equation (Rosenbluth et al., 1957) (interaction of other species ignored):

$$\nabla_v^2 h = -8\pi f(v), \qquad \nabla_v^2 g = h.$$

Knowing f, one can use standard finite difference techniques to calculate h, and then the same techniques can be used to calculate g.

A code was set up to relax the Fokker–Planck equation in just this way, and, indeed, it worked for the equation in the complete velocity space. But when the loss cone was added, a numerical instability always developed. The exact origin of this instability is not known, but it seemed to be related to an inability to supply the right sort of coefficients to smooth out sharp peaks in the distribution, which would grow as the calculation was advanced.

The second attempt at a different method involved the expansion of the term $|v - v'|$ in orthogonal polynomials of v/v', $\cos \theta$, and $\cos \theta'$ when $v < v'$, and of v'/v, $\cos \theta$, and $\cos \theta'$ when $v > v'$. The expansion used was similar in form to that given in Eq. (28) of BenDaniel and Allis (1962). Terms up to tenth order in v'/v (or v/v') were retained in the expansion.

This attempt met with the same fate as that outlined just previously; in fact, the nature of the numerical instability that occurred was very similar.

A faster method of computing the coefficients could save time in the case of problems without space dependence. However, in problems with space dependence, calculation of the coefficients involves a relatively small fraction of the total run time. Therefore, for these problems, one need not place a great premium on efficient methods of calculating them.

Appendix D. Solution of the Difference Equations

We first convert the difference equations to the form

$$
\begin{aligned}
-(\alpha_{i,j} + \varepsilon_{i,j})f^{n+1/2}_{i,j+1} + (\alpha_{i,j} + \beta_{i,j} - \tfrac{1}{2}c_{i,j} + \rho)f^{n+1/2}_{i,j} \\
- (\beta_{i,j} - \varepsilon_{i,j})f^{n+1/2}_{i,j-1} = \psi^n_{i,j}, \\
-(\gamma_{i,j} + \zeta_{i,j})f^{n+1}_{i+1,j} + (\gamma_{i,j} + \delta_{i,j} - \tfrac{1}{2}c_{i,j} + \rho)f^{n+1}_{i,j} \\
- (\delta_{i,j} - \zeta_{i,j})f^{n+1}_{i-1,j} = \chi^{n+1/2}_{i,j},
\end{aligned}
\tag{D1}
$$

where

$$
\alpha_{i,j} = \frac{1}{\Delta v_j}\left(\frac{a_{1i,j}}{\Delta v_{j+1/2}} + \frac{b_{1i,j}}{2}\right), \quad \beta_{i,j} = \frac{1}{\Delta v_j}\left(\frac{a_{1i,j}}{\Delta v_{j-1/2}} - \frac{b_{1i,j}}{2}\right),
$$

$$
\gamma_{i,j} = \frac{1}{\Delta\theta_i}\left(\frac{a_{3i,j}}{\Delta\theta_{i+1/2}} + \frac{b_{2i,j}}{2}\right), \quad \delta_{i,j} = \frac{1}{\Delta\theta_i}\left(\frac{a_{3i,j}}{\Delta\theta_{i-1/2}} - \frac{b_{2i,j}}{2}\right),
$$

$$
\varepsilon_{i,j} = \frac{a_{2i,j}}{4\,\Delta v_j\,\Delta\theta_{i-1/2}}, \quad \zeta_{i,j} = \frac{a_{2i,j}}{4\,\Delta v_{j-1/2}\,\Delta\theta_i}, \quad \rho = 2/\Delta t,
$$

$$
\psi^n_{i,j} = \gamma_{i,j}f^n_{i+1,j} - (\gamma_{i,j} + \delta_{i,j} - \tfrac{1}{2}c_{i,j} - \rho)f^n_{i,j} + \delta_{i,j}f^n_{i-1,j}
$$
$$
+ \varepsilon_{i,j}(-f^{n+1/2}_{i-1,j+1} + f^{n+1/2}_{i-1,j-1}) + \frac{a_{2i,j}}{4\,\Delta v_j\,\Delta\theta_{i+1/2}}
$$
$$
\cdot (f^n_{i+1,j+1} - f^n_{i-1,j+1} - f^n_{i,j+1} + f^n_{i,j-1}) + S_{i,j},
$$

$$
\chi^{n+1/2}_{i,j} = \alpha_{i,j}f^{n+1/2}_{i,j+1} - (\alpha_{i,j} + \beta_{i,j} - \tfrac{1}{2}c_{i,j} - \rho)f^{n+1/2}_{i,j} + \beta_{i,j}f^{n+1/2}_{i,j-1}
$$
$$
+ \zeta_{i,j}(-f^{n+1}_{i+1,j-1} + f^{n+1}_{i-1,j-1}) + \frac{a_{2i,j}}{4\,\Delta v_{j+1/2}\,\Delta\theta_i}
$$
$$
\cdot (f^{n+1/2}_{i+1,j+1} - f^{n+1/2}_{i-1,j+1} - f^{n+1/2}_{i+1,j} + f^{n+1/2}_{i-1,j}) + S_{i,j}.
$$

To solve these equations, we evaluate

$$
E^n_{i,j} = \bar{A}^n_{i,j}/(\bar{B}^n_{i,j} - \bar{C}^n_{i,j}E^n_{i,j-1}),
$$

$$
F^n_{i,j} = (\psi^n_{i,j} + \bar{C}^n_{i,j}F^n_{i,j-1})/(\bar{B}^n_{i,j} - \bar{C}^n_{i,j}E^n_{i,j-1}),
$$

where

$$\bar{A}^n_{i,j} = \alpha_{i,j} + \varepsilon_{i,j}, \qquad \bar{B}^n_{i,j} = \alpha_{i,j} + \beta_{i,j} - \tfrac{1}{2}c_{i,j} + \rho,$$

$$\bar{C}^n_{i,j} = \beta_{i,j} - \varepsilon_{i,j}.$$

The $E^n_{i,j}$'s and $F^n_{i,j}$'s are evaluated along a line of constant i; once they are computed, $f^{n+1/2}_{i,j}$ can be computed along the same line from the formula

$$f^{n+1/2}_{i,j} = E^n_{i,j} f^{n+1/2}_{i,j+1} + F^n_{i,j}.$$

Note that each $E^n_{i,j}$ and $F^n_{i,j}$ depends on the values of $E^n_{i,j-1}$ and $F^n_{i,j-1}$, while each $f^{n+1/2}_{i,j}$ depends on the value of $f^{n+1/2}_{i,j+1}$, so the process is one of sweeping out and back on each line of constant i.

On the next half time step, we evaluate

$$E^{n+1/2}_{i,j} = \bar{A}^{n+1/2}_{i,j} / (\bar{B}^{n+1/2}_{i,j} - \bar{C}^{n+1/2}_{i,j} E^{n+1/2}_{i-1,j}),$$

$$F^{n+1/2}_{i,j} = (\chi^{n+1/2}_{i,j} + \bar{C}^{n+1/2}_{i,j} F^{n+1/2}_{i-1,j}) / (\bar{B}^{n+1/2}_{i,j} - \bar{C}^{n+1/2}_{i,j} E^{n+1/2}_{i-1,j})$$

where

$$\bar{A}^{n+1/2}_{i,j} = \gamma_{i,j} + \zeta_{i,j}, \qquad \bar{B}^{n+1/2}_{i,j} = \gamma_{i,j} + \delta_{i,j} - \tfrac{1}{2}c_{i,j} + \rho,$$

$$\bar{C}^{n+1/2}_{i,j} = \delta_{i,j} - \zeta_{i,j}.$$

Now the computation proceeds back and forth on lines of constant j, and we have

$$f^{n+1}_{i,j} = E^{n+1/2}_{i,j} f^{n+1}_{i+1,j} + F^{n+1/2}_{i,j}.$$

The reason that part of the calculation of the mixed derivative term can be done implicitly is that, as we calculate implicitly in the v-direction on a line of given i, we already have the values at $i - 1$ at the advanced time $t = t^{n+1/2}$. A similar situation exists as we progress in j while differencing implicitly in θ. This allows us to evaluate $\psi^n_{i,j}$ and $\chi^{n+1/2}_{i,j}$ from (D1), even though they contain terms at the advanced times.

Note that the explicit part of the mixed derivative calculation is such as to "balance" the approximation on each side of the point in question; that is, calculation of the term on an i line during the first half time step involves an implicit calculation at $i - 1$ and i, and an explicit calculation at i and $i + 1$, etc.

So far, the term cf in Eq. (53) has been treated half implicitly and half explicitly. Variations on this feature from one extreme to the other have been investigated, but to no apparent advantage.

Since the boundary conditions are considerably different for the two cases with and without a loss cone, they must be considered separately. First, consider loss-cone boundary conditions in the absence of a potential, which are somewhat simpler. At $v = 0$ ($j = 1$), at $\theta = \theta_{LC}$ ($i = 1$), and at the maximum v value ($j = J$), we must have $f = 0$. The first two conditions are satisfied if we use $E_{i,1}^n = F_{i,1}^n = 0$ and $f_{1,j}^{n+1/2} = 0$ on the first half time step, and $E_{1,j}^{n+1/2} = F_{1,j}^{n+1/2} = 0$ and $f_{i,1}^{n+1/2} = 0$ on the second half time step. The last is satisfied if we set

$$f_{i,J} = 0 \tag{D2}$$

at all times in the procedure outlined above for the solution of the difference equations. Our other boundary condition is that the distribution be symmetric about the point $\theta = \pi/2$. This is obeyed if $f_{I+1,j} = f_{I-1,j}$. This condition can be directly applied after the calculation for the first half time step has been completed up through $i = I$. Furthermore, it is easy to show that it will be satisfied when the computation is carried out implicitly in the θ-direction if we apply the formula

$$f_{I+1,j}^{n+1} = (E_{I-1,j}^{n+1/2} F_{I,j}^{n+1/2} + F_{I-1,j}^{n+1/2})/(1 - E_{I-1,j}^{n+1/2} E_{I,j}^{n+1/2})$$

These last considerations on the symmetry about $\theta = \pi/2$ also hold if no loss cone is present; i.e., if the problem is to be solved in the complete velocity space. The same is true of the condition (D2) on the distribution function at the maximum value of v. However, the boundary conditions at $v = 0$ require special consideration. They are:

$$f(0, \theta) \text{ must be the same for all } \theta, \tag{45}$$

$$\partial f/\partial v(0, \pi/2) = 0. \tag{46}$$

It has been found that a good way to impose these conditions when computing implicitly in v is to first solve the difference equation implicitly at $\theta = \pi/2$ ($i = I$), using the relations $E_{I,1}^n = 1$ and $F_{I,1}^n = 0$, which yields the result $f_{I,1}^{n+1/2} = f_{I,2}^{n+1/2}$, an approximation to condition (46). This allows one to advance the function at $v = 0$ and $\theta = \pi/2$, i.e., to obtain $f_{I,1}^{n+1/2}$. Then one can solve the equations at all other values of θ by using the conditions $E_{i,1}^n = 0$ and $F_{i,1}^n = f_{I,1}^{n+1/2}$ to satisfy (45). After the second half time step, (45) and (46) are satisfied by putting $f_{i,1}^{n+1} = f_{I,2}^n$. At $\theta = 0$ ($i = 1$), we require $\partial f/\partial \theta = 0$. After differencing implicitly in v, one approximately satisfies this condition by setting $f_{1,j}^{n+1/2} = f_{2,j}^{n+1/2}$. When differencing implicitly in θ, the same effect is obtained by using $E_{1,j}^{n+1/2} = 1$ and $F_{1,j}^{n+1/2} = 0$.

These methods of imposing boundary conditions when solving problems in the complete velocity space have proven to be applicable to other problems, e.g., heat conduction problems in polar coordinates.

ACKNOWLEDGEMENT

This work was performed under the auspices of the United States Atomic Energy Commission.

REFERENCES

BENDANIEL, D. J. (1961). *J. Nucl. Energy, Pt. C* **3**, 235.
BENDANIEL, D. J., and ALLIS, W. P. (1962). *J. Nucl. Energy, Pt. C* **4**, 31.
BERNSTEIN, W., CHECHKIN, V. V., KUO, L. G., MURPHY, E. G., PETRAVIC, M., RIVIERE, A. C., and SWEETMAN, D. R. (1966). In "Plasma Physics and Controlled Nuclear Fusion Research," Vol. II, pp. 23–44. IAEA, Vienna.
BING, G., and ROBERTS, J. E. (1961). *Phys. Fluids* **4**, 1039.
CHANDRASEKHAR, S. (1942). "Principles of Stellar Dynamics." Pergamon Press, Oxford.
COENSGEN, F. H., CUMMINS, W. F., ELLIS, R. E., KOVAR, F. R., and NEXSEN, W. F., JR. (1967). Plasma containment in the $2X$ experiment. Rept. UCRL-70656 Preprint. Lawrence Radiation Lab., Livermore, California. Presented at the *Intern. Conf. on Plasma Confined in Open-Ended Geometry, Gatlinburg, Tenn., Nov. 1–3*, 1967.
FOWLER, T. K., and RANKIN, M. (1966). *J. Nucl. Energy, Pt. C* **8**, 121.
FUTCH, A. H., JR., HECKROTTE, W., DAMM, C. C., KILLEEN, J., and MISH, L. E. (1962). *Phys. Fluids* **5**, 1277.
FUTCH, A. H., Jr., DAMM, C. C., FOOTE, J. H., FREIS, R. GORDON, F. J., HUNT, A. H., KILLEEN, J., MOSES, K. G., POST, R. F., and STEINHAUS, J. F. (1966). In "Plasma Physics and Controlled Nuclear Fusion Research," Vol. II, pp. 3–22. IAEA, Vienna.
HASTINGS, C., JR. (1955). "Approximation for Digital Computers," p. 175. Princeton Univ. Press, Princeton, New Jersey.
KAUFMAN, A. N. (1956) USAEC Doc. TID-7520, Pt. 2, p. 387.
KILLEEN, J., and FUTCH, A. H., JR. (1968). *J. Comp. Phys.* **2**, 236.
KILLEEN, J., HECKROTTE, W., and BOER, G. (1962). *Nucl. Fusion Suppl. Pt.* **1**, 183.
KRYLOV, V. I. (1962). "Approximate Calculation of Integrals." Macmillan, New York.
MARX, K. D. (1968). Solution of a spatially dependent Fokker–Planck equation for mirror-confined plasmas. Ph.D. Thesis, Univ. of California, Davis, California...
MONTGOMERY, D. C., and TIDMAN, D. A. (1964). "Plasma Kinetic Theory," pp. 19–20. McGraw-Hill, New York.
PEACEMAN, D. W., and RACHFORD, H. H., JR. (1955). *J. Soc. Ind. Appl. Math.* **3**, 28.
POST, R. F. (1961). *Phys. Fluids* **4**, 902.
POST, R. F., and ROSENBLUTH, M. N. (1965). *Phys. Fluids* **8**, 547.
POST, R. F., and ROSENBLUTH, M. N. (1966). *Phys. Fluids* **9**, 530.
ROBERTS, J. E., and CARR, M. L. (1960). Rept. UCRL-5651-T. Lawrence Radiation Lab. Livermore, California.
ROSENBLUTH, M. N., MACDONALD, W. M., and JUDD, D. L. (1957). *Phys. Rev.* **107**, 1.
SIMON, A. (1955). "An Introduction to Thermonuclear Research," Pergamon Press, Oxford.
SPITZER, L., JR. (1962). "Physics of Fully Ionized Gases," 2nd ed. Wiley (Interscience), New York.
YUSHMANOV, E. E. (1966). *Zh. Eksperim. i. Teor. Fiz.* **49**, 588 (English Transl: *Soviet Phys.—JETP* **22**, 409).

Author Index

Numbers in italic indicate the pages on which the complete references are listed.

A

Abernathy, F., 194, *210*
Allis, W. P., 423, 427, 429, 442, 485, *489*
Amsden, A. A., 214, 216, *239*, 342, *417*
Appleton, J. P., 356, *417*
Armstrong, T. P., 16, *27*, 35, 55, 62, 72, 73, 81, *84*, 89, 94, 100, *133*, 310, *338*
Artsimovich, L. A., 392, *417*
Ashby, D. E., 341, *417*
Auer, P. L., 341, *417*

B

Backus, G., 37, *84*
Baldwin, D. E., 127, *133*
Barnes, G. H., 345, *417*
Beach, A. D., 341, 342, 370, 390, 416, *417*
BenDaniel, D. J., 423, 427, 429, 442, 457, 469, 470, 485, *489*
Berk, H. L., 16, *27*, 34, *84*, 88, 89, 98, 99, 100, 127, *133*, 310, *338*
Bernstein, I. B., 45, 70, 74, 77, *84, 85*, 354, *420*
Bernstein, W., 429, *489*
Bethe, H. A., 192, *211*
Betrand, P., 94, *133*
Bing, G., 422, 429, *489*
Birdsall, C. K., 1, 2, 17, 21, *27, 28*, 136, 162, 185, *210*, 242, 243, 254, 256, *257, 258*, 309, 326, 330, *338*
Birmingham, T., 10, 14, *28*
Bobrovskii, G. A., 392, *417*
Bodin, H. A. B., 341, 342, 370, 390, 416, *417*
Boer, G., 435, 464, *489*
Book, D. L., 88, 127, *133*
Boris, J. P., 159, 184, *210*, 382, 414, *417*
Bottoms, P. J., 343, 394, 398, 400, 413, *418, 419*
Bragrimovskii, K. A., 383, *417*
Brauch, D. F., 181, *211*
Bray, K. N. C., 356, *417*
Brawn, R. M., 345, *417*
Brettschneider, M., 265, *305*
Broaddus, T., 55, 73, *85*
Buneman, O., 1, *28*, 89, *133*, 155, 157, 181, *210, 211*
Bunting, C. A., 341, 342, 370, 390, 416, *417*
Butler, T. D., 216, 218, *239*, 343, 398, 401, 411, *418*
Buzbee, B. L., 157, 161, *210*, 228, *239*
Byers, J. A., 2, *28*, 181, *210*, 291, 294, 296, 303, 304, *305*

C

Carpenter, J. P., 343, 394, 398, 413, *418*
Carr, M. L., 422, 446, 454, *489*
Chandrasekhar, S., 70, *85*, 290, *305*, 431, *489*
Chapman, S., 352, *418*
Charney, J. G., 300, *305*
Chechkin, V. V., 429, *489*
Chorin, A. J., 168, *210*
Chu, C. K., 341, *418*
Cochran, W. T., 139, *210*
Coensgen, F. H., 453, *489*
Colgate, S. A., 389, *418*
Comisar, G. G., 70, *86*, 343, *419*
Conte, S. D., 245, *257*
Cook, J. L., 218, *239*, 401, *418*
Cooley, J. W., 136, 139, 145, *210*
Coudeville, A., 343, 398, *418*
Cowling, T. G., 352, 414, *418*
Cramer, H., 41, *85*
Crownfield, F. R., 55, 73, *85*
Cummins, W. F., 453, *489*

D

Damm, C. C., 282, 283, 290, *305*, 429, 435, 444, 451, *489*
Dancy, D. J., 341, 342, 370, 390, 416, *417*

491

AUTHOR INDEX

Dawson, J. M., 1, 2, 7, 10, 11, 14, *28,* 89, 116, *133,* 242, 257, *257, 258*
Decker, J. F., 75, *85*
Denavit, J., 71, *85*
De Packh, D. C., 34, *85,* 90, *133*
Dickman, D., 234, 239, *239*
Dory, R. A., 90, *133*
Doucet, H., 81, *85*
Doyle, B. W., 71, *85*
Drummond, W. E., 45, 56, 74, *85,* 119, *133*
Dubois, D. F., 82, *85*
Duchs, D., 341, 343, 356, 391, *418*
Dyachenko, V. F., 401, *418*
Dykhne, A. M., 392, *420*

E

Eldridge, O. C., 1, 2, 10, *28*
Ellis, R. E., 453, *489*
Engelmann, F., 45, 55, 74, *84, 85*
Evans, W. M., 256, *258*

F

Favin, D. L., 139, 210
Feix, M. R., 1, 2, 10, 16, *28,* 35, 55, 58, 68, 69, 70, 71, 72, 73, *85,* 94, 99, *133*
Feld, B. T., 192, *211*
Ferguson, J. P., 389, *418*
Filippov, N. V., 343, 394, 398, *418*
Filippova, T. I., 343, 394, 398, *418*
Fisher, D. L., 341, *419*
Fisser, H., 341, *418*
Fjortoft, R., 300, *305*
Foote, J. H., 282, 290, *305,* 429, 444, 451, *489*
Forsen, H. K., 342, *419*
Forsythe, G. E., 162, 163, 169, *210*
Fowler, T. K., 90, *133,* 423, 438, *489*
Freeman, J. R., 394, 395, 396, *418*
Freidberg, J. P., 78, *85*
Freis, R., 282, 290, *305,* 429, 444, 451, *489*
Fried, B. D., 245, *257*
Fromm, J. E., 136, 168, *210*
Furth, H. P., 389, *418*
Fuss, D., 17, 21, 27, 162, 185, *210,* 254, 256, *257,* 309, 326, 330, *338*
Futch, A. H., Jr., 282, 283, 290, *305,* 423, 429, 435, 444, 451, 456, *489*

G

Galeev, A. A., 342, *420*
Garabedian, P. R., 380, *418*
Gardner, C. S., 90, *133*
Gartenhaus, S., 56, *85*
Gary, S. P., 72, *85*
Gentleman, W. M., 139, *210*
Gentry, R. A., 136, *210*
Gill, S., 59, *85*
Gilmer, R. M., 341, *420*
Godunov, S. K., 383, *417*
Goldenbaum, G. C., 341, *420*
Goldstein, H., 314, *338*
Golub, G. H., 157, 161, *210,* 228, *239*
Gorbunov, E. P., 392, *417*
Gordon, F. J., 282, 290, *305,* 429, 444, 451, *489*
Gorman, D., 56, *85*
Gould, R. W., 37, 73, *85*
Grant, F. C., 16, *28,* 35, 55, 58, 68, 69, 70, 71, 72, 73, *85*
Greene, J. M., 1, *28,* 77, *84*
Grewal, M., 2, *28*
Griem, H. R., 341, 356, *418*
Griffin, W. G., 357, *419*
Gross, R. A., 341, *418*

H

Hain, G., 341, 342, 365, 387, 394, 397, 400, *418, 420*
Hain, K., 341, 342, 343, 365, 366, 368, 370, 380, 387, 394, 397, 400, *418, 420*
Hardcastle, R. A., 341, *420*
Harding, R. C., 35, 55, 78, *85,* 310, *338*
Harlow, F. H., 136, *210,* 256, *257, 258,* 342, *417, 418, 419*
Harris, E. G., 77, *85*
Hasegawa, A., 1, 2, *28*
Hastings, C., Jr., 446, 459, *489*
Heckrotte, W., 265, 283, *305,* 435, 464, *489*
Helms, H. D., 139, *210*
Henins, I., 216, *239,* 343, 398, 401, 411, *418*
Hertweck, F., 343, 353, 368, 369, 370, 392, 394, *419, 420*
Hess, R., 257, *258*

AUTHOR INDEX

Heywood, G. C. H., 341, 342, 370, 390, 416, *417*
Hide, R., 414, *418*
Hinnov, E., 355, *419*
Hinton, F. L., 73, *85*
Hirsch, R. H., 71, *85*
Hirsch, R. L., 192, *210*
Hirschberg, J. G., 355, *419*
Hirshfield, J. L., 75, *85*
Hobbs, G. D., 357, *419*
Hockney, R. W., 17, 21, *28*, 136, 141, 161, 162, 163, 177, 181, 185, 187, 190, 192, 194, 195, 197, *210*, *211*, 256, *258*, 293, *305*, 345, 382, *419*
Hohl, F., 99, *133*, 163, 168, 177, 181, 195, *210*, *211*
Holmes, L. S., 341, *420*
Hoyt, H. C., 341, *420*
Hsi, C. G., 89, 116, *133*, 242, *257*
Hunt, A. H., 282, 290, *305*
Hurwitz, H., Jr., 341, *417*

I

Iiyoshi, A., 341, *420*
Imshennik, V. S., 401, *418*
Ivanov, D. P., 392, *417*

J

Jackson, E. A., 80, *85*
Jackson, J. D., 246, *258*
Jahoda, F. C., 216, *239*, 343, 398, 401, 411, *418*
Janes, G. S., 192, *211*
Jefferey, A., 345, 348, *419*
Jolas, A., 343, 398, *418*
Jones, T. J. L., 357, *419*
Judd, D. L., 424, 485, *489*

K

Kaenel, R. A., 139, *210*
Kahn, H., 225, *239*
Kamimura, T., 136, *210*
Kasahara, T., 297, *305*
Kato, M., 345, *417*
Kaufmann, A. N., 353, 379, *419*, *420*, 427, 437, *489*
Keck, J. C., 355, *419*

Kellogg, P. J., 14, 16, *28*, 35, 38, *85*, 266, *305*
Kenward, M. R., 341, 342, 370, 390, 416, *417*
Kerst, D. W., 342, *419*
Kilb, R. W., 341, *417*
Killeen, J., 89, *133*, 186, *211*, 224, *239*, 265, 267, 274, 281, 282, 283, 290, *305*, 341, *419*, 423, 429, 435, 444, 451, 456, 464, *489*
King, R. E., 342, *420*
Kirillov, V. D., 392, *417*
Knorr, G., 35, 38, 50, 78, *85*, 89, *133*, 310, *338*, 356, *419*
Kolb, A. C., 341, 391, *418*, *419*
Kooyers, G. P., 181, *211*
Köppendorfer, W., 341, 342, 365, 387, 394, 397, 400, *418*
Kovar, F. R., 453, *489*
Kronauer, R., 194, *210*
Kruskal, M. D., 77, *84*
Krylov, V. I., 474, *489*
Kuck, D. J., 345, *417*, *419*
Kulstrud, R., 14, *28*
Kuo, L. C., 282, *305*
Kuo, L. G., 429, *489*
Kurihara, A., 294, *305*
Kuznetson, Z. I., 392, *417*

L

Landau, L. D., 32, *85*
Lane, F. O., 394, 395, 396, *418*
Lang, W. W., 139, *210*
Langdon, A. B., 1, 2, 18, *28*, 185, *210*, 242, 243, 256, *257*, *258*
Lapidus, A., 394, *419*
Lax, P. D., 372, 373, *419*
Leavens, W. M., 65, *85*
Leith, C. E., 264, 275, *305*
Lenard, A., 70, *85*
Levy, R. H., 181, 192, 194, *211*
Lewis, H. R., 310, 332, 335, *338*
Lewis, P. A. W., 145, *210*
Lilly, D. K., 293, 294, *305*
Lomax, R. J., 73, *85*
Long, J. W., 343, 398, *419*
Longmire, C. L., 292, *305*
Low, F. E., 78, *85*, 314, *338*

M

McCartan, J., 341, 342, 370, 390, 416, *417*
MacDonald, W. M., 424, 485, *489*
McKee, C. F., 185, *210*, 242, 256, *257*
McWhirter, R. W. P., 341, 357, 391, *419*
Makin, B., 355, *419*
Maling, G. C., 139, *210*
Malmberg, J. H., 37, *85*
Marshall, J., 216, 223, *239*, 343, 398, 401, 411, *418*
Martin, R. E., 136, *210*
Marx, K. D., 458, 467, 474, 479, *489*
Mather, J. W., 343, 394, 398, 400, 413, *418, 419*
Mawardi, O., 223, *239*
Melendez, K. J., 310, 332, 335, *338*
Meskan, D. A., 343, *419*
Mihran, T. G., 257, *258*
Miller, R. H., 176, 186, 195, *211*
Minardi, E., 55, *85*
Mirnov, S. V., 392, *417*
Mish, L. E., 283, *305*, 435, *489*
Mjolsness, R. C., 308, *338*
Montgomery, D. C., 32, 35, 56, 72, 73, 78, 81, *84, 85*, 310, *338*, 424, *489*
Morgan, P. D., 343, 344, 394, 398, *419, 420*
Morozov, A. I., 218, *239*
Morse, R. L., 17, 21, *28*, 89, 100, 116, *133*, 216, 218, 227, 228, 229, 230, 231, 234, *239*, 252, 254, 256, *258*, 309, 326, 327, 330, *338*, 343, 398, 401, 411, *418*
Morton, K. W., 263, 295, 297, *305*, 341, 343, 344, 347, 351, 361, 364, 368, 369, 373, 376, 383, *419, 420*
Moses, K. G., 282, 290, *305*, 429, 444, 451, *489*
Murphy, E. G., 282, *305*, 429, *489*

N

Nakayama, P. I., 342, *418, 419*
Neil, V. K., 265, *305*
Nelson, D. E., 139, *210*
Newton, A. A., 341, 342, 370, 390, 416, *417*
Nexsen, W. F., Jr., 453, *489*
Niblett, G. B. F., 341, *419*
Nielsen, C. E., 34, *85*, 99, *133*
Nielsen, C. W., 89, 100, 116, *133*, 157, 161, *210*, 228, 229, 230, 231, 234, 239, *239*, 252, 254, 256, *258*, 309, 326, 327, 330, *338*
Northrop, T. G., 290, *305*

O

Oberman, C., 10, 14, *28*, 73, *85*
Ohkawa, T., 342, *419*
Okuda, H., 185, *210*, 242, 243, 256, *257, 258*
Oliphant, T. A., 341, 391, *419*
O'Neil, T. M., 37, 73, *85*, 94, *134*
Oxenius, J., 55, *85*

P

Parkinson, M. J., 341, *420*
Pasco, I. K., 341, 342, 370, 390, 416, *417*
Patou, C., 343, *419*
Paul, J. W. M., 341, *420*
Peaceman, D. W., 447, *489*
Peacock, N. J., 343, 344, 394, 398, *419, 420*
Peacock, R., 341, 342, 370, 390, 416, *417*
Pearlstein, L. D., 78, *86*
Petravic, M., 282, *305*, 429, *489*
Phillips, N. A., 293, *305*
Pines, D., 45, 56, 74, *85*, 119, *133*
Potter, D. E., 344, *419*
Post, R. F., 282, 290, *305*, 422, 427, 429, 444, 451, 457, 465, *489*
Prendergast, K. H., 176, 186, 195, *211*
Puri, S., 185, *211*

R

Rachford, H. H., Jr., 447, *489*
Rader, C. M., 139, *210*
Raether, M., 80, *85*
Rampel, S. J., 224, *239*
Rankin, M., 423, 438, *489*
Razumova, K. A., 392, *417*
Ribe, F. L., 341, *420*
Richtymer, R. D., 263, 295, 297, *305*, 341, 343, 344, 347, 351, 361, 364, 368, 369, 373, 376, 383, *420*
Riviere, A. C., 429, *489*

AUTHOR INDEX

Roberts, J. E., 422, 429, 446, 454, *489*
Roberts, K. V., 16, *27*, 34, *84*, 89, 98, 99, 100, *133, 134*, 159, 184, *210*, 310, *338*, 341, 342, 343, 344, 356, 359, 361, 365, 368, 369, 375, 376, 377, 382, 387, 392, 393, 394, 397, 400, 414, *417, 418, 420*
Roberts, P. H., 414, *419*
Roberts, S. J., 341, 342, 343, 365, 369, 387, 392, 394, 397, 400, *417, 418, 420*
Robinson, B. B., 354, *420*
Robinson, D. C., 342, *420*
Rompel, S. L., 89, *133*, 186, *211*, 265, 267, 274, 281, *305*
Rosenbluth, M. N., 291, 292, *305*, 341, 379, *420*, 422, 424, 465, 485, *489*
Rowlands, G., 127, *133*
Runge, C., 141, *211*

S

Sadowski, W. L., 35, 55, 72, *86*
Saenz, A. W., 32, *86*
Sagdeev, R. Z., 45, 58, 74, *86*, 119, *134*, 342, *420*
Sande, G., 139, *210*
Schluter, J., 341, *418*
Schneider, W., 343, 353, 368, 370, 394, *419*
Schupp, A. A., 342, *419*
Sessler, A. M., 34, *85*
Shanny, R. A., 1, *28*, 89, 116, *133*, 242, *257*
Shapiro, V. D., 185, *211*
Shcheglov, D. A., 392, *417*
Sheffield, J., 341, *420*
Shkarafsky, I. P., 354, *420*
Shonk, C. R., 227, 229, *239*
Simon, A., 291, *305*, 437, *489*
Simmonet, A., 343, *419*
Smith, C., 1, 2, 7, 10, *28*, 257, *258*
Speer, R. J., 343, 394, 398, *419, 420*
Spitzer, L., Jr., 350, *420*, 426, 459, *489*
Steinhaus, J. F., 282, 290, *305*, 429, 444, 451, *489*
Strelkov, V. D., 392, *417*
Sturrock, P. A., 185, *211*, 314, *338*
Symon, K. R., 34, *85*
Sweetman, D. R., 282, *305*, 429, *489*

T

Taussig, R. T., 341, *418*
Taylor, E. C., 70, *86*
Taylor, J. B., 359, *420*
Thomas, J. D., 335, *338*
Tidman, D. A., 32, *85*, 424, *489*
Titchmarsh, E. C., 37, *86*
Toomre, A., 198, *211*
Tuck, J. L., 239, *239*
Tukey, J. W., 136, *210*

V

Van Paassen, H. L., 343, *419*
Varga, R. S., 165, 167, 168, *211*
Vedenov, A. A., 45, 58, 74, *86*, 119, *134*
Velikhov, E. P., 45, 58, 74, *86*, 119, *134*, 392, *420*
Veronis, G., 160, *211*
Vinogradov, V. P., 343, 394, 398, *418*
von Neumann, J., 300, *305*, 343, *420*

W

Wadhwa, R. P., 181, *211*
Wang, D., 185, *210*
Wasow, W. R., 162, 163, 169, *210*
Watson, J. L., 341, 342, 370, 390, 416, *417*
Watteau, J. P., 343, 398, *418, 419*
Weiss, N. O., 89, *134*, 341, 343, 344, 361, 368, 369, 376, 377, 392, 393, 394, *420*
Weiss, P. B., 265, *305*
Weissglas, P., 55, *86*
Weitzner, H., 37, *86*
Welch, P. D., 139, 145, *210*
Wendroff, B., 373, *419*
Wilcock, P. D., 343, 394, 398, *419, 420*
Williams, A. H., 343, 400, *419*
Wolf, G. H., 341, 342, 370, 390, *417*
Wong, D., 242, 243, 256–258
Woods, C. H., 90, *134*

Y

Yaneko, N. N., 383, *420*
Young, D. M., 380, *420*
Yu, S. P., 181, *211*, 257, *258*
Yushmanov, E. E., 427, 428, *489*

Subject Index

A

Accuracy, 53
Advection, 368
ALGOL, 414
ALICE, 282, 429, 451
Astron, 90, 186, 224, 267

B

Boltzmann equation, 23, 224, 312
Boundary conditions, 6, 9, 39, 43, 163, 270, 357, 389, 415, 441

C

Cloud-in-cell (CIC), 226, 309
Collisional damping, 15
Collisional phenomena, 10, 14, 69, 185
COMPASS, 145
Computers
  CDC 1604, 10
  CDC 3600, 103
  CDC 6600, 103, 139, 145, 146, 154, 162, 167, 178, 180, 183, 202
  CDC 7600, 345, 414
  GE 625, 61
  IBM 1130/1800, 160
  IBM 7044, 61, 79
  IBM 7090, 139, 161, 164, 183, 184, 187, 190, 192, 194, 414
  IBM 360/65/67, 7, 61, 139, 146, 154, 159, 180, 183, 202, 399
  IBM 360/91, 184, 345, 414
  ICL KDF9, 61, 103, 184, 414
  ILLIAC IV, 345
  SC 4020 (film recorder), 192, 194
Computing times, 8, 21, 60, 146, 154, 159, 164, 167, 178, 180, 183, 190, 194, 202
Confined plasmas, 234
Conservation, 41, 330, 346

Convergence, 164, 173
Courant condition, *see* Numerical stability

D

Debye shielding, 92
Difference schemes, *see also* Finite difference method
  explicit, 344, 370, 376
  implicit, 288, 360, 365
  Lax-Wendroff, 264, 344, 369, 373
  leapfrog, 111, 263, 295, 344, 415
  Peaceman-Rachford (ADI), 274, 447
  upstream-downstream, 263, 274
  vector difference notation, 384
Diffusion, 252, 375
Dispersion relations, 114
Double cycle reduction (DCR), 155, 159

E

E-layer, 267
Electrostatic sheet model, 2
Energy check, 53
Equations of motion, 3, 7, 30, 220
Equilibrium
  distribution, 116
  thermal, 22
Errors, 59, 63, 107, 154, 169, 301

F

Fast Fourier transform (FFT), 145
Finite difference method, 139, 259, 262, 273, 287, 293, 360, 378, 438, 444, 447
Finite number of particles, 186, 325
Finite size particle, 16, 25, 242
Fluid model, 186, 349
Fokker Planck equation, 424
FORTRAN, 59, 103, 141, 145, 154, 159, 180, 183, 202, 414

Fourier analysis cyclic reduction (FACR), 146, 159, 160
Fourier-Fourier expansion, 35

G

Galaxy model, 195

H

Hamilton's principle, 314, 322

I

Initial conditions, 39, 44, 55, 67
Instability
    bump-on-tail, 44, 58, 64, 73, 116
    computational, 112, 297
    diocotron, 194
    hydromagnetic, 404
    Kelvin-Helmholtz, 194, 303
    Rayleigh-Taylor, 91, 302
    weak cold beam, 24
Iterative method, 138, 164, 235

L

Lagrangian, 320
Landau damping, 15, 37, 45, 72, 78, 82, 94, 246
Leapfrog method, 111, 214, 375, 415
Longitudinal plasma oscillation, 244

M

Magnetohydrodynamics (MHD), 339
Mirror confinement, 425
Monte Carlo, 225

N

Noise, fluctuations, 10, 22, 31, 79, 185, 231
Numerical methods, 4, 7, 100, 106, 109, 116
Numerical stability, 111, 274, 296, 341, 358

O

One-dimensional model, 4, 260, 326, 340, 365, 387, 429

One species model, 3, 301

P

Particle-in-cell (PIC), 17, 213, 224, 254, 309
Particle model, 186
Periodic systems, 176, 228
Plasma oscillations, 3, 93, 244
Plasma gun, 190, 214, 218
Potential, 136, 247, 318

R

Recurrence relations, 143, 151
Relaxation method, 138, 164, 380
Relaxation time, 13
Rod model, 266

S

Scattering, 248
Shocks, 221, 344
Simulation, 17, 30, 228, 250
Smoothing, 17, 232, 242
Successive-over-relaxation (SOR), 138, 164, 235, 344, 380

T

Three-dimensional calculations, 228, 251, 345, 366
Time reversibility, 6, 53, 64
Transform methods, 34
Truncation error, 42, 63, 65, 137, 225
Two-component plasma, 7, 481
Two-dimensional calculation, 137, 183, 190, 216, 250, 266, 282, 290, 326, 343, 366, 392
Two-species model, 2, 7
Two-stream instability, 44, 50, 72, 91, 97, 227, 332

V

Vector potential, 318
Vlasov equation, 16, 26, 31, 56, 88, 260, 307

W

Water bag model, 34, 87, 224, 310

QA
401
M514
v.9

DEC 21 1972